Philadelphia Stories

AMERICA'S LITERATURE OF RACE AND FREEDOM

Samuel Otter

OXFORD
UNIVERSITY PRESS
2010

OXFORD
UNIVERSITY PRESS

Oxford University Press, Inc., publishes works that further
Oxford University's objective of excellence
in research, scholarship, and education.

Oxford New York
Auckland Cape Town Dar es Salaam Hong Kong Karachi
Kuala Lumpur Madrid Melbourne Mexico City Nairobi
New Delhi Shanghai Taipei Toronto

With offices in
Argentina Austria Brazil Chile Czech Republic France Greece
Guatemala Hungary Italy Japan Poland Portugal Singapore
South Korea Switzerland Thailand Turkey Ukraine Vietnam

Copyright © 2010 by Oxford University Press, Inc.

Published by Oxford University Press, Inc.
198 Madison Avenue, New York, New York 10016
www.oup.com

Oxford is a registered trademark of Oxford University Press

Library of Congress Cataloging-in-Publication Data
Otter, Samuel, 1956–
Philadelphia stories : America's literature of race and freedom/Samuel Otter.
p. cm.
Includes bibliographical references and index.
ISBN 978-0-19-539592-1
1. American literature—Pennsylvania—Philadelphia—History and criticism. 2. Literature and history.
3. American literature—19th century—History and criticism. 4. Philadelphia (Pa.)—History—19th century.
5. Philadelphia (Pa.)—In literature. I. Title.
PS255.P5O88 2010
810.9'3587481103—dc22   2009029086

1 3 5 7 9 8 6 4 2
Printed in the United States of America
on acid-free paper

For Caverlee,
Again and always

ACKNOWLEDGMENTS

I began to write this book after arriving at the Library Company of Philadelphia to research a different one. At the Library Company, I encountered not only the inexhaustible archives of the institution founded by Benjamin Franklin in 1731 but also the virtuosity of Phillip Lapsansky and James N. Green. Both men generously shared their resources and knowledge. The more I read, the more I realized that there was a story before me, or rather an array of stories, forming a tradition that had gone unrecognized by literary scholars. Without the Library Company and its remarkable staff, this book would have been inconceivable.

At a crucial early stage, Cindy Weinstein invited me to present work-in-progress at the Caltech-Huntington Seminar Series in American Studies, where I received valuable encouragement and advice from her, Martha Banta, Jennifer L. Fleissner, Catherine Jurca, and Christopher Looby. Toward the end of my writing, T. Scott McMillin invited me to deliver the Oberlin Lectures in British and American Literature, endowed by the late Andrew Bongiorno at Oberlin College. This opportunity clarified the book's arguments and structure, and allowed me to benefit from the responses of the Oberlin faculty, including Gillian Johns, Warren Liu, Mayumi Takada, and Sandra Zagarell. I am grateful to the University of California and to the Berkeley English Department and its recent chairs, Jeffrey Knapp, Janet Adelman, Catherine Gallagher, and Ian Duncan, for supporting this project. Fellowships were provided by the University of California President, the Berkeley Chancellor, the Townsend Center for the Humanities, and the Andrew W. Mellon Foundation.

I am honored to have Dorothy Hale, Jeffrey Knapp, and Nancy Ruttenburg as colleagues and friends. Their intellectual seriousness and personal generosity have served as an inspiration during my years in the profession and my work on this book. I am indebted to Dori for a keen reading of the entire manuscript. Her detailed comments enabled me to understand what I was claiming and to write a much better introduction.

I am grateful for invitations to present arguments from the book that were extended by Una Chaudhuri and Phillip Brian Harper at New York University; Jennifer Fleissner and Scott Herring at the University of Indiana, Bloomington; Philip Gould and Deak Nabers at Brown University; Gordon Hutner at the University of Illinois, Urbana-Champaign; Gavin Jones at Stanford University; Amy Kaplan at the University of Pennsylvania; Robert S. Levine at the University of Maryland; Christopher Looby at UCLA; Ilana Pardes at the Hebrew University of Jerusalem; and Takayuki Tatsumi at Keio University in Tokyo. Books need annealing, and whatever is persuasive in this book owes much to the critical engagement of these scholars and the substance of these occasions. I have benefited also from the responses of many others, including Dorri Beam, Nancy Bentley, Lauren Berlant, Stephen Best, Mitchell Breitwieser, Glenda Carpio, Christopher Castiglia, Wai Chee Dimock, Betsy Erkkila, John Ernest, the late Jay Fliegelman, Michael T. Gilmore, Jay Grossman, David Henkin, Donna Hunter, Robert S. Levine, Christopher Looby, Colleen Lye, Sharon Marcus, Ross Posnock, Kent Puckett, Carl Smith, John Stauffer, Julia Stern, Eric J. Sundquist, Leonard Tennenhouse, Bryan Wagner, and Robert K. Wallace. The intellectual coordinates of this book have been plotted in relation to the scholarship of Eddie S. Glaude Jr., Saidiya Hartman, Emma Jones Lapsansky, Gary B. Nash, Carla L. Peterson, Patrick Rael, Eric J. Sundquist, and Julie Winch.

Shannon McLachlan, my editor at Oxford University Press, has been as supportive and enthusiastic as any author could wish. She found the perfect readers for the manuscript, whose detailed reports improved this book. She and Brendan O'Neill, the assistant editor, along with Brian Desmond as production editor, Joy Matkowski as copy editor, and Mark A. Mastromarino as indexer, have deftly shepherded the manuscript and its author through the stages of publication. Aaron Bady, Peter Goodwin, Sean X. Goudie, Jennifer Greiman, Hsuan L. Hsu, Cody Marrs, Leonard von Morzé, and Margaret Ronda expertly assisted with research for the book. Margaret and Cody also tested its ideas at the later stages, and Cody labored heroically in helping to prepare the final manuscript. One could not ask for more talented and generous colleagues.

Part of chapter 4 was first published in *American Literary History* 20.4 (Winter 2008): 728–52. I consulted archives not only at the Library Company of Philadelphia but also at the Historical Society of Pennsylvania, the American Antiquarian Society, the New York Public Library, and the Frederick Douglass Papers at Indiana University-Purdue University, Indianapolis. Robin L. Condon, Assistant Editor at the Frederick Douglass Papers, and Diane M. Lucas, Head of Reader Services at St. John Fisher College, aided in locating elusive copies of *Frederick Douglass' Paper*. Permission to reproduce illustrations in this book were granted by the Clements Library at the University of Michigan, the Huntington Library, the Library of Congress, the Library Company of Philadelphia, and the Historical Society of Pennsylvania. At the Library Company, Erika Piola, the Assistant Curator of Prints and Photographs, and Nicole Joniec, the Print Department Assistant, were especially helpful in arranging for images to be photographed and in answering questions about their histories.

The support of my family has been key, and thanks are due to Marjorie Otter, Nelson Otter, Ruth and Philip Rubinstein, and William and Marion Sherry for the love and perspective they have provided. Still so much a part of my life, though gone, are Jeanne and Robert Otter and Sara and Sturges Cary. No acknowledgment can measure what they have given to me. My dedication makes clear that nothing would be possible without—that life is full because of—Caverlee.

CONTENTS

Introduction: Philadelphia Stories, 1790–1860   3

ONE   Fever   25
    Mathew Carey, Absalom Jones, Richard Allen, and the Color of Fever   29
    Ministers and Criminals: Richard Allen, John Joyce, and Peter Matthias   40
    Benjamin Rush's Heroic Interventions   46
    Mathew Carey's Fugitive Philadelphians   52
    Charles Brockden Brown's Experiments in Character   58

TWO   Manners   71
    Hugh Henry Brackenridge, and the Irrepressible Teague   73
    Edward W. Clay's "Life in Philadelphia"   81
    "The Rage for Profiles": Silhouettes at Peale's Museum   89
    Philadelphia Metempsychosis in Robert Montgomery Bird's
       Sheppard Lee   95
    "The Peculiar Position of Our People": William Whipper and
    Debates in the Black Conventions*   107
    Disfranchisement and Appeal   118
    Joseph Willson's Higher Classes of Colored Society in
       Philadelphia   123

THREE   Riot   131
    "Doomed to Destruction": The History of Pennsylvania Hall   138
    The Portraiture of the City of Philadelphia, and Henry James's
       American Scene   157
    The Mysteries of the City: George Lippard, Edgar Allan Poe   165
    The Fiction of Riot: George Lippard, John Beauchamp Jones   182
    The Condition of the Free People of Color   202

FOUR Freedom   211
      The Struggle over "Philadelphia": Mary Howard Schoolcraft, Sarah
          Josepha Hale, Martin Robison Delany, William Whipper, and
          James McCune Smith   212
      Frank J. Webb's The Garies and Their Friends: *"A Rather*
      Curious Protest"   224
      Still Life in Georgia   230
      History and Farce   237
      Parlor and Riot   244
      Philadelphia Vanitas   252
      The Social Experiment in Herman Melville's Benito Cereno   266

      Coda: John Edgar Wideman's Philadelphia   279

      Notes   289

      Bibliography   343

      Index   371

Philadelphia Stories

Introduction: Philadelphia Stories, 1790–1860

It is one of the strangest and most humiliating triumphs of human
selfishness and prejudice over human reason, that it leads men to
look upon emancipation as an experiment, instead of being, as it is,
the natural order of human relations.
—Frederick Douglass, "The Black Man's Future in
the Southern States" (1862)

My goal in this book is to make Philadelphia as crucial to our understanding of
U. S. literary history as Boston, Concord, or New York. Between the Constitution
and the Civil War, Philadelphia was seen by residents and observers as the laboratory for a social experiment with international consequences. The city would be
the stage on which racial character would be tested and possible futures would be
played out for the United States after slavery. It would be the arena in which
various residents would or would not demonstrate their capacities to participate
in the life of the city and nation. In Philadelphia lived one of the largest and
most influential free African American communities in the United States. For
members of this group, who are at the center of the stories and debates in this
book, the years between 1790 and 1860 were marked by social and economic
achievement, political backlash, violence, decline, and resistance. The Philadelphia
experiment in freedom produced a literary tradition of peculiar forms and

3

intensities that remains largely unacknowledged. Verbal performance and social behavior assumed the weight of race and nation, as a new national literature was shaped by debates around key terms—character, conduct, narrative—that were both political and literary. But while political and literary interests overlapped, they were not identical, and the writers of Philadelphia concentrated on the gap between the social world and its figuration, making that gap both topic and substance in their work. To appreciate the achievements of these writers, we need to understand the historical situation of their literary performances and the ways in which aesthetic power was related to particular questions of limit, essence, and possibility. The rhetorical instabilities and excesses in this literature were generated, but not bound, by the Philadelphia "experiment."

As Frederick Douglass signaled in the words I have used as an epigraph, the very notion of freedom as an experiment, rather than a natural right shared by human beings, was preposterous and tautological: "one of the strangest and most humiliating triumphs of human selfishness and prejudice over human reason." He added: "Slavery, and not Freedom, is the experiment; and to witness its horrible failure we have to open our eyes, not merely upon the blasted soil of Virginia and other Slave States, but upon a whole land brought to the verge of ruin." This book will reorient perspectives on the nineteenth-century literary landscape by focusing on the city positioned near the border between South and North, the first large eastern city above the boundary surveyed in the 1760s by Charles Mason and Jeremiah Dixon that, with the Missouri Compromise of 1820, became the dividing line between slavery and freedom. In his 1862 speech, Douglass anticipates emancipation during the Civil War, but his words are retrospective as well as prospective and include in their scope Philadelphia, the place that he had remarked in 1848 "more than almost any other in our land, holds the destiny of our people."[1] The Philadelphia portrayed by the writers in this book, located at the extremity of freedom, will be distinguished by this sense of cynosure and destiny, this mixture of urgency and absurdity.

Experiment

The historian Mary P. Ryan has described antebellum U.S. cities as laboratories for democratic practice, and historians such as Erica Armstrong Dunbar, Emma Jones Lapsansky, Gary B. Nash, and Julie Winch have distinguished the Philadelphia setting. The city was founded in the late seventeenth century as part of the Quaker William Penn's Holy Experiment in religious toleration and representative government. In the third quarter of the eighteenth century, Quakers such as

John Woolman and Anthony Benezet, drawing upon a history of uneasiness with racial slavery among some of the membership, argued for the need to disengage from the system and to prepare those who had been enslaved for liberty. In 1775, Philadelphians founded the Quaker-dominated Society for the Relief of Free Negroes Unlawfully Held in Bondage, the first organization of its kind in North America. Adding "The Pennsylvania Society for Promoting the Abolition of Slavery" to its title after the Revolution, the group expanded its membership and included such figures as Benjamin Franklin and the eminent physician and reformer Benjamin Rush. In 1776, the Philadelphia Yearly Meeting announced that it would disown Quakers who did not free their slaves.[2]

The Pennsylvania state assembly passed the first "Act for the Gradual Aboli-tion of Slavery" in 1780. Although the act left many subjugated for a long period, freeing those born into slavery after its passage only at age twenty-eight, and although it continued to permit the buying and selling of slaves, outlawing only their import, the legislation helped to bring about the decline of the sys-tem. It prompted some owners to free their slaves in the present or in their wills, the Abolition Society purchased slaves and liberated them, and other states developed their own gradual abolition laws.

Philadelphia became the intellectual source for arguments endorsing the shared humanity (but not necessarily identical capacities) of whites and blacks and for arguments supporting the environmental basis of racial characteristics. Samuel Stanhope Smith, a leading member of the city's American Philosophical Society, gave prominence to such arguments in his *Essay on the Causes of Variety of Complexion and Figure in the Human Species,* first published in 1787 and revised in 1810.

In the 1780s and 1790s, Philadelphia's free black residents established institu-tions that would help to define the community. Led by the ministers Absalom Jones and Richard Allen, they established the Free African Society in 1787, which was the first independent black mutual aid organization in the United States, and the pioneering African churches, St. Thomas (Episcopalian) and Bethel (Meth-odist) in 1794.

From the 1790s through the 1850s, many Philadelphians obsessively reflected upon their city, with hope or horror, viewing it as the testing ground for freedom. In the late summer and fall of 1793, when Philadelphia was devastated by a yel-low fever epidemic, civic and medical authorities, including Benjamin Rush, sum-moned the city's free blacks to serve white residents as nurses and carriers of the dead. They invoked the city and state's history of support for abolition, interra-cial working relationships, and a mistaken belief that African Americans were not susceptible to infection. At the time, Philadelphia was the temporary capital of the new nation. Its State House had been the setting for the Declaration of Independence, adopted by the Second Continental Congress in July 1776, and for the Constitution, approved by state delegates in September 1787. In this historic, symbolic city, the yellow fever epidemic of 1793 became a spectacle of character and destiny regarded by a national audience, a spectacle that would be turned into a contested story about racial performance to be told again and again.

The city became the destination for waves of European immigrants, especially from Ireland, Germany, and England, for Africans escaping from the American South or taken from the Caribbean (in the 1790s, many planters fled to the city with their slaves from Saint Domingue during the hemisphere's other late-eighteenth-century revolution), and for those already in the North seeking a new space of freedom. It appears repeatedly as the crossing point in narratives of slavery. "Philadelphia" was the address on the wooden crate holding Henry "Box" Brown, which was mailed from Richmond, Virginia, in 1849, in the famed postal escape. At the climax of the first part of *Running a Thousand Miles for Freedom; or, The Escape of William and Ellen Craft from Slavery* (1860), the first glimpse of city lights is compared to the sight of the cross that relieved the burdens on John Bunyan's Pilgrim—but due to legal vulnerability and white hostility, the protagonists must flee from this "city of refuge" to Boston. In *Incidents in the Life of a Slave Girl* (1861), Harriet Jacobs describes how her protagonist Linda Brent, on her first stop northward after enslavement in North Carolina, experiences release. She receives the support of Philadelphia's African American Vigilant Committee and is moved by her exposure to a new visual authority, when, for the first time, she sees portraits of African American children. Linda also suffers constraint. Boarding a train to New York City, she is forced to ride in a segregated car with an uncouth mixture of people. For many writers, black and white, Philadelphia will involve a measured freedom and the quandaries of status. The city is sanctuary and trap in the narratives of black antislavery enterprise collected by the Philadelphian William Still in his post–Civil War anthology, *The Underground Railroad* (1872).[3]

In the first half of the nineteenth century, white hostility escalated toward blacks in the city and statewide, while a nascent black middle class evolved. In 1805, white celebrants attacked blacks who had joined a July Fourth commemoration in the square across from Independence Hall. Racial tensions were heightened by economic decline (severe in 1816–1823 and 1837–1842); by conflict among male laborers, especially between immigrant Irish and free blacks; by white fears about black poverty, crime, achievement, and population increase in the city during the early decades of the nineteenth century; by outrage over interracial sexual contact, stoked by the press; and by the specter of a Caribbean revolution that might extend to the United States. Legislation barring the entry of free

African Americans to the state of Pennsylvania or regulating the movement of current residents was proposed, but defeated, five times between 1805 and 1814, and an effort to deny access was attempted once more in 1831. The city maintained its prominence in debates about the status of racial difference, now serving as the forum for Samuel George Morton and the "American school" of ethnology, whose adherents contended that such differences were inherent and hierarchical. African American men were largely shut out of professions such as law and medicine and from jobs in the developing machine, foundry, and textile industries. They occupied positions in skilled trades such as catering, barbering, and hairdressing, and some owned their own businesses. Many men were laborers; many women were domestics.

African American social aspirations became the object of caricature and defense. Debates unfolded between whites and blacks and within black groups about moral reform, proper conduct, and the merits of political activism. Philadelphia was the setting for five of the first six national black conventions held in the 1830s, and young Philadelphians strongly influenced the proceedings. Attendees considered issues of emigration, colonization, education, career, temperance, moral reform, racial consciousness, and social "elevation." African Americans in the city sought to influence opinion and shape behavior within and beyond their communities through a variety of print media, including petitions, sermons, speeches, essays, and public letters. The "condition" of the city's African Americans became the preoccupation in a series of reports and counterreports from the 1830s through the 1850s, prepared by Pennsylvania Abolition Society, the Society of Friends, and their opponents. These reports diagnosed the condition of freedom for both blacks and whites. In May 1838, a mob, decrying abolition and racial amalgamation, set fire to Pennsylvania Hall, recently opened as the city's preeminent space for advancing social reform. (This is the scene depicted in the cover illustration of this book and discussed in chapter 3.) The next fall, after extended public dispute, the voters of Pennsylvania narrowly ratified an amendment that revised the state constitution, which in 1790 had granted the franchise to "every freeman" who was at least twenty-one years old and had paid a state or county tax. Now, between the word "every" and the word "freeman," voters inserted the adjective "white."

Over the decades, the majority of African Americans settled in the southern districts of the city, the racially and economically diverse area that straddled Cedar or South Street, which Emma Jones Lapsansky has labeled the "Cedar neighborhood." In the 1830s and 1840s, its African American residents and their homes, benevolent societies, and churches became targets for rioters. Violence flared in the major outbreaks of 1842 and 1849. According to some observers, the tensions between Irish and African American laborers were encouraged by Anglo elites. The riots were partly a backlash against the city's role in the expanding abolition movement. The American Anti-Slavery Society had been founded there in 1833, and the Pennsylvania Anti-Slavery Society in 1837. The riots also were fueled by economic crisis. The Panic of 1837 led to six years of depression, and the 1841 collapse of the Bank of the United States, in Philadelphia, caused acute local hardship. Poverty became an increasingly visible feature in the cityscape and an audible concern among reformers. Most African American residents, whose vocational alternatives and economic circumstances had been declining since the early nineteenth century, saw their positions further erode. At the same time, leaders persisted in their efforts to consolidate an African American presence in the city through churches, mutual aid societies, schools, libraries, and literary associations. A minority of the minority population strove to maintain their vulnerable status as members of what the mid-century African American chronicler Joseph Willson described as the "higher classes of colored society in Philadelphia." In popular culture, debate, census, ethnography, riot, and fiction, the city and its African American residents were the focus of an extended meditation on freedom in the United States.[4]

The public sphere in Philadelphia developed through a series of violent episodes that were interpreted as tests of individual, racial, and civic character. The border status of the city, its symbolic value and political history, its resilient African American population, and the circumstances of extremity provoked inquiries that unfolded in a range of texts over seven decades. A publishing center in the early national period, the city produced a body of writing that reflected on its status. Books and pamphlets about Philadelphia were distributed by an influential group of entrepreneurs, many of whom had begun their careers as printers and then joined with local capitalists to build the industry and expand their markets. Publications also were financed by smaller establishments or private individuals who helped to disseminate the textual city. Under threat, urban life seemed newly legible: as a limit outside the self that shaped identity, as a felt excess that resisted such limits, and as a possibility for transformation. Freedom, like coercion, was negotiated in the details of urban life. In this setting, literature, and especially literary fiction with its scrutiny of conduct and context, played a striking role. In the middle of the nineteenth century, Philadelphia came into fiction, and fiction became Philadelphian. In this book, I analyze the historical circumstances and structures of regard that brought Philadelphia and literature into proximity—and more: that made them crucial to an understanding of one another.

Writers shared a sense that Philadelphia was the place where, in concentrated form, a peculiarly American experiment was being conducted. As will become evident over the course of this book, various writers used the term "experiment" or metaphors of trial and testing in their accounts of Philadelphia. "Experiment" is the term invoked by W. E. B. DuBois in his pioneering work of sociology, *The Philadelphia Negro*, appearing at the end of a century in which this city was treated as a social and racial laboratory. For DuBois, the predominantly African American Seventh Ward (which included the earlier Cedar neighborhood) at the core of his meticulous study epitomized "our national experiment and its ensuing problems" and "the experiment in Pennsylvania." Behind this late nineteenth-century Philadelphia fixation—the summons of the white patrons who commissioned DuBois's study and DuBois's complicated response—lies the history and literature that will be taken up in the following chapters.[5]

Place

When, in 1833, the Scottish traveler Thomas Hamilton described his frustration with Philadelphia, he invoked (with some vehemence) what by then had become a platitude about its regularity, even rigidity. He imagined the city as a location determined by grids and limits: "Philadelphia is mediocrity personified in brick and mortar. It is a city laid down by square and rule, a sort of habitable problem,—a mathematical infringement on the rights of individual eccentricity,—a rigid and prosaic despotism of right angles and parallelograms."[6] While Hamilton's view is formulaic, setting right angles against personal eccentricities, he offers a resonant way of thinking about the city as laboratory—"a sort of habitable problem"—which acknowledges that hypotheses about freedom are lived by those who move through its spaces and encounter networks of imperatives, enticements, and prohibitions. Such movements redraw boundaries and establish alternative maps of the city.

Visitors associated Philadelphia with its rectilinear design, first projected by William Penn and his surveyor Thomas Holme in their "Portraiture of the City of Philadelphia," circulated in a 1683 advertising pamphlet for the colony (Figure I.1). From the start, this plan had been altered by residents who subdivided lots and clustered in sectors, rather than obeying the directives of the imagined city. Observers continued to remark upon the relative orderliness of the streets in the urban core. Until the merging of Philadelphia with its surrounding districts in 1854, the city proper extended only to the borders of the original charter, an area of two square miles between the Delaware River in the east and the Schuylkill in the west. According to the cliché, Philadelphia was defined by symmetry and discipline. The city's perpendicular array of streets and squares and its numbering,

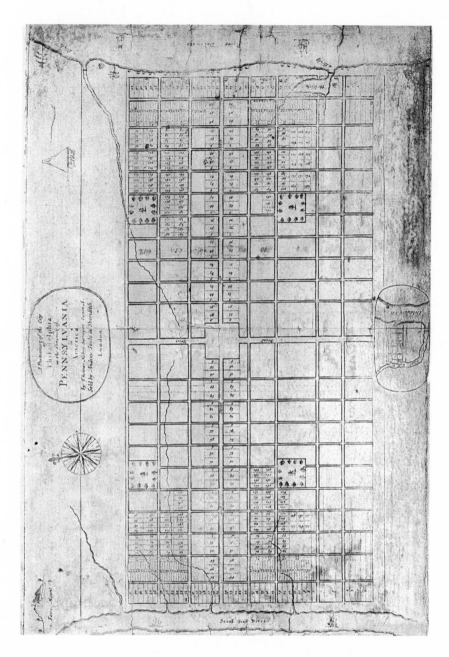

FIGURE I.I Thomas Holme, "A Portraiture of the City of Philadelphia in the Province of Pennsylvania in America" (1683). Courtesy of the Library Company of Philadelphia.

rather than naming, of north-south routes frequently were linked with the rectitude of its founder and its Quaker inhabitants. Sometimes the geometry was
admired, but often travel writers described an excess of uniformity: "too many
right angles and straight lines to be altogether pleasing to the eye" (Frances
Wright in 1819), "the most regular town that was ever built" (Mrs. Basil Hall in
1827), "too much regularity and too nice precision" (Nathaniel Parker Willis in
1831), "extreme and almost wearisome regularity" (Frances Trollope in 1832),
and "distractingly regular" (Charles Dickens in 1842). In these remarks—"too
many," "the most," "too much and too nice," "extreme and almost wearisome,"
"distractingly"—the surplus unsettles the invocations of "regularity." Philadelphia writers, inhabiting the city's problems of race and class, sought to capture
this systematic excess, and they associated it with the energies of the social
"experiment." Many of them used the grid to disorient and reposition their readers. They twisted the trope. Figurative play with the grid helped to structure literary responses to Philadelphia, as writers charted the gap between abstract and
actual space. Some marked that gap as hypocrisy and were provoked to satire;
others indicated the possibility of future correspondence; and others, with whom
we will be most concerned, explored inordinate surfaces.[7]

Benjamin Franklin, the most famous Philadelphian, whose irony, contrivance,
and vigorous negotiation of status in the public arena (the effort to gain "Credit"
and "Character," the regard for "Appearances") influenced later writers discussed
in this book, appears to be making a joke about the renowned grid, when, in the
second part of his autobiography, he reproduces an example from his "bold and
arduous Project of arriving at moral Perfection." Franklin explains that he devised
a method of habituating himself to virtue through a course of incremental progress transcribed in a small volume that he carried with him. The program would
take thirteen weeks (one for each of the virtues) and could be repeated four times
a year. In his memoir, he reproduces a sample from his "little Book." On the page,
in a lattice formed by axes denoting the seven days of the week and thirteen virtues, Franklin shows how he tried to improve his performance (Figure I.2).
Focusing on "Temperance," he had managed to keep those precincts clear of the
black spots he used to record his faults of the day. In the absence of blemishes,
he would register and savor his improvement. This sample week, although he succeeded with "Temperance," Franklin had difficulties with "Industry," "Frugality,"
"Resolution," and, most visibly, "Silence" and "Order."[8]

The local irony here is that, on the ruled page that Franklin hoped would bring
structure to his life, he marks continuing trouble with "Order." The larger irony
is that Franklin, seeking to chart the growth of his moral self on the surface of a
page, records how impulse and errancy interfere with even the most symmetrical

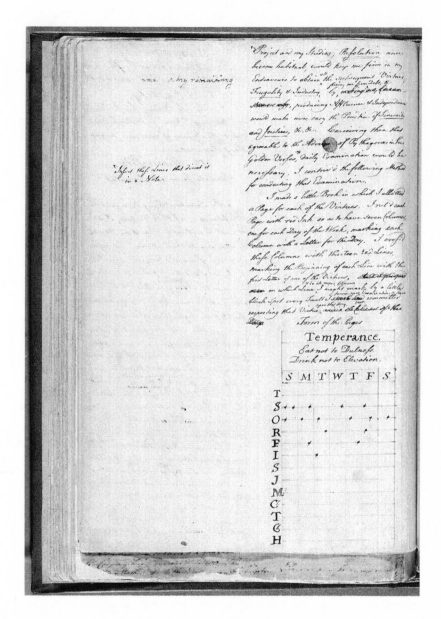

projects. Before he developed a system of wiping out his spots with a wet sponge, Franklin had scraped them off, and this repeated action tore many holes in his pages: material reminders of the fragility of his system and of the risk that time, measured as repetition, might erode rather than fulfill. Franklin's memoir page is an elaborate surface: lettered, lined, marked, simulating the pages in his virtue book. This surface contains projection and insufficiency, matrix and stain, scheme and pretense, imitation and asymptote—the coordinates of desire. Franklin's calendar of virtues resembles Penn and Holme's grid turned on a vertical axis, and blotched. Like Franklin, many of the writers in this book will plot their stories of Philadelphia, individual, social, and often urgently racial, according to a grid of expectations and limits. They also will articulate a historical surface, responding to particular events and demands and to an evolving urban geography.[9]

In the literature of Philadelphia, the dynamic between Penn and Holme's grid and specific locations and experiences resembles the dialectic between "space" and "place" in the arguments of cultural geographers such as Yi-Fu Tuan, Doreen Massey, and Tim Cresswell. Rather than setting "space" (viewed as abstract and objective) against "place" (seen as particular and subjective), the cultural geographers explicate a defining interaction. "Place," especially in the work of Massey, is the term used to describe a site where the abstract and the particular converge and where boundaries are formed through distinct linkages between inside and outside. Locations are produced in a field of pressures. They are sites not of fixity but of vigor and conflict. In words that will resonate with the kind of close textual reading endorsed in the next section of this introduction, Massey writes that "what gives a place its specificity is not some long internalized history but the fact that it is constructed out of a particular constellation of social relations, meeting and weaving together at a particular locus."[10]

Traditionally, American studies critics have lingered over "place," surveying regional character (New England or the South, for example) or highlighting cities such as New York, Los Angeles, Chicago, or Boston, which have been understood to play major roles in literary and political development. Recent work in American studies has been influenced by the new cultural geography, producing analyses that join local, regional, national, and international venues. In *Philadelphia Stories*, I bring together historical work on race, character, and politics in Philadelphia, the emphasis on the local in American Studies, the cultural geographers' insistence on circulation and implication, and a respect for aesthetic complexity and surprise. I argue for a Philadelphia that revises our sense of literary place.[11]

"Philadelphia" is on the border between North and South, rhetoric and violence, promise and betrayal. It is a "place" in several senses: a location whose coordinates situated it at the chiasmus between slavery and freedom; a locale in which specific conflicts between and within groups were played out; and a scene of affects identified with freedom: Holy Experiment, Declaration, Constitution, Abolition, Underground Railroad. In another sense, "place," considered as appropriate social and racial position, became a vivid topic in early national Philadelphia. The testing of its abstractions made the city palpable. Philadelphia was not reducible to but also inextricable from the nation. It was a city of porous boundaries and unstable parts. Its spatial complexities and local urgencies generated the stories of race and freedom that are the topic of this book. Writers narrated Philadelphia as an event, the place where racial status was disputed and civic identity forged, while the country, and a transatlantic audience, watched.[12]

Philadelphia was distinctive but not, of course, unique. In other northern cities, such as New York, Boston, and Washington, D.C., freedom was under scrutiny, and questions of race and status were prominent. In other places, local history unfolded in rhythms of black advance and white reaction. In New York, for example, the state legislature passed a series of limited emancipation acts, beginning in 1785. The growth of an influential free black community, the forming of a middle class, and a public campaign against slavery led by African Americans was met with white retaliation. Severe limits were placed on black male suffrage through state constitutional changes passed in 1821 and then reaffirmed in 1846. Racial riots erupted, with particular force in 1834 (the same year, and one month earlier, than the riot in Philadelphia) and in 1863 (the devastating draft riots during the Civil War). In New York, though, which some observers viewed as the most southern of northern cities, there were fewer coalitions across racial lines than in Philadelphia during the same period.[13]

Stories of place and race could be told about these other cities, and some have been, especially in the case of New York, but they would be different stories. In Philadelphia, geography, symbol, history, politics, demographics, epidemiology, caricature, riots, meetings, and treatises helped to incite a fascination with the city as urban cauldron in which the racial destiny of the nation would be played out. Historians have recovered the consciousness of Philadelphia as a distinctive place. What we have not recognized, and what this book hopes to make visible, is that this sense of place sustained a literary project that tested the "experiment" itself.

Literature

Scholars typically have dismissed the idea of a consequential body of writing associated with Philadelphia, apart from the contributions of isolated writers such as Benjamin Franklin, Charles Brockden Brown, Edgar Allan Poe, and the sensational novelist George Lippard. The last major literary history of the city, written by Ellis Paxson Oberholtzer, was published in 1906, and, while useful, its mode is popular description rather than analysis. In the monumental collaboration *Philadelphia: A 300-Year History*, published in 1982 on the anniversary of the city's founding, Nicholas B. Wainwright wrote that "Philadelphia failed to produce literary figures of lasting renown," and Nathaniel Burt and Wallace E. Davies held that Franklin's *Autobiography* and Owen Wister's early-twentieth-century novel *The Virginian* were the only classic works to have emerged from Philadelphia. In the small cluster of books published in recent decades on the city in North American literature, Philadelphia is mentioned occasionally, as emblem of urban depravity, but never in distinction or with an awareness of tradition.[14]

Literary critics have begun to attend to Philadelphia. In *Voicing America* (1996), Christopher Looby notes that Benjamin Franklin, Charles Brockden Brown, and Hugh Henry Brackenridge, the three writers at the center of his argument about linguistic self-consciousness in the new nation, were all Philadelphians. Looby examines debates about language in the city during and after the Revolution. The verbal import that he identifies also characterizes the exchanges about behavior during the yellow fever epidemic of 1793 and the controversies over disfranchisement that I will take up in chapters 1 and 2. In *The American Manufactory* (1998), Laura Rigal argues that the productive character of individuals was continuously on display in Philadelphia, forming a visual and literary culture in tandem with divisions of labor. According to Rigal, that exhibition took many forms: commemorative parades, museums, architecture, natural science, autobiographies, paintings, engravings, periodical essays, and poems. Strenuous displays of character (including questions about where character resides) will preoccupy many of the writers that I discuss. In *October Cities* (1998), Carlo Rotella analyzes novels about postindustrial change in Philadelphia's South Street neighborhood after World War II. He focuses on racial, ethnic, and class encounters, which often turned violent, and on the tensions between local and metropolitan authority. In chapter 3, we will see the literary boundaries of the city take shape in narratives of riot, concerned with the area around South Street. Such narratives are precursors to Rotella's twentieth-century novels.[15]

The Philadelphia tradition bridges the gap that persists in U.S. literary histories between the late-eighteenth and mid-nineteenth centuries. In scholarship, teaching, and anthologies, the critical narrative usually halts in the 1790s with the sentimentalism of Susanna Haswell Rowson and Hannah Webster Foster and the gothicism of Charles Brockden Brown and then picks up again in the 1820s with the transatlantic sketches of Washington Irving and the historical novels of James

Fenimore Cooper and Catharine Maria Sedgwick. The period between 1800 and 1820 tends to be disregarded, as though unpopulated by writers. On a conceptual level, literary scholars who analyze the 1840s and 1850s (where the professional interest still converges) often do so without a sense of development. Beginning with the literature and history of these years, they validate an originality that points forward to modernism, or they recur to earlier periods for their continuities (the politics of the American Revolution or the theology and ideology of Puritan New England), skipping the antecedent decades of the nineteenth century. In recent scholarship, individual writers have been retrieved from the gap, such as Rebecca Rush, Tabitha Gilman Tenney, Leonora Sansay, and John Neal, but analysis of their work usually has not involved a suturing of literary history. From the perspective of Philadelphia, the interval between the 1790s and the 1840s and 1850s is spanned and filled, as writers across a range of genres assess the city's experiment in freedom with a consciousness, and often a critique, of progress.[16]

The literature of Philadelphia offers an alternative to racial allegories, showing the intertwined African and European American social energies in the mid-Atlantic region. In this place, and in the narratives of this book, African American and European American writers draw from exclusive but shared histories. They address racially specific audiences but seek to thwart color lines. An immersion in literary place can expand our understanding of relation. A close reading also can be wide and deep.

Much of the writing about Philadelphia is distinguished by a set of rhetorical instabilities, notable in the fiction but present also in a range of allied narrative forms, including chronicles, satire, political debate, and documentary history. In relation, these texts gather complexity. I will join the familiar (novels, short fiction, and essays by Charles Brockden Brown, Edgar Allan Poe, Herman Melville, Henry James, and John Edgar Wideman) with the relatively well known (fiction by Hugh Henry Brackenridge, George Lippard, and Frank J. Webb and nonfiction by Martin Delany) and the unknown or the rarely interpreted, often in forms not considered sufficiently "literary": correspondence by Benjamin Rush, the fever accounts of Mathew Carey, metempsychic fiction by Robert Montgomery Bird, the records of the black national conventions, the essays and letters of William Whipper, studies prepared by the Pennsylvania Abolition Society, riot novels by Lippard and John Beauchamp Jones, a textual memorial for a symbolic building, and a recipe for turkey without bones. I also will examine visual artifacts: the caricatures of Edward W. Clay, the silhouettes made at Charles Willson Peale's Museum, prints, book covers, and frontispieces. In these patterns and circuits, I argue, the literature of Philadelphia develops. As we shall see, questions about temporality—whether the passage of time implies advance, stasis, regress, continuity, rupture, cycle, or apocalypse—become a defining aspect of the tradition.

Stories of the Philadelphia experiment derive aesthetic power from the ways they register and reflect upon its consequences. These stories of probation and scrutiny take up the violence whose impossible ideological task (the attempt to fix racial position) helps to generate their rhetorical excess. These are stories about storytelling, about the effort to determine sequence, reveal character, and construct point of view. And in these stories, narrative perpetually is at risk of unraveling. Writerly acts of self-articulation turn into narrative struggles over race and nation. Texts are riddled with positional antagonisms, social maneuverings, and self-justifications. The intensities of conflict prevent any authoritative story from cohering. The usual novelistic setting forth of the differences between the represented social world and the language used to describe it (named in the modern theoretical vocabulary by terms such as "story versus discourse" or "materiality versus ideology") is doubled by local concerns with the rift between the practice and the rhetoric of freedom. The contested nature of African American freedom disrupts proportionality, and the city's vaunted grid and the textures of its literature are skewed.

Although gothic modes are employed in Philadelphia literature, they do not correspond to the political or racial gothic sometimes described by Americanist critics, in which the repressions of a slaveholding democracy manifest themselves in haunting figures of blackness. (Such figures become the topic of debate in yellow fever narratives.) The Philadelphia writings convey a different kind of excess, produced not by antithesis and absence but by the demands of freedom. Much of the writing about Philadelphia shares a condition of verbal strain. This is a literature about surfaces: skin (chapter 1 on yellow fever narratives); manners (chapter 2 on debates about racial character); maps, streets, parlor floors (chapter 3 on riots); and tabletops (chapter 4 on the rituals of freedom). These surfaces are associated with distortion: infected bodies, exaggerated gestures, trapdoors, and volatile banquets. One reason the tradition may have been overlooked is that its surfaces, in order to be legible, require awareness of their political stakes. Yet to appreciate this literature, we also need to recognize the uneven relationships between its formal and historical registers. Its characteristic excesses proceed from, but are not bound by, the Philadelphia experiment.[17]

The Philadelphia surfaces require an eye for detail, structure, process, and context. Such a regard is not unlike the alertness to "place" called for by cultural geographers, provisionally defined by relations between inside and outside and local and distant, involving struggle rather than stable identities. These dynamics suggest that geographers and literary critics might learn from their respective approaches and that Philadelphia might offer a particularly revealing example of literary place. In construing its surfaces, I hope to avoid, or at least to manage, the spatial dilemmas of literary criticism, in which the text recedes into the background (the allure and risk of historicism) or dominates the foreground (the allure and risk of formalism).[18]

In this book, I employ close textual reading as a method of historical understanding. Most literary critics take note of details in the works they interpret, and in this sense they read closely, but I have in mind proximities that have not been featured in recent historical analyses of nineteenth-century U.S. literature. In their shift to history and politics, some literary critics have rushed to translate the specifics of representational practice into meaningful abstractions. I pause, and insist on the details, savoring literary difference and historical recalcitrance. In such close encounters, I locate the strange within the normative and the normative within the strange, and I argue that such incongruities hold the potential for transformation. The strangeness I describe may be the object, then and now, of distress or hilarity (or both at the same time) or of puzzlement or queasiness or awe. Many varieties of instability are on display in the literature of Philadelphia: wavering tonalities, rhetorical discontinuities, inordinate signification, generic mixtures, stories that eclipse their boundaries, and words that possess an uncanny agency. I will examine the workings, not of unseen power, but of lived experience—or, to describe my investment more precisely, of experience as refracted through and considered in literary terms. The designation "literary," for me, indicates verbal structures that are complex, reflexive, unsettling, and surprising, gathering their fullest meanings over time and in pattern—the "tradition" to which I have referred in these opening pages. We all have our aesthetic investments, we all make our judgments and take our pleasures, and these are mine. They are values that I hope not only to display but also to justify over the course of this book.

Chapters

The four chapters—"Fever," "Manners," "Riot," and "Freedom"—advance chronologically from the 1790s to the 1850s. They move from the yellow fever epidemic of 1793 to disfranchisement in 1838, the riots of the 1840s, and the assessments of past, present, and future in the 1850s. The chapter titles refer to events and issues, and they point to multiple temporalities: sequential, simultaneous, and cumulative. The trials of character and city in "Fever" are repeated in the other chapters. In both "Fever" and "Riot," outbreaks of violence provoke efforts to diagnose and treat racial disorder. In "Manners" and also in "Riot," decorum is crucial. In "Freedom," as well as "Fever," Philadelphia is distinguished by a peculiar memento mori. The chapters describe various relationships between literature and history. In "Fever" and "Riot," social calamity leads to narrative struggle; in "Manners," speculations on character influence legislation; in "Freedom," history is subject to literary analysis. The slight imbalance between "Fever" and "Riot," titles that name events (which became associated with ideas about race, conduct, and nation), and "Manners" and "Freedom," titles that refer to ideas about identity and agency (which became associated with events), points to the dialectic between place and concept that this book will explore.

In the first chapter, "Fever," I argue that the premises and tropes of much writing about Philadelphia emerged in the debates surrounding the epidemic of 1793. In the second chapter, "Manners," I analyze the obsessions with social performance in the early nineteenth century and especially in the 1830s, which came to a head with the 1838 vote to disfranchise African American men. In the next chapter, "Riot," I show how Philadelphia was given fictional shape, how its boundaries were defined through violation, in accounts of the riots in the late 1830s and the 1840s. In the final chapter, "Freedom," I evaluate the reflection across genres in the 1850s about the significance of Philadelphia. At the apex is Frank J. Webb's novel, *The Garies and Their Friends* (1857), a singular appraisal of freedom's qualities. Across the chapters, I develop both narrative and analytical lines, connecting various stories and moving toward a sustained reading of Webb's novel, which is, in many ways, *the* Philadelphia story.

In "Fever," I discuss the multiple narratives of the 1793 yellow fever epidemic. The publisher Mathew Carey struggled for accuracy and sought to vindicate the city, in the scrupulous versions of his *Short Account of the Malignant Fever*, unfolding across the decades (four versions in 1793, one in 1794, and another in 1830). Carey's increasingly long *Short Accounts* are emblematic of the stories told about Philadelphia: riddled with justification and antagonism, refusing to cohere, exceeding their boundaries. In the "Narrative of the Proceedings of the Black People, during the Late Awful Calamity in Philadelphia," issued in the wake of the epidemic, the ministers Absalom Jones and Richard Allen defended the conduct of African Americans who were called to serve and then charged with extortion and theft. Jones and Allen fixed on a telling paragraph in Carey's *Short Account*, which reverberates for two hundred years. (It spurs John Edgar Wideman to write his short story "Fever," published in 1989.) The physician Benjamin Rush wrote daily letters to his wife, Julia, in which he described his medical service and his identifications with the afflicted and the accused. In the fictional *Arthur Mervyn; or, Memoirs of the Year 1793* (1799–1800), Charles Brockden Brown incorporated Carey, Rush, and the debates about fever. All of these writers exorbitantly narrated social experiment in the midst of crisis. They consider a knot of issues that distinguish Philadelphia texts: the city as specimen, the diagnosis and treatment of urban disorder, the trials of character, the qualities of action, the status of race, the vehemence of prejudice, the effects of position on interpretation, and the potency of stories.

In "Manners," I turn to several genres related to the Philadelphia experiment: early national picaresque narratives that tested the character of their characters, sketches that linked deportment to destiny, and essays and speeches on social elevation. In *Modern Chivalry* (1792–1815), Hugh Henry Brackenridge's narrator satirized his foil, an Irish American servant who endures various trials in pursuit of status and vocation, and he conducted thought experiments in which racial positions were exchanged. In "Life in Philadelphia," an internationally popular and widely imitated series of etchings first issued between 1828 and 1830, Edward W. Clay mocked social posturing, especially among on the city's rising African Americans. In *Sheppard Lee* (1836), a tale of Philadelphia metempsychosis, Robert Montgomery Bird turned the novel of manners inside out. The spirit of Bird's hapless protagonist uneasily occupies the bodies of others, traversing the stations of class and race, as the author imagines the internal struggles that precede individual social performance. Both Clay and Bird treated African Americans as limit cases.

At the five national black conventions held in Philadelphia in the 1830s, participants discussed whether the obstacles to their advancement in northern states resulted more from "condition" (degraded status) or "complexion" (racial prejudice). After the 1838 vote to disfranchise African American men in Pennsylvania, William Whipper altered the terms of the debate. Rejecting his earlier stance that rights would accrue through moral reform, he proposed a model of conduct as tactic, exerted in a society perceived as battlefield or courtroom. In *Sketches of the Higher Classes of Colored Society in Philadelphia* (1841), Joseph Willson countered the images of African Americans in Clay's burlesques and the arguments for disfranchisement. Willson provided his readers with strategic glimpses of the parlors of the "higher classes," whose members attempted to preserve community on the edge of violence.

In "Riot," I argue that Philadelphia assumed literary substance in portrayals of violence: the antiabolitionist riot of 1838, during which the imposing Pennsylvania Hall, committed to free inquiry and social reform, was destroyed, and the racial outbreaks of 1842 and 1849, which targeted African American property, institutions, and persons in the Cedar neighborhood. In documentary history and sensational fiction, the city's buildings, streets, and neighborhoods were materialized in their ruin. Writers elaborated on the famous grid, tracing not the stock gap between ideal and lived city but a constitutive violence. The editors of the memorial *History of Pennsylvania Hall* (1838) included prints, letters, speeches, poetry, an official police report, and a critique of that report, in an effort to preserve the meanings of the structure. George Lippard inflected the gothic protocols of the European city mystery genre with Philadelphia's topography, politics, and history. He granted the city a scandalous and unprecedented fictional visibility. In the trajectory from *The Quaker City* (1845) to *The Nazarene* (1846) and *The Killers* (1850), Lippard approached historical violence in Philadelphia, finally depicting the events of 1849, including African American resistance. Through riot, he developed an aesthetics of place, involving suspended, violent figures and techniques of spatial disproportion. Contemplating Philadelphia, writers such as Edgar Allan Poe and, later, Henry James relished the incongruities between aesthetics and history and questioned attachments to place.

In his novel *The City Merchant* (1851), John Beauchamp Jones invoked the struggles among Anglo, Irish, and African Americans and merged the riots of 1838, 1842, and 1849. As several writers would in the 1850s, Jones reflected on the city's social experiments and assessed the state of the nation. He offered a fantasy of violent expulsion as the remedy for a misguided, disastrous African American liberty. Jones defended the conduct of riot, which he portrayed as strategic targeting to enforce subjection. His novel disputed the censuses and studies based upon them (in 1838 and 1849), whose backers, the Pennsylvania Abolition Society and the Society of Friends, ventured evidence of social progress. These studies certified Philadelphia's African Americans as the urgent and proper topic of research, a community whose status would reveal the prognosis for the nation. The reports were used by W. E. B. DuBois in preparing his landmark *The Philadelphia Negro* (1899), which appeared at the end of a century of speculation about the character of the city.

In "Freedom," I begin with the appraisals of Philadelphia made in the early 1850s. In her "Letters on the Condition of the African Race in the United States" (1852), Mary Howard Schoolcraft, citing the reports of the 1840s, declared social failure. Sarah Josepha Hale used Philadelphia to epitomize the urban North in her novel *Liberia; or, Mr. Peyton's Experiments* (1853), in which she tested a sequence of possible locations and futures for emancipated slaves. Hale combined a romantic racialism about life in the South with an unsparing analysis of northern prejudice and its psychological (and even spatial) effects. As did Hale, Martin Delany concluded that freedom was not possible for Africans in America and recommended departure. Hale advocated colonization in Liberia, while Delany proposed emigration to Central and South America and the West Indies. In the central section of his *Condition, Elevation, Emigration, and Destiny of the Colored People of the United States* (1852), Delany recorded the achievements of the

Philadelphia entrepreneurs, but he maintained that such efforts had been answered by the Fugitive Slave Act of 1850, which reinforced both southern captivity and northern constraints. In the late 1850s, trading public letters with the New York doctor James McCune Smith in *Frederick Douglass' Paper,* William Whipper evaluated Philadelphia since the 1830s, cataloguing economic and political decline and confessing despair.

Entering such debates, Frank J. Webb published in London *The Garies and Their Friends* (1857), a novel about those who strove in Philadelphia and about the anomalies of freedom. In the North, according to Webb, African Americans were neither free nor enslaved, or both free and enslaved, a condition that Saidiya V. Hartman has described as a "burdened individuality," resulting from "the double bind of equality and exclusion."[19] The genres shaped by the Philadelphia experiment—fictional tests, sketches of manners, reports on character, and narratives of violence—intersect in Webb's critique of the post-Independence prospect that African American virtue and discipline would secure legal rights and economic success. Webb alluded to two key violations: the disfranchisement of 1838 and the riots of 1842 and 1849. According to Webb's narrative of achievement and backlash, the experiment has not been conducted in good faith. The political rules have been changed. Economic and social progress has bred resentment, not acceptance. *The Garies* is a novel of complicated manners, framed by an elusive, disorienting narrator. On the levels of character (the strenuous civility of the protagonists), scene (the graphic violence of the riot chapters), and rhetoric (insinuating and overdone), Webb details the social texture of African American Philadelphia: a fragile, labored surface defined by violence. He endorses and mourns his characters, sympathizes with and satirizes them. Rather than yielding to the imperative to demonstrate character and earn acknowledgment, Webb meditates on that demand, its history and consequences, and what he identifies as a temporal pattern of regressive advance.

I finish this chapter with a twist, suggesting how regard for the distinctive literary space of Philadelphia can deepen our understanding of other works. Webb's novel helps to illuminate features of Melville's exacting novella *Benito Cereno* (serialized in 1855, published in book form in 1856): the unexpected social comedy, the emphasis on manners, and the intimacy of violence. We might think of *Benito Cereno* as an inverted and transposed Philadelphia story in which Africans under slavery force their captors to perform their freedom, while they themselves, seeking freedom, perform their servitude. Both Melville and Webb examine junctures of decorum and violence, showing how characters act under extraordinary pressure. Both render overwrought surfaces in meticulous prose. With a curious humor, they reflect on position and interpretation, entangling their readers. Together, for all their differences, *The Garies and Their Friends* and *Benito Cereno* outline the edge between freedom and slavery.

If the example of Melville suggests that Philadelphia narratives can clarify other American writings, the work of John Edgar Wideman shows that the tradition continues to evolve. In a coda, I discuss the shared concerns and different tones of Wideman's short story "Fever" (1989) and his novels *Philadelphia Fire* (1990) and *The Cattle Killing* (1996). In all three, Wideman turns over in his mind the characters and events of the 1793 yellow fever epidemic, and he connects them with a late-twentieth-century urban disaster, the 1985 MOVE bombing. In 1985, Wilson Goode, the first African American mayor of the city, presided over an administration that dropped an explosive device on the home of the radical African American separatist group MOVE and destroyed a neighborhood. Wideman is preoccupied with the links and discrepancies between the two crises and with the figure of the minister Richard Allen, both leader and servant, in the anomalous position of a "free black." In *Philadelphia Fire*, with disbelief, Wideman recounts the persistence of social experiments in the post–Civil Rights America of the 1970s and 1980s. Riffing on the famous grid, he considers the entice-ments of Philadelphia, then and now, for protagonists, authors, and critics. Wide-man, like Webb, reflects over years of Philadelphia writing, recapitulates, and projects.

The literature of Philadelphia between the Constitution and the Civil War suggests that we do not quite know what we mean by "respectability," "bour-geois," and "uplift"—terms that have been used to classify the positions of Afri-can American leaders and writers in the later nineteenth and the twentieth centuries. I am indebted in this book to the efforts of literary critics such as Carla L. Peterson and historians such as Patrick Rael and Eddie S. Glaude Jr. who, revaluing terms and contexts in the North before the Civil War, have ana-lyzed, rather than labeled, the debates. They have qualified the charges of acqui-escence leveled against "respectability": that such approaches imitated "white" middle-class values of industry, frugality, circumspection, and moral purity in a bid for social acceptance, patronizing the masses and surrendering to the domi-nant culture. As Peterson has written, "to criticize [the] ideology of racial uplift as bourgeois or conservative is to misunderstand the dynamics of social change." As we will see, literature in and about Philadelphia by a range of writers, black and white, extends these revisions even further. Such literature unsettles our formulas.[20]

As I have argued in this introduction and will elaborate in the following pages, "Philadelphia" stands for a place, a history, a tradition, a method, and, with some extravagance, a version of the "literary." In "Fever," we will examine the impact of words and the uneasy correspondence between parts and wholes. In "Manners," we will look into the status of characters and readerly identifications. In "Riot," we will test the reach of irony and press the relationships between the local and the generic and between history and aesthetics. In "Freedom," somewhat obsessively, we will see how far close reading can get us and dwell upon the burdens of excess. Assembling a Philadelphia tradition, I make a case for the depth of surfaces and the peculiar substance of forms. We will find literature in unlikely places.

CHAPTER ONE

Fever

While affairs were in this deplorable state, and people at the lowest
ebb of despair, we cannot be astonished at the frightful scenes that
were acted, which seemed to indicate a total dissolution of the
bonds of society in the nearest and dearest connexions. Who,
without horror, can reflect on a husband, married perhaps for
twenty years, deserting his wife in the last agony—a wife unfeelingly
abandoning her husband on his death bed—parents forsaking their
only children—children ungratefully flying from their parents, and
resigning them to chance, often without an enquiry after their
health or safety—masters hurrying off their faithful servants to
Bushhill, even on suspicion of the fever, and that at a time, when,
like Tartarus, it was open to every visitant, but never returned
any—servants abandoning tender and humane masters, who only
wanted a little care to restore them to health and usefulness—who,
I say, can even now think of these things without horror?
—Mathew Carey, A *Short Account of the Malignant Fever*
(Nov. 30th, 1793)

Nature's poisons here collected,

Water, earth, and air infected— O,

what a pity

SUCH A CITY

Was in such a place erected!

—Philip Freneau, "Pestilence" (1793)

In the late summer and early fall of 1793, while thousands were dying in Philadelphia, while most who remained in the city hid in their homes and those who ventured out did so chewing garlic or smoking cigars or pressing vinegar-soaked handkerchiefs to their faces, while European American doctors labored to treat patients and debated causes and cures and speculated about the physiological differences between whites and blacks, while African American volunteers cared for the sick and carted and buried the dead, while there seemed to be, in the words of the publisher Mathew Carey, "a total dissolution of the bonds of society in the nearest and dearest connexions," while all this was going on, *Aedes aegypti*, the female yellow fever mosquito, was silently and invisibly spreading the virus, puncturing the skin of its victims, drawing and mixing blood. Not until 1901 did doctors demonstrate the process by which mosquitoes transmitted the yellow fever virus from infected persons to healthy ones.

During the 1793 epidemic, more than four thousand people died, approximately one tenth of the city's population, almost one fifth of those who remained in the city. One half of Philadelphia households were deserted at the peak of the fever, in September and October. Many government officials and city safety officers fled, as did residents who had the means or the money. The state and municipal governments disintegrated. Public services were dangerously reduced. Responsibility for managing the city fell to the mayor, who remained, to a Citizen's Committee he appointed, and to black and white volunteers. The extremities in Philadelphia were national news. As the physician Benjamin Rush wrote in his *Account of the Fever* (1794), with characteristic fervor, "The United States wept for the distresses of their capital." The medical and social crisis in Philadelphia led to reflections over the character of residents, city, and nation. There was concern about the vulnerability of national boundaries, worry that the fever had spread to the mainland United States from revolutionary Saint Domingue. Authorities debated the sources of the epidemic (miasma or contagion), the proper response (to remain or to flee), and the treatment (stimulants or depleting treatments such as purging and bloodletting). Doctors examined the effects of the disease upon the human body, some arguing that African Americans were immune.[1]

In November 1793, in a surprisingly consequential paragraph in the first two editions of his *Short Account of the Malignant Fever*, the Irish American publisher, editor, and writer Mathew Carey criticized black nurses and carriers of the dead, charging that some had seized opportunities for extortion and theft. In late January 1794, the African American ministers Absalom Jones and Richard Allen responded with their own "Narrative of the Proceedings." They argued that Carey discounted black assistance and exaggerated black misconduct, and they assailed him for leaving the city and profiting from the crisis. Carey responded, defending his actions in a public letter in April and ultimately revising his comments about African American participation in the final edition of the *Short Account*, published in 1830. Between August and November 1793, the physician and signer of the Declaration of Independence Benjamin Rush wrote almost every day to his wife, Julia, who had been sent with their younger children to stay with family in the relative safety of New Jersey. In these letters and in his *Account of the Bilious Remitting Yellow Fever* (1794), Rush dramatized his own performance during the epidemic and reflected upon the course and nature of disease. The lives and texts of these four writers were entangled during the fever months and beyond.

Two of the four men developed symptoms of the fever and survived. Rush suffered continuously, with attacks on September 15, October 5, and, most seriously, October 10. Allen became sick in late September and recovered over several weeks at the impromptu hospital established at Bush Hill, north of the city. Carey, after visiting Bush Hill in mid-September, feared that he had contracted the illness, although he admitted in his *Autobiography* that he may have "only fancied" the effects, which dissipated the next day.[2]

None of the three seemed able to get the events of 1793 out of his system. Rush wrote about them obsessively in letters, medical essays, his *Account*, and his autobiography, *Travels through Life*. Rush wrote *Travels* partly to vindicate his actions during the epidemics of 1793 and 1797 to his children. Allen appended the "Narrative of the Proceedings" to his 1833 *Autobiography*, which was reprinted in at least ten editions. Carey published six versions of his account of the fever, scrupulously revised: one in October of 1793, three in November, another in January 1794, and then a final edition in March 1830. In an April 1794 public letter, continuing to defend his position, Carey reprinted his paragraph on African American service and several paragraphs from Jones and Allen's response. In his *Autobiography*, which appeared toward the end of his life, Carey reproduced a long passage from the *Short Account* about social disintegration in Philadelphia during the epidemic and immediately followed it with a confession of personal vigor: "It is a curious fact, which I leave physiologists to account for, that some of the most happy and tranquil hours of my existence, were passed during the prevalence of this pestilence." Carey suggested that his calm state of mind had to do with release from the burdens of his publishing business and with the fraternity established among the members of the mayor's committee, who "became a band of brothers."[3]

Carey's remarks resonate with Rush's statement to his wife, Julia, in a September 8, 1793, letter: "Through infinite goodness, I am preserved not only in health but in uncommon tranquility of mind." Rush's composure stemmed from the gratitude he had received from the patients whom he heroically served and from his confidence that his disputed treatments for the fever—copious purging and bleeding—had proven successful. In his autobiography, though, written seven years later, after he had been accused of weakening and even killing his patients and charged with arrogance, obstinacy, and profiteering, Rush wrote that "the lapse of years has not much lessened the painful recollection of the events of that melancholy year."[4]

Although 1793 was not the most costly epidemic in Philadelphia's history— the yellow fever epidemic of 1699 or the influenza pandemic of 1918 resulted in greater loss of life, proportionally and absolutely—it certainly has been the most written about by participants, historians, novelists, and poets.[5] Part of the reason may have to do with the city's status as symbol of the American Revolution, temporary capital of the new nation, metropolis, immigration hub, and publishing center. Part of the reason—the part that is the focus of this chapter—has to do with the crucial social "experiment" underway in Philadelphia, in which the capacities of the city's residents and the status of freedom were under scrutiny, and the future of the nation seemed to be at stake.

In 1793, under the pressure of yellow fever, the terms of that experiment were altered. In the chaos of the epidemic, vulnerability was shared. Not only African American ministers and volunteers were under probation but also Anglo sons of the Revolution and Irish entrepreneurs. During the fever, in the laboratory of character that was Philadelphia, roles were reversed, borders traversed, allegiances complicated. Color became prominent: not only white and black but also the symptomatic jaundice of skin and eyes and the purple of hemorrhages. What was inside came out violently in the effects of the fever, which often included bleeding from the nose and mouth and the vomiting of a black substance, and in the corporeal exposure of the many dissections performed in the medical capital of the new nation. Recently, Phillip Lapsansky, Julia Stern, Philip Gould, and Joanna Brooks have recognized the importance of the exchange between Carey and Jones and Allen for the development of an early national literature.[6] Yet those who have commented on the dispute have tended to choose sides, arguing either that Carey was balanced in his characterizations and Jones and Allen overreacted (as some earlier historians did) or that Jones and Allen exposed Carey's racism (as recent literary critics have done). The stances are not so simple, and the context is wider than has been acknowledged. Bound by the fever, Carey, Jones, Allen, and Rush debate issues of partiality, identification, history, narrative, and conduct. They prepare the literary terrain for Charles Brockden Brown's fictions about the yellow fever, especially his novel *Arthur Mervyn* (1799–1800), with which this chapter ends. Brown turns his novel into a metonymy of the epidemic. Its redundant parts are linked in the relationship of diagnosis and false racial cure. His title protagonist embodies both the charges leveled against African Americans and the heroic services they rendered. He flaunts both Rush's exalted sense of his achievements and the failings arraigned by his critics.

In these stories, "Philadelphia" is imagined under threat and rupture. Character is exposed. These stories about race and performance during 1793 set the terms for a volatile tradition of writing about freedom in the United States.

Mathew Carey, Absalom Jones, Richard Allen, and the Color of Fever

Born in Dublin in 1760, Mathew Carey fled to America in 1784 to avoid prosecution for his writings in favor of Irish Catholics and against the British government. Arriving in Philadelphia with little money, he, like Benjamin Franklin, parlayed his political contacts to advance his publishing business. In the late 1780s and early 1790s, with his Irish publishing experience as a model, Carey helped to create a national American audience by establishing distribution networks and widely marketing his periodicals *Columbian Magazine* and *American Museum*. His accounts of the 1793 yellow fever were popular across the country and in Europe. The first version was a twelve-page pamphlet titled "A Desultory Account," published on October 16, 1793, at the peak of the epidemic. The "Desultory Account" set the pattern for the series: remarks on the origin of the fever; reports on its development; criticism of the measures taken by neighboring states to protect themselves from Philadelphia's residents; speculation about African American conduct; insistence that readers be given an accurate, rather than exaggerated, picture of how the crisis was affecting the city; praise of the mayor's committee; lament over the disputes among medical professionals; and a list of the dead.[7]

In the "Desultory Account" and in the expanded *Accounts of the Malignant Fever*, issued in 1793 and 1794, Carey expressed concern with "the magnifying tongue of rumour." He deplored the corrosive effects of false stories on Philadelphia's reputation, citizens, and economy. Carey saw his own texts as antidotes to such unhealthy narratives. He would describe "the real state of our city" and thus restrain damaging speculations.[8] Yet this therapeutic goal begins to falter in the first edition of the *Short Account*, published on November 14, which includes the statement on African American conduct that will proliferate uncontrollably. The difficulty (shared by Carey, Rush, and the Philadelphia medical community) has to do with a mistaken sense of who was and was not susceptible to the yellow fever. In the first two editions, immediately after his paragraph on African American nurses and carriers of the dead, as if justifying his criticism of those who took advantage when they should have served gratefully, Carey quoted a Dr. Lining. Analyzing the yellow fever in South Carolina, Dr. Lining had argued that African Americans were immune: "'There is something very singular in the constitution of the negroes . . . which renders them not liable to this fever'" (I, 22:77–78). Carey reported that African Americans in Philadelphia did indeed contract the fever, but he added that "the number seized with it was not great; and, as I am informed by an eminent doctor, 'it yielded to the power of medicine in them more readily than in the whites'" (I, 2:78).

The "eminent doctor" was Benjamin Rush, whose influence—and also, as we shall see, absence of influence—on Carey's paragraph was eventful. Carey probably found his extract from Dr. Lining in the *American Daily Advertiser,* where Rush had published it on September 3. He received his comparative diagnosis of the fever from Rush in a letter dated October 29. Apparently, Rush was writing in response to a request from Carey for information and advice that he could use in expanding the "Desultory Account" of October 16 into the *Short Account* of November 14. Rush had publicized the Lining quote as part of a public assurance to white Philadelphians that employing blacks as attendants would be safe and wise. He had explained to African Americans in Philadelphia that "a noble opportunity [was] now put into their hands, of manifesting their gratitude to the inhabitants of that city which first planned their emancipation from slavery, and who have since afforded them so much protection and support, as to place them, in point of civil and religious privileges, upon a footing with themselves."[9]

Rush had made a similar argument about service, also invoking Lining, in a letter to Richard Allen in early September. Jones and Allen themselves evoked an implicit social contract with advance in status hinging on the continued demonstration of character, in the advertisements they placed for nurses and buriers. In their "Narrative of the Proceedings," however, Jones and Allen made clear that they did not share the "privileges" of citizens, although they hoped future generations of Africans in America would. The two ministers extended their public offers of assistance after a September 5 meeting of their Free African Society, the first African American benevolent organization in the United States, which they had formed in 1787. They privately had volunteered their services to Philadelphia's Mayor Clarkson on September 6.[10]

The debate over vulnerability to the yellow fever in 1793—over singular or shared human constitutions—was a harbinger of the ethnological debates of the 1830s, 1840s, and 1850s, when Philadelphia became the center of the "American school" of racial science. Rush soon realized his error in spreading Lining's claim of black immunity. As he acknowledged in his *Account:* "It was not long after these worthy Africans undertook the execution of their humane offer of services to the sick, before I was convinced I had been mistaken. They took the disease, in common with the white people, and many of them died with it. . . . A large number of them were my patients. The disease was lighter in them, than in white people" (97). Rush's diction suggests some of the ironies circulating during the fever. Service could be fatal. The disease might be seen not only as lighter in blacks but also as lightening. Typically, Rush is more graphic in his letters to his wife, Julia, moving from "No one of them has died with it, and I suspect none have been affected" (September 6) to "The Negroes are everywhere submitting to the disorder. Richard Allen, who has led their van, is very ill. If the disorder should continue to spread among them, then will the measure of our sufferings be full" (September 26).[11]

Modern medical historians argue that African Americans in Philadelphia did die in smaller numbers, corresponding to their populations, than white residents. They conjecture that those who had migrated from the southern United States, the West Indies, or Africa previously had been exposed and had developed some resistance. In 1793, the need for aid was so urgent and the belief that African Americans seemed constitutionally suited for service was so deeply held that, even as the number of casualties mounted during the weeks of September and October, civic authorities did not reconsider their summons. The hypothesis of black immunity persisted after the epidemic, not only among European American doctors but also among at least one African American chronicler, Benjamin Banneker, despite the conspicuous evidence of injury.[12]

African Americans continued to be associated with the yellow fever, not only geographically and epidemiologically but also in terms of history, literature, and skin. The fever may have contributed to the defeat of the French during the revolution in Saint Domingue. Fever and race are yoked across nineteenth- and twentieth-century American fiction, in Brockden Brown's *Arthur Mervyn* (1799–1800), Harriet Wilson's *Our Nig* (1859), Frank J. Webb's *The Garies and Their Friends* (1857), Frances E. W. Harper's *Iola Leroy* (1892), William Faulkner's *Absalom, Absalom!* (1936), and John Edgar Wideman's "Fever" (1989) and *The Cattle Killing*

(1996). The enduring association may have to do with the resonant events of 1793 and also with the figurative links between fever, color, and exposure. These links are made literal by Rush in his misguided speculation in a 1799 treatise that black skin color might result from a disease such as leprosy. Meant, as he explained in a letter to Thomas Jefferson, to convince readers to treat African Americans with "humanity and justice" (as well as to reinforce the taboos against miscegenation), Rush's argument quarantined sympathy and pathologized environmental arguments about human variation. Such a diagnosis contrasted with the intimate identifications he expressed during the fever months. It seems to be a perverse act of benevolence, reversing the exemption from disease that he had advertised in 1793. Frederick Douglass parodied the link between black skin and yellow fever in his essay "Colorphobia in New York!" (1849). Equating fever and racism, Douglass identified a new population of sufferers. He expressed his sympathy for the unfortunate white victims of "colorphobia," a perceptual disease which he described as "malignant," an "epidemic," and a "strange plague." Outlining the physical and mental symptoms of this fever, Douglass advised that the infected be treated with ridicule and indignation.[13]

In 1793, the narrative fever intensified with one small, unstable paragraph. In the first edition of *A Short Account of the Malignant Fever*, published on November 14, Mathew Carey wrote the following:

> At an early stage of the disorder, the elders of the African church met, and offered their services to the mayor, to procure nurses for the sick, and to assist in burying the dead. Their offers were accepted; and Absalom Jones and Richard Allen undertook the former department, that of furnishing nurses, and William Gray, the latter—the interment of the dead. The great demand for nurses offered an opportunity for imposition, which was eagerly seized by some of the vilest of the blacks. They extorted two, three, four, and even five dollars a night for attendance, which would have been well paid by a single dollar. Some of them were even detected in plundering the houses of the sick. But it is wrong to cast a censure on the whole for this sort of conduct, as many people have done. The services of Jones, Allen, and Gray, and others of their colour, have been very great, and demand public gratitude. (I, 2:76–78)

This is the paragraph, reprinted in the second edition of *A Short Account*, to which Jones and Allen respond with measured fury in January 1794 and which goads John Edgar Wideman's fiction in the late twentieth century.

Both Jones and Allen were born into slavery, Jones in Delaware in 1746 and Allen in Philadelphia in 1760. Allen was sold to a farmer in Delaware. Both were permitted by their masters to purchase their freedom with the income from their labor. In 1792, after being asked to move to segregated pews during prayers at St. George's Methodist Episcopal Church, where they both served as lay preachers, Jones and Allen led their African American congregants out of the church. Supported by Benjamin Rush, they began efforts to establish the first independent African church in the United States. Along with William Gray, Jones and Allen in 1793 organized Philadelphia's black residents to serve during the crisis: as nurses who visited the sick at home or staffed the hospital at Bush Hill, as carters and buriers of the dead, and as bleeders and purgers according to Rush's directions. As John Edgar Wideman has remarked, the fever dissolved and refigured boundaries: "people who would never dream of having a black person enter their front door, let alone their bedroom, were now dependent on a black person who was wielding a knife and who entered the bedroom and opened a vein."[14]

Jones and Allen shared with Carey a desire to "declare facts as they really were" ("Narrative of the Proceedings," 3) and to offer a textual remedy for pernicious stories, but they saw Carey's Short Accounts as part of the problem. They argued that, in seeking to heal the city, he had inflicted a new wound. He had disseminated nationally a slander about African American character that had been restricted to the precincts of Philadelphia. Jones and Allen make clear that Carey had not been the first to accuse black nurses and carters of profiting from disaster: "We feel ourselves sensibly aggrieved by the censorious epithets of many" (5). Carey had indicated as much in his own caveat: "it is wrong to cast a censure on the whole for this sort of conduct, as many people have done" (I, 2:77). Carey's airing of the charge impelled Jones and Allen to print. In safeguarding some of Philadelphia's citizens, they asserted, he stigmatized others.

Although Jones and Allen did not reproduce Carey's words on African American conduct—and one suspects this was deliberate, a refusal to give them further currency—his paragraph was at the center of their "Narrative of the Proceedings of the Black People, during the Late Awful Calamity in Philadelphia in the Year 1793: and a Refutation of Some Censures, Thrown upon Them in Some Late Publications," brought out at their own expense in January 1794. They argue that African Americans in Philadelphia responded to public "solicitation" and to Dr. Rush's "call" for help at the risk of their lives, without seeking fee or reward (3, 5). The two ministers select their words very carefully throughout the "Narrative." Here they suggest an initial stage of appeal that Carey had omitted. They assert that black suffering was great during the epidemic, but unknown to most whites. They accuse Carey of understating service, magnifying abuse, and failing to understand the contexts in which the events and his words acquired meaning. They strive to make visible the aspects of the fever they insist he has overlooked.

A few pages into their "Narrative," the two ministers display and resist the pressure of Carey's words:

> We feel ourselves hurt most by a partial, censorious paragraph, in Mr. Carey's second edition, of his account of the sickness, &c. in Philadelphia . . . where he asperses the blacks alone, for having taken advantage of the distressed situation of the people. . . . Had Mr. Carey been solicited to such an undertaking, for hire, *Query,* "what would *he* have demanded?" but Mr. Carey, although chosen a member of that band of worthies who have so eminently distinguished themselves by their labours, for the relief of the sick and the helpless—yet, quickly after his election, left them to struggle with their arduous and hazardous task, by leaving the city. It is true Mr. Carey was no hireling, and had a right to flee, and upon his return, to plead the cause of those who fled; yet, we think, he was wrong in giving so partial and injurious an account of the black nurses; if they have taken advantage of the public distress? Is it any more than he hath done of its desire for information. We believe he has made more money by the sale of his "scraps" than a dozen of the greatest extortioners among the black nurses. . . . That there were some few black people guilty of plundering the distressed, we acknowledge; but in that they only are pointed out, and made mention of, we esteem partial and injurious; we know as many whites were guilty of it; but this is looked over, while the blacks are held up to censure.—Is it a greater crime for a black to pilfer, than for a white to privateer? (6–7)

Jones and Allen repeatedly use the word "partial" to characterize Carey's account. Carey is partial in celebrating the heroism of white but not black citizens. They juxtapose many scenes in which poor blacks display their "humanity" and "sensibility" with those in which some whites gouge prices, steal possessions from the sick, and abandon their responsibilities (8, 16, 9–10, 15–16). Jones and Allen seek to modify Carey's alignments of character with color. Reworking Carey's signature paragraphs about the "total dissolution of the bonds of society in the nearest and dearest connexions," they describe the efforts of African American spouses, parents, children, nurses, and carriers of the dead to reconstitute these bonds during the crisis. Jones and Allen's African American "ministers"—clergymen such as themselves but also an array of residents who offer support during the fever—stand in implicit contrast to Carey's lone representatives: "The corpses of the most respectable citizens, even of those who did not die of the epidemic, were carried to the grave, on the shafts of a chair, the horse driven by a negro, unattended by a friend or a relation, and without any sort of ceremony. . . . Many men of affluent fortunes, who have given daily employment and sustenance to hundreds, have been abandoned to the care of a negro" (*Short Account,* 3:33, 34–35).

Often in fever narratives, African American figures were linked with neglect, apprehension, and death. In his *Account of the Bilious Remitting Yellow Fever*, Rush gave such figures the status of omens or knells: "A black man, leading or driving a horse, with a corpse on a pair of chair wheels, with now and then half a dozen relations or friends following at a distance from it, met the eye in most of the streets of the city at every hour of the day, while the noise of the same wheels passing slowly over the pavements, kept alive anguish and fear in the sick and well, every hour of the night." Rush asks a rhetorical question: "What medicine could act upon a patient who awoke in the night, and saw through the broken and faint light of a candle, no human creature, but a black nurse, perhaps asleep in a distant corner of the room, and who heard no noise, but that of a hearse conveying, perhaps, a neighbor or friend, to the grave?" In this scene, it is as though the glimpse and the sound—again a coupling of blackness and reverberation—themselves constituted symptoms of a fever, which no medicine could palliate. "Black nurse" is separated from "human creature" and rhymed with "hearse." Rush's "but" ("no human creature, but a black nurse") implies an uneasy connection between the terms.[15]

These figures of alienation in Rush's *Account* are markedly different from the familial ascriptions in his letters to Julia. On October 15, for example, during his most severe attack of the yellow fever, Rush describes his gratitude for the care given him by his servant Marcus (never named in the *Account*), who has slept in his room and fed him (715–16). Like Mathew Carey's proliferating editions, Rush's stories of the fever unfold over time in several forms: medical history, personal narrative, and letters. The most revealing features often lie in the turns from one form to another. The differences between the African American figures in Rush's *Account* and his letters may have to do with his sense of private versus public discourse and with the differences between writing in the midst of the fever, when Rush's letters are charged with ardor and possibility, and writing in more clinical retrospection. The figurative pattern in the *Account* also may suggest the currency of such images during and after the fever, a publicity that Carey, intentionally or not, encouraged. Such figures continue to circulate at the end of the decade, despite Jones and Allen's efforts to dispel them, in Charles Brockden Brown's novel of 1793, *Arthur Mervyn*.

According to Jones and Allen, Carey is partial in elevating a few blacks but condemning the mass. His "compliment" to themselves and to William Gray, they suggest, is complicated: "By naming us, he leaves these others, in the hazardous state of being classed with those who are called 'the vilest'" (11). In his paragraph, Carey had repeated but also altered the information he received in Rush's letter of October 29. Rush offered both praise and blame. When Rush criticized black nurses ("Many . . . it is true were ignorant, and some of them were negligent"), he immediately qualified the complaint: "but many of them did their duty to the sick, with a degree of patience and tenderness that did them great credit." He thus avoided distinguishing between individuals and the group, and he made no mention of black attendants demanding exorbitant fees. He lauded Gray and Allen ("In procuring nurses for the sick, [they] were indefatigable, often sacrificing for that purpose whole nights of sleep without the least compensation"), Allen ("extremely useful in performing the mournful duties which were connected with burying the dead"), and Allen and Jones (for administering Rush's cherished treatments—bleeding and purging—and "recover[ing] between two and three hundred people"). Jones and Allen object to what they perceive as Carey's specifying of them as exceptions to the "vilest of the blacks."[16]

Carey, they assert, is partial also in criticizing those who remained in the city, while he himself left. So precise about dates elsewhere in the "Narrative," Jones and Allen here strategically omit mentioning any specific interval and imply that Carey quit the city for a prolonged time in order to safeguard himself and to avoid serving on the citizen's committee. In his April 1794 "Address to the Public," Carey insists that, although he did leave for the last two weeks in September to settle outstanding business in Maryland and Virginia, he returned "about the beginning of October," when the ravages of the fever were even greater. Carey's supposed desertion is the weakest of Jones and Allen's retorts. It registers their anger at his insinuations about those who remained in the city.[17]

Jones and Allen protest that Carey singles out blacks for criticism of advantages taken by both blacks and whites. He does not acknowledge that market forces were largely responsible for the prices paid to nurses. The demand was great and the supply small, and so those in need offered higher prices. Inflation, not racial predilection, led to the exorbitant fees.[18] Jones and Allen turn Carey's scenario and syntax against him. The great demand for nurses, they argue, led many of the most prominent whites to seize the opportunity for imposing on poor blacks—the "kind of assurance" that they were unlikely to be infected or die ("Narrative of the Proceedings," 3)—to secure their assistance: "Thus were our services *extorted at the peril of our lives,* yet you accuse us of extorting *a little money from you*" (13). The idea of "service" is key here. Black labor during the fever opened possibilities for new kinds of movement and access. Yet Carey and others seemed to be suggesting that events in the fall of 1793 confirmed beliefs about African American disqualification. Fueling the exchange is the tenuous line between service and slavery: Jones and Allen's memory of their own bondage, subordinated labor in northern cities, and larger debates over emancipation.

Carey is partial, they insist, because he does not recognize or does not acknowledge the momentous social and political contexts in which he prints his words. In satisfying the public's "desire for information," he also has contributed to its prejudices (7). As Jones and Allen put it, "The bad consequences many of our colour apprehend from a partial relation of our conduct are, that it will prejudice the minds of the people in general against us . . . for we conceive, and experience proves it, that an ill name is easier given than taken away. We have many unprovoked enemies, who begrudge us the liberty we enjoy, and are glad to hear of any complaint against our colour" (8, 11). In a decade of deliberation over the rights and capacities of African Americans to participate in the new nation, "information" about racial conduct was an urgent commodity, and the consequences of "partiality" could be especially "injurious." Jones and Allen juxtapose the crimes of "pilfering" and "privateering": the taking of a few extra dollars for dangerous work and the grand profits acquired by marketing a scarce item—precious information—during the calamity. Alluding to the lawful pirates who had been involved in the international slave trade since the seventeenth century, the term "privateering" expands their comparison to include local and systemic violations: the extortion of money and the appropriation of lives.[19]

Jones and Allen press Carey relentlessly because, for them, his paragraph epitomizes the skewing of debate about community and polity. Carey's "partialities"—stressing European American fortitude and distress, isolating African American criminality, splitting rather than joining residents in crisis, offering sensational details without an appreciation of their political consequence—fortify a racial common sense against which they struggle. Their refrain "partial" may evoke the divisions in Article I, section 2, of the U.S. Constitution, the "all other persons" (African Americans under slavery) who were to be considered "three-fifths" of a person for representation and taxation. Insisting that Carey acknowledge the contexts and impact of his terms and refusing fractions, Jones and Allen contribute to a wider logomachy.

In his April 1794 public letter, Carey defends himself against a writer with the pseudonym "Argus" who charged that he had fled Philadelphia after his election to the mayor's committee, returning only when censured, and that he balked at serving the poor. Carey also responds acridly to Jones and Allen. He portrays the African American ministers as "indecent, unjust, and ungrateful" (5). He uses the tools of his trade to reprint the last few sentences of his paragraph from the *Short Account* with strategic capitals and italics: "BUT IT IS UNJUST TO CAST A CENSURE ON THE WHOLE, FOR THIS SORT OF CONDUCT, AS MANY PEOPLE HAVE DONE. *The services of Jones, Allen, and Gray, and others of their colour, have been very great, and* DEMAND PUBLIC GRATITUDE." Carey accurately draws attention to his cautions against judging a group on the basis of individual conduct and to his praise of black service. He employs his printed characters to defend his own character.[20]

Yet Jones and Allen have read Carey with different emphases and with frames of reference wider than the single page. Their point, made through a suggested pun of their own, is both technological and ideological. They argue that print—repeating words, circulating innuendo, propagating stories—can stamp human character. The debate between Carey and Jones and Allen is a debate about emphasis, exclusion, context, and agency. It is a debate about capitalizing, italicizing, and naming. Given Carey's own explicit motive for distributing his accounts of the fever—to counter a "proneness to terrific narration" that was destructive to individuals and to the city (*Short Account*, 3:56)—Jones and Allen may have felt especially frustrated by his portraits of African American conduct.

In his April rejoinder, Carey contends that the language he had used in his paragraph was that of an "advocate," rather than an "enemy": "Does this deserve railing or reproach? Is it honourable for Jones and Allen to repay evil for good?" And Carey's annoyance is understandable, even though critics attempt to dismiss it or explain it away. As Phillip Lapsansky has observed, Carey probably believed that he had written as a supporter, or at least as a balanced observer, as the political reformer he was, antislavery and pro-Irish. Of course, these two stances do not preclude, and may even help to explain, his portrayals in the *Short Account*, given the competition for jobs and status among Philadelphia's working-class African Americans and Irish in the late eighteenth century. Carey's vehement initial resistance to Jones and Allen also may have resulted from his own sense of embattled marginality. During his early years in Philadelphia, he, an Irish Catholic, had been viciously attacked.[21]

Carey is in some ways reminiscent of Melville's Captain Delano in the novella *Benito Cereno* (1855), who himself has been too swiftly dismissed by his critics. For both, their partiality is more complicated than the words that have been used to label it: "racism" or "liberalism." Melville examines how his character, his readers, and, uncannily, his modern critics manage not to see what is before them, how they look through jaundiced eyes and are tempted to incomplete judgments. As Carey earnestly writes, defending the *Short Account* in his April letter: "I thought it a duty I owed the city in which I lived, and indeed to the united states generally, to give a candid and full statement of affairs as they really stood, without bias or partiality" (3). This kind of insistence on partial impartiality fascinates Melville. As we shall see, Mathew Carey, unlike Captain Delano, changes his mind.

In the last part of their "Narrative," Jones and Allen convey the precarious contexts in which they write. In five sections that follow their story, they meticulously address different audiences.

In a letter to "Mathew Clarkson, Esq., Mayor of the City of Philadelphia," Jones and Allen respectfully deny that they had stolen the beds of the deceased. They explain that they had buried or burned them to avoid further infection. They ask the mayor for a "certificate of your approbation of our conduct" and emphasize that he had urged them to persevere during the epidemic despite the risk and their despair. Following their letter to Clarkson, they print a statement from the mayor praising the "diligence, attention and decency of deportment" of Jones and Allen and those employed by them (18–19).

With irony and anger, they deliver "An Address to those who keep Slaves, and approve the Practice." They make explicit the comparison between the small crimes during the fall of 1793 in Philadelphia and the entrenched national practice of chattel slavery. They contend that black inferiority is imposed through systems of social oppression and false representation. Invoking the Philadelphia setting, they argue that new circumstances will give the lie to incapacity: "We believe if you would try the experiment of taking a few black children, and cultivate their minds with the same care, and let them have the same prospect in view, as to living in the world, as you would wish for your own children, you would find upon the trial, they were not inferior in mental endowments" (19–20). With Jesus as a model, they forgive their oppressors, as they wish to be forgiven for their sins. Yet this forgiveness does not connote assent: "were we to attempt to plead with our masters, it would be deemed insolence, for which cause they appear as contented as they can in your sight, but the dreadful insurrections they have made, when opportunity has offered, is enough to convince a reasonable man, that great uneasiness and not contentment, is the inhabitant of their hearts" (21). The pronoun shifts here—the "we" of Jones and Allen who are imagined pleading with their masters, the "they" who are not content in slavery, the "you" who hold slaves or support the system—link free and enslaved, North and South, present and past, in a syntax of warning. They who "appear as contented as they can in your sight" would seem to apply to Jones and Allen, as well as to those in bondage.[22]

"To the People of Colour" in slavery, Jones and Allen express sympathy. They remind them that they themselves had been captives, and they counsel patience and reliance upon God. "To the People of Colour" in the free states, they advise restraint. They describe the calculus of obligation to each other, to those in slavery, and to their enemies, as well as their friends. They stress that the cause of freedom depends on their bearing.

In "A Short Address to the Friends of Him Who Hath No Helper," they evince to sympathetic white friends "an inexpressible gratitude." Jones and Allen thank such readers for their support in liberating Africans in America. They value their empathy: the ability to "feel our afflictions" and "sympathize with us in the heart-rending distress," their "tear of sensibility" and "righteous indignation" (23).

Jones and Allen's concluding addresses underscore the fact that their entire text serves as a demonstration of character and a testament of their own sensibility. The divided addresses indicate the fractured and charged discursive terrain they must negotiate: the disparate audiences; the personal, collective, and national stakes; the pressures on each sentence and word. Many of the fever texts, including Carey's *Accounts*, Rush's letters, and Jones and Allen's "Narrative of the Proceedings," surpass their boundaries. Their stories cannot be contained by the usual forms. This excess takes a particular shape, fused with an urgent decorum, in the addresses that extend beyond Jones and Allen's narrative.

Jones and Allen negotiate stance and limit. Their mixture of bitterness and entreaty, sense of discursive probation, riven audiences, high rhetorical stakes, and concern with black elevation all will be echoed in the mid-nineteenth-century writings of Frederick Douglass, Harriet Jacobs, and Frank J. Webb and the later nineteenth-century fiction of Frances Harper and Charles Chesnutt. Some who have written about the "Narrative of the Proceedings"—and many of the critics of what has come to be known as the tradition of African American "uplift"— tend to fault, or at least express discomfort with, what is perceived as an acceptance of the master's capitalist, bourgeois, or sentimental terms. Such critics see capitulation and tainted imitation. Often these appraisals are based on a loaded choice between words and acts, resistance and supplication, the pure and the diluted. Sometimes the options are critically rehabilitated by a spatial revelation: behind the mask of deference lies the authentic demand. These choices seem false. They are inattentive to history, detail, and the difference made by the past. Jones and Allen's "Narrative of the Proceedings"—literary and political, terms that for them are reciprocal rather than antagonistic—may help us to rethink the literature of "respectability."[23]

Ministers and Criminals: Richard Allen, John Joyce, and Peter Matthias

In an effort to understand Jones and Allen's "Narrative," we might wish to consider its relation to a contemporary genre with which it bears surprising resemblances: the African American criminal confession. Jones and Allen's text draws on various genres: plague narrative, sentimental narrative, sermon, petition (collective written appeals from African Americans to the state legislature date back

in Pennsylvania to at least 1781 and continue throughout the nineteenth century), protest pamphlet (Jones and Allen's is considered the first in a long series),
and black idealist history (the "Narrative" was a model for writers who defended
the race against misrepresentation and provided alternative stories).[24]

Criminal narratives were a subset of the gallows literature popular in America
and England in the eighteenth century. Issued as broadsides or pamphlets, they
sometimes contained execution sermons, last words, and poems by or about the
executed criminal. With the explicit goal of disciplining their audiences, criminal
narratives, like all literature that exposes transgressive behavior in order to condemn it, risked their displays. Although ministers and judges labored to control
responses (publishers, as time went on, tried less hard), there was no guarantee
that the wrong lessons might not be drawn. These texts often were marked by a
tension within the narrative or among the documents: a rhetorical struggle
between the accused and his or her amanuensis, or the ideological strain of details
that did not rest easily in their interpretive frames. In the case of black criminals,
authorities sometimes implied that merely to be an African in America was to
have violated the law. Criminal narratives share with Jones and Allen's "Narrative
of the Proceedings" an association between blackness and criminality, split
addresses, a discursive probation, and a verbal intricacy.[25]

"Sketches of the Life of Joseph Mountain" (1790) reads like an inverted
Philadelphia experiment, in which the achievements of character are scandalous,
and invigorating. After passing the first seventeen years of his life as a servant in
a Philadelphia household, Mountain sailed for London and began a fifteen-year
career as a renowned European thief and highwayman. He reveled in his status.
Returning to North America, he was apprehended in Connecticut for stealing
five dollars and then whipped repeatedly. He was mortified at the affront to his
dignity and fame. On his way to New York, he meets and "wantonly injures" an
"innocent girl." Mountain admits (or admits through his amanuensis, probably
the justice David Daggett) doing wrong, but he balks at the charge of rape. The
editor alludes to the invasive rhetoric of Mountain's "confession": "the facts
related were taken from the mouth of the culprit." Mountain's confession pivots
on questions of who takes what from whom, and why. In the most ambiguous
moment in the text, he is presented as dwelling on his compulsion to linger at the
scene of his offense:

When her cries had brought to her assistance some neighbouring people, I still
continued my barbarity, by insulting her in her distress, boasting of the fact, and
glorying in my iniquity. Upon reflection, I am often surprized that I did not
attempt my escape; opportunity to effect it frequently presented before I was

apprehended. Yet, by some unaccountable fatality, I loitered unconcerned, as tho'
my conduct would bear strictest scrutiny. The counsel of heaven determined that
such a prodigy in vice should no longer infest society. (300)

This passage is riddled with questions. What is the status of the "I" here, mediated
through Daggett? What is the relationship between Mountain's own humiliation
and his abuse of his victim? Why does he remain? To relish his dominance and
provoke his punishment, as he implies, but also it seems that he stays for reasons of
pride, even dignity—"as tho' my conduct would bear the strictest scrutiny"—as
though there were a system within which his actions might seem justified, a system
as yet "unaccountable" except for its "fatality." The last line of the quoted passage,
shifting to the diction of emphatic judgment ("counsel of heaven," "prodigy in
vice," "should no longer infest society"), seems molded by the authority of the legal
amanuensis. The shift lends credibility to the surprise and the hint of twisted rectitude as indicating the attitudes of Mountain. The discourse of judgment asserts
itself as though to inoculate readers against the preceding sentence and its suggestions about Mountain's conduct being somehow appropriate or at least understandable. The verbal tensions here raise the possibility, in this heavily mediated text, that
some words may still abide in the mouth of the culprit.[26]

Like Jones and Allen's "Narrative," the "Address of Abraham Johnstone," published in Philadelphia in 1797, explicitly directs its rhetoric to different audiences: Johnstone's confession addressed "To the People of Colour," his dying
words to "Good People All," and a letter to his wife, Sarah. Like Jones and Allen
(and given this and other similarities, it seems plausible that he was influenced by
their "Narrative"), Johnstone refutes charges and also meditates on testimony:

> I most earnestly exhort and pray you ["the People of Colour"], to be upright, and
> circumspect in your conduct . . . a combination of circumstances that at this juncture
> of time concur[s] to make it of importance to our colour for my unfortunate unhappy
> fate however unmerited or undeserved, may by some ungenerous and illiberal minded
> persons, but particularly by those who oppose the emancipation of those of our
> brethren who as yet are in slavery, be made a handle of in order to throw a shade over
> or cast a general reflection on all those of our colour, and the keen shafts of prejudice
> be launched against us by the most active and virulent malevolence.

Alone among the black criminal narrators, Johnstone writes with apparently minimal interference, proclaims his innocence, and uses his conviction to indict his
accusers. A brief preface, referring to Johnstone in the third person, explains that,
with the following documents, readers "may be enabled to form an opinion of
the true character, and guilt of the man." The editor invites readers to sit in

judgment, strongly implying that an injustice has been done. In preface and texts, Johnstone's "Address" decries capital punishment and especially perjury, a legal form of what Jones and Allen termed Mathew Carey's "injurious account." The preface asserts that Johnstone offers "a singularly uncommon and peculiar case as there was not positive evidence to the act." In his "Address to the People of Colour," Johnstone impugns the testimony under oath that has condemned him for the murder of Thomas Read, another black man, in New Jersey.[27]

Johnstone links perjury to pestilence, as he imagines the fate of his accuser: "Perjury, like poison, most certainly destroys the guilty taker . . . instead of health, rottenness will seize his bones, every chronic disease, and every fierce malady will afflict him . . . and sickness, sorrows, and all the catalogues of human plagues will sink him to the grave" (25). According to Johnstone, false stories infect and consume. Born in Delaware, released from slavery after his master's death, and in danger of being reenslaved while working as an indentured servant, Johnstone fled to New Jersey. Once there, he contracted the flux—"(it being the time of the Philadelphia sickness) . . . people feared that it was the fever I had gotten"—and suffered prejudice. "Many reports circulated to [his] disadvantage" about his infection and his character (he was repeatedly suspected of theft), and he found it difficult to secure lodgings (34–36).

The truth, Johnstone maintains, is that he did not commit the crime. He is a victim of his position. He has been framed because of the property he held, his success in cultivating it, and the envy and hatred generated by this success. Resisting the equation of achievement with offense and the presumption of his guilt, he insists that "some whites (with all due deference to them) [are] capable of being equally as depraved and more generally so than blacks or people of colour" (7). Having been sentenced, Johnstone admonishes. Like Jones and Allen, he deliberates on race and transgression.

As the most eminent African American clergyman in Philadelphia in the late eighteenth and early nineteenth centuries, Richard Allen preached execution sermons for the city's black prisoners. In 1808, Allen himself compiled two criminal narratives, "The Confession of John Joyce" and "The Confession of Peter Matthias," which included his own sermon and detailed the trial and execution of two African American men in their mid-twenties. Joyce and Matthias had been convicted of murdering Sarah Cross, a white shopkeeper and widow about fifty years old, and stealing her money and property. Allen occupied all sides of the law. In 1793, he had felt himself tainted by charges of extortion and malpractice leveled by Mathew Carey and others. In 1808, he had been detained as a fugitive slave; although technically free, he was threatened with return to bondage. As a minister, he preached to those the law had condemned.[28]

Both of Allen's "Confessions" include an "Address to the Public, and People of Colour" (Allen's sermon), the "Substance of the Trial" (excerpted from a newspaper report), the "Address of Chief Justice Tilghman, on Their Condemnation," and supplementary paragraphs describing the prisoner's finally contented trip to the gallows. The separate editions contain the different confessions of Joyce and Matthias, as told to Allen. There is a remarkable aspect to the "Confessions," taken together. Woven in the texture of preacherly warning, journalistic indictment, judicial rebuke, and defendants' admission is the enigmatic figure of Peter Matthias. Despite the sealed coffin engraved at the top of the Matthias document, in visual parallel with the word "CONFESSION," both Matthias and Joyce insist that Matthias was not present during the murder, contradicting the testimony of a young witness, the thirteen- or fourteen-year-old Anne Messinger. Her account, in which, through a keyhole, she witnessed Joyce strangle Cross, includes the parataxis that "Peter was in the room with Joyce" after the murder and leaves Matthias's role unclear. Although Judge Tilghman maintains in his "Address" that both men received an "impartial trial," the newspaper article reports that Benjamin Rush delivered a ninety-minute speech against the death penalty and that the judge had instructed the jury that he believed this was a case of murder in the first degree and that "the extension of mercy did not fall within their province" (419).[29]

As amanuensis, Allen lets stand Joyce's repeated assertions of Peter's innocence and the truth of both confessions in all their parts. Allen also records, in a footnote to Joyce's confession, a hint that Joyce was pressured by the city's mayor to implicate Matthias: "IT is to be remarked, that after the Prisoner had given his confession, he was visited by the Mayor, who closely interrogated him as to the guilt of his fellow prisoner." Allen reports that Joyce twice concedes to the mayor that Peter was present at the murder, but as soon as the mayor leaves, he retracts his statements and begs the Lord's forgiveness.[30] Like Joyce, Matthias insists that he had left the house and returned to find that Joyce had killed Mrs. Cross. The discrepancy between confession and verdict is highlighted by Allen's reprinting the same documents in the Joyce and Matthias texts: sermon, trial account, judge's censure, and final hours of the criminal. Matthias's "confession"—that is, his refusal to confess—marks the only salient difference. He admits not to murder but to spending a misguided evening with the inebriated Joyce, when he should have been playing his violin at Jenny Miller's in Pine Alley. Both Joyce's and Matthias's avowals support Matthias's innocence. Both are framed by his condemnation.

In his "Address to the Public, and People of Colour," reprinted twice, Allen exhorts his readers to avoid drunkenness, stealing, and harlotry. In these sermons on the necessity of faith and discipline, Joyce and Matthias seem linked as examples of sin leading inevitably to the gallows. Yet in their own confessions and in Allen's note, the two men are disconnected spatially (Joyce in Mrs. Cross's house, Matthias outside) and in terms of their responsibility for the murder. Within the formal requirements and stock phrases of the execution sermon and criminal confession, Allen leaves a record of dissent. Matthias's guilt by association resonates with the indictments of African American character during the 1793 epidemic. In response to those charges, Allen had refused distance and elevation. Publishing the "Confessions" of Joyce and Matthias, he uses his position as intermediary, amanuensis, and editor to raise, or at least to suggest, questions about the intransigence of the system that has judged Peter Matthias.[31]

A different version of events is presented in a criminal narrative titled "The Fate of Murderers: A Faithful Narrative of the Murder of Mrs. Sarah Cross, with the Trial, Sentence and Confession of John Joyce and Peter Mathias, Who Were Executed Near Philadelphia on Monday 14, March 1808." Printed in the same year as Allen's "Confessions," and probably at the same time, this pamphlet also supplied information to an avid public in the wake of the trial and executions. On its cover, "The Fate of Murderers" displays an engraving of two figures hanging side by side on the gallows, equating the fate and guilt of Joyce and Matthias. The text begins with a preface, invoking Shakespeare, Pope, Dryden, and Milton, that supports, with regret, the death penalty as necessary to curb iniquity. The anonymous writer points to the examples of Joyce and Matthias, whose punishment serves as a negative example for readers. There follows a report on the discovery of Sarah Cross's body, the arrest of the criminals, and the recovery of her property, and then a longer account of the trial from the same newspaper source used by Allen.

"The Fate of Murderers" omits the confessions of Joyce and Matthias, substituting for these documents two final paragraphs, each given a page, evaluating the characters of the two men. (The details in these paragraphs indicate that whoever compiled "The Fate of Murderers" was familiar with Joyce's and Matthias's statements but chose not to reprint them.) Joyce is praised for conceding his guilt, atoning for his crime, welcoming his punishment, and seeking the mercy of God. Matthias is described as spending his last days "occupied in prayer," but faulted for continuing to deny "his participation in the guilt" and expecting to receive a pardon. Such hopes, readers are told, were "strongly urged by the clergymen of his own colour, and by several others who attended him." At the end, "he became in some measure reconciled," confessed to Richard Allen, and asked for all to pray for God's mercy on him. Allen's formal and rhetorical maneuvers in the "Confessions" become sharper in the context of the sweeping judgments rendered in "The Fate of Murderers." Yet though "Fate" suppresses indications that the two men might not be equally guilty of the murder, it registers Matthias's denials, even as it censures them. The diction leaves unspecified the content of his fervent prayers and the exact "measure" of his reconciliation. The details suggest what Allen himself was unwilling or unable to disclose: that some African American clergy believed the accused when they insisted that Matthias was not directly involved in the murder, and they expected, or at least hoped, that the authorities would reach the same conclusion after reviewing the evidence and then spare him from death.[32]

Linking Jones and Allen's yellow fever text with African American criminal narratives and with Allen's own "Confessions" of John Joyce and Peter Matthias gives us a fuller sense of the verbal performances. Rather than capitulating, masking, or defying, the writers and speakers in these pamphlets seize the tenuous opportunities of emancipation, and they fiercely negotiate, at the level of the word, for status and authority. In these texts, the boundaries are crossed between deference and resistance, rumor and perjury, and ordinary and capital sentences. At the start of the literary tradition spurred by the Philadelphia "experiment," in the "Narrative" of 1793 and the "Confessions" of 1808, is the conspicuous, elusive character of Richard Allen.

Benjamin Rush's Heroic Interventions

An influential teacher and essayist, as well as one of the city's leading physicians, Benjamin Rush heroically remained in Philadelphia throughout the 1793 epidemic. He treated patients, announced his remedies, and battled the medical establishment. He advocated the depleting treatments of purging and bloodletting, thus weakening many of those under his care. Against many skeptics, he maintained that the fever was of domestic, rather than imported, origin. In actuality, the 1793 fever was both: imported from the West Indies and then transmitted locally by mosquitoes. Rush returned again and again in his writings to his controversial role in the Philadelphia epidemics of the 1790s.

Rush emerges as a character—no, that is too mild: Rush strenuously enacts his character in the daily letters he wrote to his wife, Julia, who remained in New Jersey during the fever months. These letters are intense and revealing, and they offer a different narrative texture from his more public, retrospective *Account of the Bilious Remitting Yellow Fever* (1794) and *Travels through Life* (written in 1800). In his stories of the fever, Rush, like Mathew Carey and many other Philadelphians in 1793, turned to Daniel Defoe's fictional *Journal of the Plague Year* (1722) for advice about how to come to terms with the epidemic. When he compared what he had witnessed with "histories I had read of the plague," in a letter to Julia, Rush probably had in mind Defoe's book (August 25, 1793; *Letters*, 2:640). He owned a first edition of Defoe's *Journal*, which he dated June 10, 1790. This copy, now in the collections of the Library Company of Philadelphia, is heavily marked and annotated. On the last page, front and back, he devised his own alternative table of contents, with topics and page numbers.[33]

In his letters from the plague year, Rush charts the ebbs and surges. In an early letter, he invokes Psalm 78: "It is indeed as I had expected. The disease has awakened like a giant refreshed by wine" (September 8; *Letters*, 2:655). He details the mounting public despair, the exposure and distress of the poor, his own euphoria at uncovering the depleting "cure," and the public service of his disciples and servants and of the African American community. Rush describes how the fever invaded his home, infecting everyone, ultimately killing three of his pupils and his sister. He ministers to the sick in their homes and in his parlor. Overwhelmed by suffering, he describes his perseverance. Reading Rush's letters, one realizes how much has happened—that the fever already had reached its peak—by the time Mathew Carey published his "Desultory Account" on October 16.

To an astonishing extent in these letters, Rush makes personal and literary his struggles against the fever. He compares his writing to the release of blood, as though composing the letters had been part of the treatment for his own fever. The letters to Julia resemble an epistolary novel, in which character is revealed in installments and events and sentiments are given the effects of immediacy. Rush tells stories of the fever and also the story of his attraction to his wife, which he compares to the force of gravity (October 21; *Letters*, 2:721–22). On display in the letters are their frustrated plans to meet, her continually deferred homecoming, and his ardor on the eve of her return.[34]

Rush's letters to Julia are part conversion narrative. He writes on November 8 that he wishes his dispatches to contain "a faithful narrative" of his experience during the fever. By "faithful," of course, he means full and accurate. (He is about to tell her that he had concealed how serious his fever was during the second week of October.) But the adjective also evokes the theological terms he uses to describe the discovery and effects of his "cure" for the fever, "the triumphs of mercury, jalap, and bloodletting" (September 11; *Letters*, 2:659). Rush claims in his letters and in his *Account* that all of the usual remedies had failed to diminish the fever. The medical professionals were baffled in their theories and mistaken in their practice. And then, one day in September, he opened a book that had been given to him by the late Benjamin Franklin, and he had an epiphany. In this volume, a 1741 account of the yellow fever written by a Dr. Mitchell, the answer was revealed: evacuation, to which Rush added bloodletting (*Account*, 197–203). Since Rush believed that all disease overstimulated the body, and especially the blood vessels, he prescribed therapies that severely depleted the quantity of blood and bile.

According to modern historians, Rush's ideas and the contemporary debates over etiology and treatment for the yellow fever were part of the incoherent response by doctors who did not understand the principles of viral infection. The Philadelphia medical establishment was caught between two paradigms. Older theories held that disease resulted from imbalances in the body's four humors, while newer "solidist" hypotheses maintained that illness was caused by excessive irritation of the body's tissues, manifested in the blood vessels and nerves. Many people were infected in Philadelphia in 1793 (estimates range between 50 and 90 percent of those who remained in the city), and most survived, not as the result of Rush's radical treatments or his opponents' alternatives, but because of the responses of their own immune systems. Although twentieth-century medicine has been able to control the disease through systematic vaccination and programs to eradicate mosquitoes, there remains no cure. Medical historians have been unable to determine the degree of hazard presented by Rush's remedies.[35]

Many of Rush's contemporaries had no such uncertainties. His Princeton classmate Ebenezer Hazard compared him with the zealous, parochial Dr. Sangrado in Le Sages's picaresque *Gil Blas*, who treated all complaints by recommending copious bleeding and the drinking of large quantities of hot water. As Hazard put it, alluding to Le Sage and also to the fictional Moorish king reputed to possess a helmet of pure gold that rendered its wearer invulnerable: "[Rush] is a perfect Sangrado, and would order blood enough to be drawn to fill Mambrino's helmet, with as little ceremony as a mosquito would fill himself upon your leg." From a modern perspective, Hazard's mention of mosquitoes is ironic, given the discovery in 1901 that the insect carried the yellow fever virus. In 1793, mosquitoes were spreading the disease by performing on a minuscule level the same operation—bloodletting—that Rush pursued on a large scale in his remedy.[36]

Rush published his cure on September 12. Writing to Julia, he announced that the discovery had "infused a vigor into my body and mind" (September 6; *Letters*, 2:653). Along with the gratitude of his patients, it had acted like a "cordial to his soul" (September 6 and September 8; *Letters*, 2:653, 655). In his *Account*, he gives an even stronger version of the effects: "Never before did I experience such sublime joy as I now felt in contemplating the success of my remedies. It repaid me for all the toils and studies of my life" (204). Rush practiced and preached his cure with the vehemence of the converted. He tirelessly attended the sick, bleeding and purging in vast quantities. He struggled with unbelievers in the newspapers and on the streets. He made astounding claims for his power to heal: "I now save 29 out of 30" (letter to Julia on September 5; *Letters*, 2:650–51); "all would recover probably, had I time to attend closely to them after the expulsion or extinction of poison by the mercury" (September 8; *Letters*, 2:655); "I think I was the unworthy instrument in the hands of a kind Providence of recovering *more* than ninety-nine out of an hundred of my patients before my late indisposition" (letter to John Rodgers on October 3; *Letters*, 2:696–97). During the fall of 1797, in an effort to discredit Rush's authority during a subsequent outbreak of the fever, his fellow physician William Currie circulated an image of Rush as the deranged doctor preacher of 1793. In an unsigned attack on the pages of the *Gazette of the United States*, Currie wrote: "That his mind was elevated to a state of enthusiasm bordering on phrenzy, I had frequent opportunity of observing—and I have heard from popular report, that in passing through Kensington [a district north of the city] one day with his black man on the seat of his chaise along side of him, he cried out with vociferation, 'bleed and purge all Kensington! drive on boy!'"[37]

Part of the humor in Currie's image comes from his pun on "purge." Currie suggests that the good doctor takes the preacher's mission to cleanse his congregation a bit too literally. Modern observers have tended to explain Rush's excessive faith in purging and bloodletting in ideological terms: Rush as Democratic-Republican, believing in local origins and in depleting remedies, or Rush as nascent Federalist, in favor of controlled bloodletting and regulated passions. These assessments take their cue from Rush himself, who argued after the fact that his system was democratic, that is, accessible to and practiced by different classes, races, and genders. Rush also claimed that those who disputed his medical opinions were hostile to his republican politics. Yet such glosses, then and now, tend to reduce to identifiable political stances the unstable combination of medicine, politics, psychology, theology, and literature that shaped Rush's conduct during the fever. Rush's heroic medical interventions—his own Philadelphia experiments—were bound up with his sense of undaunted masculinity, his fondness for narratives of conversion and deliverance, and his anxieties about an environment suffused with fever. This knot of concerns would be taken up by Charles Brockden Brown in his novel *Arthur Mervyn*.[38]

To his medical *Account of the Bilious Remitting Yellow Fever* (1794), Rush appended a personal narrative, whose terms evoked popular stories of deliverance from shipwreck, war, captivity, and famine. In the *Account* and especially in his letters to Julia, Rush interprets his own deliverance in complicated ways. At the start of his September 10 letter to Julia, he writes that his name should be Shadrach, Meshach, or Abednego, invoking the miraculous preservation in Nebuchadnezzar's "burning fiery furnace" (Daniel 3). (Jones and Allen cite the same biblical story, in a more modulated fashion, at the start of their "Narrative of the Proceedings.") Rush's alignments with the Savior range from the conventionally humble (October 6; *Letters*, 2:705) to the self-aggrandizing (October 28; *Letters*; 2:729). And he revels in his own prowess, aspiring to "intrepidity in the use of the lancet" (*Account*, 226). As the letters unfold, Rush seems to swell with the fever, to brandish his lancet like Excalibur against his nemeses.[39]

Unlike Shadrach, Meshach, and Abednego—but like Mathew Carey and Richard Allen—Rush is transformed by his experience. He is physically altered by the fever:

> From my great intercourse with the sick, my body became highly impregnated with the contagion. My eyes were yellow, and sometimes a yellowness was perceptible in my face. My pulse was preternaturally quick, and I had profuse sweats every night. These sweats were so offensive as to oblige me to draw the bed-cloths close to my neck to defend myself from their smell. ("Narrative," in *Account*, 341)

> From all these sources, streams of contagion were constantly poured into my house, and conveyed into my body by the air, and in my aliment. ("Narrative," in Account, 353)

> Every room in our house is infected, and my body is full of it. My breath and perspiration smell so strongly of it. . . . My eyes are tinged of a yellow color. This is not peculiar to myself. It is universal in the city. (Letter to Julia, September 13; Letters, 2:663)

From his intimacy with the sick, from the food he eats, from the walls of his house, from the surging air—from the streams not of grace but of infection—Rush is penetrated and soaked with fever.

In the "Narrative" part of his *Account*, Rush describes not only physical but also perceptual effects: an unusually slow consciousness of the passage of time, in which "the herse and grave mingled themselves with every view I took of human affairs" (358). His vulnerability and metamorphosis open him, in the letters to Julia, to identifications with the African American residents of his household and of the city. These affinities did not originate with the epidemic. Rush was an early abolitionist and a supporter of Jones and Allen's plan for an African church. In 1788, he had written to his friend Jeremy Belknap in Boston, somewhat theoretically: "I love even the name of Africa, and never see a Negro slave or freeman without emotions which I seldom feel in the same degree towards my unfortunate fellow creatures of a fairer complexion. . . . Let us continue to love and serve them for they are our brethren not only by creation but by redemption" (*Letters*, 1:482–83). Yet his experience of the fever personalizes such attachments and renders them volatile. His empathy can be condescending and self-serving. Yet these flaws do not invalidate the gestures. Rush responds to calls for support like those made by Jones and Allen in the "Address to the Friends" section of their "Narrative of the Proceedings." The identifications of European Americans and African Americans with and against one another during 1793 are part of the continuous positioning, the opening and closing of individual and civic possibilities, in the new nation.[40]

If Mathew Carey depicts the "total dissolution of the bonds of society" and Absalom Jones and Richard Allen chronicle how African Americans played the roles of absent spouses, parents, and children, Benjamin Rush describes the extension of his family during the fever. "Sickness and distress have at last reached our family," he writes to Julia on September 22 (*Letters*, 2:674). "Our family" includes not only his mother and sister but also his black servant Marcus, a mulatto boy Peter, and three of his pupils who were living in his house. During the fever months, everyone in the house became sick, was nursed, and in turn nursed others. While Rush was ill, his pupils and servants became doctors to his patients. During his most severe attack of the fever, Rush writes to Julia of his servant's care for him: "Marcus has slept in the room with me for some time past, chiefly of late to hand me a little food in the middle of the night, for I have become so much a child, or an old man, in constitution that I am obliged to eat often or I become weak and fainty. . . . I cannot tell you how much we all owe to Marcus. His integrity, industry, and fidelity deserve great praise" (October 14; *Letters*, 2:715–16). This last sentence, applauding Marcus's "integrity, industry, and fidelity," could be taken out of context and placed in the mouth of a slaveholder, typifying a master's regard. Yet "freedom" in Philadelphia, although not the opposite of slavery, is also not equivalent to it, and the receptivity Rush describes in his letters should not be dismissed.[41]

Rush's ties to African Americans in Philadelphia in 1793 have to do with his politics, his respect for assistance given to the community and to his family, a shared vulnerability to the fever, and also his sense of persecution. Like Jones and Allen and like Carey, Rush was accused of profiteering. Like them, he felt himself to be a victim of rumor and innuendo. Rush was charged with taking credit that was due to others, with acting precipitously and lethally, and with endangering the lives of Philadelphia's white citizens by employing uneducated blacks as his medical assistants. In a letter to John Rodgers written in October 1797, during a subsequent outbreak of yellow fever, Rush alluded to a new wave of personal attacks and made a surprising claim for a signer of the Declaration of Independence: "The persecutions of that memorable year 1793 have lately revived against me and with accumulated asperity. . . . Ever since the year 1793 I have lived in

Philadelphia as in a foreign country" (*Letters*, 2:794). One way of making sense of such expressed alienation is to link it with a statement Rush made to Julia in a September 10, 1793, letter written during the early course of the epidemic and in the flush of his cure, the same letter that began by proposing that henceforth he should be called "Shadrach, Meshach, or Abednego." Rush writes: "My African brethren are extremely useful in attending the sick. I met a good woman of their society a few days ago at the foot of a pair of stairs. 'Hah! Mama,' said I, '*we black* folks have come into demand at last.' She squeezed my hand, and we parted" (*Letters*, 2:658). During the fever, Rush discovers, as Jones and Allen do, from a different but not mutually exclusive position, how exacting the demands of service can be.

Mathew Carey's Fugitive Philadelphians

Over six versions and thirty-seven years, Mathew Carey alters his story of the fever. As writer, editor, and publisher, he supervised the content and technology of production. While Jones and Allen had a degree of control over their "Narrative of the Proceedings," whose printing they had funded, Carey wielded authority over his entire series. Even for a writer such as Carey, who often revised and reprinted his own work, the arc from the "Desultory Account of the Yellow Fever" in October 1793 to the 1830 *Brief Account of the Malignant Fever* is exceptional. Across the editions, Carey corrects mistakes and incorporates public responses. He expands, deletes, and reorders, adjusting diction, typography, and design. Given his scrutiny of process and detail, the various changes are telling. Carey shares with Jones and Allen an appreciation of verbal substance and consequence, and this is one reason that the words of the three men became so closely entwined.

Jones and Allen were by no means Carey's only critics. A copy of the third edition of the *Short Account*, published on November 30, 1793, originally owned by John Beale Bordley, a Maryland agriculturalist and lawyer who had moved to Philadelphia in 1791, contains extensive marginal notes, underlinings, insertions, and proposed cuts. Carey's impulse to get the fever right seems contagious. Bordley debates Carey on a range of topics: dates, facts, weather, the causes of the fever, and the behavior of residents. Bordley's reactions to Carey's paragraph on black conduct fill the lower half of the left margin. He corrects Carey on the roles played by Jones and Allen and William Gray. He testifies to Gray's honesty, apparently sensing, as Jones and Allen will, that Carey's remarks on "the vilest of the blacks" undermine his praise of specific individuals. Bordley's overwrought copy suggests the vigorous response produced by Carey's fever texts, which the publisher attempted to gauge in his evolving *Accounts*.[42]

Over time, Carey meticulously revised the paragraph that Jones and Allen excoriate in their "Narrative of the Proceedings." African American carriers of the dead had made a brief appearance in his initial "Desultory Account" published on October 16. He had included a long quote from a New York City newspaper that described corpses being carted and buried by blacks. On the next page, he invoked an ominous, solitary figure: "there have been very many instances, in which as soon as a person was seized with the fever, he was immediately abandoned by friends and the nearest relations, and resigned to the care of perhaps a single negro" (5). The "partial, censorious" paragraph (as Jones and Allen described it) on the "opportunities for imposition" seized by African Americans first appeared in the November 14 and November 23 editions of Carey's *Short Account* (76–77). In a subsequent paragraph, Carey speculated on black immunity to the fever, quoting Dr. Lining ("There is something very singular in [their] constitution" [77–78]). He also qualified this claim but then paraphrased an unnamed "eminent doctor" (Benjamin Rush, with whom Carey had corresponded): "'it yielded to the power of medicine in them more easily than in the whites'" (3:78).

In revising his "Desultory Account," Carey expanded from twelve to almost one hundred pages. In the third edition, published on November 30, he began to tinker with the context of the paragraph on African American conduct. He moved the paragraph on black resistance to the fever before the "opportunities for imposition" paragraph and combined them, thus providing a rationale for African American service. As a suture for the two paragraphs, he added a sentence that cannot have pleased Jones and Allen. He described the "very salutary effect" of the "error" about immunity, since whites were able to procure nurses, and "the sufferings of the sick" were diminished (3:78). Carey saw advantage for white residents where Rush, in his October 29 letter to Carey, had discerned African American credit: "The merit of the blacks in their attendance upon the sick is enhanced by their not being exempted from the disorder" (*Letters*, 2:731).

By the fourth edition, published on January 16, after the epidemic had subsided, the *Short Account* had expanded to 164 pages, including a burgeoning list of the dead. Although this edition appeared a week before Jones and Allen's pamphlet, Carey's changes in his paragraph on black performance suggest that he already had heard their criticisms or similar assessments. He describes the tasks performed by Jones, Allen, and Gray more generally, avoiding inaccuracy about their roles. After the phrase "the vilest of the blacks," he places a cross directing his readers' attention to a note at the bottom of the page that, for the first time, extends the racial field: "The extortion here mentioned, was very far from being confined to the negroes; many of the white nurses behaved with equal rapacity" (4:63). Although subordinated to the text, this note represents an important shift, notwithstanding Carey's dismissal three months later of Jones and Allen's "Narrative" as "undeserving of notice" ("Address of M. Carey to the Public," 5).[43]

In the last edition, published in March 1830 and reduced to ninety-two pages, Carey finally concedes to Jones and Allen. He revises his notorious sentence. It now reads: "The great demand for nurses, afforded an opportunity for imposition, which was eagerly seized"—not by "some of the vilest of the blacks" but—"by some of those who acted in that capacity, both coloured and white" (5:68). In the body of the *Short Account*, rather than a note, Carey no longer restricts the misconduct he describes. Syntactically, he joins black and white nurses in offense but also in service. In their "Narrative," Jones and Allen complain, "Had Mr. Carey said, a number of white and black wretches eagerly seized on the opportunity to extort from the distressed, and some few of both were detected in plundering the sick, it might extenuate, in a great degree, the having made mention of the blacks" (11). Thirty-six years later, Carey says just this. He acknowledges his partiality, at least implicitly, and he seeks to correct the record. After almost four decades, Carey still was reflecting on the fever and revising his paragraph.

No evidence exists to suggest that Allen was aware of the changes or that he felt vindicated. Jones had died in 1818, and Allen would die in 1831, the year after Carey's final *Account* appeared. In Allen's posthumous *Autobiography*, his and Jones's 1794 "Narrative of the Proceedings" was reprinted with its original censure of Carey intact.

Carey and Jones and Allen struggle over one paragraph. Yet in that paragraph, both sides see a world of significance. That paragraph is altered in the exchanges between Carey, Rush, Jones, and Allen. It is shaped by and in turn shapes the discourse of fever.

The paragraph on African American conduct is part of the intricate, evolving form that is the *Short Account*. Over time, the relationship among the parts shifts, while the structure remains. Carey's reports begin and end providentially, with the announcement that Philadelphia, scourged for its pride, ultimately has been delivered. In all of them, Carey portrays social disintegration through scenes of distress and heroism featuring middle- and lower-class white citizens. The episodes of breakdown generate warnings about the dangers of "terrific narration" (3:56), which are substantiated in Carey's tales about the discriminatory acts of other cities and states. Fearing contagion, other localities proscribe Philadelphians, guarding boundaries in transport and commerce. Dissolution—terrific narration—discrimination. Then Carey reviews the comparative susceptibility of different groups to the fever, concluding this sequence of thought with the paragraph on African American conduct. As though infected by the rumor and bias that have preceded it, despite Carey's attempted inoculations, this paragraph seems to propel what comes next.

What comes next is a series of remarkable incidents, anecdotes, and comments about life during the fever. In earlier editions, this material appears toward the end of the narrative. In the third edition, it follows the story proper and is gathered into two chapters entitled "Desultory Facts and Reflexions,—A Collection of Scraps" (3:83–110).

Across the twenty-seven pages of these two chapters, Carey considers the pleasures of an ordinary funeral, the disarray in Philadelphia graveyards, the behavior of landlords, and the malfunction of clocks and watches. He delineates spatial changes during the fever: ironically, the jail, strictly administered, became a refuge, and the churches, teeming with believers, were incubators of mortality. Many of these "scraps" consist of anecdotes that Carey has heard or evidence about the potency of stories during the fever. Some postmasters in other states took hold of mail from Philadelphia with tongs, immersing the letters in vinegar before they would handle them. Several subscribers to Philadelphia newspapers instructed their servants to sprinkle the periodicals with vinegar and dry them at the fire. An old gravedigger, who imagined he was immune to the fever because he had lost his sense of smell, opened a grave and inhaled a stench that killed him within a day or two. Prodigies were circulated: stories about mysterious voices heard in the streets of Philadelphia and two angels who conversed with the watchmen.

Sometimes Carey's items seem random, and other times they cluster. In the second chapter of scraps, there are two anecdotes about transporters of the sick who pursue their reluctant charges or who arrive at the Bush Hill hospital only to find their vehicles empty, as well as a tale about a carter of the (mistakenly) dead whose freight awakens. There are two stories about spurned coffins that ultimately welcome their owners. Although Carey gestures toward reassuring episodes and statistics, the emphasis in these "desultory" chapters is on the poignant and the lurid. The Rev. Henry Helmuth, who published his own fever narrative in 1794, distinguished between the pleasures of distress ("in sadness itself the heart finds sometimes a kind of voluptuous satisfaction") and the "divine sadness" he himself sought to elicit. Regardless of whether Helmuth had Carey's prominent accounts in mind, he points to the allure of such texts.[44]

In the most extended cluster of scraps, Carey depicts many scenes in which the white citizens of Philadelphia have been mistreated in other places because of their association with the fever. A few pages earlier, Carey judiciously reports that Philadelphians themselves had been known to overreact against emigrants from other towns during times of pestilence. He counsels his readers not to "indiscriminately vilify" those who take precautions against Philadelphians (3:92). Yet such balance is overwhelmed by the pages describing "the inhumanity . . . experienced by Philadelphians from strangers" (3:96).

On roads leading from the city, Philadelphians are refused food and shelter. They are forced from stagecoaches and not allowed to disembark from ferries. In Easton, Maryland, a wagon full of goods is burned, and a female passenger is tarred and feathered. In a New Jersey town, the residents establish a patrol to guard against Philadelphians. In Virginia, they enforce a twenty-one-day quarantine. When Philadelphians die abandoned on the road, they are buried with contrivances that keep their corpses at a distance. Ships from Philadelphia are denied supplies and turned away. Near Baltimore, a tavern keeper refuses to house or board Philadelphians. Near Newark, a fence is built on either side of a house in which a Philadelphian lies ill. At the Bordentown, New Jersey, bridge, a Philadelphia girl conceals her civic identity so that she may enter the town. A Philadelphia father returning to his lodgings after burying his daughter finds his furniture on the road and his access barred. The sequence ends with the curious image of a boy who, believing that tar was a preventive, had tied a rope dipped in tar around his neck. He awoke in the night, "half strangled and black in the face. He may with justice be said to have nearly choaked himself, to save his life" (3:101).[45]

In these scenes, fear distorts perception and behavior. Boundaries are secured. "Philadelphia" is imagined as separate from Easton, Baltimore, and Bordentown. With repetition and under discrimination, the term "Philadelphian" in the third edition takes on the aspect of a discrete group or class, almost an ethnicity. And these are not just Philadelphians but "fugitive Philadelphians" (3:95; also 99, 49). Their distinctiveness has been forged in their dislocation. Carey generates sympathy for the plight of these fugitives. He calls for unity between those who remained and those who fled and for a combined effort in "cleansing and purifying our scourged city" (3:109).[46]

In these iterations, there are resonances that exceed Carey's intention. There are stories within and without his stories. Carey seeks to refute the aspersions cast on Philadelphians and the injuries done to Philadelphians by a troubled society. Yet through these scenes of intolerance—"our citizens were proscribed in several cities and towns—hunted up like felons in some—and debarred admittance in others, whether sound or infected" (3:73)—there also circulate figures that Carey largely leaves out of his accounts. In many of the scenes, the term

"Philadelphian" could be replaced with the term "African American" (or the term "Irish American"), while preserving the message about the contagion of prejudice. "Philadelphians" are formed in a similar cauldron of discrimination. The venues could be transposed beyond the city and its environs. "Yellow fever" could be doubled by "black skin," as if Rush's theory of skin color as disease had been confirmed. (One thinks of Abraham Johnstone, judged on the basis of fears about his tainted character.) Carey may avoid explicitly representing the black victims and heroes of Philadelphia or his own sense of vulnerability, but such figures haunt his scenes of quarantine. They are like the figures Toni Morrison describes in her essay "Unspeakable Things Unspoken." "Certain absences," she writes, "are so stressed, so ornate, so planned, they call attention to themselves . . . like neighborhoods that are defined by the population held away from them." Such claims are made vivid in the literal borders, fugitives, and circuits of Carey's *Short Accounts.*[47]

In earlier editions of the *Short Account*, the scenes of bigotry against Philadelphians are contained within paragraphs (1, 2:78–97). In the third edition, each scrap is suspended on the page, divided from the others by a gap and ornamental design (3:83–110). The episodes unfold in a phantasmical sequence. In the fourth edition, Carey begins to tame his images (4:70–94). He includes a note of apology at the beginning of the section. He alters words to diminish some of the unsettling effects. He adds two paragraphs toward the end that draw out an analogy between the citizens of Philadelphia and an army, both of which rally after an initial rout (4:92). In the fifth and final edition, published in 1830, he eliminates the breaks and visual devices, returns to continuous paragraphs, and reduces the scenes depicting lost, lunatic, or beleaguered Philadelphians (74–92).

Across the editions, while Carey represents Philadelphia's collapse and rebirth; while he speculates on the cause, treatment, and development of the fever; while he defends the city and its inhabitants against pernicious rumor, advocates for those who left, responds to charges that he had unfairly judged the performances of black volunteers, and sketches the experiences of dislocation and intolerance; while Carey tries to account for character and conduct during the emergency, the list of the dead swells and presses on all that comes before. At first, it appears on only two pages, numbered by day and then by religious denomination ("Desultory," 11–12). In the early editions of the *Short Account*, there are four pages of names ("a few of the most noted inhabitants of Philadelphia, who have died since the first of August") and four pages of burial charts, tallying the dead by church and denomination (1, 2:100–3). Then, in the third edition, after charts of the burials by month in the different graveyards, sixteen pages are covered with the names of those who have perished. This list is alphabetized and categorized according to the place of interment: Protestant, Catholic, or Quaker church, Potter's Field. The names are squeezed onto the pages in tiny print. Some of the dead are given surnames, some only first names, and some the names of their husband or parents or employer or owner. Some are defined by their profession, others by their race (appendix 1–16).

In the fourth edition, the list runs over forty pages. After five pages of burial charts, there are thousands of names in alphabetical order (113–17, 121–63). The list begins, as Phillip Lapsansky has pointed out, with "Abigail, a negress." Carey has abandoned any effort to group by category. The masses of the dead have overwhelmed the previous grids, divisions, and headings. This necrology was one of the reasons for the popularity of Carey's texts. Readers inside and outside Philadelphia scanned the inventory to see who appeared and who did not. In the fourth edition, Carey tabulates the deceased, with a total of 4,041, but he advises that this number "is not given as fully complete and accurate" (121). The casualties ultimately balk accounting. The list of the dead is part of the dynamic of medical speculation, narrative, vignette, polemic, and enumeration that constitute Carey's increasingly long *Short Accounts*.[48]

Obsessively revising, Carey devotes himself to concerns about proper borders, equilibrium and excess, the relation of parts to wholes, and individual, civic, and national constitution. His *Short Accounts* are not therapeutic, as some have construed them. He does not merely seek to normalize or to regulate. Instead, Carey's texts form a body of work, meticulous and excessive, that develops over time and that enacts the issues it considers. Carey's *Short Accounts,* Jones and Allen's "Narrative of the Proceedings of the Black People during the Late Awful Calamity in Philadelphia," and Benjamin Rush's letters to his wife, Julia, together form a sustained treatment of the disorder in Philadelphia. They also serve as the framework in which we can appreciate the conceits and techniques in Charles Brockden Brown's fever novel, *Arthur Mervyn*.[49]

Charles Brockden Brown's Experiments in Character

Issued in two parts in 1799 and 1800, Brown's *Arthur Mervyn; or Memoirs of the Year 1793* echoes Mathew Carey's *Short Account of the Malignant Fever.* According to Dr. Stevens, who narrates the first part of the story told by the young Arthur, during the fever, "The usual occupations and amusements of life were at an end. Terror had exterminated all the sentiments of nature. Wives were deserted by husbands, and children by parents." Mervyn goes on to describe the ways in which fear and misunderstanding led to estrangement and the unnecessary loss of life. These words and images are close to Carey's set piece on the fever and the depictions in Brown's other fever stories, "The Man at Home," thirteen sketches that appeared in the winter and spring of 1798, and the novel *Ormond*, published in 1799.[50] In Carey's final *Account*, published in 1830, he returns Brown's acknowledgment. In a footnote to his paragraphs describing the city's distress, Carey writes, "The novel of Arthur Mervyn, by C. B. Brown, gives a vivid and terrifying picture, probably not too highly coloured, of the horrors of that period" (5:25). This exchange suggests the reach of fever narratives across time and genre. Brown himself contracted and recovered from yellow fever, and his mentor, Elihu Hubbard Smith, died of the infection in New York in 1798. Brown's own experience of the fever in New York and his knowledge of the epidemic's impact on Philadelphia spurred his career as a writer. His protagonist, Arthur Mervyn, explains that he was drawn to Philadelphia and the fever by the extravagant, compelling stories and the "sublimity" of great danger. He "ardently pursues" the fever in his imagination, "recommended by some nameless charm" (130). Brown links imagination and fever repeatedly. In "The Man at Home" and *Ormond*, "the force of imagination" activates the dormant illness of Baxter, who has observed the mysterious burial of a fever victim. In *Arthur Mervyn*, the fever stimulates Arthur's escalating conjecture. Although Mervyn's responses are not identical with his author's, Brown himself ardently pursues the fever in fiction and essays. Like Mathew Carey and like Benjamin Rush, Brown seems to have been oddly buoyed by the fever.[51]

Critics have linked Brown and Carey, arguing that the two writers encourage virtuous behavior, or prescribe therapeutic narratives, or display models for the proper distribution of knowledge. Some have suggested that, in the character of Arthur Mervyn, Brown was appraising Benjamin Rush's "self-righteous" heroism during the 1793 epidemic. In his novel, Brown does present characters who seem to endorse Rush's viewpoints in the debates about the origin and nature of the fever. Dr. Stevens treats Arthur without fear and maintains his own health through a regimen of cleanliness and diet. Arthur's companion Medlicote insists that the disease is not contagious or imported but instead the product of "a morbid constitution of the atmosphere, owing wholly or in part to filthy streets, airless habitations and squalid persons" (159–61). Yet Brown's addition of "squalid persons" to this list implies the dangers of mobility and importation. In *Arthur Mervyn*, Brown repeatedly and vertiginously links Philadelphia's "morbid constitution" and tainted "atmosphere" (161) to streets, dwellings, bodies, money, and texts that circulate between the mainland and the plantations and upheavals of the West Indies and particularly Saint Domingue, often cited by importationists as the likely source of the epidemic. Brown figures such circulations in the remarkable image of the missing Watson, who wears 10,000 pounds sterling in bills of exchange in a leather belt around his waist and under his clothes, the profits from the sale of an estate in Jamaica, sold in fear of insurgency and war (240–44). The tangled crimes of the villain Welbeck bind the economies of Philadelphia and the West Indies.[52]

As critics have recognized, the symbolic meanings of the fever proliferate in Brown's writings. He invites exegeses of the fever as irrationality, sympathy, conspiracy, egocentrism, revolution (American, French, Haitian), sexual anxiety, market economy, and racism.[53] Brown not only provides a range of allegorical options but also stages his own debate about fever hermeneutics in the eleventh sketch of "The Man at Home." The narrator and his friends Harrington and Wallace are discussing the swift nocturnal killings carried out over four months in an ancient Greek colony in Italy on the orders of a secret tribunal of a ruling faction. Harrington compares this classical tyranny—inscrutable, prolonged, and costly—to the recent assault of yellow fever on Philadelphia, and he suggests that more suffering is produced by unknown causes than by malignant human passions. Wallace rejects the analogy, saying that he himself has benefited from the fever. Forced to leave the city and his grueling work in his store on Water Street (where, historically, the first cases of the fever appeared in late August), he went to the countryside, lived a healthier life, and met a beautiful and virtuous young woman whom he married and who brought a dowry of 300 pounds a year.

The narrator's stance in this debate about the resemblance between fever and tyranny is left unclear, and the signals are mixed. Even before the question of analogy or allegory is raised by the characters, the narrator links the biological and the civil through a pun on "intestine commotions," which joins disturbances internal to a country with those internal to a body (81).[54] How or whether we get from one "inside" to the other is not explained. The debate between Harrington and Wallace is followed by a sketch in which the narrator literalizes the cliché of love as a disease, portraying the world as "one vast hospital" (87), and then offers a riddling analogy in which sleep is described as an epidemic. These connections seem to be conceits, rather than arguments. Although the stories of fever told by the narrator in the second, fourth, and fifth sketches warn of misplaced curiosity and an imagination that activates the fever, the narrator, like Wallace, like Arthur Mervyn, and like Constantia Dudley in *Ormond*, benefits from the epidemic. In *Arthur Mervyn* especially, Brown disseminates various meanings of the fever and does not choose among them. Fever breeds conjecture, and conjecture can kill, as it does Baxter in "The Man at Home" and *Ormond*, or can redeem, as it does Arthur Mervyn.

Fever generates allegories in Brown's fiction and also produces formal effects. Critics have sought to explain the redundant correspondence between the first and second parts of *Arthur Mervyn*. One way to understand the relationship is to think about the first part as diagnosis and the second part as cure, or attempted cure, and to recognize that other fever texts—Carey's *Short Accounts*, Jones and Allen's "Narrative of The Proceedings," and Benjamin Rush's letters, *Account*, and "Narrative"—are also fractured, recursive, and exorbitant. The fever that afflicts Arthur is described in a memorable scene at the threshold of a room in which a stricken man lies. Arthur ingests the fever, and it consumes and delivers him:

> As I approached the door of which I was in search, a vapour, infectious and dead-ly, assailed my senses. It resembled nothing of which I had ever before been sensi-ble. Many odours had been met with, even since my arrival in the city, less insupportable than this. I seemed not so much to smell as to taste the element that now encompassed me. I felt as if I had inhaled a poisonous and subtle fluid, whose power instantly bereft my stomach of all vigour. Some fatal influence appeared to seize upon my vitals; and the work of corrosion and decomposition to be busily begun. . . . This incident, instead of appalling me, tended rather to invigorate my courage. The danger which I feared had come. I might enter with indifference, on this theatre of pestilence. I might execute without faultering, the duties that my circumstances might create. (144)

Possibly echoing the suffusions of fever described by Benjamin Rush in his 1794 "Narrative," Brown describes Arthur as infected and invigorated. Acknowledging his vulnerability, Arthur imagines himself to be unmoored from his fate and character and to be entering a new field of determination. Interpreters have dif-fered on the course of the narrative fever in *Arthur Mervyn*. Norman Grabo has described Arthur's story as "therapeutic," offering progress from individual drive and sexual dominance to one of civic responsiveness, following Dr. Stevens's prescription of candor. More recently, Bryan Waterman describes Arthur as find-ing a cure for the narrative illnesses of rumor and decay by taking control over the story in the second part. In contrast, Teresa Goddu has insisted that Brown demonstrates in *Arthur Mervyn* that narrative is infectious and unstable.[55]

Carroll Smith-Rosenberg and Sean X. Goudie have pointed to the ways in which Brown represents Arthur as seeking a cure for instability by securing his difference from the African American characters in the book. In Brown's novel, as in Carey's narrative, isolated African American figures tend to be linked with service and mortality. Soon after he enters the city, Arthur sees a hearse, driven by a black man, with two white attendants. Medlicote tells the story of how the merchant Thetford summoned a black man to cart one of his servants to the Bush Hill hospital, despite her slight illness and vehement protests. An indigent black woman is the only one left to care for Thetford's doomed wife and child.

(As though Arthur has imbibed Carey's partiality along with the fever, he describes her as not very diligent in her duties.) A "faithful black" remains with Medlicote to tend to his needs after his landlady and her daughter have fled (161).

In a reflexive sequence, Arthur appears to resolve his insecurities through racial contrast. In Welbeck's mansion, after seeing himself in a mirror dressed in French finery, Arthur's concerns about the uncertainty of appearances are dispelled by a "summons to breakfast, obsequiously delivered by a black servant" (51). Arthur seems to be assuaged by the consolations of status. But then, in Thetford's former abode, Arthur discovers a ransacked cabinet and sees in a mirror a tawny, scarred apparition, dressed in the livery of a servant. When Arthur turns to face the figure, he is struck unconscious. Taken for a victim of the fever, he is almost placed in a coffin by three hearse attendants whom he had met upon his entry into the city.[56]

On a coach to Baltimore, where he hopes to restore money and papers recovered from Watson to their legal owners, shortly after Arthur has taken over the narration, his looking glass is not a mirror but an ethnology text:

> I mounted the stage-coach at day-break the next day, in company with a sallow Frenchman from Saint Domingo, his fiddle-case, an ape, and two female blacks. The Frenchman, after passing the suburbs, took out his violin and amused himself with humming his own *tweedle-tweedle*. The monkey now and then mounched an apple, which was given to him from a basket by the blacks, who gazed with stupid wonder, and an exclamatory *La! La!* upon the passing scenery; or chattered to each other in a sort of open-mouthed, half-articulate, monotonous, and sing-song jargon. . . . As to me my thought was busy in a thousand ways. I sometimes gazed at the faces of my *four* companions, and endeavored to discern the differences and samenesses between them. I took an exact account of the features, proportions, looks, and gestures of the monkey, the Congolese, and the Creole-Gaul. I compared them together, and examined them apart. I looked at them in a thousand different points of view, and pursued, untired and unsatiated, those trains of reflections which began at each change of tone, feature, and attitude. (370)

This scene has a contrived quality to it (and that is saying a lot, given Brown's penchant for artifice). The stage has been set with a representative cast of types: a Frenchman from Saint Domingue, whose sallow color links him with the yellow fever and who, like many of his fellow colonials, may have fled from his West Indian plantation to Philadelphia to escape revolution; a monkey, whose presence on the coach is never quite explained; and two black women, who may or may not belong to the Frenchman. While the fiddle-case and violin are accompanied by possessive pronouns, the relationship, if any, of the monkey and the women to the Frenchman is left obscure, although he does reprimand the monkey using a proper name. The only passenger other than Arthur to be given a name is the monkey, and that name (Dominique) evokes the island of revolution (Saint Domingue or Santo Domingo). Arthur attempts to arrange the types before him in a familiar order. As Sean X. Goudie argues, Arthur's comparative scrutiny suggests Jefferson's *Notes on the State of Virginia* (1787) and Charles White's *Account of the Regular Gradation in Man* (1799). The scene is particularly reminiscent of Pierre Camper's *Dissertation Physique* (1791), with its visual calibrations of skull structure and facial angle. So close is Arthur's study to Camper's illustrations charting the sequence from ape to black to white that the Dutch anatomist seems a passenger on the Baltimore coach.[57]

Looking systematically from face to face, establishing relationships, and testing racial hierarchies, Arthur, who soon will apprentice himself to Dr. Stevens, practices his ethnological faculties. Yet despite claims that Arthur fixes differences, the results are far from definitive. As he stares at faces and attempts to determine relations in the moving coach, his "thousand different points of view" are not resolved. The passage contains various possible relations, rhetorically figured as sameness (the Frenchman's *"tweedle-tweedle"* and also the black women's *"La! La!"*), overlap (the slant rhyme of the women's "sing-song"), and divergence (Arthur's assessments of "stupid wonder" and "jargon"). As if the walls of the Baltimore coach cannot contain his speculations or satisfy his visual desires, Arthur looks out and appraises the passing landscape and then looks inward and forward, reflecting on the events that have transpired and the tasks that await him.

In this book structured by repetition, the pattern of attempted racial "cure" is prominent. It continues after the Baltimore coach, with Arthur looking through a window and recognizing the attractive features but alienating hue of a black girl, and then Arthur imagining that two black men who are commanded by their mistress to escort him from her home waver because of racial regard: "Their habitual deference for every thing *white*, no doubt, held their hands from what they regarded as a profanation" (379). "No doubt"—but, then again, maybe a great deal of doubt. Brown does not provide narrative assurances that Arthur's distinctions are stable or that the authority they seem to impart is not illusory.

In *Arthur Mervyn*, the contrasts sometimes work in reverse. When Arthur enters Philadelphia, it is the two white hearse attendants, not the black driver, who, "with a ferocious indifference to danger or pity," banter coldly about the death of the family whose bodies they carry (140). In the context of Mathew Carey's accounts, Arthur's behavior during the fever—going in and out of houses, taking things that don't belong to him, seeking to do good but to profit, too—echoes the charges leveled against black nurses and carriers of the dead. In Brown's Arthur, who eagerly seizes the opportunities presented by the fever, and in Carey's fugitive Philadelphians, racial distinctions blur and twist. The racial cure in *Arthur Mervyn* seems to be part of the problem, a false inoculation against the social and economic turbulence diagnosed in the first part of the book. The scene in the Baltimore coach purports to reveal while it conceals. The scrutiny of faces is part of a larger experiment in character at the center of the fever story that Brown tells in *Arthur Mervyn*.[58]

Such an experiment is embodied in the figure of the missing Watson, who has 10,000 pounds in bills of exchange concealed under his clothing. Not only the person of Watson and not only the bills he carries but also his character remains in circulation. Dr. Stevens's friend Wortley describes the state of affairs: "If he [Watson] be dead, and if the bills are not to be recovered, yet, to ascertain this will, at last, serve to vindicate his character. As long as his fate is unknown, his fame will be loaded with the most flagrant imputations, and if these bills be ever paid in London, these imputations will appear to be justified" (243). Watson is the object of speculation. In Brown's novel, the fever reveals character as the product of individual acts, public regard, and systemic effect. The intricacies of character—a term that both classifies and evaluates, that is both referent and sign—are made vivid.

A prominent method of discerning character, on display not only in the Baltimore coach scene but also throughout the book and especially in the second part, is the attempt to gauge face value. Arthur prides himself on his skill in "tracing distinct characters" as a copyist (21) and also in reading faces. Echoing the physiognomical disclosures about the character of Falkland in William Godwin's *Caleb Williams*, a source for *Arthur Mervyn*, Brown has Arthur describe how illness and perspicacity render Welbeck's face legible: "Health had forsaken his cheeks, and taken along with it those flexible parts, which formerly enabled him to cover his secret torments and insidious purposes, beneath a veil of benevolence and cheerfulness" (335).[59] Beneath the pliant shroud of flesh, Arthur discerns the revelations of bone. Part two of *Arthur Mervyn* begins with Dr. Stevens appraising Arthur's own character: his "inimitable and heroic qualities," his courage that was "the growth of benevolence and reason," his "pure intentions" (219). Yet Dr. Stevens praises too much, and soon the doubts that fuel the second part of the story are expressed: "Surely the youth was honest. His tale could not be the fruit of invention; and yet, what are the bounds of fraud? . . . Had I heard Mervyn's story from another, or read it in a book, I might perhaps have found it possible to suspect the truth; but, as long as the impression made by his tones, gestures and looks, remained in my memory, this suspicion was impossible" (229).

Dr. Stevens explains that Arthur's presence convinced him of the young man's honesty, but, of course, the reader occupies the positions that Stevens describes as generating suspicion: hearing the story from another and reading it in a book. As Stevens continues testifying to Arthur's character, assurance is again given and then at least partially withdrawn: "Wickedness may sometimes be ambiguous, its mask may puzzle the observer; our judgment may be made to faulter and fluctuate, but the face of Mervyn is the index of an honest mind. . . . He that listens to his words may question their truth, but he that looks upon his countenance when speaking cannot withhold his faith" (229–30). Faces may divulge, in contrast to obfuscating words, yet Arthur's words are all that readers have. Later in the second volume, in the chapter that precedes Arthur's journey in the Baltimore coach, Mrs. Wentworth expresses doubt about her ability to determine Mervyn's character from his face or his words: "but there must be other proofs besides an innocent brow and a voluble tongue, to make me give full credit to your pretensions" (363).[60]

Arthur's "pretensions"—how he puts himself forward, the claims he makes about himself, whether he is to be regarded as sincere or feigned—have been a focus for the book's interpreters. Brown stages this debate in the novel itself. In his narration, Dr. Stevens weighs the evidence about Arthur's character, admitting, as readers of *Arthur Mervyn* must: "It was possible, however, to find evidence, supporting or confuting his story" (230). Mrs. Althorpe ponders Arthur's behavior, "which betrayed a mixture of shrewdness and folly, of kindness and impudence" (236). Critics divide in their evaluations of Arthur's character, following the divergent lines of R. W. B. Lewis, who portrayed Arthur as a "foolish young innocent: the first of our Adams," and Warner Berthoff, who described Arthur as a "chameleon of convenient virtue" and "an invincible moral sharper." Those who maintain Arthur's virtue often invoke external support: Brown's statements about writing in his essay "Walstein's School of History" (Norman Grabo), moral philosophy (Emory Elliot), William Godwin's politics and ethics (Dorothy J. Hale), republicanism (Michael Warner), and late-eighteenth-century medical knowledge (Bryan Waterman). Yet these alignments are unsettled in Brown's inconsistent text and by what Dr. Stevens refers to as Arthur's "nervous eloquence" (229). Although Michael Warner concludes that Brown regarded *Arthur Mervyn* "as different from public treatises only insofar as the convenience of narrative allows him to 'methodize his own reflections,'" the novel itself—with its splintered points of view, tangled stories, proliferating metaphors, strange comedy, and gaps between intention and consequence—seems most unlike a treatise.[61]

In some ways, the experiments in character in *Arthur Mervyn* resemble those in Godwin's *Caleb Williams*. In both books, a young protagonist has promised to keep the secrets of an older man who has committed a crime. Such a promise subjects the young man's motives and conduct to doubt. Under public scrutiny, the youth undergoes a trial that demonstrates that his character is not exclusively his own possession. At the end of *Caleb Williams,* Caleb announces that, as the result of his curiosity and his exposure of Falkland, he himself has thwarted his aim: "I now have no character that I wish to vindicate." Yet Godwin's allegory of power and his analysis of master and slave dynamics are more fully sustained, and his continuous first-person point of view lends more stability to his novel's meanings than Brown's stories within stories in *Arthur Mervyn.* Across the three volumes of *Caleb Williams,* the narrative progresses toward its conclusion. Across the two volumes of *Arthur Mervyn,* the narrative starts and stops, advances and returns. As Dorothy J. Hale argues, Godwin emphasizes tyranny, while Brown emphasizes reform; *Caleb Williams* tends toward the tragic, while *Arthur Mervyn* ends in a kind of triumph.[62]

As in Carey's *Accounts,* Jones and Allen's "Narrative of the Proceedings," and Rush's letters and personal narrative, the yellow fever in *Arthur Mervyn* transforms Philadelphia—the symbolic space of Declaration and Constitution—into a laboratory for testing character and evaluating freedom, in which "race" is seen as crucial. The figures and issues of 1793 circulate through *Arthur Mervyn.* Like Mathew Carey, Brown employs a structure of shifting temporalities to describe the potency of stories during and after the fever, and he conveys the urgency of determining which stories are true and which are false. Like Carey, Mervyn insists on his impartiality, but such a stance is complicated by his myopia. Carey, Jones and Allen, and Brown all stage a debate about conduct during the fever in texts that open their terms to radical appraisal.

Like Benjamin Rush, Arthur Mervyn strenuously enacts his character and becomes the focus of public debate, inside and outside his text. Both Rush and Mervyn are described as being viscerally and psychically transformed by the fever, vulnerable and in circulation, ultimately annealed by the experience. While Rush fervently identifies with African Americans in Philadelphia, Arthur is moved to clinical detachment. Both advertise their virtue. Brown's portrayal of Arthur combines Rush's self image, on display in his public letters and personal narrative, and the figure criticized by his adversaries. In one of the novel's oddest scenes, Arthur delivers a little speech on his character, after a bullet has nicked his left ear and just missed his forehead. The bullet has emerged from a pistol fired by a woman in a house of prostitution into which Arthur has intruded in search of Clemenza, whom Welbeck has abandoned along with his child. Arthur immediately gleans a lesson for himself about being more cautious in the future when he confronts passionate women brandishing firearms. He advises her to discipline her responses, and then he justifies his conduct: "I am incapable of any purpose that is not beneficent; but, in the means I use and in the evidence on which I proceed, I am liable to a thousand mistakes. Point out to me the road by which I can do you good, and I will cheerfully pursue it" (330). Needless to say, his assailant does not take him up on his offer. This scene captures Rush's heroic, destructive, self-dramatizing, supremely confident zeal. Brown seems fascinated in *Arthur Mervyn* by this kind of character in action and under fever.[63]

The association of Mervyn with Rush does not solve the riddles of *Arthur Mervyn*, but it does point to a more complex set of virtues in the protagonist than many critics grant, and it elucidates Brown's pattern of exposing character in a specific location (Philadelphia) and under historical pressures (the yellow fever). It suggests a way to appreciate what kind of book *Arthur Mervyn* is. We might read Brown's fever narrative as an experimental novel, not unlike Emile Zola's late-nineteenth-century naturalist version, in which the writer as scientist analyzes the conditions necessary for the occurrence of social phenomena. Zola writes in 1880:

> in society as in the human body there is a solidarity which links the different members, the different organs together so that if an organ becomes infected many others are tainted, and a very complex illness becomes evident. Thus in our novels when we experiment on a grave infection which poisons society we proceed like the experimental doctor; we seek to find the simple initial determinism in order to arrive at the complex determinism which has ensued.[64]

In *Arthur Mervyn*, Brown shares Zola's sense of organicism, although he emphasizes a republican, and acutely Philadelphian, sense that the health of the whole depends on the character of its individual members. Brown's society, like the society Zola describes, suffers from a "complex illness." Yet when Brown examines the disorder, his aim is not to trace it to its root cause but to test the character of his characters. Brown evaluates Arthur's progress: his ardor for exposure, his partial impartiality, and the consequences of his zeal.

In *Arthur Mervyn*, we might say that Brown is an "experimental moralist," to use Zola's term. He shares something of the later naturalist detachment and fascination with inevitability. In the essay "Walstein's School of History" (1799), Brown sounds a bit like Zola when he writes that the "physician" and the "moral reasoner may discover principles equally universal in their application"—but, of course, Brown's republican and Zola's naturalist principles are not the same. In "Walstein's School of History," Brown outlines a fictional historian's approach to storytelling: "By exhibiting a virtuous being in opposite conditions, and pursuing his end by means suited to his own condition, he believes himself displaying a model of right conduct, and furnishing incitements to imitate that conduct, supplying men not only with knowledge of just ends and just means, but with the love and the zeal of virtue." Here, as several critics have pointed out, we have the plot and character of *Arthur Mervyn*. Yet this passage is often taken as though it were transparent. According to Brown, the historian places on exhibit not only character but also the terms of assessment. The writer *believes* himself to be displaying a model of right conduct and those beliefs, too, are subject to inquiry. We might view *Arthur Mervyn* as an experimental republican novel, in which readers are drawn into the trials of character during the fever and are asked to consider evidence, actions, and points of view, as they were in the public debates about Mathew Carey, Absalom Jones and Richard Allen, and Benjamin Rush.[65]

If Carey, Jones and Allen, and Rush set the stage for Brown's book, *Arthur Mervyn* itself points from fever narratives toward a Philadelphia genre that will become conspicuous in the first decades of the nineteenth century. Critics have puzzled over the last part of the novel, in which the story takes a domestic turn and Arthur shifts his affections from the fifteen-year-old country girl Eliza Hadwin to the twenty-five-year-old wealthy English divorcée Ascha Fielding, to whom he becomes betrothed. Does Arthur's impending marriage signify patriarchal victory or dependence? A tribute to, or the spoils of, virtue? A sentimental elevation, or a capitulation to the market?[66]

Another kind of question to ask might be: What is the relationship between the fever story and the sentimental comedy that follows? Although the yellow fever has subsided in the last part of the book, Arthur's personal fervor has not. Although he insists that he speaks with candor—"I felt no scruple on any occasion, to disclose every feeling and every event" (397)—Arthur still does not seem to know his feelings or recognize the consequences of his actions. Repeatedly in this last part of the book, Arthur's emotional obliviousness is inflicted upon Ascha. He tells Ascha, whom he is fond of calling "mamma," about Eliza (397, 415, 429). When he shows her their letters, she blushes. When he suggests that Ascha behave as Eliza's elder sister, she cries. When he wonders what he can do to make her happier, she briefly glances at him with "sweet and solemn significance" (429). When he asks her if there is any way in which he can be wholly hers, she chokes. After a conversation with Dr. Stevens, in which Arthur is made to realize that Ascha is not the "exact counterpart" or "type" of the woman he desires as a wife but the person herself (407, 432), at first he keeps his distance but then he follows her to the countryside, where, after a night spent throbbing on a precipice, he elaborately confesses to an increasingly uneasy Ascha the infamy and guilt and crime of . . . his love for her. In his relationship with Ascha, Arthur is continually underestimating her responses or overdoing his.[67]

Arthur also persists in his bodily inquiries. "There is no book," he explains, "in which I read with more pleasure, than the face of woman" (403). Arthur may not be able to tell from Ascha's face that she loves him, but "a peculiarity in [the] expression" of her eyes conveys to him the "secret" that she is Jewish. Similarly, Dr. Stevens's extrudes her ethnicity, as he tries to provoke Arthur into defending Ascha by caricaturing her features: "But she is a foreigner: independent of controul, and rich. . . . But then she is unsightly as a *night-hag*, tawney as a moor, the eye of a gypsey, low in stature, contemptibly diminutive, scarcely bulk enough to cast a shadow as she walks, less luxuriance than a charred log" (432). When Ascha tells the story of her life to Arthur, she says that her father was a Portuguese Jew "with few of the moral or external qualities of jews" (416). She recounts the demand of her first husband's father that she convert to the English church, and her relief at the prospect. If Ascha and her father do not possess the "moral or external qualities of jews," it is hard for the reader to tell what kind of "secret" Arthur discerns from her eyes. PAscha's "dark and almost sallow" complexion links her visually with the African Americans who served during the epidemic and with the European Americans who were stricken.[68]

The movement from fever to manners, the revelations of race, and the experiments in character in *Arthur Mervyn* all point to Philadelphia's peculiar genres of manners: Hugh Henry Brackenridge's satire *Modern Chivalry*, Edward W. Clay's images of "Life in Philadelphia," Robert Montgomery Bird's metempsychic novel *Sheppard Lee*, the minutes of the black national conventions, and Joseph Willson's *Sketches of the Higher Classes of Colored Society in Philadelphia*. In these early-nineteenth-century works, deportment is linked to destiny, and social behavior and verbal performance assume the weight of race and nation. The story of these genres is the focus of the next chapter.

CHAPTER TWO

Manners

There must doubtless be an unhappy influence on the manners of
our people produced by the existence of slavery among us.
—Thomas Jefferson, "Query XVIII: Manners,"
Notes on the State of Virginia (1787)

Critics and fiction writers have long debated the viability of the novel of manners in the United States. In the nineteenth century, during the first century of American democracy, the argument goes, there may not have been a sufficiently developed social history and class hierarchy to support an indigenous novel of manners. There may not have been the pressure of convention on character and the valuing of gesture, tone, and ornament needed to provide "texture," as Henry James would describe it, in the fictional renderings of American society.[1]

This social and generic skepticism itself forms a native tradition, extending from J. Hector St. Jean de Crèvecoeur to James Fenimore Cooper, Alexis de Tocqueville, Nathaniel Hawthorne, and James. In his epistolary fiction *Letters from an American Farmer* (1782), Crèvecoeur's narrator contrasts American with English prospects. In America, there "are no aristocratical families, no courts, no kings, no bishops, no ecclesiastical dominion, no invisible power giving to a few a very visible one, no great manufactures employing thousands, no great refinements of luxury." In the preface to his novel of Europe, *The Marble Faun* (1860), Hawthorne lamented the challenges faced by the American writer: "No author, without a trial, can conceive of the difficulty of writing a Romance about a country where there is no shadow, no antiquity, no mystery, no picturesque and gloomy wrong, nor anything but a common-place prosperity, in broad and simple daylight, as is happily the case with my dear native land." James famously quotes Hawthorne in his critical biography *Hawthorne* (1879), during a discussion of Hawthorne's note-books, and then inflates the catalogue of "the absent things in American life—especially in the American life of forty years ago": "No State, in the European sense of the word, and indeed barely a specific national name. No sovereign, no court, no personal loyalty, no aristocracy, no church, no clergy, no army, no dip-lomatic service, no country gentlemen, no palaces, no castles, nor manors, nor old country-houses, nor parsonages, nor thatched cottages nor ivied ruins; no cathe-drals, nor abbeys, nor little Norman churches; no great Universities nor public schools—no Oxford, nor Eton, nor Harrow; no literature, no novels, no muse-ums, no pictures, no political society, no sporting class—no Epsom nor Ascot!"[2]

Yet James and the others doth protest too much. (James's own escalation and anticlimax suggest parody.) The catalogues of American absence evoke the trope of New World colonial innocence in Montaigne's essay "Of Cannibals" and Gonzalo's speech in Shakespeare's *The Tempest*. Building on these tropes upon tropes, some twentieth-century critics, such as Lionel Trilling and Richard Chase, have asserted a preference among nineteenth-century U.S. writers for the prose romance over the novel of manners. These writers describe social isolation rather than engagement; they pursue ideas through elaborate symbols, rather than exam-ining customs and class differences. Although the arguments of Trilling and Chase have been countered by a generation of "New Americanists," who analyze them as mystifications of American social reality, neither old nor new American-ists have paid much notice to manners in U.S. literature before the Civil War. In the mid-twentieth century, Ralph Ellison suggested an alternative to the insistent negations. In "The World and the Jug," with Hawthorne, James, and Trilling in mind, he inverted the trope, and in several of the essays collected in *Shadow and Act*, he described the plenitude of his African American childhood in Oklahoma City. He used this location as the unlikely site for restoring social texture to the historical imagination. We might consider Philadelphia, especially in the years between the Constitution and the Civil War, as offering another alternative to the declaration of absence.[3]

In Philadelphia, as we have seen in the narratives of 1793, debates pivoted on questions of conduct and character. In his life and writings, Benjamin Franklin had helped to create a public arena in which individuals were taught to be acutely conscious of their social performances. Franklin recounted in his memoir how he performed his frugality and industry, in set pieces such as the entry into Philadelphia, with his teenage self parading down Market Street, a roll of bread under each arm and one stuffed in his mouth, and the young entrepreneur transporting paper through the streets of Philadelphia in a wheelbarrow so that merchants would appreciate his labors. Instructing readers on the virtues of understatement and the value of appearances, Franklin offered an amalgam of conduct book, courtesy book, and etiquette manual. Readers were shown a model of behavior in which moral character was both natural and acquired, substantial and formal. In the ultimate irony, Franklin presented a model that eluded imitation. His autobiography was a "how-to-succeed" book whose directives only its author, an extraordinarily skilled and well-connected maneuverer in a patronage society, could fulfill. It was a guide to crafting appearances that unsettled the relationship between character and performance. The ironies and tensions on display in Franklin's memoir reverberated in the nineteenth-century literature of manners in Philadelphia.[4]

This literature takes different forms, which this chapter considers in relation: Philadelphia picaresque fiction, such as Hugh Henry Brackenridge's *Modern Chivalry* (1792–1815) and Robert Montgomery Bird's *Sheppard Lee* (1836), in which authors test their characters; "Life in Philadelphia," Edward W. Clay's internationally popular series of etchings lampooning black social aspirations, which first appeared in the late 1820s; a different visual revelation of character found in the silhouettes cut at Charles Willson Peale's Museum; Robert Purvis's "Appeal of Forty Thousand Citizens" (1838), in which the history of conduct is marshaled to protest African American disfranchisement; and Joseph Willson's *Sketches of the Higher Classes of Colored Society in Philadelphia* (1841), an outsider's view of politics and manners published at the beginning of a spectacularly violent decade for the city. In the 1830s, with the rise of the black convention movement in Philadelphia and its debates over respectability and with the rewriting of the state constitution in 1837–38 and the vote of 1838 to deny African American men the right to vote, the topic of social behavior took on conspicuous urgency. The literature of manners in Philadelphia reflected on the depths of character and participated in the struggle over rights.

Hugh Henry Brackenridge, and the Irrepressible Teague

At the end of the last volume of *Modern Chivalry*, Hugh Henry Brackenridge's satire of politics, race, ethnicity, and faith in the new nation, the narrator explains that "a key" to its hundreds of pages "will be found in the history of the times; and especially of that of the state of Pennsylvania." Over the course of the seven volumes, which appeared in parts from 1792 until 1815, the narrator invokes Brackenridge's own personal history: a stinging loss to William Findley, an Irish ex-weaver, during the 1787 election for representatives to the Constitutional Convention; his tactical support of the farmers on the western Pennsylvania frontier during the 1794 Whiskey Rebellion against the federal excise tax (a move that satisfied neither government nor farmers); and controversies over his tenure as a justice on the Pennsylvania Supreme Court. In *Modern Chivalry*, Brackenridge assesses his own experiences, and he seeks fictional revenge. Yet the "history of the times" is found not only in Brackenridge's biography and in Pennsylvania state history but also in the book's literary experiments. At the center of *Modern Chivalry*, giving this shapeless book its dynamism, Brackenridge places his two protagonists, the aging, bookish Captain John Farrago, a model of propriety, and his ambitious Irish servant, Teague O'Regan. In the first parts (the bulk of volumes 2, 3, and 4), Farrago and O'Regan are subjected to fictional tests of character in Philadelphia, and O'Regan's status as a citizen is gauged. Many of the subsequent events and digressions in the book are marked by this Philadelphia sojourn.[5]

Brackenridge repeatedly invokes the pairing of Don Quixote and Sancho Panza, and he aligns his book not only with Cervantes but also with Horace, Lucian, Le Sage, Swift, Rabelais, Sterne, and Smollett. He imagines Cervantes in America. He transposes the bond between Quixote and Panza and the satiric correction of fantasy to the social laboratory of Philadelphia and its issues of slavery, human diversity, and civil rights. Brackenridge uses reason and ridicule to temper what he views as the extravagances of democracy, particularly the risks of demagoguery and mob rule. He supports the republican virtues of humility and self-denial and the moderating influences of a representative and divided form of government. The narrative tracks, and risks becoming derailed by, Farrago's social experiments.[6]

From his bitterness at losing to an Irish candidate in the voting for the Constitutional Convention, the Scots-Irish immigrant Brackenridge conceived the remarkable Teague O'Regan, who becomes the object of his narrator's and Captain's manipulations for over two decades. Introducing O'Regan, the narrator tells us that he "shall say nothing of the character of this man, because the very name imports what he was," and during the narrative, the redundant "Teague O'Regan" is often supplanted by the epithet "bog-trotter" (6). Yet, rather than self-evident, O'Regan is a surprising force. He drives events in *Modern Chivalry*, and other characters are fascinated with his attributes. He almost becomes a state legislator, a philosopher, a preacher, and an Indian chief. In Philadelphia, O'Regan is an actor, a candidate for state employment, and a cynosure for the ladies, igniting "a kind of Teagueomania" (230). Appointed an excise officer in a remote district of the state by the president, he is tarred and feathered by a mob, and his presence incites a local uprising (evoking the Whiskey Rebellion). Still tarred and feathered, he is captured by hunters, returned to Philadelphia for exhibit, and acquired by the American Philosophical Society. On loan to the French for study, he is liberated during their revolution, admired by the multitudes, and, as an Esquimaux Indian, joins the famous cavalcade of the Frenchman Anacharsis Cloots. Back in the United States, he becomes an editor, a successful (if ghost-written) memoirist, a seller of patent medicines, a judge, an inadvertent hero in a military campaign against the Indians, and a camp meeting entertainer. Dressed as a panther, he is displayed as a beast who can speak and serves as evidence in a fierce controversy over whether to extend the franchise to the animal kingdom.

In some of these instances, O'Regan aspires and pretends. In other cases, he is inveigled or exploited. Farrago often misleads his servant, placing him in vulnerable circumstances from which he must extricate him. Again and again, the imaginative energy of the book focuses on repositioning O'Regan and then examining his conduct and the responses of others to his trials of status. O'Regan's character is the enigma that animates these scenes and generates their repetition. Despite the narrator's initial announcement that he "shall say nothing of the character of this man, because the very name imports what he was," Teague O'Regan's surplus Irishness prompts his verbosity. Teagueomania is experienced not only by the ladies in Philadelphia but also by his master, Farrago, and by the narrator and author. Everybody wants O'Regan. And part of their desire has to do with his protean ethnic and racial identity. Irishman, Indian, man or beast, Esquimaux, panther—O'Regan is moved into and through various racial and even species predicaments during his vocational odyssey. In part 2 of *Modern Chivalry*, the narrator defends himself from charges that he has unfairly singled out "*the Irish nation.*" He explains that "the character of the Irish clown . . . 'has more stuff in it,'" and that "[t]he American has in fact, yet, no character" (405). Such a defense helps to explain the fixation with O'Regan, as the narrator and the Captain test the material of character.[7]

Running away from his master, O'Regan becomes a Philadelphia stage actor, taking on the parts of a witch in *Macbeth* and of the Irishman Darby in John O'Keefe's comic opera *The Poor Soldier*. As Darby, O'Regan enacts his type. The actor's calling glosses the function of O'Regan in the narrative, moved from role to role, eliciting reactions from different audiences. The Captain decides to present him at the president's levee as a candidate for state office. The positive response leads Farrago to subject O'Regan to formal training in movement so that he will be able to cut a successful figure in high society. He is given lessons by a French dancing master, whose thick accent and nervousness about Irish brutality combine with O'Regan's brogue and inability to tell his right from his left foot to produce a series of literal missteps, culminating in a tangle and fall with Monsieur Douparie, who resigns his commission. Farrago determines to serve as O'Regan's instructor in manners. He prohibits various behaviors associated with his class and ethnicity: no belching or breaking wind, scratching, chewing tobacco, spitting, talking with a full mouth, or singing bawdy songs. Across the volumes of *Modern Chivalry*, Brackenridge plays with O'Regan's labored attempts to improve his status, which reveal the gap between manners and nature. Again and again (and again), recognition is dangled before O'Regan and then withdrawn.

O'Regan's minimal and temporary progress in assuming the social graces in Philadelphia, as well as the cachet bestowed upon his blunt speech and the rumor that a high office for him is close at hand, makes him the toast of society, especially its principal ladies. Within ten days, Teagueomania has taken hold of the city, as women project their desires upon "Major O'Regan." Brackenridge satirizes the political culture in Philadelphia, the nation's temporary capital, where the public, marked as female, is seduced by office seekers whose influence mounts as they exchange favors. O'Regan loses his social footing after the Captian reveals his identity to the family of a Miss Mutchkin, who is on the verge of accepting his proposal of marriage. Instead of evening tea, O'Regan receives the blows of a porter's cudgel when he arrives at the Mutchkin household.

As in many of the episodes in *Modern Chivalry*, here Farrago is implicated in O'Regan's imposture and punishment. He sets up O'Regan, establishing and then undermining him. Farrago continually savors the social disturbance, flinches, and then intervenes to expose and deliver O'Regan so that he can be subjected to another trial. Teagueomania thus signifies a wider disorder than indicated in Brackenridge's ephemeral, if deft, satire of capital politics in the 1790s. The *Modern Chivalry* scenario—the exacting, compromised social experiment in freedom, with ethnicity and race as catalysts and disintegrating lines of authority—is repeated across many of the genres of Philadelphia writing between the Constitution and the Civil War.

In the chapters about Philadelphia, the narrator associates the beleaguered Teague with African American residents of the city. In search of O'Regan, before finding him on stage, Farrago attends a lecture at the American Philosophical Society, delivered by an African American servant or slave (it is not clear which) Cuff, whose name, like Teague's, supposedly fixes his type. In dialect, Cuff argues that all men were originally black and that racial differences have been caused by the effects of climate. Here Brackenridge reworks the environmental arguments of Samuel Stanhope Smith, a prominent member of the Philosophical Society whose *Essay on the Causes of the Variety of Complexion and Figure in the Human Species* was first published in 1787. The narrator speculates on "the diversity of the human species" (117), dismissing various theories (the biblical curses on Cain or Ham or Babel, the effects of climate) and proposing his own: that Adam was white and Eve was black and that this and subsequent miscegenation produced the varieties of human color. For Brackenridge, the absurdity seems to lie in theorizing about racial difference, rather than in acknowledging its presence. In the 1830s, in works such as the novel *A Sojourn in the City of Amalgamation* (1837), racial mixing in Philadelphia will become the topic for Juvenalian satire. In part I, volume 2 of *Modern Chivalry*, issued in 1792, such intermingling among the biblical parents is advanced with a gentler irony.

After Farrago sees Teague on stage, he considers purchasing an African American slave as his replacement. Mentioning this plan at breakfast at his tavern, he is engaged in debate by a Quaker. The Captain holds that in nature and history "the great law is Force" (134). Human beings can and should dominate other human beings, as they dominate animals, as long as the subordinated creatures are given sufficient rest and nourishment. "The fact is," he explains, "a state of liberty is an unnatural state. Like a bone out of place, the mind, in an individual, or political capacity, seeks the condition of a master or servant; avoiding, as the particular propensity may be, the one or the other" (136). Farrago confesses that he would rather have a white person as a slave, "especially in the summer season, as being a more light and airy colour," and concedes that, given the law of "domination and subjection," he himself might become a slave in turn (137). This defense of slavery, with its respectable, brutal logic, is one of the points at which the distance between Farrago's "chivalry" and his author's modernity seems greatest.

The irony is deepened by the narrator's support of Farrago in the following chapter. If the theft of persons from Africa were morally wrong, the narrator explains, then the entire system of slavery would be corrupt and would contaminate all who participated in it. If this were the case, then those who were enslaved should be emancipated immediately. Since Christian churches, with the exception of the fanatical Quakers, uphold slavery, it cannot be immoral. Gradual abolition, like that provided for in the law of Pennsylvania, is preferable to giving immediate freedom to slaves, since "those who have got them could not do without them, no more than a robber could do without the money that he takes"— but gradual abolition is "the whim of the day" and a "phrensy." The only consistent principle is to believe in the "right of absolute subjugation" of people of all colors and nations or in absolute emancipation (139). Opposed to African American men voting in Pennsylvania, the narrator worries that pettifogging lawyers might invoke the 1790 state constitution, "by which it is established that 'all *men* are born equally free and independent'" (140). Such misguided arguments would lead to habeas corpus petitions, the acknowledgment that slaves are not property, and their release.[8]

When the tarred and feathered O'Regan is returned to Philadelphia and exhibited, Brackenridge gathers the associations with race, ethnology, law, and property. Before O'Regan is purchased from the hunters, two members of the Philosophical Society write a treatise (which the narrator includes) on the behavior and appearance of the creature. They ponder how to classify it and decide that it represents a new species, located somewhere between bird and beast or beast and human (318–21). The chief justice of Pennsylvania issues a writ of habeas corpus to O'Regan's keepers, demanding that they account for his imprisonment, if he is a man. (This protection was denied to those accused of being escaped slaves, according to the federal law of 1793.) The court empanels a jury to resolve O'Regan's status but denies a motion insisting that half of the jurors be beasts. Rejecting the argument that the creature speaks with a brogue and so must be human (counterevidence is presented from Aesop's *Fables* and *The History of Reynard the Fox* that beasts can speak), the court instructs the jury to decide in favor of the keepers and the habeas corpus petition is rejected.

In Brackenridge's disorienting satire, O'Regan occupies the position of the norm. Terrified, resilient, immutable, Teague remains constant while the society around him contorts and reveals itself. On the one hand, O'Regan's imperviousness to change would seem to reinforce his stereotypical limits. Yet O'Regan's fixity is remarkably portable, and it stimulates the necessities and upheavals of the plot, the apparently infinite series of resituations in which the Irishman's limits are tested and his compatriots are exposed. Teague's finitude is excessive and seems to require perpetual demonstration. The Philadelphia philosophers try, but fail, to classify him. O'Regan pleads with them not to dissect him (Farrago has warned him that this is what philosophers do), and they assure him that they want only to observe his "external structure" (322). The ethnological and legal absurdities in Brackenridge's Philadelphia proceed from deductions about interiority based on such external structures: tar, feathers, anatomy, posture, and accent. Manners for Brackenridge (but not, as we shall see, for all of the Philadelphia writers who follow) betray the gap between performance and nature, but O'Regan's nature is specified to the point of collapse. The court declares him property, but then, in France, after the tar and feathers have worn off his backside, his lack of breeches is mistaken by the mob for political commitment (he is seen as a literal "sans culotte" [324]), and he is set free. On the pages of *Modern Chivalry*, O'Regan's intransigence appears revolutionary.

The Captain and narrator often assert the importance of status and hierarchy in the new democracy: "There is nothing makes a man so ridiculous as to attempt what is above his sphere," says Farrago to the weaver Traddle, who is running for election to the state legislature against a man of education, echoing Bracken-ridge's own experience in 1787 (14). "It is indeed making a devil of a man to lift him up to a state to which he is not suited," reflects the narrator (20). Weighing the lessons of *Modern Chivalry*, the narrator concludes, "The great moral of this book is the evil of men seeking office for which they are not qualified. The pre-posterous ambition of the bog-trotter, all points to this" (611). Toward the end of the book, overlooking his own complicity, Farrago reassures himself that O'Regan has been satisfied with his place, except when others have misled and confused him.

Yet what exactly is O'Regan's "sphere," "state," or "office"? What are his enti-tlements or exclusions? O'Regan's impropriety gives the book its verve. Originat-ing in Brackenridge's loss to William Findley in 1787, the character of the Irish upstart first appeared in satires he published in the *Pittsburgh Gazette* in 1787 and 1788, then in his poem *The Modern Chevalier*, then as a minor character at the beginning of *Modern Chivalry*, and then in the pivotal role of Teague O'Regan across the volumes.[9] Brackenridge's literary revenge produced a surprising result. Over the decades, the stereotype seems to have taken on a life of its own, transfix-ing its creator.

At the end of *Modern Chivalry*, Brackenridge returns to the figures and issues in the Philadelphia sojourn and offers his most sustained conceit: a debate over whether the right of suffrage should be extended to beasts (635–719). Although these chapters are located in a new state, in which Farrago serves as governor, Brackenridge invokes the Pennsylvania context. The chapters hinge on the pun that debates about property qualifications are at the same time debates about whether property is qualified to vote. While Farrago is governor, a plan is advanced that beasts should be allowed to cast ballots and to serve as legislators: "The people were naturally led from the idea of property giving the right of suffrage, to that of the property itself exercising this right; and herds and flocks propria persona, coming forward viva voce, or with a ticket; and this by an association of ideas, introduced that of being capable of being elected" (665). Brackenridge personifies the agency of property implied by its requirement, and he logically suggests that property itself—not land but horses, sheep, rams, oxen, and cattle—should be allowed to exercise the right it enables. When animals come to vote "in propria persona," questions are raised about human properties and proprieties.

Blurring the line between property and persons, Brackenridge clarifies the differences. Human beings, the narrator explains in a chapter relatively unmarked by satire, can be improved. Animals cannot, beyond a certain limit. Human beings are capable of rationally acquiring language, they can think metaphysically, and they have ideas about the past and hopes and fears for the future. They can participate in and modify civil government (685–88). In an earlier volume, the narrator had praised democracy. Quoting Thucydides, he defended a respect for the multitude, rather than the few; equality before the law, including equal rights of office and of suffrage to all male citizens, regardless of means (privileges that should be extended to immigrants, including the Irish); distinctions of virtue, rather than wealth; freedom of opinion; and mutual respect (530–37, 506–9).

The figure of O'Regan confirms but also complicates these stances. Although he seems ineducable, the narrative holds out the slim possibility that in the next episode things might work out differently. And his humanity is measured not by his susceptibility to improvement but by other capacities: his resilience and his persistence, an ineradicable, irresistible presence. The energies of a Teague O'Regan balk every effort to contain or elevate him. Although the Captain and narrator repeatedly endorse moderation against excess, O'Regan's superfluity continues to fascinate over the pages of this extravagant book, and it serves as an outlandish instance of the irreducible human nature upon which Brackenridge founds his philosophical and political distinctions.

Yet the satire of the beast franchise is not so easy to read. A visionary philosopher tests the idea that beasts are capable of development. He establishes an academy where squirrels study algebra and are taught to play the fiddle and cattle are instructed in legislative debate. O'Regan is captured by two young men with a cart, who dress him in an animal skin and parade him as a speaking panther (duplicating his earlier tarred and feathered display in Philadelphia), in support of the claim that animals should participate as citizens. The people insist on the perfectibility of beasts and experiments are designed to assess their capacities. ("Experiments" is Brackenridge's term, used on 682, 683, 701, 702, 704, and 710.) A monkey is appointed clerk of the court, and dogs are admitted to the bar (where they bark in argument). O'Regan, in his own skin, is adduced as an example. Ultimately, Governor Farrago wins the debate by arguing that if beasts are to be given the rights of citizenship, "we should have them set free as we done the negroes": "Now if cattle . . . oxen, and horses become entitled to equal privileges, we could not treat them as beasts of burden, or use them for the draught; much less could we knock down a pig, or shoot a deer, or take the skin off a bear; nor even ride a horse, but on condition of taking turns, and letting him sometimes ride us. Who of you would be hitched in a sled, or stand at the tongue of the wagon for a whole night champing cut straw, and rye meal, or bear the whip of the carter in the day time?" (713).

As in the passage linking slavery to robbery during the Philadelphia chapters, here the analogy between racial slavery and animal subjugation emphasizes violence and registers concern about the prospect of reversal, in which the free would become bound. The satire works against racial slavery, black or white, but is double-edged. Farrago wins the debate over beast elevation through his analogy with emancipation, but the victory comes with a cost, or at least a question. Many citizens in Farrago's new state are persuaded that beasts cannot be given "equal privileges" like the "negroes" because then they would either have to lose their own privileges or share the burden and pain of servitude. The argument plays upon the citizens' ambivalence about the status of African Americans. Beasts should not be manumitted because their subjection is necessary for the freedom of their owners. Brackenridge's irony suggests that this is a vicious system, but it is the distressing prospect of freedom (and the perceived consequences of gradual abolition in states such as Pennsylvania) that turns the citizens against reform. The narrator and author (and in the later volumes of *Modern Chivalry*, their perspectives tend to converge) may think that racial slavery should be abolished, but the citizens that Farrago addresses are not so sure and seem uneasy with the local consequences.

What are the entitlements and exclusions of African Americans in the state of Pennsylvania and its leading city, Philadelphia? How do slavery and freedom define and alter one another? What happens to abstract rights as they become the focus of struggle on the pages and streets of the city? These questions, the satiric mode, and Brackenridge's scenario—in which character is tested in a series of experiments in freedom—are at the center of Philadelphia's literature of manners before the Civil War.

Edward W. Clay's "Life in Philadelphia"

"Preposterous ambition" is the phrase Brackenridge uses to describe the spectacle of Teague O'Regan's misguided efforts, concocted across the volumes of *Modern Chivalry* (611). "Preposterous ambition" also preoccupies Edward W. Clay, whose satirical etchings, with the series title "Life in Philadelphia," gained international renown in the 1830s and 1840s. Originally issued between 1828 and 1830, these hand-colored prints were widely imitated. Clay's images had sources in British urban illustrations of the 1820s, such as those by George and Robert Cruikshank for the popular *Life in London* (1820); in French Orientalism, whose examples he saw and copied during a stay in Paris; and in comic scenes and types from American theater. Clay reaffirmed Philadelphia's reputation as America's fashionable city, and he emphasized a racial edge. (Three of the era's most prominent racial caricaturists were Philadelphia natives: Clay and also James Thackera and David Claypoole Johnston.) A few of the etchings lampoon white Philadelphians promenading on the city streets, but the majority—and the images that engaged the public—focus on African Americans.[10]

A pseudo-gentleman with gloves, top hat, and cane, seeking an audience with Miss Dinah, bends down to place his card on a tray extended by a young woman from her position on the cellar steps. In dialect, a young man with arms akimbo prompts a sumptuously dressed and coiffed Miss Florinda to compliment him on his new striped shirt. She does, mentioning that she had seen him wear it on New Year's Day during a procession for the abolition society, and comparing him to "Pluto de God of War." A woman in a dress with an elaborate floral pattern and a hat with a vast brim and streaming ribbons, crowned with floral encrustations, inquires of a white dry goods merchant if he carries any flesh-colored silk stockings. Assuring her that he does have "von pair of de first qualité!" he holds up a pair of dark stockings. A woman in a ballooning dress and a hat strewn with bows holds a guitar in her lap and gazes with yearning at her beau in tight pants, coat, and tails, who holds his gloved hand to his chest and serenades her in dialect. She praises his singing as "con a moor [rather than con amore], as de Italians say!!" The dominant note of the series is sounded in an exchange between two characters, when Mr. Cesar, in topcoat, vest, chains, and high collar, asks Miss Chloe how she is finding herself in the hot weather, and she, almost eclipsed by her various accoutrements, replies, "Pretty well I tank you Mr. Cesar only I aspire too much!"[11]

Chloe's exorbitant aspirations are visible in her finery and audible in her diction. The unpleasant humor of these prints often turns on what Clay illustrates as inappropriate emulation. His African American figures attempt to wear the clothes, strike the poses, and speak the language of a white rising class, yet their efforts fall short, and this gap becomes the space of ridicule. Clay features the strains in social performance. No matter how hard his figures try, no matter the expense or rehearsal or care for detail, Clay reveals in scene after scene how the clothes and words don't fit and the postures look absurd. Manners cannot raise African Americans in Philadelphia above their natural limits. The desires of Chloe and the other figures yield perspiration rather than elevation—and they don't seem to know the difference. Clay satirizes what he views as inadvertent burlesque of white affectations, and this double parody may help to explain the appeal of these prints. They offer European American viewers the reassurance that their own performances are more successful and their own positions more secure. Such reassurances would overlap with the satisfactions of the contemporary minstrel stage and its popular black dandy character, Zip Coon. Clay published his series at the end of two decades of rapid population growth and economic stagnation in Philadelphia, charges of poverty and criminality against the mass of African Americans, resentment at the achievements of an emerging black higher class, support for colonization, and increasing public violence.[12]

Yet the images of "Life in Philadelphia" register more than anxiety and hostility. We can acknowledge their offense but also recognize their distinctiveness when compared with Clay's imitators and his own later prints on related subjects. Several historians have reprinted Clay's images, adducing them as transparent racial caricature, but more is on display in the series than such a use implies. The images are undeniably racist, suggesting that inherent difference governs individual and group attainment and restricts the possibilities for African Americans. As we shall see, contemporary African American observers such as Joseph Willson, bristling at their popularity, sought to repudiate their message and insist on alternatives. Yet the visual textures of "Life in Philadelphia" are replete with detail and indicate a broader satire of all social performance as mimicry. Ultimately, they raise questions about who is parodying whom.[13]

Clay lavishes attention in the prints that emphasize black figures. The few images of white characters are comparatively abstract and listless. In the eighth plate of the series, a white dandy flirts with a woman encased in an unadorned cloak and bonnet, whose broad curves obscure any expression of stance or posture (figure 2.1). The effect is similar in an early, apparently unpublished image from the series, "Going Home from a Tea-Fight" (1825). In this ink and watercolor piece, two of three characters are entirely hidden beneath the smooth geometrical forms of their coats and hats. The face of the third figure, a young white woman on the left, smiles at the viewer from the cave of a large bonnet. In vivid contrast, the African American images supply detail about the cut and fold of garments, props, gestures, and domestic or public settings. Attributes often are exaggerated, but rarely twisted to the extremes found in the "Life in Philadelphia" versions produced by others in New York or London or in Clay's own later "Practical Amalgamation" series of lithographs (1839), which offer a sneering portrayal of abolition as interracial sexual congress.[14]

We can appreciate the difference by contrasting Clay's single-sheet hand-colored etchings with the reduced black-and-white designs that appeared in the *New Comic Annual,* a small volume published in London in the 1830s. This London "Life in Philadelphia" offers nine small wood engravings (some images taken from Clay, others from a "Life in New York" series he inspired), now framed by

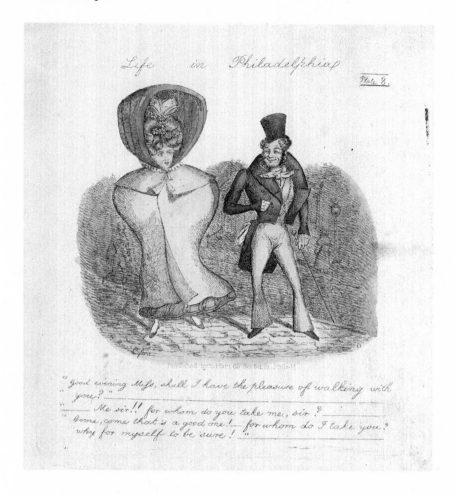

FIGURE 2.1 Edward W. Clay, "Life in Philadelphia," plate 8: "Good evening Miss, shall I have the pleasure of walking with you?" (circa 1830). Courtesy of the Library Company of Philadelphia.

a story. Traveling on a stagecoach, the narrator overhears a debate about abolition, during which a thin gentleman describes "the result of my experiment" in freeing slaves and sending them to New York. As the gentleman tells his anecdotes about the ludicrous spectacle of African American freedom, the writer for the *New Comic Annual* loosely strings together situations and dialogue provided by Clay and his followers. Dispersed in the text are miniature versions of "Life in Philadelphia," stressing facial caricature. Clay's precision and misalignments are lost, and the jokes come too easily.[15]

In Clay's "Philadelphia," racial and social hierarchies are asserted and under-mined. In the eleventh plate, for example, the joke about the silk stockings cuts several ways (figure 2.2). In response to the woman's query—"Have you any *flesh* coloured silk stockings, young man?"—the salesman holds up a pair of dark stockings. Here "flesh coloured" is not conventional pink but a shade that

FIGURE 2.2 Edward W. Clay, "Life in Philadelphia," plate I I: "Have you any *flesh* coloured silk stockings, young man?" (1829). Courtesy of the Library of Congress.

reflects the woman's own skin. The joke pivots on this discrepancy. Viewers are supposed to imagine that the woman, ostentatiously, either asks for pink stockings and is offered dark ones or considers dark a fashionable color. The dark choice also may have been made by the salesman. Viewers are reminded that color renders some aspirations ludicrous. Yet several visual aspects complicate the joke. Since the print focuses on the moment of display, knowledge is withheld about what either the salesman or the woman thinks about the connection between request and response. The woman raises the lens on her necklace, paralleling the gesture of the salesman who holds the stockings, but this viewing instrument is held below eye level. The characters look at one another without expressing any reaction to the proposed sale. The print centers on these suspended gestures and linked gazes. The distinctions between the two figures are not clear. While the salesman himself is "flesh coloured," he also speaks in a French-inflected dialect ("Oui Madame! here is von pair of de first qualité!"), while the woman inquires in arch, standard English. He, too, is overdecorated. His thick, curled hair pulls his face along a horizontal axis, exaggerating his prim appearance; he wears a tight jacket, patterned vest, white shirt, and pink neckcloth. Clay makes fun of African American and French American social ambitions, and he lances the prestige of French culture and commodities in early national Philadelphia. On the wall behind the salesman hang various textiles, offering a palette of blues, pinks, and grays. In this print, ultimately, it is hard to discern a hierarchy of color privilege ("first qualité!") or to establish a standard of "flesh."

In the space of this dry goods shop, flesh is overwhelmed by apparel. Only the face of the woman is visible, given in profile. Her green hat transforms the shape of her head, yellow gloves cover her hands, and her gray boots rise above the lower hem of her dress. A tight floral design proliferates across the billowing green skirts and bodice and the sweeping brim and crown of her hat. The dress and hat vertically dominate the frame. Organic in color, pattern, and flow, they seem more alive than any of the posturing humans.[16] (A vibrant yellow dress and hat, attached to another dark face, wait in the background, at the threshold to the shop.) In several other prints, Clay represents space more abstractly and distorts facial features more conspicuously than he does in the silk stockings image, and his racialist intentions seem clearer. Yet in this image and across the series, in the pageant of costumes (cut, fold, pattern, layer, ornament, gather, and bustle) and props (canes, umbrellas, eyeglasses, fans, and handkerchiefs), the targeting of racial pretense also becomes a broader and deeper study of Philadelphia social masquerade. Clay's eye for detail competes with his ideology. And his purpose—to reduce black aspiration to farcical mimicry—gets tangled in layers of parody whose effects may exceed his intent.

The flamboyance in "Life in Philadelphia" has multiple sources, including European American middle-class imitation of upper-class behavior, African American rituals such as elaborate balls (plate 5 in the series) and Masonic splendor (two black Masons appear in their regalia in plate 6), and African American working-class blazon in dress and movement. In diaries, travelers' accounts, and the pronouncements of cultural arbiters, both white (the Pennsylvania Abolition Society) and black (ministers and civic leaders), observers in Philadelphia in the first half of the nineteenth century debated African American public appearance. As Shane White and Graham White describe the situation, "the attaining of freedom in the North sparked an exuberant cultural display, as newly liberated blacks deliberately, consciously, and publicly tested the boundaries of freedom." Although this exuberance was largely a feature of working-class culture, and sometimes the object of disapproval for African American leaders, members of the "respectable" class themselves were criticized by white authorities for their parades and balls. Manners became a form of expression and experiment.[17]

Yet who is parodying whom in Clay's "Philadelphia"? Clay mocks both blacks and whites for their pretense. Some of his figures seem to be members of Philadelphia's African American "higher classes" (as Joseph Willson will describe them in 1841), who strive to imitate European American protocols. This category would include the woman in the silk stockings print and the man who extends his calling card to the servant in the cellar. Others could be members of higher or lower classes, such as Miss Florinda and the man in the striped shirt or the serenaders "con a moor." In one print, the seventh in the series, Clay portrays tensions across African American classes. An older, well-dressed man, who supports the administration of John Quincy Adams, chastises a barefoot boy in torn and patched attire, who is celebrating the recent election of Andrew Jackson and victory for the Democrats. Clay derides the "preposterous ambition" of his African American figures, but his details imply additional stories. When we see the meticulous finery adorning the bodies of Clay's African American characters, we might be glimpsing the sartorial play before his eyes in Philadelphia in the 1820s, a mixture of class desire and African American satire, in ratios impossible to recover. Clay parodies African American figures who may, in turn, be making fun of their white models, such as the troupers in Washington Square or the attendees at the Fancy Ball that Clay himself represents in his series. These figures, in turn, may have been influenced by African American extravagance in the public spaces of Philadelphia.[18]

Clay's "Life in Philadelphia" offers a spectacle of parody all the way down. Unlike Brackenridge in *Modern Chivalry*, whose Teague O'Regan possesses a democratic force of character that persists across his ill-fitting roles, Clay's characters seem defined by their presumption and dominated by fashions whose promise of status can never be secured. The phrase "life in Philadelphia" itself came in vogue to describe a society constituted by imposture, whose emblems were the African American dandy and dandizette.[19] In Clay's graphic comedy of manners, individuals are the product of mimicry, and African Americans are depicted as imitations of imitations. Rather than revealing an interior or acquiring prestige, manners— enticing surfaces—appear to be all there is to character. The denizens of Clay's Philadelphia "aspire too much," and the gaps and strain (and allure) in their social performances are exposed. In Benjamin Franklin's Philadelphia, a strategic display of enterprise might lead to worldly success. Habits of industry, discipline, and virtue might secure character. In Clay's Philadelphia, ambition seems, by definition, preposterous, and character entirely an unstable accrual of surfaces.

Clay's images endured long after the original series appeared. In his early-twentieth-century history *The Negro in Pennsylvania*, Edward Raymond Turner noted an unfortunate exhibit in the symbolic center of the city: "See the ridiculous colored prints by Charles Hunt and by I. Harris . . . in the museum of Independence Hall, Phila. These pictures ridicule the brilliant, colored clothes of the negroes, and their aping the importance of the white people." In the early 1830s, Charles Hunt had etched versions of Clay's images that had been redrawn by William Summers for the English publisher Harrison Isaacs. Turner mentions the contemporary show at Independence Hall during his narrative of white backlash against the "great mass of the negroes of Pennsylvania" in the decades before the Civil War. He objects to such ridicule but indicates that the prints may convey a mimesis and exuberance with some historical basis. Turner's diction and syntax—"their aping the importance of the white people"—makes it hard to tell whether he means to criticize an original social blunder or Hunt and Summers's misconstruals. The word "aping" conceals his approach to mimicry, containing both possibilities: that such performances were deluded, failed imitations or that such performances were strategic repetitions, signifying on rituals of white importance. If it is difficult to fix Turner's attitude toward the embellishment represented in the prints, it is impossible to know why those images were hanging in Independence Hall at the beginning of the twentieth century or how those who viewed them responded. Were they exhibited or received as history or humor, as on target or misguided, at the expense of the artist or his subjects? This mixture, and the presence of caricature in Independence Hall, distinguishes "life in Philadelphia."[20]

"The Rage for Profiles": Silhouettes at Peale's Museum

In the early national years, Philadelphia was known for two distinctive types of visual portrait: the caricatures of Clay and the silhouettes manufactured at Charles Willson Peale's Museum. These forms provided different ways of thinking about line, color, and character. In 1802, Peale had introduced a new attraction at his museum, then located in the vacant State House (later to be renamed Independence Hall). The "physiognotrace" was a machine that replicated the profile of a sitter. Designed by John Isaac Hawkins, an Englishman living in Philadelphia who became Peale's business partner, and based on earlier versions in Europe and America, the physiognotrace could be operated by the sitter, another guest, or a trained attendant at the museum. As the operator manipulated a brass index along the subject's profile, the mobile arms of the machine moved a steel point that incised a miniature version of that outline on a folded sheet of paper at the top of the machine (figure 2.3). Then the paper would be removed and the outline cut from the middle. When the paper was unfolded, the sitter would have four copies of the silhouette, one in each of the hollow quadrants. These hollow likenesses could be separated and mounted on a dark-colored background. Many sitters framed their portraits or assembled images in family albums. Traditionally, silhouettes had been traced by hand from a subject's shadow or drawn from observation. Typically, they were black forms, positive shapes cut out and placed against a white ground. Peale's likenesses, on the other hand, were defined by empty space, their forms clarified by the dark ground. The physiognotrace, eliminating color and dispensing with the role of the painter or sketch artist, seemed to offer visitors to the museum a direct transcription. The machine was an immediate success, with thousands of silhouette portraits cut during its first year of operation, and it continued to attract visitors and purchasers for several decades.[21]

What Peale described in an 1803 letter as "the rage for profiles" among visitors to his museum has been explained in several ways. Silhouettes offered an alternative to the oil portrait, a cheap and fast way for visitors to acquire a self-image. They appealed to a renewed taste in Europe and America for the linear forms of Greek classical art and to a curiosity about faces as the registers of character, influenced by Johann Casper Lavater's theories of physiognomy. Lavater's *Essays on Physiognomy* (1775–78) was translated into English and published in several editions in England and America, including variants such as *The Pocket Lavater* (1800). Lavater instructed his readers how to discern identity from the features and outlines of the face. Peale and his children, many of

FIGURE 2.3 "The Physiognotrace," illustrated by Charles Willson Peale in a letter to Thomas Jefferson, January 28, 1803. Courtesy of the Library of Congress, Manuscripts Division, Papers of Thomas Jefferson.

whom were artists, depicted character in silhouettes, portraits, and miniatures. Peale himself kept a "Profile Book," composed of the "block heads" discarded from physiognotrace images, and sought to advance the study of human types.[22]

At the end of the "Long Room" of the old State House, operating the physiognotrace soon after it had been installed and cutting out the profiles that the machine etched with its steel point, was Moses Williams, an African American who had been Peale's slave. Peale had freed Williams's parents in 1786 in accordance with the 1780 Pennsylvania Act for the Gradual Abolition of Slavery. Under its terms, the son was bound until he reached the age of twenty-eight. Peale had emancipated him a year early, in 1802, around the time he gave Williams authority over the physiognotrace. Writing years later, Rembrandt Peale, one of the sons, claimed that Williams was freed ahead of schedule because of his dexterity and accuracy as a producer of silhouettes and the income he brought to the museum. (Visitors paid a small fee for paper, on top of the museum admission, and optional charges for operating and cutting, if they wished to avail themselves of Williams's labor.) Moses Williams remained at the museum, earning a living from silhouettes, for two decades.[23]

Williams's name is associated with the only two known Peale Museum silhouettes of African Americans: "Moses Williams, cutter of profiles" and "Mr. Shaw's blackman" (figures 2.4 and 2.5). Both images are hollow-cut with outlines drawn by the physiognotrace. Williams is the subject of the first, attributed to Raphaelle Peale, another son given an illustrious name, and Williams may have produced the second. Neither image bears an operator's or cutter's signature, nor did any of the Peale Museum silhouettes. Many of the Peale silhouettes were blind-stamped with a spread eagle and "Peale's Museum," but this mark does not indicate who made the profile. Gwendolyn DuBois Shaw speculates that Williams may have traced his own image. Although the designers remain elusive (and it is not clear that "designer" is the pertinent concept for these forms, the result of both human and mechanical hand), the identities of these two sitters are inscribed in their captions. These portraits of African American men suggest the differences between silhouette and caricature, and they set forth the particular visual dynamics of the hollow-cut profiles turned out by the thousands at Peale's Philadelphia museum.[24]

In the Peale silhouettes, character is reduced to outline, but in contrast to the exaggerated features in Clay, the physiognotrace lends restraint. The person holding a pair of scissors could embellish the mechanical lines (and whoever cut the paper for "Moses Williams" did alter hairline and necktie), but such adjustments are minor in the silhouettes from Peale's Museum now held by the Library Company of Philadelphia. In "Moses Williams" and "Mr. Shaw's blackman," as well as in the profiles of European American subjects made at Peale's Museum such as a "Mr. Shaw" (who may or may not be the owner of the "blackman") and an 1820 image of "Edward Clay Portrait Painter" (figure 2.6), each face is

Moses Williams, cutter of profiles

FIGURE 2.4 "Moses Williams, cutter of profiles," attributed to Raphaelle Peale, Peale Museum, Philadelphia (after 1802). Courtesy of the Library Company of Philadelphia.

distinguished by the lines that contour the voids over which the paper is laid. The differences in head shapes are eclipsed by the visual similarities. Between "Mr. Shaw" and the "blackman," there is a slight fullness of lip, a few degrees in the angle of the forehead, and a wave in the hair, but were it not for the caption identifying race and announcing possession, the viewer of these two profiles would find it difficult to ascertain identity or conclude who owned whom. Between "Edward Clay," who would go on to produce "Life in Philadelphia" and become a leading graphic artist in the decades before the Civil War, and "Moses Williams," who in 1821 was nearing the end of his career overseeing the

FIGURE 2.5 "Mr. Shaw's blackman," attributed to Moses Williams, Peale Museum, Philadelphia (after 1802). Courtesy of the Library Company of Philadelphia.

physiognotrace at Peale's Museum and would slip into obscurity, there is a necktie, a bit of jowl, a fullness of lip, a rounded nose, an inked eyelash, and a curling ponytail, but these variations do not certify aesthetic or intellectual hierarchies. Although the captions record that the two men employed different

CUT AT PEALE'S MUSEUM, PHILADELPHIA.

E.W.C.   Ann: Ætat. 21

EDWARD WILLIAMS CLAY
·PORTRAIT · PAINTER·

FIGURE 2.6 "Edward Williams Clay," Peale Museum, Philadelphia (1820). Courtesy of Clements Library, University of Michigan.

media and techniques—"Portrait Painter" and "cutter of profiles"—the words also join them in professional regard.[25]

The silhouettes of all four men define character at the border. While such a border is present in all silhouettes, and while most silhouettes render heads a uniform dark color, the contact between pale outline and dark setting in the hollow-cuts is distinctive. These faces are not positive forms laid on light-colored paper for contrast but negative forms that shape the dark ground. This dynamic stresses the transitory quality of the image. The exquisite lines temporarily organize the void, shore against its overflow. They might easily be damaged or broken. Within these lines, the viewer does not find the pageantry of surfaces in Clay's "Life in Philadelphia." Instead, a different kind of emptiness is on display. Individual character is located on the edge, in slight inflections. The centers of these images are without color or feature: an expanse shared by the sitters but beyond delineation. David R. Brigham reports that visitors to Peale's Museum sometimes viewed the silhouettes they purchased there as keepsakes or memento mori.[26]

Silhouettes could be arranged to establish a hierarchy of types, as in Lavater; or they could be distorted, as in Clay, or labeled for ownership, as in "Mr. Shaw's blackman"; or they could be included in a bill of sale, as is the case with the cut paper and brown ink image of "Flora," an African American who passed from one owner to another in Connecticut in 1796.[27]

Yet the images from Peale's Museum, traced by the index and steel point of the physiognotrace, refuse such demonstrations. Instead, they define a shared condition.

Philadelphia Metempsychosis in Robert Montgomery Bird's *Sheppard Lee*

In *Sheppard Lee* (1836), Robert Montgomery Bird combines the vigorous ambition of Brackenridge's hapless Teague O'Regan and an Edward Clay–like regard for the aspirations of gesture, dress, and tone. For Bird, as for Clay, African Americans serve as the revealing limit case in the experiment of freedom. Bird not only considers social attitudes toward others but, in this novel of Philadelphia metempsychosis, he has his protagonist *become* those others, as Sheppard Lee's spirit takes on the forms of a middle-aged Philadelphia brewer, a dandy, an aged miser, a Quaker philanthropist, an enslaved black, and a rich young dyspeptic. Bird not only examines modes of behavior but also goes *inside* that behavior. Readers are given access to the tensions between spirit and body and to the maneuverings for status within individuals. Invoking theatrical analogies, he shows his readers the strained rehearsals within characters that precede social performance.

Bird's materialist account of character stemmed from his medical training. He received a degree from the University of Pennsylvania Medical School in 1827. After giving up his practice, he wrote several plays that were performed to acclaim in the 1830s before he turned to fiction later in the decade. In the first chapter of *Sheppard Lee*, the eponymous narrator, describing the registers of possible interest in his story, gives a digest of Bird's own pursuits: medicine, physiology, psychology, metaphysics. In the decade before his eccentric novel of manners appeared, Bird had written an apprentice play, a stage comedy set in Philadelphia entitled *The City Looking Glass* (1828), in which one of the speakers articulates a metaphor for character that Bird would develop in his later fiction. Ravin, described as "a swindling gentleman," chastises his brother for his awkward gentility. He tells him to stand up straight and keep his hands out of his pockets, and then offers further advice: "Only fancy yourself a gentleman, and you are one; for the character, like that of a poet, is oftener established by conceit rather than by natural privilege." The pun on "conceit" here is relatively easy to track in this early play, with its two male rogues, two young ladies (one of whom, a foundling, is revealed to be the daughter of a Virginia planter), and ultimate exposure of the swindlers. Although Ravin in his arrogance believes that status can be contrived, at the end of the performance "natural privilege" triumphs.[28]

In *Sheppard Lee*, the conceits are more sophisticated. Bird develops the idea of character as "conceit" in multiple ways: in his bizarre plot conception (that Lee's soul leaps from body to body), in his portrayal of Lee's inflated estimate of his own abilities, and in his unfolding of elaborate metaphors for the relationship between body and spirit. Character in *Sheppard Lee*, "established by conceit," is revealed to be an unstable trope. The book starts on a familiar note, with Lee implying that he will tell a Benjamin Franklin–like story: "it sometimes happens that circumstances conspire to elevate the humblest person from obscurity, and to give the whole world an interest in his affairs; and that man may safely consider himself of some value in his generation, whose history is of a character to instruct the ignorant and inexperienced." Lee's "circumstances"—his serial discoveries that he can transfer his spirit or soul (Bird uses the terms interchangeably) into the bodies of recently deceased persons—do not exactly elevate him. He not only rises but also falls and moves laterally and obliquely, with no coherent trajectory. His incarnations result from accident and distress. As his spirit careens from host to host, Lee finds that bodies are not cozy domiciles or pliable vessels but composed of recalcitrant stuff. And it is not clear what instruction *Sheppard Lee* might offer its readers, unless it is the (strangely literal) advice to look before you leap into bodies, invoked twice in the second volume. Published anonymously in New York, the full title of the novel was *Sheppard Lee, Written by Himself.* This guarantee, summoning the reassurances on the title pages of autobiographies and early slave narratives, affixed to a book that declares the unsteadiness of personality, raises questions about self-possession and self-expression. Which of Sheppard Lee's multiple "selves" has composed the narrative?[29]

Before he discovers an aptitude for metempsychosis, Sheppard Lee casts around for a suitable vocation. The son of a New Jersey sausage manufacturer (and yes, of course, Sheppard can be reckoned among his jumbled products), the indolent Lee ponders a career after his father dies and he turns over the management of the farm he has inherited to an overseer. Lee samples farming, game hunting, horse breeding, and racing. When his farm and his finances diminish, he tries the lottery, the stock market, politics, and courtship. He fails at all these speculations. Up until this point, Sheppard Lee's pursuits resemble the ill-fated efforts of Brackenridge's Teague O'Regan, but then the plot takes a substantial turn.

While digging for buried treasure on his farm, Lee has an accident, falls into a trance, and awakens to see his own corpse. Unable to reenter his body, he discovers that he can will himself into the dead bodies of others (entering through their nostrils!), thus reviving them. The status of the "them" is crucial in the novel, as Bird uses his protagonist's changes to meditate on the relationships between body and spirit and the location of character. In this metempsychic picaresque, Sheppard Lee searches for a corpse in which he will be content. His first venture, John Hazelwood Higginson, an arrogant, middle-aged New Jersey brewer, turns out to have gout and a shrewish wife. As (or in) Higginson, Lee travels to Philadelphia, where his host owns a domicile on Chestnut St. and a brewery in the Northern Liberties, and where most of the action of the novel will take place, with one telling exception.

Sheppard Lee's embodiments also mark the beginning of the fictional realization of Philadelphia. Bird is one of the first novelists to particularize the city: the refined Chestnut St. (71) and also the less fashionable precincts (112), the Schuylkill River to the west (97–98), and districts to the north and south, such as the industrial Northern Liberties (82) and Southwark, where African Americans lived in row houses, vulnerable to the chicanery of white landlords (124–25). All of these scenes will be amplified in the fiction of the 1840s, particularly the riot novels.[30]

After Lee's second move, into the body of the young dandy Isaac Dulmer Dawkins, he finds that he is plagued by creditors and romantic deceit. When Lee first looks at himself as Dawkins in a mirror, he sees a beard and mustache, elegant shoulders, and capering foot, and he resembles an Edward W. Clay cartoon of a European American fop. Before long, he becomes troubled by the deeds behind this façade, as he and his friends maintain their status by exploiting young men "of plebeian origin" who seek social advancement (126). The Dawkins chapters are a novelistic version of the kind of stage comedy of manners that Bird scripted in *The City Looking Glass*. Lee next enters the body of Abram Skinner, a decrepit miser and moneylender wracked by his greed and the betrayals of his designing children. Although not explicitly labeled a Jew, Skinner's name, profession, and habits suggest that Bird's readers would have made the link. Skinner's fanaticism renders this embodiment intense. Constituted by only a few exaggerated characteristics, Skinner is easy for Lee to enter but difficult to abide.

In Skinner, whose body bridges the two original volumes of *Sheppard Lee*, the novel's protagonist almost loses his identity. His "trait[s]" are "destroyed" (210). Moving into another's body never expands Lee's consciousness and always results in disappointment. Rather than Emerson's ecstatic "transparent eye-ball," a catachresis for visual authority that exceeds the body and links self with God (the essay "Nature" was published in the same year as *Sheppard Lee*), Bird describes a male spirit that proceeds through the nasal passages of others and finds itself confined and altered in their forms. The unusual narrative stance of the book, in which Lee, whose perspicacity is limited wherever he is located, tells the stories of his incarnations in unreliable retrospect, makes it impossible to discern whether Bird means to suggest that Skinner's caricature reflects or produces the narrator's quandary. In Skinner, is Lee's problem that such characters are limited, that such characters are represented as stereotypes, or that stereotypes are the only kind of types there are?

Eager for a different body and a life of generosity and virtue rather than self-ishness, Lee leaps into the zealous Quaker philanthropist Zachariah Longstraw, after the Good Samaritan unfortunately has been killed by a convicted felon whom he sought to assist. Bird revels in mocking the benevolent reform of Long-straw, fueled by "the delight of self-approbation" and a misguided belief in human perfectibility (245). In Longstraw, Lee feels a magnanimity in his breast "which burnt on until it became at last a general conflagration of philanthropy" (257). Such enthusiasm makes him vulnerable to swindling by his associates and to injury from the many ungrateful objects of his charity. Lee as Longstraw insists that he is the friend of the African freeman in Philadelphia (his tenderness marked by racial slurs) but no abolitionist (although he is theoretically opposed to slavery). Even so, Yankee peddlers, associating his beneficence with antislavery zeal, kidnap him and take him south, intending to sell him in Louisiana, where they have heard that there is a lucrative market for abolitionists.

On the verge of being lynched at an election day rally in Virginia (the candidate calls for an "'orderly and dignified'" murder [324]), Lee transfers his spirit from Longstraw into the corpse of a black slave, variously referred to as "Tom," "Tommy," and "Thomas." In the most complicated passage of the book, to which I will return, Lee reluctantly, in Virginia rather than in Philadelphia, occupies a body at the center of antebellum political debate and the limits of its imagination. As "Tom," Lee experiences an unprecedented, overdetermined contentment. This idyll is ruptured by abolitionist propaganda, which instigates a violent revolt. Hanged for his part in the slave uprising, Lee/Tom is unearthed by young anatomists, who restore him through galvanic experiments. Avoiding a second hanging, he then enters the body of a young man, Arthur Megrim, who had expired in terror at the sight of his revival. In Megrim, a dyspeptic and hypochondriac, Lee suffers from delusions that he has been transformed into a coffee pot, dog, icicle, chicken, loaded cannon, clock, and hamper of crockery, and he also believes that he has been elected emperor of France. In this last body, Lee's character comes unhinged. Megrim's physician, a Dr. Tibbikens, offers a homeopathic cure for his figurative overload. He literally treats him as though he were his substitutions, attempting to heat the human coffee pot over a fire, beating the dog, melting the icicle, wringing the neck of the chicken, and so on. "In short," Lee as Megrim explains, "there was no conceit entered my brain which Dr. Tibbikens did not cure by a conceit" (394–95).

Finally, encountering the corpse of Sheppard Lee on display as an embalmed mummy, Lee looks at his face, breaks the glass of the exhibit case, grasps his hand, and wills himself into his own or, rather, his former body. (The preceding sentence indicates the descriptive challenges posed to the critic by Bird's novel.) Lee flees attempts to preserve him anew and another lynching, this time threatened by an outraged audience who feel they have been cheated by the mummy's vitality. Reunited with his body, he runs back to New Jersey. Once home, he finds that his farm has been successfully managed by his relatives in his absence. His brother-in-law tries to convince Lee that he has been there all the time, suffering from hallucinations during the long convalescence after his accident. Lee insists on his seven changes and plans to issue a narrative of his adventures. The novel ends with Sheppard Lee having found industry and discipline and proclaiming comfort in his body and with his status. He has learned to shun envy and ambition and to create his own happiness. Yet all that has come before troubles this consonance. *Sheppard Lee* depicts not just social insecurity but an even more radical corporeal disorder.[31]

Bird draws on an early national variant of the picaresque narrative (forerunners in the United States would include Royall Tyler's 1797 *The Algerine Captive* and Brackenridge's *Modern Chivalry*), novels that flaunted Philadelphia as the arena for social conflict and satire (such as Tabitha Gilman Tenney's 1801 *Female Quixotism* and Rebecca Rush's 1812 *Kelroy*), theatrical comedies of manners (including Bird's own *City Looking Glass*), and visual parodies of social behavior (such as

Clay's "Life in Philadelphia"). In Bird's narrative, the protagonist travels only between New Jersey, Philadelphia, and Virginia, but within that space, he migrates along the stations of class and race. Sheppard Lee's corporeal journeys are rooted in Philadelphia, with its scrutiny of manners and experiments in freedom. Bird may have taken his conceit not only from the fashionable interest in metempsychosis but also from the British novel of circulation, such as Charles Johnstone's *Chrysal; or the Adventures of a Guinea* (1760–65) and Thomas Bridges's *Adventures of a Bank-Note* (1770–71). In these stories, objects narrated their passage from owner to owner and situation to situation. As Sheppard Lee circulates, his value diminishes. He discovers that his identity depends on particular embodiments. Rejecting theology and metaphysics, Bird offers a series of metaphors that develop a materialist argument about the relation between body and spirit.

About to enter into the recently deceased brewer Higginson, Sheppard Lee imagines that the human body is a "tenement," a "natural dwelling" in which the "feeble factions" of spirit and body would join and the spirit would "claim" its place (52). Unfortunately, such comfortable metaphysics are belied by his discovery that the qualities of spirit are contingent on the material it inhabits. Lee finds that the spirit does not dwell in the body like the owner of a home. Inside Higginson, Lee possesses "two different characters," which struggle for dominance (59). As Dawkins, ashamed of his conduct, Lee regrets that "men's bodies are not like the dry-goods dealers' boxes in Market-Street, to be stumbled into at any moment" (127). He narrates his growing awareness that the "associations of the mind" depend on bodily causes (140). Here Bird invokes the associationist psychology of John Locke, George Berkeley, David Hartley, and Thomas Brown, with a twist. The contents of Sheppard Lee's consciousness are formed not just by the memory of sensory impressions linked by such principles as contiguity, similarity, and frequency. Sheppard Lee's "great experiment" in metempsychosis teaches him that the sensation of having a body gives substance to thought (212). When Lee exists in a "new body," he acquires almost a "new mind," which barely retains its "original character" (140).

In the oddest somatic figure of the book, Bird describes the orientation of spirit in body with a strategically prosaic image. Lee distinguishes between strong minds, which might be capable of transcending their medium (although no such minds are represented in the book), and weak ones: "ordinary spirits lie in their bodies like water in sponges, diffused through every part, affected by the part's affections, changed with its changes, and so intimately united with the fleshly matrix, that the mere cutting off of a leg, as I believe, will, in some cases, leave the spirit limping for life" (141). This passage is filled with jokes about materialism. The body is neither a sacred container nor a corrupt vessel but, well, a sponge: a porous substance that soaks up or wipes out. As the simile expands, matter and spirit exchange qualities. Sponges acquire affections and spirits limp. These jokes deflate notions that elevate or detach spirit from body. As an alternative, Bird presents a physiology in which the two are uneasily bound in a "fleshly matrix." Lee finds that different bodies have different textures. They have varying degrees of porousness and resistance. He struggles to maintain distinctions between his spirit and the bodies he occupies. He continually risks being absorbed. Across the narrative, the conceit of being able to enter and leave bodies at will and the final hint that Lee has dreamed it all seem fantasies of escape from the discovery that spirits are diffused in bodies.

In an 1836 review of *Sheppard Lee*, Edgar Allan Poe complained about Bird's handling of metempsychosis. According to Poe, the author should have shown how the various bodies contrasted with Lee's *"unchanging"* character, but in stead "the hero, very awkwardly, partially loses, and partially does not lose, his identity, at each transmigration."[32] Yet the textual evidence suggests that this "awkwardness" is deliberate. For Bird, character is contingent. It depends on the material out of which it is made. The action in the novel takes place most vividly within Sheppard Lee's bodies, rather than in the often hackneyed, if amusing, encounters between Lee and others. In Philadelphia, Bird pushes the novel of manners to its limits. He turns it inside out. Rather than taking one side or the other in the traditional debate about whether manners are natural or acquired, whether manners express inner virtue or are signs of self-interest, Bird probes the substance of character and of characters. Lee feels the pressure of internal, rather than external, conventions. He cannot pull a Benjamin Franklin and successfully manipulate his appearances because his interior is embattled.[33]

Later in the novel, Bird's metaphors amplify the discomfort. Tainted by the miser Skinner's rascality, Lee explains that "a man's body is like a barrel, which, if you salt fish in it once, will make fish of everything you put into it afterward" (209). Embarrassed by his benevolent monomania and susceptibility to fraud while in the body of the philanthropist Longstraw, he hopes to be more careful: "'Yea, verily, I will next time be certain I am not putting my soul, as the pickpocket did his hand, into a sack of fish-hooks'" (305). Bodies are figured as tainting and barbed, but in this novel there is no alternative for the soul, which Bird associates with a hand, and a thieving hand at that. It is an image that, with its idiosyncratic violence and tinge of blasphemy, might be found in an Emily Dickinson poem: the soul steals a body that is riddled with a thousand punctures.

In *Sheppard Lee*, Bird stages the instability of character, viewed as the product of internal tensions, in the register of farce. In his next novel, *Nick of the Woods, or The Jibbenainosay* (1837), he presents it as melodrama. *Nick of the Woods* tells the story of

Nathan Slaughter, a Pennsylvania Quaker who, on the Kentucky frontier, is transformed by vengeance into the "Jibbenainosay," a slayer and desecrator of Indians. Nathan's transformations, unlike Sheppard Lee's, are involuntary: "great and unexpected," "extraordinary," "sudden." As "Nick of the Woods," Nathan's spirit is possessed by revenge, and in his actions he mirrors the violence of the Indians who killed his family and are terrorizing settlers. Bird obscures distinctions between Native American and European American violence, and he suggests "something essentially demoniac in the human character and composition." The narrative is driven by the seizures that alter the protagonist, as he swells into the "Jibbenainosay" and diminishes into Nathan. In these two novels, Bird evaluates male conceits, and especially the presumption that character is stable and transcendent.[34]

In *Sheppard Lee*, too, there are rhythms of character. As Lee moves from body to body, he experiences the weight of flesh in the gout-ridden bulk of the brewer Higginson, then the seductive veneer of the fop Dawkins, the cramp of the miser Skinner, the aggrandizement of the philanthropist Longstraw, the inertia and revolt of the slave Tom, the deluded exchanges of the hypochondriac Megrim, and finally the overstated contentment in his "own" body at the end of the book. In the African American Tom, the reach and limits of Sheppard Lee's "great experiment" (212) are dramatized.

Lee's movement into Tom is redundant and reductive. It is redundant because Lee already has been treated like a slave in his role as the philanthropist Longstraw—kidnapped, bound, and threatened with lynching. Earlier in the plot, while in Philadelphia, he had been treated like a free black. After harboring a fugitive slave, who had robbed him and then been jailed, Longstraw was targeted by an African American mob, who blamed him for the fugitive's misfortune and burned down his house. (Or maybe, Bird suggests, the arsonist was Longstraw's assistant Abel Snipe, who had purchased an insurance policy on the dwelling.) In a series of dizzying exchanges, Longstraw harbors a fugitive slave and then becomes the object of black, not (historically) white, violence, with a hint of white conspiracy. According to Bird, Longstraw's philanthropy renders him vulnerable to those with whom he identifies, culminating in his misguided abolitionist zeal.

Lee's movement into Tom is reductive because this Virginia slave is a blatant device even in this book of stereotypes. When Lee takes "a survey of my physiognomy" in a fragment of mirror in his tidy hovel and sees Tom, he sees the black face, immense red lips, and large white eyes of racist caricature (331). No other character in the book is limned with such visual hyperbole. When Lee dreams as Tom, he imagines a tableau of indolence. His experience of leisure and of his master's affectionate treatment produces a "revolution in [his] feelings" (335). Enslaved, he discovers fulfillment: "I was satisfied with my lot—I was satisfied even with *myself*" (342). In Tom, he becomes an indifferent, lovable scoundrel. Echoing proslavery arguments, he reports that his responsibilities as a chattel slave are less burdensome than the labors of white wage slaves in New Jersey and that his master was more oppressed than his bondmen. Unlike the other forms Lee occupies, whose traits goad his spirit to activity, Tom's body depletes his character. As Tom, Lee undergoes two "revolutions": from distress to contentment and then, through the sense of injury generated by abolitionist propaganda, from contentment to revenge (335, 345, 355). Tom is first the happy slave and then the murderous slave, following the anxious trajectory represented in popular and political culture in the wake of Nat Turner's 1831 revolt.

Bird finds it difficult to imagine any interior life or social context for Tom, comparable to the musings and predicaments he devises for the others, even within the constraints of their types. This limit is wrapped in an evasion, because the logical body for Lee to enter would not have been a Virginia slave but a member of Philadelphia's African American aspiring classes. This would have been logical, given the setting of the book, its status concerns, and the visibility of such figures in the popular culture of the 1830s. Bird conspicuously withholds this incarnation from his protagonist and swerves his narrative south to avoid it.

In *Sheppard Lee*, Bird meditates on character and also, sometimes explicitly and sometimes inadvertently, on fiction, and specifically on identification. Bird insists that different characters have different consistencies, which allow Lee easier or more strenuous access and produce different kinds of involvements. This dynamic applies not only to the protagonist but also to the author and his (and to readers and their) degrees of identification. Bird suggests an analogy between Sheppard Lee's experience in other bodies and the ability of readers to associate themselves with different characters. Readers are drawn into the characters and stories of Abram Skinner and Zachariah Longstraw and also pulled out of them, as Sheppard Lee realizes his is "a borrowed existence" and he seeks other attachments (226). Inhabiting characters is represented as an act of will that is conditioned by substance. Bird suggests that it is easier to identify with types than with more elaborate characters, yet also that such types can present unexpected resistance. Some types inertly or perfectly represent a category (such as the slave Tom), and others possess attributes that impede: black and free, say, or female. Sheppard Lee never occupies a woman's body, white or black. Unlike the smoother transactions in sentimental fiction, which often are accompanied by the belief that such engagement will improve the reader, in Bird's novel inhabiting characters is an awkward, recalcitrant business.[35]

It would be easy to read and dismiss the "Tom" chapters in *Sheppard Lee* as part of the torrent of racist caricature in the 1830s. These chapters point to defenses of slavery and rebukes of abolition. (In his review of the book, Poe admires Bird's anti-anti slavery stance.) Yet the politics and aesthetics in this novel are not so neatly aligned, and the satire in *Sheppard Lee* is more difficult to construe. The portrayal of Tom is bound up with Bird's exposure of all characters as limited. All are the product of weak spirits diffused in flawed bodies. In the novel, no character successfully or fully represents himself to others or even to himself. Characters are revealed as caricatures, whose excesses issue from their bewildered, contested depths. Although Tom is shown to be hindered by his body, his abilities determined by his features in ways consonant with nineteenth-century racial science, these burdens are shared by others, contrary to the privilege of disembodiment often claimed for European American men in political theory and popular debate.[36]

Bird easily could have undermined Lee-as-Tom's report of the abolitionist pamphlets that incite discontent and revolution by presenting that episode in dialect. "Tom" is surrounded by African American characters who speak in Bird's version of substandard English. We might read the absence of dialect in "Tom" as further evidence of Bird's distance from this character, since in Lee's other incarnations, Bird makes attempts, some more successful than others, to show the ways in which language is altered in different bodies and contexts. But even so, that distance has the effect of sustaining, rather than impugning, the case against slavery. The pamphlets, Lee-as-Tom tells the reader, invoke God and the Declaration of Independence in contending that freedom and equality are natural rights. They alter the enslaved Africans' sense of their treatment. Lee-as-Tom comes to understand the way his master's young son rides and pummels him not as "child's play" but as abuse (358). Before the pamphlets, this mastery is extravagantly portrayed as endearment and welcomed by "Tom." After the pamphlets, he is "enraged" (358). Although Bird implies that this shift is the misguided result of external incitement, the youngster's behavior and "Tom"'s response are depicted as unhealthy from the start. In these scenes, it is as though Lee-as-Tom has an insight akin to that expressed by Thomas Jefferson in *Notes on the State of Virginia.* In response to Query XVIII about "the particular customs and manners that may happen to be received in that state," Jefferson devotes his answer to the corrupting effects of slavery on social behavior, particularly on domestic nurture and pedagogy: "There must doubtless be an unhappy influence on the manners of our people produced by the existence of slavery among us. The whole commerce between master and slave is a perpetual exercise of the most boisterous passions, the most unremitting despotism on the one part, and degrading submissions on the other. Our children see this, and learn to imitate it; for man is an imitative animal."[37]

Bird had secured fame as a playwright with *The Gladiator*, first performed in New York in 1831, in which his hero Spartacus, the freeborn Thracian who becomes a Roman slave, musters his fellow captives to rebellion in eloquent blank verse. The playwright's discomfort with slavery continues in the work of the novelist but in altered form, no longer insulated by the distant past. In the "Tom" chapters of *Sheppard Lee*, racial slavery in the present is addressed not in classical tableaux and measured diction, but in warped conduct.

Any reading of Bird's "Tom" satire must confront the pattern in the novel in which contentment is associated with platitude and delusion. This is the case at the end, when Sheppard Lee tells his readers that, back home in New Jersey, he awakens to find that his farm has prospered, his family has missed him, and he now feels satisfied with his condition. Given the vividness of struggle that distinguished Lee's various embodiments, his exceptional complacency as the slave Tom seems singularly unpersuasive. Why should readers be less skeptical about Tom's complacency than they are about Longstraw's philanthropy? The turn to racial revolt at the end of the Virginia sequence is more in line with the model of internal turmoil that Bird exposes in Lee's other bodies than it is with the illusory contentment of "Tom" under slavery or Lee as "himself" at the end of the novel.

Bird indicates skepticism, or at least narrative anomaly, when he has Lee-as-Tom attempt to explain his embrace of slavery, despite his initial dread. Perhaps, he thinks, he is content because he has embraced an "African" love of the present and now, suffering from a "defect of memory," cannot recall his former state. Perhaps his mind was "stupified," rendering him unable to understand "the evils of my condition." Or perhaps his new circumstances were appropriate to "my mind and nature." (Of course, in the case of Lee-as-Tom, the referent for "my" remains obscure or multiple.) "The reader," Lee explains, "may settle the difficulty for himself, which he can do when he has read a little more of my history" (341–42). The narrative hiatus and overture are unusual in this text. Although Bird skews the evidence and appears to maintain that slavery as actually practiced in the South is less objectionable than slavery understood in the abstract, he hesitates and provides conflicting signals. In this novel about bodies, property, and agency and about the reach and limits of identification, slavery and revolt occupy the ambivalent center. The flaws of this ambitious, erratic novel are part of the dynamic it explores.

When Bird represents "free" African Americans in his earlier drama or later fiction, he does so from the outside and with disapproval, even resentment. In *The*

City Looking Glass (1828), the phrase "more impudence than a Philadelphia negro" is used to exemplify social breach, and Bird includes a vignette of a European American man who extends his arm to a well-dressed Philadelphia lady passing him on the street one evening and then discovers, with alarm, that her face is black.[38] Staging the misalignment between costume and visage and playing this exposure for shock and laughs, *The City Looking Glass* resembles Clay's "Life in Philadelphia."

In Bird's *Adventures of Robin Day* (1839), the bearing of African Americans on the streets of Philadelphia collides with the hapless young protagonist's self-regard as a citizen and a man. Philadelphia offers Robin Day a series of rebuffs and debasements, prompting his announcement toward the end of his stay that he is "now heartily sick of the City of Brotherly Love." Shortly after his arrival, deciding to move along the street aggressively like everyone else, he has the first of several discomfiting public encounters with African Americans: "[I] had just begun to conceit myself almost a citizen, and to fancy that every body else so considered me, when my equanimity received a blow from the wheelbarrow of a black porter; who, coming up from behind, whistling Yankee Doodle with a vigour that drowned the creaking of his wheel, tumbled me into a lot of pottery arranged along the pavement." Robin's "conceit" that he is a citizen (again Bird hinges his displays of character on that word) is literally overturned by the arrogance of a black porter, immersed in a patriotic anthem of resistance, who acts as though he, too, can command the streets.[39]

A short time later, Robin is knocked over by an African American woodsplitter who, clinking his tools and chanting his wares, is oblivious to his presence. Then he is pitched into a cellar by a third black man. Of "the deportment of the coloured gentlemen of Philadelphia," Robin concludes that "they were, next to the pigs, the true aristocracy of the town, or, at least, of the streets thereof. . . . The insolence of the black republicans was to me astonishing, though not more so than the general submissiveness with which I found it endured." Seeing a black porter upset a white lady with his carriage, Robin can no longer countenance racial affront, and "boiling over with indignation," he strikes him. Next he is jostled by a "black fellow . . . dressed like a dandy, though of the shabby genteel order, his hat cocked smartly on the side of his head, a rattan in his hand, with which he thwacked his boots at every second step, with a swaggering gait, and a look that said as plainly as if labeled in show-bill letters on his nose, which was the broadest part of his countenance, 'Get out of my way, white man!'" Robin again retaliates, stinging and blinding him with the contents of his snuff box, and relishing his triumph. Such episodes, in which African American publicity is viewed as incitement, will become common in the history of the Philadelphia riots of the 1830s and 1840s and in fiction about violence in the city, extending to twentieth-century novels such as Jack Dunphy's *John Fury* (1946) and Pete Dexter's *God's Pocket* (1983).[40]

For Robin Day, and evidently for his author, the presence of African Americans on the streets of Philadelphia, claiming their right to join in the public life of the city, expressing themselves in costume, vocation, and music, is received as an assault on the status of white citizens. Indifference to superior rank is interpreted as belligerence. The young black man with cocked hat, swinging his rattan, and promenading down the street is figured, in Bird's vehement image, as though he were advertising racial defiance ("in show-bill letters on his nose") and goading conflict ("'Get out of my way, white man!'"). In Philadelphia, manners involve self and group expression and social negotiation, and also take on the forms of combat. African American enterprise comes to be seen not only as "preposterous" but also as aggressive. Like Clay, Bird in his satire preserves details of African American expressive culture, but in *Adventures of Robin Day*, there is more rancor than in "Life in Philadelphia." Since Bird imagines African American freedom as insolence, it is not surprising that he would choose a Virginia slave, rather than a Philadelphia dandy, for Sheppard Lee's black embodiment. "Tom"'s evacuated interior may have seemed more tolerable and less alien terrain than the characterological affront presented by members of the African American aristocracy.

Bird swerves south and avoids placing Sheppard Lee in the body of one of the "higher classes of colored society in Philadelphia," to use the title phrase from Joseph Willson's 1841 sketchbook of African American manners. With this swerve, this denial, this limit to the "great experiment" (212) of character in *Sheppard Lee*, the novel comes closest to the debates in Philadelphia during the 1830s. These debates about citizenship, race, and conduct began with the black national conventions held in Philadelphia in the first half of the decade and culminated in the 1838 referendum that deprived African American men of the right to vote. We now turn to this history and then to Willson's *Sketches*, in which manners and politics are joined.

"The Peculiar Position of Our People": William Whipper and Debates in the Black Conventions

The first Convention for the Improvement of the Free People of Colour in the United States was held in Philadelphia in September 1830. The specific impetus for the 1830 meeting was trouble in Cincinnati, where, responding to strife between white laborers and black immigrants seeking jobs, authorities had revived laws restricting black rights and requiring blacks to register and post a $500 bond or leave within thirty days. African Americans in Cincinnati discussed the feasibility of emigrating to Canada and approached other communities for guidance and support. Richard Allen, now the seventy-year-old bishop of the African Methodist Episcopal Church, seized the initiative from New Yorkers and called for a national meeting to be held in Philadelphia. Five of the first six national conventions were held there (1830–1833 and 1835, with the 1834 meeting held in New York), and the sessions were dominated by young Philadelphia men.[41]

More generally, the convention movement began as a secular development of the black church's concern with self-reliance and moral improvement. The meetings were a venue for grappling with the challenges faced by African Americans, free and enslaved, as well as a response to heightening northern repression. The gatherings had multiple audiences. They were occasions for exchange and display among those present and for addressing the working classes, European American supporters and opponents, and especially beginning with Henry Highland Garnet's "Address to the Slaves of the United States of America" (1843), those in bondage. Pageants of deliberation, the meetings served as a riposte to the satires of African American conduct in the urban North. Key issues taken up in the first phase of the movement included emigrating to Canada, anticolonization (and specifically resistance to the efforts of the American Colonization Society), education, temperance, moral reform, and social "elevation." The Philadelphians were associated, especially by their detractors (and most sharply by their critics in New York), with a misguided enthusiasm for moral improvement at the expense of political engagement.[42]

At the 1834 and 1835 conventions, the Philadelphians, and William Whipper in particular, laid the groundwork for what came to be called the American Moral Reform Society, a controversial group that held meetings between 1836 and 1841. Samuel E. Cornish, writing in *The Colored American*, the New York periodical he founded, described the organizers of the 1837 American Moral Reform convention as "wealthy and intellectual" and "visionary in the extreme." Whipper and Robert Purvis were "vague, wild, indefinite and confused in their views. They created shadows, fought the wind, and bayed the moon, for more than three days." We will return shortly to Whipper's arguments about morality and social performance and to the charges that such "Philadelphia" concerns were immaterial and irrelevant. The Moral Reform Society splintered the convention movement, and there were no national meetings again until 1843. In the 1840s and 1850s, several state conventions were held, including two in Pennsylvania (Pittsburgh in 1841 and Harrisburg in 1848). When the national conventions were revived between 1843 and 1855 (with a final meeting in 1864), leadership had shifted to New York and to the West, and the agenda turned to specific projects of racial advance and to the wider politics of abolition, black nationalism, and emigration.[43]

In the minutes of the conventions, usually issued in pamphlet form, debates often hinged on the terms "condition" and "complexion." To what extent was the plight of free African Americans the result of their degraded status? To what extent did it result from prejudice against their color? Arguing for the value of agricultural employment, the minutes of the 1841 Pittsburgh state convention reported that "prejudice is not against *color*, but against *condition*; therefore improve the condition, and you destroy the prejudice." Could prejudice be overcome through economic advancement? Moral improvement? The public display of responsibility? How could moral and economic efforts strengthen African American communities internally, regardless of their reception by white observers?[44]

Analyzing the issue of caste, a report included in the minutes of the 1847 national meeting in Troy, New York, signed by Frederick Douglass and others, described "the peculiar position of our people." The adjective "peculiar" was often attached to discourse about status. Samuel Cornish, defending the necessity of black institutions, explained that "our condition in the community is a peculiar one, and that we need SPECIAL EFFORTS and special organization, to meet our wants, and to obtain and maintain our rights." His adversary in these debates, William Whipper, used the term to insist on differences internal to the ostracized group: "The peculiarity of our situation leads the current of our thoughts into many channels, with the hope that we may devise some new method to procure our elevation. When we meet in convention we severally bring with us our peculiar habits of life, our different degrees of education, our prejudices in favor of this or that measure, so that often our dialects are so different we can scarcely understand each other." Another of Whipper's opponents, who signed his articles in the *Colored American* with the pen name "Sidney," used the word to emphasize a shared response: "Whenever a people are oppressed, peculiarly (not complexionally,) distinctive organization or action, is required on the part of the oppressed, to destroy that oppression." For "Sidney," African Americans were a group defined by the rigid barriers they confronted.[45]

The "peculiarities" of African American freedom in the North during the early and mid-nineteenth century are manifold. Legally free, African Americans were subject to discrimination and regulation, and after the revised Fugitive Slave Act of 1850, legal kidnapping. They possessed some civil rights but few political rights. Many African American males in Pennsylvania were "free men," but not (in the struggle over the franchise, which pivoted on diction and etymology in the

1790 state constitution) "freemen." Represented as monolithic, their urban communities in the North had ramified economically and socially and often were split by debate. Bound by prejudice, African Americans also were divided by status, ambition, city, region, and the Mason-Dixon Line. On probation and under scrutiny, explicitly in Philadelphia with its experiment in freedom, they were poised between the abstract natural rights granted in the Declaration of Independence and the disavowal of those rights in U.S. legal and social practice. African Americans in the North in the decades before the Civil War were neither free nor enslaved or both free and enslaved.[46]

Such a "peculiar position" influenced the debates about "condition" and "complexion" in the annual meetings, and the intricacies of these exchanges were sometimes glossed over by the participants and have been obscured by modern historians. Terms such as "moderate" and "conservative," used to describe the stance of the moral reformers, or antitheses between "deference" and "demand" and between manners and action misrepresent the thought expressed at the conventions. "Condition" and "complexion" were not exclusive alternatives. Instead, condition was often colored.[47]

The example of the unorthodox William Whipper shows how surprising those debates can be and how the 1838 denial of the franchise in Pennsylvania altered views. Whipper's ideas were easily caricatured by his opponents. One of the leading figures in African American Philadelphia in the 1830s, he played a dominant role in the first phase of the black convention movement. Whipper insisted on the priority of moral regeneration for all Americans. His stewardship of the American Moral Reform Society and the *National Reformer*, the monthly periodical he edited between September 1838 and December 1839, provoked criticism not only from Samuel Cornish and others in the black press in New York and Pittsburgh but also from within Philadelphia circles. The absence of any term designating "color" in the title of the society was deliberate, since Whipper argued in the 1830s and 1840s that such distinctive nomenclature perpetuated the tropes of racism. Agreeing that African Americans were an oppressed caste in a racist nation, he also insisted, along with the Garrisonians, that exclusive organizations violated moral law. The proper responses to social violence were spiritual recoil and an awakening to Christian benevolence and universality. Whipper did not abjure every use of racial designation, but in language proposed at the 1835 national meeting held in Philadelphia, he recommended "as far as possible, to our people to abandon the use of the word 'colored,' when either speaking or writing concerning themselves; and especially to remove the title of African from their institutions, the marbles of churches &c."[48]

Taking willful pleasure in his iconoclasm, repeatedly proclaiming the virtues of *"free discussion,"* Whipper would not surrender the issue despite, or maybe because of, the eloquent (and increasingly exasperated) rebuttals by Cornish, "Sidney," and others. Whipper's opponents argued the need for self-consciously African American enterprise, and they labeled his stance as counterproductive and detached from the sentiments of the vast majority. Wickedly, he published a series of three letters in 1841 to Charles B. Ray, then the editor of the *Colored American,* applauding a resolution passed by an Albany meeting in 1840 that called for the removal of all laws and systems "founded in the SPIRIT OF COMPLEXIONAL CAST." Whipper suggested that "the Albany Convention of Colored Citizens" had violated its own decree in title and spirit, and, referring to the *Colored American,* he "humbly hope[d] that the principles of the resolution will fall on its distinctive title and grind it to powder." Although his polemic cost him support for his American Moral Reform Society and exposed him to public attack, Whipper continued to spurn what he considered to be racial exclusivity. The American Moral Reform Society held its sixth and last annual meeting in August 1841. Whipper was involved in several state and national meetings in the 1840s and 1850s and contributed articles to the black press, but after the demise of his Moral Reform Society he focused on his business career, joining in partnership with the lumber and coal merchant Stephen Smith and amassing a personal fortune. He used his elevation to aid fugitive slaves by donating funds and operating a major Underground Railroad station for more than twenty years in Columbia, Pennsylvania, where he had moved in 1835, near the border with the slave state of Maryland. During the 1850s, Whipper softened his arguments against racially distinctive groups and voluntary emigration.[49]

Whipper and others developed an analysis of conduct and consequence that does not easily fit the evaluations of many modern critics, who, until recently, have tended to describe nineteenth-century African American moral reform as insulated from the politics of slavery and civil rights and as beholden to the values of a white middle-class. As Patrick Rael has demonstrated, African American leaders in the North "cofabricated" a discourse of manners with other Americans. Evelyn Brooks Higginbotham and Eddie S. Glaude Jr. have argued that the "politics of respectability" was an intricate and shifting rejoinder to American racism. Yet even these new appraisals, welcome as they are, might not be sufficient for understanding the arguments of figures such as Whipper and the turmoil of antebellum debate in Philadelphia, which forms a prehistory to later nineteenth-century ideas about "uplift." We might pause, look closely at the Philadelphia texts, and entertain the possibility that they compel our understanding. Across his speeches, the addresses he prepared for the national and state meetings, and his periodical essays, William Whipper considers the implications of "character."[50]

From the beginning, in his earliest speeches delivered in Philadelphia before the Colored Reading Society (1828) and the Colored Temperance Society (1834), Whipper argued for individual discipline and "ambition" as means to bolster the position of African Americans in the North and to undermine slavery. He insisted on the "moral force" of character—that its cultivation and display would help to reorder American society. Whipper's vehemence has sources in the practical virtue urged by Benjamin Franklin and in the moral fervency of the Second Great Awakening, including the Garrisonianism of the 1830s. Yet Whipper revises, rather than imitates. In the early speeches, he criticizes his listeners for "an indifference in ourselves relative to emancipating our brethren from universal thralldom." He distinguishes among free African Americans: those who have accumulated property and are insulated by their relative comfort; those in a "middle class" who are occupied with acquiring the "necessaries of life"; and those in a "lower class" whose debasement, according to Whipper, threatens to confine them in ignorance and servitude. Whipper folds arguments against slavery and prejudice into a call for universal moral reform, acknowledging that listeners might object to his statement that "negro slavery . . . is but a concomitant" to intemperance. Yet he also elucidates the "peculiar situations" of African Americans in the North, caught in a system of profit and debasement, and the acute dilemma of being marked with "a badge of complexional degradation." Given the "balance of power" that favors the whites and their eagerness for proof of differences in character, as well as color, Whipper urges, as will many of his peers, that African Americans must be "superior in morals," "more pure than they, before we can be duly respected."[51]

Samuel Cornish described this comparative burden in March 1837, in the pages of his *Colored American:*

> [s]hould we establish for ourselves a character—should we as a people, become more religious and more moral, more industrious and prudent, than other classes of community, it will be impossible to keep us down. This we should do, we are more oppressed and proscribed than others, therefore we should be more circumspect and more diligent than others. . . . We owe it to ourselves and we owe it to the poor slaves, who are our brethren. . . . On *our* conduct, in a great measure, *their* salvation depends. Let us show that we are worthy to be freemen.

For Cornish and Whipper, the display of character is vital to the struggle. We might reduce this investment to complicity or assimilation, but in the 1830s many African American leaders, especially those in Philadelphia, maintained that such efforts had both internal and external value. They would help to strengthen an embattled community and also demonstrate the virtues that would press upon white observers the natural rights of African Americans. The moral reformers wavered between asserting those rights and suggesting that they must be earned or confirmed. This instability—exemplified in Cornish's adjective "worthy"—often sharpened the debate about the terms of the Philadelphia social experiment. Cornish describes an exacting fulcrum in which more is required of those who have less. The burden of conduct is sustained not only for the individuals themselves and for all those in freedom but also for those under slavery whose deliverance, according to Cornish, is tied to the achievements of his peers.[52]

"Acting for ourselves," in the words of James Forten Jr., who delivered an address at the 1837 American Moral Reform Society meeting, is also acting for and on other selves, and given its urgency and potential impact, such labor should never cease: "we should be careful in all our walks, lest we should give the appearance of truth to the illiberal charges brought against us; we must not remain quiet or inactive, but approach as near to perpetual motion as possible." In the court of public opinion, indictments hover, and conduct is weighed as evidence. Forten rebuffs the charge of inferiority, explaining that degradation is the product of a vicious system. He describes moral reform, and particularly advancement through education, as a maneuver in a struggle: "proscription cannot live where it lives; the oppressor must wither under it, and be compelled to lift his murderous foot from off the neck of the oppressed." The foot on the neck (a metaphor we will see again) debases and chokes. Thwarting ascent, it mocks the condition of the subjected. Forten was the eldest son of James E. Forten (1766–1842), the African American Revolutionary War veteran whose sail-making business, real estate holdings, and investments made him one of Philadelphia's wealthiest and most respected citizens. The father was the first president of the American Moral Reform Society, and the son was its secretary. James Forten Sr. was often invoked by abolitionists as an exemplar of freedom's possibilities.[53]

"Elevation," then, is one movement in a complex structure with multiple pressures and effects. The hopes of the Fortens, Cornish, and Whipper in the mid-1830s may have been overstated (and Whipper after 1838 will change his mind about the priority of "elevation" in the struggle for freedom), but their stance cannot accurately be reduced to o pting for "condition" over "complexion." Whipper and Cornish acknowledge the prejudicial circumstances in which they articulate "character." Cornish describes the confluence of forces and gazes in an 1837 editorial comment in the *Colored American:* "The position we hold in community is a prominent one—all eyes are upon us." "We" here is both indefinite (African Americans generally) and precisely felt (the conspicuous burdens of the rising classes). The "community" and the scrutiny are understood to be manifold: various parties are watching and waiting, with hope, desire, skepticism, dread, envy, or animosity. Cornish marks out an intensely public space through which his characters move, riddled with expectations.[54]

In an address "To the American People," printed in the minutes for the 1835 national convention held in Philadelphia, at which the American Moral Reform Society was organized, and then again in the minutes for the 1837 meeting of the Reform Society itself, Whipper both spurs his audience to improve their characters and bristles at the requirements for demonstration. Like Jones and Allen's yellow fever "Narrative of the Proceedings," the pamphlets containing the minutes of the black conventions incorporated different forms, and their documents addressed several audiences. Minutes often included declarations of sentiment; arguments and votes on resolutions; surveys of the "condition of the free colored population"; and reports on schools, agricultural cooperatives, a black press, and, especially in the 1840s and 1850s, abolition and bigotry. They contained speeches directed to black, white, and "American" audiences and to state legislatures. As the movement developed, the conventions and their minutes became more elaborate.

Whipper begins his address "To the American People" by outlining a system in which law, custom, and bias deprive African Americans of educational and economic opportunities and social advancement. Scorned for their backwardness and depravity, African Americans then are "tauntingly required to prove the dignity of our human nature, by disrobing ourselves of inferiority, and exhibiting to the world our profound Scholars, distinguished Philosophers, learned Jurists, and distinguished Statesmen." For Whipper, moral reform is necessary to fortify a proscribed group and also serves as the inevitable, galling response to the demand that the oppressed display their entitlement to the "inalienable right" of "universal liberty" already granted by God and confirmed in the Declaration of Independence. One of the motions he promoted at the 1835 meeting recognizes "the Christian forbearance practised by our people" during the riots of August 1834 that targeted black homes, churches, and a Masonic hall. Proper conduct, according to Whipper, is a volatile mixture: an individual good, a communal necessity, the reply to a taunt, and a threat. "We pray God that we may lawfully multiply in numbers, in moral and intellectual endowments," explains the "Declaration of Sentiment" published in 1835 and 1837, "and that our visages may be as so many Bibles, that shall warn this guilty nation of her injustice and cruelty to the descendants of Africa, until righteousness, justice and truth shall rise in their might and majesty, and proclaim from the halls of legislation that the chains of the bondsman have fallen, that the soil is sacred to liberty, and that without distinction of nation or complexion she disseminates her blessings of *freedom to all mankind.*" The prayer that "visages may be as so many Bibles" suggests the ways in which religion, demeanor, enterprise, and justice are intertwined in the views of the moral reformers.[55]

Neither Hugh Henry Brackenridge's unruly democratic force nor Edward W. Clay's veneer of self-interest, the debate over manners in Whipper's Philadelphia brings together a Christian emphasis on conduct as a sign of grace with a republican belief, sharpened by prejudice, that virtue merits the rights of citizenship. Whipper's account of manners resembles that given by Absalom Jones and Richard Allen in their "Narrative" and by Allen in his sermon on the condemned John Joyce and Peter Matthias—a decorum on the edge of judgment, a discipline honed by probation and violence. Like Robert Montgomery Bird in his novel *Sheppard Lee* (whose social array excluded the "higher class" types who participated in the black conventions), Whipper describes manners as the product of debate, within and without, about the substance of character. For Bird and for Whipper, manners involve urgent negotiations about status, authority, and survival. They test the reach and limits of identification.

In "Our Elevation," an 1839 essay in the *National Reformer,* Whipper repudiates his earlier stand that moral improvement necessarily preceded full civil and political rights. He changed his view after the October 1838 vote in Pennsylvania to disfranchise African American men. The pressure of the debate is felt in the allusions to "freemen" and the "disfranchised" in the minutes of the American Moral Reform Society meeting held during the summer of 1837, and the controversy and its aftermath are explicit topics in the pages of Whipper's *National Reformer.* Some historians date a shift in thinking among Philadelphia's African American leaders about "elevation" to the "Appeal to the Colored Citizens of Philadelphia" delivered at the 1848 state convention held in Harrisburg and signed by Whipper. They describe a move from "condition" to "complexion," from concern with status to an acknowledgment of the barriers of prejudice. Yet the 1848 "Appeal" contains several passages from Whipper's 1839 "Our Elevation." In 1848, Whipper develops his postdisfranchisement arguments and gives them a wider publicity, but in continuity with, rather than radical departure from, the earlier essay.[56]

After the 1838 vote, in "Our Elevation," Whipper bitterly rejects the claim that African Americans "must first be elevated" and must demonstrate their capacities before being granted full civil rights. This insistence is "a fatal error that has long been entertained by many gifted and philanthropic minds, viz. that our religious, moral, and intellectual elevation would secure us our political privileges. We aver that it will not." Instead of securing their rights, the progress of

African Americans in Pennsylvania has marked them for attack. Their display of character has made them vulnerable. With this formulation, Whipper preserves the terms but exposes the assurances and reverses the outcome of the Philadelphia social experiment. Usually combative, Whipper now concedes: "We now utterly discard it [the doctrine that elevation should precede the full rights of citizenship], and ask pardon for our former errors." He does not cast aside the need for moral reform, which he maintains is indispensable for the present and future welfare of the community, but he rejects the idea that such efforts are "constitutional requirements" for the franchise. In the Declaration of Independence and the Bill of Rights and by their Creator, African American men have been granted the same political rights as white men. Racial prejudice—"our complexion alone"—"furnishes the apology" used to deny these rights.[57]

Rather than "humbly begging the white man to 'elevate us,'" Whipper makes a different request: "All we ask of them is, that they take their 'feet from of[f] our necks,' that we may stand free and erect like themselves." The image of feet on necks, symbolizing political oppression, was used in the 1830s not only by James Forten Jr. to describe racial tyranny (as we have seen in his address at the 1837 American Moral Reform Society meeting) but also by Sarah Grimké, in her 1838 *Letters on the Equality of the Sexes and the Condition of Women*, to evoke the despotism of gender: "I ask no favors for my sex. I surrender not our claim to equality. All I ask of our brethren is, that they will take their feet from off our necks, and permit us to stand upright on that ground which God designed us to occupy." Whipper uses the image to expose the bind of elevation, in which the subjugated are pressed down and urged to rise and political rights are denied on the basis of a color that trumps character. "We need new terms for the vindication of our rights," Whipper writes in 1839. "We, too, have been allured by false idioms." The "false idiom" is not moral reform but the implied social contract, held out to African Americans in Philadelphia since the 1793 yellow fever epidemic, in which the exhibition of character would earn political and civil rights: the idiom of accomplishment and recompense.[58]

In elaborating his ideas about condition and complexion in the 1848 "Appeal to the Colored Citizens of Pennsylvania," Whipper and his cosigners, most of whom were Philadelphians, asserted that disfranchisement had opened a new phase of struggle, more explicitly political. Conduct still was key but now was seen as part of a strenuous forensics, in which African Americans would defy prejudice in words and acts. The 1848 convention in Harrisburg had been called to devise effective strategies for removing the term "white" from article 3, section I, of the revised Pennsylvania state constitution, which outlined the requirements for suffrage. According to the signers of the "Appeal," "condition"—"integrity of character, connected with all the characteristics which render men good and great"—had become the "pretext" for denying the franchise to African American men, whereas the actual reason was racial prejudice. If "condition" were the "standard," they argued, then the example of the accomplished and wealthy James E. Forten, "a *model* man," would have settled the debate. Instead, Forten was dismissed as an anomaly. The signers of the "Appeal" rejected "condition" as the "*standard*" for civic participation; instead, it was "only a *means.*"[59]

They specify the kind of means they have in mind, using a legal analogy. The signers compare the position of free African Americans with that of Somersett, the African slave who had been brought from Virginia to England by his master, escaped, been recaptured, and then was freed, in a landmark 1772 decision by Lord Mansfield, the chief justice of the King's Bench. Lord Mansfield held that, in the absence of positive law supporting slavery, slaves were free when they set foot on English soil. Unlike Somersett, who was an ocean apart from the system that oppressed him and who was represented by expert counsel in a court based on principles of justice, Africans who remain in America "are situated in the midst of our jurors, where every possible opportunity is presented for prejudging our cause." While "the evidence that was required in the Somersett case was *language,* in our case it will be *actions.*" The signers resist this burden of conduct, even as they acknowledge its inevitability. Altering the texture of the Philadelphia experiment, they maintain that rights will have to be won through public debate, in which character will serve as a kind of language, a rhetoric of gesture and tone that will form part of the struggle for authority. "Every man should consider," they warn, "that from this time forward the eyes of his jurors will be upon him, and if we would avoid any unjust cause of offence, in a case involving dollars and cents, how much more careful ought we to be where the great stake is our rights and privileges as citizens."[60]

For Whipper and his cosigners and, as we soon will see, for Joseph Willson in his *Sketches of the Higher Classes of Colored Society in Philadelphia,* "manners" are not only a sign of moral virtue and an instrument for group solidarity but also an explicit tactic of political struggle. Manners are not a ticket for admission or a performance to be rewarded, but a field of contention. The signers uneasily receive the terms of evidence and the scrutiny of the jurors, but they insist that those terms and that scrutiny do not prescribe their movements or predetermine an outcome. They deny that "we . . . need to be elevated before we are enfranchised" but recognize they will have to strive to get the voters of Pennsylvania to "take their feet off our necks." They hold that political rights should be theirs on the basis of religion and the American Revolution but concede that they will have to fight for those rights in the court of public opinion. They resolve that "we need moral and intellectual cultivation as a means through which we may be able to enlist the advocacy of our friends and influence the minds of our opponents."[61]

A "means" not a "standard"—this emphasis on character as evidence and tactic is not rebellion, and it is not the only strategy for achieving racial justice available in the 1840s, but it is also not capitulation. The Philadelphians describe an arena that extends to the church, the parlor, the literary and benevolent society, and the tax rolls, a field in which society resembles a courtroom or battleground. This is a literary as well as a political field, in which the two domains intersect at the nodes of character and conduct. In this field, a modern critical opposition between deference and demand seems too blunt a tool to grasp the complexities of social action among the Philadelphians. Whipper and his cosigners counseled discipline, not docility, and resistance in the acts of everyday life, not obeisance in the hopes of receiving favors. They did not conceal their anger behind a shrewd mask of compliance. Instead, they insisted on the expressiveness and trenchancy—the depth—of their surfaces. They argued for altering the public debate through strenuous engagement.[62]

Their analogy with Somersett describes the space through which African Americans move as juridical, in which actions are weighed as evidence, and the analogy also joins the conditions of slavery and freedom, implying a persistence of scrutiny and vulnerability, a freedom akin to probation. The signers warn that if they can be disfranchised, so, too, can "the *poor* of *every nation*" and "whole *political* parties." The burdens of conduct and the prospect of degradation may be shared, peculiar not to a people but to those living in the United States in the mid-nineteenth century.[63]

Disfranchisement and Appeal

The disillusion and fury of African American leaders at the passage of the Pennsylvania referendum in 1838 denying African American men the right to vote was exacerbated by the hinging of the dispute on the construal of a single word in the 1790 state constitution—"freeman"—and by the closeness of the final tally. The convention that met to revise the constitution did not have disfranchisement as its original goal. Instead, the delegates assembled in May 1837 in Harrisburg to curtail the powers of the governor, abolish lifetime offices, and expand access to the ballot. The issue of African American eligibility came up before the summer recess with a proposal to insert the word "white" before the word "freeman" in article 3, section I, of the 1790 Pennsylvania state constitution. The section read: "In elections by the citizens every freeman of the age of twenty-one years, having resided in the state two years next before the elections, and within that time paid a state or county tax, which shall have been assessed at least six months before the election, shall enjoy the rights of an elector."

The initial proposal to insert a racial qualification was withdrawn, but the debate erupted during the fall, after a case was filed in Bucks County by a defeated Democratic candidate for local office, who claimed that his opponent had won with illegal votes cast by blacks. The plaintiff argued that blacks should not have been allowed to vote. In December 1837, Judge Fox of the county court ruled that African Americans were not "freemen," as defined in the 1790 state constitution, and thus could not participate in elections. By January 1838, the amendment to restrict suffrage had gathered support at the convention. Benjamin Martin of Philadelphia explained that "it must be apparent to every well judged person, that *the elevation of the black, is the degradation of the white man*" and that any effort to amalgamate the two races would "alter the order of nature" and "bring about the war between the races."

The delegates argued over whether the inserting the word "white" clarified, altered, or violated the intentions of those who wrote the 1790 document. Ultimately, the change was supported on January 20 by a vote of 77 to 45. The meeting adjourned in February, and the popular vote on ratification was set for the following October. Before that vote, Chief Justice Gibson of the Pennsylvania Supreme Court handed down a decision in the case of William Fogg, an African American property owner and taxpayer who had been prevented from voting in 1835 and sued in lower courts. A judge in a local Court of Common Pleas had decided in his favor. Chief Justice Gibson, in a harbinger of the 1857 decision in *Dred Scott v. Sandford,* found that African Americans, while free men, were not legally "freemen" entitled to political privileges and that the state could deny them the vote on the grounds of their natural inferiority. On October 9, 1838, the new constitution was ratified, with the word "white" incorporated in article 3, section 1, by a narrow margin, 113,971 for and 112,759 against.[64]

As in the 1794 exchange between Absalom Jones, Richard Allen, and Mathew Carey about conduct during the yellow fever epidemic, the 1837–38 franchise debate turned on conflicting interpretations of words and their contexts. In 1837–38, the dispute over race, history, and citizenship pivoted on the word "freeman" and on the relationship between a "freeman" and a "free man." Did the state constitutions of 1776 and 1790, which granted voting rights to "freemen," include African Americans? Did the 1780 Act for the Gradual Abolition of Slavery, which mandated a passage from indenture to liberty, confer political rights? Did the Declaration of Independence or the Federal Constitution regard free African American men as citizens? A free man might not be enslaved, but is he a freeman according to English law? Is he a person entitled to the benefits accorded to citizens?

The debates in 1838 were complicated by evidence that in the decades after independence, some African Americans had been permitted to vote in elections, mostly in rural areas, but not, say, in Philadelphia, where their numbers might have influenced outcomes. The slim triumph (1,212 votes) for the revised 1838 constitution probably would have been a defeat if African American men in Philadelphia had cast their ballots. In the historian Julie Winch's view, African Americans in Philadelphia, such as the influential James Forten Sr., "saw voting rights as rights better left untested" in the years before 1837. The Pennsylvania efforts to restrict the franchise for blacks, while extending it for whites, were part of a wider pattern of "reform" in which many northern states rewrote their constitutions to disfranchise African American men or raised obstacles to their exercise of the privilege.[65]

African American leaders in Philadelphia and Pittsburgh were outraged by the claims that free men were not to be considered freemen. They appreciated the irony in the reaction that Benjamin Martin had cast as natural fact: that many European American citizens of Pennsylvania apparently perceived African American elevation as occurring at their expense, that progress seemed to be leading not to tolerance but to estrangement. In several petitions, they expressed their astonishment and frustration, and they sought to alter the outcomes first of the state convention and then of the plebiscite.

In July 1837, the constitutional reformers in Harrisburg received, with some umbrage, a "Memorial of the Free Citizens of Color in Pittsburgh and Its Vicinity Relative to the Right of Suffrage." Signed with close to eighty names, the "Memorial" opened with a statement of disbelief that in the year 1837, citizens of Pennsylvania might impose a complexional requirement for exercising the franchise. The document quoted extensively from the preamble to the 1790 state constitution, which argued against prejudice and slavery, and then detailed the "moral, social, and political condition" of African Americans in Pittsburgh, including churches and Sunday schools; moral, literary, and benevolent societies; property and jobs held; and taxes paid.[66]

In early January 1838, the constitutional reformers were presented with a "Memorial to the Honorable, the Delegates of the People of Pennsylvania in Convention at Philadelphia Assembled," signed "on behalf of the people of color in the city and county of Philadelphia" by Charles W. Gardner and Frederick A. Hinton, both of whom were prominent advocates of self-improvement and abolition. Gardner and Hinton offered ten arguments against confining the vote to the "white freeman," invoking theology, the Declaration of Independence,

Pennsylvania's distinguished history of supporting liberty, the principles of consent of the governed and no taxation without representation, and the benefits African Americans had contributed to the larger society.[67]

In March 1838, shortly after the revision had been approved and before the October referendum, a meeting of African Americans in Philadelphia at the First African Presbyterian Church endorsed an "Appeal of Forty Thousand Citizens, Threatened with Disfranchisement, to the People of Pennsylvania." It had been drawn up by a committee of seven eminent Philadelphians, led by the antislavery activist Robert Purvis, the son-in-law of James Forten Sr. Signed by Purvis, the pamphlet was designed to sway voters against the new constitution. Insisting that African American men in Pennsylvania had exercised the right to vote since 1790, Purvis and his committee supplement many of the arguments in the earlier, briefer "Memorials." They condemn disfranchisement as the act of a "despot majority," insisting on their allegiance to state and country despite the proposed offense. They assess legal records and contemporary debate about the term "freeman." Refuting the analyses and citations in the *Fogg* case, they argue that history, diction, syntax, and logic all prove that the term "freeman" in 1790 included colored men.[68]

To demonstrate the progress that African Americans have made in freedom, the "Appeal" marshals statistics about population, real and personal estate, income, tax payments, churches, schools, teachers, libraries, and benevolent associations, most of them culled from a report on "The Present State and Condition of the Free People of Color, of the City of Philadelphia and Adjoining Districts," issued earlier in the year by the Pennsylvania Society for Promoting the Abolition of Slavery. Statistics had been amassed and employed in polemics about race and freedom since the late eighteenth century, by the Quaker abolitionist Anthony Benezet and the Abolition Society and, beginning in the nineteenth century, by black leaders such as James Forten Sr. The Abolition Society reports of 1838 sought to influence the decision about the franchise. The first was dated January 5 and the second April 4, and they were published together as "The Present State and Condition." Compiled by the white reformers of the society with the assistance of the African American minister Charles W. Gardner, the reports, filled with details and numbers, made the case for African American character.

At the beginning of the April document, the authors of "The Present State and Condition" note that in the interval between January and April, despite the first report having been sent to the delegates, they had voted to restrict the franchise and to uphold the denial of a fugitive slave's right to a jury trial. "The Present State and Condition" is formally split by the convention vote to disfranchise. The authors reaffirm the need to circulate information and the strategy of vindicating through statistics. Yet the document itself, registering the vote, reveals the limits of evidence in the face of prejudice and the difficulties of authenticating human equality. Once the concession is made that statistics can justify rights, the numbers will be open to dispute and bias, and the status of citizens will remain insecure. Throughout the nineteenth century, including reports on the condition of African Americans in Philadelphia published in 1838, 1849, and 1856, and culminating in W. E. B. Dubois's 1899 inquiry, *The Philadelphia Negro* (which itself draws upon the earlier research), Philadelphia was seen by protosociologists and then the emerging profession as the site whose African American residents might hold the key to understanding and overcoming the dilemmas of freedom in the United States.[69]

On its own terms, the "Appeal of Forty Thousand Citizens," the most substantial of the petitions against disfranchisement, which was honored in African American and antislavery circles, delivers a forceful argument on the basis of law, statistics, justice, and history, including the service of African Americans during the yellow fever epidemic of 1793. Yet neither the "Appeal" nor the two earlier "Memorials" to the 1837–38 convention succeeded in derailing the efforts to alter the state constitution. Set against the backdrop of the dozens of memorials and petitions to the citizens of Pennsylvania and the state legislature (offered, for example, at the black state conventions in Pittsburgh in 1841, Harrisburg in 1848, and Pittsburgh again in 1865), "The Appeal of Forty Thousand Citizens" fits a pattern of ceremonial, frustrated address. African American men in Pennsylvania did not gain, or regain, the vote until 1873, after the Civil War. In 1855, eighteen years after disfranchisement, a committee of seven, signing on behalf of the "Colored Citizens of Philadelphia," published a "Memorial of Thirty Thousand Disfranchised Citizens of Philadelphia, to the Honorable Senate and House of Representatives." Repeating the arguments and updating the statistics from earlier petitions, the signers castigated the "Reform Convention" for perpetrating a travesty that had helped to inaugurate a period of economic decline and racial violence.[70]

Over the decades, with repetition and with no sign that the legislature intended to remove the adjective "white," the African American memorials gather resentment, and the rhetoric takes on an edge of bitter disbelief. The 1838 debate was the closest the petitions came to having an impact on the legal requirements for suffrage. As early as 1843, in an address delivered at the National Convention of Colored Citizens held in Buffalo, Samuel H. Davis lamented: "We have petitioned [for our rights] again and again, and what has been the result? Our humblest prayers have not been permitted a hearing. We could not even state our grievances.

Our petitions were disregarded; our supplications slighted, and we spurned from the mercy-seat, insulted, abused, and slandered; and this day finds us in the same unhappy and hopeless condition in which we have been for our whole lives." In the parade of appeals, the stances take on formulaic qualities, and the decorum of entreaty, however forceful, reaches an impasse.[71]

Joseph Willson's *Higher Classes of Colored Society in Philadelphia*

In the chapter on politics in his 1841 *Sketches of the Higher Classes of Colored Society in Philadelphia*, Joseph Willson condemns the posture of supplication, first in mild tones, using the language of romance and law: "almost, if not entirely, deprived of political rights and power . . . they [the people of color in Pennsylvania] must appear altogether in the attitude of suitors; and show themselves very humble in the exercise of even that prerogative." Then, more strongly, he evokes a residual sense of "class" as rank in order to describe the archaic character of democracy in mid-nineteenth-century Pennsylvania: "Thus it is necessary for the people of color to keep up an incessant *begging* of their *rulers* to legislate in their behalf; and with what effect is well known to all." "Well known to all" is the fact of disfranchisement, voted into law three years before the publication of Willson's *Sketches*. Disfranchisement and bigotry shape Willson's book of Philadelphia manners. Echoing the language of Purvis's 1838 "Appeal of Forty Thousand," Willson refers to disfranchisement as "the tyrannical act of the ever memorable 'Reform Convention.'" The mixture of politics, conduct, sobriety, and censure distinguishes Willson's treatment of social surface.[72]

Willson views African American "higher class" society in Philadelphia from the position of a self-described outsider, "as it would be found by a stranger visiting" (89). He was not exactly a stranger, since he had lived near the city for years by the time his book appeared in 1841, but he cast himself as more of an observer than a participant. He refers to himself on the title page only as "a Southerner." (A notice of the book in the *Pennsylvania Freeman* in October 1841, identifying the writer as "our talented young friend Joseph Willson," suggests that his authorship was an open secret.) Willson was born in Augusta, Georgia, in 1816 or 1817 to a Scots-Irish banker and his African American servant, who had been freed by her master. Facing increasing legal restrictions on free people of color in Georgia, Willson's mother left for Philadelphia in the early 1830s, supported by funds she had inherited from the banker, which were administered by a white guardian. Willson and his family lived in the unincorporated Spring Garden district north of the city for fifteen years. They were one of the few black families in a largely white neighborhood, composed mostly of residents of German, English, or Irish ancestry. After his mother's death in 1847, Willson moved with his family to Moyamensing Township just south of the city, bordering the Cedar Street neighborhood. This racially diverse area was the center of African American Philadelphia. In 1854, he relocated to Cleveland, Ohio.[73]

Willson writes in his preface that he has two goals in representing "colored society in Philadelphia": "first, to remove some of the unfounded prejudices from without; and secondly, to correct certain abuses which are known to exist among themselves" (79). He structures his volume in terms of this dialectic of outside and inside. The chapters move from the general social characteristics of African Americans in Philadelphia (shared with other groups), to the "higher classes," to discord among its members, to their social intercourse and domestic rituals, to the politics of moral improvement and disfranchisement, and finally to a catalogue of literary groups, libraries, and schools. Willson dissects, instructs, compliments, and reproves his audiences. He hopes that the access he provides will have consequences.

We might say, with Karl Marx, that Willson is defending his class interests, aligning himself with the bourgeoisie. Or we might say, with Pierre Bourdieu, that Willson is attempting to legitimate distinctions between middle- and lower-class values, seeking to mark off his group with symbolic capital. Or we might say, with the historian Stuart Blumin, that Willson is expressing an awareness of and desire for membership in a white American middle class, distinguished less by its relations to the means of production and more by its cultural beliefs and economic circumstances. Or we might say, with the historian Kevin K. Gaines, that Willson is engaged in a bid for acceptance from white authorities by imitating dominant notions of respectability and by separating his group from the black masses. Yet in doing so, we would be misapprehending the kind of book Willson has written.[74]

In his *Sketches*, Willson does not seek to isolate the "higher classes" or to gain white approval. It is not clear what name to use for Willson's "class" or to what extent he considers himself part of the group he describes. Even Julie Winch, the historian who edited Willson's book and reprinted it for the first time since 1841, seems unsure about nomenclature. Instead of the original title, *Sketches of the Higher Classes of Colored Society*, Winch offers a new one, taken from an 1828 passage in *Freedom's Journal*: "Should a stranger desire to see the elite of our people, he must visit Philadelphia."[75] Winch calls her edition *The Elite of Our People*. Yet Willson himself deliberately does not use the term "elite" to designate the focus of his study. Keenly aware of his potential readerships—a white audience that he hopes to educate, a fracturing black audience to whom he counsels respect and unity, and a readership beyond Philadelphia that is weighing the experiment of freedom in this symbolic city—Willson selects his words very carefully.

Joseph Willson's small volume disturbs our understanding of race and class in Philadelphia in the mid-nineteenth century, and beyond. It exposes what Raymond Williams has called the "essential ambiguity" of the term "class." Williams argues that "class" describes at the same time group (a social or economic category), rank (a comparative social position by birth or mobility), and formation (a perceived economic relationship). Whatever class Wilson's higher classes belong to, the modifiers "middle" or "elite" do not accurately describe their situation. Literary critics have begun to rethink a vocabulary of "class." One way to advance this goal would be to recognize the ways in which Joseph Willson's *Sketches* resists modern labels and continues in the early twenty-first century to negotiate its status and to press for subtler terms of analysis.[76]

From the start, Willson distinguishes between what some of his readers may anticipate and what he will present:

> The idea of "Higher Classes" of colored society is, it must be confessed, a novel one; and will, undoubtedly, excite the mirth of a prejudiced community on its annunciation . . . there are [those] who like to see their neighbors' merits caricatured, and their faults distorted and exaggerated [who] will expect burlesque representations, and other laughter exciting sketches, and probably be thereby led to procure this little volume for the purpose of gratifying their *penchant* for the ludicrous. Now, while I desire not to put anything in the way of its *sale*, be the motive for purchasing it what it may, yet all such are informed—but they must first procure it before they can possess the information!—that they will find upon perusal, that they had indulged in a very erroneous impression. (79)

Willson writes "Higher Classes"—not "elite"—signifying a relative, rather than superlative, position. "Higher," he asserts, is not defined in strictly economic terms and does not involve shades of color. With an emphasis that will have literary consequence for Frank J. Webb's later novel, *The Garies and Their Friends*, Willson associates the "boundary" (86) that defines the higher classes with home ownership: "What, therefore, I would have the reader understand by the designation 'higher classes,' as here applied, consists of that portion of colored society whose incomes, from their pursuits or otherwise, (immoralities or criminalities of course excepted,) enables them to maintain the position of house-holders, and their families in comparative ease and comfort" (87). (Julie Winch estimates that this definition would have applied to at most 5 percent of the total black population in Philadelphia.) What it means to "hold" a house is key for both Willson and Webb: owning property but also establishing a threshold and supervising a domestic realm. In addition to possessing a home, membership in the higher classes entails personal responsibility, social commitment, and intellectual cultivation. Willson writes that he uses the term "class" not to introduce "invidious distinctions" but for "perspicuity" (82)—so that his readers can appreciate social complexity in African American Philadelphia.[77]

At the start, Willson raises issues of perspective. He will offer "sketches," rather than the "burlesque representations" of racial audacity disseminated by Edward W. Clay and others in the late 1820s and 1830s. Alluding to such cartoons, Willson suggests that he will provide a different glimpse of "Life in Philadelphia." Those who have a *"penchant,"* a cultured taste, for caricature will find their desires gauged and thwarted. Willson will introduce other modes, and as he delights in informing such readers (who already have purchased his book), he will make them pay for the privilege and for their indulgence. Later in the volume, he complains about viewers who form "an opinion of the beauty of the landscape merely by the heavy shading in the fore-ground of the picture" (97). He seeks to correct such myopia by giving his readers a depth of field.

By "sketches," Willson means not only a counterportrayal of African American domestic life and social exchange but also a *quality* of representation. He will exhibit "society in a body" (89), rather than the individual distortions found in popular culture. He will describe contours, rather than details, and patterns of behavior, rather than individual acts. In doing so, Willson may hope to avoid deepening the rifts within and across African American groups in Philadelphia and elevating specific individuals at the expense of the group. Given the context of violence, especially the riots of 1834 and 1838, Willson also may use generality to protect individuals by refusing to name them in his pages. He explains that he does not wish to cater to the appetite of "the monster public" (82) for ridicule and exposure.[78]

Willson makes clear that he will not make available a stable or penetrating view. There will be an indistinctness to his distinctions. He has "merely glanced" at African American society in Philadelphia (79). He will not be offering a statistical report, guidebook, or ethnology treatise. In his first chapter, Willson does reprint facts about benevolent associations, mechanics, and finances from the 1837 "Minutes and Proceedings" of the American Moral Reform Society on "the progress and present state of the colored population," and he devotes his last chapter to the particulars of black literary societies in Philadelphia. Yet while the opening and closing chapters evoke the promise of statistics to affirm character, the intervening pages give only partial disclosures. The higher classes exist, and Willson hopes that such an acknowledgment will diminish the partiality of white readers, but he will not provide a transparent display. Neither the character nor characters of the higher classes are so easily apprehended. For the book's different audiences in 1841, white and black, expert and amateur, the interplay of identity and anonymity and inside and outside knowledge would have been part of the reading experience.

For modern readers, Willson's editor, Julie Winch, furnishes a different kind of access in more than fifty pages of meticulous notes. Where Willson gestures, Winch locates: particular streets, neighborhoods, churches, and schools; specific ministers, doctors, and painters; literary allusions; family genealogies, immigrations and migrations, social rivalries, and domestic rituals. When Willson does mention individuals in his last two chapters, listing delegates to the first black convention and members of libraries and literary societies, Winch elaborates on the lives of the Morels, the Whippers, the Purvises, the Fortens, the Hintons, and the Casseys. The list of delegates alone generates fifteen pages of small print in the endnotes. Winch's details become part of Willson's text. They are drawn into its perceptual dynamics. On Willson's pages, what kind of access do we have to the higher classes?

Willson invites readers into their parlors, manipulates expectations, and obscures the view. Those parlors become crucial and impalpable spaces. In the fourth chapter, on the *"home condition"* of the higher classes, Willson gestures toward their furnishings—the "sofas, sideboards, card-tables, mirrors, &c.&c."—but refrains from giving "an elaborate statement or inventory" (98). He suggests that his readers can supply the details from other fashionable rooms they have seen or envisioned. He describes the social rhythms of the higher classes: the formal visits, the strict reciprocities, the adherence to protocol, the abstinence from strong drink, the evening entertainments including musical recitals and conversation in which women as well as men play leading roles, the parties during which "the greatest order and neatness of management is observed" (100). The higher classes express themselves, manifest their intellectual refinement, and practice virtue, but this behavior does not take place in a vacuum. Willson intimates that the parlor serves as a refuge from a publicity that might expose young men and women to assault: "Very little out-door amusement is resorted to, as walking or riding excursions; but the reason of the non-observance of these, and one which is quite sufficient to prohibit them, is readily traceable to its proper source" (99). The prolix negative here ("but the reason of the non-observance of these") captures at the level of the phrase the strenuous parlor performances, the ways in which conduct takes place at the border between "observance" and "non-observance." In obeying the rules, Willson's higher classes violate the norms. The danger that keeps the young men and women in their parlors is so obvious as not to need specifying ("readily traceable to its proper source"), like the "effect well known to all" of disfranchisement (103), although one imagines that the obviousness may have signified differently for Willson's various audiences.

A few pages later, Willson describes how "the peculiar circumstances by which they are surrounded" enter the intimate precincts of the "higher classes":

> The exceedingly illiberal, unjust and oppressive prejudices of the great mass of the white community, overshadowing every moment of their existence, is enough to crush—effectually crush and keep down—any people. It meets them at almost every step without their domiciles, and not unfrequently follows them even *there*. No private enterprise of any moment,—no public movement of consequence for the general good,—can they undertake, but forth steps the relentless monster to blight it in the germ. But in the face of all this, they not only bear the burthen successfully, but possess the elasticity of mind that enables them to stand erect under their disabilities, and present a state of society of which, to say the least, none have just cause to be ashamed. (101)

Even in the houses they hold, behind fastened doors, animosity weighs on the gestures of the higher classes. It alters the space through which they move. Willson's own characteristic verbal decorum is ruptured here. He materializes prejudice (as a mass that threatens to crush), personifies it (as following, even stalking), and gives it a melodramatic cast (a "relentless monster"). In his portrait of the higher classes, Willson examines how conduct is formed in a field of pressures. The sense that a ubiquitous prejudice tests the elasticity of mind and body links the higher classes (who may have some defense, but no escape) with other classes.

Their parlors represent an effort to practice rituals, ornament interiors, and maintain community on the edge of violence. Their eloquent surfaces are the product of arduous effort. Willson hopes that this society and his portrayal will "speak loudly against the injustice that is done them" and that "positive knowledge" and "practical demonstration" will help to alleviate intolerance and "secure [the] estimation" that will lead to "entire enfranchisement" and the "quiet, undisturbed possession of their civil liberty" (99, 119). Such hopes dissolved in the riots of 1842 and 1849, when the persons and structures of the higher classes were assailed. Willson's book stands at the end of ten years of debate over conduct and politics, which began with the Philadelphia convention movement in 1830, divided over the American Moral Reform Society, and was revised in Whipper's post-1838 arguments about "condition" as a "means," rather than a "standard."

When Willson repeatedly admonishes the members of the higher classes to avoid disputes and when he calls for "honesty, courtesy, self-respect" (110), he not only offers moral instruction as a good in itself but also reminds his African

American readers of wider struggles. He laments the absence of the unity and concerted action he imagines was present in the early years of the black convention movement. (The 1831 meeting, which took place before Willson moved north, is enshrined in his fifth chapter.) He even suggests that fractures among the higher classes might have contributed to the popular vote for disfranchisement. When he remarks on the jealousies and rivalries, geographical preferences (especially South versus North), and conflicting attitudes toward the white majority, Willson indicates the diversity within, and not only between, groups of African Americans in Philadelphia. In contriving their status, the higher classes also have succeeded in replicating the strife that comes with social distinction. Willson values such cleaving as a sign of social development, but he also attempts to rectify its excesses, which he views as undermining the exemplary force and political efficacy of the higher classes.

Willson insists that social distinctions are not important as "pretences to superiority," but only when founded in the "true and just standard—the MIND;—the *mind*, as developed in the goodness—the virtue—of its possessor" (90). Willson's "virtue" links self-cultivation with group solidarity and security. He condescends to "the hewers of wood and the drawers of water" (97, evoking Joshua 9.21), but he does not dismiss them or discount the possibility that they may be or may become virtuous. He seeks to distinguish the higher classes from "the vicious and worthless" (102), but he also believes that the lower classes can be inspired to rise. Like several other nineteenth-century African American writers, Willson argues that differentiations are properly made according to shifting notions of class, rather than fixed ideas about race. Ambition in Willson's *Sketches* is neither preposterous (as it is for Edward W. Clay) nor offensive (as it is for Robert Montgomery Bird), but human. Willson's mid-nineteenth-century higher classes do not form "the aristocracy of the Negro population" that W. E. B. DuBois famously criticizes in Philadelphia at the end of the nineteenth century as self-absorbed and detached from contact with and responsibility for the masses.[79] Instead, Willson insists on a depth of field and shared social space, even as he appreciates distinctions.

Willson's *Sketches of the Higher Classes* is difficult to classify. The book is an amalgam of journal, travel narrative, report on the "condition," and courtesy, conduct, and etiquette manual. Like the Pennsylvania Abolition Society reporters, Willson describes populations and institutions, but he relies on sketches, rather than statistics, and the distance he maintains from the objects of his study veils, as well as clarifies. As in the older literature of courtesy, Willson addresses an "upper-class" audience and instructs his readers in virtue, tying manners to morals, yet his African American higher classes occupy an acutely unstable position.

As in the conduct books, Willson encourages the development of "middle-class" character, an effort with particularly high stakes for African Americans in Pennsylvania, who are striving for citizenship rights in the wake of disfranchisement. He does not write different books for men and for women, as did many conduct writers in the nineteenth-century United States. Although Willson does sometimes split his address along gender lines, he emphasizes a shared racial position. As in the etiquette manuals, Willson acknowledges decorum as a consequence of social interdependence. Yet unlike the writers of etiquette manuals, he refrains from giving advice about specific situations and promoting exact rules. Rather than furnishing a guide to elevation, Willson seeks to invigorate the higher classes and grant them a strategic prominence. *Sketches,* then, promotes a tenuous security, rather than mobility. Willson's book engages the high-stakes politics of information in Philadelphia in the 1830s and 1840s.[80]

Willson's *Sketches* was not the only African American manners book before the Civil War. Cyprian Clamorgan's *The Colored Aristocracy of St. Louis* (1858) reminds us that Willson's complex earnestness was only one tone, his higher classes one demographic, and postdisfranchisement Philadelphia one location in a diverse array. "Aristocracy" is Clamorgan's chosen term, and he revels in it. He describes the free people of color in St. Louis who have money and use their wealth to maneuver for social and political influence. More brazen and satiric than Willson's *Sketches,* Clamorgan in his *Colored Aristocracy* flaunts a delightful superficiality, in which manners are unhinged from morals. He parodies white society and also seeks to establish a colored equivalent. The texts of Willson and Clamorgan point to an unexplored landscape of manners in nineteenth-century U.S. literature.[81]

Published in 1841, joining manners and violence, Willson's *Sketches of the Higher Classes* appeared on the verge of the spectacular riots of the 1840s that brought Philadelphia into fiction.

CHAPTER THREE

Riot

Whoever shall write a history of Philadelphia from the Thirties to
the end of the Fifties will record a popular period of turbulence
and outrages so extensive as to now appear almost incredible.
—Charles Godfrey Leland, *Memoirs* (1893)

In 1829, 1834, 1835, 1842, and 1849, racial riots erupted in Philadelphia that,
along with the antiabolitionist disorder of 1838 and the ethnic and religious
disturbances that culminated in riots during the summer of 1844, earned the city
notoriety as, in the words of the anonymous author of one of the fictional "mysteries of Philadelphia" published before the Civil War, "the queen of violence." In
the 1830s and 1840s, and until the merging of the city and county of Philadelphia in 1854, the city's jurisdiction extended only from the Delaware River in the
east to the Schuylkill River in the west and from Vine Street in the north to Cedar
or South Street (the name was officially changed to South Street in the 1850s).
This was the grid of William Penn's original charter, comprising only two square
miles. More people resided in the outlying districts than in the city itself. The
upper classes and skilled workers, largely white and Protestant, tended to live in
the original precincts of the city, while the poor, including large numbers of Irish
Catholic immigrants, were in areas to the north and the south: the Northern

Liberties, Kensington, Moyamensing, Southwark (figure 3.1). Many African Americans lived in the racially and ethnically mixed Cedar neighborhood or South Street corridor, approximately fourteen blocks long and two blocks wide, that overlapped the southern border of the city. Here were the homes, churches,

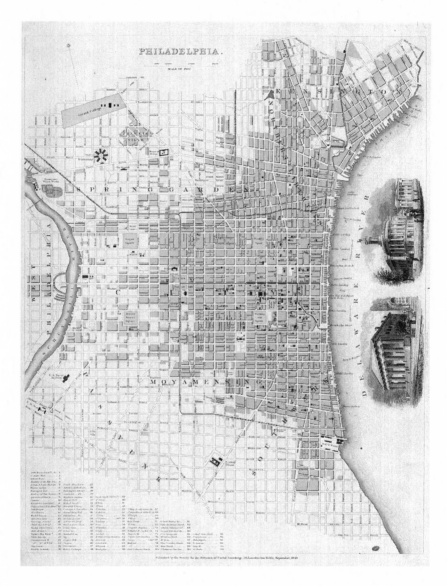

FIGURE 3.1 Map of Philadelphia (1840), published by the Society for the Diffusion of Useful Knowledge. Courtesy of the Library Company of Philadelphia.

benevolent societies, and cultural institutions described by Joseph Willson in his *Sketches of the Higher Classes of Colored Society in Philadelphia.*[1]

The violence of 1834, 1835, 1842, and 1849 focused on African American property and persons in the Cedar neighborhood. Its streets were vertically segregated. That is, residents—African, English, Irish, German, and Dutch—lived in clusters and tended to consider themselves apart, but they were not spatially isolated in discrete blocks or subneighborhoods. In 1850, the area was approximately 28 percent Irish and 25 percent black. The neighborhood included the relatively prosperous homes and civic establishments on Lombard Street and the notoriously crowded dwellings on Bedford Street. White property owners and middle- and lower-class blacks in the Cedar neighborhood were outnumbered by what the historian Emma Jones Lapsansky has described as a "rootless white community." Given the diversity and vigor of the neighborhood, Lapsansky writes, "The wonder is not that there were riots, but that riots were not more frequent, more violent, and more widespread."[2]

Historians have analyzed various causes for the Philadelphia violence, notable for its sustained intensity in a period when disturbances occurred in many American cities. In Philadelphia, the mixture seems to have been especially volatile: technological change (the city led the industrial revolution in the United States), factory servitude, a rapid increase in the white laboring population, an economic depression that lasted with occasional recoveries from the late 1830s until the early 1850s, an expanding gap between rich and poor, inadequate housing, and political incompetence and corruption. Races, ethnicities, and religions struggled over economic resources, living and working space, sexual contact, and political authority. They disputed stories about the riots as well, and particulars of setting and plot accrued ideological weight.[3]

Here are some of the details:

On August 12, 1834, there were reports of a clash between whites and blacks in a building that housed a popular carrousel, the "Flying Horses," on Cedar Street above Seventh. A group of white men, many of them young and lower working class, some of them Irish, most of them from the neighborhood, attacked and destroyed the building, and then targeted black residences on St. Mary's Street in the city and Bedford and Baker streets in Moyamensing Township to the south. As white New Yorkers did during the riots of July 1834, white Philadelphians signaled to rioters that their homes were to be spared by placing candles in their windows. Such acts raised questions among those who later debated the riots about whether there was a conspiracy.

On the evening of August 12 and for the next two nights on the edge of the city and the areas south, African Americans were under siege. Mobs attacked two black churches, a black Masonic hall, an interracial tavern, private homes, and individuals they encountered in the streets. Members of both the lower and higher classes were assaulted, and many fled across the Delaware River to New Jersey. The majority of those whites present during the riots were spectators who offered encouragement to the smaller number of active participants. Dozens of houses were ransacked, and property was thrown into the streets and destroyed. One person was killed. Within the city limits, Mayor John Swift attempted to restrain the disorder. In the southern areas outside the city proper, the authorities were less effective. (In 1835, Mayor Swift came under criticism when he enforced discipline within the city but failed to stop or condemn rioters who targeted houses occupied by blacks south of Cedar Street in Moyamensing.) The commit-tee appointed to investigate the riots in 1834 named, among its causes, white laborers' beliefs that they were unable to find jobs because of the preference for black workers shown by some employers, the forcible rescue by blacks of those arrested as fugitive slaves, and the boisterousness of African American church services.[4]

On May 17, 1838, at the corner of Sixth and Haines streets, below Sassafras or Race, in the northeastern part of the city, a mob set fire to Pennsylvania Hall, which had been dedicated only three days earlier. The hall, the largest in the city with a grand auditorium on its second floor adorned with gaslit chandeliers, had been built with funds from stocks offered to a diverse public. Pennsylvania Hall was to have been the venue for social reform. In its first and only days, lectures had been given on topics such as temperance, the status of Native Americans, colonization, women's rights, and especially slavery and abolition. The Pennsyl-vania Anti-Slavery Society and the Anti-Slavery Convention of American Women held meetings. Participating in the opening days were the abolitionists William Lloyd Garrison, Angelina and Sarah Grimké, Lucretia Mott, and Maria Weston Chapman. African Americans were seated in the hall, and whites and blacks, men and women, socialized inside the building and on the streets.

In the days following its dedication, posters appeared and leaflets were circu-lated denouncing the rumored program of immediate emancipation and racial "amalgamation." After the riots, the New York *Commercial Advertiser* reported: "The immediate cause of this popular outbreak is said to have been the ridicu-lous and ostentatious amalgamation of colors in Ches[t]nut street, during the hours of fashionable promenading." Fueling the social outrage was the sight of the light-skinned Robert Purvis helping his darker-skinned wife Harriet, the daughter of James Forten, from her carriage.[5] Pennsylvania Hall was destroyed dur-ing a season of controversy about race and citizenship in Philadelphia. In January, the state constitutional "reform" convention had voted to insert the adjective "white" into the requirements for voting; in March, African Americans in the city had adopted the "Appeal of Forty Thousand Citizens, Threatened with Disfranchisement"; and the following October, Pennsylvania's voters would ratify the exclusion.

On the evening of May 16, Angelina Grimké's speech was interrupted by hissing from members of the audience, and outside Pennsylvania Hall, a crowd gathered and stones were thrown through the windows. At the close of the evening session, African Americans were assaulted as they left. The managers requested protection from Mayor Swift, but he explained that he did not have either the legal authority or sufficient police to defend the building or attendees. On the 17th, in response to the rising threats, the evening program was canceled. That night, the doors were battered down. Furniture was smashed and used as kindling, fires were set in the second-floor auditorium, and gas pipes were broken in order to intensify the flames. Books and pamphlets were tossed into the street. Volunteer firemen doused the nearby buildings but did not attempt to stop Philadelphia Hall from burning, either because they feared reprisals from the mob or because they sympathized with the arson. Before a crowd of thousands who had encouraged the rioters (by one estimate, 10,000; by another, 25,000 to 30,000), the interior of the building was consumed, with the damage confined to the Hall. Some reported that a shout of triumph was raised when the roof collapsed.

The next night, a mob set fire to the Shelter for Colored Orphans, run by the Quakers, north of the city limits, but the building was saved by the local police magistrate and volunteer firemen. The following evening, the Bethel Church on Sixth and Lombard (founded by Richard Allen), in the south of the city, was attacked but sustained only minor damage. The offices of the *Public Ledger*, whose editors had condemned the riots, were threatened. The police committee report, issued two months later, exonerated the mayor from charges that he had acted improperly and concluded that Pennsylvania Hall was *"doomed to destruction"* by its owners and their backers, who had allowed the structure to be used for promulgating morally offensive doctrines and had encouraged interracial mixing, a spectacle bound to provoke the community. The abolitionist press featured the story of Pennsylvania Hall's destruction, and its ruins endured in the city for eight years.

On the morning of August 1, 1842, a major offensive against African Americans in the Cedar neighborhood, including the homes and institutions of the "higher classes," began with an attack on a black temperance parade held by the Young Men's Vigilant Association on the anniversary of West Indian emancipation. It was reported that onlookers were indignant at a banner held by the temperance marchers, which showed a black man pointing with one hand to the broken chains at his feet and the other to the word "Liberty" over his head.

A rising sun and a foundering ship were pictured in the background. Some saw in the image the burning towns of Saint Domingue and an incitement to slave revolt. When the marchers reached the white working-class areas of Southwark, around Fourth and Fifth and Shippen and Plum streets, they were met by insults and paving stones. The mob chased the paraders into the streets where black residences were numerous, and they attacked houses and their occupants in the courtyards and alleys around Lombard Street. After shots were fired at the rioters from a dwelling in Bradford's Alley, the building was entered and its inhabitants assaulted. That evening, rioters burned down the Second African Presbyterian Church on St. Mary's Street and Smith's Beneficial Hall on Lombard Street, which had been erected by the lumber merchant Stephen Smith as a meeting place for African American groups. A reporter for the Philadelphia *United States Gazette*, echoing the structural fatalism associated with Pennsylvania Hall, observed that Smith's property was "doomed to destruction."[6]

On the following day, black residents of the neighborhood sought refuge in the central police station or fled across the Delaware River to New Jersey. In the southwest of the city, at the Schuylkill River docks, gangs composed mostly of Irishmen set upon blacks who were reporting for work and also charged a sheriff's posse sent to restore order, while attacks in the Cedar neighborhood continued. After Mayor Swift called out seven militia companies, the streets were finally quieted. In the days after the riot, a grand jury agreed with white petitioners in the neighborhood that the black temperance hall on Bedford Street, from which the procession had started and which had survived the riot, presented a danger to their own safety and property, and the edifice was demolished by law. The grand jury also found that the riot had been provoked by the temperance marchers. Ultimately, the owners of the Second Presbyterian Church and Smith's Beneficial Hall were awarded damages by the Pennsylvania Supreme Court.

Three weeks after the riot, responding to an inquiry from a friend in Massachusetts for a report on the events, Robert Purvis confessed in a letter his inability to comply: "I know not where I should begin, nor how, or when to end in a detail of the wantonness, brutality, and murderous spirit of the Actors, in the late riots, nor of the Apathy and *inhumanity* of the *Whole* community in regard to the matter. Press, Church, Magistrates, Clergymen and Devils are against us. The measure of our sufferings is full. 'Mans inhumanity to man, indeed make countless millions mourn.' From the most painful and minute investigation, in the feelings, views and acts of the community—in regard *to us*—I am convinced of our utter and complete nothingness in public estimation. . . . And the bloody *Will* is in the heart of this community to destroy us."[7] Purvis's despair at the hostility, not just of the rioters but of civil society in Philadelphia, is echoed, as we have seen in the previous chapter, by others who reflected in the aftermath of disfranchisement and violence.

On election night, October 9, 1849, a mob, including members of the Irish Catholic gang known as the Killers of Moyamensing, attacked the California House, a building at the corner of Sixth and St. Mary's streets in the Cedar neighborhood. The structure housed a tavern that attracted interracial patrons and was owned by a mulatto man who had married a white woman. The California House had been the object of threats that autumn and in the days leading up to the attack. The rioters overwhelmed those who attempted to safeguard the building, invaded, dismantled furniture, and used it as kindling. They tore out the gas fixtures to increase the blaze. The mob obstructed the work of the volunteer firemen, cutting hoses and shooting at them, wounding many and killing two. For hours, they battled African American defenders, firemen, and city watchmen. More than thirty buildings in the neighborhood burned, either through the spreading fire or by targeted destruction. Two African Americans were slain. Militia companies arrived and finally quelled the violence by mid-morning the next day.

The loss of lives and property in this latest spectacle of riot in 1849 helped to spur the move toward consolidating the city and the county of Philadelphia with the goals of strengthening law enforcement and fire protection and extending the tax base to provide services for the expanded industrial urban center. In 1854, the original city of two square miles was joined with the six boroughs, nine districts, and thirteen townships surrounding it, becoming a jurisdiction of 129 square miles. The riots of the 1830s and 1840s helped to make Philadelphia the modern city that we recognize.[8]

The riots of 1838, in which Pennsylvania Hall was theatrically burned, and of 1834, 1842, and 1849, in which widespread damage was inflicted on African Americans in the Cedar neighborhood, were analyzed in a variety of genres, including public reports, travel narratives, documentary collections, and fiction. The Philadelphia novel in the 1840s and 1850s develops in the context of this violence. Writers superimposed the disorder of the riots against Philadelphia's renowned urban grid, conveying not just irony and hypocrisy but also distinctive spatial patterns, temporal rhythms, and rhetorical textures.

Philadelphia first assumes novelistic specificity—streets are traversed in detail, buildings are invested with character, neighborhoods are defined by their breach, the city is plotted in relation to the unruly districts that lie outside its authority—in novels of riot and corruption such as George Lippard's *The Quaker City* (1845), *The Nazarene* (1846), and *The Killers* (1850) and John Beauchamp Jones's *The City Merchant* (1851). In such works, and in their nonfictional cognates, such as the Pennsylvania Abolition Society's reports on the "Condition of the Free People of

Color" in 1838 and 1849, which are split by riots, and the *History of Pennsylvania Hall,* which documents the contested history of one building opened and destroyed in May 1838, the city comes to be represented as a distinct location, rather than a generic or merely symbolic space. The racial riots of the 1830s and 1840s became an integral part of the Philadelphia social experiment, as the Cedar neighborhood was celebrated and assaulted. In document and fiction, a social space is analyzed in which the raising of a temperance banner is viewed— and possibly intended, although not necessarily in the same ways for participants and observers—as a sign of revolution.

"Doomed to Destruction": *The History of Pennsylvania Hall*

Although the title *History of Pennsylvania Hall* may seem like an overstatement and two hundred pages unwarranted for a structure that burned three days after its dedication, the compilers of the volume mean to tell a complex narrative about the recent past that they insist has consequence in the present and for the future. The book appeared in late 1838, several months after the riots. It begins with a stock, if powerful irony: the rioters destroyed a building consecrated to free inquiry in William Penn's city of toleration. By the last pages, this irony has been turned into a literary and political critique of official stories and narrative bias. *History of Pennsylvania Hall, Which Was Destroyed By a Mob, on the 17th of May, 1838* was published without an author on the title page but has been attributed to Samuel Webb, a Quaker who served as the treasurer of the Pennsylvania Hall Association. (An opening notice "To the Public," followed by Webb's name, explains that the "Managers of the Pennsylvania Hall Association" compiled the volume.) The book begins with a visual image of the hall, then a verbal portrait and a defense of its reputation, followed by a documentary chronology of its opening days, a narrative of its demise, and finally a long appendix reprinting contradictory views of the events. Containing lithograph, mezzotint, wood engraving, ekphrasis, letters, speeches, poetry, narrative, a police committee report, and a textual appraisal of that report, the book mixes genres to transmit its unorthodox history. Gift book, epitaph, and indictment, the *History of Pennsylvania Hall* suggests that the fate of this building reveals the temper of the city.[9]

Like the conspicuous architecture in the gothic fiction of Horace Walpole, Ann Radcliffe, Matthew Lewis, and Charles Brockden Brown, Pennsylvania Hall is invested with psychological and political significance. (During his Philadelphia sojourn from 1838 to 1844, Poe would emphatically draw out the analogy between structure and psyche in the "Haunted Palace," a poem embedded in his story "The Fall of the House of Usher," first published in *Burton's Gentleman's Magazine* in the year following the destruction of Pennsylvania Hall.)[10] The building at the center of *History of Pennsylvania Hall* reveals the mind of its owners and its assailants and also, with an explicitness uncommon to gothic stories, the content of debates about slavery, abolition, and freedom in the 1830s.

The events in May 1838 seemed historic not only to the managers of Pennsylvania Hall but also to many observers. The *History* sold in both paper and cloth editions. The assault on the hall was covered extensively by the abolitionist and the proslavery press. It was invoked by George Lippard in his novel *The Quaker City* (1845) and his unfinished "Eleanor; or, Slave-Catching in the Quaker City" (1854) and by J. B. Jones in his novel *The City Merchant* (1851). Ellis Paxson Oberholtzer spotlights the events of 1838 in the chapter titled "'Black Letters'" in his *Literary History of Philadelphia* (1906).[11]

The *History of Pennsylvania Hall* opens with a frontispiece image of the new building, dominating the intersection of Sixth and Haines streets (figure 3.2). The design for the print has been attributed to the Swiss artist J. C. Wild, who, during a brief stay in Philadelphia in 1837–38, created with J. B. Chevalier a series of lithographs featuring the city's prominent buildings, especially those erected during the boom of the 1830s. A historian of lithography in Philadelphia has suggested that the frontispiece may have been copied

FIGURE 3.2 Frontispiece image of Pennsylvania Hall, attributed to J. C. Wild, from *The History of Pennsylvania Hall* (1838).

from a drawing of Pennsylvania Hall made by the architect Thomas S. Stewart. Reproducing an existing likeness would have been necessary if the frontispiece image had been produced after the destruction of the building. The view from the corner in the opening lithograph emphasizes the expanse and symmetry of the hall, "about sixty-two feet front, by one hundred feet deep; and forty-two feet from the ground to the eaves," as the eulogy to "this beautiful building," following the title page, informs the reader (3).[12]

While the prose introduction to Pennsylvania Hall details its elaborate interior and costly furnishings, the frontispiece view, and the two subsequent images, concentrate on its surfaces. Opposite the title page with the building's undoing— "DESTROYED BY A MOB"—proclaimed in capital letters stands Pennsylvania Hall at daytime, across an expanse of street, in all its neoclassical splendor. A fanlight is set in its pediment. Its name has been carved on the architrave. Pilasters and windows extend on either side of the edge presented to the viewer. Its entrance is flanked by two sets of latticed bow windows. The hall is presented in immaculate contrast to the smaller, shaded buildings on either side. This is "Virtue's shrine" and "Liberty's abode," "Sacred to Freedom," in the words of John Greenleaf Whittier's poetical "Address" read on the second day and printed in the *History* (59), as well as separately.[13] In the foreground of the lithograph, groups of small human figures, often paired and always well dressed, echo the building's regularity. A man walks with two women on either side of him, who sport the same outfit; one carriage proceeds to the right and another to the left; two apparently identical women stand on either side of a lamppost; two similarly attired gentlemen stroll alongside the left flank of the building; a pair of figures walks toward them from the end of the same block; a man and a woman gaze at the hall.

With its choreographed streets and symmetrical architecture, the frontispiece offers an especially tidy, insulated version of Philadelphian uniformity. From this perspective, Pennsylvania Hall is constituted by grids. The sides of the building are divided into rhythms of columns and windows. Each window itself is an epitome of the grid, its frame and lattice contriving in miniature Penn and Holme's famous plan of the city. The design is repeated across the façade and left side of the building. If the artist and lithographer created the print after the destruction of the hall, they, and the compilers of the *History*, seem to have aimed for strategic overstatement. Through its juxtaposition with the title page and its hypersymmetry, this first image not only prepares readers for the violation of order but also suggests its artificiality.

That violation is depicted in the other two prints on view in the book, separated from each other by only a few pages in the later section titled "Destruction of the Hall." The first, an exquisite mezzotint and engraving by John Sartain, shows the burning of the edifice. The second, a wood engraving by J. A. Woodside Jr. and R. S. Gilbert, displays its charred shell. Arriving in Philadelphia from England in 1830, Sartain popularized mezzotints in the United States and presided over a family of engravers and artists. He had joined the Philadelphia Anti-Slavery Society in 1835 and may have been among the onlookers who saw the hall burn on the night of May 17, 1838. The caption to his print in the *History* notes that the scene was "Drawn from the spot & Engraved by J. Sartain." Sartain views the building from the opposite perspective of the frontispiece lithograph. He represents the hall from the left, at night and in flames (figure 3.3). The symmetry of its construction and its spatial prominence are occluded by the intervening buildings. A fireman directs a thin white stream onto the roof of the adjacent building, above the center of the image, and wisps of water slide down and over the eaves. Sartain's portrayal reinforces contemporary accounts, which described the limited efforts of the firemen and their aim of preserving the surrounding buildings while letting Pennsylvania Hall burn.[14]

In Sartain's image, the crowd occupies the foreground and is depicted as though it were a theatrical audience. At the left, men (this audience seems to be exclusively male) sit or climb on a structure to get a better view, as an inebriated figure leans back against the post. In the center, several men gather around and on

FIGURE 3.3 John Sartain, image of Pennsylvania Hall in flames, from *The History of Pennsylvania Hall* (1838).

a fire engine. At the lower right of this pyramid of figures, two men exchange words or glances, one of them with his leg raised as though dancing a jig. Their tiny illuminated faces become visible as masks or skulls. At the right of the image, rows of top-hatted men gaze at the burning façade of the hall, possibly the "gentlemen of property and standing" who often formed part of the antiabolition mobs during the violence of the 1830s, as Leonard L. Richards has shown.[15] In this dark, crowded mezzotint, it is hard to distinguish among rioters, gentlemen, firemen, and spectators. This obscurity appears to be strategic: a prospect that implicates all the figures. The rising and falling rhythms of the crowd serve as a counterpoint to the escalating roofs of the buildings, which reach an apex in the upper story and pediment of Pennsylvania Hall, with flames emerging from the fanlight and from the spaces where the windows and their lattices used to be. Fire and smoke obscure the name of the building. The shadows of the night, rendered in subtle gradations by the mezzotint rocker, are interrupted by the blaze from the windows and the glow ascending from the roof. The shadows are accented by patches of subdued light, which correspond to the rhythms of the crowd and suggest a vulnerable, tentative contrast: the luster of gas lamp at the left, the illuminated stream of water from the hose at the upper center, and the glowing side of the building at the right.

Sartain's mezzotint portrays violence as theater, staged at a distance, but the power of the image lies in its instability. From the empty windows of Pennsylvania Hall, there emerges an incandescent energy, whose combustible force—glimpsed at the front, rear, and top of the building—might engulf the scene. The dark structures in the left half of the image block the view. Such cushioning augments the intensity of the blaze, imparting a depth and pressure to the surface of the print. In moving from the frontispiece lithograph commemorating Philadelphia's radiant temple of freedom to Sartain's night piece thronged with shadowy hordes and defined by the luminosity of flames, the compilers of the *History of Pennsylvania Hall* turn Sixth and Haines streets into an intersection in hell. And Sartain's image may owe some of its power to its visual invocations of hell in the famous mezzotints by the British artist John Martin for Milton's *Paradise Lost*, first produced in the 1820s and reprinted in the 1830s.

The third and final print in the *History*, Woodside and Gilbert's wood engraving, returns viewers to the perspective of the frontispiece, depicting the hall from the right, across the open street, centering on the angle formed by the front and side of the building (figure 3.4). Given the correspondences between the first and third prints, it seems likely that Woodside and Gilbert had the frontispiece image in mind. Although the composition is similar, the details mark a vivid contrast. Woodside and Gilbert emphasize the hollow shell that the building has become.

FIGURE 3.4 John A. Woodside Jr. and Reuben S. Gilbert, image of Pennsylvania Hall after the riot, from *The History of Pennsylvania Hall* (1838).

Through the vacant frames, they present the white sky in the central windows of the upper story and the scorched interior. The classical lines have been broken by the open asymmetry of the windows and the torn facing, stained by fire. The surface of the building, now damaged, takes up even more of the image than in the frontispiece. The engraving tool has been used to score and gouge the exterior and interior walls. The frontispiece represented, in modulated tones, an immaculate temple whose sanctum remained hidden, but Woodside and Gilbert expose a ruin whose disfigured emptiness is its revelation. This disclosure escapes those represented in the image: only a few passersby are shown on the street, and none of them looks at the building.[16]

This final stark engraving seems to fulfill, in the present and with unexpected consequences, Whittier's predictions about the hall in his "Address," printed eighty pages earlier in the *History.* Whittier had imagined a jubilee time when no one in the United States would be in bondage, the trumpet of heaven would sound, and the vestiges of the building would become a site of pilgrimage for the descendants of those who had fought against slavery: "The pencil's art shall sketch the ruined Hall,/The Muses' garland crown its aged wall,/And History's pen for after times record/Its consecration unto FREEDOM'S GOD!" (62). Yet as represented in the *History,* Pennsylvania Hall is "crumbling in decay" not in the distant future but three days after its opening. The "pencil's art," in the form of the wood graver, already has pictured the ruins, and "History's pen," wielded by the managers of Pennsylvania Hall, has preserved not "consecration" but dese-cration. In the pages of the *History,* Whittier's future has been retracted into a present whose only clear signs are violence and wreckage. The book is filled with such rearticulations, juxtaposing the events, documents, and images of Pennsyl-vania Hall.

With its sequence of images depicting how the temple of freedom swiftly became a ruin, the *History* offers an accelerated version of the allegorical canvases popular in the United States in the 1830s, most prominent among them Thomas Cole's *The Course of Empire,* five large oil paintings done between 1834 and 1836 and first displayed in New York in the autumn of 1836. Cole's images share land-scape features—a harbor surrounded by hills and a boulder atop a mountain—used as focal points to tell a story of nature's triumph over wealth, corruption, and despotism (with at least a nod to the Jacksonian years). As time passes from spring sunrise to autumn noon to winter sunset, viewers are presented with the disinte-grating cycle of history. Although the compilers of *The History of Pennsylvania Hall* left no record of their intentions, they seem to have arranged a visual sequence that draws part of its intensity from Cole's recent achievement but also reorients his figures. Whereas Cole portrays a generic European history, employing details from archaic periods and classical Greece and Rome, the compilers focus on one street corner in Philadelphia in the year 1838. They diminish Cole's centuries into the passage from a Thursday to a Friday. Such limits may seem provincial, but the compilers mean their details to suggest a larger scale and a wider story.

Rather than a *Course of Empire,* they exhibit a *Course of Riot.* The devastation of the hall is not the inevitable unfolding of a natural cycle, but the result of coor-dinated violence and official negligence. In terms of print technology, the sequence progresses backward from the most recent to the earliest, from litho-graph to mezzotint to wood engraving, from stately lines on stone to scraped and burnished metal to stark cuts in wood. Technique amplifies the narrative of vio-lent reversion. The images in the *History* infuse the *vanitas* theme, what Cole calls "the mutation of earthly things," with political content. The mob replaces nature as the agent of destructive change, and the images suggest what the words in the text will make explicit: that the building was not, in the words of the police report, "doomed to destruction," but willed to it. Whereas Cole elevates his *Course of Empire* to the level of allegory, the compilers fasten their critique of democracy to a single building. In ruins, this structure gathers significance, becoming a dialectical counterpart to the nearby steeple of the venerated State House, locus for the Declaration of Independence and the Constitution.[17]

Outside the pages of the *History,* there is a fourth image in the "Course of Riot." A few days after the violence, the firm of Philadelphia lithographer J. T. Bowen printed and colored the broadside "Destruction by Fire of Pennsylvania Hall, on the night of the 17th of May." Recently arrived from New York, Bowen rushed the print to market. J. C. Wild may have drawn the picture that was transferred to stone, although the hall is represented as lower and more horizontal than in the frontispiece to the *History*, which also has been attributed to Wild. Whoever drew "Destruction by Fire" offered a sensational rejoinder to the lithographed declarations of Philadelphia civic achievement in the 1830s (many of them drawn by Wild himself and reissued by Bowen in 1838).[18]

In this large print, nine and one half by fourteen inches, the hall has exploded into flames (figure 3.5). Night turns into day. The corner view presents the flames swirling out of the windows on the façade and right side in volatile symmetry, an infernal version of the famous Philadelphia grid. The yellow and orange are contrasted with the billowing smoke and the darkened surface of the building. The

Destruction by Fire of Pennsylvania Hall,

On the night of the 17th May.

Published by J. T. Bowen, 94 Walnut Street.

Entered, according to the Act of Congress, in the year 1838, by J. T. Bowen, in the Clerk's Office of the District Court of the Eastern District of Pennsylvania.

FIGURE 3.5 "Destruction by Fire of Pennsylvania Hall, on the night of the 17th May," published by J. T. Bowen (1838).

artist has not represented the architrave and pilasters, as though the riot has stripped Pennsylvania Hall and Philadelphia of their classical pretensions. Through the fanlight and from the roof, the flames curve and twist and spark, illuminating the darkness like fireworks. (A reporter for the *Philadelphia Inquirer* had written on May 18: "Every window vomited forth its volume [of flame], and the roof cracked, smoked and blazed before the progress of the devouring element.")[19] In the left foreground, a fireman atop an engine directs his hose on adjoining roofs. In the right foreground, a mob of top hats watches the blaze. Several well-dressed male figures raise their hats in salute. As in Sartain's mezzotint, this crowd is exclusively male. In the front, right of center, a gentleman walks and looks to the left, possibly at the fire engine. Another gentleman walks to the right but turns his head outward and to the left, away from the spectacle, jaded or oblivious.

The ignited building dominates the center, but the violence is portrayed as oddly contained, evoking the orderly destruction reported in some of the newspaper accounts. The flames proceed vertically up the sides and from the roof into the sky, leaving unscathed the structures on either side and producing no agitated movement among the firemen or alarm in the mob. The central foreground is mostly empty, except for a dog walking to the left and the strolling gentleman. The human figures to the right and the left form diagonals that complement the receding diagonals of the building's sides, thus directing attention to the intersecting lines at the front corner of the building in the lower center of the image. Yet the effect is also to open up a distance between viewer and spectacle, with that empty space as a forestage. This potent mixture of destruction and beauty, havoc and quarantine, may help to explain the market for images of the 1838 riot.

Although other images of Philadelphia riot were produced, such as the lithograph tableau sanctifying the death of the young Protestant George Shiffler during the anti-Catholic violence of 1844, several images of Pennsylvania Hall were offered to the public: not only Bowen's "Destruction" but also the three prints included in the *History of Pennsylvania Hall.*[20] On the bottom of the last page of the *History*, there is an advertisement: "A few Plates, similar to those contained in this book, have been printed on larger paper, suitable for framing. They may be had at the Anti-Slavery Office, No. 29 N. Ninth street" (200). The notice indicates some of the reasons that customers might have been moved to purchase images of the hall—to support the abolitionist cause, to commemorate the loss—and we might speculate on other reasons that the events of May 17, 1838, lent themselves to domestic exhibit. The target was a symbolic building, and the violence on that night was restricted to one edifice, a concentrated assault.

Yet the phrase "suitable for framing" is curious. When is it appropriate to frame images of riot? How is violence properly cropped? Who would buy such pictures, and where in the home would they hang? The appeal of the 1838 images may have to do with architectural symbol, political impulse, visual spectacle, and the iconography of loss, but their suitability also may have to do with how the events were presented. Missing from these pictures, and from most of the pages of the *History of Pennsylvania Hall*, are the African American residents of the city whose access to the building and appearance outside it enraged the crowds. In the prints, and especially in Bowen's vivid "Destruction," the riot of 1838 is framed as a conflict among white men about abolition, and the violence, while intense, is confined to a single street corner. Such visual economy is both potent and partial. The riots of 1838 and 1844 generated images, but very few illustrations exist of the riots of 1842 or 1849, which were directed at Philadelphia's African Americans.[21]

The owners of the printing firms may not have seen these events as suitable for framing because of the carnage or the extent of the damage or the African American topic, assuming that there would not be a market for such images among their customers. In African American parlors, at least as represented in Philadelphia novels, prints did hang on the walls, but these are portraits rather than scenes of riot (and, as we shall see, whose portrait hangs where becomes a literary motif). No African American represents the devastating riots until the novelist Frank J. Webb. In his 1857 *The Garies and Their Friends*, the focus of the next chapter, Webb offers a composite picture, taking details from 1834, 1842, and 1849. There seems to have been an asymmetry of regard for violence in Philadelphia. In his meticulous novel, which reflects on decades of the city's history, Webb expresses a different awareness of political and geographical salience. There is no Pennsylvania Hall and, for that matter, no Independence Hall.

After the frontispiece lithograph and a verbal defense of Pennsylvania Hall, the compilers of the *History* include a section titled "Opening of the Hall," in which they reprint letters read at the start of the dedication ceremonies from prominent invitees who were unable to attend but offered their qualified support.[22] The *History* contains documents that question the character of the building and challenge the polemic of its managers. In letters from the abolitionists Theodore Dwight Weld and William Jay, approval is tinged by astonishment at the necessity for a public space dedicated to "free discussion" and skepticism that such freedom can be sustained in the political environment of the 1830s. Jay points to the absurdity of cordoning off an area for open debate, especially in the city of William Penn and the Declaration of Independence. Weld meditates on the word "free": "The empty *name* is everywhere,—*free* government, *free* men, *free* speech, *free* people, *free* schools, and *free* churches. Hollow counterfeits all! FREE! It is the climax of irony, and its million echoes are hisses and jeers, even from the earth's ends. FREE! *Blot it out.* Words are the signs of *things.* The substance has gone! Let fools and madmen clutch at shadows. The husk must rustle the more when the kernel and the ear are gone!" (8).

Like Absalom Jones and Richard Allen who in 1794 struggled with a single paragraph on African American conduct written by Mathew Carey during the yellow fever epidemic, and like Robert Purvis who in 1838 castigated the proposed insertion of "white" before "freeman" in the Pennsylvania state constitution of 1838, Weld anchors his political argument in the qualities of words. For Weld, the word "free" epitomizes the formal contradictions in the United States, in which a nominal liberty is proclaimed in the face of chattel slavery and intensifying constraints on speech. Weld denounces the recent unpunished murder of the abolitionist Elijah Lovejoy in Alton, Illinois; the gag rules renewed by the House of Representatives that tabled antislavery petitions; and the maneuvers in the Senate that inhibited debate. He argues that the word "free" has been emptied, incessantly repeated in contexts that violate its meaning. Punning on the term "ear," he uses the metaphor of corn to describe the desiccated incantations of "freedom," when the word has lost its referents and listeners no longer can hear it: "the husk must rustle the more when the kernel and ear are gone." Such formulations cast doubt on the efficacy of his own rhetoric. And the irony in the *History* only begins with Weld's sense of hollowing repetition. Its climax is reserved for the book's intricate appendix.

Jay's astonishment and Weld's skepticism are combined in the next letter, dated January 19, 1838, written by the former President John Quincy Adams, who decorously and firmly refuses to speak at the opening ceremonies that spring. Adams had completed his term in 1829 and then was elected to the House of Representatives, where he acted as a determined opponent of the gag rules. He explains that he will not participate because the "freedom of speech in the city of Penn" is "AN ABSTRACTION" (12). As African American leaders in New York had in the 1830s and Frederick Douglass would in the 1840s, Adams criticizes the residents of Pennsylvania and especially Philadelphia for what he sees as their quietism on the topic of slavery. On the national level, he blames Pennsylvanians, through their Democratic congressional delegation, for suppressing debate in Congress. If he traveled to Philadelphia and spoke his "whole mind," Adams explains, he would offend his hosts and his audience. He imagines a series of charges they would direct at him. He is redundant, avowing the "self-evident truths" of the Declaration to those "sick of the sound." He is meddling in the *"peculiar institutions of the South."* He is "a *fanatic,* he is an *incendiary,* he is an *abolitionist!*" His censure will provoke the South to dissolve the Union (11). This escalating hostility, articulated at the start of the *History*, foreshadows and partially explains the outbreak in May. Adams insists that Philadelphia needs a genuine revival from within, rather than an outsider coming to preach about human rights or the pomp and ceremony of a new hall.

The bulk of the volume consists of speeches, remarks, and debate in sequence as they occurred on May 14th, 15th, 16th, and 17th, culminating in the riot. The first oration, which incited sharp responses from other participants, especially William Lloyd Garrison, was delivered by the eminent Philadelphia lawyer David Paul Brown. In his address, which runs thirty-three pages and reportedly took two hours to deliver, Brown is the epitome of moderation, insisting that slavery is an evil but scrupulously avoiding any action to end it. Slaves should be freed, in time. When they are freed, they should not yet be granted civil or political rights. Slavery is evil, but disunion would be a greater evil. The opposing parties should acknowledge that the conflict over slavery is a "fraternal struggle" and soften their animosities (18). Although Brown hesitates at the prospect because he fears that enslaved African Americans are unprepared for freedom ("they might surfeit in the excess of joy"), he advises a strategic call for "immediate emancipation" in order to negotiate an end to slavery: "We will not quarrel as to a month, or a year, or twenty years, if our antagonists will only concur with us, in reducing the liberation of the slaves to an actual certainty" (29). He concludes with a series of gentle imperatives for his audience: "Let us be ever discreet . . . [and not] foment factions . . . let me implore you to persevere in your enterprise, but with all becoming tenderness and sympathy. . . . Virtue, it is true, is always fearless, but always cautious. . . . On the other hand, be not too tame neither" (33–35).

Brown seeks a middle ground. His compromises and contortions seem part of a sincere effort to advance the cause while preserving amity. Temporizing, he responds to the violence of the debate over slavery and to the threats that verbally and soon literally would surround Pennsylvania Hall. (The reader of the *History* comes to understand the turbulent context in which invective is hurled against such restraint.) Garrison asserts that such sincerity risks yielding to the forces it claims to resist and may have more to do with self-concern and intra-group solidarity than with Africans under slavery and social change. In remarks delivered the next day and the day after that, printed in the *History*, Garrison laments the "hateful spirit of caste" that has prevented the managers from inviting "a single colored brother" to their platform (70). He maintains that Pennsylvania Hall needs a "new dedication," purged of the "fatal heresies" of Brown's opening address (71, 118). Brown had "seized the dagger of expediency, and plunged it to her [Liberty's] heart!" (71). With characteristic fervor, Garrison announces that he hates the words "'caution' and 'prudence,' and 'judiciousness.'" Playing the role of the New England outsider that Adams had declined, Garrison echoes his complaints: "there is too much quietude in this city," and Philadelphians need to experience a "moral earthquake" (71–72).

Two decades later, Herman Melville would satirize the type of accommodation Brown represents: the counsel of firmness and discretion, fearlessness and caution, the amorphous hope that the end of slavery will become an "actual certainty" sometime in the future. Melville casts such maneuvering as a confidence trick, a semblance of politics, in his portrait of the Herb Doctor, who advertises his ambivalence: "'If by abolitionist you mean a zealot, I am none; but if you mean a man, who, being a man, feels for all men, slaves included, and by any lawful act, opposed to nobody's interest, and therefore, rousing nobody's enmity, would willingly abolish suffering (supposing it, in its degree, to exist) from among mankind, irrespective of color, then am I what you say.'"[23]

While Brown equivocates on abolition, he is unyielding in his criticism of the efforts underway to alter the Pennsylvania state constitution and disfranchise African American men. Four months earlier, the state convention had voted to insert the word "white" in the 1790 constitution. Brown rejects the change, describing it as "a sacrifice to the prejudices and clamors of the South" (27). Arguing for the moral equality of whites and blacks, he tells an anecdote about a legal case in which he had been involved and, in doing so, provides a sequel to an earlier story, one of the many histories within the *History*.

Brown explains to his audience that almost twenty years ago he had been asked to defend a man accused of being an "alleged slave" (28). During a private conference with the accused, he was stunned when the man told him that his name was "Peter Mathias"—the same name as the man who had been executed thirty years ago, along with John Joyce, for the murder of Sarah Cross. Given the publicity of the case, Brown assumes that the middle-aged members of his audience, like himself, will recognize at once the name "Peter Mathias." (Now forty-eight, Brown would have been thirteen years old when the trial took place in 1808.) We remember Peter Matthias as the tenacious presence in Richard Allen's pamphlets, the "Confession of John Joyce" and "Confession of Peter Matthias," discussed in chapter 1. He was the criminal who refused to confess, the figure who would not fulfill the dictates of the genre. Brown recalls that Matthias "was supposed to have been coerced into the crime" of murder (28), although, as we have seen, Allen suggested that John Joyce had himself been coerced into implicating Matthias.

Brown is taken aback by the reappearance of the executed Peter Matthias. He explains to his audience (with, one assumes, some dramatic license and a possible reference to one of the plot twists in Robert Montgomery Bird's recently published *Sheppard Lee*) that the figure before him seemed to verify rumors that Matthias had been rejuvenated by a galvanic experiment shortly after his death. "Peter Mathias" unravels the mystery for Brown by explaining that his name actually is John Johnson. He had been imprisoned (for assault and battery) at the same time as Matthias thirty years ago. On the morning of Matthias's hanging, the condemned man had given his legal papers to Johnson, who was still enslaved, with the following advice: "'John, you are a slave, I am free; here are my freedom papers; I am going where I shall not want them—they may be of use to you, take them, change your name to Peter Mathias, and if your master ever should claim you, show these papers, and they will protect you.'" Brown uses the story to reinforce the horrors of slavery, and he adduces Matthias's gesture as an example of heroic generosity. But he also reports that, as "an honorable advocate," he "could not take advantage of such an artifice" and (in a development worthy of Mark Twain's courtroom in *Pudd'nhead Wilson*) that he was compelled to expose Johnson's decades-long impersonation of a free man and return him to slavery (28).

Brown's telling of Johnson's story in his dedicatory address at Pennsylvania Hall is replete with Philadelphia ironies. On the verge of being executed for a crime he insisted he did not commit, the "free" Peter Matthias had transferred his name and legal identity to an enslaved man. Dead for many years, Matthias has lived on. After three decades, Brown reveals an alternative set of dying words—not the stock, if poignant, acceptance of fate recorded by Allen in his "Confession," but the achievement of a persistence beyond the gallows. If the story is accurate, the name and documents did protect Johnson for three decades, but then they betrayed him when he confided his imposture to a lawyer who remembered the 1808 events and attached his name to that of a notorious transgressor. Discoursing on racial equality and freedom, Brown tells an anecdote in which law and morality require him to deliver to slavery a man who had lived "free" for decades, without acknowledging contradiction. The chiasmus of freedom and slavery to which Frederick Douglass would give enduring rhetorical form in an apostrophe to the readers of his 1845 *Narrative of the Life* ("You have seen how a man was made a slave; you shall see how a slave was made a man"), here, in this anecdote, has its terms crossed. "'John, you are a slave, I am free,'" Matthias purportedly tells Johnson, and then bestows a tenuous deliverance upon him, which over time becomes the fulcrum for Johnson's subjugation and Matthias's return.

As the trajectory of debate in the *History* moves from Brown's address to lectures on temperance, Whittier's paean to the hall, speeches on emancipation and Indian rights, Garrison's call for moral upheaval, arguments in favor of colonization, invective against the gag rules, and defenses of abolition, the exchange of views in the hall is punctuated by mounting violence. Stones are thrown against and through the windows on the second and third days of the meetings. Garrison's remarks on the third day are frequently interrupted by shouts and hisses from the audience and tumult from men who have broken into the lobby. In the climactic oration of the volume, delivered by Angelina Grimké Weld, the acts of the mob rupture her sentences, and the editors signal the rising turmoil in bracketed descriptions within and at the end of paragraphs. Grimké faced hostility on a variety of fronts: as an abolitionist, as a southerner who had betrayed her region's investments, and as a woman speaking in public on controversial matters before a mixed audience. She remarks on her position as an exile from South Carolina, knowing and testifying to the evils of slavery, who has come to Philadelphia only to find indifference. Amid the disorder of the evening, she observes that the "spirit of slavery" knows no boundaries (123). It pervades the North, animates the mob, and distorts the audience that is listening to her. She turns Pennsylvania Hall into an architecture both sentimental (revealing the corruptions of the heart) and gothic (vulnerable to both internal division and external threat, haunted by a vicious system). As the crowd expresses its outrage and this House of Usher teeters on the brink, she declares, "There is no such thing as neutral ground" (125).[24]

The editors build toward "The Destruction of the Hall," the final section before the appendix, but understate the event itself. They recount the public agitation, deflecting responsibility from the city's residents with hints about the leading roles played by "strangers from the South" (137). They blame Mayor Swift and the sheriff for not properly responding to entreaties from the managers. They accuse Swift of implicitly encouraging the actions of the mob by demanding that the events on the evening of May 17 be canceled, requesting the keys, and leaving the triumphant crowd gathered around the building. The burning of the hall is described in a single sentence: "This [the attack] was done by forcing open the doors, and carrying papers and window-blinds upon the speaker's platform, where they set fire to them, and turning the gas pipes towards the flames thus increased their activity, and in a few hours the building was consumed" (140). Sartain's mezzotint and Gilbert and Woodside's wood engraving are left to convey the damage. For the editors, the noteworthy history of the hall lies not in the fiery spectacle—which J. T. Bowen would feature in color—but in its aftermath.

The last fifty-five pages of *The History of Pennsylvania Hall*, a quarter of the book, are taken up by an appendix in which the editors arrange documents with a variety of perspectives on the riot. On these pages, any effort to insulate

Philadelphians from responsibility for the violence comes undone. Extracts from newspapers in New Orleans, Augusta (Georgia), and St. Louis, in which correspondents savor the wreckage, are followed by two abolitionist poems, "The Tocsin," by the Boston antislavery poet and Unitarian pastor John Pierpont, and "The Pennsylvania Hall," which had been published anonymously in the *Pennsylvania Freeman*. The southern accounts highlight the orderliness and integrity of the mob and condemn the specters of racial mixing and social unrest that helped to fuel the riot. The "horrid tragedy of St. Domingo" is evoked (167). In the New Orleans paper, the reporter describes the sounds of that night: the cry of fire, the State House bell pealing in alarm (one of the provocations for Pierpont's "Tocsin"), and the "loud shout of joy" with which the assembled crowd welcomed the flames (168). The Augusta correspondent depicts a sanctified blaze (as will the novelist J. B. Jones in his 1851 historical novel of the Philadelphia riots, *The City Merchant*): "The devouring element assumed an aspect which to me it had never worn before; it seemed to wear, combined with its terrible majesty, *beauty and delight*. To witness those beautiful spires of flame, gave undoubted assurance to the heart of the Southron, that in his brethren of the North *he has friends who appreciate him*, and who will defend him, though absent, at any, and at every hazard" (170).

"Those beautiful spires of flame" are reminiscent of the ambivalence in Bowen's ravishing "Destruction by Fire of Pennsylvania Hall," with its oddly contained and alluring violence. The "spires of flame" evoke the prominent tower of the State House and its Independence Hall, suggesting alignment rather than contrast. For the Augusta reporter, the flames arising from Pennsylvania Hall convey the reassurance that Philadelphians will support the rights of southerners to their "peculiar institution." The flames signal a reciprocity between independence and slavery, or possibly a consummation of the former in the latter.

Such an alarm is sounded at the beginning of Pierpont's caustic "Tocsin":

Wake! children of the *men* who said,
"All are born free"!—Their spirits come
Back to the places where they bled
In Freedom's holy martyrdom,
And find *you* sleeping on their graves,
And hugging there your chains—ye slaves!
(171)

The customary summons to abolitionist readers is followed by an italicized gap between the present-day children ("*you*") and the Fathers of the Revolution ("the *men*"). The declaration of the Fathers ("All are born free") is accented by the poet's (not the fathers') exclamation point and interrupted by the caesura that marks the lapse between then and now and points to the troubled return of the spirits. Not only have the children forsaken the original commitment of the Fathers, but they have become insensible. In the turn at the end of the stanza, the poet conjures the progenitors' sight of the children languishing on their graves, holding tight, for comfort and with tenderness, to the chains that bind them. The addressees of the poem are not only children, but "slaves." "Ay, dream, while Slavery's foot is set/So firmly on your necks," the poet goads in the next stanza, employing the trope of constraint used by contemporary advocates for human rights.[25]

The Pennsylvania Hall remembered in "The Tocsin"—"Go, then, and build yourselves a hall,/To prove ye are not slaves, but men!/Write 'FREEDOM' on its towering wall!/Baptize it in the name of PENN"—is distinguished by the poet's skeptical imperatives and the charge of insufficient labor. Build, write, baptize—all of these enterprises are shown to be flawed (the burden of "prove" remains uncertain), and they end in "a smouldering heap!" (172). The poet as prophet looks forward to the triumph of the slave power and to the iniquity of the North as signs that God will unleash his justice and wrath on the entire country. In Pierpont's jeremiad, the vision of divine requital eclipses the loss of one building in Philadelphia in May 1838 and the delight, lament, and sarcasm gathered in the appendix.

"The Tocsin" reverberates more deeply than the hackneyed images and stock reassurances at the end of "The Pennsylvania Hall," the poem that follows it: "the singing birds," "glad sunshine," "balmy breezes," rejoicing "'franchised slaves," and "blue welkin," all linked by Noah's rainbow, God's "promise-sign" that follows "the raging storm" and "rushing waters" (174). Or maybe not. It is impossible to know what the compilers of the *History* had in mind in joining the two poems. Did they lack taste? Did they, or their readers, find cliché as potent as ingenuity? Did they mean to offer two alternatives without making a choice? Or did they intend to skew that choice? Was their point that their readers could influence the future—judgment or promise—through their own actions? Such is the puzzle and allure of the documentary collage in *The History of Pennsylvania Hall*.

The appendix and the *History* end in the particulars of syntax and diction, reminiscent of the close verbal struggle between Mathew Carey and Absalom Jones and Richard Allen after the 1793 yellow fever epidemic. Reprinting the "Report of the Committee on Police" that had been issued in July 1838, the compilers of the *History* superimpose a critique of its distortions through typography and footnotes. They stress words by placing them in italics and capitals. In notes, identified through a series of asterisks and daggers, notes that sometimes ascend more than halfway from the bottom of the page and compete for space with the text, the editors raise questions and present counterevidence. On the pages of the *History*, the official version of the riot appears under a scrutiny that literally transforms it. The report had vindicated the mayor's conduct and the inability of the police to quell the violence. It blamed the managers of the hall and abolitionist interlopers for offending the public, and it came close to excusing the violence as a justifiable response. The compilers dispute these findings and defend themselves against insinuations that they did not adequately safeguard their property or fully cooperate with the inquiry. They admit a reluctance to participate that stemmed from their belief that the committee had skewed its procedures and reached its judgments in advance, serving as "at once the accused and the accuser, the counsel, the witnesses, the judge, the jury, and the executioner!" (177).

The editors reserve their most emphatic mark—the icon of a pointing hand, known as a printer's fist—for the phrase *"doomed to destruction,"* which appears twice in the report and which they italicize both times (179, 188). After the first instance, they place a dagger guiding the reader to the bottom of the page, where they reproduce the words after the icon, capitalizing "DOOMED." Italics, capital letters, printer's fist—the editors redundantly contend that the destruction of Pennsylvania Hall is not a story of fate or providence, acknowledging the temptation to construe the *History* according to such formulas. As the documents unfold, they tell a story not of destiny but of politics and bias—a struggle whose outcome was far from certain and whose meaning remained contested.

The editors focus on the report's qualified endorsement of the riot and assignment of blame, which are printed shortly after the first avowal that the hall was *"doomed to destruction"*:

> But, however deeply the Committee may deprecate and censure the existence of that feeling [this violent outrage upon private rights and private property]; however impossible it may be for them in any manner to justify or excuse it; they owe it to the cause of truth, to declare that this excitement, (heretofore unparalleled in our city), *was occasioned** by the determination of *the owners* of that building and of their friends, to preserve in openly promulgating and advocating in it *doctrines repulsive to the moral sense*† of a large majority of our community; and to persist in this course against the advice of friends, heedless of the dangers which they were encountering, or *reckless of its consequences to the peace and order of our city.*‡ (180, with italics and footnote marks inserted by the editors of the *History*)

The first note, signaled by the asterisk after *"was occasioned,"* quotes remarks by the editor of the *Pennsylvania Freeman* (John Greenleaf Whittier), who compared the report's blaming the victims of the riot to "the cool audacity of a Catherine Medicis, charging the criminality of the massacre of St. Bartholomew's upon the hunted and outraged Huguenot." Whittier's allusion to historical allegations that Catherine de Médicis had instigated the infamous slaughter in 1572 reinforced the suspicion that authorities may have conspired to promote the May 1838 assault. It is a hyperbolic comparison—the ruin of a building placed alongside the murder of thousands—but the overstatement registers the distress among the supporters of the hall at the inversions of censure and acquittal in the police committee report. In their second note, after *"doctrines repulsive to the moral sense,"* the editors point out that the crowd expressed its "moral" distaste on the night of May 17 through arson. After *"reckless of its consequences to the peace and order of our city,"* the editors deny the charge of irresponsibility and demand that the committee specify the "doctrines" that had threatened Philadelphia. They refuse to accept the proposition that morality can be determined by a referendum of the mob.

The verbal scrutiny becomes even more pointed in the next section of the appendix, where the editors reprint an assessment of the police investigation by an observer of the Philadelphia events, Charles Hammond, in the *Cincinnati Daily Gazette.* Hammond takes apart the same sentences as the editors, highlighting the logic whereby police inertia is excused because of the determination of the rioters, whose actions are in turn justified as an understandable response to abolitionist goading. Hammond suggests a different explanation: "The actors were excited by vulgar brutality, that indulges a rooted malice against the black man's elevation in society:—*the lookers on were chained into inactivity by the avarice of trade.* COTTON AND SUGAR BEREFT THEM OF MORAL SENSE, AND SUBSTITUTED COLD AND HEARTLESS CALCUATIONS OF SOUTHERN MARKETS AND SOUTHERN VISITERS" (198).

Until this point in *The History of Pennsylvania Hall,* the story told has largely been about the conflicts between whites in the North and the South and within Philadelphia about slavery, abolition, and miscegenation. From his perspective as an outsider, Hammond sees a backlash against the progress of some African Americans in the city. For the attackers, Pennsylvania Hall had become a symbol of that advance and of its impact on debate in Philadelphia. Such an analysis would link the 1838 riot with the violence of 1842 and 1849, when African Americans and their property became explicit targets. For the audience that witnessed the burning and supported it through inaction (or applause), the hall represented the specter of interference with commercial interests that bound Philadelphia to the South. Although Hammond separates the two groups into "actors" and "lookers on," the motives he describes—prejudice and avarice, elevated by the police report into a "moral sense"—combine in his materialist account of the "excitement" that fueled the riot (196–97). Hammond adduces the figure of the police, who had mingled in the crowd during the night of conflagration but could not identify any of the perpetrators: "They witnessed the crime—they saw, they mixed with those engaged in its commencement, progress and completion, and they remained in blind ignorance of the criminals!" (199). The *History* culminates with this image of expert witnesses to an illuminated crime who were unwilling or unable to record what they saw.

In the appendix, the editors get between and behind the words in the official report. In doing so, they transform the usual ironies. If the *History of Pennsylvania Hall* begins with the historical irony that a building dedicated to free inquiry has been targeted by a mob in William Penn's city of toleration, then draws narrative power from the tragic irony of a destruction known to all its readers, and veers toward a situational irony in which the compilers occupy a position of superior knowledge, it ends with an appendix that complicates such distances—an irony of verbal texture in which judgment is interlaced with prejudice and the efficacy of insight remains in doubt.

The Portraiture of the City of Philadelphia, and Henry James's *American Scene*

Those who analyze violence in Philadelphia before the Civil War—journalists, travel writers, novelists—often invoke William Penn and Thomas Holme's famous grid plan, the 1683 "Portraiture of the City," and the town's vaunted rectitude to define the gap between ideal and reality (see figure I.I). In the wake of the 1838 riots, a reporter for the *Liberator*, preparing readers for an account of "Tremendous Excitement in Philadelphia! Riot and Arson!" makes the conventional gesture with a disparaging extravagance:

> What sobriety of behaviour, what an air of tranquility, what order and regularity, on the part of its inhabitants! All is square-built, judicious, prudent, complacent, comfortable. The very animals in the streets tread along the pavements deliberately—for even *animal* excitement is deemed pernicious "agitation," though God designs it for good. Those broad, cleanly, far-reaching streets, extending undeviatingly from the Delaware to the Schuylkill,—those stately, beautiful blocks of buildings, with marble door-steps, and marble fronts, and marble porticoes, (peradventure some of their occupants have marble hearts, polished like a mirror, but cold and stone-like,)—those ornamental squares, the joint achievements of Nature and Art, where dead spires of grass are springing into life at the resurrection call of Spring, and

buds and blossoms are covering the nakedness of parental branches with more than filial dutifulness—how all these serve to make Philadelphia the queen of American cities!

Anticipating the gothic exposures of the "city mysteries" written about Philadelphia in the 1840s and 1850s, the reporter for the *Liberator* describes a measured surface that masks a fundamental disarray. The city's prudence will be unveiled as hypocrisy and its judiciousness as complicity. "Animal excitement" will be unleashed. The "queen of American cities," as the reporter dubs her, will be unveiled as "the queen of violence," in the words of the anonymous narrator of *The Mysteries of Philadelphia* (1848). Or as a columnist for the *Liberator* proclaimed after the "Horrible Affair" of August 1842, comparing city with harlot in a stock feature of the urban gothic, "Let her cognomen henceforth be, 'the city of fiendish malignity,' instead of 'the city of brotherly love.'"[26]

Yet the "mysteries" of Philadelphia amplified in fiction, essays, and public reports during the riot years often go beyond such etymological reversal and the platitude about Penn and Holme. Such ironies are too easy, securing distance between interpreters and action and bypassing history. And they misrepresent the actual topography of the city. In contrast to the reticulation imagined in 1683 (which from the start had been altered by the uneven settlement of Philadelphia's residents, with their divergent needs and desires), by the 1840s many of the original lots had been divided into labyrinths of alleys and courts that branched off from secondary pathways. Narrow three-story row houses filled these spaces or backed up against the rear walls of larger buildings facing the street. Edifices that once housed the affluent had been converted into boarding houses and tenements. The city proper was bordered on the north and south by working-class suburbs whose populations had increased at a much faster rate. In these suburbs, the patterns of the city—houses crowded into alleys and courts—were reproduced.[27]

This was the landscape of riot. During the years of economic depression, outside the boundaries of city authority, violence erupted in Kensington to the north, with its Irish immigrant laborers, and in the Cedar neighborhood and Southwark and Moyamensing to the south, with African Americans and Irish, many of them poor, living in close quarters. The simple things to write about Philadelphia were that behind its façades lay a secret world of depravity and that its orderly streets covered a multitude of sins. George Lippard, who became notorious as the popularizer of the sordid "Quaker City," would say these things again and again. But Lippard, as we shall see, also pressed such exposures beyond the clichés he helped to market. Drawing upon Philadelphia's mid-nineteenth-century cityscape and the riots of 1838, 1842, and 1849, he transformed the prominent grid into a surface of vulnerability, a network of trapdoors that served as figures for an urban space—streets but also parlors—riddled with violence.

Dating back to Charles Brocken Brown in *Arthur Mervyn* (1799–1800) and continuing to the present with John Edgar Wideman in *Philadelphia Fire* (1990), novelists of Philadelphia often have construed their fictional city partly in response to the symmetrical commitments of Penn and Holme's imagined grid. Writers have not only charted deviations from the grid (the easier ironies just suggested) but also incorporated the design in their urban anatomies.

One of the most sophisticated riffs on the "Portraiture of the City of Phila-delphia" is offered by Henry James in *The American Scene* (1907), a collection of essays describing his tour of the eastern coast of the United States in 1904–05. James had returned to America after living on the Continent and in England for more than twenty years, announcing in his preface that he viewed the sights with a "freshness of eye, outward and inward" and in "a state of desire." The chapter on Philadelphia appears more than halfway through the book, which is organized in a sequence extending from north to south, New England to Florida. James begins with an extravagant flourish, laying the groundwork for the turns that will follow. Philadelphia "was the American city of the large type, that didn't *bristle* . . . essentially couldn't and wouldn't ever . . . no movement or process could be thought of, in fine, as more foreign to her genius." (The running title James selected for this page in the first English edition, providing an odd, arch slogan for the city, was "The Indisposition to Bristle.") Philadelphia was distinguished by "an admirable comprehensive flatness," "the absence of the note of the per-petual perpendicular," and "the principle of indefinite level extension." It was an inbred city, "not a place but a state of consanguinity . . . a society in which every individual was as many times over cousin, uncle, aunt, niece, and so on through the list, as poor human nature is susceptible of being." Philadelphia "would be, of all goodly villages, the very goodliest, probably, in the world; the very largest, and flattest, and smoothest, the most rounded and complete."[28]

Philadelphia, in James's conceit, is not a porcupine. (The narrator specifies the animal that "bristles" a few sentences later, and the city as porcupine—New York "bristles" in *The American Scene*—is only one in a series of eccentric metaphors carefully developed over the book.) Philadelphia's surfaces are not barbed and do not register fear or irritation. Instead, the city resembles a coin: flat, smooth, rounded, complete. Philadelphia resembles a coin because of its mercantile his-tory but also because of the investments of its citizens in placid exteriors and in maintaining a social homogeneity that permits an insular exchange. Such invest-ments have produced, according to James's narrator, a surface consistency. And a narrowness. As he remarks, with a dig at the founder: "To walk her streets is to note with all promptness that William Penn *must* have laid them out—no one else could possibly have done it so ill" (585). James's observer explains that he came to savor the streets of Philadelphia "just in proportion as they conformed, in detail, to the early pattern—the figure, for each house, of the red-faced old gentleman whose thick eyebrows and moustaches have turned to white; and I found myself detesting them in any instance of a new front or a new fashion" (585). The orderly streets and Georgian brick façades of the old town cultivate particular kinds of regard in James's narrator, especially a longing for repetition associated with the familiar and the superannuated.

The grid not only constricts but also attenuates: "From the moment it [the "narrowness"] was in any way corrected the special charm broke—the charm, a rare civic possession, as of some immense old ruled and neatly-inked chart, not less carefully than benightedly flattened out, stretching its tough parchment under the very feet of all comings and goings" (585). James's narrator invokes Penn and Holme's design and possibly Benjamin Franklin's table of virtues. (Later in the chapter, he describes Franklin's image as imprinted on the city, with Joseph Siffred Duplessis's famous portrait "working as some sudden glimpse of the fine old incised seal . . . that had originally stamped all over, for identification, the comparatively soft local wax" [597]). The "special charm" and "civic possession" of Philadelphia are compared to chart or map that sustains those who walk upon it. Such pedestrians are aware of the grid beneath their feet and its vulnerability to "correction." As they traverse the streets, such awareness enhances the "charm." The parchment may be "tough," but the narrator's metaphor also suggests a tenuous foundation. As the citizens of Philadelphia walk on this surface and receive its impressions, they in turn press upon it and wear it down. Here James fashions a lucid image of how habit can both deepen response and undermine position. His narrator confirms the allure of "Philadelphia": "This was an image with which, as it furthermore seemed to me, everything else consorted—above all the soothing truth that Philadelphia was, yes, beyond cavil, solely and singly Philadelphian" (585). Giving voice to a distinctive urban provincialism, James's narrator asserts the tautology of proper noun and adjective. Likening the city to yet another grid, he employs modifiers and a concluding alliteration that do not seem entirely benign: "the vast, firm chess-board, the immeasurable spread of little squares, covered *all* over by perfect Philadelphians" (586).

The narrator does offer a cavil or two. Immediately following the sentence about the "singly Philadelphian," he acknowledges that "there was an interference absent, or one that I at least never met" in Philadelphia. He is referring to immigrants from Europe, the "grosser aliens" whose "disconcerting" presence he had described in the earlier New York chapters of *The American Scene* (585). In the

Philadelphia chapter, the narrator suggests that "they may have been gathered, in their hordes, in some vast quarter unknown to me and of which I was to have no glimpse; but what would this have denoted, exactly, but some virtue in the air for reducing their presence, or their effect, to naught?" (586).

A similarly dematerializing "virtue in the air" also seems to have operated on the narrator's view—or lack thereof—of African Americans in Philadelphia. This is a surprising omission, given African American prominence not only in the city and its portrayals but also in W. E. B. DuBois's recent *The Philadelphia Negro: A Social Study* (1899)—and given the fact that James's narrator (somewhat equivocally) praises DuBois and his *The Souls of Black Folk* (1903) toward the end of the section on Charleston. Although DuBois had been born in Massachusetts and held undergraduate and graduate degrees from Harvard (where he studied under Henry James's brother William), the narrator relegates *The Souls of Black Folk* to the status of a rare "'Southern' book of any distinction" (697). He controversially evaluates black service in the Richmond chapter, but does not seem to view African Americans as part of the "American scene" in the North generally or in Philadelphia specifically. In a virtuoso analysis of "thinking" in *The American Scene*, Sharon Cameron argues that "James empties the landscape" and "others are gotten out of the way" so that consciousness can dilate. She rightly insists that James is interested in neither psychological realism nor historical archive, but her formulation overstates the case. It does not account for the distinctive resistances to consciousness in the book (some "landscapes" are less empty, and some "others" do present themselves), the narrator's acknowledging—and not just mobilizing— the limits of his discernment, or the ways in which aesthetic perception is joined with historical insight.[29]

Manipulating his image of Philadelphia as a coin, James revises the spatial dynamics of the grid, showing the constitutive role of violence. Although James has in mind not the riots of the 1830s and 1840s but political corruption in the early twentieth century, his figurative portrait of Philadelphia and his description of manners sharpened by injury resembles the city depicted in Frank J. Webb's mid-nineteenth-century novel, as we shall see in the next chapter. James's narrator explains that a "discordant voice" "superfluously, rather tactlessly, dropped into my ear" details about criminal behavior, which transformed his picture of the city. The "discordant voice" is an aesthetic boon, refining the narrator's consciousness of urban surface.

His surprise seems disingenuous. That Philadelphia offered "one of the most lurid pages in the annals of political corruption" (587) could hardly have come as news to James or to his American readers, given the city's notoriety and the conspicuous pages on the topic written by Lincoln Steffens for *McClure's Magazine* and published in his 1904 collection, *The Shame of the Cities*. "Corrupt and Contented" was Steffens's title for his chapter on Philadelphia, which may have provided James with his key terms. James's narrator inflates the suddenness of his insight—"this presentation, as in a flash, of the other side of the medal"—but such effects serve to underline his studied innocence and the complexity of the figurative space he describes:

> The place, by this revelation, was two distinct things—a Society, from far back, the society I had divined, the most genial and delightful one could think of, and then, parallel to this, and not within it, nor quite altogether above it, but beside it and beneath it, behind it and before it, enclosing it as in a frame of fire in which it still had the secret of keeping cool, a proportionate City, the most incredible that ever was, organized all for plunder and rapine, the gross satisfaction of official appetite, organized for eternal iniquity and impunity. (587)

The "revelation" here is not the usual exposure of depth (upper and lower) or the illumination of darkness (lights and shadows) found in urban sensationalism. Instead, the narrator outlines an elaborate parallel space. Although "distinct," the genial society and the rapacious city exist in intimate proximity—not "within" or "above" but "beside," "beneath," "behind," and "before." Struggling to find the appropriate preposition, the narrator offers a series of linked intensives connoting relations on all sides. These terms constitute a set of defining pressures, not a grid against which characters' actions are plotted or a chart beneath the feet, but a space—we might call it a literary space—in which gesture, word, and tone are understood in relation to the contexts that surround and inform them. Characters discern their positions with various degrees of cognizance and complicity. The "mysteries" of James's city have to do with the effort to interpret the "exchange" between the polite and the corrupt. As his narrator puts it, "the interesting thing to get at, for the student of manners, will ever be just this mystery of the terms of the bargain" (588).

The Philadelphia "bargain" is understood differently by Absalom Jones, Richard Allen, William Whipper, Joseph Willson, and Frank J. Webb. Rather than the willingness of an upper class to tolerate political misconduct in return for economic profit and social detachment, these writers describe the charged relationship between social performance and civic recognition in an explosive setting. Some of these earlier writers do imply an elite capitulation to slaveholding interests, and Lippard explicitly indicts the upper classes. Yet despite the differences in time and circumstance, James and the earlier writers, especially the novelists Lippard and Webb, share an appreciation of "Philadelphia" as the place where the relationships between manners and violence are flaunted. James invokes the metaphor of a "slumbering volcano" that had circulated in the mid-nineteenth century to describe the precariousness of a society erected on the foundations of human slavery (the invocation may be deliberate or the metaphor may come with its own history):

> And if it be asked, I may add, whether, in this case of social Philadelphia, the genius for life, and what I have called that gallantry of it above all, wouldn't have been better shown by a scorn of *any* compromise to which the nefarious City could invite it, I can only reply that, as a lover, always of romantic phenomena, and an inveterate seeker for them, I should have been deprived, by the action of that particular virtue, of the thrilled sense of a society dancing, all consciously, on the thin crust of a volcano. It is the thinness of the crust that makes, in such examples, the wild fantasy, the gay bravery, of the dance—just as I admit that a preliminary, an original extinction of the volcano would have illustrated another kind of virtue. (588–89)

The narrator here, as in the portrayal of the genial society and the iniquitous city, ratchets up the melodrama, but his interest lies not in cosmic evil or in pyrotechnics, but in the "dance," the specifics of maneuver. His hyperbole conveys the social intensities, the pressures of context on performance.[30] "Philadelphia" describes the vivid space of compromise and insecurity, distinguished by its frangibility and by the complicated agency ("all consciously" but also "wild fantasy") of its actors. The narrator explains that the knowledge of political corruption, instead of disconcerting him, "added the last touch of colour to my framed and suspended picture" (587).

If James's narrator can be accused of aestheticism (and stressing his manipulations and satisfactions, he seems to *want* to be accused), it is a peculiar aestheticism not divorced from history but steeped in it. The narrator values the circumstances that produce extremity. He is willing, almost eager in his overstatement, to accept a venality that will heighten his awareness of the perilous dance. Whipper and Webb never gauge slavery in comparable ways. To make the comparison is to feel the differences between the positions and interests of James in the early twentieth century and of Whipper and Webb in the mid-nineteenth. And yet . . . the literary appetites of James's narrator in *The American Scene* and Webb's narrator in *The Garies and Their Friends* are not all that dissimilar. Both narrators seize on opportunities to frame, suspend, and evaluate conduct in a Philadelphia where corruption and violence are "beside, beneath, behind, and before" action, and both tell their stories with an irony whose extravagance seems part of the system they analyze. Both narrators are connoisseurs of apprehension, weighing gesture and tone on the thin crust of the volcano. James's narrator associates the city with a subdued and insistent memento mori that we also will find in the works of Lippard and Webb: "I could note that nowhere so much as in Philadelphia was any carking care, in the social mind, any uncomfortable consciousness, as of a skeleton at the banquet of life, so gracefully veiled" (588). Writers often represent knowledge in Philadelphia as omnipresent and obscured.

The coin of Philadelphia, according to James's narrator, appears smooth and complete viewed from only one angle, the perpendicular. To appreciate its value—or, we might say, to read it properly—the observer must turn it over and over again and regard it obliquely and in motion and relation. Such a movement from surface to surface reworks ideas about "flatness" and "extension" with which the narrator began. The "flatness" of Philadelphia is neither uniform nor featureless nor calm. Nor does it cover secret depths. The genial society is not the veneer beneath which lies the corrupt city. Instead, the parallel surfaces of the city contain its depths, a set of relations between historical circumstances and human action manifested in social—and for James and Webb, literary—texture.

When the narrator, at the end of the chapter, describes the "Pennsylvania Penitentiary," the massive prison whose "cellular system" of solitary confinement, initiated by the Quakers, had been praised by Tocqueville in the 1830s and condemned by Dickens in the 1840s, as the only "excrescence on this large smooth surface," the image seems redundant and belated, since he already has figured an urban pattern in which structures emerge and recede. The narrator himself theatrically repeats such a gesture when he defends his "imagination" against a "swarm" of "suggestions" that the prison raises about Philadelphia's "cynicisms and impunities." He attempts to soothe the potential rupture by comparing penitentiary to country club ("a sunny Club at a languid hour"), but his terms don't quite cohere: "The only thing was that, under this analogy, one found one's self speculating much on the implied requisites for membership" (600–1). At the end of the chapter, the gothic penitentiary (James's narrator stresses "its ancient grimness, its grey towers and defensive moats," "drawbridge," and "portcullis") seems less an excrescence on the smooth surface of the city and more a figure stamped on its coin, an element in a pattern of obverse and reverse in which the gothic and the domestic, the violent and the mannered, the archaic and the modern, correspond in their contradictions.[31]

In *The American Scene*, James's eccentric narrator does not provide anything that resembles a conventional history or traveler's account of Philadelphia. Not only is William Penn disparaged but the revolutionary founders are sidelined. Admiring the wainscoted chambers of the old State House, the narrator imagines that architecture gave rise to independence: "One fancies, under the high spring of the ceiling and before the great embrasured window-sashes of the principal room, some clever man of the period, after a long look round, taking the hint. '*What* an admirable place for a Declaration of something!'" (594). Benjamin Franklin's "aged, crumpled, canny face" (but not his biography or writings or politics or inventions or civic activism) hovers over the city (597). Immigrants from Europe are out of sight, and African Americans seem to be out of mind. Instead of chronology, archive, or travelogue, James offers an aesthetics of place. Elsewhere in the book, in a passage from one of the New York chapters that is echoed in the Philadelphia chapter, his narrator reflects on the amalgam of event and imagination that gives form to history: "I draw courage from the remembrance that history is never, in any rich sense, the immediate crudity of what 'happens,' but the much finer complexity of what we read into it and think of in connection with it" (506; also see 593).

"What 'happens'" is not explicitly represented in *The American Scene*, but it also is not absent. James works into his figures an involved urban space—surfaces that are "beside, beneath, behind, and before"—whose strenuous dances, volatile intimacies, and exquisite innocence he links to twentieth-century political corruption. Few writers can match James's devotion to the "mysteries of his own sensibility" (593), and other writers on Philadelphia work out different ratios between "what 'happens'" and "what we read into it," but the dialectic of city and sensibility, rearticulation of the grid, and intricate historicism mark a range of writings about the city.

The Mysteries of the City: George Lippard, Edgar Allan Poe

Philadelphia was the setting, even the obsession, for the first and most popular of the American "city mystery" novels, George Lippard's scandalous *The Quaker City; or, the Monks of Monk Hall: A Romance of Philadelphia Life, Mystery, and Crime*, published in serial installments in 1844 and 1845 and as a book in 1845. The "mystery" and the "crime" in Lippard's Philadelphia fictions—*The Quaker City* and its unfinished sequel *The Nazarene* (1846), and also *The Killers* (1850) and "Eleanor; or, Slave Catching in the Quaker City" (1854)—often include antagonism and conspiracy that Lippard portrays as leading to the riots of the 1830s and 1840s.

Lippard spent most of his relatively short life in Philadelphia. (He died at age thirty-one of tuberculosis.) Abandoning legal studies, he pursued a career as a writer, first as a news, police, and courtroom reporter on the *Spirit of the Times* and then as a writer and editor for the weekly *Citizen Soldier*, supplying political columns, literary criticism, and satire. Between 1844 and 1854, he published a series of novels and dozens of stories, essays, and lectures. Lippard's novels fall into two broad categories: idealized legends of the American Revolution and graphic mysteries of the mid-nineteenth-century city, especially Philadelphia and New York. (Philadelphia is the template for Lippard's urban portrayals.) Across his career, the two kinds of stories are linked, as he narrates how the democratic potential of 1776 was violated in the elite urban corruptions of the 1840s and 1850s. In his last years, Lippard focused on developing the Brotherhood of the Union, a labor organization he founded in 1849. His sensational tales of depravity and violence brought Philadelphia into fiction. Lippard publicized its architecture, neighborhoods, boundaries, social conflicts, and riots. As the writer of one of Lippard's obituaries wrote in 1854, in a notice appended to a chapter of his serialized story "Eleanor": "his struggles in boyhood, and until his death, have been identified with our city."[32]

Lippard saw himself as the heir to a Philadelphia gothic tradition and the American interpreter of the newly popular genre of the European city mystery. He inscribed the second edition of *The Quaker City* "to the Memory of Charles Brockden Brown." In the late eighteenth century, Brown had imbued the landscapes of rural Pennsylvania (*Edgar Huntly*), the suburbs of Philadelphia (*Wieland*), and the city itself (*Arthur Mervyn*) with turbulent history and aberrant psychology. In 1848, Lippard wrote an impassioned tribute to Brown, in which he identified with the earlier writer's difficulties in sustaining an audience for his art. On the back wrappers of *The Quaker City*'s original parts, Lippard associated (and distanced) his story from its European counterpart: "Commenced long before 'Mysteries of Paris' appeared, the Romance, in some respects, bears the same relation to Philadelphia that the 'Mysteries' do to Paris." Although Lippard's "Monk Hall," the headquarters of Philadelphia's debauched elite, owes a debt to such novels as Matthew Lewis's *The Monk* (1796), it is Eugène Sue's *Les Mystères de Paris*, a bestseller on both sides of the Atlantic, that served as his main literary incitement. Locating gothic excess in the modern city, Sue offered a potent mixture of sexual titillation, aristocratic perversity, class struggle, histrionic violence, and appeals for social reform, which Lippard sought to translate from Paris to Philadelphia. (G. W. M. Reynolds's *Mysteries of London*, issued in weekly numbers from 1844 until 1856, achieved phenomenal success as well.) The blend of sensation and reproval in these inexpensive city mysteries had wide appeal and prompted vehement criticism. The responses of the public altered these writers' sense of vocation. Sue, Lippard, and Reynolds each experienced what Michael Denning has termed, expanding remarks by Peter Brooks, "conversions through one's fiction." Each became more active in working-class politics.[33]

Lippard insists that his *Quaker City* had priority over Sue's *Paris*, and this claim is difficult to evaluate. *Les Mystères de Paris* appeared in a French periodical in 1842 and 1843, was serialized in English in the New York *New World* in 1843, and then was printed as a book in 1844, the same year Lippard began publishing install-ments of *The Quaker City*. It seems unlikely that his work on the story "com-menced long before" Sue's *Les Mystères*, even if we regard Lippard's city reportage, starting in early 1842, as the background for his novel. It is more likely that Lippard asserts priority to avoid the charge of imitation.[34]

Questions about imitation and translation and about the particular and the general haunt the city mysteries, a formulaic genre that purports to represent distinct urban locations. There were mid-nineteenth-century mysteries not only of Paris, Philadelphia, and London but also of Berlin, New York, Boston, New Orleans, St. Louis, San Francisco, Cincinnati, and Lowell (Massachu-setts), among others. In Lippard's Philadelphia, as in Sue's Paris, readers find mansions, secret chambers, hypocrisy, financial intrigue, prostitution, seduction, and revelation. In George G. Foster's Philadelphia, readers find, well, New York. In late 1848 and early 1849, the journalist Foster published in the New York *Tribune* "Philadelphia in Slices," a sequel to his popular "New York in Slices" columns that recently had finished running in the same newspaper. In one of the sketches ("Dandy Hall"), a lair of iniquity that Foster locates in Southwark just south of Philadelphia, is clearly modeled on Lippard's "Monk Hall." Not only does Foster recycle fiction as fact but he also recycles Philadelphia as New York. Por-traying grotesque, lascivious interracial dancing in Pete Williams's notorious dance hall in the Five Points neighborhood of lower Manhattan in *New York by Gaslight* (1850), Foster lifts entire sentences from "Dandy Hall." In Foster's journalistic mysteries, the cities of Philadelphia and New York appear to be "sliced" from the same pie.[35]

Given the allure and reach of the tropes of urban exposure in the modern city mysteries and their lineage in European gothic fiction, which often was set in the past and outside the city, Lippard's insistence on the singularity of his *Quaker City* seems even less persuasive. When is Philadelphia like Paris? Like London? Like New York? Like seventeenth-century Madrid? Sue, Lippard, Reynolds, and those who followed them all repeated and innovated gothic practices. They were faced with a distinctive form of the challenge posed by literary tradition. They claimed to be revealing the mysteries of "X," where "X," the proper name of a city, stood for features that were both inherited and contrived. In his note on the back wrap-pers of *The Quaker City*, Lippard gestured toward the enigmas of the genre: "the Romance, in some respects, bears the same relation to Philadelphia that the 'Mys-teries' do to Paris." Insisting on priority, Lippard offers a qualified analogy. "In some respects" his book "bears the same relation." But what are those "respects" and how are "some" and "the same" defined? The "relation" may be "the same," but neither Lippard's nor Sue's novels document their titular cities with any more fidelity than James's *American Scene* reported on Philadelphia, New York, Boston, or Richmond. Lippard signals the literary difference by invoking the term "Romance," but, in so doing, he also sharpens the issue: what relation does "Romance" bear to urban place?

Leslie A. Fiedler posed a related inquiry in his introduction to a 1970 reprint of Lippard's *The Monks of Monk Hall*: "But what *is* specifically American about Lippard's fiction? What, in fact, had he added to or subtracted from the already established European tradition?"[36] Fiedler responded along the lines of his by-then influential arguments about American sexuality and domesticity. Lippard figured seduction—he understood social injustice—as an assault of the impious on the American family. In a variant of Fiedler's question, we might ask what, if anything, is specifically Philadelphian about Lippard's *The Quaker City*, *The Nazarene*, and *The Killers?*

Across theses novels, Lippard develops an aesthetics of place, inflecting the gothic protocols with Philadelphia's distinctive geography, politics, and history, especially the history of its riots. He insists on the urgency of appreciating the city's peculiarities. Although "aesthetics" may seem a misplaced term for the sensationalist potboilers Lippard rushed to print (and although the turn from Henry James to George Lippard in this chapter might dislocate a vertebra or two in the reader's neck), Lippard's novels cultivate a fictional awareness of the city's boundaries and of the affinities between manners and violence.

In *The Quaker City*, Lippard himself contends (he is in a state of perpetual contention) that he is pursuing aesthetic goals suitable to his urban materials. Defending his interest in exploring the caverns of Monk Hall and the psyche of a gruesome character named Devil-Bug against an imagined oversensitive male critic (a feminized strawman he mercilessly parodies), Lippard's narrator labels his approach the "grotesque-sublime." The term alludes to Victor Hugo's manifesto of French Romanticism, in the preface to his play *Cromwell* (1827). Hugo had argued that for modern writers the sublime and the grotesque were obverses, rather than opposites. The modern arts were distinguished by mixtures of the high and the low. (Hugo's influence on Lippard may extend further, since Quasimodo from his 1831 *Notre Dame de Paris* seems a likely model for Devil-Bug.) Lippard invokes Hugo's authority to justify his own breaches of decorum and his concern for the outcast and the monstrous, but he seems to have had more than Hugo in mind.[37]

Introducing the "grotesque-sublime" during Devil-Bug's pilgrimage into the abyss of Monk Hall, Lippard's narrator conjures the etymology of the term "grotesque." From the Italian "opera or pittura grotesca," meaning a work or painting resembling that found in a grotto, the word referred to the wall paintings and ornaments in first-century buildings revealed when streets were dug up in late-fifteenth-century Rome. These images blended human, animal, and vegetative forms, and over time "grotesque" acquired not only descriptive but also negative connotations and came to be associated with an uneasy mix of horror and humor. Lippard seeks to transvalue the negative and to exploit the uneasiness. As Devil-Bug climbs down beneath the floors of Philadelphia's Monk Hall, the narrator justifies his own pursuit of the "grotesque." His own literary descents, the narrator implies, are part of broader movements that may involve ascents: intense readerly experiences that alter composure and provoke insight—responses that we might call, with some hyperbole and recalling the emphasis of Longinus on linguistic transport, an urban gothic "sublime." Lippard provides not only an aesthetic term—"the grotesque-sublime"—but also a characteristic spatial texture for his Philadelphia excavations. Rather than departures from the famous grid of symmetry and propriety, he represents a foundational instability linked to the city's political history and contemporary social violence.

Lippard's narrator in *The Quaker City* regularly summons the commonplaces about the city's declension and hypocrisy, but the novels transmit more elaborate stories. The narrator tells his readers that an old lawyer, from whom he received the documents on which he has based his story, confided to him that "'whenever I behold [Philadelphia's] regular streets and formal look, I think of the Whited Sepulchre, without all purity, within, all rottenness and dead men's bones'" (3). Toward the climax of the book, the narrator proclaims that "the city which William Penn built in hope and honor,—whose root was planted deep in the soil of truth and peace, but whose fruits have been poison and rottenness, Riot, Arson, Murder and Wrong,—will put on its face of smiles" (540). Lippard advertises such familiar duplicity in the ironic title of the book itself: instead of tolerance, his *Quaker City* will reveal "Mystery" and "Crime." Yet Lippard's Philadelphia complicates such parables of exposure. In Lippard's "American Scene," readers are given "the immediate crudity of what 'happens,'" as James termed it (and Lippard revels in his own calculated vulgarity), but there also is a "finer complexity" that emerges from his obsessive urban regard. Although Lippard and James may seem to inhabit different literary planets, both writers encourage an appreciation of Philadelphia's fraught surfaces and contribute to a distinctive urban aesthetics.

The central arena in *The Quaker City* is "Monk Hall," a huge mansion located in the Southwark district. Lippard's narrator explains that Monk Hall had been erected by a wealthy foreigner before the Revolution. The building has lost its original grounds and now is hemmed in by dilapidated frame houses and the modern city's labyrinth of alleys and courts. The narrator emphasizes the significance of the mansion ("No reader who wishes to understand this story in all its details will fail to peruse this chapter" [46]) and also its literary entailments when he directs attention to the adjacent buildings: "a printing office on one side and a stereotype foundry on the other" (48). A relic of the city's past, the hall is the headquarters for the new aristocrats of Philadelphia who dominate society through their professional sway: judges, lawyers, ministers, businessmen, doctors, and magazine owners and editors. Here these "monks" (the term registers an ambient anti-Catholicism) carouse and plot. They feast in a chamber whose visual emblems are paintings of an inebriated Bacchus and a sleeping, nude Venus. Presiding over their table is the effigy of a monk with long black robes raising his goblet in a toast; the monk's cowl reveals a skull.

Monk Hall resembles one of Poe's macabre ritual chambers in "King Pest" (1835), "Ligeia" (1838), or "The Masque of the Red Death" (1842). This affinity may reflect the influence of Poe's fiction on Lippard. The writers knew one another in the 1840s. Lippard acclaimed Poe's originality and creative vision in print, aided him on his last visit to Philadelphia when he sought financial help, and defended him against slander and false praise after his death in 1849. Poe wrote Lippard in 1844 about his early novel *The Ladye Annabel*, saluting his imagination but warning about a carelessness in detail and style. Lippard included the prominent writer's letter in his novel *Herbert Tracy* (1844). Identifying himself with Poe's literary concerns and professional struggles, as he did with Charles Brockden Brown, Lippard traced a genealogy for the Philadelphia gothic.[38]

A comparison between Lippard and Poe suggests the two writer's different understandings of aesthetics, place, and history. Poe lived and worked in Philadelphia from 1838 until 1844, during a key phase in his career. His stay was bracketed by outbreaks of violence. He arrived in the spring or summer of 1838, in proximity to the burning of Pennsylvania Hall, and he left for New York in the spring of 1844, before the nativist riots involving Protestants and Catholics that summer and after the 1842 attacks on the black temperance parade and the Cedar neighborhood. "Philadelphia" may circulate through the fiction he published in the city's *Graham's Magazine* between 1840 and 1845: the specter of fever and misguided efforts at insulation ("The Masque of the Red Death"), the struggle to discern character in an urban environment ("The Man of the Crowd"), the savagery of consanguine strangers ("The Murders in the Rue Morgue"), and the absurd experiment in freedom ("The System of Doctor Tarr and Professor Fether").[39]

London is the ostensible setting for "Man of the Crowd" (1840), but the narrator's zeal for typology may be linked to the "American school" of racial science, led by the Philadelphian Samuel George Morton, and the mood "of keenest appetency" with which he views passersby through a coffeehouse window

may owe a debt to the Philadelphia fixation with the public appraisal of character. The inexplicable city and its diabolical emblem, the old man, serve as immediate precursors to the uncovering of urban mystery in the works of Sue, Lippard,
and Reynolds. Paris is the venue for "The Murders in the Rue Morgue" and also
"The Mystery of Marie Rogêt" (whose murder was based on the notorious case
of Mary Rogers in New York), but the concatenation of razor, ape, mimicry, and
violence in "Rue Morgue" (1841) may play on anxieties about African American
social mobility in Philadelphia, as some have argued. Foils to "The Man of the
Crowd," these two Inspector Dupin stories offer not the bane of opacity but
fantasies of urban legibility.[40]

Although situated in the "extreme southern provinces of France," "The System of Doctor Tarr and Professor Fether" (1845) offers a perversely comic fable
about authority, liberty, and retribution in America. If Poe's allusions (including
the partial date "18–," the "southern provinces," and the heavy-handed pun in
the "tar and feather" title) point to a racial allegory, the details of the story refuse
to align. Are the asylum inmates who pretend to be free, have imprisoned their
keepers, and can barely restrain themselves from enacting the reductio ad absur-
dum of their delusions meant to represent European American lower classes or
African Americans under southern slavery or in northern freedom? Are the misguided officials, who instituted a "system of soothing" that banned punishment
and granted the inmates "much apparent liberty," meant to be northern social
reformers or southern liberals? Or since they have been tarred and feathered and
are at first taken by the narrator for monkeys or apes when they escape from their
cells, are they blackened as well? The story seems to endorse no "system," neither
the benevolence of the administrators nor the revenge of the inmates.

The comically obtuse narrator of "Tarr and Fether" doesn't get it. He does
not perceive what is happening before his eyes. But beyond the fact that inmates
and keepers have switched roles, it is not clear, in terms of politics, region, or
race, what it would mean to get the story, or even what it is. Poe wickedly places
readers in the position of the narrator and (as Melville will do in his novella
Benito Cereno) tempts them into assuming an unwarranted superiority. Displacing
identifications and withholding clear markers, "The System of Doctor Tarr and
Professor Fether" permits itself to be read as, among other possibilities, a satire
of the misguided experiment in northern freedom for African Americans, distinguished by ludicrous performance, as it was for Edward W. Clay and others. Yet,
however the roles are cast, Poe's satire is more gentle than vicious. Except for tar-
ring and imprisoning the authorities (whose punishment may not be entirely
undeserved), the inmates are represented as eccentric rather than savage. The
story is told in the register of comedy, rather than horror.[41]

Although Poe's Philadelphia stories may contain such associations, he typically portrays composite, rather than specific, urban spaces, withholding or refusing firmer attachments. His locations are often transposed and eclectic. None of the stories mentioned here is explicitly set in Philadelphia. As a writer, and unlike Robert Montgomery Bird, George Lippard, or Frank J. Webb, Poe does not think through the circumstances of a historical place.

Poe stages his aesthetic distance in "Morning on the Wissahiccon," a minor sketch given the title of a specific locale, the renowned topography to the west of Philadelphia. The piece appeared in a gift book titled *The Opal*, dated 1844. Poe borrowed some of his material from an 1835 essay, "The Wissahiccon," that had been published in the *Southern Literary Messenger* and reprinted in an 1836 anthology, *The Philadelphia Book; or Specimens of Metropolitan Literature*. But Poe provides a final twist. In this familiar and inspiring setting, the narrator meditates on nation (an American sublime), history (the decline from a romantic past to a utilitarian present), and nature (in the form of a majestic elk who comes into his line of sight on a rocky cliff and incites a passionate identification). Unfortunately, these reveries are punctured when the elk turns out to be a pet belonging to an English family who own a nearby villa. The narrator watches as their "negro" servant places a halter around its neck. (Poe's narrator never comments on the implausibility of an elk as an appropriate house pet.) To complicate the affinities for place, Poe's verbal sketch is introduced by an engraving of a deer, not an elk, on a crag overlooking river scenery that resembles the Hudson River as much and maybe more than it does Wissahickon Creek.

Various aspects of Poe's "Morning on the Wissahiccon" combine to reinforce among observant readers a skepticism about the value of local sentiments. The engraving may have been a stock image, not a particular landscape near Philadelphia. It does not depict the wildlife that Poe describes. And uncertainty remains about whether Poe created his words in response to the image, or the image followed the words, or both existed independently and were merely juxtaposed in the gift book. Such disorienting effects between the covers of *The Opal: A Pure Gift for the Holy Days* (even in the register of private joke) probably would have been agreeable to Poe, whose scenery, including his urban scenery, seems designed to perplex identification.[42]

Joan Dayan has asserted that Philadelphia's controversial Eastern State Penitentiary, with its gothic aspect and discipline of silence and separation, looms over Poe's fiction: his "decors of lavish, medieval ornament, gates of iron, crenellated towers and picturesque effects, premature burials, and the singular torments of narrators who experience unnatural solitude and dark phantoms owe their force to his knowledge of the excesses of the Pennsylvania System of prison discipline." Such connections seem plausible, given Poe's residence in the city and the salient debates about prison reform, but they also seem oblique, rather than crucial, to the meaning of the stories. Such contexts do not explain the fiction, or they have less explanatory force than they do in the case of Lippard. This is not to argue that location is unimportant for understanding Poe's stories, that Poe is concerned with aesthetics and Lippard with history, or that Poe's imagination roams freely while Lippard's is moored; instead, I am suggesting that different writers consider location and history in different ways and with varying degrees of specificity. In this book, I focus on writers who represent a distinctive Philadelphia that they engage with a sense of tradition and consequence.[43]

Poe's elusive, synthetic topographies are worth remembering when we turn to *The Quaker City*. Lippard fills the conventions of the gothic novel and city mystery with the social history of Philadelphia. Monk Hall is a gothic castle situated in the mid-nineteenth-century United States and wedged in the alleys and courts that had proliferated to accommodate a burgeoning working-class population. Three stories above ground are inhabited by the "monks," and three below are the domain of thieves and murderers over whom Devil-Bug presides. Lippard's Monk Hall is an interpretive map of Philadelphia elaborated in three dimensions: the authoritative old city layered upon the southern, purportedly lawless districts (Southwark and Moyamensing), now become intimately subterranean, with the upper and lower chambers joined by staircases and passageways. The façade of Monk Hall presents a mass of black and red brick with pillars and an elaborate cornice fashioned into the visages of satyrs, a precipitous gable, and rows of strangely molded chimneys. It appears to be both an anti–Independence Hall (which was famed for its stately Georgian brick design) and a travesty of neoclassical civic pride, whose epitome in early-nineteenth-century Philadelphia was the massive Doric temple of the Second Bank of the United States. Reflecting on the character of Philadelphia, Lippard describes the reactionary persistence of elite dominion and conspiracy. In the symbol of Monk Hall, the famous grid is pivoted, skewed, excavated, and undermined, as Lippard uses architectural space to impart urban devolution.

Lippard bases his story in *The Quaker City* on an actual scandal, the 1843 murder by Singleton Mercer of Mahlon Heberton, who had promised marriage to Mercer's sister but then raped her. Mercer was acquitted by the jury at his trial. In Lippard's novel, the rape of Mary Arlington by Gus Lorrimer takes place in the chambers of Monk Hall and is avenged by her frenzied brother Byrnewood. In the three compressed days of his narrative, Lippard adds various plots having to do with strategic female adultery, a lost and restored daughter, women manipulated by a charismatic leader, surprise genealogies, working-class desires, forgeries,

robberies, murders, dissections, and conflagrations. He provides an array of characters, some hackneyed and others vivid in their hyperbole: the relentless striver
Dora Livingstone, the (repulsive but audacious) antihero Devil-Bug, the elite
impostor Colonel Fitz-Cowles (who resembles Poe's prosthetic "Man That Was
Used Up"), diabolical or obsequious African American servants, unscrupulous
editors (Buzby Poodle), mercenary Jews (Gabriel von Gelt), and lascivious Protestant preachers (F. A. T. Pyne).

Critics have attended to Lippard's genres, his sensationalism, his politics, and
his treatments of sexuality and gender in the novel, but not to the qualities of the
city he represents in this and subsequent books. Michael Denning has written
persuasively about Monk Hall as a "figurative reduction of Philadelphia," a tele-
scoping of class and sexual relations, but for him the "figurative" comes at the
expense of the particular. Comparing *The Quaker City* with the New York journalism of George Foster, Denning asserts that Lippard depicts "very little in the way
of urban topography, very little local color." Yet in *The Quaker City*, Lippard names
streets, provides directions, and transforms the city's grid; in *The Nazarene*, he
defines neighborhoods through their invasion; and in *The Killers*, Philadelphia
becomes visible in riot. What turns out to be most "Philadelphian" about
Lippard's writing is his figurative rendering of its violent history, his delineation
of a literary topography that models, rather than reduces, specificity.[44]

The novel begins at night on the streets of Philadelphia, with a view of the
State House. The male characters adjourn to an oyster cellar on Chestnut Street,
where Byrnewood Arlington and Gus Lorrimer make a wager about the virtue of
the young woman with whom Gus has an assignation that night (she turns out to
be Byrnewood's sister Mary). Four hours earlier, the narrator tells his readers, a
woman (the ill-fated Mary) had rushed down Third Street toward Monk Hall.
Lorrimer and Arlington stand in the glare of a gas lamp at the corner of Eighth
and Chestnut streets, then walk down Eighth to Walnut and then south on Thirteenth, and enter the house of an astrologer who foretells the killing of one of
the men by the other. As the plot unfolds, the narrator follows the movements of
characters along Front Street, then west on Chestnut to Third, a couple of blocks
from the State House clock (35); into a mansion on South Fourth Street (39)
and a massive hotel on Chestnut Street (151); along Walnut and then down
Seventh and into an alley, ending in front of a decrepit, once-stately residence in
a southern district (198–99); down Third to a side street and then a dark alley
and into a lecture hall (260–61); down Fourth Street (286); along the streets of
Southwark (347); on Chestnut to Sixth near the State House (408); to marble
steps on South Third Street (416); up Fourth Street toward a warehouse (416);
along Independence Square, Chestnut, and Walnut, then south and into an alley

and a door at the side of a mansion that leads to a dissecting hall (426–36); back to the large hotel on Chestnut Street (548); down Chestnut, turning south at Third, and standing in front of the Girard Bank (562); then down Walnut Street to the wharf and onto a ferry that travels the Delaware River between Philadelphia and Camden, New Jersey, and the murder of seducer by brother (563–68).

In *The Quaker City*, Lippard plots his Philadelphia along an axis with the State House and its Independence Hall in the north and Monk Hall in the south as foci. Characters are repeatedly pulled down toward Southwark and from main streets into side streets and alleys. The narrator never mentions Cedar or South Street, the lower border of the city. Such blurring of lines is another way for Lippard to insist on the layered intimacy between the old city and the newer districts, the "higher" and "lower" parts, figured in the metonymy of Monk Hall. The bell of Independence Hall punctuates the action of the novel, tolling to deliver a heavy-handed reminder about Lippard's narrative: "There is a wild music in the sound of that old bell. It rings like declension and the wages of the voice of a warning spirit, when heard in the silence of night. . . . That sound, speaking from the heighths of Independence Hall, strikes over the Quaker City like the voice of God's Judgment" (346–47). The knell also accents the temporal compression and dilation of the narrative (three days over six hundred pages) and conveys the weight of past and future on the novelistic present. Lippard embellishes the prestigious east-west streets, Walnut and especially Chestnut, with its mansions, shops, and promenading crowds, even as he directs notice and action south along Third and Fourth streets and into the alleys of Southwark and the cloisters of Monk Hall. The pit beneath Monk Hall serves as the inverted counterpart to the State House spire and an analogue for Lippard's pervasive images of urban decay: corpses, skeletons, skulls, leading up to the apocalypse of Devil-Bug's dream about the city in 1950.[45]

In the trapdoors that structure and connect the spaces in Monk Hall, Lippard provides a striking image for the vulnerable surfaces over which his characters move. A series of hinged floor panels, underneath the carpet and triggered by springs, extends in a vertical line from the garret to the first floor and through the underground stories. The springs are calibrated so that a single footstep may cause the trapdoor to pivot and send the victim hurtling down. As one of the characters familiar with the system explains, in words that describe not only the interior surfaces but also the public streets of Lippard's Philadelphia, "In such cases no man could stride across the floor without peril of his life" (61).

Lippard delivers the sensational payoff for this setup in an episode where Byrnewood Arlington, in Monk Hall, is tricked by Devil-Bug into activating one of the trapdoors. The room has been arranged to simulate domestic comfort: ornamented with false bookcases, an outmoded sofa, and a table offer-ing a meal of cold chicken and (drugged) wine. With one misstep, this "quiet supper room" fissures: "And yet the very moment Byrnewood's heel, pressed against the trifling object, the floor on which he stood gave way beneath him, with a low rustling sound, half of the Chamber was changed into one black and yawn-ing chasm, and the lamp standing on the table suddenly disappeared, leaving the place wrapt in thick darkness" (120, 121). He attempts but fails to maintain his balance on the verge: "For a moment his form swung to and fro, and then his feet slid from under him; and then with a maddening shriek, he fell" (122). Although Arlington will live to avenge his sister, this image of mundane peril lingers as urban metaphor: the sense that in Lippard's coiled Philadelphia, a slight gesture or the weight of a heel might result in catastrophe.

Lippard's power as an urban novelist resides in such images, which often are distinguished by suspension and violence. The remarkable second part of his *Empire City* (1850) takes place on a train careening north toward New York. Lippard manipulates time and space and has his narrator make clear that the vehicle—a "meteor," "monster," "demon-steed," and "steam devil"—is not only symbolic but also historical, representing "The Nineteenth Century!" Its trajec-tory (having passed Philadelphia and on its way to New York) suggests the dis-placement of the Quaker City by the Empire City at mid-century, as does the novel's advance from the 1820s to the 1840s. With "hot coals burning at its iron heart," "woe to the helpless, who linger on its iron track," "its terrible progress," and its derailment, the train serves as an emblem of the industrial city. The nar-rator explores its segregated spaces and the array of types who inhabit them. If this were all, if Lippard simply offered a metaphorical train and stock characters, then we might consider *The Empire City* a diverting mid-nineteenth-century ship—or rather locomotive—of fools. But this is just the beginning.[46]

The narrator stops and reverses time and prolongs the calamity with the effect that it presses upon the movements in every scene. The wreck is given a literal cause (a log on the track) but also overlapping figurative registers, as the narrator enters the different cars and sets episodes of larceny, robbery, seduction, and slave hunting against one another. The characters on the train refer to Philadelphia as a pivotal station, where plots have been contrived, swindles and debaucheries initiated, and African Americans have escaped and are tracked and caught and escape again. After the log is set down, the narrator goes back thirty minutes, describes scenes in the cars, halts the train, and reverses it on its tracks. He uses the vehicle of his metaphor to portray heterogeneous contiguities and disrupted temporalities under the pressure of violence. This is a texture of representation associated in Lippard's writing with the urban centers of Philadelphia and

New York. In the fractured reversions of *The Empire City*, Lippard's train crashes not once but three times, and each time the aftermath is elided. The narrator ostentatiously prepares for the derailment, just as the narrator in *The Quaker City* elaborately stages Byrnewood Arlington's fall through the trapdoors of Monk Hall, but then both narrators swerve from picturing their catastrophes, instead suspending the images of collapse over their narratives, ominous and unresolved.

Urban apocalypse does descend two-thirds of the way through *The Quaker City*, in the form of Devil-Bug's vision of Philadelphia in 1950. Titled "The Last Day of the Quaker City," this exorbitant set piece, a Philadelphia riot to end all riots, imagines the divine vengeance inflicted on the city for its defiance of the Quaker and Revolutionary founders' ideals. In Devil-Bug's 1950, a royal dwelling has been erected upon the ruins of Independence Hall with marble quarried from Girard College. (Funding for a school to educate poor white orphan boys, granted in an 1831 bequest of the merchant and financier Stephen Girard, was tied up in lawsuits over Girard's will, becoming a cause célèbre for Lippard. The institution would not open until 1848.) A jail and gallows have been constructed in Washington Square. On the day before the royal procession, the dead arise from their graves and join the revelers, who remain oblivious to their warnings. In the sky over Philadelphia hangs a black cloud with letters of fire that spell "WO UNTO SODOM," which serves as a refrain for the chapter. A pale spirit (possibly a relative of the spirits who took Charles Dickens's Scrooge on his tour of past, present, and future in the 1843 *Christmas Carol*) lifts Devil-Bug so that he can see on the Delaware River fleets of coffins with burning skulls on their prows, manned by corpses engaged in battle. The scene changes, and Devil-Bug observes a column of dead moving over the river, lamenting those who will expire on the morrow and celebrating the victory of the poor. Devil-Bug is taken back to the streets of the city, where the reinstallation of the king is being celebrated. When the marchers—royalty, clergy, and judges—at last recognize the figures of death accompanying them, they cry out in horror. The "slaves of the city, white and black," "the slaves of the cotton Lord and the factory Prince" smile and greet their redeemers (389). Mansions sink into the ground, vapor emerges from the seething earth, and Devil-Bug, on a high column, witnesses a primal, fatal struggle between a father, his daughter, and her lover. Then he looks down, with glee, at Philadelphia reduced to ashes.

Moving from the sidewalks of Philadelphia crowded with the rich and the poor to an elevated view of corruption, then higher to a stance from the east across the Delaware, down again to attend the parade of the living and the dead, and then up once more to behold the city's ruin, Lippard's narrator alternates the urban perspectives in vogue in the United States and northern Europe at mid-century, which the historian John F. Kasson has called "bird's eye" and "mole's eye" views. From the bird's-eye view, taken from an architectural high point or an imaginary stance in the air (often delivered in panoramic lithographs), the metropolis was converted into harmonious design (the fantasy of the Philadelphia grid materialized). Neither congestion nor social hierarchy nor poverty was visible. From the mole's-eye view, on the ground and steeped in details (the vantage assumed by "mysteries" fiction and journalism), the city was depraved and incoherent. In "Devil-Bug's Dream," Lippard takes the reader on a tour of Philadelphia that moves between sky and ground, with the aerial perspective magnifying the terrestrial exposures and furnishing vistas not of progress but of apocalypse. In this version of his "grotesque-sublime," Lippard twists the elevated panorama to the objectives of the city misery.[47]

The urban disclosures in "Devil-Bug's Dream" gain some of their melodramatic force from the European *danse macabre* (Lippard's souped-up version of the leveling march) and from biblical appeal: the burning of Sodom and Gomorrah in Genesis, the warnings about declension from Jeremiah, and the portents and fulfillments of Revelation. Yet Lippard also outlines a specifically modern apocalypse, a dance of death set in Philadelphia, in which vulnerability is tied to economic inequality, class antagonism, and vehement local history. The details of struggle and riot are processed through his extravagant trapdoors, doomed locomotives, and heaving sidewalks. These are gothic devices, Calvinist tropes, and also images of the volatile surfaces in nineteenth-century Philadelphia.

Particularizing Lippard's conventions and animating the city he depicts across his novels in the 1840s are the riots. In *The Quaker City* (1845), he represents a Philadelphia defined by violence, alludes to the events of 1838, 1842, and 1844, and envisions the ultimate riot. In *The Nazarene* (1846), he lays the groundwork for a depiction of the 1844 clashes between Protestants and Catholics but stops short. In *The Killers* (1849), rushed into print only three weeks after the California House outbreak, Lippard supplies the payoff for his earlier deferral. In this novel, which announces on its title page that "the deeds of the Killers, and the great Riot of election night, Oct. 10, 1849, are minutely described," historical violence compels the novelist's meticulous attention to neighborhoods, alleys, courts, and boundaries that become lucid in their breach.

In *The Quaker City*, allusions link the different riots. An editor boasts about the recent issue of his "Ladies Western Hemisphere and Continental Organ," which contains a "comic" engraving: "Nigger church on fire, with the Sheriff and Court looking on, to see that it is done in an effective manner*'" (277). Lippard refers to the burning of the Second African Presbyterian Church in the Cedar neighborhood during the riot of 1842 and to suspicions that authorities then, and in

1838, had countenanced the destruction. In an asterisked note, Lippard explicitly connects the two riots: "*See the charge of a certain Judge, in which he instructs the Grand Jury to present a certain Hall as a nuisance, because it was threatened by a mob, and, therefore, it endangered the surrounding property. It was owned and used by Negroes for benevolent purposes. This latter fact furnishes sufficient apology for any act of outrage in a city where Pennsylvania Hall was burnt by the whole population, because the object for which it was built happened to be unpopular" (277). Lippard joins mob action (the burning of the Second African Presbyterian Church) with legal decree (the order to destroy a black temperance hall in the aftermath of the 1842 riot) and public consensus about targets (with a pointed reference to the audience of thousands who witnessed the ruin of Pennsylvania Hall), in order to map a characteristic pattern of riot in Philadelphia. Here gothic conspiracy records history: the tacit and explicit support for violence.

The allegation is reinforced in *The Quaker City*, when a minor character explains his troubles with the law: "'Why you see, a party of us one Sunday arternoon, had nothin' to do, so we got up a nigger riot. We have them things in Phil'delphy, once or twice a year, you know? I helped to burn a nigger church, two orphans' asylums, and a school-house. And happenin' to have a pump-handle in my hand, I aksedentally hit an old nigger on the head. Konsekance wos he died. That's why they call me Pump-Handle'" (482). The racial riot is "got up," that is, initiated according to a plan. As Pump-Handle (whose name commemorates his fatal tool) explains, such affairs occur in the city with regularity. The targets are familiar—the institutions of the African American rising classes—and he casually, almost habitually, refers to civic brutality. In Lippard's apparent (but not irrational) hyperbole, Pump-Handle reports that he was convicted and sentenced and then the judge, jury, and opposing counsels appealed to the governor, who granted him a pardon.

Lippard has a character named Luke Harvey deliver a speech during which he commingles details and offers a portrait of Philadelphia as the domain of riot:

> "One day [Justice in the Quaker City] stands grimly smiling while a mob fires a Church or sacks a Hall, the next, ha, ha, ha, it hurries from its impartial throne, and pastes its placards over the walls of a Theatre, stating in pompous words, and big capitals, that THE TRUTH *must not be told in Philadelphia!* . . . Come into court, Humanity, and point to the blackened ashes of the Asylum, the School House, and the Hall! . . . Justice in the Quaker City . . . has laughed pleasantly while riot after riot, went howling through the town; it has chuckled gaily as it bade assassin after assassin, go scatheless from its bar; it has grown violent in its glee, as it beheld its judicial halls, soiled by the footsteps of corruption; and,

now and then, it has crept from off its lazar-throne, and arrested an editor who raised his voice for the right; or stopped a play, that dared speak out for the truth!" (205–6)

With self-indulgent capitals and italics, Lippard here alludes to the furor outside the Chestnut Street Theatre in November 1844, when a mob gathered to prevent the opening of a dramatic version of *The Quaker City* and to threaten its producers. Lippard had written a script for a five-act melodrama based on his story, which was still being issued in parts. Behind the orchestrated outrage probably were Singleton Mercer (the historical source for Lippard's avenging Byrnewood Arlington) and other prominent Philadelphians who saw themselves caricatured in Lippard's story. The mayor pressured the managers of the theater to cancel the performance, the mob gathered, and "The Quaker City" was withdrawn. Thus Lippard's novel itself almost provoked a riot.[48]

Toward the end of *The Quaker City*, Lippard's narrator compares a huge fire set by Devil-Bug on a country estate to the spectacular burning of a church that he witnessed, evoking the destruction of two Catholic churches in the Kensington riots in May 1844. As Luke Harvey says, "riot after riot." References to 1838, 1842, and 1844 course through the novel, lending substance to Lippard's figures of violence. With a memory of the upheavals during the 1830s and 1840s and of Robert Purvis's lament in the wake of the 1842 attacks ("I know not where I should begin, nor how, or when to end in a detail of the wantonness, brutality, and murderous spirit of the Actors, in the late riots, nor of the Apathy and inhumanity of the Whole community in regard to the matter"), we might treat Lippard's gothic and sensationalist clichés as, in part, a search for forms that might adequately express riot, forms that themselves bring a potent literary history, which Lippard, in turn, freights with local significance.

Lippard shows little interest in the members of the city's free African American communities except as servants. On display in *The Quaker City* are Muskito and Glow-worm, the infernal attendants at Monk Hall; the domestic Thomas, "who looked as though he had been born in his grey and velvet livery, with but the power of saying yes ma'am, no ma'am" (253); and the beautiful Creole slave boy Dim, who imitates his master Fitz-Cowles (who himself is revealed at the end of the book to be the son of a Creole slave). There are no African American mechanics or caterers or barbers or sailmakers or merchants or financiers or homeowners. For good or ill, there are no African American pretenders to respectability, the types that Edward W. Clay had made famous in "Life in Philadelphia." The absence of such characters is manifest, resembling Robert Montgomery Bird's elision in his catalogue of Philadelphia types in *Sheppard Lee*. The absence is also puzzling, given the continued scrutiny of the African American middle and "higher" classes in periodicals, reports, and political debate.

In "Philadelphia in Slices" (1848–49), Lippard's contemporary, George Foster, sketched a largely favorable picture. In the ninth "Slice," Foster explained that "we should be guilty of a glaring omission if we failed to notice so important a feature of the city as its Colored Population. It may be, too, that the facts we shall offer and the observations we shall make will afford some slight assistance to those who wish to form honest and just opinions respecting the condition of the Colored Race in contact with free whites." Foster remarks that African Americans in Philadelphia are divided into many classes and that their "better class" compares favorably with the equivalent group of whites. He describes fraternal, educational, and benevolent organizations and the mixture of classes in the Lombard Street or Cedar neighborhood. He comments on the fraction of African Americans who are in relative comfort and the great majority who live in poverty, owing to their former enslavement or the constraints of freedom. After speculating about Africans in racialist terms (they are "addicted to music and dancing" and evince a distinctive power of sympathy and imitation that corresponds to "the female sex or the minor key in the grand analogy of the universe"), Foster turns to what he labels a "fact" that has been demonstrated in Philadelphia: "the progressive development of the colored race . . . their innate self-progress and . . . the active benevolence which exist among its members."[49]

In Lippard's encyclopedic *Quaker City*, there is no evidence of debate over the terms or conduct of the Philadelphia social experiment. Its consequences, though, are registered in the tension and violence that suffuse daily life, especially in the presence, through figure and allusion, of the riots directed at antislavery efforts and black achievement. Lippard's narrator vilifies chattel slavery, as well as what he and others termed "wage slavery," and he sides with the abolitionist victims of 1838 and the African American casualties of 1842. In later works such as *The Empire City* (1850) and "Eleanor; or, Slave Catching in the Quaker City" (1854), his narrators will castigate the reinforced Fugitive Slave Law that was included in the political Compromise of 1850. (Philadelphia was the venue for the first case tried under the new law.) Like many labor reformers, though, Lippard was uncomfortable with the abolitionist movement, insisting on the priority of support for the white working class and concerned about the threat to national unity. In chapter 4 of "Eleanor," he may be reflecting on that ambivalence and on his own literary evolution when he has the Quaker Elijah Carwin declare, "'I am no Abolitionist. I never liked their sectarian spirit. I am ashamed to say, that some years ago, I stood in a street of this city, among the city authorities, all unconcerned spectators of the burning of Pennsylvania Hall. Until the Fugitive Slave

Law, I thought of slavery as an evil afar off . . . my attention was occupied by the hideous White Slavery of England . . . But the Fugitive Slave Law woke me up, as it did hundreds of thousands of others . . . that Black Slavery is the very embodiment of all the evils of White Slavery, multiplied *ad infinitum.'*"[50]

As Lippard's literary career develops across the 1840s and into the 1850s, the riots of 1844 and especially 1849, as well as the trespasses of the Fugitive Slave Law, provoke him to define his city and embody historical violence.

The Fiction of Riot: George Lippard, John Beauchamp Jones

In his preface to *The Nazarene* (1846), the unfinished novel published after *The Quaker City*, Lippard trumpets his ambition: "My task is an iron one; somewhat stern, somewhat terrible, somewhat difficult. To portray the scenes of two successive riots, when all that is barbarous in religious war, all that is horrible in arson or murder, all that is terrible in the spectacle of graves torn open, living men shot down like dogs, churches laid in ashes, was enacted in Philadelphia."[51]

With this prelude and with the date he invokes in the book's subtitle ("A Revelation of Philadelphia, New York, and Washington, in the Year 1844"), Lippard signals that he will offer a fictional account of the ethnic and religious violence in the summer of 1844. These riots were the product of rising Protestant nativism and anti-Catholicism, debates about which Bibles were to be read in public schools, incitement by politicians and newspapers, and working-class economic rivalry. In May, violence flared in the Kensington district north of the city. After Protestant nativist meetings were interrupted by a group of Irish Catholics and the teenage George Shiffler was killed, dozens of Irish homes were attacked. Groups battled, and there were numerous casualties on both sides. Shiffler was immediately treated as a Protestant martyr, his death used as a rallying cry and commemorated in broadside and lithograph. In one widely circulated image, Shiffler was shown on one knee, blood dripping down the front of his shirt over his heart, as he clutched an American flag. Mobs burned the Hibernian Hose Company's firehouse in Kensington, two Catholic churches (St. Michael's in Kensington and St. Augustine's in North Philadelphia), and a female seminary (in Kensington). A grand jury held that Irish Catholics were responsible for the violence. In July, a mob attacked the Church of St. Philip de Neri in Southwark and fought state militia in the neighborhood over several days. An estimated five thousand troops were called up. By the time the struggle ended, more than thirteen civilians and two soldiers had been killed, and dozens wounded. The Kensington and Southwark riots of 1844 spurred the effort to consolidate the various jurisdictions of Philadelphia County into one municipal entity and, according to the historian Sam Bass Warner Jr., shifted the city's politics from the revolutionary legacy of class discord (merchant versus mechanic) to divisions along the lines of ethnicity and race.[52]

A broadside song sheet, titled "Philadelphia Riots," undated but probably issued in the aftermath of the May events, links the riots of 1834, 1842, and 1844 through culpability. Written in dialect, with the refrain "I guess it wan't de niggas dis time," the lyrics blame the Irish for the Kensington violence and, through epithet, blame African Americans for previous assaults, while holding the city authorities culpable for not protecting the "Natives." The singer adopts a minstrel perspective to scapegoat Irish Catholics and African Americans as responsible for the violence largely inflicted upon them.[53]

Lippard's own allegiances in *The Nazarene* are complicated. The plot, whose various developments are never resolved, involves secret societies (including Catholic intrigue and a nonsectarian group called the Brotherhood), financial and political malfeasance, a satanic bank president who stokes Protestant and nativist fanaticism for his own gain, the swindling of Indians out of their recompense for land sold to the federal government, and attempts to obstruct the bequest of Stephen Girard (to whom the book is dedicated). In a cameo role, the aged Andrew Jackson makes a noble appearance. Before the narrative breaks off, the reader is taken back to Palestine in A.D. 30 and then to Renaissance Italy, as part of a digression on the history of the "Wandering Jewess." It is not hard to see why Lippard left the story unfinished, since in his "effort to portray the scenes of two successive riots" in Philadelphia, he has introduced a tangle of seemingly incompatible actions. Michael Denning has suggested that Lippard's inability to get to the riots has causes that are both formal (the predictable limits of the urban gothic with its oblique secrets) and historical (Lippard's conflicted response to the ethnic splintering of class politics in Philadelphia during the 1840s). Yet while plausible, such explanations do not acknowledge the illuminating aspects of his failure or the substance of the framework he establishes.[54]

In setting up the 1844 riots, Lippard's plots are too narrow and too broad. He suggests that the circumstances were arranged by a few individuals to augment their power and wealth, imputing the conflict among white laborers to capitalist deviltry. But he also links the events to vast developments of, one has to admit, uncertain relevance: historically speaking, the Wandering Jewess probably did not play a significant part in the Kensington riots. Lippard apprehends the synchronic and diachronic aspects of the riots, but he reduces the local and reaches too far back for the historical. The conspiracy of financiers may epitomize an upper-class role in the violence, and ethnic legend may convey the abiding structures of social hierarchy and the fervent, almost erotic persistence of bigotry, but in *The Nazarene*, Lippard has difficulty representing what happened in May and June 1844.

Yet, as in *The Quaker City*, Lippard in *The Nazarene* brings Philadelphia into the novel, not through stock characters and gothic plots, but through his manipulations of figurative space. In *The Nazarene*, the narrator delineates Kensington to the north and Southwark and Moyamensing to the south, elucidating the demographic and economic tensions within these poorer areas and the explosive boundaries they formed with "the City Proper" (166).

On the southern borders of the city, the narrator describes a group of inebriated medical students from the South, staggering down an alley lined by tenements. He imagines a nightmare promenade of the neighborhood's residents: "Creeping from the damp cellars, crawling from the narrow doors, staggering forth from the dens where maddening drugs were sold, these creatures would lay their loathsome shapes in the sunlight, along the curb, or over the sidewalk, clustering together in groups of wretchedness and squalor. White and black, young and old, man and woman, were mingled in the hideous prospect. . . . These were the Heathens of the Quaker City . . . the Lepers of Philadelphia" (138–39). The medical students are in search of Columbiana Hall, a decrepit blue frame structure housing a tavern run by Peter Crow, formerly a lawyer and now a seller of corpses and tracker of runaway slaves. Inside the murky room, the students ask a black fiddler to play a tune, and they dance with an assortment of degraded women. Later in the chapter, in a scene that presages the kind of ritual conflict between white and black that Lippard will represent in *The Killers*, the students are accused of being "kidnapers" by the African American denizens of Columbiana Hall, and they retort by punning on their vocation and threatening to "'dissect these subjects!'" (160–61). A fight with knives and clubs is barely avoided.

At the beginning of the next chapter, the narrator invites his readers on an unprecedented fictional tour of the northern districts. Moving from Southwark and Moyamensing to Kensington, "traversing the heart of the city," the disembodied narrator chronicles the industrial sector of Philadelphia, as though he were accompanying the reader: "Do you see. . . . Do you hear. . . . Let us look. . . . Here we behold. . . . Let us enter" (166–69). The direct address here is not new, of course, since the rhetoric of urban exposure had become a staple of city mysteries novels and reportage, but no one before Lippard had displayed such meticulous literary regard for Philadelphia's geography. The narrator spotlights a huge textile factory where cotton grown under slavery in the South is processed on steam looms by an army of gaunt men, women, and children. These workers, he explains, are "slaves" of the northern *"Manufacturer or the Monopolist"* (166–67). He then takes his readers down Germantown Road, turns at Master Street, points out a market house, a red brick schoolhouse, and a few paces to the east, Second Street, the walls of St. Michael's Church, and, just beyond, the Catholic seminary, popularly known as the "Nunnery." He is preparing the stage for the riots: "These localities are worthy of your serious recollection, for let me tell you, in a few days this quarter of Kensington, will become the scene of strange and terrible events" (168). Although *The Nazarene* ends before the two Catholic establishments are burned, the narrator bears witness to structures that no longer exist.

Continuing the tour, he guides readers west to a triangular block, an "island" of houses formed by the intersection of Washington, Cadwallader, and Jefferson streets (168–69). He advances north along Cadwallader, past a crumbling brick domicile, noting the sound of looms even during the night. Every twenty paces, he looks westward into a series of ruined courtyards. On the east side of the street, in the center of the triangle, the narrator pauses at a stunted dwelling whose bricks are shored with planks of timber, and he enters the only inhabited apartment, going through a narrow door and into a large room, barely lit by a cheap candle. There is a weaver's loom, a bed, a chair with a broken pitcher on it, and, above the candle, a plaster image of Christ on the cross. (The narrator's gloss on that image—Christ as the emblem of a suffering laborer who will be redeemed—appears to give the book its title.) In this room, the narrator finds an impoverished family of Irish weavers who will assume roles in the story's prolif-erating lines. Yet the striking aspect is not the Dickensian squalor, but the pains-taking treatment of Philadelphia's urban space: the directions (one can follow the narrator's route on a mid-nineteenth-century map); the relationships between street, alley, and court; the merging of domestic and industrial space; and the aura of imminent destruction.

The narrator specifies these places in anticipation of the riots that will devas-tate the neighborhood. The buildings are clarified by a fictional time that under-scores their transience. The streets described had been the scene for the pivotal events of the May 1844 riots. The interrupted nativist meetings were held in an open lot at the southwest corner of Master and Second streets. The market house in Washington Street above Master, known as the "Nanny-Goat Market," had been used as a fortress against the sheriff's posse by striking weavers during a riot in 1843 and would be used as a refuge by nativists in 1844. Across the street, on the eastern side of the triangular block described by the narrator, was the Hibernian Hose Company building, from which shots had been fired at the nativists and which the mob burned down. The fire spread from this house along both sides of Cadwallader Street, the west side of Washington, and the south side of Jefferson, consuming many buildings on the triangle and also destroying the market house. Fighting spread from Washington, down Cadwallader and Germantown Road, and up to Jefferson Street.

Philadelphia had been mapped in the series of *Stranger's Guides* and *Philadelphia as It Is* volumes, which first were published in the early nineteenth century and appeared regularly in the middle decades. These volumes were manuals for identifying the city's buildings and navigating its streets. But the most prominent fictional treatments of the city had been in the registers of allegory and satire, as was the case with Brackenridge's *Modern Chivalry* and Bird's *Sheppard Lee*. For Brackenridge and Bird, Philadelphia was meaningful as a setting, but except for landmarks such as Independence Hall and the American Philosophical Society and emblematic avenues such as Chestnut, they did not detail streets or neighborhoods, nor did they attend to the relationships between the city and its surrounding districts. As Lippard narrated urban violence across the 1840s, he became more and more interested in those relationships. Philadelphia had emerged in fiction in Charles Brockden Brown's *Arthur Mervyn*, defined through crisis, as it had been in the earlier yellow fever narratives of Mathew Carey, Benjamin Rush, Absalom Jones, and Richard Allen. In the 1840s, Lippard identified peculiar histories, spaces, and temporalities and sought to extend the range (to quote the subtitle of one of H. S. Tanner's *Stranger's Guides*) of "everything interesting in the city and suburbs of Philadelphia."[55]

When the narrator moves from southern to northern districts—"Traversing the heart of the city, we will hurry some two miles northward from the State House" (166)—he follows the trajectory of those rioters who advanced from Southwark and then through downtown Philadelphia and the area called Northern Liberties to Kensington, without any interference from city authorities.[56] The friction between modes and locations in *The Nazarene* gives Lippard's Philadelphia its distinctive plots and narrative energies. He represents Kensington as a burgeoning capitalist "North," whose emblem is the factory and whose mode is realistic narrative. Southwark and Moyamensing are an iniquitous "South," bound to slavery and transmitted in the register of the gothic. Philadelphia is clarified and undermined by its investments in these linked systems of oppression, as Lippard insists on wider contexts for understanding his city. Its grid ramifies into alleys and courts of implication. Such spatial instabilities (local terrain epitomizes the strains between South and North as the borders of the city are traversed by riot) and temporal stresses (in retrospect and prospect, violence seems omnipresent) lend a historical cast to the Philadelphia memento mori depicted by Lippard.

In *The Nazarene*, Lippard imparts a tenuous materiality to the city as he approaches, but does not reach, the riots of 1844. In *The Killers*, published three years later, he finally portrays riot in Philadelphia, not in Kensington during the summer of 1844, but in the southern areas during 1849. He swerves from, but then returns, spectacularly, to the city's African Americans. The title page promises "A Narrative of Real Life in Philadelphia, in Which the Deeds of the Killers, and the Great Riot of Election night, October 10, 1849, are Minutely Described." Lippard's "real life," of course, contains much invention, but his title also indicates something about his literary practice and about the development of the Philadelphia novel that might not be as obvious: the generative relationship between riot and fictional particularity.

The title of the novella refers to the notorious gang that dominated the eastern part of Moyamensing in the late 1840s and early 1850s. Composed of young Irishmen, many of whom were members of a volunteer firemen's group, the Killers had more than three hundred followers. They instigated the 1849 California House riots, partly out of prejudice (the tavern served a racially mixed clientele and was run by a mulatto man and his white wife) and partly out of economic struggle, in an attempt to displace black men from unskilled jobs sought by the Irish. Lippard invents a character who leads the Killers, Cromwell D. Z. Hicks, and features him on the title   page, along with two other fictional protagonists, Don Jorge, a Cuban who schemes to advance the trade in slaves, and "the Bulgine, the celebrated Negro Desperado of Moyamensing," who defends against the Killers' assault. Lippard presents the 1849 riots through the lens of his obsessions, setting events against a backdrop of attempted rape, financial chicanery, and the intrigues of slavers.[57]

The convoluted publishing history of the story told in *The Killers* suggests that Lippard believed there would be an audience (or several) eager to read about the Philadelphia riots. With impressive speed, he began serializing *The Killers* in the December 1, 1849, issue of his *Quaker City Weekly*, only seven weeks after the events. At the same time, according to David Faflik, Lippard was rushing into print a shorter version, with a different title, altered names, and transposed passages. With a copyright date of 1849 and a publication date of 1850, *The Life and Adventures of Charles Anderson Chester, the Notorious Leader of the Philadelphia Killers* appeared almost at the same time as *The Killers*. In 1851, *The Killers* was reprinted, under a different title, as *The Bank Director's Son, A Real and Intensely Interesting Revelation of City Life. Containing an Authentic Account of the Wonderful Escape of the Beautiful Kate Watson, from a Flaming Building in the City of Philadelphia*. This was the only one of the three texts that bore Lippard's name on the title page. The texts of *The Killers* and *The Bank Director's Son* are identical, but the title pages imagine different audiences. *The Killers* addresses those with some knowledge of the events, who would recognize the name of the gang and the occasion of the riots, and emphasizes masculine violence. *The Bank Director's Son* aims at those interested in a more general urban exposure penned by the scandalous originator of the American city mystery, with no mention of the riots and "Philadelphia" subordinated. Such readers might be enticed by the story of filial relationships and the escape of "The Beautiful Kate Watson" from a flaming building. Neither "Kate Watson" nor her incendiary plight was "authentic," despite the blazon. All three texts combine fact, artifice, and politics to capitalize on potential markets for the story of the 1849 riots.[58]

The *Life and Adventures of Charles Anderson Chester*, like *The Killers*, bills no specific author, an omission that reinforces the purported documentary aspect of the story. (*Chester* lists no writer, *The Killers* only a sober vocation: "By a Member of the Philadelphia Bar.") *Chester* also invents a leader for the Killers, giving him a different name, and records an alternative date for the October 1849 riots, October 11 rather than 10, which appears in the title of *The Killers*. Neither, it turns out, was the actual date of the California House riot, which occurred on the election night of October 9. Whether the result of haste or strategy, the discrepancies on the title pages open a gap between history and fiction and underline Lippard's contrivances. In *Chester*, the narrator focuses on the riot. The Cuban character is eliminated, as are the financial and slave trading plots, the indictment of northern merchants as "Killers," and the censure of authorities for their failure to deal effectively with the rioters. With awkward exposition used to suture the text taken from *The Killers*, the condensed *Charles Anderson Chester* presents a timely, narrow account of the 1849 riots as an instance of local misbehavior and family dysfunction. To confirm its "factual" basis, *Chester* appends a list of those killed, wounded, or taken into custody during the riots (some names are actual, some fabricated). The narrator also tacks on a lesson for America's youth, who are urged to "learn wisdom" from the demise of the title character. The substance of that wisdom is never divulged and is hard to fathom, unless it runs something like (the needless) "don't join a violent gang and foment a riot."

All three texts contain engravings. *The Killers* includes an image of gang members and another of a woman looking in a mirror. *Chester* has a frontispiece with white and black figures battling in front of a burning California House, a title page image of Charles Anderson Chester ostensibly "taken from a daguerreotype," and the black avenger "Bulgine" standing over a white victim. *The Bank Director's Son* offers the "Bulgine" again with raised knife and foot on a prostrate body, a woman commanding a man to leave her house, and the leader of the Killers, with an accomplice, threatening another man. None of these pictures is especially noteworthy, with the exception of the tableaux of racial violence involving the "Bulgine," to which I will return, but *Chester* does include an additional image, one that illustrates the city rather than characters or events.

On the verso opposite the first page of chapter I, there appears a map of the eastern part of Philadelphia and the districts of Moyamensing and Southwark. The map is inverted so that the southern areas are at the top and the city is at the bottom (figure 3.6). The vaunted grid, here divided into asymmetrical patterns

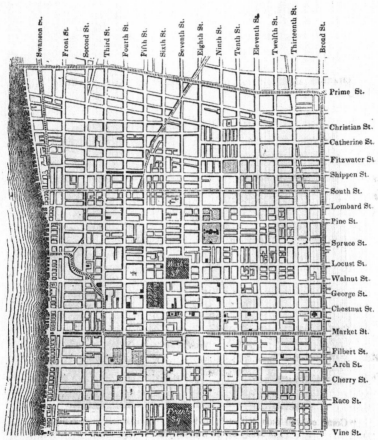

MAP of the City and Districts of Moyamensing and Southwark, from the river Delaware to Broad street,

† ‡ The scene of Riot at Sixth and St. Mary streets.

FIGURE 3.6 "Map of the City and Districts of Moyamensing and Southwark, from the river Delaware to Broad street," from *The Life and Adventures of Charles Anderson Chester*, by George Lippard (1850). Courtesy of the Library Company of Philadelphia.

that extend into Southwark and Moyamensing, appears like a maze. The truncated map, with only two of the city's squares (Franklin and Washington), dispenses with Penn and Holme's original proportions. Two daggers mark "the scene of Riot at Sixth and St. Mary streets" in the upper third of the image, on the border between city and suburbs. The map at the beginning and the list of the dead at the end of *Charles Anderson Chester* lend a veneer of reality. Yet the plan of streets indicates both fidelity (an exactness of reproduction) and tactic (the customary directions are reversed). The facing pages of image and text suggest that the coordinates for riot will be plotted. The novella will allow readers to view the city from a different perspective. To my knowledge, this is the first map attached to a work of Philadelphia fiction. With daggers pinpointing the scene of the 1849 riot, it invites readers to see *Charles Anderson Chester* as a "Stranger's Guide," not to public buildings or places of amusement, but to urban disorder.

While the violence located in *Charles Anderson Chester* is contained within a few city blocks and within individual biographies, *The Killers* presents a systemic outbreak. Characteristically, Lippard reduces and expands the contexts for his events. On the one hand, he presents the assault on the California House at Sixth and St. Mary's streets as a cover for kidnapping schemes. Agitation is stoked on an election night, when alcohol flows and brawls are common, so that a rich merchant of Walnut Street and a young woman (the beautiful Kate Watson) can be seized. On the other hand, the agents of conspiracy have ties to fathers implicated in profits from the slave trade, who wish to reengage the United States in that international traffic. And so Lippard seems relatively uninterested in the persons and property of African Americans in the Cedar neighborhood, the targets in 1849. Yet in dwelling upon finances and enslavement, he also points to the continuities between slave traders (the fathers) and race rioters (the sons), situating the events that occur on a discrete Philadelphia night in systems of commerce that extend across the eastern seaboard and into the Caribbean. The disproportion—the stress on foreground and background that implies a turbulent middle zone—and the pattern of discernment and disregard give the story, and many of Lippard's urban stories, a curious intensity. However we might evaluate his conspiracies and alibis, Lippard's proposals in book after book that his actors in riot are part of larger scripts and that violence covers multiple interests reproduce an aspect of the historical circumstances in Philadelphia.

Preparing for riot in *The Killers*, Lippard's narrator turns the Cedar neighborhood into "the Barbarian District":

> It was that District, which partly comprised in the City Proper, and partly in Moyamensing, swarms with hovels, courts, groggeries—with dens of every grade

of misery and drunkenness—festering there, thick and rank, as insects in a tainted cheese. It cannot be denied that hard-working and honest people, reside in the Barbarian District. Nor can it be denied that it is the miserable refuge of the largest portion of the Outcast population of Philadelphia County. . . . Here, huddled in rooms thick with foul air, and drunk on poison that can be purchased for a penny a glass, you may see white and black, young and old, man and woman, cramped together in crowds that fester with wretchedness, disease and crime. (35–36)

In his zeal to disclose the extremes of poverty, Lippard skews the geographical space in which the 1849 riots occurred, and he advances the evolving popular caricature of the neighborhood. He contracts its diversity to its most destitute residents and to a phantasm of noxious heterogeneity. By the early 1850s, such conceits will pass freely, and sometimes indistinguishably, between fiction and reportage. The narrator's sketch of "the Barbarian District" immediately precedes his summary of the riot, and it echoes his earlier portrayals of the areas south of the city: "Runnel's Court," "Dog Alley," and the "Den of the Killers." The October 1849 riots did take place in a region "partly comprised in the City Proper, and partly in Moyamensing," as the narrator indicates, but he makes it seem as though the violence were centered in streets notorious for their poverty and racial intimacy (such as the unnamed Bedford Street). Instead, in 1849, as in 1834 and 1842, the damage tended to be concentrated in the sectors where African Americans owned property. Either through ignorance or design, Lippard restricts his narrator's chronicle of the neighborhood to "tenements and hovels" (36).[59]

Yet there is more to Lippard's riot. After setting his scene, the narrator presents the violence by mixing journalistic review, melodramatic vignettes, and symbolic tableaux. From a reportorial perspective, the narrator recounts how a group of men and boys dragged a burning wagon down St. Mary's Street toward Sixth, "principally inhabited by negroes," and was fired upon. The mob then attacked the California House, whose defenders had prepared themselves after weeks of threats. The barroom was destroyed, and gas fittings were ripped out to fuel the blaze. Members of the Killers took aim at the volunteer fire companies that rushed to the scene, shooting dow one man. As the fire spread to other houses, men fought throughout the night, giving the area an "appearance of a sacked and ravaged town" (36), until the military finally arrived in the morning. As reporter, the narrator separates fact from rumor, describes events and locations, and refrains from taking sides. Once the riot begins, he casts both Irish and African Americans as partners in ferocity, while treating the fireman as embattled heroes. He records how the attackers singled out African Americans and denounces the city authorities for their lack of response. As though marking this perspective, the narrator assures his readers after his last words as reporter that "all this may be read in the daily papers of October 1849" (49).

Then Lippard uses his fiction to supplement those daily pages. After the chapter in which most of the reportage is given, the narrator switches to his own plots within the official story. Kate Watson is kidnapped by Black Andy or "the Bulgine," who has been enlisted for the task by the Killers. The leader Cromwell Hicks knocks Andy unconscious. Hicks's father, whose "wealth—such was the popular rumor—had been acquired at a time when the slave trade was as legal, moral, and religious, as stock gambling at the present day" (11), reveals that another character, the mechanic Elijah, is his son, while the slave trader Jorge Marin looks on. Lippard signals that he knows such scenes are over the top when he has Marin laugh at the spectacle of family disclosure: "It's as good as a play. If they'd only sing it, we should have an Opera on the spot!" (40). "Opera" is what Lippard adds to riot or, rather, what he shows to be an aspect of riot's performance: the loaded gestures, the tangled plots, the consciousness of audience, the elaborate settings and postures that circulate in its aftermath (the burning hall, the fallen martyr). Lippard illuminates—makes entertaining as well as disturbing—the knot of race, ethnicity, sex, commerce, and class that helped to generate the riots of October 1849.

In two theatrical scenes featuring Black Andy, Lippard alters the conventions. Andy, the proprietor of a saloon in Moyamensing, is introduced, with Lippard's penchant for cliché, as a huge man, "black as the ace of spades," with a torn face and "fists that might have felled an ox" (28)—a vehement engine, confirming his sobriquet, "the Bulgine," the name for a small locomotive used on the docks. When he seizes Kate Watson and she recoils at his face not once but twice, readers appear to be greeted by the familiar, potent specter of the vulnerable white female threatened with black assault. While this image lingers, the narrator also makes clear that Black Andy loses interest in his kidnapping assignment, and later he "instinctively determines to save her" from harm (47). Andy turns against those who have enlisted him in their schemes. In a tableau of African American militancy, Lippard depicts Andy standing above the supine body of the gang leader Hicks, whom he has stabbed to death: "And over him, triumphant and chuckling stood the negro, '*Bulgine*'—the knife which he shook, dripping its red drops, upon his black and brawny arm" (42). The illustrators of both *The Life and Adventures of Charles Anderson Chester* and *The Bank Director's Son* engraved this scene, and publishers offered it after the title page in both versions.

On the pages of *Charles Anderson Chester*, F. O. C. Darley, the prominent illustrator who had done the frontispiece for one of the editions of Lippard's *Quaker City*, casts Andy in a pose that confronts the reader. One hand is lowered with a knife, and the other raised in a fist. His foot is on Anderson's chest. As David Faflik has noticed, Darley signed this image in the blood trickling from the gang leader's body. The illustrator for *The Bank Director's Son* offers a less direct view. Andy, with his foot on the back of the prostrate leader's head, lowers one hand in a fist and raises a knife in the other hand to defend himself against a gang member descending the stairs at the left. These gestures reverse those in Darley's earlier engraving. In *The Bank Director's Son*, the black figure is pivoted sideways to face his adversary rather than the viewer. This artist depicts a more traditionally noble figure and orients the violence within the frame.

In his verbal portrait of Black Andy triumphant, Lippard seems to be alluding to the circumstances of that October evening when African Americans who had fortified the California House resisted the assault and then, after their eviction, continued the struggle during the night in the streets. Instead of George Shiffler, the Protestant martyr of 1844, mortally wounded and on one knee, Lippard and his illustrators display Black Andy with his foot on the body of a Killer as a token of 1849. The character is part animal, part avenger, part hero (his name in *Charles Anderson Chester* is "Black Herkles"), an unstable compound of Lippard's attitudes about race and violence. Immobilizing the Killers and later, in a second tableau, poised on the edge of a burning roof (an analogue for the California House), Andy is neither servant nor slave, but an epitome of defiance—the only such African American in Lippard's Philadelphia riot fiction. Another of Lippard's figures of suspension and excess, he is the cynosure in the last part of *The Killers*.

This is how Lippard finally tells the story of riot in Philadelphia: "minutely," as the title page of *The Killers* promises, itemizing district, street, and event, but also hyperbolically, inventing vast plots and mounting spectacular tableaux. The riots in Lippard's fiction—Devil-Bug's urban apocalypse in *The Quaker City*, the Kensington setup in *The Nazarene*, the California House payoff in *The Killers*—generate meanings that outstrip the forms he uses to convey them. As he juxtaposes modes, shifts registers, and pulls out all the stops, Lippard seems aware of this dynamic and also subject to it. We might simply conclude that he was a hack writer and no kind of artist. To do so, though, would be to overlook the literary project that he sustains across the 1840s, however unevenly (and unevenness has its own aesthetic and historical interest). His effort to represent Philadelphia is inseparable from his effort to represent violence. Seeking literary ways to articulate a historical "frame of fire" (as Henry James would term it), Lippard narrates boundaries under assault, streets that must be defended, and a society in which a false move, the presumptions of class or race, might cause a parlor to disintegrate or a thoroughfare to erupt. This is a city that riot makes visible.

In *The City Merchant; or, The Mysterious Failure* (1851), John Beauchamp Jones telescopes the violence of the late 1830s and the 1840s to tell a story about Philadelphia whose climax restores an order premised on racial subservice. Jones's novel participates in an extensive reflection on Philadelphia's history during the 1850s. In *The City Merchant*, a racist novel, Jones more deliberately articulates his political, economic, and racial plots than does Lippard, and he advocates riot as a social strategy. The Philadelphia experiment ends in carnage, and the city's African American residents are viewed as instigators and legitimate targets. They are at the center of debate for Jones, as they will be in works by Mary Schoolcraft, Sarah Josepha Hale, Martin Delany, and Frank J. Webb that will be taken up in the next chapter.

Jones was an editor, journalist, and popular novelist who was born in Baltimore, spent his early life in Kentucky and Missouri, and lived in or near Philadelphia during 1839–40, 1845, 1847–48, and 1857–61. His first three sojourns in the city were adjacent to major outbreaks. In *The City Merchant*, his third novel, he condenses the time between 1838 and 1842 and between 1842 and 1849, offering a fantasy of sacred violence (Jones's construal of the burning of Pennsylvania Hall) and racial exile (combining the disfranchisement of 1838 and the displacement of 1842).

In his preface, Jones explains that he has written a historical novel whose urgency his audience, inside and outside Philadelphia, will recognize: "In regard to the principal events of this story, and upon which most of its details are made to depend, it can hardly be necessary to say they were real occurrences, and actually transpired in the order in which they are related. Matters of so recent occurrence, and of such startling notoriety, cannot have been forgotten by anyone of mature age." With a significant exception (he backdates the ruin of Pennsylvania Hall so that it can precede the financial panic of 1837), Jones does relate events in sequence, but he also accelerates and conflates them. He generates a narrative of abolitionist interference and compulsory violence that justifies racial hierarchy. Published in the aftermath of the unstable political Compromise of 1850 between North and South, which included an invigorated Fugitive Slave Law, Jones aligns himself with the southern states and imagines Philadelphia as the site that confirms the bonds between Saxon and Celt and the failures of African American liberty. Transforming the archive of riot, Jones proposes a theory of social and economic history.[60]

The City Merchant begins on February 1, 1836, on Market Street in Philadelphia, between Second and Sixth. This "great commercial mart" is bustling with salesmen and with the delivery of goods from warehouses on Front Street. Conjuring the past, the narrator reassures his readers that despite the altered buildings and the fortunes that have been made and lost between then and now, commerce still thrives. "Perhaps, after all," he wonders, "Time treads as lightly and mows as tenderly here as elsewhere. We shall see" (14). Preparing for the escalation to come, he invokes the early-and mid-1830s. Andrew Jackson had vetoed the congressional rechartering of the Bank of the United States, which was headquartered in Philadelphia with Nicholas Biddle as president. Jackson withdrew the bank's deposits and assigned the funds to state banks, which issued large quantities of paper currency, expanded credit, and helped to fuel an economic surge. The narrator warns about the illusory speculations of the businessmen on Market Street, who sought to prosper "in defiance of the rules regulating the real value of commodities in accordance with the amount of money in circulation" (15). Across the novel, Jones elaborates a dichotomy in which the excesses of financial speculation are linked with abolition, social reform, and Philadelphia's African Americans and set against Anglo-Saxon prudence.

The first half of the book dramatizes the economic register of this argument. Edgar Saxon, a patrician dry goods merchant, stands apart from the unsound investments of Market Street. He converts his stock and his notes into gold or silver, appearing to his colleagues to fail in his business but actually protecting his estate against the impending crisis. Saxon discusses recent history with the banker Nicholas Biddle, who appears as a character in the novel. The dry goods merchant explains that he was on Biddle's side during the struggle with Jackson over the Bank of the United States, and he predicts a collapse of the financial system. Readers learn that Saxon is a Whig, and that his porter, Paddy Cork (who, like his employer, bears the name of his type), is a Democrat who supports Jackson's political heir, Martin Van Buren. Paddy will learn that the Democrats only seek to exploit him for their own gain. After a politician reprimands him for his involvement in the burning of Pennsylvania Hall because the event might cost the Democrats abolitionist swing votes in the free states, Paddy renounces all political attachments. When he does, Jones gestures toward the riots of 1844: "'How do I know,'" Paddy says, "'that the nixt trick of party will not be to raise the hue and cry against the Catholics and Irishmen?'" (144).

In the second half of *The City Merchant*, the racial plot dominates, as Jones retells the stories of the 1838 and 1842 riots, joining them in a narrative of political scheming, African offense, and Saxon backlash. The shift to the racial plot would seem to indicate that economic turmoil aggravates social tensions in the city. But by the end of the novel, cause and effect seem to be reversed, as the vigorous reimposition of hierarchy points to economic solvency and sectional reunion. With the riots, *The City Merchant* gains descriptive force. Economic disquisitions in placid interiors are replaced by graphic action and fervent rhetoric. The two plots ramify and then entwine.[61]

In Jones's telling, the riot of 1838 is the fault of northern politicians who connive to undermine the power of southern states by agitating for the end of slavery. They heighten sectional divisions and promote a false equality between whites and blacks. Almost without warning, the racial plot erupts in the middle of a chapter, when Saxon's nieces, Alice and Eda, are accosted by two mulatto men who offer the young ladies their arms and laugh at their refusal and discomfort. The young men are part of the social carnival and "unwonted jubilation" (128) that accompany the meeting of abolitionists. Echoing the public outrage at the specter of miscegenation that helped to generate the attack on Pennsylvania Hall, Jones's narrator observes: "And for several days great strapping negro fellows were seen promenading the streets in sociable attitudes and familiar converse with white women; while white men walked the pavements with sooty-faced African women hanging on their arms!" (130). Jones does not need to name "the Hall in Sixth Street" where the violence will occur, confident that after a dozen years his allusions will remain fresh in his readers' minds.

The narrator mentions that Lucretia Mott and Abby Kelley have delivered speeches at the convention, and for good measure, he adds George Thompson, the English abolitionist, who had lectured against slavery in the United States in 1834–35 and 1850 but who was not in Philadelphia in May 1838. The narrator describes, on Chestnut near the corner of Thirteenth, Frederick Douglass walking alongside Lucretia Mott, even though Douglass did not gain his prominence as a speaker until 1841. (He escaped from slavery in Maryland in 1838.) Here Jones probably invokes the recent scandal over Douglass's walking on Broadway in New York City with two white female friends in May 1849.[62] The references to Thompson and to Douglass are part of Jones's method of superimposing the present on the late 1830s and early 1840s to show continuity and to justify his racial politics. He changes the year from 1838 to 1836 so that the riot can be followed by—and in the logic of the narrative help to provoke—the election of the Democrat Martin Van Buren in late 1836 and the financial panic that began in 1837.

Jones is knowledgeable about the details and debates surrounding Pennsylvania Hall, which he incorporates in *The City Merchant.* He emphatically takes sides, repeating the charges that abolitionists goaded the violence though interracial displays and through their fanatical sentiments, which Jones repeatedly characterizes as "incendiary," as though the reformers themselves set fire to the hall. Embodying the public, the character Paddy defends the Saxon girls' honor, and he pummels the two men. He, in turn, is knocked to the ground by a blow and then avenged by other Irishmen. Irish and African Americans battle in the streets until the police arrive. Later that day, Paddy harangues passersby up and down Market Street about the social affront, and he secures the agreement of the captains of the fire companies to withhold their assistance. When that evening the "motley congregation" comes up to the hall "to chant incendiary verses and utter blasphemous prayers," objects are thrown at them, and they respond with taunts. A "stream of vociferous men" enters the hall and breaks up the furniture but harms no one. Furniture and tracts are placed in the center of the room and ignited. Seeing that the fire "did not burn in unison with his eager desires," one champion ruptures the gas pipes to fuel the blaze. (He is pictured in an engraving, a rare illustration of the inside of Pennsylvania Hall during the riot.) The fire companies arrive, go through the motions of preparing to control the fire, and take no action. The mayor and his posse attempt to detain the leaders of the mob, but the mayor is restrained and told, in the words of the 1838 police report that Jones endorses and that the compilers of *The History of Pennsylvania Hall* had condemned, that the building "was doomed to destruction" (138–41).

And then Jones offers the most eloquent passage in his novel:

> Thousands and tens of thousands were now assembled to witness the grand spectacle. And when the roof fell in, and an immense volume of flame ascended high up in the air, the whole canopy of heaven was so brilliantly illuminated that the stars faded away, as if the sun itself had burst from the center of the earth. The chimneys and timbers fell within the walls, as if there was some supernatural avenger co-operating with the mortals, and indicating that every vestige of the unholy edifice, and naught else, should be consumed. Not a breath of wind wafted a burning brand in the direction of other houses. The mighty shower of sparks ascended far up in the blue vault, and descended again to the place from which they emanated. (141)

In this counterhistory of Pennsylvania Hall, Jones presents holy sanction for the public will, illuminating the darkness. Jones's riot is focused and disciplined, almost an act of piety. The pillar of fire that arises from the "unholy edifice" and the fall of sparks reveal a concord between earth and heaven. The "doom" of the hall is now articulated as prophecy, a welcome fire next time. Here Jones may be reinterpreting the imagery in Pierpont's "Tocsin" and the poem that followed it, "The Pennsylvania Hall," which the managers had included in the appendix to their *History*. He describes the burning of the hall as a sign, not of divine wrath against the backsliding children of the Founders who had allowed slavery to flourish, but of divine approval at a return to the original commitment to racial subordination. In this aspect and others, Jones seems to be writing *The City Merchant* with a copy of the *History of Pennsylvania Hall* close at hand.

In his paragraph on the destruction of the hall (a singularly lyrical moment in *The City Merchant*), Jones looks back from the perspective of 1851 to the year 1838 as the harbinger of a decade of riot initiated by abolitionists and the African Americans they had emboldened. Through his historical fiction, Jones substantiates the ardor voiced by the correspondent from Augusta, quoted in the appendix of *The History of Pennsylvania Hall*: "The devouring element assumed an aspect which to me it had never worn before; it seemed to wear, combined with its terrible majesty, *beauty and delight*. To witness those beautiful spires of flame, gave undoubted assurance to the heart of the Southron, that in his brethren in the North *he has friends who appreciate him*, and who will defend him, though absent, at any, and at every hazard" (*History of Pennsylvania Hall*, 170). The citizens of Philadelphia will protect southern interests and promote sectional harmony. Riot punishes audacity. Jones's ekphrasis conjures the Augusta correspondent's "beautiful spires of flame" and also J. T. Bowen's colored lithograph "Destruction by Fire of Pennsylvania Hall," published shortly after the riot, with its haunting violence. Jones enlists the flames in Bowen's ambivalent image for the southern cause.[63]

Reanimating the violence of 1838 for debates in the 1850s, Jones also furnishes subplots that forge links between 1838 and 1842 to promote white solidarity and black exclusion. In Jones's 1838, the riot has its specific origin in the bellicosity of the two mulatto men who confront Alice and Eda Saxon on Chestnut Street. Paddy Cork comes to the women's defense, and he and his fellow countrymen, who call themselves the Avengers, burn Pennsylvania Hall. Jones thus turns the 1838 events, which took place in the northern part of the city and in which Irish residents did not play a conspicuous role, into a rehearsal for his version of the 1842 riots, when Irish and other working-class men attacked the Cedar neighborhood to the south. He also gestures toward 1849, when the Irish gang, the Killers, fomented disorder around the California House.

In *The City Merchant*, after the burning of the hall, Edgar Saxon and his family are apprehensive until they realize that Paddy and his Avengers were responsible. With this understanding, "they resigned themselves to sleep with feelings of assured security" (142). Jones's riots teach that "the free colored man" must submit to his unequal status in American society. If not, writes Jones, reversing the terms in Matthew 19.6, he will defy a consecrated racial alienation: "he will find both the Saxon and the Celt arrayed against him. What God has put asunder let no man attempt to join together" (195). At the end of the novel, Paddy remains a subordinate, but he has been conscripted as an ally against the forces of reform and African American progress.

Jones brings 1838 and 1842 together in time, as well as agency and target. He closes the distance between the two riots. After Jones's Pennsylvania Hall is burned, the Democrat Van Buren is elected president, and, as Saxon had expected, financial panic ensues. In the logic of the novel, these political and economic circumstances indicate that the violence in 1838 has not restored proper stability, and more extreme measures are warranted. The mulatto subplot is developed, as the narrator explains that the two men, John and Henry, are cousins of a woman named Olivia, passing for "white," who reveals to her son Billy that she had been a slave in Virginia. A proslavery wish fulfillment, Olivia preaches natural inferiority as God's will. She is against education for African Americans in the North, since her own experience of Philadelphia freedom has taught her that as her awareness increased, she became increasingly discontented. (Robert Montgomery Bird had made the same point in the Virginia sections of his *Sheppard Lee*, and Sarah Josepha Hale will repeat it in her 1853 novel, *Liberia*.) Billy becomes a spy for the Saxons. John and Henry are determined to avenge their chastisement, and they, along with hundreds of other African Americans in the southern part of the city, are planning to retaliate for the destruction of Pennsylvania Hall.

Olivia warns her son to seek refuge after they make their move, gesturing toward an impending racial catastrophe: "'They are hated by all the white laborers and menials in the city, and all of them will combine on some occasion to exterminate them. Yes, here, in the north, the time may come, perhaps must come, when the blood of enfranchised Africans will flow through the streets'" (164). Here, as in Lippard's *Quaker City*, Philadelphia is imagined as the scene of urban apocalypse, but now in racial terms: not divine justice against the elite on behalf of the impoverished, but the war of resident upon resident, an ordained struggle between white and black. The term "enfranchised" conveys the unresolved status of the "Africans." In the Philadelphia context, as Jones surely knew, it referred both to the emancipation granted in the 1780 Pennsylvania Act for the Gradual Abolition of Slavery (a state of quasi-freedom that his novel further circumscribes) and to the right of African American men to vote, nullified when the revised state constitution was adopted in 1838.

The resentful mulatto characters John and Henry kidnap the Saxon daughters, and the narrator describes a furious carriage ride crisscrossing from Walnut Street to Thirteenth, then Spruce, Twelfth, Pine, and St. Mary's (the scene of the 1849 riots), where they transfer to another vehicle, which takes them further south to Queen and Sixth streets. A medical student from Virginia succeeds in overpowering the girls' captors. (Southern medical students often appear in the city's antebellum literature, reflecting the prominence of its medical institutions and the presence of the South.) He barricades himself and the young women in a house on Queen Street. They come under attack by an African American mob, as Jones switches the racial positions. A rescue party is formed, consisting of Saxon, a group of Virginia medical students, and the police captain and his forces. They battle on the narrow streets with an increasing number of African Americans, who have been armed and incited by abolitionists under the influence of northern politicians. Paddy and his men arrive, and they liberate Alice and Eda.

Thousands of men continue to fight, and many are killed. Jones's narrator evokes the details of the 1842 and 1849 riots, as African American homes are entered, their occupants dislodged, furniture is smashed and thrown on the streets, and the buildings are set aflame. Fire companies arrive but are dissuaded. The leader of the working-class Avengers strikes an epic pose on the roof of the burning house in which Alice and Eda were held, and he bellows to the firemen to cease, in a scene that may be Jones's answer to Lippard's defiant Black Andy in *The Killers*. Women in their homes assail the "white portion of the rioters" with "every description of projectile from the windows, fluid, granite, and metallic" (192). The Avengers target such domestic loopholes and demolish or burn the structures.

In the morning, companies of militia arrive and are assailed by both sides. As the white combatants dominate, the authorities urge blacks to relinquish their homes and leave the area. The military lines the streets, forming a cordon for the refugees. In his rendering of the 1842 flight of African Americans from the Cedar neighborhood, Jones presents a vision of internal exile:

> For many hours, interminable columns of the motley fugitives defiled along the avenues running parallel with the river; and many thousands of them found refuge on the opposite side of the stream in New Jersey. Many of them were innocent of any participation in the outrages which caused the outburst of popular fury; but all partook of the danger, as an indiscriminate massacre was threatened; and they were urged to avert the catastrophe by a precipitate flight.
>
> It was a painful scene to witness the weeping women and children thronging the streets, flying from their homes with such articles of dress and other movables as they could bear on their backs, and one which will not be soon forgotten. (193–94)

Jones's narrator laments the suffering of black residents and acknowledges the disproportionate response of whites who rioted. While disproportionate, though, the severity is not represented as unwarranted. Led by the Avengers with the imprimatur of Edgar Saxon, the counterriot is viewed as a necessary rejoinder to African American impudence. The ultimate responsibility lies with those in the North who, speculating on the inferior character of African Americans, have encouraged their circulation in "freedom" and threatened national stability. Violent excess is the unfortunate but unavoidable result of such misguided investments. The narrator makes clear in the following chapter that the riot demonstrates that African

Americans, whether in slavery or freedom, must be kept "in subjection." Those who surrender, who are "industrious" and "faithful," will be accepted by the dominant society and protected from harm (195). But the narrator has a warning and a prognosis for "the worthless, the indolent, the impudent, and the dishonest among them, who cluster together in obscure streets and filthy alleys, against whom the prejudice existed, still exists, and must ever exist": "the time will come when legislative enactments will be invoked to drive them beyond our borders."

The narrator describes his regret that "a slave should escape from a kind master, to become a miserable object of charity here, a tenant of the Almshouse, or an inmate of the Penitentiary" (196). "Here" is the literary place that Jones has designed *The City Merchant* to elucidate: a Philadelphia whose social failures— degenerate neighborhoods, indigent residents, and audacious lawbreakers—are marked as conspicuously African American, signs of the ruinous experiment in freedom. "Here" there are no African American higher or middle classes or even a natally free population. The narrator imaginatively converts all African Americans into fugitives from slavery who endure a dismal liberty.

Jones's complex version of riot in Philadelphia is disturbing and informative. Although we might be tempted to dismiss *The City Merchant* for its twisting of fact according to prejudice, the novel confirms aspects in other accounts and also discloses features that some narratives understate or avoid. As had George Lippard and the editors of *The History of Pennsylvania Hall*, Jones depicts the strategic performances of violence, the reticence of authorities, the complicity of elites, the official blaming of the victims and partial acquittal of the instigators. Jones emphasizes what Lippard had overlooked in favor of his preference for a conspiracy against the white working class: that the riots of 1842 and 1849 were assaults on black property and community. He pushes the violence south, beyond the borders of Philadelphia proper, to quarantine the city, but he also shows that homes were targeted not to divert public notice from other misdeeds, as Lippard would have it in *The Killers*, but as an end in itself and part of a continuing effort at subjection. Jones registers the communal intensities of African American resistance, including the household items turned into projectiles by female occupants, a plot detail that Frank J. Webb also will employ in his rendition of the violence. Lippard, on the other hand, concentrates defiance in the solitary, histrionic figure of Black Andy.

Jones narrows the gap between the antiabolitionist riots in 1838 and the antiblack riots of 1842, and he frames both in terms of the Irish gang violence against African Americans in 1849. He turns the working-class Irish into Avengers and joins them with the elite Saxons, overstating solidarity across ethnic and class lines but anticipating how, as Noel Ignatiev would put it, the Irish "became white."[64] Given Jones's racial logic, it is not surprising that he elides the riots of

1844, when Protestants and Catholics took up arms against one another. Instead, he shows Saxons and Irish, Philadelphians and Virginians, uniting to rescue young Saxon women held captive in the southern districts. Such juggling distorts history but reveals ideology and also presses us to consider that "conspiracy," vivified in Lippard's and Jones's novels, may not be an inaccurate term to describe the experience (and maybe also the facts) of riot in Philadelphia in the 1830s and 1840s. Taken together, the different portrayals of Lippard and Jones convey patterns of riot that seem as distinctive as the city's venerable grid.

In the fantasy of *The City Merchant*, riot is the antidote to freedom. As Saxon recommends, during an exchange about slavery and abolition after the riots, "'we should devise the means of ridding ourselves of the curse of a pauper, nay, a profligate and dangerous free negro population in our midst'" (206–7). Freedom here is viewed as profligacy—extravagant, improvident, promiscuous, depraved— a "curse" that the novel substantiates and then banishes. The second riot in *The City Merchant* is, like the first, accompanied by financial panic, this one transatlantic, but at the end of the novel Jones's narrator points to a renewed stability following the harsh and necessary adjustments. While many of his peers lose their fortunes because of their misplaced confidence in the market, the judicious Mr. Saxon, who had foreseen the calamity and retained only hard currency, now is able to buy at vastly reduced prices, and he reaps huge profits and restored security in the aftermath of the riots.

In what appears to be a late, extraneous subplot, the narrator informs his readers that a certain Miss Lofts, the superannuated inhabitant of a mansion on Arch Street, tries a bit of social engineering, under the influence of abolitionists. She invites "a select party of colored gentlemen and ladies" into her house, but they cannot figure out how to behave, she finds them unpleasant, her white servant girls quit, her black servants refuse to wait on them, and she herself must cater to the guests. (This fleeting reference to an incongruous "select party" is the only glimpse of Joseph Willson's "higher classes of colored society" in the novel.) After the ordeal, Miss Lofts "came to the conclusion that it would be best to be a philanthropist only in theory" (223). Transformed by riot, the political speculations and social experiments that earlier in the novel were represented as imperiling civic and national order have been reduced to a Philadelphia absurdity.

The Condition of the Free People of Color

When John Beauchamp Jones has his character Edgar Saxon in *The City Merchant* adduce Philadelphia's southern districts, almshouses, penitentiary, and "the worthless, the indolent, the impudent, and the dishonest" (195) to prove the debacle of freedom, he is invoking years of reports that investigated the status of African Americans in Philadelphia. These studies, mentioned toward the end of the last chapter, examined poverty, mortality, and crime rates, property ownership, tax rolls, occupations, prisons, churches, and benevolent societies.

Among these documents were "The Present State and Condition of the Free People of Color" and "Trades of the Colored People," prepared by the Pennsylvania Abolition Society in 1838 and based on a census of African Americans in the city and surrounding districts taken in 1837; "On the Effects of Secluded and Gloomy Imprisonment on Individuals of the African Variety of Mankind, in the Production of Disease" (1843), written by Dr. Benjamin Coates; "A Statistical Inquiry into the Condition of the People of Colour" (1849), based on an 1847 census directed by the Society of Friends; "Ten Years' Progress: or A Comparison of the State and Condition of the Colored People in the City and County of Philadelphia from 1837 to 1847," prepared by a committee of the Pennsylvania Abolition Society, ascribed to one of its members, Edward Needles, and based on data from the two African American censuses; "The Mysteries and Miseries of Philadelphia" (1853), which combined reportage and sensationalism; and "Statistics of the Colored People of Philadelphia," drawn up by the Pennsylvania Abolition Society and based on a third census, this one focusing on education and jobs (1856; issued in a second edition in 1859, with a letter about prisons and crime). Over twenty years, three censuses scrutinized African Americans in Philadelphia. (The manuscript of the 1838 census alone takes up several volumes.) There were no comparable studies of other groups in the city, no reports with titles such as "The Present State and Condition of the Irish" or "The Present State and Condition of the English in Philadelphia."[65]

W. E. B. DuBois illustrated the condition of quandary at the start of his *The Souls of Black Folk* (1903), when he expressed the unasked question he felt posed to him by "the other world": "How does it feel to be a problem?" *Souls* appeared four years after DuBois issued his own professional inquiry, *The Philadelphia Negro: A Social Study* (1899), in which he relied on the three antebellum censuses and subsequent reports. DuBois's patrons, seeing African American indigence and crime as a threat to the city, had charged him with "ascertain[ing] every fact which will throw light on this social problem." In response, DuBois rearticulated that "problem," mixing statistics, ethnography, social history, maps, charts, and interviews to describe, in his words, "the Negro group as a symptom, not a cause; as a striving, palpitating group, and not an inert, sick body of crime; as a long historic development and not a transient occurrence." DuBois felt pressure to confirm what his sponsors believed was the inherent degradation of

Philadelphia's African American residents. Instead, he highlighted several factors to explain social distress, including the legacy of slavery, racial prejudice, and disadvantage in economic rivalry with European American immigrants. He recommended a program of moral reform and social action. *The Philadelphia Negro* tops off a century of regarding African Americans in the city as a "problem" to be diagnosed and treated.[66]

In the late 1840s and the 1850s, reports on both sides, those arguing for progress and those arguing for failure, treated Moyamensing Township—where in 1848, in the southwest part of the Cedar neighborhood, a third of the African Americans in Philadelphia County lived between South and Fitzwater streets from Fifth to Eighth—as the locus of poverty and vice. Whether the reports concluded that Moyamensing was representative or anomalous, they saw in it the depths of the city's social problems. Reports and fiction influenced one another. Both genres sought to expose Philadelphia's "mysteries." The novelists George Lippard, John Beauchamp Jones, and, as we shall see in the next chapter, Sarah Josepha Hale and Frank J. Webb all participated in the debate about the "condition of the free people of color." Although many of the fictional city mysteries produced in the wake of Lippard's *Quaker City* tend to be generic exposés, lacking his elaborate immersion, the stories told within and across the investigative reports disclose Philadelphia's specific histories of violence and reform.[67]

The dates of the first major studies—1838, 1843, 1849—are juxtaposed in uncanny counterpoint to the outbreaks of riot. The Pennsylvania Abolition Society report of 1838, which strove to demonstrate the character of free African Americans and thwart disfranchisement, was, as we have seen, followed by the burning of the abolitionist Pennsylvania Hall and the vote to restrict the state constitution. After the riots of 1842, which devastated the Cedar neighborhood, Benjamin Coates offered a thesis before the American Philosophical Society about the inordinate mortality of African Americans in the city, who were unsuited, he argued, in terms of habits and climate, for life in the North. The riots of 1849 disrupted the Society of Friends and Abolition Society's case for a decade of improvement. Reports and riots unfold in a tangled irony of earnestness, vehemence, achievement, overstatement, and denial.

The modern historian Theodore Hershberg has identified a gap between rhetoric and facts within the reports themselves. Analyzing the censuses in 1837, 1847, and 1856, Hershberg argues that, notwithstanding the progress asserted in 1849 and 1856, the data manifest a considerable socioeconomic decline. Comparing 1837 and 1847, Hershberg notes the persistence of extreme poverty; an increase in job discrimination, with the vast majority of men working as unskilled laborers and women as domestic servants (and a growing number of skilled artisans unable to practice their trades); a 10 percent decrease in per capita value of personal property; a small decline in per capita wealth; a reduced number of property holders; and intensifying residential segregation. Statistics, of course, do not convey a full or transparent picture. Stressing the resiliency of the Cedar neighborhood, Emma Jones Lapsansky cites evidence in the data that property ownership among African American residents of means increased between 1837 and 1847. Joseph Willson, the author of *Sketches of the Higher Classes of Colored Society in Philadelphia*, moved in the late 1840s from the northern suburb of Spring Garden to the Cedar neighborhood, buying a house in Moyamensing.[68]

Hershberg and, before him, W. E. B. DuBois remark on the hyperbole of those who evaluated the "condition" and "progress" of African Americans in Philadelphia. According to the two historians, the reporters, consciously or not, in their admirable campaign against slavery and defense of the city's black residents, obscured the social damage. They broadcast achievements, which were remarkable in context, but in doing so they also understated obstacles and limits. The reports on "the condition," like the minutes of the black national conventions, are intricate documents, whose arguments played a substantial role in the Philadelphia debates. The writers of the reports expressed the faith that "by comparing the present with past periods of their history, such information would enable all concerned in vindicating the character and rights of this oppressed people" ("Statistics of the Colored People," 3). This is a faith, earnest and by the mid-1840s outmoded, that would spur individuals and organizations to extraordinary activity, but it also was a faith embarrassed by history.[69]

The reports magnify the progress of a community under assault and also indicate a more complicated trajectory: a Philadelphia rhythm of advance shadowed by retreat. The reports on the "condition of the free people of color," along with the African American petitions directed to the state legislature to restore the franchise, eloquently rehearse statistics and appeals. The two genres sometimes converge: The 1856 Pennsylvania Abolition Society report ends by quoting facts about personal and real estate, beneficial societies, and a decrease in crime rates among African Americans that appeared in the 1855 "Memorial of Thirty Thousand Disfranchised Citizens of Philadelphia." Yet the reiterations and the violent counterpoints imply suspension rather than forward movement.

The riots of the 1840s are palpable in the 1849 Society of Friends's "Statistical Inquiry" and the Pennsylvania Abolition Society's "Ten Years' Progress." Toward the beginning of the "Statistical Inquiry," the reporters, who present their evidence with less skewing toward progress than those in the Abolition Society, assess the reasons for the sharp decline in the rate of population increase among blacks in Philadelphia and its adjoining districts between 1837 and 1847, while during the same period there was a significant rate of increase in the white population. This fact, which qualified the arguments for improvement, was featured in both documents from 1849. The Society of Friends reporters emphasize riot and joblessness: "the mobs of 1842, which drove away many of the people of colour; and the great increase of poor emigrants from Europe, who have supplanted them in employments, which a few years ago were altogether in their hands" (7).[70]

The riots of early August 1849 intervened between the writing of the "Statistical Inquiry" and the publication in November of "Ten Years' Progress." In an opening section, the writers of "Ten Years' Progress" incorporate the events. After noting the diminished population increase, they reproduce the passage about the 1842 attacks from the earlier "Statistical Inquiry," discuss poverty and overcrowding, and then interrupt their account. Stressing the moment of writing, they call out to African American readers:

> The foregoing paragraph was written at a time when, to all appearance, you were living in the quiet enjoyment of your peaceful homes—having, in great measure, recovered from the distress you had suffered by the mobs which the Friends speak of as having contributed to keep the colored population of our city from increasing in number, as might have been expected. And now we come to you again, to sympathize with you, to mingle our tears with yours, on account of the late terrible outbreaks of lawless violence to which many of you have been exposed. We are distressed on your behalf, and scarcely know how to address you on the subject. (5)

The riots fissure the space between paragraphs here. Their intrusion suggests a pattern (recovery followed by renewed assault) and also the intimacies between reform and disorder. Defending the success of African Americans in Philadelphia, the reporters inadvertently expose their vulnerability. The property and institutions heralded in the reports became the focus of indignation. "And now we come to you again": approaching iambic tetrameter, this line evokes the ritual of advocacy and condolence. We come to you again, in friendship, with sympathy, after another outbreak, bearing statistics and advice. "We . . . scarcely know how to address you on this subject": this moment of doubt is conspicuous in a genre that relentlessly extends the unhesitating counsel of patience and moderation.

The two 1849 documents share with each other and with Lippard's *The Killers* (1850) a portrait of "the infected district in Moyamensing" ("Statistical Inquiry," 39; "Ten Years' Progress," 14). The last quarter of the Society of Friends's "Statistical Inquiry" catalogues the straitened living conditions of some in the

economically and racially mixed neighborhood. The reporters decline to treat the
notorious area as a synecdoche for the condition of African Americans: "It is in
this district and in the adjoining portion of the City, especially Mary street and
its vicinity, that the great destitution and wretchedness exist, which have been
supposed by some, to be prevalent among the greater part of the colored population of Philadelphia" (33). Instead of elevating the district to representative
status, the Friends seek to cordon it off. They excerpt a letter written by the
coroner, Napoleon B. Leidy, outlining in relatively dispassionate terms the mortality and unhealthy living conditions of the black poor, and then insert a lurid,
anonymous narrative of a visit to the area. Statistics segue into coroner's report
and then gothic tour, with more than a touch of Lippard's *Quaker City*. Insisting
on the respectability of the great number of African Americans, the committee
establishes borders determined by class rather than race: "The degradation and
wretchedness which mark the infected district in Moyamensing, are foreign to the
real character of our coloured population, to whom it would be doing a gross
injustice, not to point out clearly the broad line of separation"
(39; quoted in "Ten Years' Progress," 14).

The movement from statistics to gothicism, the distinguishing of borders, and
the effort at quarantine in the Society of Friends report recapitulate the ways in
which Philadelphia came to fictional life in the late 1830s and 1840s. This development occurred in a range of overlapping genres, including documentary histories, sensational and historical novels, and analyses of the "condition of the free
people of color." These genres were marked, and many of the texts were preoccupied, by the riots. An 1853 pamphlet offers a striking example of how reports
and fiction coalesced. "The Mysteries and Miseries of Philadelphia, as Exhibited
and Illustrated by a Late Presentment of the Grand Jury, and by a Sketch of the
Condition of the Most Degraded Classes in the City" bears the title of the fictional genre that Lippard inherited from Eugène Sue and shared with G. M. W.
Reynolds. It begins with a grand jury report of a visit to Moyamensing, then
reprints a journalistic tour through the neighborhood, which is indebted to the
city mysteries, and finishes with statistics about increasing rates of crime and
imprisonment. In subjecting Philadelphia to "graphic description" (2), the
unnamed editor of the pamphlet conflates genres, bringing together various
forms of urban exposure.[71]

Recounting their trip to residences in Baker and Strafford streets, the members
of the grand jury describe unfurnished apartments that resemble dark cells, into
which people of both sexes and all ages, "the most depraved class of our population," are crowded (6). They recommend that strong action be taken to eliminate
these "dens of misery," including the establishment of a house of correction that

would offer discipline and labor (7). The editor then includes an article from the Philadelphia *Evening Bulletin*, written by a reporter named Casper Souder Jr. After reading the grand jury findings in their initial printing, Souder had determined to visit this part of the Cedar neighborhood and inform his readers about "the real condition of the 'infected district'" (11). Obtaining a guide and a guard, Souder inspected the streets. In his exposé, "The Mysteries and Miseries of Philadelphia," which gives the pamphlet its title, he begins by invoking his readers' familiarity with the "graphic descriptions" and "dens of misery" (jury report and gothic tour share the phrases) in Sue's Paris, Dickens's London, and New York's infamous Five Points district (12). Souder will introduce his readers to similar areas in Philadelphia.

He explains that he is describing not just a Baker Street or a Small Street, about whose wretchedness readers may have heard, but an entire neighborhood adjoining and blighting the "city proper": "It occupies an area of many acres, and comprises in its bounds many streets, scores of alleys, and courts almost without number" (13). He names various pathways that deviate from the original grid and conjures the threat they pose: "the district is a cancerous sore, and its roots permeate adjacent comparatively healthy portions of the city, threaten to infect and poison other parts, and spread still wider the foul blot" (13). The sense of threat that pervades Souder's "Mysteries" is a response to social decline in the 1840s and also a product of the riots: a view of the neighborhood as an economic and racial affront that demands severe measures. He treats the neighborhood as a contaminated zone of grog and junk shops, barrooms, hovels, morbid racial and sexual intimacies, and appalling scenes. As a range of contemporary observers attested, poverty and crime were evident in some parts of southern Philadelphia and northern Moyamensing, but Souder transforms the entire neighborhood into an emblem of social collapse. Distinctions are nowhere to be seen.

Souder does provide glimpses of interest, but mostly he presents his characters and scenes as interchangeable with one another and with sensationalist codes. At one point, introducing the Irish proprietor of a grog shop, he invites his readers to "Imagine the filthiest, ugliest, and most uncouth of hunchbacks; fancy a sinister, villainous expression of countenance, with an eye in which cunning, avarice, sensuality, and cruelty are indicated" (15)—to imagine, in other words, a character like George Lippard's Devil-Bug.

Souder's "Mysteries and Miseries of Philadelphia" returns us to Lippard's urban gothic but without his proliferating contexts, suspended figures, or encyclopedic indictments. Souder's exposures are given in the discourse of contagion and defense, as he warns of outbreak. The joining of grand jury "Presentment" and gothic "Mysteries" reminds us of the claims of urban fiction to uncover the truth behind and beneath surfaces and of the often generic qualities of its revelations. It also suggests the mixture of reportage, verdict, caricature, and fiction in the literary debates about "freedom" in Philadelphia in the 1850s, to which we turn in the next chapter.

CHAPTER FOUR

Freedom

On the whole, it was an American supper, got up regardless of
expense—and whoever has been to such an entertainment knows
very well what an American supper is.
—Frank J. Webb, *The Garies and Their Friends* (1857)

"The coloured man . . . in Pennsylvania . . . has always been viewed as a *quasi* freeman only—deriving his imperfect freedom from the will of the white community,
and enjoying it under their government rather by *toleration* than *right*," wrote the
lawyer John F. Denny in 1834, four years before the state constitutional convention and the citizens of Pennsylvania denied the right of African American men
to vote. Denny cited some of the imperfections of freedom, asserting that blacks
were restricted to menial jobs and were not permitted to hold public office or to
vote except for the "generous" customs in some parts of the state. They did not
have "the capacity to attain" "the qualifications that bestow that valuable property of the citizen." They did not possess "'a sufficient evident common interest
with and attachment to the community.'" (Here Denny is quoting the 1776
Pennsylvania "Frame of Government.") Nor could they form such an attachment,
when "the reward which it meets is nothing but social and civil degradation."[1]

As if in answer to Denny, and to decades of contention about race, status,
capacity, and interest, Frank J. Webb published in 1857 *The Garies and Their Friends,*

a complex work of historical imagination, whose action begins in the late 1830s and ends in the mid-1850s. A novel of strenuous civility, graphic violence, and peculiar humor, combining William Whipper, Joseph Willson, George Lippard, Harriet Beecher Stowe, and Martin Delany, *The Garies and Their Friends* redraws the debate about "condition" versus "complexion." Webb tells the story of the Philadelphia experiment from the perspective of the mid-1850s, when circumstances had deteriorated even further for African Americans. His narrator both endorses and mourns his protagonists' conduct. Webb interprets the social texture of antebellum Philadelphia and, by implication, the United States: the imperative to prove character, the edge of violence that defines behavior, the achievements of "quasi freedom." This chapter focuses on Webb's subtle and fierce literary history, the consummate Philadelphia story, but first considers what "Philadelphia" meant in the 1850s to writers who reflected on the city.

The Struggle over "Philadelphia": Mary Howard Schoolcraft, Sarah Josepha Hale, Martin Robison Delany, William Whipper, and James McCune Smith

"Philadelphia," for Mary Howard Schoolcraft, the South Carolina native who defended slavery and the Fugitive Slave Act of 1850, is the location where one searches for evidence of racial equality and answers to questions about whether fugitive slaves and African Americans under freedom can "become respectable, dignified, and wealthy ladies and gentlemen." In her pamphlet "Letters on the Condition of the African Race in the United States," published in 1852 and nominally addressed to her brother during her stay in Washington, D.C., Schoolcraft represents Philadelphia as an unmitigated social failure. She assures her readers that most northerners reject abolition and share ideas about black inferiority. With individual dispatches between September and November 1851 and a publication date of 1852, Schoolcraft's "Letters" may have been written partly in response to Stowe's *Uncle Tom's Cabin,* whose installments began appearing in the *National Era* in June 1851 and came out as a book in March 1852. Instead of humanity under assault in Kentucky and New Orleans, Schoolcraft portrays degraded hopes in the symbolic city of Declaration and Constitution.[2]

Employing the language of the urban sensationalists, Schoolcraft announces that she will "hold up the curtain of misery" and reveal the corruption hidden from polite observers. Unlike the journalistic reports of Lippard and Foster, these mysteries of the city are delivered secondhand. In her fourth and final letter, devoted to Philadelphia, Schoolcraft explains that she had hoped to see for herself the consequences of an abolitionist fanaticism that sought "to inveigle the colored people from their happy home, in the warm sunny South, to come to the North to gain suicidal freedom," but her husband (the ethnologist Henry Rowe Schoolcraft) prevented her from visiting the poorest districts. Instead, she gives her readers access through statistics and descriptions culled from the urban reports of the 1840s. Schoolcraft quotes from Benjamin Coates, who had concluded in an 1843 study that the disproportionately high black mortality rates in the Eastern State Penitentiary resulted from "intellectual and moral weakness and decay," and she includes long excerpts from the gothic tour of the infamous courts and alleys of Moyamensing at the end of the 1849 "Statistical Inquiry into the Condition of the Free People of Colour."[3]

Yet Schoolcraft misrepresents the latter source. The 1849 "Statistical Inquiry," conducted under the direction of the Society of Friends, had supported Philadelphia's black community. Its writers hoped to confirm social and economic progress and show the unreasonableness, if tenacity, of white prejudice. Emphasizing that the conditions in Moyamensing were shared by both races, the reporters classed the majority of African Americans with respectable members of society. Schoolcraft excerpts only the horrors of Moyamensing and recounts stories she has heard of intemperance, pestilence, and overcrowding. She erases distinctions that the "Statistical Inquiry" had hoped to establish. Schoolcraft does impart an economic distress that the statistical reporters, in their advocacy, tended to understate. Yet hers is a skewed record. Reviewing the information compiled by gentlemen in Philadelphia, "designed to give the most flattering accounts" of free black progress in the North, she discovers, instead, "the hopeless desolation" that advanced her cause. For Schoolcraft, Philadelphia is a social laboratory that offers exploited African Americans the opportunity for self-destruction, a "suicidal freedom."[4]

For Sarah Josepha Hale, editor, novelist, women's historian, and longtime resident, Philadelphia is a critical station in the quest to determine the proper future for emancipated African Americans. That quest is figured in the subtitle of her *Liberia; or, Mr. Peyton's Experiments* (1853). The plot follows a sequence of trials, arranged by Charles Peyton, a Virginia owner grateful to his slaves for their fidelity during social upheaval. Peyton decides to set an example for other slaveholders and demonstrate that African Americans can flourish beyond the plantation. With the advice of his wife, he tests a series of alternatives for his slaves in freedom: a farm in Virginia, the northern city of Philadelphia, a settlement in Canada, and finally (with success) the African colony of Liberia. On the title page, Hale is listed as editor of the volume, a designation pointing to the mix of fiction, document, and polemic, and to the ways in which early Philadelphia novels are often tied to politics. The book ends with a sixty-page appendix in support of the African colony, including reprinted letters from white colonizationists and black emigrants, the Liberian Declaration of Independence, the first article of its Constitution, and addresses given by its president. Responding more explicitly to Stowe's *Uncle Tom's Cabin* than had Schoolcraft in her "Letters," Hale in *Liberia* makes an unambiguous case for benevolent paternalism. She diagnoses northern racism as irredeemable and endorses the remedy of African colonization, one of the alternatives t o which Stowe had gestured at the end of her novel.[5]

Mr. Peyton's experiments turn out as one might expect, under the pen of a southern sympathizer. On the Virginia farm, on their own, African Americans decline. Balked by the specter of white superiority, indolent and improvident, they are unable to take care of themselves. In Philadelphia, the harsh climate and northern racism intensify their suffering and endanger their lives. In Canada, they encounter an unfamiliar terrain and people, hard labor, and continuing prejudice. The chapters point north, outlining a trajectory of frustration, until the move across the Atlantic to Liberia, where at last thwarted African potential can be expressed. If the results of Hale's experiments are unsurprising, her analyses of agency and limit and her mix of bias, reform, and social critique retain, as Susan M. Ryan puts it, "the capacity to embarrass modern readers." Like many Philadelphia texts, Hale's novel unsettles our judgments of race and class. In *Liberia*, Hale exonerates the southern system, but she also provides one of the most unsparing and precise accounts of northern racism to be found in pre–Civil War U.S. literature, spotlighting the City of Brotherly Love.[6]

Early in the Philadelphia chapter of her book, when she reintroduces Clara, a former slave of Peyton's who has relocated to the city, Hale shows the persistent appeal of the images in Edward Clay's "Life in Philadelphia." Peyton reluctantly has allowed Clara, her brother Americus, her husband Ben, and their daughter Madge to settle in Philadelphia, worried about the effect of urban temptations on their susceptible natures. Virginia Peyton, strolling on fashionable Chestnut Street with her husband, admires an elegantly attired lady walking in front of them and remarks: "just notice in what perfect keeping every part of her dress is; that light, stone-colored silk, and white crape shawl, and tasteful white bonnet. I think I shall take her for my model." When Clara turns around, Hale gives a spin to Clay's jokes. The Peytons are "astonished," as Hale carefully selects her adjective, indicating surprise, amazement, and perplexity. But the scene is not played for easy laughs. Before chapter's end, the reader will be shown that there is a lack of fit between Clara and her aspirations in Philadelphia, but when she turns on Chestnut Street, there is no burlesque of the incongruity between her attire and visage or staging of the Peytons' recoil. Instead, Hale seems interested in both Clara's status and the divergent responses of Charles and Virginia.[7]

Hale's Clara is a more restrained figure than the woman in Clay's "silk stockings" print (discussed in chapter 2), and this difference signals a complicated sympathy in her Philadelphia chapter. A few pages after the Chestnut Street encounter, Hale stages a debate between the Peytons about the decorum and usefulness of Philomathean Society meetings in the city, at which African Americans discuss topics ranging from poetry to affairs of state. When Hale writes that Virginia Peyton "hardly knew whether to laugh or be indignant at the absurdity of the whole affair," she seems to evoke the spectrum of responses to Clay's images, but she also portrays Charles as respecting the desire for intellectual improvement and the expressiveness of style and fashion (83). When Virginia visits Clara at her home on South Street in the Cedar neighborhood, she is impressed by the "exquisite order" and cleanliness (81). In the parlor, Hale's narrator describes the carpet, furniture, and ornaments, especially the framed engraving of a preacher named Mr. Wiley, "a solemn-looking colored clergyman, in a white cravat and spectacles, with one hand resting on the Bible, and the other grasping a manuscript sermon" (80). Such rooms and their presiding deities will be featured in Webb's *The Garies and Their Friends*, as they were in Stowe's *Uncle Tom's Cabin*. Here, in Hale's portrait, sobriety and piety function as a check on extravagance and offer the possibility of limited success in the urban North.

In revealing moments, Hale combines her interests in fashion and deportment with her appraisal of racial conduct in Philadelphia. (By the time she published *Liberia*, she had been the editor of *Godey's Lady's Book* for sixteen years and also was the author of prominent housekeeping and etiquette manuals.) Hale represents an excess in Ben's gestures and in the bearing of Clara's friend Amanda Fitzwater, whose sources and consequences Webb will explore in his novel. When the Peytons admire Clara as she walks in front of them before she turns around, Ben, working as a coachman for a gentleman in Walnut Street, drives by in the box of a carriage and smiles at her acknowledgment. Seeing his old master and mistress, Ben's response is to "take off his hat with a peculiar flourish, meant to express a great deal, and to give Clara a significant look as he drove by" (77). Hale's diction ("peculiar," "a great deal," "significant") indicates, but does not specify, the abundant content of these gestures and the ambiguities expressed in this charged field. (As we have seen and will see again, the word "peculiar" has its own strange life in the antebellum literature of Philadelphia.) Hale stresses that, in Philadelphia, not only Charles and Virginia Peyton but also Clara and Ben react in complex ways to the realignments of class and race and to each other. The Peytons are disoriented but not entirely dismissive. Clara and

Ben are pleased with their new opportunities and anxious for the imprimatur of their former masters but uncomfortable at being evaluated. Linked by their pasts, the four characters are bound in a web of scrutiny, expectation, and judgment. Hale gives prominence to her African American characters but recognizes the shared, unstable ground of assumptions over which both black and whites characters move.

When Amanda Fitzwater steps into Clara's parlor, Hale extends her social analysis: "and a little black woman, round, plump, and consequential, with her chin thrown up in the air by the exertion of maintaining a proper dignity of deportment, entered with a roll of music in her hand" (81–82). The energy needed to maintain a stance and to move through space is figured here in Amanda Fitzwater's extended chin. Keeping her chin up requires a practiced effort, underlined by her theatrical, even musical, entrance. Amanda is "consequential" because she may have an inordinate regard for herself, and Hale has some predictable fun at her expense, but she also is "consequential" because her movements register Hale's appreciation of what Saidiya Hartman has called the "burdened individuality" of African Americans under freedom: liberated but encumbered, laboring under a double bind of emancipation and subordination. Hale does not dwell on inappropriate posturing; instead, she analyzes her characters' responses to the forces that press upon their bearing.[8]

Hale's narrator delivers an unsparing portrayal of intolerance in the North. She describes a tyranny of law and custom: "even when in outward forms justice was done to them, the spirit with which its enactments was [*sic*] carried out was often so oppressive, that they derived but little satisfaction from its decrees" (86). The relative idyll of the opening scenes in the Philadelphia chapter is followed by turmoil. Readers are told of a shoemaker who long ago had been attacked and blinded in his home by neighbors who had become enraged by his success. After an "anti-slavery fair" is held in Philadelphia, tensions rise (87). When Clara's brother Americus reluctantly escorts home a white woman who had been spending the evening with his employer's family, he fears for his safety. As they head toward the southern parts of the city, he is attacked by a crowd of volunteer firemen, who target him for his public intimacy and also his finery: "there was not an article of his apparel, from his carefully tied cravat down to his brightly polished boots, that did not cost him several severe bruises from the jealous mob" (91). Americus pays a price in blows for each item in his array. With this formulation, Hale suggests a continuity between the satires of African American public display and the vehemence of rioters who treated aspiration as offense. At the same time that disturbances erupted around the "anti-slavery fair," the narrator reports, "an old feud between the lowest class of laborers and the colored race had broken out afresh in the suburbs of the city . . . in which the blacks were almost invariably the sufferers rather than the aggressors" (87). Americus learns that an acquaintance of his has been fatally beaten by "a whole gang of Killers and Bouncers" in Moyamensing (92). The scapegoating of the North is too easily achieved here, tied to Hale's vindication of the South, but she potently invokes details of the riots of the 1830s and 1840s.

Like Jones in his earlier *The City Merchant* and Webb in his later *The Garies and Their Friends*, Hale strategically manipulates her history. The rebellion that threatened the Peytons in Virginia at the start of the narrative might refer to Gabriel Prosser's plan in 1800 to invade Richmond, seize the armory, and distribute weapons among the slaves, which was cut short by informers, or to Nat Turner's 1830 assault on his master's family and other whites, which spread panic throughout the South. The "anti-slavery fair" and targeting of interracial mixture evoke the opening of Pennsylvania Hall in 1838 and the attack on the California House in 1849, and the violence in the suburbs recalls the riots of 1834, 1842, and 1849. Yet, seeking to present Liberia as the providential answer to the failed experiments, Hale shows Charles Peyton devising his plan for African colonization after the events in Philadelphia and Canada, when he visits Washington, D.C., during December 1816. This location and date mark the establishment of the American Colonization Society, which began to promote Liberia as a colony in 1822. The Liberian nation was declared in 1847. In Hale's novelistic time, the experience of Philadelphia in the 1830s and 1840s leads inevitably to the founding of Liberia in the 1820s.

Hale's African American characters are punished for their ambitions. The responsibility is partly theirs (extravagance and folly) and partly the city's. She provides the by-now requisite scene of literary discovery in the festering alleys of Moyamensing. Two young ladies, on a tour of the area led by a ragged girl who turns out to be Clara and Ben's daughter Madge, encounter in a cellar the ruined parents and their dead newborn. As Hale represents it, the decline of Clara and Ben results mainly from an unyielding prejudice. Ben is exhorted by the missionary Mr. Lyndsay to buck up: "'No person who does their duty . . . is ever despised, no matter what his color may be,'" he insists, venturing advice that is belied by the events of the chapter in which he appears. Ben responds: "'But people for the most part don't stop to ask if I do my duty. They see that I ain't a white man, and push me out of the way'" (110–11). In Hale's riposte to the social prospects sketched by Joseph Willson, she has Ben tell of an African American elite in Philadelphia (alluded to but never represented in the novel), for whom elevation has bred isolation. Money will not buy intimacy with whites, and it separates them from the majority of blacks. Hale's Philadelphia teaches that racism places severe limits on black progress, thwarting and distorting achievement. Only in Africa, toward the end of the book, does Ben feel "'like a man'" (224).

Hale's conclusion is not all that different from the one reached by Martin Robison Delany in his *The Condition, Elevation, Emigration, and Destiny of the Colored People of the United States* (1852), published in the year between Schoolcraft's "Letters" and Hale's *Liberia*. Delany argues for voluntary black emigration to Central and South America and the West Indies, rejecting Liberia as an artifact of the slave power, manufactured by the American Colonization Society. He shares Hale's belief that freedom in the North is impossible to achieve. Of course, Delany furnishes a different access to life in Philadelphia. Like Joseph Willson, he explains in his preface that he has written his book to counter false impressions and offer a black perspective: "The colored people are not yet known, even to their most professed friends among the white Americans; for the reason, that politicians, religionists, colonizationists, and abolitionists, have each and all, at different times, presumed to *think* for, dictate to, and *know* better what suited colored people, than they knew for themselves."[9]

Delany writes that African Americans occupy a "peculiar position" in the United States (42). Like other politically degraded classes in other countries, they form a nation within a nation. The pivot in his argument for emigration is his reprinting of the 1850 Fugitive Slave Act, which strengthened the provisions of the congressional law of 1793 (161–69). The 1850 act denied the accused a jury trial and the right to testify in self-defense, punished citizens who did not uphold the law, and provided bounties to federal officers who issued arrest warrants. Delany verges on equating freedom and slavery for African Americans in the United States. Both "freemen" and "bondmen" are prohibited from voting or holding office; both are denied civil, religious, and social rights, except those granted them by sufferance of their masters; both exist "as mere nonentities among the citizens, and excrescences on the body politic." The only difference is that free men are "defacto masters of ourselves and joint rulers of our own domestic household" (44–45). Even that difference erodes over the course of Delany's *Condition*. Evaluating U.S. society in the 1850s, he insists (possibly with the riots of the 1840s in mind) that the "fundamental right" articulated by Chief Justice Gibson of Pennsylvania—"Every man's house is his castle, and he has the right to defend it unto the taking of life"—was not intended for African Americans (172). (This right, including the transformation of home into fortress, will dominate Webb's portrayal of African Americans under siege in *The Garies and Their Friends*.) "We are slaves in the midst of freedom," Delany asserts. The 1850 Act epitomizes for him the vulnerability of Africans in America, as he adds (with strategic overstatement): "The slave is more secure than we; he knows who holds the heel upon his bosom—we know not the wretch who may grasp us by the throat" (170–71). Debasement, insecurity, and pervasive threat all impel black emigration.

Delany engages the debate about "condition" versus "complexion," prominent since the national conventions of the 1830s. He alludes to those meetings early in his book, when he pays tribute to the efforts of black leaders in Philadelphia, with some distance from his nostalgia: "Twenty years ago, when the writer was a youth, his young and yet uncultivated mind was aroused, and his tender heart made to leap with anxiety in anticipation of the promises then held out by the prime movers in the cause of our elevation" (45). Now, in the 1850s, from the vantage of a more cynical present, his mind cultivated by the experiences of disfranchisement, riot, and the Fugitive Slave Act, Delany judges the unfulfilled promises of "elevation" and argues for the need to recognize the plight of Africans in the United States, who are "aliens to the laws and political privileges of the country" (173). Racism has made their "condition" intolerable within its borders.

At the core of his book, Delany honors black enterprise, despite systemic hostility. He records military, economic, literary, and professional success, belying the claims of those such as John Denny who insisted that blacks could not be citizens because of their incapacities and their lack of "'sufficient evident common interest with and attachment to the community.'" Over almost a hundred pages, Delany brandishes those attachments. At the beginning of his catalogue of accomplishment, he puns on the terms "interest" and "investment": "The legitimate requirement, politically considered, necessary to the justifiable claims for protection and full enjoyment of all the rights and privileges of an unqualified freeman, in all democratic countries is, that each person so endowed, shall have made contributions and investments in the country. Where there is no investment there can be but little interest" (75). African Americans should share in the profits of citizenship because of their financial, civic, and patriotic investments. Such expenditures should accrue public interest, binding them to the larger community and validating their rights.

Delany's catalogue hinges on the Philadelphian entrepreneurs: the sail manufacturer James Forten, the financier Joseph Cassey, the lumber and coal merchants and real estate speculators William Whipper and Stephen Smith, the famed restaurateur Henry Minton, whose tables were "continually laden with the most choice offerings to epicures" and who presided over a "shrine of bountifulness" (119–20). Yet the inventory is followed by chapters on disfranchisement and the Fugitive Slave Act and then several chapters advocating resettlement. In the structural and historical logic of Delany's book, incorporated in his title, African Americans responded to their degraded "condition" by serving colony and nation and participating in all aspects of the developing society. They redundantly substantiated their character. This "elevation" produced not acceptance but intensifying bias and constraint. The only hope for advancement lies outside the country. Such "emigration" is the "destiny" proposed by Delany. For him, Philadelphia epitomizes this narrative of assurance, enterprise, betrayal, and retreat. The book that began as Delany's effort to "make each [race] acquainted" (38) with the other turns into a farewell.[10]

Across his chapters, Delany alters the meaning of the term "condition." Near the start, arguing for the importance of professional knowledge, Delany advises, "What is necessary to be done, in order to attain an equality, is to change the condition, and the person is at once changed" (70). He urges discipline, a commitment to education, literary atta inments, and practical efforts in business. If African Americans extend their investments in the country, they will suture their interests with those of its people and will be entrusted with the privileges of citizens. Even at this stage in his narrative, though, echoing the tempered hopes of the black national conventions and the American Moral Reform Society, Delany represents a "condition" not swiftly mutable or simply responsive to self-making, but wrought in: "The degradation of the slave parent has been entailed upon the child, induced by the subtle policy of the oppressor, in regular succession handed down from father to son—a system of regular submission and servitude, menialism and dependence, until it has become almost a physiological function of our system, an actual condition of our nature" (72). Here Delany revises the legal formula that in slavery *partus sequitur ventrem*: "the condition of the child follows the condition of the mother." He describes servitude as practically a biological inheritance and a danger to manhood. The condition of African Americans threatens to be inextricable from the subordination inflicted because of their complexion. When Delany dwells in his last chapter on the need for African Americans to avoid menial labor, exhorting his readers as had Whipper and the other moral reformers in Philadelphia, such a stance not only reflects class alignments but also bolsters a polemic against reinforcing the state of dependence.

While the 1838 disfranchisement altered Whipper's views, the 1850 Fugitive Slave Act recast Delany's call for "elevation," as he represents it in *The Condition*. Whipper pictured a mordant struggle with conduct as a tactic in the courtroom of public opinion and a weapon on the social battlefield. Delany invokes the tropes of Exodus. He dismisses the rivalry between African American leaders in New York and Philadelphia, when he likens the debate between "two respectable colored ladies" over which metropolis was superior to a contest between slaves over whose master is the finest gentleman (199). By the end of his book, history, psychology, physiology, law, and prejudice all combine to make freedom untenable for Africans in the United States. Their "condition" describes a status and also, in the title pun that Delany extends across the volume, a constitutional and Constitutional disability. Quoting "the talented Mr. Whipper," Delany asserts that "our children . . . 'cannot be raised in this country, without being stoop shouldered'" (220). Delany's concluding acknowledgment of Whipper, in which he pivots "elevation" and impediment, suggests that the perspectives of the "assimilationist" and the "nationalist" may not have been as antagonistic as they seem to modern observers.

At the end of his book, Delany argues for progress through independent labor, self-discipline, and education, but he insists that it must take place on a different foundation: not in Philadelphia, where achievement is met with disfranchisement; not in Liberia, under the thrall of the American Colonization Society and the slave power; not in Canada, whose people share a European heritage with the United States and will be influenced by their repressive goals—but in Central and South America and the West Indies, where there exist large colored populations and a diminished risk of American influence. The "condition" that must be "changed" is the residence of blacks in the United States (70). According to Delany, they do not need better jobs or more temperance societies. They need a new country: "We love our country, dearly love her, but she don't love us—she despises us, and bids us begone, driving us from her embraces" (216). From a distance, through the force of their example, the settlers can exert pressure on the system of racial slavery in the United States, "as the redemption of the bondman depends entirely upon the elevation of the freeman" (218). Delany understates the agency of the former and overstates the impact of the latter, but this flourish caps his effort across the book to explain the reciprocities of slavery and freedom.

While Delany recorded his frustration and advised departure, William Whipper expressed despair. In 1854, he published a letter in *Frederick Douglass' Paper*, admitting his weariness with the continuing debate about whether "condition" or "complexion" was at the root of white intolerance. Whipper argued that prejudice did not originate in the slave states (as William Wells Brown maintained, supporting the argument for "condition"), nor did it arise from caste differences (as the Rev. Beriah Green held). Instead, Whipper points to a historical record of color prejudice with "its foundation in human selfishness, pride and ambition." He concludes that "this prejudice is of very ancient birth, that it has pursued different nationalities down the long catalogue of ages, that it is older than American slavery and that the latter derived its existence from an organic action of the former."[11] This sense that prejudice has a relentless history and agency, that African Americans are subject to forces beyond southern authority and the federal government, fuels his pessimism in a remarkable exchange with the

New York doctor and essayist James McCune Smith, which appeared in *Frederick Douglass' Paper* between the spring of 1858 and the winter of 1859.

McCune Smith had published a column in April 1858, in which, like so many other African American writers, he confronted the events of the 1850s: the Fugitive Slave Act, efforts to bar African Americans from western territories in the Free Soil movement and to extend slavery in the battles over popular sovereignty in Kansas and Nebraska, and the 1857 Supreme Court decision in *Dred Scott v. Sandford*, which declared that African Americans, slave or free, could not become citizens or sue in federal court, maintaining that they "had no rights which the white man was bound to respect." McCune Smith reflected on present, past, and future. Quoting Coleridge's "Rime of the Ancient Mariner"—"Alone, alone, all alone"—he tried to find the proper term to describe his strange detachment from current events. Is it "apathy," he wonders? No, the feeling is keener: a "despair." He contrasts this state with the "holy expectation" and "beatific joy" that African Americans had experienced a quarter of a century earlier, when antislavery efforts had been reinvigorated under the influence of William Lloyd Garrison and the prospect of interracial "brotherhood" had seemed conceivable. Now, in the late 1850s, with intolerance and slavery ascendant and progress arrested, blacks alone must work to compel the recognition of shared humanity. They must not confuse despair at the failure of whites to accomplish the work of reform with despair that reform is not possible. McCune Smith evokes African American isolation and then urges his readers to understand it as an inevitable phase. As those in slavery continue to resist their bondage and influence the national debate, his readers in the North must work for social change.[12]

In Pennsylvania, Whipper seems to have found the opening paragraphs of McCune Smith's essay particularly resonant. He answered in a letter that appeared in the June 4, 1858, issue. Joining McCune Smith's terms, doubling the effects of insensibility and hopelessness, Whipper cites Macauley's *History of England* and describes himself, like the condemned Monmouth, like the other "'free blacks' of Pennsylvania," as having "imbibed the 'apathy of despair.'" Whipper reviews the decline for African Americans in Pennsylvania since the 1830s. They have moved from an undefined civil status favorable to their development and a patriotic attachment to a state with an illustrious antislavery history, through the Pennsylvania court cases of the 1830s, the referendum that led to disfranchisement in 1838, and the national ostracism in *Dred Scott v. Sandford*, to their present circumstances, in which "faith in the future ought to be considered an illusion."

Whipper reconsiders his own faith in moral reform before 1838, invoking, after more than twenty years, the stinging words of Samuel Cornish. In the New York *Colored American* in 1837, Cornish, as we have seen in chapter 2, had described the Philadelphia leaders as "visionary in the extreme." He had added that they were "not sufficiently self-sacrificing to merit [the] appellation" "fanatical." In 1858, Whipper writes: "If I were at this moment hopeful with regard to the future condition of our people, under all the surrounding circumstances, opinions, and practices of the rulers in the National and State governments, I would not find fault with others for regarding me as visionary and fanatical." (He misremembers the label of "fanatical" as having been applied, instead of strategically withheld.) Whipper (sort of) concedes that Cornish was right, now if not then, about his own misguided ideals and indefinite goals. Whipper employs a conditional tone and layered temporality: if he were at this moment (1858) hopeful (which he is not), then he would not find fault with others (namely Cornish) for regarding him as visionary (which Cornish did in 1837). Whipper is still quarreling with his detractors from long ago and still rethinking the legacy of moral reform, but the sense of irony that always had been mixed with his earnestness now dominates.[13]

From the perspective of 1858, Whipper sees that his confidence in the transformative force of character had been misplaced, and he acknowledges the gap between hope and fulfillment, but he implies that these recognitions could have been achieved only over time. "Free blacks in Pennsylvania . . . have been rapidly advancing in religious and moral culture, science and mechanism," but their achievements have bred resentment. If the choice is between retreating into ignorance in order to regain a hollow civil and political freedom or yielding to an "apathy" prompted by the ironies of elevation, then he will choose apathy and irony. In a second letter published in *Frederick Douglass' Paper* on July 2, Whipper defended his choice by outlining the caustic rhythms of history in Philadelphia. Those who still believed in a promise that had been repudiated were suffering from a "popular delusion." They were unable to see what was in front of their eyes. In their retrospections, Delany, Whipper, and Webb all trace, with different tones and consequences, the double-edged progress of freedom from the 1830s to the 1850s, in which African Americans struggled to advance and their status was undermined, in which investments led to the accrual, not of interest, but of enmity.[14]

Two months later, in August 1858, McCune Smith lambasted Whipper over "the 'apathy' problem" and rejected his narrative of backlash. African American men in Pennsylvania had been deprived of only one right, the right to vote, because of public misrepresentation, a "juggle" in which the proponents of disfranchisement featured "the lowest haunts and dens of vice and filth presented by the worst class of Philadelphia free blacks" (here McCune Smith sounds a bit like Casper Souder reporting on the alleys of Moyamensing), rather than "the parlors of the moral and cultivated free blacks" (here he sounds like Joseph Willson), who constituted a majority. Blacks in Pennsylvania continue to possess many other rights of citizenship, including the right to hold property, be included in the census, intermarry, have a passport, and take an oath in a court of justice. Whipper and his peers should concentrate less on making money and cultivating morals (the charges New York relished hurling at Philadelphia) or waiting for "an unwritten miracle" to deliver them. Instead, they should lower themselves into the political arena and exert their influence without scruples. They should use their standing and financial resources to coerce officials and regain the vote. Such "moral degradation" would be good for them and is necessary for the political elevation of any people. McCune Smith's reply to Whipper has more to do with satire and regional feud than with sociology or history. Yet he has a serious purpose. He rejects Whipper's fatalism, and he means to turn apathy and despair to political ends.[15]

Whipper responded again in *Douglass' Paper* on September 3, 1858, disputing McCune Smith's list of rights held by African Americans in Pennsylvania and accusing him of distorting his positions. Whipper writes that he had not charged blacks with degradation but with being degraded, and he invites McCune Smith to visit the state and "examine into the condition of the free blacks for himself." In the final letter of the exchange, McCune Smith reports that he has been to Philadelphia three times, including an appearance at an exasperating convention in 1855 that Whipper had helped to organize, which had induced a headache and turned his dark hair gray. He would not be returning any time soon.[16]

Much of the debate about Philadelphia in the 1850s—its status as case study, the history of its social experiment, its volatile freedom, the impact of northern prejudice, the rift between promise and betrayal, the demands on its white and black residents, the gauging of prospects, the disillusion and jaunty determination—is absorbed and transformed in Webb's historical novel. *The Garies and Their Friends* links the Philadelphia genres: fictional tests of character, reports on the condition of the free people of color, sketches of manners, and narratives of violence. It is a book that is at once retrospective and climactic.

Frank J. Webb's *The Garies and Their Friends*: "A Rather Curious Protest"

The Garies and Their Friends was published in London in 1857 by G. Routledge, the chief promoters of American authors to the British public. The novel originally appeared in two editions, an expensive blue cloth volume, blind-stamped and lettered in gilt, and a cheaper edition, bound in thin yellow boards. The two editions suggest that Routledge imagined the book would appeal to both elite and popular audiences. A full-column advertisement in the London *Athenaeum* announced: "As a very large demand is anticipated for this Work, orders should be forwarded immediately," and a later notice in *Lloyd's Weekly Newspaper* reported that the demand for the book had delayed its publication.[17] Both editions contained two brief prefaces, one by Henry Brougham, who had helped to pass the British Slavery Abolition Act of 1833, and the other by Harriet Beecher Stowe, who had published *Uncle Tom's Cabin* five years earlier in 1852. Thus *The Garies and Their Friends*, which has been disparaged by several modern critics for evading the topic of slavery, came to the public in 1857 with impeccable abolitionist credentials.

Frank J. Webb was born in Philadelphia in 1828 and seems to have lived on the margins of Philadelphia's African American "higher classes." The riots of 1838, 1842, and 1849 spanned his childhood and young adulthood. We have scant evidence of his life before his marriage in 1845. His wife, Mary, became celebrated for her public readings of literary works, especially Stowe's *Uncle Tom's Cabin* and Longfellow's "Hiawatha." Mary performed during tours in northern cities in late 1855 and early 1856 and in England in late 1856, where Frank arranged for the publication of *The Garies*. In 1858, the Webbs traveled to Jamaica for Mary's health, and Frank worked in the Kingston post office. After she died in 1859, he remarried. He returned to the United States in 1869, clerked for the Freedmen's Bureau in Washington, D.C., attended law school at Howard University, and published fiction, poetry, and essays in the African American weekly *New Era* in 1870. In an 1870 letter, Webb mentions a five-hundred-page second novel entitled *Paul Sumner* that he had submitted to Harper's, but the novel never appeared in print, and no manuscript has surfaced. He spent the last twenty-five years of his life in Texas as a post office employee and an educator. Two daguerreotypes exist that may represent the Webbs, but the attributions are questionable, and it is not clear that the same individuals appear in the different images. These traces—slight biography, lost second novel, incongruous photographs—seem appropriate for the elusive narrator of *The Garies and Their Friends*.[18]

It was not unprecedented for African American writers to sign up with British firms, given the prominence of abolitionist circles and the protection of copyright laws. (William Wells Brown's novel *Clotel* had been brought out with the London house of Partridge and Oakey in 1853.) Although we have no evidence that *The Garies* was issued in the United States before a reprint edition in 1969, Webb's novel did circulate among African American readers in the middle of the nineteenth century. A long review from the London *Daily News* was republished on the front page of *Frederick Douglass' Paper* in December 1857. In the inaugural and early issues of the *New Era*, several of Webb's bylines informed readers that he was the "author of 'The Garries'" [*sic*]. He was heralded as "Frank J. Webb, Esq., a colored man, author of the somewhat famous book entitled '*The Garries*,' published in London in 1858, with prefaces by Lord Brougham and Mrs. Stowe, and extensively read in England and this country." The misspelled title, incorrect date, and qualifying adverb ("somewhat" famous) raise questions about just how "extensively" *The Garies and Their Friends* was read. They also point to its uncertain status in our histories of nineteenth-century literature.[19]

Webb tells the stories of three families. Clarence Garie, a wealthy white planter and slave owner, moves north from Georgia to Philadelphia with his family at the urging of Emily, the mixed-race woman with whom he has fathered two children. She wants them and the baby she is carrying to grow up in a free state. They are befriended by the Ellises, an industrious African American couple and their three children. The father, Charles, is a carpenter. The mother, Ellen, takes in laundry and sewing, and their daughter, Esther, also sews. The bedraggled son, Charlie, resists being put out to service and ultimately matures into the reputable "Charles." Their other daughter, Caroline or Caddy, obsessively cleans and orders the Ellis home. The names "Esther" and "Caddy" evoke the striving outsiders in the recently published *Bleak House*, and Webb reworks Dickens's concerns with deportment and respectability.[20] The Garies end up as targets for the machinations of George Stevens, an unscrupulous white lawyer who engineers a riot designed to force blacks from their homes so that he and his cronies can reap a real estate windfall. Having discovered that he is Garie's cousin and only surviving heir, Stevens plots his murder to inherit his vast estate. During the riot, the Ellises take refuge with the wealthy black entrepreneur Walters, who has converted his mansion into a fortress. A mob invades the Garies' home. Mr. Garie is shot, Emily dies of exposure, her child is stillborn, and only their two children, also named Clarence and Emily, survive. The elder Ellis, on his way to warn the Garies, is attacked and maimed.

In the following years, the younger Clarence Garie attempts to pass for white in the town of Sudbury. Charlie Ellis struggles to find employment despite prejudice. Walters marries the strong-willed Ellis daughter, Esther, and Emily Garie marries Charlie, now Charles. At the wedding of Emily and Charles, including an elaborate supper, the remnants of the Garie and Ellis families and their friends gather to celebrate their fragile achievements. McCloskey, an Irishman who had been blackmailed into helping Stevens execute the riot, confesses his role on his deathbed and reveals that Stevens murdered Garie and that he has preserved

Garie's will, now in a trunk in his hospital room. In New York, Stevens, facing arrest for his crimes, leaps from a window to his death. The patrimony is transferred from Stevens's children to the Garie heirs. Clarence Garie, on the verge of marrying the white Anne Bates, is ravaged by guilt. After being exposed as "black" by Stevens's son and humiliated by Anne's father, he returns to Philadelphia and dies of consumption at his sister Emily's home. In a postscript, we are told by the narrator that the Garie and Ellis survivors are happy and productive.

In 1937, Benjamin Brawley, one of the first twentieth-century critics to comment on *The Garies*, described the novel as "somewhat apart from other works of the period." This difficulty in fitting Webb's book into the usual categories has persisted. Arthur P. Davis, who wrote opening remarks for the 1969 reprint that introduced Webb's novel to later twentieth-century readers, set the tone and terms for much of its subsequent reception. He praised *The Garies* for its technical superiority and credited Webb with many firsts. He had written the first African American novel to emphasize free black lives in the North, to portray a "mixed marriage," to include a mob, to treat the "color line" ironically, and to feature the theme of "passing for white." Yet Davis also faulted Webb for the "desperate efforts [of his characters] to imitate the best white people in manners, speech, morality, and business" and for his lack of "a frontal attack on slavery" or clear support for abolition. These charges echo those made in the mid-nineteenth century against the Philadelphia higher classes. Davis labels the novel a "typical nineteenth-century melodrama." He concludes that Webb was "not a strong protest writer," and *The Garies* "has a tendency to be a 'goodwill book,'" seeking approval from a white audience.[21]

More recently, Blyden Jackson, in his *History of Afro-American Literature* (1989), judging the novel a sellout to Americanism and capitalism, has described it as a "rather curious protest." Curious it is, and, joining several recent critics who have turned their attention to *The Garies*, I will spend time trying to account for the novel's historical and rhetorical strangeness. *The Garies* is not about acquiescence but about resilience, and Webb's disposition is mordant rather than conciliatory. As Phillip S. Lapsansky wrote in the early 1990s, "Webb's novel has suffered from 133 years of political incorrectness." Like another Philadelphia text, Joseph Willson's *Sketches of the Higher Classes*, which may have been one of Webb's sources, *The Garies and Their Friends* continues to negotiate its status.[22]

By the time she wrote her preface, Stowe had been involved professionally and personally with the Webbs for at least a couple of years. She had written a theatrical version of *Uncle Tom's Cabin*, titled *The Christian Slave*, for Mary Webb to perform, and Frank had edited the text and composed a biographical sketch about Mary for its London publication. When the Webbs traveled to England, Stowe wrote letters of introduction. In his biographical preface, Webb explains that Mary's tour of *The Christian Slave* was strategic. Winning the acclaim of the English guardians of culture, they sought to persuade an audience in the United States of "the right to compete [with our fair-skinned oppressors] in the world of art for the prizes it offers." Webb envisions a day when "genius will be no longer considered as the exclusive attribute of one race or another, but a gift distributed with an impartial hand by our beneficent common Father." The publication of *The Garies* in London in 1857 formed part of this international undertaking.[23]

According to Stowe, the key question posed, and answered in the affirmative, by Webb's novel is "Are the race at present held as slaves capable of freedom, self-government, and progress?" (xix). Contemporary British reviewers disagreed about the success of Webb's literary performance. Presuming that his goal was to show that "the negroes possess intellect not inferior to that of the whites, and that similar cultivation would result in equal intelligence, which is evidenced by the condition of the coloured population of Philadelphia," a writer for the London *Sunday Times* concluded, in September 1857: "Of the capabilities of the race, the manner in which Mr. Webb wields his pen sufficiently testifies." On the other hand, the critic for the London *Athenaeum*, mentioning in October 1857 that *The Garies* was "interesting, and well written," explained that these qualities, and the success of African Americans in Philadelphia, resulted from the "admixture of European blood . . . so that the question intended to be at once raised and answered by this work—whether slaves are capable of self-government—is not fairly stated."[24] For these reviewers, Stowe's preface has set the terms for evaluating Webb's novel: does it or does it not it show the race "capable of freedom"?

The questions that Webb asks are different. They are questions about the social and political contexts in which such a formulation could have meaning and about the qualities of freedom for all in such circumstances. Stowe renders hypothetical the capability that Webb takes for granted. Yet he understands that Mary's theatrical efforts and his literary efforts inevitably will play a role in wider debates about race, freedom, and citizenship. Webb may be conscious of the necessity, but he also appreciates the absurdity, of confirming natural rights and verifying human equality. The British assessment of *The Garies* reprinted in *Frederick Douglass' Paper* shares Webb's distance: "As to the question which Mrs. Stowe . . . says it elucidates, it is one which we never thought of asking." The reviewer goes on to label doubts about capability "bosh" and "nonsense."[25] Webb grapples with a question whose premise he rejects, and his answer is riddled with ironies. In *The Garies*, he is both earnest and incredulous.

Lord Brougham, in his preface, quotes from a letter Stowe had sent to one of her friends. Brougham reports her as writing that Webb "shows what I long have wanted to show; what *the free people of colour do attain,* and what they can do in spite of all social obstacles" (xvii). Stowe may have long wanted to represent free communities, but she restricted her ambit in the 1850s to the South and to slavery. In the preface to *The Key to Uncle Tom's Cabin,* the volume in which she defended her famous novel against attacks on its credibility, she explained that she had planned to include in the *Key* a "whole department" on "the characteristics and developments of the colored race in various countries and circumstances," but, for reasons of length, was forced to delete it. The closest she comes in her novel to imagining the kind of freedom to which African Americans might aspire is when she represents the "higher circle" of house servants on the St. Clare plantation, characters such as Jane, Rosa, and Adolph. Adolph clothes himself in his master's discarded finery and has "fallen into an absolute confusion as to *meum tuum* with regard to himself and his master." Depicted with affectionate condescension, Stowe's Adolph could have stepped from the pages of one of Edward W. Clay's gentler satires of free African American pretense in "Life in Philadelphia."[26]

In both *Uncle Tom's Cabin* and her later novel *Dred: A Tale of the Great Dismal Swamp* (1856), Stowe is intrigued by European American characters who preside over attempts to instruct the enslaved. In the New Orleans of *Uncle Tom's Cabin,* the New England Calvinist Ophelia attempts to mold the obstinate young Topsy, who has been purchased by her cousin Augustine St. Clare to test her pedagogical commitments. In *Dred,* Edward Clayton, at the Magnolia Grove plantation in South Carolina, teaches slaves to read and write, while his sister Anne provides uniforms and inculcates discipline.[27] Stowe gestures at freedom in both books and provides glimpses of contentment in the North or in Canada. In *The Garies and Their Friends,* Webb surveys this lacuna, relocating attention from South to North and from cabin to parlor, detailing the spaces of freedom. In response to Stowe and also, it seems likely, to Sarah Josepha Hale, Webb interprets the Philadelphia experiment from the point of view of its African American subjects.

In her preface to *The Garies,* Stowe makes clear to the novel's British audience what "Philadelphia" means: "This city, standing as it does on the frontier between free and slave territory, has accumulated naturally a large population of the mixed and African race . . . they form a large class—have increased in numbers, wealth, and standing—they constitute a peculiar society of their own, presenting many social peculiarities worthy of interest and attention" (xv). Stowe emphasizes Philadelphia's border status, the distinctiveness of its African American residents, and its importance for considerations of national destiny. She does not explain what she thinks is "peculiar" about this Philadelphia society, although she repeats the word and its cognates several times in her brief foreword.

Stowe's "peculiar" here resonates with the scene in Hale's *Liberia,* in which the character Ben doffs his hat on a Philadelphia street with "a peculiar flourish, meant to express a great deal." The adjective reminds us of the "peculiar" status of free blacks described by William Whipper, Samuel Cornish, Frederick Douglass, and Joseph Willson and of the "peculiar power" of metempsychosis wielded by Robert Montgomery Bird's Sheppard Lee. Etymologically, the word derives from the Latin "peculiaris," or private property, from "peculium," referring to "that which is one's own." At its root is the word "pecu," or cattle. This etymology helps to account for the term "peculiar institution" as a euphemism for chattel slavery. The Oxford English Dictionary lists the first recorded use of "peculiar institution" in 1842, although it appears earlier, for example in the 1838 *History of Pennsylvania Hall.*[28]

The word "peculiar" raises questions about property, authority, character, distinction, and anomaly. Its implications often exceed its particular use. The word has lives of its own. In *The Garies and Their Friends,* Webb harnesses its energies and extends its reference. The forms of "peculiar" ricochet throughout his text, associated with the practice of slavery and the predicament of his African American and European American characters in the North. In his novel, the condition of all who move through Philadelphia is represented as "peculiar."[29]

Still Life in Georgia

The Garies and Their Friends begins in Georgia, on a plantation near Savannah, in the late afternoon, when "a Family of peculiar Construction," as the first chapter title describes them, gathers for tea. This scene frames the action of the novel and will be hinged to the final supper in Philadelphia, celebrating the wedding of the younger Emily Garie and Charles Ellis. At the start of *The Garies and Their Friends,* Webb sets an uncommon table:

> It was at the close of an afternoon in May, that a party might have been seen gathered around a table covered with all those delicacies that, in the household of a rich Southern planter, are regarded as almost necessaries of life. In the centre stood a dish of ripe strawberries, their plump red sides peeping through the covering of white sugar that had been plentifully sprinkled over them. Geeche limes, almost drowned in their own rich syrup, temptingly displayed their bronze-coloured forms just above the rim of the glass that contained them. Opposite, and as if to divert the gaze from lingering too long over their luscious beauty, was a dish of peaches preserved in brandy, a never-failing article in a Southern matron's catalogues of sweets. A silver basket filled with a variety of cakes was in close

proximity to a plate of corn-flappers, which were piled upon it like a mountain, and from the brown tops of which trickled tiny rivulets of butter. All these dainties, mingling their various odours with the aroma of the tea and fine old java that came steaming forth from the richly chased silver pots, could not fail to produce a very appetising effect. (1)

Despite the narrator's guarantee about the appealing qualities of this scene, its excesses (and especially the facts revealed when readers are introduced to the human beings at the table) induce at least a slight queasiness. In Webb's Southern plantation still life, the inanimate objects—spilling over their boundaries, revealing their interiors, tempting viewers—seem to be alive. The tender skins of the strawberries are "peeping" through the enveloping sugar, offering florid glimpses. As the verb "peep" implies, the strawberries themselves might be regarding the diners, furtively or playfully. The limes, not just any limes but Geeche limes from the Low Country region of South Carolina and Georgia associated with the Gullah people and their durable African customs under slavery, are nearly overwhelmed by the luxurious syrup they produce. Their "bronze-coloured forms" tantalize. Rivaling their "luscious beauty" are the peaches in brandy, placed "as if to divert the gaze" from the limes, but the aesthetic intent here is left obscure. What is the status of the "as if"? Who or what is the agent? Did the "Southern matron" seek the diversion, or someone else, or the narrator, or even the fruit itself?

Ripe and peeping strawberries, enticing and drowning limes, diverting peaches, seeping corncakes—nothing is still in this picture. The silver baskets and the rims of glass barely contain these exorbitant products. The delicacies here are figured as inviting, vulnerable bodies. Some strange visceral comedy or drama of manners, race, sex, pleasure, and economics is being played out across the table even before we meet the "rich Southern planter" and the "Southern matron." As the chapters unfold, the narrator shows how food becomes a medium of struggle, culminating in the final supper, which extends the opening tableau and breaks its frame.

The "rich Southern planter" is Clarence Garie, whom the narrator informs us did not "attract more than ordinary attention" (1). The same cannot be said about the "lady of marked beauty" who sits "opposite to him . . . presiding at the tea-tray" (2). The narrator encourages scrutiny:

The first thing that would have attracted attention on seeing her were her gloriously dark eyes. They were not entirely black, but of that seemingly changeful hue so often met with in persons of African extraction, which deepens and lightens with every varying emotion. Hers wore a subdued expression that sank into the heart and at once riveted those who saw her. Her hair, of jetty black, was arranged in braids; and through her light-brown complexion the faintest tinge of carmine was visible. As she turned to take her little girl from the arms of the servant, she displayed a fine profile and perfectly moulded form. No wonder that ten years before, when she was placed upon the auction-block at Savanah, she had brought so high a price. Mr. Garie had paid two thousand dollars for her, and was the envy of all the young bucks in the neighbourhood who had competed with him at the sale. (2)

Flesh and fruit are linked here, since the woman, too, is composed of appealing surfaces ("gloriously dark eyes," "jetty black" hair, "light-brown complexion," "fine profile and perfectly moulded form"). Such outlines again suggest glimpses of an interior: "through her light-brown complexion the faintest tinge of carmine was visible." Her eyes reveal (her emotional state, possibly her "African extraction") but also penetrate and fix ("a subdued expression that sank into the heart and at once riveted those who saw her"). Like the commodities on the tea table, she has been purchased and forms part of the planter's array. We learn about her status through the decorous, jarring mid-sentence volta of "the auction-block at Savanah" and the remembered spectacle of the "young bucks" who eagerly sought to acquire her. Again the narrator complicates his appetizing effects, suggesting how desire and pleasure are bound to, but not limited by, a system of exploitation.

The "marked beauty" of the woman distinguishes her and also indicates that she has a price. The amount—$2,000—restates the sum paid in Stowe's *Uncle Tom's Cabin* and *The Christian Slave* for the young Cassy. In Stowe's novel, the character discloses her value to Tom in an impassioned speech. In Stowe's play, the actress Mary Webb would have delivered the lines. In Webb's novel, social violence emerges through the twisting of an apparently placid verbal surface. The woman at the tea table is differentiated first by race, then class, then caste. She has a name, "Emily," which is withheld until a line of dialogue, several paragraphs later, when Mr. Garie recounts to his guest, Mr. Winston, a "dark-complexioned gentleman" (a freed slave who turns out to be Emily's cousin), the disapproval of a northern acquaintance, Mr. Priestly, at his "speaking of Emily as my wife" (3, 4).[30]

Garie speaks of Emily as his wife, but she is not legally his wife, nor is she the conventional "Southern matron" governing table and home that readers were led to expect in the opening scene. The narrator does not clarify matters for another hundred pages, at which time Garie's "kind-hearted" old Uncle John warns him that he will be exposed to public disgrace if he lives in Philadelphia with his "mulatto mistress" (99, 101). Uncle John advises him to remain in Georgia where he can cohabit with her or dismiss her as he pleases. Garie defends his relationship, arguing that he considers Emily to be his wife, even if state law prohibits a legal recognition. Before then, the narrator repeatedly has used the term "wife" to refer to Emily, reflecting Garie's cognizance of their bond and also the slave owner's myopia, with the possible effect of misleading the reader (13, 53, 56, 58, 59). Finally, at the start of the chapter in which Clarence and Emily are married by a minister in Philadelphia, after another clergyman has refused to perform the service, the narrator intervenes: "To Emily Winston we have always accorded the title of Mrs. Garie; whilst, in reality, she had no legal claim to it whatever" (133). This kind of discrepancy typifies the narrator's performances throughout the book. A sly guide to the plantations of Georgia and the streets and parlors of Philadelphia, he continually and decorously shifts the ground under his characters and readers.

Emily's children, a girl and a boy, alongside her at the table in the opening scene, are not easily identifiable by any racial mark. The little girl "showed no trace whatever of African origin" and, as for the boy: "The critically learned in such matters, knowing his parentage, might have imagined they could detect the evidence of his mother's race, by the slightly mezzo-tinto expression of his eyes, and the rather African fulness of his lips; but the casual observer would have passed him by without dreaming that a drop of negro blood coursed through his veins" (2–3). The racial judgments of both the expert (who imagines evidence) and the amateur (who is oblivious) are suspect here. The instability and palpability of racial distinctions are confirmed in an exchange between Mr. Garie and Mr. Winston at the tea table. Winston tells a story about his being received as "white" while in New York and in the company of Mr. Priestly, who boasted of his ability "to detect evidences of the least drop of African blood in any one" (4). As Garie laughs uproariously at the fact that Priestly had asked Winston to squire his daughter Clara to church and to fancy balls, the merriment (described as a "contagion") endangers the girl held by Emily, "who almost choked herself with the tea her mother was giving her, and who had to be hustled and shaken for some time before she could be brought round again" (3–4). No mention is made of either Winston or Emily delighting in the joke about racial masquerade or the spectacle of black men and white women in public. In this novel, laughter almost always comes with an edge.

The tea table scene begins with a profusion of delicacies and segues into auction blocks and choking babies. The words, like the items on the table, bristle with significance. The opening tableau is the first of many set-pieces in the book that structure its development, including a plantation arbor, an elite urban parlor, a city stroll, the home as castle, a race riot, and a wedding supper. These scenes are linked by the narrator's slow, uneasy disclosures, his disorientations and reorientations, an intricate sympathy for his protagonists, and contrivance and irony.

A few chapters after the tea table, Webb creates similar effects, when Clarence and Emily are lounging in an arbor a short distance from the house. Under a canopy of trees, from which Georgia moss sways gently, washed in the scent of blossoms, "Mr. and Mrs. Garie sat looking at the children, who were scampering about the garden in pursuit of a pet rabbit which had escaped, and seemed determined not to be caught upon any pretence whatever" (53). Everything is lovely in this happy plantation scene, except that "Mr. and Mrs. Garie" are not married, the children who are scurrying after their pet are themselves property, the loving father is insensitive to their danger, and the mother is oppressed by their condition.

Prodded by Garie, Emily finally expresses her anxieties:

"Are they not beautiful?" said Mr. Garie, with pride, as they bounded past him. "There are not two prettier children in all Georgia. You don't seem half proud enough of them," he continued, looking down upon his wife affectionately.

Mrs. Garie, who was half reclining on the seat, and leaning her head upon his shoulder, replied, "Oh, yes, I am, Garie; I'm sure I love them dearly—oh, so dearly!" continued she, fervently—"and I only wish"—here she paused, as if she felt she had been going to say something that had better remain unspoken.... "I wish they were not little slaves." (53)

Like the pet rabbit her children pursue, Emily seems "determined not to be caught upon any pretence whatever." The "pretence" she resists here is that, in the luxury of Garie's estate, with the kindest of masters, she and her children are not slaves. Webb stresses the mixture of tenderness, dependence, and constraint in their relationship. In response to Clarence's playful chiding that she is not sufficiently pleased with their children, Emily not so playfully urges him to remove the family to the "free States" (55), where those children (including the baby she reveals to him she is carrying) will not be liable to sale in the event of his demise. Emily also wishes to move north to Philadelphia because she longs for companionship, especially female companionship, in the "pleasant social circle" of African Americans that her cousin Winston has described (57). Though myopic, Garie is not portrayed as blind, and despite his loyalty to the South and his concern about northern prejudice, he accepts Emily's distress and finally agrees to try the "experiment of living in the North" (58).

The arbor scene is reproduced in the only illustration that exists for *The Garies and Their Friends.* The picture appears on the cover of the inexpensive edition issued by Routledge in 1857 (figure 4.1). Beneath the title block, which prominently bills the preface by Mrs. Stowe and gives the wrong middle initial for Frank Webb ("C." rather than "J.," a mistake not repeated within the covers of the book), is a colored engraving of Emily and Clarence lounging in their arbor. Her head rests on his shoulder, a river prospect unfolds in the right background and the two children run after that telltale rabbit in the foreground. In some ways, the image closely follows the text; in others, it diverges from it. The artist has hatched lines in the faces of the children to indicate hue, despite the narrator's caution. Emily, too, is rendered dark, while Garie's pinkness is apparent: the lines on his face indicate shadow. The cover features the Garie family on the plantation, maintaining the odd emphasis in the book's title, even though the Garies move north to Philadelphia a quarter of the way into the narrative, after which Webb dwells on other characters, including the Ellises, Walters, and Stevens.[31]

It would seem that the illustrator merely has reproduced the comfort of Webb's arbor, except that in the upper left and right corners, leaning against the pediment that holds the title, we find two unexpected characters. On the left is a slouching white-faced figure in red coat and hat and white pants with jagged red stripes. He holds the handle of a whip, whose cord dangles into the image, almost touching the canopy of leaves. On the right is a dark-faced (but also pink-limbed) figure in a simple red outfit who rests his head on his hand. The links of a chain hang down, possibly from his unseen foot or from the "E" at the end of Stowe's name. Neither figure matches any character in Webb's novel. The figure on the left evokes a plantation overseer. His gesturing whip and also his trousers associate him with the scene below. The trousers, white with red stripes, reminiscent of the U.S. flag, display the same pattern worn by Clarence Garie. The red coat of the overseer at the top left is similar to the outfit of the dark-faced personage at the top right and also similar to Garie's jacket and to the children's garb. Thus the two figures on opposite sides of the title, evoking overseer and slave, loom over the view and rhyme with its space. The whip and chain gesture toward the ties.

Below the title, British readers are tempted with the delights of plantation fiction, but the entire image suggests wider contexts and harsher frames. The cover manifests the racial identities of Emily and her children, emphasizes the plantation, invades the arbor, displays the hierarchies of slavery, and clothes these insinuations in the American flag. The illustrator has responded to the motives in Webb's early scenes, with a regard for his technique that few critics, then or now, have shown. The engraving avoids, however, Webb's principal concern in the novel: the experiment in freedom that unravels in Philadelphia.

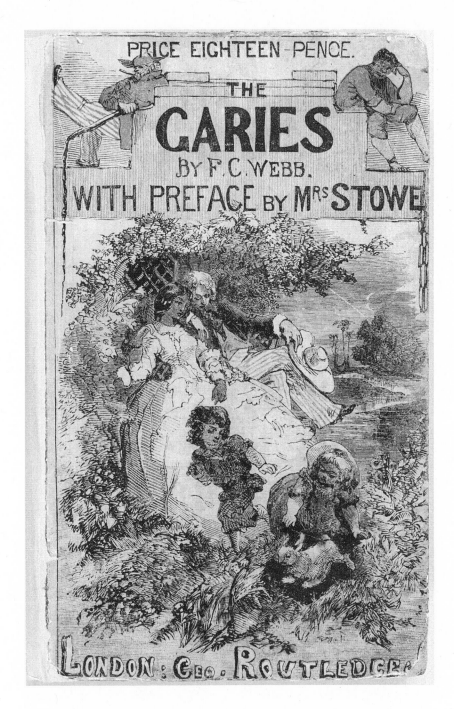

FIGURE 4.1 Cover illustration from the "yellowback" edition of *The Garies and Their Friends*, by Frank J. Webb (G. Routledge, 1857).

History and Farce

We can estimate the chronological parameters of Webb's novel through his "suggestive historicism," to use Robert S. Levine's phrase. With a plot of escalating bias and a riot that evokes the 1842 outbreak, Webb seems to have placed the action of the first three-quarters of the novel in the years following disfranchisement, that is, post-1838. Allusions suggest that most of the novel is set in Philadelphia before the merging of city and county in 1854. Stevens's Irish pawn McCloskey expresses surprise that his blackmailer wishes him to lead the mob to Garie's home, which is "away up there in the city limits!" (180), and the mayor tells Walters that he will be unable to protect any of the buildings on a list of targets except for Walters's house because they are "out of my jurisdiction" (202). The last quarter of the novel takes place "many years" later, in a present time in which characters who had been juveniles have married or are about to be married (309). *The Garies,* then, implies a story time that centers on the 1840s and extends to the mid-1850s.[32]

Although Webb never refers to a date, he meticulously provides the names of street after street. Insinuated in time, *The Garies and Their Friends* is anchored in space—or so it seems. Of course, we find Chestnut Street, "the fashionable part of the city," with its "line of shops" and "aristocratic quarter" (19–20), and the old State House bell strikes the hours (38). The Cedar neighborhood is prominent in Stevens's hit list, including addresses in "Baker-street, Bedford-street, Sixth, Seventh, and Eighth Streets" (196), but Webb does not stigmatize Baker and Bedford, as did J. B. Jones in *The City Merchant* and Casper Souder in "The Mysteries and Miseries of Philadelphia." Readers are told that the Ellises flee to Walters's mansion during the riot because their own home "was quite indefensible (it being situated in a neighbourhood swarming with the class of which the mob was composed)," a description that evokes the racially mixed Cedar neighborhood with its Irish workers, although no address is given for the Ellis home (203–4). The narrator provides the names, and often the numbers, of streets that had not become familiar allegories in Philadelphia reportage and fiction. Mr. Ellis's carpentry shop is at 18 Little Green-street (41). The Garies home is at 27 Winter-street in the northwestern part of the city (64–65, 117). Mr. Walters's house is at 257 Easton-street, at the corner of Shotwell (196, 199, 200). When Walters exhorts the mayor to defend the homes on Stevens's list of targets, when Stevens instructs McCloskey on which routes the mob should take and where they should strike, and when father Ellis attempts to go from Walters's house to Garie's in order to warn him, only to be attacked himself, readers are supplied with abundant detail about urban space in Philadelphia, inflected by riot.

The addresses are gratuitous, since they have no function in the plot. British readers, and most American readers, would not have perceived any significance in 18 Little Green, 27 Winter, or 257 Easton streets. These numbers lend the homes an illusory substance. And some of the crucial streets recorded in *The Garies* seem not to have existed at all. Easton and Shotwell, where Mr. Walters and his friends safeguard his home during the riot, are not listed in any contemporary map or directory. Given that Walters's residence is located within the city limits and that Stevens directs the rioters to proceed from the south to get there, his neighborhood may correspond to the Lombard Street area in southeast Philadelphia, where the wealthy sailmaker and abolitionist James Forten Sr. had lived for decades, until his death in 1842. Invented streets with exact addresses contribute to an unstable specificity in the novel.[33]

Webb skews his history as well as his space. Absent from his Philadelphia are the public controversies over moral reform and colonization and emigration. The black national gatherings in the city are never mentioned, nor is disfranchisement, nor the Fugitive Slave Act. The prominent African American churches— Episcopal, Presbyterian, Methodist, and Baptist—are barely visible, with only glancing references to the (presumably Episcopal) minister who marries Clarence Garie and Emily and "the coloured Episcopal church" (234). Instead of reproducing such details, Webb pursues a different sort of history.

The Fugitive Slave Act may not be mentioned in the novel, but it is resisted. When Emily's cousin George Winston visits Philadelphia, the black waiters at his fancy hotel mistake him for a white Southerner. One of them, adopting a servile dialect and posture, enacts the role of a former slave wistful for his plantation and "'kind marster'" (39). He endeavors, unsuccessfully, to cadge some funds, which he and his fellow waiters hope to apply to the Vigilance Committee, formed to shelter and assist escaping slaves. Webb's narrator enjoys both Winston's indignant response and the satirical game the waiters play with their southern marks. Rather than the "incessant *begging* of their *rulers*" that Joseph Willson laments in the years after disfranchisement, Webb scripts calculated blandishments.[34]

Disfranchisement may not be mentioned in *The Garies*, but the effects of exclusion are omnipresent. Mrs. Ellis, Caddy, and Mr. Walters take a "'dreadful long walk'" (as Mrs. Ellis describes it), "a very long walk" (the narrator reinforces), to the house that Mr. Walters has in mind for the Garies, because blacks are not permitted to ride on the omnibuses (64–65). Mrs. Bird and Charlie Ellis are removed from the first-class section on a train to New York and forced to travel in the "negro car" (as a gentleman on the train refers to it) or "the nigger car" (as a bystander more bluntly puts the matter [110–11]). Mrs. Stevens forces the teacher of the two mixed-race Garie children to expel them from school. Walters tells a story about deacons in a "white" church who pulled up the floor from under a pew that had been obtained by a black man so that he could not take his seat, evoking the infamous removal of Richard Allen, Absalom Jones, and other worshippers from St. George's Methodist Church in 1792. Even the dead are not spared, since Clarence and Emily Garie, victims of the riot, cannot be buried together in the same cemetery. When Charlie Ellis undertakes a quest for employment, he discovers that he is acceptable only as a servant. Starting an apprenticeship with Mr. Blatchford, a banknote engraver and abolitionist, Charlie is fired by his employer after the other employees refuse to work alongside a "nigger" (297–98). The elder Ellis advises Winston, who considers passing for a white man, that, if he settles down in Philadelphia, "'you'll have to be either one thing or the other—white or coloured. Either you must live exclusively amongst coloured people, or go to the whites and remain with them'" (44).[35]

In representing Philadelphia in the 1840s, Webb assumes the stance of those such as William Whipper who, in the wake of disfranchisement, recognized the force of prejudice yet continued to support "elevation" as a way of advancing personal security and group solidarity and as part of the struggle for rights, but no longer with the faith of the early 1830s that such efforts would guarantee inclusion. Webb's deepest interest in *The Garies* lies with those characters who remain and fight, rather than those such as Mr. Winston who, after touring the northern states in search of a place where he would be able to establish himself in business, decides to leave the country and is dropped from the narrative, or those who deny their racial ties, such as the younger Clarence Garie. The narrator understands Clarence's reasons for "passing" in the aftermath of the riot, during which his father had been murdered and he had watched his mother die. Yet he also records the objections of the investor Walters, who concedes, with a sneer, "'that in our land of liberty it is of incalculable advantage to be white,'" but warns that Clarence always will be vulnerable to exposure and opprobrium (275). And the narrator amplifies the melodrama: "We, too, Clarence, cast a tear upon thy tomb—poor victim of prejudice to thy colour!" (391). Yet he reserves his most sustained regard for those who struggle in Philadelphia.

Readers are introduced to the city through the Ellises, "a highly respectable and industrious colored family" (16). At the Ellis tea table, there are no silver baskets, finely engraved decanters, or overflowing receptacles, as there were on the Garie plantation. Instead, the narrator pictures a china teapot, "which received its customary quantity of tea," no more and no less. This table, too, is precarious, but the Ellises attempt to guard against its vulnerability. The brewing pot has been "carefully placed behind the stove pipe that no accidental touch of the elbow might bring it to destruction" (17). Rather than piling up a mountainous array of fruit and cakes, the Ellises consume quantities of nutritious and hearty food, here warm cornbread and cool butter. Both pleasure and sustenance are their aims. The Ellises appreciate their edibles. While reluctantly serving as a waiter at a dinner party given by his employer, Mrs. Thomas, the young Charlie Ellis corrects a bigoted dinner guest who denies the "antiquity of the use of salad" by removing a volume of Chaucer from the bookshelf and quoting a relevant passage (6).

Webb's early Philadelphia scenes evince a social comedy different from the satires of the gap between reach and grasp found in Brackenridge's *Modern Chivalry*, Clay's "Life in Philadelphia," and Bird's *Sheppard Lee*. Webb flaunts the ways in which his characters undermine their menial roles or enact the rituals of respectability with a telling vehemence. Critics of the book hardly ever discuss its social and physical comedy, associated with Charlie and his friend Kinch and also with Charlie's sister Caddy. The humor in these scenes pivots on the intimacy between manners and violence. Those who write about Webb's novel stress themes of racial passing, the red herring of assimilation, the spectacular ferocity of the riot, or the assault on the reprobate Stevens by a group of volunteer firemen who mistake him for a member of a rival company and blacken him with tar. Yet so much of the action of Webb's book takes place on the level of gesture and tone, and so much of its meaning lies in the negotiations and consequences of small details. In the subtleties, Webb discovers inordinate significance.

Charlie's resistance to service under Mrs. Thomas plays out the disparagement of such labor as a "badge of servitude," expressed by a range of African American leaders from Richard Allen at the first national convention in 1830, to Martin Delany at the 1848 meeting in Rochester, New York, and in his 1852 *Condition*, to Frederick Douglass in his 1853 editorial "Learn Trades or Starve."[36] Webb has his character Walters level the familiar charge that working as a servant perpetuates dependence. Instead, Walters urges, young boys should become small entrepreneurs and learn to profit from the economy. Webb identifies himself with these attitudes through Walters's speech and Charlie's recalcitrance and also in the affectionate disdain with which he limns the misguided products of African American service, such as Mrs. Thomas's attendants Aunt Rachel and Robberts, who perform their roles without irony.

Bound to Mrs. Thomas, Charlie wages a campaign against his employer in the minutiae of everyday life: soiling his uniform, disputing with the other servants, using the pet cat as a weapon, turning the drawing room and the dinner table into arenas of indignity. Mrs. Thomas, of working-class descent and French affectation, craves membership in the "ton"—she, rather than the Ellises, is represented as the pretender. At one of her grand meals, Charlie, dressed in his livery, attaches a pin to the elbow of his sleeve so that when he removes the cover from the soup tureen he hooks his employer's cap and wig and, with one movement, sweeps them off her head, exposing her short white hair and red face. Many of the gestures in Webb's book resemble this one, their smooth trajectories often taking surprising turns. As the characters move, the narrator delineates the field of constraint and choice, and the ways in which the two dovetail. Performing his obligations, Charlie asserts an elbow room. He serves, resists, and is punished, initiating events that lead to his return home.

The Ellis's obsessive daughter Caddy loves to scour. Of plain appearance and "a rather shrewish disposition," she is "indefatigable . . . never so happy as when in possession of a dust or scrubbing brush; she would have regarded a place where she could have lived in a perpetual state of house cleaning, as an earthly paradise" (16). Anticipating a visit from Mr. Winston, Caddy springs into action. She makes sure that the little parlor in the Ellis home is the perfection of order, bringing it to "an astonishing state of cleanliness" (45). She arranges ornaments at exact distances from the corners of the mantelpiece, burnishes the looking glass until it is immaculate, and places the doors "in a state of forwardness to receive their expected guest" (45). In charge of preparing the house that the Garies will occupy when they arrive from Georgia, Caddy harries two old cleaning women when she detects streaks on the windows and "infinite small spots of paint and whitewash" on the floors (85). Toward the end of the book, she supervises the domestic arrangements for Charlie and Emily's wedding and supper, tyrannizing Walters's staff and driving the entrepreneur from his own home. On the last page of the book, we are told that she and Kinch have married and have a little girl named Caddy, her mother's pride: "a wonderful little girl, who, instead of buying candy and cake with her sixpences, as other children did, gravely invested them in miniature wash-boards and dust-brushes, and was saving up her money to purchase a tiny stove with a full set of cooking utensils. Caddy declares her a child worth having" (392). In this final glimpse, there is humor, burden, and uncertainty. Caddy bequeaths to her Caddy a disposition and a set of investments whose effectiveness in securing a future order remains open to question.

Webb portrays Caddy's exertions as a complex response. She furiously tries to maintain order in her domain. Her labor is so strenuous because of her passion for symmetry and her anxieties about scrutiny (visitors are imminent: like her poised doors, Caddy is always in a "state of forwardness to receive") and because of the pervasive threats to African American homes. Her insecurities are marked by both class and race. Like Sarah Josepha Hale's Amanda Fitzwater, Webb's Caddy displays in her gestures the energy required to maintain her position. He represents her incessant activity as negotiating the demands of social performance in Philadelphia, an attempt to organize a space in which she and her family can abide. Her efforts to preserve order—arranging, dusting, scrubbing—appear to be without end, as Webb indicates when his narrator informs his readers that before Caddy's eyes were "infinite small spots of paint and whitewash." Not "infinitely," which would emphasize her perspicuity, but "infinite," hinting that she may never be able to safeguard her home. The "infinite small spots of paint and whitewash" suggest that racial difficulties in Philadelphia may be indelible and septic. The protective character of Caddy's labors is dramatized on the night of the riot, when she uses her prowess to defend the Walters mansion. With the assistance of her young friend Kinch, she boils kettles full of hot water and cayenne pepper and delivers the scorching contents onto the heads of those who are about to breach the front door with their axes. When Walters runs upstairs to discover the source, Caddy proudly displays her weapon: "'This,' said she, holding up a dipper, 'is my gun'" (214).[37]

Caddy's dignity often is undercut by the slapstick comedy that accompanies her endeavors. Preparing tea for her father and Mr. Winston, who are expected shortly, she covers her silk dress with an old petticoat. When she notices a "beggar boy" drawing with charcoal on her pristine steps, she demands that he cease, and he laughs and puts his thumb to his nose (46). Grabbing a broom, she steals around the side of the house and brings her weapon down upon the head, not of the boy, but of a startled Mr. Winston, pushing his hat down over his eyes. With the details of petticoat and crushed hat, Webb indicates the flimsy shield of attire and the thin line between decorum and pratfall.

Often in *The Garies*, an excess of good form leads to amusing or violent consequences and sometimes to both at once. While Caddy is readying the Garies' new home, her brother Charlie is given the task of bringing her a kettle with her favorite meals. Dawdling to play marbles, he mistakenly picks up a similar container belonging to one of the other boys, with a much inferior dinner. Vexed at being deprived of her meal, Caddy takes a hairbrush and hits Charlie or, as Webb puts it, "belabour[s] him without mercy" (88, repeating a similar usage on 77). He trips on the carpet and tumbles down a long flight of stairs, breaking his arm. Ill with a fever for days, he becomes delirious, to Caddy's anguish. In this scene, her ardor spills into attack. She inflicts her discipline on her younger brother with almost fatal results. In the wake of the riot, Caddy directs her rage outside her family and community. Talking with Charlie, she calls white people "'devils'" (267), and later, despite the remonstrances of her sister Esther, she says that she wished they did not exist. She wields her sewing needle as though it were a voodoo implement: "'Oh! well, I don't like any of them—I hate them all!' she continued bitterly, driving her needle at the same time into the cloth she was sewing, as if it was a white person she had in her lap and she was sticking pins in him" (300).

As the Ellises, Walters, and their allies prepare to defend Walters's mansion, the scene parallels Caddy's earlier domestic arrangements: one sets one's house in order so that one can receive guests or withstand the assault of a mob. The difference between the two in Webb's city is not as great as it might seem.

Just before the carnage, there is a Shakespearean or Dickensian interlude of low comedy. Kinch, hoping to project an aura of aggressive masculinity, has out-fitted himself in an old sword that he has discovered in the attic. He trips over it, falls down the stairs, collides with a table, and overturns a pan of sticky batter, which covers his head and back. Caddy helps him comb the batter from his hair and wash it from his face. This scene provides a counterpoint not only to the riots that follow but also to an earlier chapter ("Mr. Stevens Falls into Bad Hands"), in which the villainous lawyer has his face covered with tar. Maneuvering in the lower parts of the city to arrange the violence, Stevens buys a coat from Kinch, who is minding his father's used-clothing store. Unfortunately for the lawyer, this "coat . . . of peculiar cut and colour" (186) turns out to belong to one of the city's notorious volunteer fire brigades. (The narrator implies that Kinch knows that he is dressing Stevens for trouble.) During his peregrinations, Stevens crosses the territory of a rival company and provokes its members, who beat and gag him and paint his face. Darkened and with swollen lips (having been pummeled into a caricature), he is taken for black and humiliated by a group of intoxicated young white men, some of whom he recognizes. At home, he painfully removes the tar, along with a good deal of the skin from his face. Thus Webb's narrator subjects Stevens to his own racist treatment, and he extends the vulnerability of life in Philadelphia. To wear the wrong coat on the wrong street is to risk one's life. Kinch has an easier time removing the layer of batter that covers his face than Stevens has scraping off his tar, but characters in *The Garies* are con-tinually victims of their surfaces, despite their attempts to disguise or protect themselves.

The social comedy in *The Garies*, which often turns into farce and mixes with tragedy, is "belaboured" (77, 88). Webb puns on the contiguities of labor and violence in his overwrought Philadelphia: Charlie being forced into service and resisting, Caddy scouring the house and scourging her brother, Caddy preparing a kettle to burn the mob, the modest success of the Ellises and the prodigious achievements of Walters opening them to attack.

In his novel, Webb presents an African American twist on Lippard's Philadel-phia as Monk Hall, riven by class struggle and venality, composed of a series of "trap-doors." As we have seen in the previous chapter, in Lippard's *Quaker City*, "no man could stride across the floor without peril of his life." A "quiet supper-room" disintegrates, and Byrnewood Arlington falls into the abyss.[38] Webb's characters—the Ellises, the Garies, Walters, Stevens—walk across their parlors or on the streets of the city, and with one false step—false in ways not revealed until after the social or racial mistake is made—they activate a hidden spring and a chasm opens. They attempt to preserve their balance on the verge. The wrong dinner kettle leads to a beating for Charlie Ellis, or a ripple in the carpet hurtles him down the stairs, or a particular coat turns into a bull's-eye for Stevens, or Garie, at home with Emily, hears the evening calm broken by cries of "'Down with the Abolitionist—down with the Amalgamationist!'" directed at him by the approaching mob (221).

With his "trap-doors," Webb evokes the turbulent history of Philadelphia that we have considered. In 1838, when the light-skinned Robert Purvis helped his darker-skinned wife down from a carriage while attending the opening ceremonies at Pennsylvania Hall, the gesture was perceived as a scandal. The moment, repeatedly invoked, was used to justify the burning of the hall three days later. In 1842, a banner held by a group of African American temperance marchers, depicting a slave whose chains had been severed and the backdrop of a rising sun, was interpreted as an affront by onlookers (some discerned a slave ship or a town in flames), who then set upon the paraders, inciting two days of violence in the Cedar neighborhood.

Giving a racial edge to Lippard's pitfalls, Webb has Walters imagine the danger he would face were he to appear on the street during the rampage: "'a certain death . . . my black face would quickly obtain for me a passport to another world'" (216). In Webb's Philadelphia, a black face risks being perceived as an invitation to deprive its bearer of his rights. His metaphor compresses the anger over segregation, disfranchisement, and riot. Walters is apprehensive that such a face may be a passport to oblivion.[39]

Parlor and Riot

The graphic riot scenes at the center of *The Garies and Their Friends* do not tear the novel open, rending its mannered surfaces and revealing hidden brutality. Instead, they offer a spectacular enactment of the violence in everyday life that has been on display, in the South and in the North, from the beginning of the narrative. In Webb's book, novels of domesticity, sensation, and reform converge, and the most insulated spaces and humble particulars are shown to bear the weight of history.

Webb does not let his readers or his characters rest comfortably, even in the most sumptuous quarters in the novel. When Garie is ushered into Mr. Walters's parlor, he becomes a surrogate for Webb's artifice:

> The elegance of the room took Mr. Garie completely by surprise, as its furniture indicated not only great wealth, but cultivated taste and refined habits. The richly-papered walls were adorned by paintings from the hands of well-known foreign and native artists. Rich vases and well-executed bronzes were placed in the most favourable situations in the apartment; the elegantly-carved walnut table was covered with those charming little bijoux which the French only are capable of conceiving, and which are only at the command of such purchasers as are possessed of more money than they otherwise can conveniently spend.
>
> Mr. Garie threw himself into a luxuriously-cushioned chair, and was soon so absorbed in contemplating the likeness of a negro officer which hung opposite, that he did not hear the soft tread of Mr. Walters as he entered the room. The latter, stepping slowly forward, caught the eye of Mr. Garie, who started up, astonished at the commanding figure before him. . . .
>
> As Mr. Garie resumed his seat, he could not repress a look of surprise, which Mr. Walters apparently perceived, for a smile slightly curled his lip as he also took a seat opposite his visitor. (121)

Garie is startled by the "commanding figure" of Walters, who resembles the portrait of a black officer that has seized his attention. Webb seems to enjoy placing his readers in the attitude of a southern planter. When Garie first enters the room, he is unsettled by the conspicuous signs of elegance. Conspicuous—but imprecise. Webb supplies adjectives ("cultivated," "refined," "well-known," "well-executed"), rather than nouns that would define Walters's taste. (As we will discover shortly, the narrator and proprietor do identify one crucial item.) It is hard to tell from this passage whether the amorphousness reflects the limits of character (Garie is impressed but doesn't know what he is looking at; Walters advertises his status with little regard for the details) or the concern of narrator or author with the effects, rather than the substance, of cultivation. In the Philadelphia novel *Aristocracy; or, Life in the City*, published anonymously in 1848, the narrator takes readers on an ecstatic tour ("Let us enter the parlor!"), during which the furnishings proclaim the security and worthiness of their owners, who are lauded as aristocrats not of wealth but of virtue: "Do not the very chairs and tables—the lounges, the foot-stools, nay, the broad bright brass stair-rods themselves—do they not all speak an unmistakable language? And do not their polished surfaces elongate into a happy smile, and seem to say—'We share it; we do! We share their joy, though they know it not.'"[40]

In contrast, Webb's narrator withholds or obscures details, playing up Garie's responses. The commodities in Walters's parlor speak in more aggressive tones and with an ambiguity they share with their owner. Like Joseph Willson in his *Sketches*, Webb gives only partial access to the domestic spaces of the higher classes. Until the end of the novel, when readers are invited to Walters's dining room to witness an extraordinary supper, the only area Webb's narrator describes in the mansion, other than the parlor, is the upstairs drawing room. On the night of the riot, it is decorated with guns, cartridges, and a powder keg. These are rooms in which Walters projects and defends his authority.[41]

In the parlor, Webb's narrator directs his readers to the walnut table and its "charming little bijoux which the French only are capable of conceiving." The bijoux indicate that Walters's tastes are deftly expressed, unlike the awkward parroting of Charlie Ellis's employer, Mrs. Thomas. They also show that Walters has the means (the economic "command") to afford such superfluities. But the "charming little bijoux" also indicate something more: an aesthetic, and not just an economic, surplus. Webb's narrator frequently savors the odd circumstance and appreciates the exquisitely wrought. He values stylistic excess.

Webb's irony, figured in the smile that "slightly curled" Walters's lip, is hard to track. In her *Key to Uncle Tom's Cabin*, Stowe describes a scene whose interpretive provocations resonate with those in Webb. She hears from a group of liberated slaves in the North about a master who had sold his nurse (whom he had promised to free) to a man renowned for his cruelty because she had fallen asleep one night during her vigil. Their tribute to the man impresses and perplexes her: "A peculiar form of grave and solemn irony often characterises the communications of this class of people. It is a habit engendered in slavery to comment upon proceedings of this kind in language apparently respectful to the perpetrators, and which is felt to be irony only by a certain peculiarity of manner, difficult to describe." Stowe is intrigued not by the easily calibrated translation of praise into censure, but by an incongruity that takes a "peculiar form" and arises from "a certain peculiarity of manner" (that word again, twice). This kind of articulation disorients the observer, forcing her to heed verbal detail and gauge aspect and meaning. Stowe may get only part of the joke, the gravity and not the guile, since, despite her sensitivity to tone and to her uncertain role as interpreter, she does not consider the possibility that the storytellers' "apparent respect" might extend to her in the present, as she treats them as native informants in her attempt to discern the habits of "this class of people." Stowe's *Key* suggests a complicated irony, the product of antebellum freedom, that may help us to understand Webb's literary manners.[42]

Before the narrator labels the "negro officer" in the portrait that fascinates Garie, he offers a picture of the businessman Walters: "above six feet in height, and exceedingly well-proportioned; of jet-black complexion, and smooth glossy skin. His head was covered with a quantity of wooly hair, which was combed back from a broad but not very high forehead. His eyes were small, black, and piercing, and set deep in his head. His aquiline nose, thin lips, and broad chin, were the very reverse of African in their shape, and gave his face a very singular appearance" (121–22). Like the portrait on the wall, the imposing Walters seems designed to challenge his viewer's appraisals. His features are the "reverse of African," but his color also inverts the racist alignment of whiteness with enterprise. Although Walters may resist typecasting, his allegiances are clear: against servility, prejudice, and racial masquerade, for entrepreneurship and profit. A composite figure, Webb's magnate evokes the Philadelphians Joseph Cassey, Stephen Smith, and especially James Forten Sr. During the 1842 riot, Forten's son-in-law Robert Purvis had guarded his home with a rifle across his knees.[43] William Whipper, a figure who eludes categories, also may have served as a model for Walters. In devising his character, Webb may have drawn on various aspects of Whipper's life, including his commitment to moral reform, advocacy of elevation as tactic and weapon, distance from institutional religion, and support of the Underground Railroad.

When Garie is leaving the parlor, he stops to look again at the portrait on the wall, and his host remarks: "'So you, too, are attracted by that picture,' said Mr. Walters, with a smile. 'All white men look at it with interest. A black man in the uniform of a general officer is something so unusual that they cannot pass it with a glance'" (122). Walters and the narrator imply that some viewers will recognize the portrait, while others will be surprised, echoing the dynamic of inside and outside knowledge in Joseph Willson's *Sketches of the Higher Classes.* Walters has arranged his parlor so that he can observe his visitors' responses to the image and evaluate their apprehensions. A measure of taste, the portrait links refinement to political awareness.

"'That is Toussaint l'Ouverture,'" Walters explains to Garie, and no further detail is necessary (123). Even those who do not recognize the face will know the name of the man who led the Haitian revolution. Walters praises the accuracy of the likeness, distinguishing it from the usual caricatures. He has attended to the imperative that would be enshrined in T. Morris Chester's "Negro Self-Respect and Pride of Race," an address delivered to the Philadelphia Library Company in 1862: "Take down from your walls the pictures of WASHINGTON, JACKSON, AND MCLELLAN; and if you love to gaze upon military chieftains, let the gilded frames be graced with the immortal TOUISSANT." Instead of the semblance that hangs on the wall in Uncle Tom's cabin (a "portrait of General Washington, drawn and colored in a manner which would certainly have astonished that hero, if ever he happened to meet with its like") or the image in Ben and Clara's modest Philadelphia dwelling in Hale's *Liberia* ("the portrait of a solemn-looking colored clergyman, in a white cravat and spectacles, with one hand resting on the Bible, and the other grasping a manuscript sermon"), Webb flaunts the uniformed black commander of Saint Domingue, supplying an alternative emblem of the parlor and a mirror for its guests.[44]

Exactly what Garie sees when he looks so intently is never put into words. Webb's narrator supplies only an equivocal line of dialogue: "'This,' said Mr. Garie, 'gives me an idea of the man that accords with his actions'" (123). Webb holds back whatever "idea" Garie has of Toussaint and whether he approves or disapproves of his "actions." The portrait hangs on the wall, as *The Garies and Their Friends* lies in readers' hands, drawing out viewers, and the narrator appreciates the show.

Walters and Toussaint are linked in the action of the novel, when the entrepreneur defends his home, which has been converted into "a temporary fortress": "the shutters of the upper windows had been loop-holed, double bars had been placed across the doors and windows on the ground floor, carpets had been taken up, superfluous furniture removed, and an air of thorough preparation imparted" (203). Along with the Ellises and other allies, Walters prevents the mob, instigated by Stevens, from entering the building and harming its inhabitants or contents. First they employ reflected light to attract the rioters; then they hurl stones on them, fire bullets, and pour down kettles of hot water. The Ellis women play significant roles. The quiet Esther learns how to load pistols with "precision and celerity," and she alone acts to save the group by removing a firebrand from the pile of cartridges on which it had landed (209). The industrious Caddy serves the recipe of blistering pepper-water that turns the mob from the door.[45]

Webb then narrates events in the streets between Walters's house in the southeast part of Philadelphia and Garie's residence in the northeast, bringing the riots of 1834, 1842, and 1849 into the city proper. Ellis, the father of Esther, Caddy, and Charlie, volunteers to warn the Garie family of their danger. Close to the Garies' house on Winter Street, he encounters a gang who shout, "'Here's a nigger! here's a nigger!'" and chase him down a blind alley (217). He climbs onto the roof of an unfinished building. He struggles to hold off his assailants with a club, but finally is overcome. The men force him to the edge, intending to throw him over. Screaming for help, he clings to the roof, but one of his attackers strikes his fingers—the fingers that enable his livelihood as a carpenter—with first the handle and then the blade of a hatchet, severing two fingers on one hand and deeply cutting the other, and Ellis falls. He is discovered by a few men who lament the night's violence, summon a doctor, and ensure that he is taken to a hospital.[46]

Webb represents a third and final scene during the riot, at Garie's house, where a mob, led by Stevens's henchman McCloskey, breaks through the front door. Assailed by stones, Garie fires his pistol and is shot in the head (by Stevens after McCloskey balks, as McCloskey reveals years later on his deathbed). For two hours, men ransack the house. The terrified Emily, who has taken refuge in a woodshed behind the house with the young Clarence and Emily, dies after a night of exposure, giving birth to a stillborn child. These chapters are among the most graphic fictional depictions of racial riot in the North before the Civil War. They constitute the only sustained literary account from an African American point of view. The English reviewers of the novel drew attention to these scenes. The *Daily News* excerpted the attacks on Ellis and the Garies; the *Sunday Times* reprinted the resistance at Walters's mansion.[47]

Like John Beauchamp Jones in *The City Merchant* but from a different standpoint, justifying rather than blaming his African American characters, Webb writes a retrospective, telescoped meditation on violence in Philadelphia, incorporating details from the riots of the 1830s and 1840s. This suturing of riot was also a feature of Philadelphia's visual culture. In "A View of the City of Brotherly Love," a lithograph from the early 1840s published by the New York firm of Henry R. Robinson, an image of William Penn, braced by an intersecting peace pipe and scroll with the motto "Wise Laws and a promt and just administration of them," is suspended over a vision of the city that brings together various locations and events in a welter of struggle (figure 4.2).

In the midground of the right half of "The City of Brotherly Love," the shell of Smith's Beneficial Hall lies across the street from Pennsylvania Hall, in flames. The hall had been built by William Whipper's partner Stephen Smith as a meeting place for black organizations and was burned during the riots of 1842, while Pennsylvania Hall had been destroyed in 1838. In the actual city of Philadelphia, the two locations were three-quarters of a mile apart.[48] In front of Smith's Hall and extending down and to the right are a cluster of small figures representing the event that ignited the 1842 riots, an attack on the black temperance parade on the anniversary of West Indian emancipation (a banner reads "LIBERTY, August 1st"). Closer to the foreground, on the right, black and white faces, limbs, and bodies are knotted in hostility, and the broken musical instruments of the marchers litter the pavement.

The print is filled with allusions to the city's history of violence: street fights, shootings, stabbings, hosings, riots. Weavers hoist their trademark, a shuttle, and troop around the corner of the burning Pennsylvania Hall. Recurrent tensions

FIGURE 4.2 "A View of the City of Brotherly Love," published by Henry R. Robinson (circa 1842). Courtesy of the Historical Society of Pennsylvania (HSP).

between the handloom weavers, many of them Irish Catholic immigrants, and Protestant nativists would help fuel the riots in Kensington during the summer of 1844. Throngs battle in front of federal and state banks, invoking the controversies over the rechartering of the Bank of the United States during the 1830s and its ruinous failure in 1841. Contorted figures occupy the niches between the pillars of the U.S. Bank.[49] At the left of the image, crowds gather in front of a building whose placard advertises both an "Irish Repeal Meeting" and "Best of Liquors at 3 cts a glass," as the artist (who is not identified) rehearses the canard about the volatile Irish mix of politics and cheap alcohol. At the right, behind the picture windows of a building marked with letters indicating the fashionable "CHES[T]NUT St.," an upper-class man and woman enact a crime of passion.

In the center foreground, a white urchin directs a stream of water from a hydrant, which passes over the head of a black boy scuffling with a white boy and splashes on the face of an angry, muscular black woman who has a raised a fist to strike a beseeching white woman in a ragged dress, whom she has grabbed by the hair. The struggles between the children visually rhyme with those of the women, suggesting a baleful inheritance. In the tableau, black woman and child are pictured as aggressors, and at least temporarily have the upper hand. The kneeling white woman reverses the famous abolitionist image of the supplicating black slave who pleads "Am I Not a Man and a Brother?"[50] In front of the women and children, in the gutter of this stage, lie bricks, an empty pail, a club, a pistol, and a long knife, emblems of the "City of Brotherly Love."

In the distance, elevated on Bush Hill, at the apex of the scene and directly under the bust of Penn, a group evokes the federal procession of July 4, 1788, in honor of the adoption of the new Constitution. The parade had begun on Third and Cedar streets (the southern area evoked by the racial clashes in the foreground and midground), traversed the city, and ended on Bush Hill to the north. From a distance, given the spare cues, the viewer of the print cannot discern whether these July 4 celebrants are marching or brawling, and whether this vista offers the contrast of past harmony or the continuity of strife.

What is clear in the turmoil is that time does not march forward. Instead, it fractures into simultaneous clusters of discord. The violence that dominates the center of the image juxtaposes different periods, incidents, and locales and spikes into other angles of conflict that extend into the distance. The artist redraws the map of Philadelphia, sketching the city as a theater of perpetual dispute. Its principal space is not one of the celebrated squares in William Penn's "green Country Towne," but a jagged triangle formed by eruptions of brutality, surrounded by the public structures that typify clashing interests. Everywhere the viewer looks, there is antagonism. At the top, above the fray, William Penn seems to be frowning, or sleeping, or to have fainted.

In some ways, Webb in *The Garies and Their Friends* presents a similar "View of the City of Brotherly Love." Manipulating sequence and event, he composes one in a series of indictments of the gap between Philadelphia's etymological promise and its historical reality. In both Robinson's print and Webb's novel, the movement of time involves violent repetition, but Webb's narrative includes a fragile progress. Webb illustrates an encumbered present, a development at the risk of collapse, but, however tenuous, there remains the possibility for change, for a measure of security and success for his African American characters. In Webb's city, past, present, and future might not be one. While the artist in Robinson's print is cynical about his antagonists, Webb depicts his strivers with a tangled sympathy.

Placing black aggression in the foreground, Robinson's print echoes the blame for racial strife found in documents such as the police report after the 1838 riot, the grand jury findings in 1842, and John Beauchamp Jones's 1851 novel, *The City Merchant*. Webb rejects such official stories. His narrator disparages the "truthless verdict" that elides culpability for the deaths of Clarence and Emily Garie, announced by an inquest whose panel includes the murderer George Stevens (229). He conjectures that whites schemed to foment violence, rehearsing the distrust in Philadelphia since the candles placed in the windows to divert rioters in 1834 and echoed in Lippard's *Quaker City* and *The Killers.* Webb represents Stevens as orchestrating the riot with his wealthy cronies and Irish subordinates in order to seize African American property and inherit Garie's fortune. He alludes to the lack of protection from city authorities during the riots. When his character Walters requests assistance from the mayor, he is told that the city might be able to supply two or three officers at most, if Walters insists, and then to safeguard only his residence. The "rising indignation at the apathy and indifference" (202) of the mayor, felt by Walters, parallels the frustration of blacks and whites with the police responses in 1834, 1838, 1842, and 1849.

Webb justifies black violence as a limited response to attack. Under siege in Walters's home, Esther loads pistols and Caddy prepares kettles. Neither resembles the Fury in Robinson's "City of Brotherly Love," who raises her prominent fist. Unlike Black Andy in Lippard's *The Killers,* Mr. Walters counters with restraint. His wealth enables a fantasy of entrepreneurial redress. Spurned at a hotel in Trenton because of his color, Walters buys the building and evicts its owner. Preserving his mansion from assault, he figuratively restores structures that had been lost to historical riot: Smith's Beneficial Hall and the African American temperance hall in 1842, the California House in 1849, and the private homes in the Cedar neighborhood destroyed in the 1830s and 1840s. In the choreographed defense at Walters's house, Webb recapitulates the black collective action during the riots of 1849.

In *The Garies and Their Friends,* the ubiquitous public violence of Robinson's "View of the City of Brotherly Love" is extended to private arenas as well. In his interiors, Webb joins the intimate and the spectacular, and he plays out the tragedy, melodrama, farce, and possible comedy of the Philadelphia experiment. The rhetorical achievement of the novel, which also is a literary historical achievement, is to convey the pressures and textures of urban space: the peculiar freedom of Philadelphia.[51]

Philadelphia *Vanitas*

In the final set piece of *The Garies and Their Friends,* Webb's narrator describes the wedding of Charles Ellis and Emily Garie in a time approaching the present, "many years" after the riot (309). The festivities are held in the home of the businessman Walters, who has married Charles's sister Esther. (They have two children.) The remnants of the Garie and Ellis families and their many friends have gathered to celebrate. The guests include a few whites, who have supported the families during the course of the narrative, playfully figured by the narrator as the "blancmange" alongside the "chocolate cream" in the inventory of desserts below. After the wedding, a meal is served and, representing the constraints of freedom, Webb pulls out all the stops:

> Then came the supper. Oh! such a supper!—such quantities of nice things as money and skill alone can bring together. There were turkeys innocent of a bone, into which you might plunge your knife to the very hilt without coming into contact with a splinter—turkeys from which cunning cooks had extracted every bone leaving the meat alone behind, with the skin not perceptibly broken. How brown and tempting they looked, their capacious bosoms giving rich promise of high-seasoned dressing within, and looking larger by comparison with the tiny reed-birds beside them, which lay cosily on the golden toast, looking as much as to say, "If you want something to remember for ever, come and give me a bite!"
>
> Then there were dishes of stewed terrapin, into which the initiated dipped at once, and to which they for some time gave their undivided attention, oblivious, apparently, of the fact that there was a dish of chicken-salad close beside them.
>
> Then there were oysters in every variety—silver dishes containing them stewed, their fragrant macey odour wafting itself upward, and causing watery sensations about the mouth. Waiters were constantly rushing into the room, bringing dishes of them fried so richly brown, so smoking hot, that no man with a heart in his bosom could possibly refuse them. Then there were glass dishes of them pickled, with little black spots of allspice floating on the pearly liquid that contained them. And lastly, oysters broiled, whose delicious flavor exceeds my powers of description—these, with ham and tongue, were the solid comforts. There were other things, however, to which one could turn when the appetite grew more dainty; there were jellies, blancmange, chocolate cream, biscuit glacé, peach ice, vanilla ice, orange-water ice, brandy peaches, preserved strawberries and pines; not to say a word of towers of candy, bonbons, kisses, champagne, Rhine wine, sparkling Catawba, liquors, and a man in the corner making sherry cobblers of wondrous flavor, under the especial supervision of Kinch; on the whole, it was an American supper, got up regardless of expense—and whoever has been to such an entertainment knows very well what an American supper is. (376–77)

It is hard to know where to begin talking about this passage or how to stop. The critic in the London *Daily News,* after excerpting the paragraphs I have quoted, in a review that caught the eye of Frederick Douglass, suggested larger implications for the meal: "Who can wonder that with such feeding indigestion should be a national institution in the model republic?"[52] As in the southern opening of the novel, this northern table overflows with provisions far beyond the needs of its diners. The items at the wedding banquet are more substantial than the decadent fare on the Georgia table and, of course, this is a larger meal, held on a ceremonial occasion, but in both scenes, the array of food is oddly personified, sexualized, and historicized.

At the wedding table, there are no slow disclosures of race and caste. The supper at Walters's house is a conspicuous accomplishment of African American Philadelphia. The wedding party and guests have survived. Family and friends have assembled. Walters and the Ellises have prospered in business and marriage to the extent that they can afford and savor this banquet. Webb evokes the distinctive food culture of mid-nineteenth-century Philadelphia. The city's passion for oysters "in every variety" was legendary, and dishes made from sea turtles or from terrapins, the marsh turtles that were a cheaper local alternative, were a Philadelphia specialty. The city was known, too, for its black hospitality and catering industries, presided over by such figures as Robert Bogle, esteemed for his terrapin dinners, and Henry Minton, whose bountiful spreads were lauded by Martin Delany in his *Condition*. Webb does not name Bogle (who died in 1837) or Minton (whose career was flourishing in the 1850s), choosing to model his portrayals in relation to local circumstances, rather than specify them. Yet the lavish spread in general and the terrapins in particular evoke the influential black caterers and restaurateurs. In *The Garies*, Webb showcases a black clientele for their expensive services, which more typically would have been solicited by affluent European American customers.[53]

Webb's diners enjoy their food and drink at the wedding supper, as they have in the previous scenes of eating at the Ellis and Walters homes in Philadelphia. At the southern tables in the novel, the fare remains largely untouched. Although the excess on display at the wedding supper complicates the guests' pleasures, it does not invalidate them. The characters are presented as having earned their sumptuousness and their release. This event is no temperance affair, like the parties approved by Joseph Willson in his *Sketches of the Higher Classes*. At this supper, distinguished by black achievement, the North seems different from the South and the end of the story appears to represent clear progress from its beginning. Yet the opening and final meals are linked by their extravagant details, and the boundary between slavery and freedom becomes porous. In both scenes, tables and diners are figured as vulnerable. Pleasure is tangible but also unsettling. Despite the narrator's reassurance, the "comforts" of the wedding supper are far from "solid."[54]

The happy ending is qualified by various plot developments. The meal is bracketed by two death scenes in which the past erupts into the present and binds the future. Before the supper chapter, but after the meal itself (Webb manipulates the story time), George Stevens, consumed with guilt and fearing arrest, jumps to his death from the balcony of his New York City mansion. His broken form resembles that of Charles Ellis, hurled from the roof years before, a victim of the events that Stevens had orchestrated. During the supper, interrupting dessert, a lawyer and minister are summoned to McCloskey's hospital room, where the dying man confesses that Stevens had paid him to help incite the riot and that he had been unable to kill Garie, an act that Stevens himself performed. For all these years, he has kept in a trunk, now in the hospital room, Garie's will. Through the proper administration of that will, Garie's estate is transferred from the Stevens family to his rightful heirs, which means that his children Emily and Clarence, whose mother insisted on moving north to spare them the condition of slavery, now become the owners of a Georgia plantation, including its slaves, whom Garie never emancipated. The narrator does not inform his readers that this inheritance has been altered, and it remains unclear whether the continued possession of slaves by those who had been born slaves is an oversight of the characters or the narrator or the author, or whether this unresolved detail is another one of Webb's sly contrivances.[55]

On the level of rhetoric and figure, even more thoroughly than in the plot, this is a strangely overdone "American supper." Waiters rush in and out of the room, but no mention in this orgy of consumption is made of where or how all of these goods were produced, no allusion similar to the "Geeche limes" in the opening scene. Cunning cooks—and "cunning" seems an equivocal trait in cooks, or even in authors—have removed the bones from the meat, leaving no visible trace of their labor. Although the skin on the turkeys is not "perceptibly broken," the birds have been sliced open and reconstructed. The capacious bosoms and delicate skin seem as though they might rupture at the touch of a diner's knife.

The narrator draws attention to the absence of bones but never explains what this absence signifies. What has been taken out? What is not being represented, or is being represented by its removal? Those who have produced this meal? African Americans in Philadelphia, the great majority of whom would not have the means for such a display? African Americans laboring under slavery in the South? Or is the turkey itself—a product of concealed, extracted, vulnerable labor—a reminder of slavery? Have the bones been removed in an attempt to banish the skeleton from this feast, to evade memories of riot and intimations of mortality? The main dish at the table may recall "The Singing Bones," an African folktale in which a poor woman who has many children cooks and serves them to her husband. One day the husband hears the bones, which the woman had removed, sing to him about their fate and the need for proper burial. In anger, he kills his wife, inters the children's remains, and lives alone for the rest of his life. Such a tale would furnish a counterpoint of loss and requital to the festivities.[56]

Is the turkey without bones a symbol of abstraction and artifice, the kinds of imaginative labor performed upon the world that enable its literary consumption? Can we read it also as an emblem for the critical sleight of hand that pulls structure from verbal substance? If so, is the skeleton "form" or "history"? If the diners strenuously reconstruct their innocence and stage their freedom, is this effort myopic, misguided, purgative, or fortifying? In what senses are the characters—and also the narrator, Webb's different readers, and the author himself—"innocent" or not? The "American supper" passage is filled with insinuations about knowledge, ignorance, and cunning.

Webb did not invent his "turkeys innocent of a bone," but he amplifies the metaphors. We can find, for example, instructions for preparing a "Boned Turkey" in Eliza Leslie's *New Receipts for Cooking*, published in 1854. Although we have no evidence that Webb knew this particular volume, Leslie's renown as a Philadelphia author and culinary expert and the popularity of her cookbooks allow us to speculate that *New Receipts for Cooking* might represent the kind of approach to food preparation that Webb incorporated in *The Garies*. Here is part of what Eliza Leslie has to say about the manufacture of her turkey:

> Next loosen the flesh from the breast, and back, and body; and then from the thighs. It requires care and patience to do it nicely, and to avoid tearing or breaking the skin. The knife should always penetrate quite to the bone; scraping loose the flesh rather than cutting it. When all the flesh has been completely loosened, take the turkey by the neck, give it a pull, and the whole skeleton will come out entire from the flesh, as easily as you draw your hand out of a glove. The flesh will then fall down, a flat and shapeless mass. With a small needle and thread, carefully sew up any holes that have accidentally been torn in the skin. . . . Stuff it very hard, and as you proceed, form the turkey into its natural shape, by filling out, properly, the wings, breast, body, &c. When all the stuffing is in, sew up the body, and skewer the turkey into the usual shape in which they are trussed; so that, if skillfully done, it will look almost as if it had not been boned.[57]

Often when literary critics turn to supposedly nonliterary sources, they describe how creative writers transform the inert materials of their culture. In Eliza Leslie's recipe, though, we already find the cunning of the cooks in preparing their meals: the exquisite perforation, the diligent scraping, the artful extraction conveyed with an odd simile that joins autopsy and undressing, dissection and fashion ("and the whole skeleton will come out entire from the flesh, as easily as you draw your hand out of a glove"), the meticulous, aggressive renovation, and the fantasy of flesh without bones. Webb has recognized the curiosity of such rituals and the extravagance of such investments, and he has extended the frame of reference from the domestic to the civic and the national. The "turkeys innocent of a bone" become the centerpieces in his "American supper."

Sexuality, not explicitly represented in the plot of *The Garies and Their Friends,* is embodied, as it was on the Georgia tea table at the start of the novel, in the inviting delicacies arrayed at the wedding supper: the tiny reed birds "which lay cosily on the golden toast," their aspect soliciting a bite, and the "brown and tempting" turkeys "into which you might plunge your knife," with "their capacious bosoms giving rich promise of high-seasoned dressing within." Like the items on the Georgia table—the ripe strawberries that peep through their coating of sugar and the Geeche limes that expose their bronze forms just above the rim of the glass—the reed birds and turkeys at the wedding supper entice viewers with their sensuous exteriors and glimpses of interior delights.

Webb here draws on a tradition of still life painting in which fruit, meat, and human flesh are visually linked—a Dutch tradition, or at least Dutch as transmitted through early-nineteenth-century Philadelphia artists, a context to which I turn shortly. At this wedding feast, he implies a sexuality that decorum may restrict him from presenting in a more direct way. His distance may be strategic as well, given the emphasis in popular culture on black avidity. Webb communicates the intense satisfaction experienced by his diners and also their involvement, as victims and possibly actors, in larger frames of oppression. There is a disconcerting quality to the scene: the items on the table seem to encourage their violation. Webb may be summoning a discordant echo of the historical warrants for the Philadelphia riots (the victims' own behavior prompted assault) or the twisted justifications for rape. He also seems to be having intemperate fun, embedding metaphors of sexuality and injury at his respectable banquet. In the opening and final table scenes, he alters the usual antislavery pictures of South and North, stressing the exposure in Philadelphia and under freedom. The aspects of the supper—endorsement of pleasure, exposure of violence, social critique, sexual humor—do not fit together seamlessly, and Webb appears to relish the excess.

The meat at Webb's supper table is figured as human, not only because its appealing surfaces resemble flesh and not only because it appears to speak, but also because it is subject to the kind of harm bodies experience in war or riot: a blade plunged "to the very hilt." Eliza Leslie advises her cooks to make sure that their knives "should always penetrate quite to the bone," and Webb emphasizes the carving knife as weapon, furnishing it with "hilt," like a dagger or sword. The supper phrase "to the hilt" repeats a description two chapters earlier, when the younger Clarence Garie, passing for white, imagines murdering George Stevens's son, who knows and will expose his secret: "As he sat there . . . he became a murderer in his heart; and if an invisible dagger could have been placed in his hands, he would have driven it to the hilt in his breast" (346). The blade and the bones at the "American supper" evoke the ritual of public violence at the center of the novel: the hatchet that cuts into father Ellis's hands as he grasps the edge of a roof, the damage produced by his fall. Ellis himself, addled and infirm, makes the connection at the wedding: "The poor old gentleman scarcely seemed able to comprehend the affair, and apparently laboured under the impression that it was another mob, and looked a little terrified at times when the laughter or conversation grew louder than usual" (372). In an earlier scene, while the festivities were being planned at the tea table, the merriment had startled Ellis, "who cried, 'There they come! there they come!' and cowered down in his great chair, and looked so exceedingly terrified, that the noise was hushed instantly" (342). The specter of riot is never far from Ellis's mind, and at the wedding and supper, he serves as a living reminder of its carnage.

When the narrator imagines the tiny reed birds at the supper importuning the guests ("'If you want something to remember for ever, come and give me a bite!'"), the diction hints, ominously or at least ambiguously, that they will have an indelible experience. But what about the "bite" will the diners be unable to forget? The enigmatic "something" may not be entirely pleasant. The line beckons but also dares. With his ardent reed birds, Webb may be rewriting the scene in chapter 13 of *Uncle Tom's Cabin*, set in the Quaker Rachel Halliday's northern kitchen, where the escaped slaves George, Eliza, and Harry find refuge: "even the knives and forks had a social clatter as they went on to the table; and the chicken and ham had a cheerful and joyous fizzle in the pan, as if they rather enjoyed being cooked than otherwise." The domestic fantasies in Stowe and Webb come with overtones of coercion, but Webb accentuates the instabilities and gives his meal a queasy agency. Those dainty reed birds may—or may not—cheerfully submit to their fate.[58]

Webb may have had other literary meals in mind, given the abundance of "American suppers."

At Judge Temple's table in Cooper's *The Pioneers* (1823), the provisions—"an enormous roasted turkey," a boiled turkey, squirrel fricassee, venison, bear, mutton, sweetmeats, cakes, pies, and decanters of brandy, rum, gin, and wine—are consumed while the guests debate the eradication of forests. As in Cooper's novel, the superfluity at Webb's table is both admirable (as a triumph in the wilderness) and disturbing (in its link to external ravage).[59]

In Irving's "The Legend of Sleepy Hollow," published in *The Sketch Book of Geoffrey Crayon* (1820), the narrator describes how the eager Ichabod Crane, surveying the livestock on the Van Tassel farm and the prospect of marriage with daughter Katrina, envisioned his own personal banquet:

he pictured to himself every roasting pig running about with a pudding in his belly, and an apple in his mouth; the pigeons were snugly put to bed in a comfortable pie, and tucked in with a coverlet of crust; the geese were swimming in their own gravy; and the ducks pairing cosily in dishes, like snug married couples, with a decent competency of onion sauce . . . not a turkey, but he beheld daintily trussed up, with its gizzard under its wing, and, peradventure, a necklace of savoury sausages; and even bright chanticleer himself lay sprawling on his back, in a side dish, with uplifted claws, as if craving that quarter, which his chivalrous spirit disdained to ask while living.[60]

In his table scenes, Webb (somewhat less genially than Irving) pictures a complex domesticity in which the origins of the feast are both insulated and emphasized by metaphors of luxurious surrender. Webb appears to overdraw Irving: the "Geeche limes, almost drowned in their own rich syrup" deepen the predicament of the "geese . . . swimming in their own gravy." The eloquent "reed-birds lay[ing] cosily on the golden toast" are more provocative versions of the "ducks pairing cosily in dishes."

The uplifted claws of Irving's rooster, seeking a mercy that his "chivalrous spirit" refused when he was alive, gesture at the trajectory from medieval to modern table manners that Norbert Elias analyzes in *The Civilizing Process* (1939). Elias argues that the establishment of manners involved suppressing the "animalic character" in the display of food. In Edmund Jephcott's translation:

> The direction is quite clear. From a standard of feeling by which the sight and carving of a dead animal on the table are actually experienced as pleasurable, or at least as not at all unpleasant, the development leads to another standard by which reminders that the meat dish has something to do with the killing of an animal are avoided to the utmost. In many of our meat dishes the animal form is so concealed and changed by the art of its preparation and carving that, while eating, one is scarcely reminded of its origin.

For Elias, decorum at the bourgeois table reflects historical changes since the Middle Ages. Social constraints have been internalized, feelings of shame and delicacy have become refined, and physical violence has been delegated to the State. This process has been forgotten, while the achievements of "civilization" have been taken for granted. For Elias, such developments are epitomized in the limits placed at the dinner table on the use of the knife, symbol of danger and death, "beset with affects," conjuring a past when it served as weapon and not merely utensil. On Ichabod Crane's table, the rooster has been arranged so that the violence of its preparation is obscured, but Irving plays up Crane's inordinate appetites.[61]

At the wedding table in *The Garies and Their Friends*, the "direction" of progress is even less clear. The meal seems part Victorian, part Medieval, part Roman. The artifice is so orchestrated—those turkeys from which cunning cooks have smoothly extracted every bone—that readers are reminded of the energy needed to sustain the illusion. The knife at the wedding supper in *The Garies* is imagined as a sword, the meat as its victim: "you might plunge your knife to the very hilt without coming in contact with a splinter." At this American supper, violence is not the distant, forgotten origin of civilized manners but their current incitement. Nancy Bentley has argued that, at the late-nineteenth- and early-twentieth-century dinner tables of Henry James and Edith Wharton, the sublimated vehemence of the elite is on display, part of a ritual contest over social power. At Webb's earlier "American supper," multiple class forces are present, exerted by African American survivors who labor to keep their surfaces intact, inflicted by working class rioters (many of them Irish American) who are portrayed as the instruments of an Anglo American elite.[62]

In designing his supper, Webb also may have turned to Melville's linked sketches, "The Paradise of Bachelors and the Tartarus of Maids" (1855). In "The Paradise of Bachelors," with a nod to Irving, Melville's narrator inflates through martial analogies the feast he shares with nine bachelors in London, whose surfeit extends into the second portrayal, "The Tartarus of Maids," which outlines the dehumanizing labor of women in a New England paper factory. In "Tartarus," Melville's narrator draws out comparisons between landscape and female anatomy, manufacture and parturition. Although the narrator insists that the second sketch is "the very counterpart" and "the inverted similitude" of the first, no firm relationship is articulated (an unsteadiness that the discrepancy between the two formulations reinforces). The bachelors are criticized but also caressed, and the maids receive both sympathy and satire, while the figurative play sometimes borders on misogyny. Banquet is hinged with factory, and the pleasures of the bachelors, their "very perfection of quiet absorption" and "remarkable decorum," are viewed in a wider frame of exploitation. Webb's narrator, too, wavers about his diners (also indulging in sexual metaphor) and engages visual practices (for Melville, the diptych; for Webb, the still life and *vanitas*).[63]

Behind Webb's supper, and possibly the other American feasts, may lie the "Trimalchio's Banquet" episode in the fragmentary *Satyricon* of Petronius. Written in the first century A.D., printed in 1664, and translated into English in 1694, the edition most readily available to Webb would have been published in 1854 as part of Henry G. Bohn's renowned Classical Library. Trimalchio, a former slave, hosts a meal whose indulgence makes Walters and the Ellises look like pikers and the "cunning cooks" seem amateurish. As the wine is poured, Trimalchio's own slaves, under his guidance and often with musical accompaniment, treat his guests to a series of culinary marvels. A boar wearing the cap of freedom is sliced open with a hunting knife and birds emerge. The belly of a Priapus figure holds an array of fruits, which squirt juice in the faces of those who touch them. Pastries are made in the shape of thrushes, a fat goose is composed of pork, and thorns are stuck in quinces so they appear to be sea urchins. The vulgar freemen indulge their appetites and exult in their host's ingenious prodigality. Trimalchio alternates between savoring the occasion, threatening his slaves, and theatrically lamenting his mortality. Critics dispute whether Petronius provides a moral critique of Trimalchio, satirizes the behavior of the freemen, or merely enjoys himself. [64]

Compared with "Trimalchio's Banquet," Webb's "American supper" is a modest affair. The extravagances of Webb's diners are tempered by their means, their earnestness, and the surrounding intolerance. They pursue respectability rather than vulgarity. Their author never questions their right to be free. Yet there are resemblances between the two meals. In both Petronius and Webb, narrators consider the exertions of their freemen. Tables overflow with implications. The free and the enslaved move in uneasy proximity. And death, albeit it in very different tones, shadows the feast.

Visually, the form that most resembles Webb's opening and final table scenes is the still life, especially as painted by the Dutch in the seventeenth and eighteenth centuries and by Philadelphians in the first half of the nineteenth century. In the Dutch images, usually oil paintings, tables were set and skewed, with their lavish contents indicating the aspirations but also ambivalences of a rising middle class. The signs of cultivated affluence were marked by reminders of transience. The images combined optical pleasure and moral intimation. Such palpable allegories were further developed in the type of Dutch still life known as *vanitas*. In these paintings, the objects arranged in seeming disorder on the tables—fruit, meat, flowers, candles, books, coins, crystal goblets, hourglasses, and skulls—incorporated a lexicon of mortality. Mundane and erudite, these objects bristled with significance. They were not "still" but in the process of consumption or decay, vivified by loss, often balanced at precarious angles or tipped over. On banquet tables, the game was skillfully displayed, often ornamented to appear as if alive. The contents of mince pies spilled toward the viewer, as though they were viscera. [65]

Still-life painting in the early United States gained prominence in Philadelphia, with works by the family of Charles Willson Peale, and especially by his son Raphaelle. Raphaelle Peale's still lifes often concentrated on a few objects—fruits, vegetables, a cut of meat—in a shallow, isolated space. Alexander Nemerov describes the uncanny embodiment of Peale's objects, which are portrayed with a regard so intense that they appear weirdly sentient. Blackberries seem to have absorbed not only the artist's mind but also his corporeal presence. A glistening cut of steak with split bone, its flesh rendered in exquisite detail, heightens the fragile meatiness of artist and observer, an effect echoed in a skull-like head of cabbage resting against it. On such canvasses, Peale intensifies the still-life and *vanitas* traditions and raises the possibility that close attention to surfaces might risk the secure distance and depths of the observer.[66]

The Dutch and Philadelphia still lifes offer a perspective on the qualities of freedom that Webb represents in *The Garies and Their Friends*. He may have seen such images on display at the Pennsylvania Academy of Fine Arts or on the walls of parlors and dining rooms in African American or European American higher class homes. The reminders of mortality are on view throughout the novel, from the skull and crossbones Kinch chalks on the back of Charlie Ellis's uniform, to the bullet hole that Walters leaves in his ceiling after the riot, to the invalid father Ellis who dreads a mob at the wedding. The book opens and closes with two hinged counterparts, the Georgia tea table, a still life whose delicacies are entangled in the slave economy, and the Philadelphia supper, a northern *vanitas* whose satisfactions come with a bite and whose emblems are the "turkeys innocent of a bone" into which knives may be plunged "to the very hilt." Across the novel, Webb presents scenes that are characterized by what we might call a still-life aesthetics: meticulously arranged domestic interiors—visions of freedom, consumption, and constraint—whose surfaces, imbued with narrative and historical meanings, invite viewers to partake of their complex pleasures. The surfeit conveys achievement as well as unease and insinuates details in broader contexts and temporalities.

Webb's verbal still lifes are influenced by the distinctive experience of African Americans in Philadelphia. The attainments of his characters are fragile, not only because of the inevitability of death (the typical *vanitas* motif) but also because of the tenacity of prejudice and the omnipresence of violence. The death that shadows his African American characters, and also his European American characters but in different ways, takes as one of its forms the historical materiality of racial enslavement in the United States, a social death whose effects pervade the North. The successes of Walters, the Ellises, and the Garies are viewed as excessive by Stevens and the rioters, who mark them for attack; by the public and private authorities in the novel, who enforce racial boundaries on streetcars, in schools, trades, churches, and cemeteries; and to some extent by Harriet Beecher Stowe and Lord Brougham, the renowned figures who introduce the book as a parable of capability and treat its characters and events as "peculiar."

At the end of the novel, the surviving African American protagonists remain in the city, in spite of disfranchisement and riot. Webb resists the voluntary emigration supported by Martin Delany and other leaders in the 1850s, the resettlement urged by the American Colonization Society and by Sarah Josepha Hale, and the expulsion imagined by writers such as J. B. Jones. (Webb himself, we might remember, moved with his family to Jamaica from 1858 until 1869, when he returned to the United States.) Like Joseph Willson in his *Sketches of the Higher Classes*, Webb enlists his novel in the politics of information, with a trans-atlantic audience in mind. He hopes that his narrative of African Americans in Philadelphia will reinforce the judgments of those who denounce prejudice and support abolition and influence the views of those who do not see or who distort the progress under freedom. Yet *The Garies and Their Friends* should not be reduced to a stance. Such position-taking does not begin to convey the range of attitudes in Webb's novel or the dynamics of his historical imagination.

Webb endorses and mourns the diners at his American supper. He sympa-thizes with them and satirizes them. Walters and the Ellises carefully negotiate status and authority in a game whose rules change as they advance, and readers are drawn into the story. As the narrator suggests, "whoever has been to such an entertainment knows very well what an American supper is" (377). Webb allows a distance between his readers and such entertainments (restricting address to "whoever has been"), perhaps indulging his British audience, but he also col-lapses that distance, implying that all of his readers, British and American, black and white, men and women, participate in the extravagant ceremonies of race and freedom.

Like the contemporary African American anti-ethnologists, Frederick Douglass in his lecture "The Claims of the Negro Ethnologically Considered" (1854) and James McCune Smith in his essay "On the Fourteenth Query of Thomas Jeffer-son's Notes on Virginia" (1859), both of whom painstakingly demonstrate the equal humanity of their race and seek to refute the ludicrous but devastating charg-es of natural inferiority, Webb balks at proving the obvious and responds with earnestness and outrage. Like his peers and his characters, he labors on. *The Garies and Their Friends* is, as I have tried to show, much more than an effort to validate capability. It is a meditation on that demand and on its backgrounds and legacies. Rather than William Whipper's "'apathy of despair,'" Webb in 1857 portray an energy of despair. He suggests that a measure of freedom still may be possible in a society in which he represents his characters as having a history of investments. This certainly is a freedom qualified by racism and inequity, as Harriet Jacobs implies at the end of her *Incidents in the Life of a Slave Girl* (1861), published on the verge of the Civil War: "We [she and her family in New York] are as free from the power of slaveholders as are the white people of the north; and though that, according to my ideas, is not saying a great deal, it is a vast improvement in *my* condition." With a similar deftness and a gesture to those "who know very well," Webb's narrator insists on degrees of freedom, even as he involves his readers in a difficult history and suggests there is no unconstrained position.[67]

Webb is skeptical about progress and, despite the four-paragraph coda to the novel, in which the narrator assures readers that the families lived for many years in domestic contentment, the sequence of episodes in the book leaves open the question of whether the future will repeat or diverge from the Philadelphia pattern of regressive advance. The African American service during the yellow fever of 1793, followed by charges of extortion and theft; the national conventions "for the Improvement of the Free People of Colour" in the 1830s, followed by the burning of Pennsylvania Hall and disfranchisement in 1838; the African American temperance parade of 1842 met with assault; the 1849 report on "Ten Year's Progress" split by riots; petition after petition to restore the vote, with no legal effect—such a pattern seems as distinctive of the city as the famously symmetrical grid outlined by William Penn and Thomas Holme in 1683.

In his still lifes, Webb presses the adjective "still," examining persistence (the choice to stay rather than emigrate), labor (the vehemence of restraint), and contradiction (the regressive advance). Still—in the future as in the past, nevertheless—perhaps foolishly, perhaps not, Webb's characters strive in the hope that their efforts will produce different outcomes, and the narrator keeps his distance.

Webb's narrator—setting and skewing his tables—does not capitulate to dominant values or recommend an elevation that is really a submission, in moves that many observers have seen as characteristic of Philadelphia's African American leaders or a wider devotion to "respectability" in the nineteenth century. These are the kinds of judgments questioned recently by literary scholars such as Carla L. Peterson, Claudia Tate, and Ann duCille, and historians such as Evelyn Brooks Higginbotham, Eddie S. Glaude Jr., and Patrick Rael. Yet Rael, at the end of his *Black Identity and Black Protest in the Antebellum North,* pulls back from his significant reappraisal. Using an analogy that will seem familiar to those who have read Webb's novel, Rael maintains that black leaders' calls for respectability were vitiated by an acceptance of elitist and masculinist values: "Eating from the ideological table of their oppressors, they became so reliant on its menu that they may have imbibed some of its more distasteful offerings."[68] As we have seen in chapter 2, the Philadelphia debates in the 1830s and 1840s were fiercely negotiated, with self and social consciousness, especially in the wake of disfranchisement. The contrasts at Rael's "ideological table" between oppressors who arrange the meal and subjugated diners who choose from its bill of fare, not always sure of what they are eating, are too neatly drawn. We might say that Rael's scene is not literary enough. William Whipper, Joseph Willson, and Frank J. Webb thwart our modern back-formations in which conduct may be purified from or reduced to ideology. Instead, they present a social field in which action is constrained but also creative.

When Werner Sollors, the editor of the only volume of Webb's collected writings, in his astute introduction skims over those table scenes in *The Garies*—"This thoroughly bourgeois novel takes delight in the culture of the Garies' and Ellises' domestic meals: a Southern dinner and a Philadelphia wedding feast are described in lavish detail"—we are alerted to the possibility that we may wish to read even more slowly and less transparently. Intricate distinctions are played out in those "lavish details."[69] When we move through books such as *The Garies and Their Friends* to claims about politics, our terms may not be as self-evident as they seem. "Thoroughly" does not acknowledge the different perspectives assumed by Webb's narrator, and "bourgeois" insufficiently marks the characters' tactical materialism and difficult pleasures.

Webb's novel refuses the opposition between "form and manner" and "substance," made then (in debates about conduct in Philadelphia) and now (in theoretical disparagements of form). Webb shows that form, his characters' and his own, is vital rather than ephemeral or symptomatic. In his novel, details of gesture, tone, and ornament are not only expressions of personal and group identity but also part of a struggle for authority, even survival. In *The Garies*, to obey the rules is to violate norms. Webb situates his forms and formalities in a depth of field that includes southern slavery and northern prejudice, the black political conventions of the 1830s and 1840s, disputes about "condition" and "complexion," the endeavors of the African American middle and higher classes, disfranchisement in 1838, riot in the 1840s, and the pessimism expressed by many in the 1850s.[70]

Webb's forms are the substance of the debates in and about Philadelphia. When he aestheticizes the Georgia tea table or the Philadelphia wedding supper, when he pauses to specify objects on the tables or the behavior of diners, when he focuses on Charlie's wayward domestic service for his employer or on Caddy's demanding labors in her own home, such representations do not evade or displace social realities, but consider them in literary terms. Webb uses verbal texture to examine position, acknowledge the contexts and temporalities for action, gauge the pressures on conduct, and suggest an excess that is neither detachable from these circumstances nor reducible to them. Webb's novel can help us see the literary register of the debates about freedom in Philadelphia. These were debates about history and form, the constitution of space, the articulation of character, the struggle for authority at the level of the word, and the burdens and pleasures of excess. Texts such as *The Garies and Their Friends* call for a close reading that is also deep and wide. They suggest that we only think we know what we are seeing when we look at surfaces.

The Social Experiment in Herman Melville's *Benito Cereno*

Webb's novel, and the writing about freedom in Philadelphia between the Constitution and the Civil War, can illuminate texts in other settings and other traditions. Take, for example, Herman Melville's novella *Benito Cereno*, published first in three installments in *Putnam's Monthly Magazine* in 1855 and then revised for *The Piazza Tales* in 1856. This story of enslaved Africans who revolt and commandeer a Spanish ship taking them to bondage in Peru, whose main events take place off the southern coast of Chile, would seem to have little to do with the debates in Philadelphia or with Webb's peculiar novel of manners. Yet both *Benito Cereno* and *The Garies and Their Friends* are retrospective works of the 1850s. Melville and Webb reorder the past, delineate an explosive present, and consider the future. Both works turn on issues of manners, character, and violence. They are linked by their inverted plots. In *Benito Cereno*, Africans under slavery force their white captors to simulate their freedom, while they themselves, seeking liberty, enact their servitude. In *The Garies and Their Friends*, free African Americans, on the border of slavery, arduously perform their freedom. Both Melville and Webb describe how black and white performances are strained and bound.[71]

Webb could have read Melville's story while he was working on his novel, since *Benito Cereno* appeared in *Putnam's* two years before *The Garies* was published. The "turkeys innocent of a bone" at Webb's American supper may have an analogue in the skeleton of the slave owner Alexandro Aranda, removed from his body and "prepared" in a way that the Spanish Captain Benito Cereno has been told but "can never divulge" (111–12). The Africans substitute Aranda's bones for the original figurehead of Christopher Columbus on the Spanish vessel. Both writers may have been responding to Stowe's *Uncle Tom's Cabin*. Yet the value of juxtaposing *Benito Cereno* with *The Garies* does not depend on influence. The two stories overlap in concern and technique. They form a diptych representing the tense freedom of the 1850s.[72]

Considering *Benito Cereno* alongside *The Garies and Their Friends* deepens our understanding of both works and indicates the significance of Philadelphia's stories beyond geographical borders. The juxtaposition helps to clarify aspects of Melville's novella that have eluded its trenchant critics: the emphasis on manners, the intimacy of violence, and the unexpected social comedy. And it suggests alternative ways of understanding the narrator's wily invitations and exacting rhetoric.

Critics have traced Melville's web of allusions to the Haitian revolution in the late eighteenth and early nineteenth centuries, the maritime slave revolts on board the American brig *Creole* in 1841 and the Spanish schooner *Amistad* in 1839, African cultural practices, American racial ethnology, and the persistence of Old World imperialism in the New. They have analyzed his reworking of the main source for *Benito Cereno*, chapter 18 of Amasa Delano's *Narrative of Voyages and Travels in the Southern and Northern Hemispheres* (1817). The actual Captain Delano, born in Massachusetts, related how, in an 1805 encounter with a Spanish ship off the coast of Chile, his sunny disposition ("It was to my great advantage, that, on this occasion, the temperament of my mind was unusually pleasant") rendered him oblivious to the elaborate masquerade in which the enslaved Africans forced their Spanish captors to pretend that they retained authority. His ignorance preserved him from harm and allowed him, once Cereno exposed the duplicity, to seize the vessel and return the Africans to bondage.[73]

Melville seems to have been intrigued by that "unusually pleasant" temperament and by the racial theater scripted by the Africans. In *Benito Cereno*, he dramatizes the sustaining failure to see what is before one's eyes. Critics have questioned Melville's proximity to or separation from Delano's consciousness, through which the narrative is focalized during most of the story. They have evaluated his oblique portrayal of the African characters, the unsparing cycle of revenge, and the meanings of his apparently equivocal, tautological prose. The quality of Melville's irony has been at the center of appraisal. Some view him as capitulating to prejudice or abdicating moral responsibility. Others insist that, detaching narrator from protagonist, he opens a space for incisive political critique. Others (more accurately, it seems to me) caution that, rather than securing distance, Melville's irony entangles characters and readers in judgment. His technique raises the stakes of interpretation. He implies, but also obstructs, analysis from the perspective of the enslaved. Skewing details, he tempts readers into an exaggerated confidence in their own acuity. In 1960, as perusal of *Benito Cereno* intensified during the U. S. Civil Rights movement, Leslie Fiedler expressed the queasiness induced in many readers by the story: on topics of race and slavery, Fiedler wrote, Melville adopts a "tone less ironical than one would expect."[74]

Both *Benito Cereno* ("less ironical than one would expect") and *The Garies and Their Friends* ("a rather curious protest") hinge their narratives on racial assumptions. Readers may anticipate certain attitudes and outcomes. Instead, Melville and Webb invite readers into their literary parlors and then dim the lights. If, as I have been arguing over these four chapters, Philadelphia stories are about the unsettled boundaries between freedom and slavery, the exposure of character under threat, the scrutiny of evidence, the depth of surfaces, a regressive advance, and social and literary experiments, then we might consider *Benito Cereno* as a kind of Philadelphia story.[75] Webb's novel helps us to see that Melville is concerned with freedom as well as slavery, expression as well as suppression, and the urgent performances of everyday life as well as the theater of rebellion.

The social experiment that Melville portrays in *Benito Cereno*, transposed to the decks of the *San Dominick*, upsets the usual hierarchies. (Melville has rechristened the actual Spanish vessel, the *Tryal*, with a variant of the name for the revolutionary Saint Domingue or Santo Domingo.) The burdens of performance and the costs of failure are shared by the Africans, whom the narrator often describes as the "blacks," and the Spaniards, whom he often refers to as the "whites." Melville heightens the ascriptions when revising his periodical story for *The Piazza Tales*, twice exchanging national terms ("Spaniards," "Spanish") for racial ones ("whites," "white").[76] If the rebel Africans fail to persuade Delano that they remain in bondage, they will be attacked by his sailors and killed or recaptured— as they are when their ingenuity is exposed. If the vanquished Spanish captain and his surviving crew fail to persuade Delano that they retain mastery, both Spanish and American sailors will face the consequences. And if Delano recognizes the imposture and discloses his awareness, the Africans will kill him.

The Spanish, under probation, are cast temporarily in the roles of black characters like those in the fiction of Robert Montgomery Bird or John Beauchamp Jones. As Cereno maintains in his deposition, appended to the narrative, the Spanish were warned not to vary from the parts that had been dictated, and they were punished for their expectations. According to Cereno, the ringleader Babo threatened that his "dagger would be alert as his eye" (109). The Africans, exercising a prescriptive authority, are cast temporarily in the roles of white elites like those in the fiction of George Lippard, J. B. Jones, and Frank J. Webb. Delano can be seen as an extreme version of characters, such as those found in Stowe and Webb, in whom benevolence, cruelty, and short-sightedness merge. From these elements and on a stage in which freedom and slavery change places, Melville fashions his violent comedy of racial manners.

And manners do seem crucial in the story, in ways that most critics have not recognized. From the start, the narrator draws attention to the behavior of the *San Dominick*—"the longer the stranger was watched, the more singular appeared her maneuvers"—and ponders "the true character of the vessel" (47, 48). Across the novella, he stresses gesture, tone, and ritual. On an elevated deck, six Africans methodically polish their hatchets, directing and punctuating the action on board ship. Babo, apparently serving his frail Spanish captain, exhibits what Delano considers to be "steady good conduct" (52). He administers cordials whenever his master coughs. He shaves Cereno with precision and affection—right after Delano insists on details about the storm that ostensibly disabled his ship (an extended scene to which we will return). At the toll of the ship's bell, Atufal, once a king in Africa and now purportedly wrapped in chains, is summoned and asked if this time he will seek his captain's pardon for an unnamed offense. The African steward Francesco obsequiously serves lunch to the two captains, keeping them under surveillance as Delano continues to inquire about the reasons for the adversity on board the *San Dominick;* all the while, Babo caresses his master's temple and insists that he take some more wine.

Captain Delano flaunts an impressive ability to smother apprehension with reassurance. Time after time, he blithely dismisses his twitches, slight twinges, "involuntary suspicion[s]" (67), and symptoms that resemble "incipient sea-sickness" (76) or "the ague" (78), often consoling himself with the sight of what he takes to be docile Africans. With each repetition and every rereading, the series becomes crueler and funnier. With a matching redundancy, Cereno falters, chokes, lowers his eyes, and recoils "like one flayed alive" (93). His body involuntarily communicates the distress that he has been forbidden to speak.

Delano inadvertently tortures Cereno, prompting several of the Spaniard's fits with his musings. Assuming that the Spanish captain is distraught over the loss of his friend Aranda, Delano commiserates: "'I think that, by a sympathetic experience, I conjecture, Don Benito, what it is that gives the keener edge to your grief. . . . Were your friend's remains now on board this ship, Don Benito, not thus strangely would the mention of his name affect you'" (61). Delano explains that he, too, had a compatriot who died at sea. He knows how Cereno feels. Well, maybe not. Readers learn in the deposition that the Africans killed their owner Aranda, removed the flesh from his body (possibly ate it), and fastened his skeleton to the prow of the ship. Below they chalked a warning to the sailors and captain if they failed to obey: "'*Sequid vestro jefe*' (follow your leader)" (49, 99, 107). "'Were your friend's remains now on board this ship,'" Captain Delano soothes—but they are: the skeleton figurehead, wrapped in canvas—and so at the mention of Aranda's name, Cereno faints into his captor Babo's arms.[77]

The narrator assures his readers that Delano is a "man of such native simplicity as to be incapable of satire or irony" (63). But the novella's interlocking perspectives—focalized through Delano, crossed with Babo, and inflected by the narrator, then rendered in legal testimony, dialogue, and the final image of Babo's head impaled at Lima—ensure that words are riddled by their contexts. As the ironies proliferate, everyone is capable of and vulnerable to satire. Delano and Cereno act out a ritual of aggressive innocence and hypersensitive experience, of candor and despair. They are uncomprehending partners in excess who help maintain the system of racial subordination. Melville, like Webb, but stressing the demands on the white characters, slows and repeats the action, as he weighs the qualities of "freedom." He seems uneasy with the forceful attainments of his black characters and less sanguine than Webb about evading a cycle of violence. Yet the story does not, as some critics hold, either embrace or reject Delano or Babo. The narrator allows us to condescend to the American official or to condemn the African rebel, but the novella shifts the ground under its characters and readers.

In revising Amasa Delano's *Narrative of Voyages and Travels,* Melville conceals the mutiny (the actual Delano had revealed the situation from the beginning) and intensifies the ferocity of the African rebels. Readers are misled during the long initial movement of the story, given through Delano's perspective, in which, to cite only a few instances, Babo is compared to a sorrowful and affectionate "shepherd's dog" and it is observed that "the negro" is "the most pleasing body servant in the world," that Babo is Cereno's "faithful personal attendant" (with the adjective "faithful" inserted for book publication), and that blacks possess "a certain easy cheerfulness, harmonious in every glance and gesture; as though God had set the whole negro to some pleasant tune" (51, 52, 53, 83). The skewing continues after the conspiracy is divulged and the narrator trumpets Delano's insight: "across the long-benighted mind of Captain Delano, a flash of revelation swept . . . the scales dropped from his eyes," and he sees "the negroes . . . with mask torn away" (99). During the brutal retaking of the ship, the narrator describes the Africans whose "red tongues lolled, wolf-like, from their black mouths" (102). This gratuitous detail and the figurative pressure at the end of the Delano section may indicate that his "flash of revelation" still leaves the good captain "benighted" and that masks lie behind masks, but it is a risky strategy in which readers are structurally and rhetorically invited to share the thrill of reenslavement.

Cereno's subsequent legal deposition underscores his partial view of the events. Its indictments also transmit the artistry of the plotters: the Ashantee hatchet polishers, whose chores left them poised to use their weapons; Babo, whose officiousness allowed him to police his master; and Francesco, who advocated serving Cereno and Delano their final meal. Embedded in the testimony is a record of Babo's desire to be taken to "any negro countries," where the Africans might regain a status and a possibility that had been obliterated in the New World (105). But such messages in the deposition are subdued, and there is no antidote provided to its distortions, as there is in, say, the counternarrative to the official story included in *The History of Pennsylvania Hall.* Melville works hard not to ensure a "correct" reading.

If we take *Benito Cereno* to be telling a kind of Philadelphia story, then the plots at first glance seem oddly turned. The "whites" labor under the shadow of "black" authority, and they are emancipated. The "blacks" put on their servitude in a bid for deliverance, and they are returned to slavery. Their experiment in freedom has been exposed as a cruel artifice, and their true character has emerged, unfitting them for progress. In such a reading, the outcome on board the *San Dominick* might seem a vicious fulfillment of the speculations in E. W. Clay's "Life in Philadelphia." Yet this is the perspective of Delano and Cereno, for whom the fantasy of subservience is dispelled through violent unmasking.

We get a different view in the shaving scene, which takes place in the ship's cuddy, into which Babo has ushered Cereno shortly after the captain's deviation from his script. The cuddy is Babo's parlor, in which the African leader manipulates the heads of his captain and audience and Melville reflects on constraint within and beyond the story. The scene is charged by the tension between a ventriloquized racial complacency and escalating images that suggest a different kind of mastery. The complacency is delivered in unstable indirect discourse that may represent Delano, a premutiny Cereno, or an interpolated reader's common sense:

> There is something in the negro which, in a peculiar way, fits him for avocations about one's person. Most negroes are natural valets and hairdressers; taking to the comb and brush congenially as to the castanets, and flourishing them apparently with almost equal satisfaction. There is, too, a smooth tact about them in this employment, with a marvelous, noiseless, gliding briskness, not ungraceful in its way, singularly pleasing to behold, and still more so to be the manipulated subject of. (83)

At odds with such narrated comfort are the props and figures. The chair in which Babo arranges Cereno "seemed some grotesque, middle-age engine of torment" (83). Delano becomes conscious that for an apron to wrap around his master, Babo has employed the Spanish flag. He almost imagines an execution: "nor, as he saw the two thus postured, could he resist the vagary, that in the black he saw a headsman, and in the white, a man at the block.... The negro seemed a Nubian sculptor finishing off a white statue-head" (85, 87).

Yet the line I have drawn between perspective and figure is too clean. In the "there is something in the negro" passage, the diction and syntax cut against the reassurance. Babo is "fit" for service "in a peculiar way," but "peculiar" suggests incongruity as well as suitability. More than that: invoking the prominence of African American barbers in northern cities, the narrator conjures the specter of ambivalent intimacy that preoccupied contemporary observers.

The author and abolitionist Thomas Wentworth Higginson described how Frederick Douglass responded in 1850 to an accusation that he and his people wanted to slash the throats of whites by "bending down graciously over [his accuser] and waving his hand a little over [his] tangled and soiled headdress, 'Oh, no, we will not cut your throats; we will only cut your hair.'"[78]

In an 1858 lecture before the New York Anti-Slavery Society, reprinted in the *Liberator*, Higginson associated shaving and insurrection: "I have wondered at the patience of the negro; I have wondered in times past, when I have been so weak-minded as to submit my chin to the razor of a colored brother, as his sharp steel grazed my skin, at the patience of the negro in shaving the white man for so many years, and yet keeping the razor on the outside of his throat; I have wondered, I say, at that, but I was foolish in making that a test of his courage. Thank God! assassination is not the highest test of courage; endurance until the time comes may be a higher. . . . We see among us the African as he is crushed by social institutions, overwhelmed by ignorance, kept back and down by poverty; we do not look at his records; we do not see what he has been, and may be again. We speak of the American slave as if he was never to do anything for his own emancipation. We forget the heroes of St. Domingo."[79]

Cyprian Clamorgan, in his *Colored Aristocracy of St. Louis* (1858), ironically confirmed the fitness of African Americans for the trade: "It will doubtless be observed by the reader, that a majority of our colored aristocracy belong to the tonsorial profession; a mulatto takes to razor and soap as naturally as a young duck to a pool of water, or a strapped Frenchman to dancing; they certainly make the best barbers in the world, and were doubtless intended by nature for the art. In its exercise, they take white men by the nose without giving offense, and without causing an effusion of blood."[80]

Although these reflections postdate Melville's story, they can help us construe the shaving episode in *Benito Cereno*. Douglass, Higginson, Clamorgan, and Melville all point to the exposed neck, the ambiguities of touch, and the delicate line between scraping and cutting. Like Douglass, Melville and his character Babo play on the opportunity for violence. As Higginson will in his lecture, Melville links small and large scales, shaving and Saint Domingue, and he worries that patience has a limit. Unlike Higginson, Melville folds violence into ordinary life. As will Clamorgan, Melville, invoking "natural" gifts, appreciates the cunning art of the shave. Melville extends the scene to the relationship between writer, narrator, and reader, as indicated in the awkward, open syntax paying tribute to a finesse that is "singularly pleasing to behold, and still more so to be the manipulated subject of."

The actual Amasa Delano had no shaving episode in his *Narrative*. Melville invents it, and he places it at the center of his story. Focused on the barber's chair, it is a version of the elaborate scenes of interpretation in *Moby-Dick* (1851) and *Clarel* (1876), in which characters reflect on a symbol (the "Doubloon" in *Moby-Dick*, the "Mar Saba Palm" in *Clarel*) from various perspectives. But the shaving scene in *Benito Cereno* lacks any stable choreography. The positions shift, and it is not always clear who is shaving whom. Cereno, in the chair, is manipulated by Babo and watched by Delano, who sees and does not see what is transpiring. The narrator encourages readers to identify with Delano and also urges distance. The implied author supplies a figurative excess, inviting readers to make interpretive moves whose benefits often come with costs. This "play of the barber" (87; Delano's phrase, voiced by the narrator), advertised as comforting, bewilders.[81]

In an exquisite reading of *Benito Cereno*'s linked rhetoric and politics, Eric J. Sundquist argues that Babo's authority, like Melville's narrative command, finds expression "in a barely suppressed revolutionary gesture." According to Sundquist, Babo does not—cannot—use his weapon. Sundquist captures the anxious, redundant qualities of Melville's prose. Meaning is suspended (asserted and then contained, balanced between opposed and equal alternatives) and progress is balked in the historical context of racial tyranny and sectional impasse. Sundquist evaluates the limits on the conduct of Delano, Cereno, and Babo: "Their stylized enactment of a rebellion contained within the illusion of mastery, as though in ritual pantomime, finely depicts the haltingly realized potential for slave revolution in the New World."[82]

While cogent, this analysis describes only part of the story that Melville tells. *Benito Cereno* is about freedom, as well as slavery, and enterprise, as well as containment—and these are aspects that Webb's *The Garies and Their Friends* can bring into relief. Sundquist and others have analyzed the "tautology," "impasse," "arrest," and "paralysis" in Melville's novella, suggesting that it registers the political deadlock over slavery in the 1850s and a failure of racial imagination.[83] Yet the allure of impasse and allegory may obscure other features. On this brutal stage and despite the proliferating double negatives, antitheses, and caveats that threaten to suspend or enervate, there is movement. It all depends on what we mean by action. Babo's gestures may not be revolutionary in their sweep, but he does use that razor:

> Here an involuntary expression came over the Spaniard, similar to that just before on the deck, and whether it was the start he gave, or a sudden gawky roll of the hull in the calm, or a momentary unsteadiness of the servant's hand; however it was, just then the razor drew blood, spots of which stained the creamy lather under the throat: immediately the black barber drew back his steel, and remaining in his professional attitude, back to Captain Delano, and face to Don Benito, held up the trickling razor, saying, with a sort of half humorous sorrow, "See, master,—you shook so—here's Babo's first blood. (86)

"Here" (at the beginning of the passage) is when Delano remarks on Cereno's barely credible account of the *San Dominick* having been at a standstill for two months, and "just then" (Babo's cut) is when the Spanish captain is about to answer. With his razor, like the "steel" to which the narrator compares it, drawing blood, Babo reinforces his authority. He underlines Cereno's vulnerability, flaunts his dripping weapon, and signals his captain, with his back to Delano, that this is *not* "Babo's first blood," but the latest maneuver in a protracted conflict.

In this scene, and throughout the long first part of *Benito Cereno*, Melville dwells on fragile surfaces: unsteady decks, crumbling balustrades, exposed necks, gestures made under extraordinary pressure. As the shave continues, Cereno repeats the lines about the ship's travails that he has been instructed to say, Babo applies his razor "at convenient times," and the narrator observes that "To Captain Delano's imagination . . . there was something so hollow in the Spaniard's manner, with apparently some reciprocal hollowness in the servant's dusky comment of silence" (87). Yet to interpret this hollowness as empty, rather than eloquent, would be to follow Delano. These manners are full of meaning.

Manners are critical in *Benito Cereno*: rendered in exacting detail, they form the substance of the novella. At the lunch table following the shave, the narrator communicates Delano's sense that Francesco's obeisance is "at once Christian and Chesterfieldian" (88). For Delano, the terms appear to signify "humble" and "refined," but their discordant histories ("Christian" manners seen as tied to morals, "Chesterfieldian" manners seen as divorced from them) and the backdrop of slavery and resistance imply that Delano does not fully appreciate Francesco's approach. Francesco is not a Christian, and Cereno alleges in his testimony that the steward had hoped to serve poison to the captains for lunch. "At once Christian and Chesterfieldian": with these uneasily yoked terms, Delano suspects (and represses) and the narrator explicates the knot of conduct in *Benito Cereno*. The narrator, through Delano's obtuseness, is fascinated by the meticulous gestures of Babo. The story ends with the image of his head, severed and fixed on a pole in the square at Lima, described by the narrator as "that hive of subtlety" (116).

As several critics have noticed, and some have censured, Melville does not attempt to represent Babo's psychic or emotional recesses. Yet while readers are not provided with access to his interior, they are given a panorama of Babo effects: the febrile Cereno, the hoodwinked Delano, the chained Atufal, the monitory hatchet polishers and oakum pickers, the skeleton figurehead with its chalked motto exchanged for the likeness of Columbus (Babo wields the emblem of mortality as satire and ultimatum), the Spanish flag converted into a bib, the face mutely and openly turned up to his captain, the encircling arm and riveted eye, the crutch, the dagger—and, most prominent of all, that hand urging the razor on Cereno's neck, poised to shave or to slice. Like Webb, Melville lavishes detail on scenes in which tiny shifts can produce catastrophic outcomes and style becomes inordinately expressive.[84]

All choices are constrained in the story, including, it would seem, the author's. Melville associates himself with the subjected mastery of Babo, who contrives fictions. According to Cereno, "the negro Babo was the plotter from first to last" (112). Melville strikes conflicting poses. He identifies with Babo's artistry but places Delano in the foreground for most of the story. He appears to understand, even as he criticizes, the American's responses. He almost justifies the revolutionary force of the Africans as the only way to counter an irredeemably vicious system. This last approach resembles the proposal of Frantz Fanon in his mid-twentieth-century analysis of colonialism, *The Wretched of the Earth*—but Melville is not Fanon. He approaches this determination in *Benito Cereno* but swerves from it.[85]

Readers are pressed to follow their leader—to make judgments about character and conduct, while the author, having arranged the play or, in Webb's terms, set the table, keeps his distance. *Benito Cereno*, like *The Garies and Their Friends*, is a story that pivots on issues of awareness, drawing readers into unexpected spaces, disorienting and implicating them.

Melville and Webb share a literary project. Both writers examine the juncture of manners and violence, and they detail a volatile freedom. After the revelation of the mutiny, during an exchange between the two captains toward the end of the story, Cereno reaches for metaphor to describe the predicament he and Delano shared: "'Do but think how you walked this deck, how you sat in this cabin, every inch of ground mined into honey-combs under you. Had I dropped the least hint, made the least advance towards an understanding between us, death, explosive death—yours as mine—would have ended the scene'" (115). As Cereno imagines it, the very ground on which they walked (which, of course, was not terra firma but the rolling deck of a ship) was "mined" (as though excavated or pitted with charges) "into honey-combs" (penetrated by holes or cavities, figuratively associated with "that hive of subtlety"). Instead of nectar, these structures contained explosives.

Cereno offers Delano the metaphor as a gesture toward fraternity, which is thwarted by Delano's amnesiac cheer and Cereno's own haunted misery. But beyond the two captains, the "'ground mined into honey-combs'" pictures the surface over which all the characters move in the story. Melville has taken the "slumbering volcano," the image used by Frederick Douglass and others, including Melville himself elsewhere in *Benito Cereno*, to evoke the precariousness of a nation built on slavery, and he has contrived an unstable amalgam of the engineered and the natural. Who or what "mined" that "honey-comb"? It is as though

Melville combined the sublimity of Douglass's volcano with the banality of Lippard's trapdoors in *The Quaker City*, southern with northern terrain, to articulate the verge of slavery and freedom.[86]

In *Benito Cereno* and *The Garies and Their Friends*, the unsteadiness of a hand, an unfortunate choice of outfit, a misplaced word, or the dropping of a hint may cause a shave to become an execution, or a dinner table to erupt. Both works include scenes of riot that clarify the more prosaic violence of their represented worlds, and in both, order is only tenuously restored, burdened by past and future. With "a sort of half humorous sorrow" (*Benito Cereno*, 86), in stories marked by odd redundancies and a curious detachment, their narrators stage a peculiar freedom (to quote Philip Fisher on *Benito Cereno*) in "the aftermath and residue of slavery."[87]

Certainly, there are differences between Melville's and Webb's narratives of freedom. In Melville's perverse social experiment on board the *San Dominick*, the roles of master and slave appear to be continually reversible. This possibility is given an emblem, the tableau on the oval stern piece of Cereno's ship: "a dark satyr in a mask, holding his foot on the prostrate neck of a writhing figure, likewise masked" (49). The satyr may be seen as Babo, with his figurative foot on the neck of Cereno; or as Delano, who "with his right foot" literally "ground the prostrate negro" to the bottom of his whaleboat after Babo attempted to stab his captain (99); or as Cereno and his friend Aranda, who, before the tale begins, have subjugated the Africans and converted them into property, which they are transporting to Peru. The masks thwart identification. Only the posture remains the same: the foot on the neck impeding elevation and utterance. As we have seen in chapter 2, a similar image had been used to typify prejudice by James Forten Jr., Sarah Grimké, and William Whipper. In veiling the agents, Melville suggests that the struggle for mastery may have no end.[88]

Delano's relentless and hilarious myopia and the systemic bias of the legal deposition point to the historical crime of slavery as the origin of this cycle of violence, but Melville's story tends to blur the differences between black and white brutality in the present and the future. In *Benito Cereno*, unlike *The Garies and Their Friends*, black violence is represented as strategic and offensive, not a limited response to a specific attack. Of course, in one story the characters are represented under slavery and in the other under freedom (however qualified), but as I have been arguing, Melville and Webb, separately and together, cross the border between the two conditions.

Juxtaposed with the Philadelphia reflections of the 1850s, which would include Delany's *Condition*, Webb's *Garies*, and the essays of William Whipper and James McCune Smith, *Benito Cereno* seems closer to Whipper's disillusion over the immutability of prejudice in his exchange with McCune Smith and to Delany's view of a destiny that lies elsewhere than to Webb's chance of progress for those who remain and strive. If Webb evaluates the demand to prove character and the absurdity of justifying natural rights, Melville, through the focalized Delano, examines that demand and that absurdity from another point of view. In a thought experiment, Melville looks through the eyes of a character like Delano and acknowledges the force and allure of ideology. In the movement from Delano's perspective to Cereno's deposition to Babo's transfixed head, Melville suggests that the freedom on display in *Benito Cereno* fails not because of African incapacity but because it is extinguished by force and because all of the performances on board the *San Dominick* are impaired by slavery and racism. The feet are never far from the necks in *Benito Cereno*; expectations are violently opened and then brutally closed. Rather than the pattern of regressive advance portrayed by Webb in *The Garies*, Melville stages a temporality in which, as the narrator indicates during the recapture of the *San Dominick*, voicing Delano's thoughts (and possibly his own), "past, present, and future seemed one" (98).

Melville tells stories of repetition but also of difference. If the events within the narrative imply a perpetual revolution of masters and slaves, the narrator's allusions, similes, metaphors, symbols, and puns require continuous reappraisals of conduct and perspective. Melville invites, and satirizes, such reappraisals in the hyperbolic knot thrown to Delano by an aged Spanish sailor: "For intricacy such a knot he had never seen in an American ship, or indeed any other. The old man looked like an Egyptian priest, making gordian knots for the temple of Ammon. The knot seemed a combination of double-bowline-knot, treble-crown-knot, back-handed-well-knot, knot-in-and-out-knot, and jamming-knot" (76). Since Captain Delano is not shown to be a connoisseur of classical lore, the resemblance between the old sailor and an Egyptian priest and the turning of the singular Gordian knot of legend into an object of nineteenth-century manufacture seem to be aspects furnished by the narrator and his author.

That author himself, of course, is a fabricator of knots. (And he may have invented, or at least renamed, the "back-handed-well-knot" and "knot-in-and-out-knot," which, unlike the others in the list, appear not to have maritime referents.) The attributes of this knot—doubling and trebling its effects, oblique ("back-handed"), and insinuating ("knot-in-and-out-knot"), fashioned under constraint ("jamming-knot")—resemble the verbal textures of *Benito Cereno*. Unlike the Gordian knot, which Alexander was supposed to have sliced in half, thus fulfilling the oracle's prophecy that he who unraveled it would go on to become the king of Asia, Melville's verbal knots frustrate swift routes to mastery. "'Undo it, cut it, quick,'" insists the Spanish sailor to Delano—but this is another one of the story's crafty incitements. Melville's knots signify differently with each subsequent reading—it seems fatuous to put it this way, of course, since such variations are part of any literary experience, but Melville amplifies the potential gaps between readings through his point-of-view gambit, narrative withdrawal, and figurative overload.

Melville's narrator (as we knew he would) provides a figure of speech for that excess, when Delano, after observing Babo with his razor over the neck of the shuddering Cereno, imagines "that in the black he saw a headsman, and in the white, a man at the block. But this was one of those antic conceits, appearing and vanishing in a breath, from which, perhaps, the best regulated mind is not always free" (85). The phrase "antic conceits" could serve as an epitome of *Benito Cereno*, referring to Melville's array: knots, padlocks and keys, feet on necks, cranial manipulations, theatrical ships, and brittle and urgent racial performances. In his novella, Melville brings the figurative to bear on the prosaic, and his lines approach the concentration of poetry. The word "antic" suggests the ludicrous and grotesque qualities of this tale about racial "conceit"—ludicrous and grotesque because this is a story about the past that is also a story about the present, enacted again and again. Melville stages repetition and imagines, in the surfeit he offers, the possibility, but no guarantee, that assumptions may change. Melville and Webb delineate freedom in the 1850s with a peculiar literary irresponsibility. To use Webb's metaphor, both writers serve extravagant literary meals: "whoever has been to such an entertainment knows very well what an American supper is" (*Garies*, 377). These stories turn on the pleasures and burdens of such knowledge.

Coda: John Edgar Wideman's
Philadelphia

We might follow the development of stories about Philadelphia after the Civil War in various directions. We could turn to Frances E. W. Harper's serialized novel *Trial and Triumph* (1888–89) about African American class distinction and communal struggle in the wake of Reconstruction, or to Owen Wister's unfinished *Romney* (1912–15), which details a corrupt European American Philadelphia afflicted by a strange complacency: "Here then was the jest: out of moderation's very heart excess had been created—too much moderation." Or we might look at Jessie Fauset's satires of manners, in which Philadelphia typifies the past and an ossified black higher class, part of her wider social critique: *There Is Confusion* (1924), *Plum Bun* (1929), and *Comedy American Style* (1933). Or we might consider David Goodis's Philadelphia noir *Down There* (1956), translated to Paris by Francois Truffaut in his film *Shoot the Piano Player,* or the post–World War II "South Street" novels, which dramatize conflicts between neighborhood and metropolis and encounters among Anglo, Irish, and African American residents: Jack Dunphy's *John Fury* (1946), William Gardner Smith's *South Street* (1954), David Bradley's *South Street* (1975), Pete Dexter's *God's Pocket* (1983), and Diane McKinney-Whetstone's *Tumbling* (1996). Or we might take up Mumia Abu-Jamal's prison writings in *Live from Death Row* (1995); Abu-Jamal was sentenced to death for the 1982 murder of a Philadelphia police officer in a controversial case still under review. Or we might read Thomas Pynchon, who, in his comic epic *Mason & Dixon* (1997), imagines a vibrant eighteenth-century colonial Philadelphia, "second only to London, as the greatest of the English-speaking cities." Pynchon represents the sojourn of the two Englishmen who, in the mid-1760s, determined the fateful boundary between Mid-Atlantic colonies that became the dividing line between states and then between slavery and freedom.[1]

Instead, we will end with the fiction of John Edgar Wideman and the trajectory from "Fever" (1989) to *Philadelphia Fire* (1990) and *The Cattle Killing* (1996). Like the Philadelphia writers of the 1850s, especially Frank J. Webb, Wideman reflects on the city and its histories, evaluates past and present, and contemplates the future. For Wideman, as for Webb, Philadelphia offers a peculiar synecdoche for the nation, a part that skews the whole. Wideman's fiction returns us to where we began—the narratives, characters, and debates of the 1793 yellow fever epidemic—and also advances us to the present. "Fever," *Philadelphia Fire*, and *The Cattle Killing* revolve around the focal points of 1793 and 1985, the yellow fever epidemic and the MOVE bombing.

On May 13, 1985, Wilson Goode, the first African American mayor of Philadelphia, ordered, or at least acquiesced to, the dropping of an explosive device on the rooftop of a building on Osage Avenue in West Philadelphia that served as the most recent headquarters for the group MOVE (short for "The Movement"). Led by John Africa (born Vincent Leapheart), the mostly African American members established an urban commune meant to stand as a rebuke to the city. Africa argued against modern technology and capitalism and for a return to modes of living closer to nature. For years, tensions had escalated between group members and police. A dispute in 1978, while Frank Rizzo was mayor, had resulted in a gun battle, during which a police officer was killed. Several members of MOVE were given long prison sentences. At a row house on Osage Avenue belonging to John Africa's sister, where the group had relocated after 1978, MOVE members stockpiled weapons and addressed their neighbors through bullhorns. In May 1985, after months of discord and complaints from the mostly black, working-class residents of Osage Avenue, city authorities decided to act against MOVE. They initiated a plan to knock down a reinforced defensive structure on the roof of the house and then use tear gas to expel the residents. After water jets failed to level the structure, the police and MOVE shot at one another for ninety minutes. Later that day, a police helicopter dropped a military-grade blasting agent on the rooftop, and within twenty minutes the building was in flames. Despite the proximity of firefighters and water cannons, no attempt was made to quell the blaze for forty minutes (in a historical echo of official inaction as Pennsylvania Hall burned in 1838). By that time, the fire had spread to adjacent buildings. Two city blocks were destroyed, and more than 250 people were left homeless. Only two in the MOVE house survived. Eleven died, including five children.[2]

Wideman had attended the University of Pennsylvania as an undergraduate between 1959 and 1963 and returned as an English Department faculty member in 1967, becoming the university's first African American professor to receive tenure. He set his third novel, *The Lynchers* (1973), in Philadelphia and, according to interviews, had long planned to write about the 1793 yellow fever epidemic, having first read Jones and Allen's "Narrative of the Proceedings" in the late 1960s. In the aftermath of the 1985 MOVE bombing and fire, Wideman's literary interests in 1793 took shape. The fever, and especially the figure of Richard Allen, preoccupied him across a short story and two novels. Like Benjamin Rush, Mathew Carey, and Richard Allen, Wideman repeatedly tells the tales of 1793. Unlike them, he does not seek justification or clarity. Instead, through his numerous focalizers, mixed genres, and extravagant tropes, he complicates historical patterns.[3]

At the end of "Fever," which up until this point has followed a character based on Richard Allen through the scenes of 1793, Wideman's narrator, in the middle of a paragraph, shifts to the late twentieth century:

> Almost an afterthought. The worst, he believed, had been overcome. Only a handful of deaths the last week of November. The city was recovering. Commerce thriving. Philadelphia must be revictualed, refueled, rebuilt, reconnected to the countryside, to markets foreign and domestic, to products, pleasures and appetites denied during the quarantine months of the fever. A new century would soon be dawning. We must forget the horrors. The Mayor proclaims a new day. Says lets put the past behind us. Of the eleven who died in the fire he said extreme measures were necessary as we cleansed ourselves of disruptive influences. The cost could have been much greater, he said I regret the loss of life, especially the half dozen kids, but I commend all city officials, all volunteers who helped return the city to the arc of glory that is its proper destiny.

Wideman evokes the kind of narrative comfort, the turning of the page from calamity to renewal, that Mathew Carey attempted at the end of his *Short Account of the Malignant Fever.* He acidly dedicates his story "To Mathew Carey, Esq., who fled Philadelphia in its hour of need and upon his return published a libelous account of the behavior of black nurses and undertakers, thereby injuring all people of my race." (Carey's disparagements of black character in 1793 are also rebuked in *The Cattle Killing.*) In a note to "Fever," Wideman writes that Absalom Jones and Richard Allen's 1794 "Narrative of the Proceedings" was a source for his "meditation on history," and he incorporates passages from their original pamphlet in his short story.[4]

The terminal comfort in "Fever" is mixed with a willful amnesia. Progress is tied to an imperative to forget. The narrator's diction and syntax hinder that imperative. Somewhere in the space after the period at the end of "the quarantine months of the fever" and before the capital letter that begins "Of the eleven who died in the fire," Wideman's narrator sutures the yellow fever epidemic and the MOVE bombing. The sentences in between—"A new century would soon be dawning. We must forget the horrors. The Mayor proclaims a new day. Says lets put the past behind us."—can be read or reread as applying to 1793 or to 1985, or both, unsettling the directive to move forward. In Wideman's fiction, 1985 is not 1793. The centuries are not erased, and the actors, events, and politics are not conflated. But they also are not separated. Readers are offered patterns whose nuances they must gauge. In *The Cattle Killing*, Wideman provides a figure for historical continuity and difference: a female entity that serially inhabits mortal bodies, based upon Ibo beliefs in the restless, consuming spirits known as "ogbanje." (Remembering Robert Montgomery Bird's metempsychic *Sheppard Lee*, we also might consider, in terms of tradition if not intention, a local aspect to Wideman's design.) Across his Philadelphia fiction, Wideman stresses the "fever" patterns: the absurd and palpable effects of "race," the tenuous effort to maintain social distinction, the anomalous figure of the "free black," the risk of internalizing prejudice, the civic violence, and the tropes of purgation and deliverance.[5]

In "Fever," 1793 and 1985 are associated as stories of urban crisis in which differences of race and class become vivid and lethal. In *Philadelphia Fire*, the protagonist, a writer named Cudjoe, is drawn back from the island of Mykonos to his native Philadelphia by a "fantasy of identification" with the lone survivor of the MOVE conflagration, a child for whom he searches but never locates. (In 1985, there were two survivors, a child and also a woman.) Summarizing the events on Osage Avenue, one of Wideman's narrators, in a reportorial voice, implies that the bombing was a municipal riot, in the historical mold, with certified acquittal (we might recall the aftermaths of 1838, 1842, and 1849): "A grand jury subsequently determined that no criminal charges should be brought against the public officials who planned and perpetrated the assault." In *The Cattle Killing*, Philadelphia in 1793 and 1985 is associated with South Africa in the mid-1850s, where the Xhosa people slaughtered their cattle in response to a young girl's prophecy that such destruction was the only way to restore their depleted herds and secure military victory against the encroaching British army. For Wideman, Philadelphia epitomizes a disorder in which violence is inflicted upon Africans from without and within.[6]

At times, Wideman's narrators verge on paranoia (from one standpoint in *Philadelphia Fire*, the MOVE bombing is viewed as genocide) or seductive tautology:

at the end of *The Cattle Killing*, Ramona Africa (the adult survivor of the MOVE fire), Nelson Mandela, Mumia Abu-Jamal, the Black Panther Huey Newton, and the murdered Civil Rights activists Andrew Goodman and James Chaney are bound together. But the histories of Philadelphia that Wideman excavates suggest that paranoia, tautology, and even apocalypse (Wideman's spectacle of "Philadelphia Fire" is reminiscent of George Lippard's "Last Days of the Quaker City") may not be unwarranted responses, even if they are not entirely reasonable. As he draws upon sources, readers are left to evaluate the different perspectives and temporalities in his fictions.

At the center of Wideman's stories about Philadelphia is the figure of Richard Allen: emancipated and subjected, leader and minion, faithful in catastrophe. In "Fever" and *The Cattle Killing*, Wideman examines Allen's position in the contexts of blame (Africans in Philadelphia accused of transmitting the infection), anomaly (claims that they were immune to the fever), entreaty (the calls to serve as nurses and carters of the dead), accomplishment (the lives saved and city preserved in 1793), and indictment (the charges that those who labored became extorters and thieves). These circumstances, Wideman has said in an interview, "seemed an archetypal configuration of the problems, the issues and many of the ironies that have dogged black-white relationships ever since." This nexus of demands, pressures, and judgments is, in the words of the Richard Allen character in "Fever" (which may conjure Melville's symbol tossed to Amasa Delano and the readers of *Benito Cereno*), "the ironical knot I wished to untangle for you" (141).[7]

In "Fever," the Allen protagonist interrogates his own conduct and debates his service with another pariah, a dying Jew named Abraham. In *The Cattle Killing*, Wideman splits the Allen character in at least three ways. He appears as an itinerant male preacher, who focalizes many of the scenes in the novel. The preacher travels to Philadelphia in the fall of 1793 to minister to the victims of the fever, to purge himself after a riot in the suburbs, and to locate the female spirit that had appeared to him earlier in the story. The narrator also imagines the historical Richard Allen meditating on the enormity of his break with St. George's Methodist Church and his audacity in founding the African Methodist Episcopal Church. He wonders whether God will follow him and his congregants into the new building, or abandon them, and he recoils at a momentary yearning to be a white man. Wideman also represents the young preacher confronting a fictional Richard Allen in the narrative itself. After a cellar housing those orphaned during the epidemic has burned, set on fire by one of the residents (an invented episode that invokes the MOVE deaths), the preacher tells Allen that he has lost his own faith. He cannot understand how the minister still believes in God and redemption.[8]

In depicting 1793, Wideman reflects on Philadelphia as the arena for an enduring social experiment in which African Americans, granted a quasi-freedom, are on probation and under scrutiny. The preacher in *The Cattle Killing* refers to the state of affairs as "this new condition white people were contriving for the so-called free blacks in the city."[9] In *Philadelphia Fire*, the most despairing and furious of the three stories, Wideman imagines the city in the 1980s as a historical cage. Discussing the Wilson Goode administration, the MOVE events, and the Civil Rights movement, Cudjoe's friend Timbo, a cultural attaché for the mayor, outlines a bleak view of racial progress. Affirmative action in the university, which Timbo calls "academic welfare," was an "experiment": "Way I look at it now they was testing us. Put a handful of niggers in this test tube and shook it up and watched it bubble" (76, 77). The invitations, according to Timbo, come with limits. In Wideman's fiction, all eyes are on Philadelphia, as they seem always to have been. One of the characters in *Philadelphia Fire*, Margaret Jones, a former member of MOVE, describes the case study that the city and its African American residents have become. With a nod to the University of Pennsylvania (where W. E. B. DuBois had written *The Philadelphia Negro* at the end of the nineteenth century), Jones worries that Cudjoe in his inquiries will be "just like the social workers and those busybodies from the University. They been studying us for years. Reports on top of reports. A whole basement full of files in the building where I work. We're famous" (20).

In *Philadelphia Fire*, the city's first black mayor is under pressure to regulate the uncivilized behavior of MOVE and forcibly reassert his dubious authority. In Timbo's words, the promise of the city has a familiar aspect:

> This city gon be Camelot, right? Our black Camelot. We're in the driver's seat, watch us go, world. . . . Possibilities here. This an old city with old money. Seemed like we might have half a chance to do our thing here, do it our way. Show everybody. A showcase city. Everybody grinning, shaking hands, making money. But shit, man. I been on the inside two years and you know what I think? I think they experimenting again. (77)

On a driving tour of Philadelphia, Timbo tells Cudjoe about a revitalized city center, a decrepit west and north, and an expanding gap between a few African Americans who are prospering and the rest, whose economic situation is dire and who resent the status quo. Wideman offers a colloquial late-twentieth-century version of the fragile surface evoked by Lippard, Webb, and James: "What's the mayor gon do when the city starts to cracking and pieces break off the edges and disappear. It's thin ice, man. Damn thin ice and we all dancing on it. We all gon fall through if the shit starts to go" (80). Wideman conveys that dance in a prose that often blends lyricism with violence. His portrait of the city in *Philadelphia Fire* is distinguished by an incredulous avowal, honed by the assault on MOVE and the ruin on Osage Avenue, possibly delivered in the register of hyperbole, possibly not, that the trials in freedom, outrageous at their inception, persist. Alert to the differences between 1793 and 1985, Wideman here conveys deadlock. (A novelist is not under the same obligations as a sociologist.) Layering past on present, he describes such racial probation, the Philadelphia experiment, as a contrived and violent tragedy of manners. His black and white characters share, asymmetrically, the blame for social failure.

In his Philadelphia stories, Wideman, like so many others, turns to William Penn and Thomas Holme's founding grid of the city to articulate its distinctive features. At the top of the broad steps leading to the Philadelphia Museum of Art on Fairmount Hill, Wideman's protagonist, the writer Cudjoe, has a vision:

He is sighting down a line of lighted fountains that guide his eye to City Hall. This is how the city was meant to be viewed. Broad avenues bright spokes of a wheel radiating from a glowing center. No buildings higher than Billy Penn's hat atop City Hall. Scale and pattern fixed forever. Clarity, balance, a perfect understanding between the parts. Night air thick and bad but he's standing where he should and the city hums its dream of itself into his ear and he doesn't believe it for an instant but wonders how he managed to stay away so long.

I belong to you, the city says. This is what I was meant to be. You can grasp the pattern. Make sense of me. Connect the dots. I was constructed for you. Like a field of stars I need you to bring me to life. My names, my gods poised on the tip of your tongue. All you have to do is speak and you reveal me, complete me.

The city could fool you easy. And he wonders if that's why he is back. To be caught up in the old trick bag again. Love you. Love you not. Who's zooming who? Is someone in charge? From this vantage point in the museum's deep shadow in the greater darkness of night it seems an iron will has imposed itself on the shape of the city. If you could climb high enough, higher than the hill on which the museum perches, would you believe in the magic pinwheel of lights, straight lines, exact proportions, symmetry of spheres within spheres, gears meshing, turning, spinning to the perpetual music of their motion? Cudjoe fine-tunes for a moment the possibility that someone, somehow, had conceived the city that way. A miraculous design. A prodigy that was comprehensible. He can see a hand drawing the city. An architect's tilted drafting board, instruments for measuring, for inscribing right angles, arcs, circles. The city is a faint tracery of blue, barely visible blood lines in a newborn's skull. No one has used the city yet. No one has pushed a button to start the heart pumping. (44–45)

Cudjoe sees laid out before him the parkway, named for Benjamin Franklin, that was cut through existing neighborhoods in the early twentieth century, a diagonal across the original grid plan with Logan Circle at its midpoint, which connected Fairmount Park and the Art Museum in the northwest to the towering Victorian City Hall erected at the center (figure 5.1). At the apex of the building stands the famous bronze statue of William Penn. From his elevated stance, Cudjoe imagines, or Wideman's narrator (one of them) imagines that Cudjoe imagines, that Philadelphia is whispering to him about the intimacy of alignment. The ownership ("I belong to you") is an illusion, a "trick," as the tenacious presence of Sylvester Stallone's Rocky Balboa suggests. In the most celebrated shot of the 1976 movie *Rocky*, on the high steps of the Art Museum, taking in the bird's-eye view, Stallone pumped his arms in clichéd and affecting triumph. Rather than "a perfect understanding between the parts," Wideman's novel exposes a pattern of enticement and betrayal. This seductive game is accented by another of the passage's jokes, the nod to Aretha Franklin's "Who's Zoomin' Who" and its erotic reversals. Despite the illusion and despite his skepticism, Cudjoe cannot resist the prospect.[10]

The city murmurs to him its need for a receptive partner to fulfill the design: "You can grasp the pattern. Make sense of me. Connect the dots. I was constructed for you." Wideman's Philadelphia speaks not only to his character Cudjoe but also to the novelist, historian, or literary critic who may be led astray by apparent symmetry and congruence, who may too hastily or too surely connect the dots. The literature of Philadelphia cautions against elevating the local, or reducing it to the national or to the global, or folding text into context, or converting past into present. It is a literature of recalcitrance and surprise, in which the particulars of form, diction, and figure register but also exceed their circumstances, and in which, as I have been arguing, such details play a substantial role in debates about the expression of character and in struggles over authority.

Wideman's Philadelphia is legible not in two rigid dimensions but as a three-dimensional surface that his metaphors render strange. At the end of the passage, the narrator shifts from the geometric to the organic—and not just the organic but the natal. Without missing a beat, the narrator moves from architect's drafting board to faint tracery, from hand to head, and from circles to circulation. He signifies on Philadelphia as the capital of the United States, the place where Declaration and Constitution were conceived: "a newborn's skull," fragile with possibility. This city may be understood as a kind of body, but not in terms of the metaphors of organic discipline sometimes invoked by cultural analysts. Wideman's flows are irregular, excessive, often blocked.

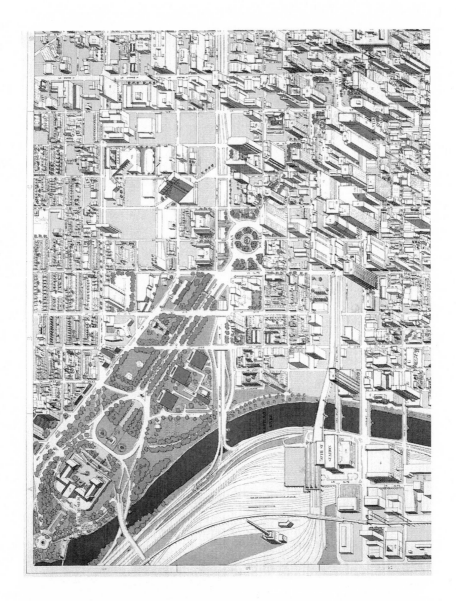

FIGURE 5.1 Philadelphia three-dimensional map: detail of northwest quadrant (1984). Courtesy of the Library Company of Philadelphia. The map has been rotated 90 degrees south, showing the east at the top. The line of sight described by John Edgar Wideman's protagonist Cudjoe, in *Philadelphia Fire*, extends from the Art Museum in the lower left (northwest) to City Hall at the upper right (southeast), connected by the Benjamin Franklin Parkway.

At the start of *The Cattle Killing*, the narrator portrays a writer (who resembles Wideman himself). As he climbs a hill in Pittsburgh to visit his father, the writer ponders the reach and limits of his imaginative access to the eighteenth century and to the young protagonist of his novel (a work which resembles *The Cattle Killing*). He worries over his connection to a boy who has been shot to death on the hill the evening before. (Again one thinks, unexpectedly, of *Sheppard Lee*, in which Bird reflects on the attachments of writers and readers to their characters.) He considers the relationships among himself, his protagonist, and the murdered boy: "*What is the name of the space they occupy now*" (13). One of the names of that space for Wideman across his fiction, and the literary space I have attempted to name in the chapters of this book—a center that is on the border, a part that is not the whole, a space in which writers across a variety of genres meticulously articulate a volatile combination of race, character, manners, violence, and freedom, goaded by a shared but fiercely contested set of events—is "Philadelphia."

NOTES

Introduction

1. Frederick Douglass, "The Black Man's Future in the Southern States: An Address Delivered in Boston, Massachusetts, on 5 February 1862," in *The Frederick Douglass Papers; Series One: Speeches, Debates, and Interviews*, vol. 3, *1855–63*, ed. John W. Blassingame et al. (New Haven, Conn.: Yale University Press, 1985), 505; "Visit to Philadelphia," *North Star* (October 13, 1848), 2.

2. See Mary P. Ryan, *Civic Wars: Democracy and Public Life in the American City during the Nineteenth Century* (Berkeley: University of California Press, 1997), 305–16ff. Ryan discusses New York, New Orleans, and San Francisco. For the historical sketch in this and the following paragraphs, I have drawn upon W. E. B. DuBois, *The Philadelphia Negro: A Social Study* (1899), intro. Elijah Anderson (Philadelphia: University of Pennsylvania Press, 1996), 10–39; Russell F. Weigley, *Philadelphia: A 300-Year History* (New York: W. W. Norton, 1982), especially Elizabeth Geffen, "Industrial Development and Social Crisis, 1841–1854," 307–362; Gary B. Nash, *Forging Freedom: The Formation of Philadelphia's Black Community, 1720–1840* (Cambridge, Mass.: Harvard University Press, 1988); Nash and Jean R. Soderlund, *Freedom by Degrees: Emancipation in Pennsylvania and Its Aftermath* (New York: Oxford University Press, 1991); Julie Winch, *Philadelphia's Black Elite: Activism, Accommodation, and the Struggle for Autonomy, 1787–1848* (Philadelphia: Temple University Press, 1988); Emma Jones Lapsansky, *Neighborhoods in Transition: William Penn's Dream and Urban Reality* (New York: Garland, 1994), and "'Since They Got Those Separate Churches': Afro-Americans and Racism in Jacksonian Philadelphia," *American Quarterly* 32.1 (Spring 1980): 54–78; and Rosalind Remer, *Printers and Men of Capital: Philadelphia Book Publishers in the New Republic* (Philadelphia: University of Pennsylvania Press, 1996). Recently, several historians have examined the roles played by African American women in the city's churches, mutual aid and antislavery societies, and print cultures (newspapers, petitions, spiritual narratives, friendship albums). See Julie Winch, "Sarah Forten's Anti-Slavery Networks," and Jane Rhodes, "At the Boundaries of Abolitionism, Feminism, and Black Nationalism: The Activism of Mary Ann Shadd Cary," in *Women's Rights and Transatlantic Antislavery in the Era of Emancipation*, ed. Kathryn Kish Sklar and James Brewer Stewart

(New Haven, Conn.: Yale University Press, 2007), 143–57, 346–66; and especially Erica Armstrong Dunbar, *A Fragile Freedom: African American Women and Emancipation in the Antebellum City* (New Haven: Yale University Press, 2008).

3. See *Narrative of the Life of Henry Box Brown, Written by Himself,* ed. John Ernest (1851; rpt. Chapel Hill: University of North Carolina Press, 2008); Brown's arrival in the city is described on pages 87–89, and the "Philadelphia" address is represented in illustrations, prints, and broadsides, which Ernest discusses in an appendix on pages 107–21. For the other entries into Philadelphia I have mentioned, see *Running a Thousand Miles for Freedom; or The Escape of William and Ellen Craft from Slavery* (1860), in *Slave Narratives,* ed. William L. Andrews and Henry Louis Gates Jr. (New York: Library of America, 2000), 724–26; Harriet A. Jacobs, *Incidents in the Life of a Slave Girl, Written by Herself,* ed. and intro. Jean Fagan Yellin (1861; rpt. Cambridge, Mass.: Harvard University Press, 2000), 159–63; and William Still, *The Underground Railroad: A Record of Facts, Authentic Narratives, Letters, & c., Narrating the Hardships, Hair-breadth Escapes, and Death Struggles of the Slaves in Their Efforts for Freedom, as Related by Themselves and Others, or Witnessed by the Author* (1872; rpt. Chicago: Johnson, 1970).

4. Travelers from abroad in the decades before the Civil War acknowledged the crucial interest of Philadelphia. The Scottish writer and reformer Frances Wright used the city as a pivot for her thoughts on the likelihood of African American progress, in her 1821 *Views of Society and Manners in America,* ed. Paul R. Baker (Cambridge, Mass.: Belknap Press of the Harvard University Press, 1963), 40–44. The historian George Wilson Pierson suggests that the Frenchmen Alexis de Tocqueville and Gustave de Beaumont, during their famous trip of 1831 and 1832, first became absorbed with questions of race in the United States after coming into contact with African Americans in Philadelphia; see *Tocqueville and Beaumont in America* (New York: Oxford University Press, 1938), 512–15. The English Quaker abolitionist Edward S. Abdy offered the respectability and subordination of the African American businessman James Forten as "'the glory and the shame' of Philadelphia," in his *Journal of a Residence and Tour in the United States of North America, from April, 1833, to October, 1834* (London: John Murray, 1835), 3:129–32. The English novelist Frederick Marryat praised the decorum of African Americans in the city (while observing their enduring intellectual inferiority to whites) and marveled, with ironic repetition, at the "degree of contempt and dislike in which the free blacks are held in all the free states of America," in his 1839 *A Diary in America, with Remarks on Its Institutions,* ed. Sydney Jackman (New York: Alfred A. Knopf, 1962), 149–51. The English Quaker philanthropist Joseph Sturge observed "that Philadelphia appears to be the metropolis of this odious prejudice [against colour], and that there is probably no city in the known world, where dislike, amounting to hatred of the coloured population, prevails more than in the city of brotherly love!" See his *A Visit to the United States in 1841* (London: Hamilton, Adams, and Co., 1842), 40.

5. W. E. B. DuBois, *The Philadelphia Negro,* 17; and see Elijah Anderson's introduction (ix–xxxvi) and also Michael B. Katz and Thomas J. Sugrue, eds., *W. E. B. DuBois, Race, and the City: The Philadelphia Negro and Its Legacy* (Philadelphia: University of Pennsylvania Press, 1998). Gary Nash uses the term "Philadelphia experiment" to describe the concern with

the results of emancipation in the city; see *Forging Freedom*, 3, 6. "Experiment" also was the term used to describe another, different scene of freedom: Port Royal in the Sea Islands off the coast of South Carolina. Between 1861 and 1865, enslaved African Americans, whose legal status was uncertain after Southern cotton plantation owners fled from Union troops, were supported (and undermined) by Northern philanthropists, abolitionists, and entrepreneurs in a trial of free labor sponsored by the U.S. government. See Willie Lee Rose, *Rehearsal for Reconstruction: The Port Royal Experiment* (Indianapolis. Ind.: Bobbs-Merrill, 1964); Elizabeth Ware Pearson, ed., *Letters from Port Royal, Written at the Time of the Civil War* (1906), rpt. as *Letters from Port Royal, 1862–1868* (New York: Arno Press and the New York Times, 1969); and (the Philadelphian) Charlotte Forten Grimké's *Journals of Charlotte Forten Grimké*, ed. Brenda Stevenson (New York: Oxford University Press, 1988), 382–511. In the broadest sense, the fascination with Philadelphia as social laboratory was a particular instance in a tradition of American experiments in place, dating back to the English founding at Massachusetts Bay and John Winthrop's alert to his fellow colonists that "wee shall be as a Citty upon a Hill, the eies of all people are uppon us." See Winthrop's sermon "A Modell of Christian Charity" (1630), in *American Sermons: The Pilgrims to Martin Luther King Jr.*, ed. Michael Warner (New York: Library of America, 1999), 42.

6. Thomas Hamilton, *Men and Manners in America* (1833; rpt. New York: Augustus M. Kelley, 1968), 337–38.

7. Wright, *Views of Society and Manners in America*, 47; Mrs. Basil Hall, *The Aristocratic Journey: Being the Outspoken Letters of Mrs. Basil Hall, Written during a Fourteen Months' Sojourn in America, 1827–1828*, ed. Una Pope-Hennessy (New York: Knickerbocker, 1931), 136; Nathaniel Parker Willis, "Pencillings by the Way," *United States Gazette* (Nov. 21, 1831), 2; Frances Trollope, *Domestic Manners of the Americans*, ed. Donald Smalley (1832; rpt. New York: Vintage, 1949), 260; Charles Dickens, *American Notes for General Circulation*, ed. Patricia Ingham (1842; rpt. New York: Penguin, 2000), 104. Penn and Holme's plan for Philadelphia first appeared in "A Letter from William Penn, Proprietary and Governor of Pennsylvania in America, to the Committee of the Free Society of Traders of that Province, residing in London" (1683); see *William Penn and the Founding of Pennsylvania: A Documentary History*, ed. Jean R. Soderlund (Philadelphia: University of Pennsylvania Press, 1983), 308–24. The design served as a model for many North American frontier cities. Emma Jones Lapsansky discusses the grid and the city's history in *Neighborhoods in Transition*, 3–29. Charles Scruggs argues that in *The Philadelphia Negro* W. E. B. DuBois gave prominence to the city's African American community, which the imagined grid had rendered "terra incognita" (DuBois's words) by the end of the nineteenth century; see *Sweet Home: Invisible Cities in the Afro-American Novel* (Baltimore: Johns Hopkins University Press, 1993), 19–24. Philip Fisher uses Thomas Jefferson's Land Ordinance of 1785, which divided the western territories of the United States into sections based on a one-mile square grid, as the emblem of a "democratic social space," in *Still the New World: American Literature in a Culture of Creative Destruction* (Cambridge, Mass.: Harvard University Press, 1999), 1–55.

8. Benjamin Franklin, *Autobiography*, ed. J. A. Leo Lemay and P. M. Zall (New York: W. W. Norton, 1986), 58–76; Franklin discusses "Credit," "Character," and "Appearances"

on 49 and 54–55, and his troubles with "Order" on 73 . The second part was written in 1784 but not published in its entirety until 1818. On the convoluted history of Franklin's manuscript and its printed versions, see Lemay and Zall's introduction, xvii–lviii, and also James N. Green and Peter Stallybrass, *Benjamin Franklin: Writer and Printer* (New Castle, Del.: Oak Knoll, 2006), 145–71.

9. Jokes about Philadelphia, then and now, often invoke the grid. Herman Melville adds "Philadelphian regularity" to his encyclopedia of clichés in *The Confidence-Man: His Masquerade* (1857), vol. 10 of *The Writings of Herman Melville*, ed. Harrison Hayford, Hershel Parker, and G. Thomas Tanselle (Evanston, Ill., and Chicago: Northwestern University Press and the Newberry Library, 1984), 72. Reproving Benjamin Franklin and neglecting his ironies, D. H. Lawrence employs metaphors of the grid (including fences, paddocks, and corrals) to portray Franklin as both the inventor and inmate of his adopted city; see *Studies in Classic American Literature* (1923), ed. Ezra Greenspan, Lindeth Vasey, and John Worthen (New York: Cambridge University Press, 2003), 20–31.

10. Yi-Fu Tuan, *Space and Place: The Perspective of Experience* (Minneapolis: University of Minnesota Press, 1977); Doreen Massey, *Space, Place, and Gender* (Minneapolis: University of Minnesota Press, 1994), with the quotation taken from page 154 of her essay "A Global Sense of Place" (1991), included in the volume; and Tim Cresswell, *Place: A Short Introduction* (Oxford: Blackwell, 2004). See also David Harvey, *The Condition of Postmodernity: An Enquiry into the Origins of Cultural Change* (Oxford: Blackwell, 1989); Edward Soja, *Postmodern Geographies: The Reassertion of Space in Critical Social Theory* (London: Verso, 1989) and *Thirdspace: Journeys to Los Angeles and Other Real-and-Imagined Places* (Oxford: Blackwell, 1996); and Henri Lefebvre, *The Production of Space*, trans. Donald Nicholson-Smith (Oxford: Blackwell, 1991). The reemergence of "place" across fields has been discussed by Paul C. Adams, Steven Hoelscher, and Karen E. Till in their introduction "Place in Context: Rethinking Humanist Geographies," in *Textures of Place: Exploring Humanist Geographies*, ed. Paul C. Adams, Steven Hoelscher, and Karen E. Till (Minneapolis: University of Minnesota Press, 2001), xiii–xxxiii.

11. Wayne Franklin and Michael Steiner call for a new attention to place in American Studies in their introduction, "Taking Place: Toward the Regrounding of American Studies," in *Mapping American Culture*, ed. Wayne Franklin and Michael Steiner (Iowa City: University of Iowa Press, 1992), 3–23. Sara Blair reviews the influence of geographical theory on literary study in "Cultural Geography and the Place of the Literary," *American Literary History* 10 (1998): 544–67.

12. John Agnew describes three aspects of "place" as locale, location, and sense of place, in *Place and Politics: The Geographical Mediation of State and Society* (Boston: Allen and Unwin, 1987), 28. Conjuring Philadelphia, postmodern writers have experimented with form in rendering the city's spatial complexities. See, for examples, Thomas Pynchon, *Mason & Dixon* (New York: Henry Holt, 1997), and John Edgar Wideman, "Fever," in *Fever: Twelve Stories* (New York: Henry Holt, 1989), 127–61; *Philadelphia Fire* (New York: Henry Holt, 1990); *The Cattle Killing* (New York: Houghton Mifflin, 1996); and *Two Cities* (New York: Houghton Mifflin, 1998). I will discuss Wideman's Philadelphia fiction in the coda to this book.

13. On New York, see Leslie M. Harris, *In the Shadow of Slavery: African Americans in New York City, 1626–1863* (Chicago: University of Chicago Press, 2003); Shane White, *Stories of Freedom in Black New York* (Cambridge, Mass.: Harvard University Press, 2002); and Christine Stansell's review essay on the Harris and White books, "Mean Streets," *New Republic* (24 March 2003), 30–34. On Boston and Washington, D.C., see George A. Levesque, *Black Boston: African American Life in Urban America, 1750–1860* (New York: Garland, 1994), and Constance McLaughlin Green, *The Secret City: A History of Race Relations in the Nation's Capital* (Princeton, N.J.: Princeton University Press, 1967). Leon Litwack discusses Philadelphia as one among many northern locations in *North of Slavery: The Negro in the Free States, 1790–1860* (Chicago: University of Chicago Press, 1961), 84–86, 100–101, 150–51, 168–69, 191–95.

14. See Ellis Paxson Oberholtzer, *The Literary History of Philadelphia* (Philadelphia: George W. Jacobs, 1906); Nicholas B. Wainwright, "The Age of Nicholas Biddle, 1825–1841," and Nathaniel Burt and Wallace E. Davies, "The Iron Age, 1876–1905," in Weigley, ed., *Philadelphia: A 300-Year History*, 299, 514. For treatments of the city in U.S. literature, see George Arthur Dunlap, *The City in the American Novel, 1789–1900* (New York: Russell and Russell, 1965); Janis P. Stout, *Sodoms in Eden: The City in American Fiction before 1860* (Westport, Conn.: Greenwood, 1976); Adrienne Siegel, *The Image of the American City in Popular Literature, 1820–1870* (Port Washington, N.Y.: Kennikat, 1981); and Richard Lehan, *The City in Literature: An Intellectual and Cultural History* (Berkeley: University of California Press, 1998).

15. See Christopher Looby, *Voicing America: Language, Literary Form, and the Origins of the United States* (Chicago: University of Chicago Press, 1996), 9–10, 35–40; Laura Rigal, *The American Manufactory: Art, Labor, and the World of Things in the Early Republic* (Princeton, N.J.: Princeton University Press, 1998); and Carlo Rotella, *October Cities: The Redevelopment of Urban Literature* (Berkeley: University of California Press, 1998), 119–201.

16. The gap remains evident in recent editions of the leading historical anthologies. The first volume of *The Norton Anthology of American Literature* (7th ed., 2007), subtitled "Beginnings to 1820," ends with selections from Tabitha Tenney's *Female Quixotism* (1801) and the 1790s are represented only by chapters from Hannah Webster Foster's *The Coquette*. The second volume, "1820–1865," begins in the 1820s with excerpts from Washington Irving's *Sketch Book*, James Fenimore Cooper's *The Pioneers* and *The Last of the Mohicans*, Catharine Maria Sedgwick's *Hope Leslie*, and poems by Lydia Sigourney. Most of its 2,600 pages are devoted to texts from the 1840s and 1850s. The first volume of *The Heath Anthology of American Literature* (5th ed., 2006), subtitled "Colonial Period to 1800," ends with Charles Brockden Brown's "Somnambulism" (1805). Only Foster's *Coquette* and Susanna Haswell Rowson's *Charlotte Temple* are reprinted from the 1790s. The second volume, "1800–1865," provides an array of openings, including Native American, Spanish American, New England, Southern, and "Narrative" (Irving, Cooper, Sedgwick). But there are almost no titles published before 1820 (although many of the included folktales and songs with later publication dates probably circulated in the early nineteenth century). A similar gap can be found in *The Norton Anthology of African American Literature* (1997), which moves from the narrative of Olaudah Equiano (1789) and the poems of Phillis Wheatley (published in the 1770s) to David Walker's *Appeal* (1829–30).

17. Stephen Best, Sharon Marcus, and their contributors examine alternative under-standings of literary surface in their special issue of *Representations* 108 (Fall 2009), entitled "The Way We Read Now."

18. For descriptions of "place" that evoke textual interpretation, see, in addition to Doreen Massey's essay "A Global Sense of Place" (cited in note 10), Adams, Hoelscher, and Till's introduction to *Textures of Place*, xiii–xxxiii. In his compelling version of historical formalism, Eric J. Sunquist seeks to do justice to both registers. Ross Posnock reviews Sundquist's career and method in "'Like but Unalike': Eric Sundquist and Literary Historicism," *Modern Intellectual History* 4.3 (2007): 629–42.

19. Saidiya V. Hartman, *Scenes of Subjection: Terror, Slavery, and Self-Making in Nineteenth-Century America* (New York: Oxford University Press, 1997), 115, 9.

20. Carla L. Peterson, *"Doers of the Word": African American Women Speakers and Writers in the North (1830–1880)* (New York: Oxford University Press, 1995), 12; Patrick Rael, *Black Identity and Black Protest in the Antebellum North* (Chapel Hill: University of North Carolina Press, 2002); Eddie S. Glaude Jr., *Exodus!: Religion, Race, and Nation in Early Nineteenth-Century Black America* (Chicago: University of Chicago Press, 2000). Evelyn Brooks Higginbotham influentially has described a "politics of respectability" in *Righteous Discontent: The Women's Movement in the Black Baptist Church, 1880–1920* (Cambridge: Harvard University Press, 1993), 185–229. Literary critics such as Claudia Tate and Ann duCille have taught us to think differently about form and class in late-nineteenth-century and early-twentieth-century African American literature by reconstructing a historical aesthetics. See Claudia Tate, *Domestic Allegories of Political Desire: The Black Heroine's Text at the Turn of the Century* (New York: Oxford University Press, 1992), and Ann duCille, *The Coupling Convention: Sex, Text, and Tradition in Black Women's Fiction* (New York: Oxford University Press, 1993). The literature of Philadelphia from the 1790s through the 1850s constitutes an anomalous precedent for this later writing.

Chapter One

1. Benjamin Rush, *An Account of the Bilious Remitting Yellow Fever as It Appeared in the City of Philadelphia, in the Year 1793*, 2nd ed. (Philadelphia: Thomas Dobson, 1794), 128. On the history of the 1793 epidemic, see J. M. Powell, *Bring Out Your Dead: The Great Plague of Yellow Fever in Philadelphia in 1793* (1949); intro. Kenneth R. Foster, Mary F. Jenkins, and Anna Coxe Toogood (Philadelphia: University of Pennsylvania Press, 1993); J. Worth Estes and Billy G. Smith, eds., *A Melancholy Scene of Devastation: The Public Response to the 1793 Philadelphia Yellow Fever Epidemic* (Sagamore Beach, Mass.: Science History Publications, 1997); Gary B. Nash, *Forging Freedom: The Formation of Philadelphia's Black Community, 1720–1840* (Cambridge, Mass.: Harvard University Press, 1988), 121–25; Julie Winch, *Philadelphia's Black Elite: Activism, Accommodation, and the Struggle for Autonomy, 1787–1848* (Philadelphia: Temple University Press, 1988), 15–17; Arthur Thomas Robinson, "The Third Horse-man of the Apocalypse: A Multi-Disciplinary Social History of the 1793 Yellow Fever Epidemic in Philadelphia," Ph.D. diss., Washington State University, 1993; and Jacquelyn

C. Miller, "The Body Politic: Passions, Pestilence, and Political Culture in the Age of the American Revolution," Ph.D. diss., Rutgers University, 1995.

2. Benjamin Rush, *Letters of Benjamin Rush*, vol. 2, *1793–1813*, ed. L. H. Butterfield (Princeton, N.J.: Princeton University Press, 1951), 664, 704, 711, and *Account of the Yellow Fever*, 343–45; Richard S. Newman, *Freedom's Prophet: Bishop Richard Allen, the AME Church, and the Black Founding Fathers* (New York: New York University Press, 2008), 85; Mathew Carey, *Autobiography* (1833–34; rpt. New York: Research Classics, 1942), 27. Both the story of the fever and the figure of Richard Allen were influential in nineteenth-century African American history; see, for examples, Robert Purvis, "Appeal of Forty Thousand Citizens, Threatened with Disfranchisement, to the People of Pennsylvania" (Philadelphia: Merrihew and Gunn, 1838), 13–14, and William Cooper Nell, *The Colored Patriots of the American Revolution, with Sketches of Several Distinguished Colored Persons: To Which Is Added a Brief Survey of the Condition and Prospects of Colored Americans* (Boston: Robert F. Walcutt, 1855), 193–95.

3. Carey, *Autobiography*, 27. In a footnote in the last version of his fever story, Carey makes similar remarks about the committee members' tranquility in the midst of the epidemic; see *A Brief Account of the Malignant Fever Which Prevailed in Philadelphia, in the Year 1793: with a Statement of Proceedings That Took Place on the Subject, in Different Parts of the United States, Fifth Edition, Improved* (Philadelphia: Clark and Raser, 1830), 30–31. On the literary aftermath of the fever for Rush and Allen, see George W. Corner, introduction to *The Autobiography of Benjamin Rush: His "Travels through Life" Together with His Commonplace Book for 1789–1883*, ed. George W. Corner (Princeton, N.J.: Princeton University Press, 1948), 1–9; Louis P. Masur, "Benjamin Rush," in *Dictionary of Literary Biography*, vol. 37, *American Writers of the Early Republic*, edited by Emory Elliott (Detroit: Gale, 1985), 264; and Phillip Lapsansky, "'Abigail, a Negress': The Role and the Legacy of African Americans in the Yellow Fever Epidemic," in Estes and Smith, eds., *Melancholy Scene of Devastation*, 75.

4. Rush, *Letters*, 2:655; *Autobiography*, 95. Memories of the 1793 fever are tenacious. Rush's pupil Charles Caldwell wrote in his *Autobiography*: "so deep and indelible is the impression produced upon me, by that memorable visitation, that, even *now*, after the lapse of more than half a century, as often as I see the two figures 93, or hear them named, some of the scenes of the calamity are revived in my memory, with a degree of freshness bordering on that which they originally possessed"; see *Autobiography of Charles Caldwell* (Philadelphia: Lippincott, Grambo, 1855), 106.

5. Susan E. Klepp, "Appendix I: 'How Many Precious Souls Are Fled'?: The Magnitude of the 1793 Yellow Fever Epidemic," in Estes and Smith, eds., *Melancholy Scene of Devastation*, 171–72.

6. See Lapsansky, "'Abigail, a Negress,'" in Estes and Smith, eds., *Melancholy Scene of Devastation*, 61–78; Julia Stern, *The Plight of Feeling: Sympathy and Dissent in the Early American Novel* (Chicago: University of Chicago Press, 1997), 219–23; Philip Gould, "Race, Commerce, and the Literature of Yellow Fever in Early National Philadelphia," *Early American Literature* 35.2 (2000): 157–86; and Joanna Brooks, *American Lazarus: Religion and the Rise of African-American and Native American Literatures* (New York: Oxford University Press, 2003), 151–78.

7. James N. Green, "Mathew Carey," in *Dictionary of Literary Biography*, vol. 73, *American Magazine Journalists, 1741–1850* (Detroit: Gale, 1988), 56–64. Green reports that Carey's fever accounts were translated into French, German, Dutch, and Italian. Poe compared Carey and Franklin in his 1836 review of Carey's *Autobiography* in *Southern Literary Messenger* 2.3 (March 1836): 203–4. Carey claims in his *Autobiography* that hundreds of copies of the second edition were sent by Philadelphia debtors to their creditors to justify their delay in making payments (25–26).

8. Mathew Carey, "Desultory Account of the Yellow Fever, Prevalent in Philadelphia, and of the Present State of the City" (Philadelphia: Mathew Carey, 1793), 3, 5. In subsequent references to Carey's fever accounts, I will give page numbers in parentheses for the "Desultory Account" and the following editions of *A Short Account of the Malignant Fever, Lately Prevalent in Philadelphia: with a Statement of the Proceedings That Took Place on the Subject in Different Parts of the United States:* Nov. 14, 1793 (1st ed.); Nov. 23, 1793 (2nd ed., which reprints the narrative of the first edition, supplying updated material in the appendices); Nov. 30, 1793 (3rd ed.); and Jan. 16, 1794 (4th ed.). The fifth and final edition was published as *A Brief Account of the Malignant Fever Which Prevailed in Philadelphia, in the Year 1793: With a Statement of Proceedings That Took Place on the Subject, in Different Parts of the United States* (Philadelphia: Clark and Raser, 1830).

9. Rush reprints his remarks in *Account of the Bilious Remitting Yellow Fever*, 96; the October 29, 1793, letter from Rush to Carey can be found in Rush's *Letters*, 2:731–32. Although the addressee was not recorded, circumstantial evidence strongly indicates that it was sent to Carey.

10. Absalom Jones and Richard Allen, "A Narrative of the Proceedings of the Black People, during the Late Awful Calamity in Philadelphia, in the Year 1793: and A Refutation of Some Censures, Thrown upon Them in Some Late Publications" (1794), rpt. in *Negro Protest Pamphlets*, ed. Dorothy Porter (New York: Arno Press and the New York Times, 1969), 20. Subsequent references will be given parenthetically. Most, but not all, of the original text can be found in Richard Newman, Patrick Rael, and Phillip Lapsansky, eds., *Pamphlets of Protest: An Anthology of Early African American Protest Literature, 1790–1860* (New York: Routledge, 2001), 33–42. Gould reprints Jones and Allen's advertisement in "Race, Commerce, and the Literature of Yellow Fever," 174; Rush reprints Mayor Clarkson's September 6 announcement in his *Account of the Bilious Remitting Yellow Fever*, 97. On the call for African American service, see Jones and Allen, "Narrative of the Proceedings," 3–4; Sally F. Griffith, "'A Total Dissolution of the Bonds of Society': Community Death and Regeneration in Mathew Carey's *Short Account of the Malignant Fever*," in Estes and Smith, eds., *Melancholy Scene of Devastation*, 54; and Robinson, "Third Horseman of the Apocalypse," 177–81.

11. Rush, *Letters*, 2:654, 684. Subsequent references to Rush's letters to Julia will be given parenthetically. On the "American school," see William Stanton, *The Leopard's Spots: Scientific Attitudes toward Race in America* (Chicago: University of Chicago Press, 1960).

12. On the difference in death rates, see, in Estes and Smith, eds., *Melancholy Scene of Devastation*, Lapsansky, "'Abigail, a Negress,'" 67; Billy G. Smith, "Comment: Disease and Community," 150; and Klepp, "'How Many Precious Souls Are Fled,'" 167–69. Describing

the fever through excerpts from a 1793 narrative, Benjamin Banneker repeated, inaccurately, that "The black people . . . were exempted in a peculiar manner from the contagion. Very few of them were taken, and still fewer died"; see "Banneker's Almanac for the Year 1795: Being the Third after Leap Year. Containing (Besides Every Thing Necessary in an Almanac,) an Account of the Yellow Fever, Lately Prevalent in Philadelphia, with the Number of Those Who Died, from the First of August till the Ninth of November, 1793" (Philadelphia: William Young). Banneker's source was "An Account of the Rise, Progress, and Termination of the Malignant Fever, Lately Prevalent in Philadelphia. Briefly Stated from Authentic Documents" (Philadelphia: Benjamin Johnson, 1793), published anonymously but attributed to James Hardie (the quoted passage appears on page 28).

13. On yellow fever and race, and also the revolution in Saint Domingue, see Robert F. Reid-Pharr, *Conjugal Union: The Body, the House, and the Black American* (New York: Oxford University Press, 1999), 72, 107, 76. Rush's conjectures about black skin color and disease, delivered before the American Philosophical Society in Philadelphia, were published in 1797; see "Observations Intended to Favour a Supposition That the Black Color (As It Is Called) of the Negroes Is Derived from the Leprosy," *Transactions of the American Philosophical Society* 4 (1799): 289–97, and also Rush's Feb. 2, 1798, letter to Jefferson, in *Letters*, 2:785–86. Frederick Douglass printed his satire "Colorphobia in New York!" in his *The North Star* (May 25, 1849); see *Frederick Douglass: Selected Speeches and Writings*, ed. Philip S. Foner and Yuval Taylor (Chicago: Lawrence Hill, 1999), 141–43.

14. John Edgar Wideman interview, "Modern Voices: John Edgar Wideman on the Yellow Fever Epidemic," *Africans in America* Web site: http://www.pbs.org/wgbh/aia/part3/3i3110.html; see also Newman, *Freedom's Prophet*, 91.

15. Rush, *Account of the Bilious Remitting Yellow Fever*, 125, 311.

16. Rush, *Letters*, 2:731. In the first three editions of the *Short Account* (all published in November 1793), Carey confuses the responsibilities of the three men during the epidemic, switching the roles of Gray and Jones. In the fourth edition, published in January, he avoids this error, writing that the three men supervised the nurses of the sick and buriers of the dead (4:63). He never mentions Jones and Allen's dispensing mercury powder or wielding the lancet. Jones and Allen distinguish responsibilities in their "Narrative of the Proceedings," 4.

17. Mathew Carey, "Address of M. Carey to the Public" (Philadelphia, April 4, 1794), 1–2. Based on circumstantial evidence, Robinson argues that Carey did not return to Philadelphia until the second week of October, in "Third Horseman of the Apocalypse," 188. Philip Freneau satirizes those who left the city, in his poem "Orlando's Flight" (1793), revised as "Sangrado's Flight" (1795), in *Poems Written between the Years 1768 & 1794: A New Edition, Revised and Corrected by the Author* (Monmouth, N.J.: Printed at the Press of the Author, 1795), 448.

18. Rush shares Jones and Allen's market evaluation in an October 1, 1793, letter to Julia; see *Letters*, 2:690–91. In his *Account of the Bilious Remitting Yellow Fever*, Rush writes of the conduct of those who remained in Philadelphia during the epidemic: "I saw little to blame, but much to admire and praise in persons of different professions, both sexes, and of all colors" (127). The author of "An Account of the Rise, Progress, and Termination

of the Malignant Fever" (1793), likely James Hardie (see note 12), reported that African Americans charged high prices for their services but explained the arrangements in terms of need, supply and demand, and "human nature" (28–30).

19. For an economic analysis of "pilfering" and "privateering," see Gould, "Race, Commerce, and the Literature of Yellow Fever," 173–81.

20. Carey, "Address of M. Carey to the Public," 5.

21. Carey, "Address of M. Carey to the Public," 5. On Carey's situation, see Nash, *Forging Freedom*, 125; Lapsansky, "'Abigail, a Negress,'" 62–63, 69; Griffith, "'A Total Dissolution of the Bonds of Society,'" 53–55; Gould, "Race, Commerce, and the Literature of Yellow Fever," 167–73; Robinson, "Third Horseman of the Apocalypse," 195–208; and Miller, "The Body Politic," 285–86.

22. Newman argues that "An Address to those who keep Slaves, and approve the Practice" was written by Allen, who took sole credit for it in his last years; see *Freedom's Prophet*, 105–14.

23. For nuanced views of "deference" and "uplift," see Newman, Rael, and Lapsansky, intro. to *Pamphlets of Protest*, 1–31, and Kevin K. Gaines, *Uplifting the Race: Black Leadership, Politics, and Culture in the Twentieth Century* (Chapel Hill: University of North Carolina Press, 1996). For analyses of Jones and Allen's "Narrative of the Proceedings," see Lapsansky, "'Abigail, a Negress'"; Brooks, *American Lazarus*, 151–78; and Newman, *Freedom's Prophet*, 78–127.

24. On African American petitions to the state legislature, see Nash, *Forging Freedom*, 63–65, 94; on pamphlets, see Newman, Rael, and Lapsansky, intro. to *Pamphlets of Protest*, 1–31; and on black idealist history, see Clarence E. Walker, "The American Negro as Historical Outsider, 1836–1935," *Canadian Review of American Studies* 17.2 (Summer 1986): 137–54, and John Ernest, *Liberation Historiography: African American Writers and the Challenge of History, 1794–1862* (Chapel Hill: University of North Carolina Press, 2004), 95–153.

25. On crime narratives and execution sermons, see *Pillars of Salt: An Anthology of Early American Criminal Narratives*, ed. Daniel E. Williams (Madison, Wisc.: Madison House, 1993); on African American crime narratives, see Richard Slotkin, "Narratives of Negro Crime in New England, 1675–1800," *American Quarterly* 25.1 (March 1973): 3–31; William Andrews, *To Tell a Free Story: The First Century of Afro-American Autobiography, 1760–1865* (Urbana: University of Illinois Press, 1988), 41–51; and Donna Denise Hunter, "Dead Men Talking: Africans and the Law in New England's Eighteenth-Century Execution Sermons and Crime Narratives," Ph.D. diss., University of California, Berkeley, 2000.

26. "Sketches of the Life of Joseph Mountain, a Negro, Who Was Executed at New-Haven, on the 20th Day of October, 1790, for a Rape, Committed on the 26th Day of May Last" (1790), in *Pillars of Salt*, ed. Williams, 299–301.

27. Abraham Johnstone, "The Address of Abraham Johnstone, A Black Man, Who Was Hanged at Woodbury, in the County of Glocester, and State of New Jersey, on Saturday the 8th Day of July Last; To the People of Colour. To Which Is Added His Dying Confession or Declaration; Also a Copy of a Letter to His Wife, Written the Day Previous to the Execution" (Philadelphia: Printed for the Purchasers, 1797), 6–7, 2. Subsequent references will be given parenthetically.

28. On Allen's detainment, see Gary B. Nash and Jean R. Soderland, *Freedom by Degrees: Emancipation in Pennsylvania and Its Aftermath* (New York: Oxford University Press, 1991), 198–99, and Newman, *Freedom's Prophet*, 159.

29. Richard Allen, "Confession of John Joyce, alias Davis, Who Was Executed on Monday, the 14th of March, 1808, for the Murder of Mrs. Sarah Cross; with an Address to the Public, and People of Colour, Together with the Substance of the Trial and the Address of Chief Justice Tilghman, on His Condemnation" (Philadelphia: Printed for the Benefit of the Bethel Church, 1808), 7–10; "Confession of Peter Matthias, alias Mathews, Who Was Executed on Monday, the 14th of March, 1808, for the Murder of Mrs. Sarah Cross; with an Address to the Public, and People of Colour, Together with the Substance of the Trial and the Address of Chief Justice Tilghman, on His Condemnation" (Philadelphia: Printed for the Benefit of the Bethel Church, 1808). The supplementary paragraphs to "The Confession of Peter Matthias" suggest that Matthias experienced a distress more acute than Joyce's. Each text included a copyright notice, reporting that Richard Allen had deposited the title on March 10, 1808, and claimed the right of proprietor. The two "Confessions" were published together, as well as separately.

30. Allen, "Confession of John Joyce," 17.

31. Newman analyzes Allen's "Address to the Public" as a rendition of moral failure, instead of racial crime; see *Freedom's Prophet*, 151–54, 200–202.

32. "The Fate of Murderers: A Faithful Narrative of the Murder of Mrs. Sarah Cross, with the Trial, Sentence and Confession of John Joyce and Peter Mathias, Who Were Executed Near Philadelphia on Monday 14, March 1808" (Philadelphia: Printed for the Purchasers, 1808), 17–18.

33. Only Benjamin's letters survive. His habit was to write in the evening, reviewing the day's events, and then write again in the morning before the letter was sent. Rush echoes Defoe in a September 22, 1793, letter to Julia (*Letters*, 2:674); he compares the number of dead in Philadelphia during 1793 with the London totals for the 1664–65 plague, in a November 25, 1793, letter to James Kidd (*Letters*, 2:746). Powell discusses interest in Defoe among Philadelphians during 1793, in *Bring Out Your Dead*, 24.

34. In his ambivalent, trenchant review of Rush's career and character, his onetime student Charles Caldwell suggests that Rush's talents were more literary than medical; see Caldwell, *Autobiography*, 319.

35. For Rush's theories about fever, see *Letters*, 2:694–700, 822–24, and his *Account of the Bilious Remitting Yellow Fever*. On contemporary views about yellow fever, see George W. Corner, "Appendix I: Rush's Medical Theories," in *The Autobiography of Benjamin Rush*, 361–66; J. Worth Estes, "Introduction: The Yellow Fever Syndrome and Its Treatment in Philadelphia, 1793," Klepp, "'How Many Precious Souls Are Fled,'"and Margaret Humphreys, "Appendix II: Yellow Fever since 1793: History and Historiography," in Estes and Smith, eds., *Melancholy Scene of Devastation*, 1–17, 163–82, 183–98.

36. Hazard's letter is quoted in Powell, *Bring Out Your Dead*, 129, and in Butterfield, ed., *Letters of Benjamin Rush*, 2:702, n. 1. In his *Account of the Bilious Remitting Yellow Fever*, Rush himself refers to mosquitoes, comparing skin lesions to mosquito bites (69) and observing that mosquitoes were present in unusually large numbers during the autumn (108).

37. [William Currie], "Respecting Dr. Rush's Conduct and Transactions during the Prevalence of the Malignant Fever of 1793," *Gazette of the United States, and Philadelphia Daily Advertiser* (6 Oct. 1797), 2. Rush's address to his fellow citizens on Sept. 12, 1793, is reprinted in *Letters*, 2:660–61.

38. On fever and the politics of the 1790s, see Jacquelyn C. Miller, "Passions and Politics: The Multiple Meanings of Benjamin Rush's Treatment for the Yellow Fever," and Martin S. Pernick, "Politics, Parties, and Pestilence: Epidemic Yellow Fever in Philadelphia and the Rise of the First Party System," in Estes and Smith, eds., *Melancholy Scene of Devastation*, 79–95, 119–46. Susan E. Klepp characterizes Powell's *Bring Out Your Dead* as a "Cold War account," pitting the forces of dogmatism and demagoguery against those of bourgeois moderation; see "'How Many Precious Souls Are Fled,'" in Estes and Smith, eds., *Melancholy Scene of Devastation*, 175–76. Rush himself suggests that his remedies are democratic in his *Account of the Bilious Remitting Yellow Fever*, 316, 325, 331, and he links resistance to his treatments to political opposition in *Letters*, 2:767, 793, 794, 824–27.

39. See Benjamin Rush, "To the College of Physicians: Use of the Lancet in Yellow Fever," printed in the *Federal Gazette* on Sept. 12, 1793, in *Letters*, 2:661–62. Rush describes his epic struggles with fellow doctors in his *Account of the Bilious Remitting Yellow Fever*. In his poem "Pestilence" (1793), Philip Freneau writes from a wider perspective: "Doctors raving and disputing,/Death's pale army still recruiting—." See his *Poems Written between the Years 1768 & 1794*, 370.

40. See Rush's letters to Jeremy Belknap (August 19, 1788), Julia Rush (July 16, 1791), Granville Sharp (August 1791), John Nicolson (August 12, 1793), Julia Rush (August 22, 1793), and the president of the Pennsylvania Abolition Society [1794?], in *Letters*, 1:481–83, 599–601, 608–609, and *Letters*, 2: 636–37, 639–40, 754–56.

41. See also Rush's letters to Julia on September 23, October 20, October 28, and November 4, 1793, in *Letters*, 2: 676–78, 719–21, 728–29, 739–40. In the "Narrative" appended to his published *Account*, written in the aftermath of the fever and based partly on his letters to Julia, Rush opens a distance between himself and his black "family." He eliminates details and replaces proper names with adjectives and nouns. Marcus becomes merely "my faithful black man" (349) and "my affectionate black man" (360).

42. John Beale Bordley, copy of Carey's *Short Account of the Malignant Fever*, November 30, 1793, now held in the collections of the Library Company of Philadelphia, 78. Bordley himself wrote a pamphlet on the "Yellow Fever" (Philadelphia: Charles Cist, 1794). Carey debated the fever beyond the pages of his *Accounts*; see, for example, his "Observations on Dr. Rush's Enquiry into the Origin of the Late Epidemic Fever in Philadelphia, Dec. 14, 1793" (Philadelphia: From the Press of the Author).

43. In the fourth edition, Carey adds that "there were scarcely any of them seized at first," indicating how mistaken beliefs about immunity might have originated, although he still insists that "the number that were finally affected, was not great" (4:63).

44. J. Henry C. Helmuth, "A Short Account of the Yellow Fever in Philadelphia, for the Reflecting Christian (1794)," trans. Charles Erdmann (Philadelphia: Jones, Hoff, and Derrick, 1794), 2.

45. In his marginalia to the third edition of Carey's *Short Account*, Bordley registers his disapproval at the mistreatment of Philadelphians (97–100).

46. In the fourth edition, published in January 1794, adding descriptions of the plague in London and Marseilles, Carey seeks to put Philadelphia on the map. In the first "Desultory Account," Carey estimates the number who fled the city at "12 or 15,000" (2) and in the third edition "at about 17,000" (3:91).

47. Toni Morrison, "Unspeakable Things Unspoken: The Afro-American Presence in American Literature," *Michigan Quarterly Review* 28.1 (Winter 1989): 11. In the Pennsylvania context, Carey's scenes of restriction evoke the policing under Congress's newly passed Fugitive Slave Act of 1793 (which arose from a dispute between Pennsylvania and Virginia) and also prefigure the state's attempts to close its border to black migrants between 1805 and 1814 and again in the 1830s. See Nash, *Forging Freedom*, 180–83, 275–76.

48. In the final edition of his *Account*, Carey omits the list of the dead, since there was no longer an audience for the news.

49. Shirley Samuels writes that Carey offers "the achievement of order through institutions of social control . . . an account that was designedly therapeutic," in "Plague and Politics in 1793: *Arthur Mervyn*," *Criticism* 27.3 (Summer 1985): 231, 233. The few critics who analyze Carey's *Short Account* treat it as though it were a single text, without reference to its different forms. Sally F. Griffith rests her argument on what she considers to be "the most compelling part" of Carey's fourth edition: "the core narrative contained in the first eight chapters." Yet it is only by excluding the "desultory scraps" and the list of the dead that she can claim the *Short Account* as "a foundation narrative in civic mythology." See her "'A Total Dissolution of the Bonds of Society,'" in Estes and Smith, *Melancholy Scene of Devastation*, 47, 56. I have tried to convey the multiplicities of Carey's text. In teaching, I usually select the third edition (Nov. 30, 1793) for its formal and rhetorical intensities. This was the last *Account* published during the fever months.

50. Charles Brockden Brown, *Arthur Mervyn; or Memoirs of the Year 1793*, vol. 3 of *The Novels and Related Works of Charles Brockden Brown*, ed. Sydney J. Krause and S. W. Reid (Kent, Ohio: Kent State University Press, 1980), 129; compare with Carey, *Short Account*, 3:33–34. Subsequent references to *Arthur Mervyn* will be given parenthetically. The first five chapters of *Arthur Mervyn* were serialized in the Philadelphia *Weekly Magazine* between June 16 and July 14, 1798; chapters 6 through 9 were serialized between August 4 and August 23. The first part of *Arthur Mervyn* was published in book form in 1799, and the second part in 1800. See Norman Grabo's "Historical Essay" in the Kent State edition of *Arthur Mervyn*, 450–62. A long excerpt from chapter 15, describing Arthur's entry into the afflicted city, was published in *The Philadelphia Book; or Specimens of Metropolitan Literature* (Philadelphia: Key and Biddle, 1836), 204–8.

51. The passages are identical in "The Man at Home" and *Ormond;* see *The Rhapsodist and Other Uncollected Writings by Charles Brockden Brown*, ed. Harry R. Warfel (New York: Scholars' Facsimiles and Reprints, 1943), 56, and *Ormond; or, the Secret Witness* (1799), ed. Mary Chapman (Peterborough, Ontario: Broadview, 1999), 93. Subsequent references to these texts will be given parenthetically. For examples of Arthur's conjectures, see chapters 14 and 15 of the first part of *Arthur Mervyn*. On Brown, his circle in New York, and

the fever, see William Dunlap, *The Life of Charles Brockden Brown: Together with Selections from the Rarest of His Printed Works, from His Original Letters, and from His Manuscripts before Unpublished*, 2 vols. (Philadelphia: James P. Parke, 1815), and Bryan Waterman, *Republic of Intellect: The Friendly Club of New York City and the Making of American Literature* (Baltimore: Johns Hopkins University Press, 2007). Robert A. Ferguson argues that the fever galvanized Brown, temporarily freeing him from familial and social constraints and giving him topic and direction, in "Yellow Fever and Charles Brockden Brown: The Context of the Emerging Novelist," *Early American Literature* 14.3 (1979/80): 293–305. Brown wrote extensively on the yellow fever in periodicals such as *Monthly Magazine and American Review, American Review and Literary Journal*, and *Literary Magazine and American Register*.

52. On Brown's *Arthur Mervyn* and Carey's *Short Account*, see Jane Tompkins, *Sensational Designs: The Cultural Work of American Fiction, 1790–1860* (New York: Oxford University Press, 1985), 90–91, and Shirley Samuels, *Romances of the Republic: Women, the Family, and Violence in the Literature of the Early American Nation* (New York: Oxford University Press, 1996), 33–43. On *Ormond* and the *Short Account*, see Cristobal Selenite Silva, "Monstrous Plots: An Epidemiology of American Narrative," Ph.D. diss., New York University, 2003), 231–51. On Arthur Mervyn and Benjamin Rush, see William L. Hedges, "Benjamin Rush, Charles Brockden Brown, and the American Plague Year," *Early American Literature* 8.3 (1974): 295–311, and Gregory Eiselein, "Humanitarianism and Uncertainty in *Arthur Mervyn*," *Essays in Literature* 22.2 (1995): 215–26. Both Hedges and Eiselein use the term "self-righteous" to describe Rush. Julia Stern suggests Jones and Allen's "Narrative" as a possible source for Brown's *Ormond*, in *The Plight of Feeling*, 219–23, 231–34. Carroll Smith-Rosenberg proposes that Brown's Dr. Stevens was based on Rush; see "Black Gothic: The Shadowy Origins of the American Bourgeoisie," in *Possible Pasts: Becoming Colonial in Early America*, ed. Robert Blair St. George (Ithaca, N.Y.: Cornell University Press, 2000), 259. Rush himself admired his colleague Edward Stevens, who tended to him during his own illness, but with whom he clashed on the proper theory and treatment of the fever; see *Account of the Bilious Remitting Yellow Fever*, 213–24. Eiselein suggests that Brown's Stevens is based on Edward Stevens. Brown uses the phrase "tainted atmosphere" twice in *Ormond* (68, 75). Robinson praises the accuracy of Brown's descriptions of the Philadelphia fever in "Third Horseman of the Apocalypse," 354–406.

53. Resisting social allegories, Bryan Waterman offers a summary statement of such critical positions, in "*Arthur Mervyn*'s Medical Repository and the Early Republic's Knowledge Industries," *American Literary History* 15.2 (2003): 219. He argues that Brown's aim is to provide "scientific and moral accuracy" (236). See also Waterman's *Republic of Intellect*, 189–230.

54. Brown repeats the pun twice in his *Address to the Government of the United States, on the Cession of Louisiana to the French* (Philadelphia: John Conrad, 1803), in which, in the persona of a "French Counsellor of State," he links it with the disease of slavery in the West Indies and the United States: "the same intestine plague" (72), "this intestine enemy" (73).

55. Norman S. Grabo, *The Coincidental Art of Charles Brockden Brown* (Chapel Hill: University of North Carolina Press, 1981), 102–6; Waterman, "*Arthur Mervyn*'s Medical

Repository," 233–36; Teresa A. Goddu, *Gothic America: Narrative, History, and Nation* (New York: Columbia University Press, 1997), 31–50 (her chapter on *Arthur Mervyn* is titled "Diseased Discourse"). Bill Christopherson describes a persistent moral ambidexterity in Arthur: "Cured though he is, Arthur may yet be a carrier"; see *The Apparition in the Glass: Charles Brockden Brown's American Gothic* (Athens: University of Georgia Press, 1993), 125.

56. Smith-Rosenberg focuses on the two mirror scenes in "Black Gothic," 249–56. Christopherson discusses the mirror scenes as evidence of white anxieties about the persistence of slavery and presence of Africans in America, in *Apparition in the Glass*, 104–11. He takes the title of his book on Brown and the American gothic from the scene in which Arthur is struck by the figure in the mirror.

57. Goudie analyzes the Baltimore coach scene in "On the Origins of American Specie(s): The West Indies, Classification, and the Emergence of Supremacist Consciousness in *Arthur Mervyn*," in *Revising Charles Brockden Brown: Culture, Politics, and Sexuality in the Early Republic*, ed. Philip Barnard, Mark L. Kamrath, and Stephen Shapiro (Knoxville: University of Tennessee Press, 2004), 74–77. Camper's illustrations are reproduced in Barbara Maria Stafford, *Body Criticism: Imaging the Unseen in Enlightenment Art and Medicine* (Cambridge, Mass.: MIT Press, 1991), 111. On the Baltimore coach scene, see also Waterman, "*Arthur Mervyn's* Medical Repository," 237–38; Goddu, *Gothic America*, 44; and Brooks, *American Lazarus*, 177.

58. Carroll Smith-Rosenberg makes a similar point about Arthur's "black" conduct, in "Black Gothic," 257, as part of her larger argument that the African American laborers and genteel European Am erican women in *Arthur Mervyn* only "bestow the appearance of coherence on the new middle-class man of commerce and industry" (245). In "Origins of American Specie(s)," Goudie argues that racial blow is followed by ethnological recovery. Robert S. Levine argues for Brown's complex and ethical treatment of racial difference in his fiction and in his two pamphlets on Louisiana. See "Race and Nation in Brown's Louisiana Writings of 1803," in *Revising Charles Brockden Brown*, ed. Barnard, Kamrath, and Shapiro, 332–53.

59. Caleb Williams describes Falkland: "every muscle and petty line of his countenance seemed to be in an inconceivable degree pregnant with meaning"; see William Godwin, *The Adventures of Caleb Williams, or Things as They Are*, ed. Maurice Hindle (1794; rpt. London: Penguin, 1988), 7. Brown echoes Godwin's description of Falkland even more closely in *Ormond:* "The features and shape sunk, as it were, into perfect harmony with sentiments and passions. Every atom of the frame was pregnant with significance" (97).

60. Sean X. Goudie, "Origins of American Specie(s)," and Hoang Phan, "The Labors of Difference: Race, Citizenship, and the Transformation of Legal and Literary Form," Ph.D. diss., University of California, Berkeley, 2004, both attend to faces in *Arthur Mervyn*. In *Ormond*, Brown's narrator explains that the protagonist Constantia Dudley has a "sixth sense" that enables her to interpret the language of features and looks (97–98) but warns about the swindler Thomas Craig: "His character was a standing proof of the vanity of physiognomy" (116).

61. R. W. B. Lewis, *The American Adam: Innocence, Tragedy, and Tradition in the Nineteenth Century* (Chicago: University of Chicago Press, 1955), 97; Warner Berthoff, introduction

to *Arthur Mervyn; or Memoirs of the Year 1793*, by Charles Brockden Brown (New York: Holt, Rinehart, and Winston, 1962), xvii; Michael Warner, *The Letters of the Republic: Publication and the Public Sphere in Eighteenth-Century America* (Cambridge, Mass.: Harvard University Press, 1990), 176.

62. *Caleb Williams*, 337. In Godwin's original manuscript ending, Falkland is not moved to confess and Caleb is still persecuted. There is even a touch of fever in *Caleb Williams:* the poet Clare dies of a malignant fever (34), and Caleb compares his own effect on those around him to an infection (279, 306). On Brown's American rendering of Godwin, see Dorothy J. Hale, "Profits of Altruism: Caleb Williams and Arthur Mervyn," *Eighteenth-Century Studies* 22 (1988): 47–69.

63. Several critics take note of the odd humor in the scene where Arthur rises from his sickbed to burn $20,000 in bills that Welbeck has (falsely) told him were forged, and then preaches to an enraged Welbeck that he has saved him from temptation (206–11); see, for example, Christopherson, *Apparition in the Glass*, 98–99. Hedges, in "Rush, Brown, and the American Plague Year," and Eiselein, in "Humanitarianism and Uncertainty," argue that Brown uses Arthur to disparage Benjamin Rush's misguided conscientiousness and debilitating sanctimony. This seems to me an incomplete view both of Rush and of Brown's attitude toward his protagonist. Although Smith-Rosenberg describes Brown's Dr. Stevens as a "barely disguised representation of Benjamin Rush," the passages she quotes from *Arthur Mervyn* describing Arthur's sense of erotic vulnerability and his intoxication during the fever ("Black Gothic," 259) evoke Rush's own self-portrayals in the narrative he appended to his *Account of the Bilious Remitting Yellow Fever* (1794) and in his letters to Julia. In *Ormond*, Brown distances his narrative from Rush's aggressive measures of bleeding and purging. Mary's stomach refuses to retain powerful evacuants, while Constantia and Lucy recover by following a gentler regimen, abstaining from food and drinking quantities of cold water (76–77, 82–83).

64. Émile Zola, "The Experimental Novel" (1880), in *Documents of Modern Literary Realism*, ed. and trans. George J. Becker (Princeton, N.J.: Princeton University Press, 1963), 179, 178. William L. Hedges suggests that Brown may have anticipated Zola's "experimental novel," in "Rush, Brown, and the American Plague Year," 308.

65. Zola, "The Experimental Novel," 178; Brown, "Walstein's School of History" (1799), in *The Rhapsodist and Other Uncollected Writings*, ed. Warfel, 146, 148. For critics who interpret Brown in *Arthur Mervyn* as strategically compelling his readers' participation, see Emory Elliott, "Narrative Unity and Moral Resolution in *Arthur Mervyn*," in *Critical Essays on Charles Brockden Brown*, ed. Bernard Rosenthal (Boston: G. K. Hall, 1981), 160; Cathy N. Davidson, *Revolution and the Word: The Rise of the Novel in America* (New York: Oxford University Press, 1986), 240–41, 252–53; Edward Watts, *Writing and Postcolonialism in the Early Republic* (Charlottesville: University Press of Virginia, 1998), 119–20; and Frank Shuffleton, "Juries of the Common Reader: Crime and Judgment in the Novels of Charles Brockden Brown," in *Revising Charles Brockden Brown*, ed. Barnard, Kamrath, and Shapiro, 88–114.

66. Bill Christopherson describes the "ambiguousness" of the marriage as "the central riddle of *Arthur Mervyn*," in *Apparition in the Glass*, 87.

67. David M. Larson describes the tone of the Arthur/Ascha relationship as deriving from "the novel of sentimental comedy," in *"Arthur Mervyn, Edgar Huntly, and the Critics," Essays in Literature* 15 (1988): 217.

68. Sean X. Goudie links Arthur's impulse to classify Ascha with his racial scrutinies in "Origins of American Specie(s)," 81.

Chapter Two

1. Henry James, *Hawthorne*, ed. Dan McCall (1879; rpt. Ithaca, N.Y.: Cornell University Press, 1997), 34.

2. J. Hector St. Jean de Crèvecoeur, *Letters from an American Farmer*, ed. Albert E. Stone (1782; rpt. New York: Penguin, 1981), 67; Nathaniel Hawthorne, *The Marble Faun: or, The Romance of Monte Beni*, ed. William Charvat et al. (1860; rpt. Columbus: Ohio State University Press, 1968), 3; James, *Hawthorne*, 34–35; see also James Fenimore Cooper, *Notions of the Americans: Picked Up by a Travelling Bachelor*, ed. Gary Williams (1828; rpt. Albany: State University of New York Press, 1991), 348–49; and Alexis de Tocqueville, *Democracy in America*, ed. and trans. Harvey C. Mansfield and Delba Winthrop (Chicago: University of Chicago Press, 2000), 578–81.

3. Lionel Trilling, "Manners, Morals, and the Novel," in *The Liberal Imagination: Essays on Literature and Society* (New York: Viking, 1950), 205–22; Richard Chase, *The American Novel and Its Tradition* (New York: Doubleday, 1957); Ralph Ellison, "The World and the Jug," in *Shadow and Act* (New York: Random House, 1964), 130–32; and also see Ellison on Trilling, James, and Hawthorne, in "Society, Morality, and the Novel," in *The Living Novel: A Symposium*, ed. Granville Hicks (New York: Macmillan, 1957), 80–84. James W. Tuttleton argues against Trilling and Chase, although the only pre–Civil War writer he discusses at length is Cooper; see *The Novel of Manners in America* (Chapel Hill: University of North Carolina Press, 1972). On the novel of manners in late-nineteenth- and twentieth-century U.S. literature, see Nancy Bentley, *The Ethnography of Manners: Hawthorne, James, Wharton* (New York: Cambridge University Press, 1995), and Susan Goodman, *Civil Wars: American Novelists and Manners, 1880–1940* (Baltimore: Johns Hopkins University Press), 2003.

4. Benjamin Franklin, *Autobiography*, ed. J. A. Leo Lemay and P. M. Zall (New York: Norton, 1986), 20–21, 49, 54. On the literature of character published in and about Philadelphia, see John F. Kasson, *Rudeness and Civility: Manners in Nineteenth-Century Urban America* (New York: Hill and Wang, 1990), 48–57, and Peter Thompson, *Rum Punch and Revolution: Taverngoing and Public Life in Eighteenth-Century Philadelphia* (Philadelphia: University of Pennsylvania Press, 1999), 114–19. Kent Puckett describes the "circuits of exchange" among courtesy, conduct, and etiquette books, in *Bad Form: Social Mistakes and the Nineteenth-Century Novel* (New York: Oxford University Press, 2008), 19–22. Franklin's memoir, a transitional text, would seem to resist the distinctions some critics have made among the three genres. For examples of those distinctions, see Michael Curtin, "A Question of Manners: Status and Gender in Etiquette and Courtesy," *Journal of Modern History* 57

(September 1985): 395–423, and Sarah E. Newton, *Learning to Behave: A Guide to American Conduct Books before 1900* (Westport, Conn.: Greenwood, 1994), 1–12.

5. Hugh Henry Brackenridge, *Modern Chivalry*, ed. Claude M. Newlin (1792–1815; rpt. New York, Hafner, 1968), 805; subsequent references will be given in parentheses. In his introduction, Newlin reviews the complicated publication history of the text (xix–xxviii); see also Christopher Looby, *Voicing America: Language, Literary Form, and the Origins of the United States* (Chicago: University of Chicago Press, 1996), 208–9, and Grantland S. Rice, "*Modern Chivalry* and the Resistance to Textual Authority," *American Literature* 67.2 (June 1995): 274–78. On Brackenridge's biography, see Newlin's introduction (ix–xix) and Daniel Marder, *Hugh Henry Brackenridge* (New York: Twayne, 1967). Philadelphia was the context and impetus for another contemporary reflection on ethnicity, race, and citizenship: the Irish immigrant Thomas Branagan's vehement case against slavery and for colonization, based on unease about aspiring, revengeful Africans in "the bowels of the Northern States." See his *Serious Remonstrances, Addressed to the Citizens of the Northern States, and Their Representatives* (Philadelphia: Thomas T. Stiles, 1805). I have quoted from page 60.

6. Sarah F. Wood discusses Brackenridge and Cervantes in *Quixotic Fictions of the USA, 1792–1815* (New York: Oxford University Press, 2005), 89–106, and William R. Hoffa considers the satiric tradition in "The Language of Rogues and Fools in Brackenridge's *Modern Chivalry*," *Studies in the Novel* 12.4 (Winter 1980): 289–300. Dana Nelson analyzes the critical potential of Brackenridge's "moderation" in "'Indications of the Public Will': *Modern Chivalry*'s Theory of Democratic Representation," *ANQ* 15.1 (Winter 2002): 23–39.

7. In the Farrago-O'Regan dyad, Looby sees Brackenridge testing nostalgic republicanism against emergent democracy, with irony directed especially at the former; see *Voicing America*, 242–46.

8. In "Thoughts on the Enfranchisement of the Negroes," published in the *United States Magazine* in December 1779, Brackenridge rejected defenses of slavery based on theology or nature and assumptions about color as a mark of servitude, and he proposed that freed slaves be resettled in colonies west of the Ohio or Mississippi rivers. The essay has been excerpted in *A Hugh Henry Brackenridge Reader, 1770–1815*, ed. Daniel Marder (Pittsburgh: University of Pittsburgh Press, 1970), 103–4.

9. On Brackenridge's portrayals of Irish character across his writings, see Newlin, introduction to *Modern Chivalry*, xx–xxiv.

10. Clay's visual sources are discussed by Nancy Reynolds Davison in her "E. W. Clay: American Political Caricaturist of the Jacksonian Era," Ph.D. diss., University of Michigan, 1980, 85–86, and also were the topic of "Reframing the Color Line: Race and the Visual Culture of the Atlantic World," an exhibit and symposium at the William L. Clements Library, University of Michigan, October 30–31, 2009. On Clay and also Thackera and Johnston, see Gary B. Nash, *Forging Freedom: The Formation of Philadelphia's Black Community* (Cambridge, Mass.: Harvard University Press, 1988), 254–59; Phillip Lapsansky, "Graphic Discord: Abolitionist and Antiabolitionist Images," in *The Abolitionist Sisterhood: Women's Political Culture in Antebellum America*, ed. Jean Fagan Yellin and John C. Van Horne (Ithaca, N.Y.: Cornell University Press, 1994), 217–220; and Shane White and Graham White, *Stylin':*

African American Expressive Culture from Its Beginnings to the Zoot Suit (Ithaca, N.Y.: Cornell University Press, 1998), 114–16.

11. Nancy Reynolds Davison, Clay's most thorough historian and interpreter, lists fourteen prints, issued separately, in the "Life in Philadelphia" series. See her "E. W. Clay," 352–55. Four of these fourteen focus on white figures. Based on my viewing of prints held by the Library Company of Philadelphia and the Library of Congress, I have described numbers 3: "Is Miss Dinah at Home?" (1828); 9: "How you like de new fashion shirt, Miss Florinda?" (n.d., probably 1828–29); 11: "Have you any *flesh* coloured silk stockings, young man?" (1829); 12: "Dat is bery fine, Mr. Mortimer" (1829); and 4: "How you find yourself dis hot weader Miss Chloe?" (1828).

12. On the racial history of Philadelphia in the 1810s and 1820s, see Julie Winch, *Philadelphia's Black Elite: Activism, Accommodation, and the Struggle for Autonomy* (Philadelphia: Temple University Press, 1988), 4–25, and *A Gentleman of Color: The Life of James Forten* (New York: Oxford University Press, 2002), 207–35; and Nash, *Forging Freedom*, 212–45. Discussing Clay's work, Davison understates the tensions during the 1820s, in "E. W. Clay," 95–96. The link between Clay's prints and the minstrel stage is made by Nash, *Forging Freedom*, 259; White and White, *Stylin,'* 116–19; and Patrick Rael, *Black Identity and Black Protest in the Antebellum North* (Chapel Hill: University of North Carolina Press, 2002), 161–65.

13. Among those who reproduce Clay's etchings or their imitations as evidence of prejudice are Nash, *Forging Freedom*, 255–59; Emma Jones Lapsansky, *Neighborhoods in Transition: William Penn's Dream and Urban Reality* (New York: Garland, 1994), 145–48; Winch, *The Elite of Our People*, 36–40; Rael, *Black Identity and Black Protest*, 159–73; Elise Lemire, *"Miscegenation": Mixing Race in America* (Philadelphia: University of Pennsylvania Press, 2002), 92–93; Martha S. Jones, *All Bound Up Together: The Woman Question in African American Public Culture, 1830–1900* (Chapel Hill: University of North Carolina Press, 2007), 18–19, and Erica Armstrong Dunbar. *A Fragile Freedom: African American Women and Emancipation in the Antebellum City* (New Haven: Yale University Press, 2008), 132–36. Suggesting that there is more to be said about these prints are Davison, "E. W. Clay," 113–14, and White and White, *Stylin,'* 114–15.

14. For other white images of "Life in Philadelphia," see, in addition to plate 8 ("Good evening, Miss"), plate 1 ("Promenade in Washington Square"), plate 2 ("Behold thou art fair Deborah"), and plate 10 ("Fancy Ball"), in the collections of the Library Company of Philadelphia. "Going Home from a Tea-Fight" was offered for sale by Cowan's Auctions in 2006; the image can be viewed at www.cowansauctions.com/past_ sales_view_item.asp?itemid=35957. Clay's African American images were copied as lithographs, prompted the series "Life in New York" around 1830, and inspired the single-sheet grotesques issued in London by Isaacs and Tregear under the title "Life in Philadelphia." The Isaacs and Tregear set included renderings of Clay's fourteen prints and six new images. On the afterlives of Clay's "Life in Philadelphia," see Davison, "E. W. Clay," 93–100. Lemire discusses and reproduces Clay's later "Practical Amalgamation" series in *"Miscegenation,"* 62–66, 94–100.

15. *The New Comic Annual, Illustrated with One Hundred Highly Amusing Cuts* (London: Hurst, Chance, and Co., n.d. [1830]), 226; "Life in Philadelphia" appears on 224–37.

16. I have described the hand-coloring in the "silk stockings" print held by the Library of Congress. The images were tinted by the publisher, according to guidelines that may have been provided by Clay. For reasons of materials or preference, the colorists (many of them women) did not always follow instructions and added individual touches. These circumstances lend additional variety to Clay's series. I am grateful to Erika Piola, Assistant Curator of Prints and Photographs at the Library Company of Philadelphia, for sharing her expertise about the making of Clay's "Life in Philadelphia."

17. On African American public display in Philadelphia during the antebellum years, see Nash, *Forging Freedom*, 217–23, and White and White, *Stylin'*, 85–124 (the quoted passage appears on 94).

18. In a historical twist, Clay's own "Life in Philadelphia" prints, which became the objects of imitation for other artists, have been confused by some modern interpreters with their (often grotesque) copies. For example, Shane White and Graham White list Clay as the artist who drew the "Life in New York" image they reproduce in *Stylin'* (95), although Davison has cautioned against the attribution, in "E. W. Clay," 93.

19. Davison mentions the use of "life in Philadelphia" as stock phrase, in "E. W. Clay," 92–93.

20. Edward Raymond Turner, *The Negro in Pennsylvania: Slavery—Servitude—Freedom, 1639–1861* (1911; rpt. New York: Arno Press and the New York Times, 1969), 139–41. Davison traces the English rendition of Clay's "Life in Philadelphia" by William Summers and Charles Hunt, in "E. W. Clay," 98.

21. On Peale's museum, see Charles Coleman Sellers, *Mr. Peale's Museum: Charles Willson Peale and the First Popular Museum of Natural Science and Art* (New York: W. W. Norton, 1980), and David C. Ward, "Democratic Culture: The Peale Museums, 1784–1850," in *The Peale Family: Creation of a Legacy, 1770–1870*, ed. Lillian B. Miller (New York: Abbeville, 1996), 260–75. On Hawkins's physiognotrace and its popularity, see David Brigham, *Public Culture in the Early Republic: Peale's Museum and Its Audience* (Washington, D.C.: Smithsonian Institution Press, 1995), 68–70; Ellen Sacco, "Racial Theory, Museum Practice: The Colored World of Charles Willson Peale," *Museum Anthropology* 20.2 (Fall 1996): 26–28; Wendy Bellion, "The Mechanization of Likeness in Jeffersonian America," MIT Communications Forum, http://web.mit.edu/comm-forum/papers/bellion.html, and "Heads of State: Profiles and Politics in Jeffersonian America," in *New Media, 1740–1915*, ed. Lisa Gitelman and Geoffrey B. Pingree (Cambridge, Mass.: MIT Press, 2003), 31–59; and Gwendolyn DuBois Shaw, *Portraits of a People: Picturing African Americans in the Nineteenth Century* (Andover, Mass., and Seattle, Wash.: Addison Gallery of American Art and University of Washington Press, 2006), 50–51. Peale explains the physiognotrace in an illustrated letter to Thomas Jefferson (January 28, 1803), held by the Library of Congress, from which figure 2.3 in this book has been reproduced. Peale's son Rembrandt reflects on the device in "Notes and Queries: The Physiognotrace," in *The Crayon: A Journal Devoted to the Graphic Arts, and the Literature Related to Them*, vol. 4 (New York: Stillman and Durand, 1857), 307–8. Rembrandt reports that the demand for the machines had diminished. Silhouettes became less popular in the 1840s and 1850s with the rise of daguerreotype photography.

22. Charles Willson Peale to Rembrandt and Rubens Peale, *The Selected Papers of Charles Willson Peale and His Family*, vol. 2, part 1, *Charles Willson Peale: The Artist as Museum Keeper, 1791–1810*, ed. Lillian B. Miller (New Haven, Conn.: Yale University Press, 1988), 537. Christopher Lukasik discusses Lavater in "The Face of the Public," *American Literature* 39.3 (2004): 426–38. On Peale, silhouettes, physiognomy, and ethnology, see Brigham, *Public Culture*, 73–75; Sacco, "Racial Theory, Museum Practice"; Bellion, "The Mechanization of Likeness," 6–13; and Shaw, *Speaking the Unspeakable: The Art of Kara Walker*, 20–22.

23. On Moses Williams, the Peale family, and the cutting of silhouettes, see Brigham, *Public Culture*, 70–71; Sacco, "Racial Theory, Museum Practice," 26–29; and Shaw, *Portraits of a People*, 44–55. Rembrandt Peale reminisces about Williams in "The Physiognotrace," 307–8.

24. In his study of Peale's Museum, Brigham reports that he can document only one African American visitor, "Mr. Shaw's blackman" (*Public Culture*, 71). Attribution of the Peale Museum silhouettes is discussed by Alice van Leer Carrick, *American Silhouettes: A Collector's Guide, 1790–1840* (Rutland, Vt.: Charles E. Tuttle, 1968), and by Shaw, *Portraits of a People*, 71. Shaw conjectures that Williams may have produced his own image on 52–53.

25. "Moses Williams, cutter of Profiles," "Mr. Shaw's blackman," and "Mr. Shaw" are in the collections of the Library Company of Philadelphia, dated after 1802; "Edward Clay Portrait Painter," likely produced in 1820, is held by the William L. Clements Library at the University of Michigan. Gwendolyn DuBois Shaw interprets the Williams image in *Seeing the Unspeakable: The Art of Kara Walker* (Durham, N.C.: Duke University Press, 2004), 24–25, and, along with "Mr. Shaw's blackman," in *Portraits of a People*, 45, 52–53. Brigham mentions "Mr. Shaw's blackman" in *Public Culture*, 71.

26. Gwendolyn DuBois Shaw glosses the visual characteristics of hollow-cut profiles, in *Speaking the Unspeakable*, 18–23. David Brigham discusses Peale Museum silhouettes as memorial emblems in *Public Culture*, 81. Revising the silhouette inheritance, the contemporary artist Kara Walker reflects on U.S. slavery and its aftermath. Walker exaggerates bodily contours for satiric effect, ruptures the elegant lines, and arranges her images in violent tableaux. For examples, see *Kara Walker: Pictures from Another Time*, ed. Annette Dixon (Ann Arbor: University of Michigan Museum of Art, 2002), and Shaw, *Seeing the Unspeakable*.

27. Gwendolyn DuBois Shaw analyzes the profile of "Flora" (in the collections of the Stratford Historical Society in Connecticut) in *Speaking the Unspeakable*, 22–23, and *Portraits of a People*, 49.

28. Robert Montgomery Bird, *The City Looking Glass: A Philadelphia Comedy in Five Acts*, ed. Arthur Hobson Quinn (1828; rpt. New York: Colophon, 1933), I, 5. On Bird's biography, see Clement E. Faust, *The Life and Dramatic Works of Robert Montgomery Bird* (New York: Knickerbocker, 1919); *Life of Robert Montgomery Bird, Written by His Wife Mary Mayer Bird*, ed. C. Seymour Thompson (Philadelphia: University of Pennsylvania Library, 1945); and Curtis Dahl, *Robert Montgomery Bird* (New York: Twayne, 1963).

29. Robert Montgomery Bird, *Sheppard Lee, Written by Himself*, ed. and intro. Christopher Looby (1836; rpt. New York: New York Review Books, 2008), 7, 247, 304. Subsequent references will be given in parentheses. The phrase "look before you leap," part of the

running joke in *Sheppard Lee*, has been available in modern English at least since Samuel Butler's seventeenth-century satire *Hudibras:* "And look before you ere you leap/For as you sow, ye are like to reap" (part 2, canto 2, 502). Literary critics have paid little attention to *Sheppard Lee*, a situation that is bound to change with the appearance of Looby's new edition, the first since 1836. In volume 1, chapter 15, of his novel *The Adventures of Robin Day* (1839), Bird parodies Franklin's ironic entry into Philadelphia, having his awkward young protagonist step off the ferry onto High Street and right into a basket of shad, greeted with curses spewed by a fishmonger.

30. In the few earlier novels set in Philadelphia, the city tends to be represented generically, rather than associated with distinctive spaces, plots, and histories. For examples, see Tabitha Tenney, *Female Quixotism* (1801; rpt. New York: Oxford University Press, 1992), which mostly takes place in a village up the Delaware River from the city, *A Journey to Philadelphia: or, Memoirs of Charles Coleman Saunders. An Original Tale. By Adelio* (Hartford, Conn.: Lincoln and Gleason, 1804), and Rebecca Rush, *Kelroy*, ed. Dana D. Nelson (1812; rpt. New York: Oxford University Press, 1992). Early novelists who depicted the 1793 yellow fever epidemic provided more detail. See Charles Brockden Brown, *Arthur Mervyn* (1799–1800), and Leonora Sansay, *Laura* (1809; rpt. Buffalo, N. Y.: Broadview, 2007).

31. According to Bird's notes, now held at the University of Pennsylvania's Van Pelt Library, he considered other roles for Sheppard Lee, including a counterfeiter, a police officer, a celebrated actor, and the president of the United States. See Looby, introduction to *Sheppard Lee*, xxvi–xxix.

32. Edgar Allan Poe, "Sheppard Lee," *Southern Literary Messenger*, September 1836, rpt. in Edgar Allan Poe, *Essays and Reviews*, ed. G. R. Thompson (New York: Library of America, 1984), 401. Poe himself employed the device of metempsychosis in stories such as "Metzengerstein" (1832) and "Ligeia" (1838).

33. Christopher Castiglia argues that the social conflicts of nineteenth-century U. S. democracy became internalized, producing a range of alienated psyches. See his *Interior States: Institutional Consciousness and the Inner Life of Democracy in the Antebellum United States* (Durham, N. C.: Duke University Press, 2008).

34. Robert Montgomery Bird, *Nick of the Woods, or The Jibbenainosay. A Tale of Kentucky*, ed. Curtis Dahl (1837; rpt. New Haven, Conn: College and University Press, 1967), 125–26, 226, 243, 327. Bird's avenger was a model for Melville's "Indian-hater" in *The Confidence-Man* (1857).

35. Catherine Gallagher argues that the desire to incarnate types fuels readerly attachments in realist fiction; see "George Eliot: Immanent Victorian," *Representations* 90 (April 2005): 61–74. The thematic and formal similarities between *Sheppard Lee* and Melville's *The Confidence-Man* (1857) suggest that Melville may have had in mind not only *Nick of the Woods* but also *Sheppard Lee* when he wrote his satire of character and type.

36. On embodiment and Bird's convoluted slavery politics in *Sheppard Lee*, see Looby, introduction, xv–xxii, xxix–xxxvii.

37. Thomas Jefferson, "Query XVIII: Manners," in *Notes on the State of Virginia*, ed. William Peden (1787; rpt. Chapel Hill: University of North Carolina Press, 1982), 162.

38. Bird, *City Looking Glass*, 30, 43.

39. Robert Montgomery Bird, *The Adventures of Robin Day* (Philadelphia: Lea and Blanchard, 1839), 171, 120–21.

40. Bird, *Adventures of Robin Day*, 124–27. My thanks to Christopher Looby for sharing his knowledge of the fiction of Dunphy and Dexter.

41. Participants in the 1830 convention voted to support emigration from Cincinnati to Canada for those who felt it was necessary but remained suspicious of the wider pressures for resettlement, especially in Liberia.

42. On the national and state black convention movements, see Howard Holman Bell, *A Survey of the Negro Convention Movement, 1830–1861* (1953; rpt. New York: Arno Press and The New York Times, 1969), and *Minutes of the Proceedings of the National Negro Conventions, 1830–1864* (New York: Arno Press and The New York Times, 1969); William H. Pease and Jane H. Pease, "The Negro Convention Movement," in *Key Issues in the Afro-American Experience*, vol. I, *To 1877*, ed. Nathan I. Huggins, Martin Kilson, and Daniel M. Fox (New York: Harcourt Brace Jovanovich, 1971), 191–205, and "Negro Conventions and the Problem of Black Leadership," *Journal of Black Studies* 2.1 (September 1971), 29–44; Philip S. Foner and George E. Walker, eds., *Proceedings of the Black State Conventions, 1840–1865*, 2 vols. (Philadelphia: Temple University Press, 1979, 1980); Winch, *Philadelphia's Black Elite*, 91–129; Eddie S. Glaude Jr., *Exodus! Religion, Race, and Nation in Early Nineteenth-Century Black America* (Chicago: University of Chicago Press, 2000), 105–67; Rael, *Black Identity and Black Protest*, 27–44; and John Ernest, *Liberation Historiography: African American Writers and the Challenge of History, 1794–1861* (Chapel Hill: University of North Carolina Press, 2004), 250–76. The term "elevation" appears regularly in the minutes of the national meetings.

43. Samuel E. Cornish, "Moral Reform Convention," *Colored American*, August 26, 1837. The disputes between Philadelphia and New York are discussed in Bell, *Survey*, 34–38, and Winch, *Philadelphia's Black Elite*, 91–129.

44. Foner and Walker, *Proceedings of the Black State Conventions*, 2:115.

45. Frederick Douglass, Alexander Crummell, John Lyle, and Thomas Van Rensselaer, "Report of the Committee on Abolition," rpt. in Bell, *Minutes*, "National Convention in Troy, N.Y., 1847," 32; Samuel E. Cornish, *Colored American* (March 29, 1838): 39; William Whipper, "Convention," *National Reformer* 1.6 (February 1839): 81; [Sidney], "William Whipper's Letters," *Colored American* (March 13, 1841): 5; rpt. in *The Ideological Origins of Black Nationalism*, ed. Sterling Stuckey (Boston: Beacon, 1972), 161. "Sidney" may have been a pseudonym used by Henry Highland Garnet.

46. On the encumbrances of freedom, see Saidiya V. Hartman, *Scenes of Subjection: Terror, Slavery, and Self-Making in Nineteenth-Century America* (New York: Oxford University Press, 1997).

47. Howard Holman Bell uses "conservative" (*Survey*, 162), and Winch uses "moderate," in contrast with "militant[s]" (*Philadelphia's Black Elite*, 108). Richard Newman, Patrick Rael, and Phillip Lapsansky qualify the opposition between "deference" and "demand"; see their introduction to *Pamphlets of Protest: An Anthology of Early African American Protest Literature, 1790–1860* (New York: Routledge, 2001), 11–18.

48. Bell, *Minutes*, "Convention in Philadelphia, 1835," 14–15. Pease and Pease refer to the "assimilationist ideas and goals" of Whipper's American Moral Reform Society, in "Negro Convention Movement," 195. Sterling Stuckey, though acknowledging Whipper's "complexities of thought and feeling," ultimately diagnoses him as a product of shame about his African ancestry; see *Slave Culture: Nationalist Theory and the Foundations of Black America* (New York: Oxford University Press, 1987), 203–11. Glaude counters that Whipper's thought should be understood as part of the subtle deliberation among African American leaders in the 1830s and 1840s over how best to confront racism in the United States; see *Exodus!* 135–42.

49. William Whipper, "Controversies," *National Reformer* 1.7 (March 1839): 99; letter to Charles B. Ray, *Colored American*, January 30, 1841, rpt. in Sterling Stuckey, *The Ideological Origins of Black Nationalism* (Boston: Beacon, 1972), 252–54. Richard P. McCormack details Whipper's career in "William Whipper: Moral Reformer," *Pennsylvania History* 43 (January 1976): 23–47. The "names controversy" is analyzed in Stuckey, *Slave Culture*, 193–244; Glaude, *Exodus!* 131–42; and Rael, *Black Identity and Black Protest*, 49–50, 107–8, 111–13. Winch discusses Whipper's role in the conventions and his American Moral Reform Society in *Philadelphia's Black Elite*, 92–129.

50. For estimations of African American moral reform, which point to the myopia of the aspiring class, see Frederick Cooper, "Elevating the Race: The Social Thought of Black Leaders, 1827–50," *American Quarterly* 24 (1972): 604–25; Jane H. Pease and William H. Pease, *They Who Would Be Free: Blacks' Search for Freedom, 1830–1861* (New York: Atheneum, 1974); and Kevin K. Gaines, *Uplifting the Race: Black Leadership, Politics, and Culture in the Twentieth Century* (Chapel Hill: University of North Carolina Press, 1996). Gary B. Nash argues that self-consciously "'respectable'" black families in early-nineteenth-century Philadelphia "displayed the cardinal virtues promoted by white society—industry, frugality, circumspection, sobriety, and religious commitment" (*Forging Freedom*, 217). On the "politics of respectability," see Evelyn Brooks Higginbotham, *Righteous Discontent: The Women's Movement in the Black Baptist Church, 1880–1920* (Cambridge, Mass.: Harvard University Press, 1993); Glaude, *Exodus!*; and Rael, *Black Identity and Black Protest*. Rael seems caught in the pun expressed in his term "cofabrication" (10), sometimes arguing for the sophisticated resistance provided by early black thinkers and at other times judging them to be imitative and complicitous. Looming over (and confusing) treatments of African American class distinction in any era is the hyperbole in E. Franklin Frazier's satire of doomed, escapist assimilators, especially his often hilarious lacerating of pretense on display in *Ebony* magazine during the 1950s; see *Black Bourgeoisie* (1957; rpt. New York: Free Press, 1997).

51. William Whipper, "An Address Delivered in Wesley Church on the Evening of June 12, before the Colored Reading Society of Philadelphia, for Mental Improvement" (1828), in *Early Negro Writing, 1760–1837*, ed. Dorothy Porter (1971; rpt. Baltimore: Black Classic Press, 1995), 115–18; "Speech Delivered before the Colored Temperance Society of Philadelphia" (1834), in *The Black Abolitionist Papers*, vol. 3, *The United States, 1830–1846*, ed. C. Peter Ripley et al. (Chapel Hill: University of North Carolina Press, 1991), 119–120, 124–27. Rael describes the influence of Franklin on northern African American leaders in *Black Identity and Black Protest*, 147–50.

52. Samuel E. Cornish, "Responsibility of Colored People in the Free States," *Colored American*, March 4, 1837, in *Black Abolitionist Papers*, 3:219–20. Discussing Whipper, James Oliver Horton and Lois E. Horton outline the political aspects of moral reform; see *In Hope of Liberty: Culture, Community and Protest among Northern Free Blacks, 1700–1860* (New York: Oxford University Press, 1997), 221–23. See also Glaude's cogent discussion in *Exodus!* 107–42.

53. James Forten Jr., "An Address Delivered before the American Moral Reform Society, Philadelphia, August 17th, 1837," in "Minutes and Proceedings of the First Annual Meeting of the American Moral Reform Society," rpt. in Porter, *Early Negro Writing*, 229, 231, 226. The English visitor Edward S. Abdy described James Forten Sr. as "well known throughout the Union for the wealth he possesses, and the probity and urbanity which mark his character, in public and private life." See his *Journal of a Residence and Tour in the United States of North America, from April, 1833, to October, 1834* (London: John Murray, 1835), 3:129–32. On the Fortens, see Winch, *A Gentleman of Color.*

54. Samuel E. Cornish, "Our Brethren in the Free States," *Colored American*, April 22, 1837.

55. William Whipper, "To the American People," rpt. in Bell, *Minutes*, "Convention in Philadelphia, 1835," 25, 28, 26; "Motion of William Whipper," rpt. in Bell, *Minutes*, "Convention in Philadelphia, 1835," 19. "To the American People" is signed by Whipper, Alfred Niger, and Augustus Price in the 1835 minutes of the national convention and by Whipper alone in the 1837 minutes of the American Moral Reform Society. The "Declaration of Sentiment," also published in both 1835 and 1837, can be found in Bell, *Minutes*, "Convention in Philadelphia, 1835," 21–25; I have quoted from 24. Porter includes the 1837 American Moral Reform Society minutes in *Early Negro Writing*, 200–248.

56. "Minutes and Proceedings of the First Annual Meeting of the American Moral Reform Society," in Porter, *Early Negro Writing*, 202, 232. Disfranchisement is a frequent topic in the pages of the *National Reformer*; see, for example, Whipper's front-page editorial, "The New Year," *National Reformer* 1.5 (January 1839): 65–66. Winch locates the shift at the 1848 Pennsylvania state convention; see *Philadelphia's Black Elite*, 162–64.

57. William Whipper, "Our Elevation," *National Reformer* 1.12 (December 1839): 180–81.

58. William Whipper, "Our Elevation," 181, 180; Sarah Grimké, "Letter II: Woman Subject Only to God," in *Letters on the Equality of the Sexes, and the Condition of Women*, ed. Elizabeth Ann Bartlett (1838; rpt. New Haven, Conn.: Yale University Press, 1988), 35. The *Colored American*, in its July 7, 1838 issue, reprinted an essay from the *Herald of Freedom* in which the writer riffs on the taunt of colonization supporters who stand on the necks and breasts of the colored people and "wickedly say to them, 'I'll step off of you, if you will creep away to Africa, before you rise'" (78).

59. "An Appeal to the Colored Citizens of Pennsylvania," in Foner and Walker, *Proceedings of the Black State Conventions*, 1:126–33; the quoted phrases are on page 128. Whipper's name is first among the signers, and the "Appeal" contains several passages from his 1839 "Our Elevation." The other names appended are Abram D. Shadd,

J. J. Dickson, J. J. G. Bias, Robert Purvis, M. W. Gibbes, and Samuel Van Brakle; the first five were Philadelphians.

60. "Appeal to the Coloured Citizens of Pennsylvania," 126, 127, 129.

61. "Appeal to the Coloured Citizens of Pennsylvania," 131, 132.

62. Eddie S. Glaude Jr. sees Henry Highland Garnet as the figure responsible for the "inversion of the languages of moral reform and . . . radicalization of the politics of respectability (as a politics with an accent on agency-as-struggle)," in *Exodus!* 161. Although historians are right to note the significance of the debate over Garnet's "Address to the Slaves" at the 1843 Buffalo, New York, convention and its printing alongside David Walker's *Appeal* in 1848, this narrative of turning points understates the trenchancy of the Philadelphians' analysis of conduct in the 1830s.

63. "Appeal to the Coloured Citizens of Pennsylvania," 128.

64. On Pennsylvania state constitutional reform in 1837–1838, see Roy H. Akagi, "The Pennsylvania Constitution of 1838," *Pennsylvania Magazine of History and Biography* 43 (1924): 301–33 (Benjamin Martin's words are quoted on 318); Charles McCool Snyder, *The Jacksonian Heritage: Pennsylvania Politics, 1833–1848* (Harrisburg: Pennsylvania Historical and Museum Commission, 1958), 96–111; and Eric Ledell Smith, "The End of Black Voting Rights in Pennsylvania: African Americans and the Pennsylvania Constitutional Convention of 1837–1838," *Pennsylvania History* 65 (Summer 1998): 279–99. On the African American franchise in Pennsylvania, see Turner, *The Negro in Pennsylvania*, 169–93, and also Winch, *Philadelphia's Black Elite*, 137–42. The Pennsylvania state constitutions of 1790 and 1838 are reprinted in *Pennsylvania Archives: Fourth Series*, ed. George Edward Reed (Harrisburg: State of Pennsylvania, 1900), 4:115–35, and *Pennsylvania Archives: Fourth Series*, ed. George Edward Reed (Harrisburg: State of Pennsylvania, 1901), 6:499–525. The provisions for male voting are found in 4:122 (1790) and 6:507 (1838). The legal case for disfranchisement was popularized in *A Familiar Exposition of the Constitution of Pennsylvania. For the Use of Schools and for the People* (Philadelphia: Uriah Hunt, 1840), 38–40.

65. On the debates about free men and freemen and the evidence for black voting in Pennsylvania, see Turner, *The Negro in Pennsylvania*, 177–87; Winch, *Gentleman of Color*, 293–301 (the quote appears on 294); and also John F. Denny, *An Enquiry into the Political Grade of the Free Coloured Population, under the Constitution of the United States, and the Constitution of Pennsylvania, in Three Parts. By a Member of the Chambersburg Bar* (Chambersburg, Pa.: J. Pritts, 1834), 21–24, and the expanded version of the *Enquiry* (Chambersburg, Pa.: Hickok and Blood, 1836), 51–60.

66. Eric Ledell Smith, "The Pittsburgh Memorial: A Forgotten Document of Pittsburgh History," *Pittsburgh History* (Fall 1997): 106–11. The 1837 "Memorial" is reprinted in this essay.

67. David McBride, "Black Protest against Racial Politics: Gardner, Hinton and Their Memorial of 1838," *Pennsylvania History* 46 (April 1979): 149–62. The 1838 "Memorial" is reprinted in this essay.

68. "Appeal of Forty Thousand Citizens, Threatened with Disfra nchisement, to the People of Pennsylvania" (Philadelphia: Merrihew and Gunn, 1838), in *Pamphlets of Protest*, ed. Newman, Rael, and Lapsansky, 132–42. The other members of the committee who

drafted the "Appeal" were Robert B. Forten, John P. Burr, James Cornish, James J. G. Bias, and James Needhan. On the context and reception of the "Appeal," see Winch, *Philadelphia's Black Elite*, 140–42, and Margaret Hope Bacon, *But One Race: The Life of Robert Purvis* (Albany: State University of New York Press, 2007), 60–65.

69. "The Present State and Condition of the Free People of Color, of the City of Philadelphia and Adjoining Districts, as Exhibited by the Report of a Committee of the Pennsylvania Society for Promoting the Abolition of Slavery, &c" (Philadelphia: Merrihew and Gunn, 1838), 22, 23, 39, 6. During the controversy over the franchise, the Pennsylvania Abolition Society also published a "Register of the Trades of the Colored People in the City of Philadelphia and Districts" (Philadelphia: Merrihew and Gunn, 1838) and an eight-page open letter "To the People of Color in the State of Pennsylvania" (Philadelphia, 1838), acknowledging the setbacks in the state convention, reassuring them of support, and counseling perseverance. On race and statistics in Philadelphia, see Nash, *Forging Freedom*, 31; Winch, *Philadelphia's Black Elite*, 80–81, and *Gentleman of Color*, 287, 299. DuBois lists the antebellum reports as sources in Appendix C, II, of *The Philadelphia Negro: A Social Study*, ed. Elijah Anderson (1899; rpt. Philadelphia: University of Pennsylvania Press, 1996), 420–21.

70. See "Memorial of Thirty Thousand Disfranchised Citizens of Philadelphia, to the Honorable Senate and House of Representatives" (Philadelphia: Printed for the Memorialists, 1855), 1–3.

71. Samuel H. Davis, "Address," rpt. in Bell, *Minutes*, "Convention at Buffalo, N.Y., 1843," 6. McBride reports eighty-one petitions on suffrage made by African Americans to the Pennsylvania state legislature between 1839 and 1851, in "Black Protest against Racial Politics," 158, n. 44; see also Turner, *Negro in Pennsylvania*, 291–92.

72. Joseph Willson, *Sketches of the Higher Classes of Colored Society in Philadelphia. By a Southerner* (1841); rpt. as *The Elite of Our People: Joseph Willson's Sketches of Black Upper-Class Life in Antebellum Philadelphia*, ed. Julie Winch (University Park, Pa.: Pennsylvania State University Press, 2000), 102–3, 111. Subsequent references will be given in parentheses. The volume was briefly acknowledged in contemporary periodicals. See *Pennsylvania Freeman*, September 8, 1841, and October 27, 1841, and the *Colored American*, September 25, 1841. DuBois lists Willson's *Sketches* in "Books and Pamphlets Written by Philadelphia Negroes," appendix C, III, in *The Philadelphia Negro*, 423; Turner mentions the book in his *Negro in Pennsylvania*, 139–40. In the "Appeal of Forty Thousand Citizens," Purvis had characterized disfranchisement as "a tyrannical usurpation which we will never cease to oppose"; see *Pamphlets of Protest*, 142.

73. *Pennsylvania Freeman*, October 27, 1841. Julie Winch details Willson's biography and the social history of African Americans in Philadelphia before the Civil War in her introduction to *The Elite of Our People*, 1–73.

74. See Pierre Bourdieu, *Distinction: A Social Critique of the Judgement of Taste*, trans. Richard Nice (Cambridge, Mass.: Harvard University Press, 1984); Stuart Blumin, *The Emergence of the Middle Class: Social Experience in the American City, 1760–1900* (New York: Cambridge University Press, 1989); and Gaines, *Uplifting the Race*.

75. The quote from *Freedom's Journal* appears in the July 11, 1828, issue; Winch uses it as one of the two epigraphs to her edition of Willson's *Sketches*.

76. Raymond Williams, *Keywords: A Vocabulary of Culture and Society*, rev. ed. (New York: Oxford University Press, 1985), 60–69. On literature and class, see *Rethinking Class: Literary Studies and Social Formations*, ed. Wai Chee Dimock and Michael T. Gilmore (New York: Columbia University Press, 1994), and Amy Schrager Lang, *The Syntax of Class: Writing Inequality in Nineteenth-Century America* (Princeton, N.J.: Princeton University Press, 2003).

77. Winch suggests the five percent figure in *Elite of Our People*, 41. On the African Amercan higher classes in Philadelphia, see, in addition to Winch, Emma Jones Lapsansky, "Friends, Wives, and Strivings: Networks and Community Values among Nineteenth-Century Philadelphia Afroamerican Elites," *Pennsylvania Magazine of History and Biography* 108.1 (January 1984): 3–24.

78. Willson's strategic reticence about naming individuals differs from the parade of African American entrepreneurs, professionals, and mechanics at the center of another Philadelphia book of character, Martin Delany's later *The Condition, Elevation, Emigration, and Destiny of the Colored People of the United States* (1852).

79. W. E. B. DuBois, *Philadelphia Negro*, 316–18.

80. For discussions of courtesy, conduct, and etiquette books, see Michael Curtin, Sarah E. Newton, and Kent Puckett, as cited in note 4 of this chapter, and also Karen Halttunen, *Confidence Men and Painted Women: A Study of Middle-Class Culture in America, 1830–1870* (New Haven, Conn.: Yale University Press, 1982).

81. Cyprian Clamorgan, *The Colored Aristocracy of St. Louis*, ed. Julie Winch (1858; rpt. Columbia: University of Missouri Press, 1999).

Chapter Three

1. *Mysteries of Philadelphia, or: Scenes of Real Life in the Quaker City, Containing an Accurate History of This Great Moral World. It Gives a Faithful Expose, Laying Bare the Vices and Iniquities of the Fashionable World. By an Old Amateur.* (Philadelphia, 1848), viii. On geography and demographics, see Elizabeth M. Geffen, "Violence in Philadelphia in the 1840's and 1850's," *Pennsylvania History* 36 (October 1969): 389–95, and "Industrial Development and Social Crisis, 1841–1854," in *Philadelphia, A 300-Year History*, ed. Russell F. Weigley et al. (New York: W. W. Norton, 1982), 352–54.

2. Emma Jones Lapsansky names and analyzes the Cedar neighborhood, in *Neighborhoods in Transition: William Penn's Dream and Urban Reality* (New York: Garland, 1994). I have quoted from page 172.

3. On the conditions in Philadelphia that led to violence, see Elizabeth M. Geffen, "Industrial Development and Social Crisis," 307–62, and "Violence in Philadelphia," 381–410, and Emma Jones Lapsansky, "'Since They Got Those Separate Churches': Afro-Americans and Racism in Jacksonian Philadelphia," *American Quarterly* 32.1 (Spring 1980): 54–78. On violence in American cities during the antebellum period, see Carl E. Prince, "The Great 'Riot Year': Jacksonian Democracy and Patterns of Violence in 1834," *Journal of the Early Republic* 5.1 (Spring 1985): 1–19, and David Grimsted, "Rioting in Its Jacksonian Setting," *American Historical Review* 77.2 (April 1972): 361–97.

4. I have taken the details for my summary of the Philadelphia riots in 1834, 1838, 1842, and 1849 from contemporary issues of the Philadelphia *Public Ledger, and Daily Transcript* and William Lloyd Garrison's *The Liberator*; Edward S. Abdy, *Journal of a Residence and Tour in the United States of North America, from April, 1833, to October, 1834* (London: John Murray, 1835), 3:316–33; Joseph Sturge, *A Visit to the United States in 1841* (London: Hamilton, Adams, and Co., 1842), 40–47; J. Thomas Scharf and Thompson Westcott, *History of Philadelphia, 1609–1884* (Philadelphia: L. H. Everts, 1884), 1:637–38, 641–42, 650–52, 660–61, 692–93; W. E. B. DuBois, *The Philadelphia Negro: A Social Study*, intro. Elijah Anderson (1899; rpt. Philadelphia: University of Pennsylvania Press, 1995), 26–30; Edward Raymond Turner, *The Negro in Pennsylvania: Slavery—Servitude—Freedom, 1639–1861* (Washington, D.C.: American Historical Association, 1911), 160–65; Sam Bass Warner Jr., *The Private City: Philadelphia in Three Periods of Its Growth*, 2nd ed. (Philadelphia: University of Pennsylvania Press, 1987), 128–52; John Runcie, "'Hunting the Nigs' in Philadelphia: The Race Riot of August 1834," *Pennsylvania History* 39 (April 1972): 187–218; Ira V. Brown, "Racism and Sexism: The Case of Pennsylvania Hall," *Phylon* 37.2 (1976): 126–36; Bruce Laurie, *Working People of Philadelphia, 1800–1850* (Philadelphia: Temple University Press, 1980), 58–66, 124–25, 130–31, 147–59; Emma Jones Lapsansky, "'Since They Got Those Separate Churches,'" and *Neighborhoods in Transition*, 130–51; Julie Winch, *Philadelphia's Black Elite: Activism, Accommodation, and the Struggle for Autonomy, 1787–1848* (Philadelphia: Temple University Press, 1988), 143–51, and *A Gentleman of Color: The Life of James Forten* (New York: Oxford University Press, 2002), 288–90; Robert S. Levine, "Disturbing Boundaries: Temperance, Black Elevation, and Violence in Frank Webb's *The Garies and Their Friends*," *Prospects* 19 (1994): 357–59; Noel Ignatiev, *How the Irish Became White* (Routledge, 1995), 124–60; and Margaret Hope Bacon, "'The Double Curse of Sex and Color': Robert Purvis and Human Rights," *Pennsylvania Magazine of History and Biography* 121.1/2 (1997): 53–76, and *But One Race: The Life of Robert Purvis* (Albany: State University of New York Press, 2007), 67–73, 98–100. The most destructive Philadelphia riots in the period occurred during the summer of 1844, in Kensington, north of the city, and involved conflicts between Protestants and Catholics, nativists and the Irish. For historical scholarship on the 1844 riots, see note 52 to this chapter.

5. "From the N.Y. *Commercial Advertiser*," rpt. in the *Liberator* 8.21 (25 May 1838), 82. In a letter to the English Quaker Joseph Sturge, Purvis described his conflicted responses at having to testify in court after the riot about the spectacle of offering his arm to his wife: "I have to say, that it was both a painful and ludicrous affair. At one time the fulness of an almost bursting heart was ready to pour forth in bitter denunciation—then the miserable absurdity of the thing, rushing into my mind, would excite my risible propensities." Sturge quotes the letter in *A Visit to the United States in 1841*, 46.

6. "The Philadelphia Riots," in *United States Gazette*, August 2, 1842, rpt. in the *Liberator* 12.32 (August 12, 1842), 126. The "rising sun" was a familiar emblem of emancipation. It appeared as the last image in the diptych masthead of William Lloyd Garrison's abolitionist weekly, *The Liberator*.

7. Robert Purvis to Henry Clarke Wright, August 22, 1842, in *The Black Abolitionist Papers*, vol. 3, *The United States, 1830–1846*, ed. C. Peter Ripley et al. (Chapel Hill: University of

North Carolina Press, 1991), 389–91. Purvis paraphrases lines from "Man Was Made To Mourn" (1786) by Robert Burns, which also were quoted with reference to the 1842 riot in the New York *Journal of Commerce*, rpt. in the *Liberator* 12.32 (August 12, 1842), 126.

8. On Philadelphia's consolidation, see Warner, *The Private City*, 155–57; Geffen, "Industrial Development and Social Crisis, 1841–1854," 359–62; and Russell F. Weigley, "The Border City in Civil War, 1854–1865," in *Philadelphia: A 300-Year History*, ed. Weigley, 363–81.

9. *History of Pennsylvania Hall, Which Was Destroyed by a Mob, on the 17th of May, 1838* (Philadelphia: Merrihew and Gunn, 1838), 4. Subsequent page references will be given in parentheses.

10. Poe's "Fall of the House of Usher" was published in *Burton's Gentleman's Magazine* 5.3 (September 1839): 145–52.

11. Ellis Paxson Oberholtzer, *The Literary History of Philadelphia* (Philadelphia: George W. Jacobs, 1906), 319–26.

12. On Wild and Chevalier, see Nicolas B. Wainwright, *Philadelphia in the Romantic Age of Lithography: An Illustrated History of Early Lithography in Philadelphia with a Descriptive List of Philadelphia Scenes Made by Philadelphia Lithographers before 1866* (Philadelphia: Historical Society of Pennsylvania, 1958), 46–50. Wainwright does not make clear on what basis he gives credit to Wild as the artist of the print used as the frontispiece for the *History of Pennsylvania Hall*. He speculates that the image may have been copied from an earlier drawing on 181–82. Martin P. Snyder briefly discusses the frontispiece lithograph and argues that Wild was the artist, based on visual similarities to his other Philadelphia prints; see "J. C. Wild and His Philadelphia Views," *Pennsylvania Magazine of History and Biography* 77.1 (January 1953): 43–44, 75.

13. Whittier's poem was printed separately as "Address Read at the Opening of the Pennsylvania Hall on the 15th of Fifth Month, 1838" (Philadelphia: Merrihew and Gunn, 1838). In some copies of the *History* (see, for example, a copy held by the Library Company of Philadelphia), the frontispiece has been colored.

14. Sartain's image follows page 136; Woodside's precedes page 141. On Sartain, see Katherine Martinez and Page Talbott, eds. *Philadelphia's Cultural Landscape: The Sartain Family Legacy* (Philadelphia: Temple University Press, 2000); for a brief discussion of the Pennsylvania Hall print, see, in this volume, Katherine Martinez, "A Portrait of the Sartain Family and Their Home," 13. In some printings of the *History of Pennsylvania Hall*, Sartain's mezzotint includes a second stream of water, entering the frame from the left, arching over the heads of the elevated spectators and onto the roof of the nearest building.

15. See Leonard L. Richards, *"Gentlemen of Property and Standing": Anti-Abolition Mobs in Jacksonian America* (New York: Oxford University Press, 1970).

16. Woodside was the son of the Philadelphia sign and fine art painter John Archibald Woodside Sr.; Gilbert was a book illustrator who lived in the city. The third print is listed in *Early American Book Illustrators and Wood Engravers, 1670–1870: A Catalogue of a Collection of American Books Illustrated for the Most Part with Woodcuts and Wood Engravings in the Princeton University Library*, intro. Sinclair Hamilton (Princeton, N.J.: Princeton University Library, 1958), 225.

17. On *The Course of Empire*, see Allan Wallach, "Thomas Cole: Landscape and the Course of American Empire," in *Thomas Cole: Landscape into History*, ed. William H. Truettner and Alan Wallach (Washington, D.C.: National Museum of American Art, 1994), 85–98. The Cole quote is on page 90. In verso and fold-out recto, Wallach reproduces the five images in their original spatial arrangement.

18. On Bowen's print, see Wainwright, *Philadelphia in the Romantic Age of Lithography*, 50, 53, 122, 125; Wainwright discusses the career of Bowen, who would become one of the nation's most prolific lithographers and colorers before the Civil War, on 46–58. As with the frontispiece lithograph in the *History of Pennsylvania Hall*, Wainwright gives no basis for attributing the "Destruction by Fire" to J. C. Wild. The two images may or may not have been drawn by him. Around 1850, a "fifth" image was added to the Pennsylvania Hall series: a lithograph bearing the title "Abolition Hall. The evening before the conflagration at the time more than 50,000 persons were glorifying in its destruction at Philadelphia May—1838. Drawn on stone by Zip Coon." Here Pennsylvania Hall, viewed from the familiar corner perspective, is the headquarters for racial mixing. In the windows and on the sidewalks and streets, blacks and whites (mostly black men and white women) mingle and embrace. We do not know to what uses this parody was employed in the early 1850s. In terms of narrative chronology, "Abolition Hall" would precede the images of destruction by Sartain and by Bowen, and purport to explain the outrages that led to the crowd's joy at the hall's demise. That images of the event still were circulating a dozen years later indicates the symbolic currency of Pennsylvania Hall. For reproductions and discussions, see Phillip Lapsansky, "Graphic Discord: Abolitionist and Antiabolitionist Images," in *The Abolitionist Sisterhood: Women's Political Culture in Antebellum America*, ed. Jean Fagan Yellin and John C. Van Horne (Ithaca, N.Y.: Cornell University Press, 1994), 226–28, and Elise Lemire, *"Miscegenation": Mixing Race in America* (Philadelphia: University of Pennsylvania Press, 2002), 88–89.

19. "Riot and Conflagration," in *Philadelphia Inquirer*, May 18, 1838, rpt. in *Liberator* 8.21 (May 25, 1838): 82.

20. The 1844 print "Death of George Shifler in Kensington" is reproduced in Gary Nash, *First City: Philadelphia and the Forging of Historical Memory* (Philadelphia: University of Pennsylvania Press, 2002), 172.

21. The 1849 riots are illustrated in George Lippard's *The Life and Adventures of Charles Anderson Chester* (1850), which includes a picture of interracial strife in front of a burning California House. Both *Charles Anderson Chester* and *The Bank Director's Son* (1851), another version of the story by Lippard, contain engravings of a fictional black avenger. These texts will be discussed later in this chapter.

22. Many of the letters appeared first in the *Pennsylvania Freeman*, edited by John Greenleaf Whittier, whose office had been in Pennsylvania Hall from March 1838 until its destruction. They also were reprinted in Garrison's *Liberator*; see "Opening of the Hall," *Liberator* 8.22 (June 1, 1838), 88.

23. Herman Melville, *The Confidence-Man: His Masquerade*, vol. 10 of *The Writings of Herman Melville*, ed. Harrison Hayford, Hershel Parker, and G. Thomas Tanselle (1857; rpt. Evanston and Chicago: Northwestern University Press and the Newberry Library,

1984), 112. Brown was a forceful defender of James Forten during his examination before the jury in the suit over damages after the destruction of Pennsylvania Hall, as reported by Forten himself in a letter to the English Quaker Joseph Sturge. The letter is excerpted in Sturge's *A Visit to the United States in 1841*, 46–47.

24. On the violence surrounding Pennsylvania Hall, see, in addition to *The History of Pennsylvania Hall*, [Laura H. Lovell], "Report of a Delegate to the Anti-Slavery Convention of American Women, Held in Philadelphia, May, 1838; including an Account of Other Meetings Held In Pennsylvania Hall, and of the Riot. Addressed to the Fall River Female Anti-Slavery Society, and Published by Its Request" (Boston: I. Knapp, 1838), and also Henry Mayer, *All on Fire: William Lloyd Garrison and the Abolition of Slavery* (New York: St. Martin's Press, 1998), 241–46. Weld's speech recently has been included in the Library of America series; see Angelina Grimké Weld, "Antislavery Speech at Pennsylvania Hall, Philadelphia, May 16, 1838," in *American Speeches: Political Oratory from the Revolution to the Civil War*, ed. Ted Widmer (New York: Library of America, 2002), 308–13.

25. "The Tocsin" was later reprinted with a series of footnotes adducing examples of the slave power's reach; see John Pierpont, *Airs of Palestine and Other Poems* (Boston: J. Munroe, 1840), 294–98, and *The Anti-Slavery Poems of John Pierpont* (Boston: Oliver Johnson, 1843), 15–20.

26. *Liberator* 8.21 (May 25, 1838), 832; *Mysteries of Philadelphia. By an Old Amateur*, viii; *Liberator* 12.32 (August 12, 1842), 127.

27. On how settlement transformed the grid, see Mary Maples Dunn and Richard S. Dunn, "The Founding, 1681–1701," in *Philadelphia: A 300-Year History*, ed. Weigley, 14–16; Geffen, "Violence in Philadelphia," 389–95, and "Industrial Development and Social Crisis, 1842–1854," 315; and E. J. Lapsansky, *Neighborhoods in Transition*, 3–34.

28. Henry James, *The American Scene* (1905), in *Collected Travel Writings: Great Britain and America*, ed. Richard Howard (New York: Library of America, 1993), 353, 580–84. Subsequent references will be given in parentheses. Before he returned to America, James negotiated for the publication of essays and a book based on his journey; while on tour in 1904–05, he gave interviews, posed for photographs, and delivered lectures. See Rosalie Hewitt, "Henry James's *The American Scene*: Its Genesis and Its Reception, 1905–1977," *Henry James Review* 1.2 (Winter 1980): 179–96, and "Henry James, the Harpers, and *The American Scene*," *American Literature* 55.1 (March 1983): 41–47.

29. Sharon Cameron, *Thinking in Henry James* (Chicago: University of Chicago Press, 1989), 6–7, 29. A critical debate has swirled around James's comments in *The American Scene* about ethnicity and race, focusing on Jews in the "New York" chapters and African Americans in the "Richmond" chapter. See, for examples, Kenneth W. Warren, *Black and White Strangers: Race and American Literary Realism* (Chicago: University of Chicago Press, 1993), 112–16, 120–23; the essays by Eric Haralson, Beverly Haviland, Sara Blair, Ross Posnock, Kenneth W. Warren, and Walter Benn Michaels in the special issue on "Race" in *Henry James Review* 16.3 (Fall 1995); Ross Posnock; "Affirming the Alien: The Pragmatist Pluralism of *The American Scene*," in *The Cambridge Companion to Henry James*, ed. Jonathan Freedman (New York: Cambridge University Press, 1998), 224–46; and the series of essays by Gert Buelens: "Possessing the American Scene: Race and Vulgarity, Seduction

and Judgment," in *Enacting History in Henry James*, ed. Gert Buelens (New York Cambridge University Press, 1997), 166–92; "James's 'Aliens': Consuming, Performing, and Judging the American Scene," *Modern Philology* 96.3 (February 1999): 347–63; "Pleasurable 'Presences': Sites, Buildings, and 'Aliens' in James's *American Scene*," *Texas Studies in Literature and Language* 42.4 (Winter 2000): 408–30 (one of the few essays to acknowledge the humor in the book); and "Henry James's Oblique Possession: Plottings of Desire and Mastery in *The American Scene*," *PMLA* 116.2 (March 2001): 300–313. James and DuBois are discussed by Kenneth Warren, *Black and White Strangers*, 112–16, 120–23, and Ross Posnock, "Henry James and the Limits of Historicism," *Henry James Review* 16.3 (Fall 1995): 275–76, and "Affirming the Alien," 240–42.

30. On the volcano metaphor for slavery, see William Gleason, "Volcanoes and Meteors: Douglass, Melville, and the Poetics of Insurrection," in *Frederick Douglass and Herman Melville: Essays in Relation*, ed. Robert S. Levine and Samuel Otter (Chapel Hill: University of North Carolina Press, 2008), 118–19. James also may have had in mind Hawthorne's rendering of the "thin crust spread over" "that pit of blackness that lies beneath us, everywhere": "It needs no earthquake to open the chasm. A footstep, a little heavier than ordinary, will serve; and we must step very daintily, not to break through the crust, at any moment." See Nathaniel Hawthorne, *The Marble Faun: or, The Romance of Monte Beni*, ed. William Charvat et al. (1860; rpt. Columbus: Ohio State University Press, 1968), 161–62.

31. Only a few critics have discussed the Philadelphia chapter of *The American Scene*. See Mark Seltzer, *Henry James and the Art of Power* (Ithaca, N.Y.: Cornell University Press, 1984), 115–25; Martha Banta, "'Strange Deserts': Hotels, Hospitals, Country Clubs, Prisons, and the City of Brotherly Love," *Henry James Review* 17.1 (1966): 7–8; and Gert Buelens, "James's 'Aliens,'" 357–63.

32. Philadelphia *Sunday Mercury* 4.7 (February 12, 1854): 2. Lippard had died on February 9; "Eleanor" appeared in the *Sunday Mercury* from January 29 through March 12. On the last page of the January 29 issue, which contained the first two chapters of "Eleanor," appeared the obituary of another prominent writer of Philadelphia, the dramatist and novelist Robert Montgomery Bird, author of *Sheppard Lee*. On Lippard's career, see David S. Reynolds, *George Lippard* (Boston: Twayne, 1982), 1–26, and also Michael L. Burduck, "George Lippard," in *Dictionary of Literary Biography*, vol. 202, *Nineteenth-Century American Fiction Writers*, ed. Kent P. Ljungquist (Detroit: Gale Research, 1999), 173–78.

33. Heyward Ehrlich quotes the statement on Eugène Sue from the back wrappers in "The 'Mysteries' of Philadelphia: Lippard's *Quaker City* and 'Urban' Gothic," *ESQ: A Journal of the American Renaissance* 18 (1st quarter 1972): 56. For excerpts from Lippard's tribute to Charles Brockden Brown, "The Heart-Broken," see George Lippard, *Prophet of Protest: Writings of an American Radical, 1822–1854*, ed. David S. Reynolds (New York: Peter Lang, 1986), 268–73. Michael Denning quotes Peter Brooks from *Reading for the Plot* in *Mechanic Accents: Dime Novels and Working-Class Culture in America* (New York: Verso, 1987), 86. On Lippard's fiction and the genre of the city mystery, see Leslie A. Fiedler, introduction to *The Monks of Monk Hall*, by George Lippard (New York: Odyssey Press, 1970), vii–xxxii; Ehrlich, "The 'Mysteries' of Philadelphia"; David S. Reynolds, *Beneath the American Renaissance: The Subversive Imagination in the Age of Emerson and Melville* (New York: Alfred A. Knopf, 1988),

82–84, 86–87; and Denning, *Mechanic Accents*, 85–87. On the genre of the American city mystery more broadly, see Ronald J. Zboray and Mary Saracino Zboray, "The Mysteries of New England: Eugène Sue's American 'Imitators,' 1844," *Nineteenth-Century Contexts* 22 (2000): 457–92; Kimberly R. Gladman, "Upper Tens and Lower Millions: City Mysteries Fiction and Class in the Mid-Nineteenth Century," Ph.D. diss., New York University, 2001; and Paul Erickson, "Welcome to Sodom: The Cultural Work of City-Mysteries Fiction in Antebellum America," Ph.D. diss., University of Texas at Austin, 2005.

34. Lippard's anxieties about literary priority developed over time into exasperation at the plagiarism of his books by other writers, including a translation of *The Quaker City* claimed by the German novelist Friedrich Gerstäcker as his own; see Reynolds, introduction to *Quaker City*, xiv, xvi.

35. Erickson provides a bibliography of more than two hundred examples of American city mysteries fiction from the 1840s and 1850s in "Welcome to Sodom." Zboray and Zboray argue that regional American city mysteries call for specific contextual analyses, rather than generic assumptions, in "The Mysteries of New England." For the transposed passages Foster used to describe the scandalous landmarks in Philadelphia and New York, see George G. Foster, "Philadelphia in Slices, 4: Dandy Hall" (November 17, 1848), rpt. in *Pennsylvania Magazine of History and Biography* 93.1 (January 1969): 40, and "The Dance-House" (1850), rpt. in *New York by Gas-Light and Other Urban Sketches*, ed. and intro. Stuart M. Blumin (Berkeley: University of California Press, 1990), 142–43. Dividing attention among Boston, New York, and Philadelphia, A. J. H. Duganne in *The Knights of the Seal; or, The Mysteries of the Three Cities* (Philadelphia: Colon and Adriance, 1845) raises questions about urban specificity within the pages of a single city mysteries novel.

36. Fiedler, introduction to *The Monks of Monk Hall*, xxix.

37. George Lippard, *The Quaker City; or, the Monks of Monk Hall: A Romance of Philadelphia Life, Mystery, and Crime*, ed. and intro. David S. Reynolds (1845; rpt. Amherst: University of Massachusetts Press, 1995), 305; subsequent references to *The Quaker City* will be given in parentheses; Victor Hugo, preface to *Cromwell* (1827), excerpted in *European Literature from Romanticism to Postmodernism: A Reader in Aesthetic Practice*, ed. and trans. Martin Travers (New York: Continuum, 2001), 45–47.

38. After initial periodical appearances, "King Pest" and "Ligeia" were reprinted in Poe's collection *Tales of the Grotesque and Arabesque* (1840); "The Masque of the Red Death" appeared in Philadelphia's *Graham's Magazine* in 1842. On the personal and professional ties between Poe and Lippard, see Reynolds, *George Lippard*, 18–19, 102–10, and *Prophet of Protest*, 256–67; and Kenneth Silverman, *Edgar Allan Poe: Mournful and Never-Ending Remembrance* (New York: Harper Collins, 1991), 414–19.

39. On Poe in Philadelphia between 1838 and 1844, see Arthur Hobson Quinn, *Edgar Allan Poe: A Critical Biography* (1941; rpt. Baltimore: Johns Hopkins University Press, 1998), 263–404; and Silverman, *Edgar A. Poe*, 129–210, 414–20. Quinn notes (and downplays) the 1838 and 1844 riots (268). The two biographers offer different ranges for Poe's arrival in Philadelphia, and no one seems to know exactly when he moved from New York. Quinn writes "sometime in the summer of 1838" (268), while Silverman offers "probably in the spring or early summer of 1838" (131).

40. Poe, "The Man of the Crowd" (1840), in *Collected Works of Edgar Allan Poe*, vol. 2, *Tales and Sketches, 1831–1842*, ed. Thomas Ollive Mabbott (Cambridge, Mass.: Harvard University Press, 1978), 507. Elise Lemire makes the (somewhat severe) argument about the Philadelphia context for "The Murders of the Rue Morgue," in *"Miscegenation": Mixing Race in America* (Philadelphia: University of Pennsylvania Press, 2002), 87–114; see also Lindon Barrett, "Presence of Mind: Detection and Racialization in 'The Murders in the Rue Morgue,'" in *Romancing the Shadow: Poe and Race*, ed. J. Gerald Kennedy and Liliane Weissberg (New York: Oxford University Press, 2001), 157–76. In his 1996 novel *The Cattle Killing*, John Edgar Wideman links Poe's "Red Death" with the Philadelphia yellow fever. One character describes to another a story, "which had become a popular parable of sorts," about a man who barricaded himself and his extended family in his mansion during the 1793 fever, in an attempt at quarantine. Indulging in lavish entertainments, all were fatally stricken. See John Edgar Wideman, *The Cattle Killing* (New York: Houghton Mifflin, 1996), 49–51.

41. Poe, "The System of Doctor Tarr and Professor Fether" (1845), in *Collected Works of Edgar Allan Poe*, vol. 3, *Tales and Sketches, 1843–1849*, ed. Thomas Ollive Mabbott (Cambridge, Mass.: Belknap Press of Harvard University Press, 1978), 1002, 1004. Compared with "The System of Doctor Tarr and Professor Feather," the reversals are much harsher and more permanent in Poe's late story, "Hop Frog; or, The Eight Chained Ourang-Outangs" (1849).

42. Poe, "Morning on the Wissahiccon" (1844), in Mabbott, ed., *Collected Works of Edgar Allan Poe*, 3:860–67. John Gadsby Chapman's engraving is reproduced in Edgar Allan Poe, *Poetry and Tales*, ed. Patrick F. Quinn (New York: Library of America, 1984), 940. Engraving and verbal sketch first appeared in *The Opal: A Pure Gift for the Holy Days*, ed. N. P. Willis (New York: John C. Riker, 1844), 249–56. On Poe's source in the earlier essay on "The Wissahiccon" and on Chapman's print, see Burton R. Pollin, "Edgar Allan Poe and John G. Chapman: Their Treatment of the Dismal Swamp and the Wissahickon," in *Studies in the American Renaissance*, ed. Joel Myerson (Charlottesville: University Press of Virginia, 1983), 245–74, and also Louis A. Renza, "'Ut Pictura Poe': Poetic Politics in 'The Island of the Fay' and 'Morning on the Wissahiccon,'" in *The American Face of Edgar Allan Poe*, ed. Shawn Rosenheim and Stephen Rachman (Baltimore: Johns Hopkins University Press, 1995), 305–29.

43. Joan Dayan, "Poe, Persons, and Property," in *Romancing the Shadow*, ed. Kennedy and Weissberg, 107. The challenge of situating Poe in historical, and specifically American, contexts is taken up by two recent critical anthologies: *The American Face of Edgar Allan Poe* (1995) and *Romancing the Shadow: Poe and Race* (2001).

44. Denning, *Mechanic Accents*, 92–93. For criticism on Lippard, in addition to the work by Fiedler, Ehrlich, Reynolds, and Denning cited earlier, see Larzer Ziff, *Literary Democracy: The Declaration of Cultural Independence in America* (New York: Viking, 1981), 91–107; Dana D. Nelson, *National Manhood: Capitalist Citizenship and the Imagined Fraternity of White Men* (Durham, N.C.: Duke University Press, 1998), 143–60; and Shelley Streeby, *American Sensations: Class, Empire, and the Production of Popular Culture* (Berkeley: University of California Press, 2002), 38–77.

45. The old State House containing Independence Hall serves as a focal point for Lippard throughout his writings and is featured in the late "Eleanor; or, Slave Catching in the Quaker City" (1854). Trinity Church occupies an analogous position in Lippard's New York novels such as *The Empire City* (1850) and its sequel, *New York: Its Upper Ten and Lower Million* (1853).

46. George Lippard, *The Empire City; or, New York by Night and Day, Its Aristocracy and Its Dollars* (1850; rpt. Philadelphia: T. B. Peterson, 1864), 45–46, 42. David S. Reynolds discusses the train scene in *George Lippard*, 46–47.

47. John F. Kasson, *Rudeness and Civility: Manners in Nineteenth-Century America* (New York: Hill and Wang, 1990), 72–80; on urban panoramas, see Hans Bergmann, *God in the Street: New York Writing from the Penny Press to Melville* (Philadelphia: Temple University Press, 1995), 41–48. J. C. Wild, the possible illustrator of Pennsylvania Hall, drew four views of Philadelphia from the State House steeple. Originally issued as "Panorama of Philadelphia," these lithographs also were bound in *Panorama and Views of Philadelphia and Its Vicinity* (Philadelphia: J. C. Wild and J. B. Chevalier, 1838), reissued in the same year by J. T. Bowen.

48. On the almost-riot over the theatrical "Quaker City," see Julia Curtis, "Philadelphia in an Uproar: *The Monks of Monk Hall*, 1844," *Theatre History Studies* 5 (1985): 41–47. Lippard's script has not survived.

49. George G. Foster, "Philadelphia in Slices, 9: The Colored Population" (January 6, 1849), rpt. in *Pennsylvania Magazine of History and Biography* 93.1 (January 1969): 60–64.

50. George Lippard, "Eleanor; or, Slave Catching in the Quaker City," Philadelphia *Sunday Mercury*, February 12, 1854.

51. George Lippard, *The Nazarene; or, The Last of the Washingtons. A Revelation of Philadelphia, New York, and Washington, in the Year 1844* (Philadelphia: G. Lippard, 1846), v. Subsequent references will be given in parentheses.

52. Warner, *The Private City*, 141–52. On the 1844 riots, see Scharf and Westcott, *History of Philadelphia*, 1:663–75; Geffen, "Violence in Philadelphia," 397–404, and "Industrial Development and Social Crisis," 356–58; David Montgomery, "The Shuttle and the Cross: Weavers and Artisans in the Kensington Riots of 1844," in *Workers in the Industrial Revolution: Recent Studies of Labor in the United States and Europe*, ed. Peter N. Stearns and Daniel J. Walkowitz (New Brunswick, N.J.: Transaction, 1974), 44–74; and Michael Feldberg, *The Philadelphia Riots of 1844: A Study of Ethnic Conflict* (Westport, Conn.: Greenwood, 1975). The Shiffler lithograph (c. 1845) is reproduced in Nash, *First City* (172), as is H. Bucholzer's 1844 image "Riot in Philadelphia, July 7th, 1844" (173).

53. The song sheet "Philadelphia Riots" was published by J. Torr, 29 South Third Street, Philadelphia; a copy is in the collections of the Library Company of Philadelphia.

54. Denning, *Mechanic Accents*, 112–14.

55. *The Stranger's Guide to the Public Buildings, Places of Amusement, Streets, Lanes, Alleys, Roads, Avenues, Courts, Wharves, Principal Hotels, Steam-Boat Landings, Stage Offices, Etc. Etc. of the City of Philadelphia and Adjoining Districts, with References for Finding Their Situations on the Accompanying Plan of the City: The Whole Alphabetically Arranged and Forming a Complete Guide to Everything Interesting in the City and Suburbs of Philadelphia* (Philadelphia: H. S. Tanner, 1828). The Library

Company of Philadelphia has among its holdings *Stranger's Guides* that date to 1810 and copies of *Philadelphia as It Is* that date to 1833.

56. Sam Bass Warner Jr. mentions the south to north route taken by many rioters, in *Private City,* 146; Scarf and Westcott describe a nativist meeting that began in the State House yard and proceeded through the State House onto Chestnut Street and then marched north to Kensington, in *History of Philadelphia,* 1:665.

57. [George Lippard listed as] A Member of the Philadelphia Bar, *The Killers. A Narrative of Real Life in Philadelphia, in Which the Deeds of the Killers, and the Great Riot of Election night, October 10, 1849, are Minutely Described. Also, the Adventures of Three Notorious Individuals, Who Took Part in That Riot, to Wit: Cromwell D. Z. Hicks, the Leader of the Killers, Don Jorge, one of the Leaders of the Cuban Expedition, and "The Bulgine" the Celebrated Negro Desperado of Moyamensing* (Philadelphia: Hankinson and Bartholomew, 1850); references to this edition will be given in parentheses. On the "Killers" gang, see Laurie, *Working People of Philadelphia,* 151–59.

58. *The Life and Adventures of Charles Anderson Chester, the Notorious Leader of the Philadelphia "Killers," Who Was Murdered, While Engaged in the Destruction of the California House, on Election Night, October 11, 1849* (Philadelphia: Yates and Smith, 1850); George Lippard, *The Bank Director's Son, A Real and Intensely Interesting Revelation of City Life. Containing an Authentic Account of the Wonderful Escape of the Beautiful Kate Watson, from a Flaming Building in the City of Philadelphia* (Philadelphia: E. E. Barclay and A. R. Orton, 1851). The publishing history is analyzed by David Faflik in "Authorship, Ownership, and the Case for *Charles Anderson Chester,*" *Book History* 11 (2008): 149–67, and also in a letter from Phillip Lapsansky to David S. Reynolds, dated March 7, 1994, held in the archives of the Library Company of Philadelphia.

59. In the 1850 census, the Cedar neighborhood crossed several wards north and south of the Cedar or South Street border of Philadelphia. Emma Jones Lapsansky analyzes the contours of the neighborhood and the spatial dynamics of Philadelphia's antebellum racial riots in *Neighborhoods in Transition,* 130–45. Lippard's narrator in *The Killers* offers an early fictional portrait of the controversial Eastern State Penitentiary (18–20), northwest of the city, echoing the disapproval of its solitary confinement expressed by observers such as Charles Dickens in his *American Notes* (1842).

60. J. B. [John Beauchamp] Jones, preface to *The City Merchant; or, The Mysterious Failure* (Philadelphia: Lippincott, Grambo, 1851). Subsequent references will be given in parentheses. Robin Grey surveys Jones's biography and literary career in "John Beauchamp Jones," *Dictionary of Literary Biography,* vol. 202, *Nineteenth–Century American Fiction Writers,* ed. Kent Ljungquist (Detroit: Gale Research, 1999), 147–58. She discusses his residency in Philadelphia in "Patronage, Southern Politics, and the Road Not Taken: Edgar Allan Poe and John Beauchamp Jones," forthcoming in *Poe Writing/Writing Poe,* ed. Jana Argersinger and Richard Kopley (New York: AMS Press). Jones pursued his interests in sectional and racial politics in a novel anticipating a civil war, issued two years before the attack on Fort Sumter, titled *Border War: A Tale of Disunion* (New York: Rudd and Carleton, 1859).

61. *The City Merchant* offers a notable example of the yearnings for intrinsic racial and economic character that Michael O'Malley analyzes in "Specie and Species: Race and the Money Question in Nineteenth-Century America," *The American Historical Review* 99.2 (April 1994): 369–95.

62. Douglass satirized the controversy over his interracial stroll in his essay "Color-phobia in New York!" printed in his *The North Star* (May 25, 1849); see *Frederick Douglass: Selected Speeches and Writings*, ed. Philip S. Foner and Yuval Taylor (Chicago: Lawrence Hill, 1999), 141–43.

63. Jones's warning about violence in Philadelphia as synecdoche for recent U.S. history was received by one of his prominent southern reviewers, William Gilmore Simms, who wrote: "The story is quite readable, not simply because of its mercantile revelations, but in consequence of the right-mindedness with which the author discusses the evils of abolition at the North, and the negro mania, which has done so much mischief North and South. A glimpse is given us of the terrible riots, which have made Philadelphia so conspicuous among the American cities, and in which the instinctive antipathies of the whites and blacks of the free States, have put them in attitudes of strife wholly beyond the operation and control of the law." See *Southern Quarterly Review* 5 (January 1852): 259.

64. See Noel Ignatiev, *How the Irish Became White*. In making his argument about ethnic assimilation and racial identification, Ignatiev focuses on nineteenth-century Philadelphia.

65. See "The Present State and Condition of the Free People of Color, of the City of Philadelphia and Adjoining Districts, as Exhibited by the Report of a Committee of the Pennsylvania Society for Promoting the Abolition of Slavery, etc." (Philadelphia: Published by the Society, 1838); "Trades of the Colored People in the City of Philadelphia and Districts" (Philadelphia: Merrihew and Gunn, 1838); Benjamin H. Coates, M.D., "On the Effects of Secluded and Gloomy Imprisonment on Individuals of the African Variety of Mankind, in the Production of Disease" (Philadelphia: John C. Clark, 1843); "Ten Years' Progress: or A Comparison of the State and Condition of the Colored People in the City and County of Philadelphia from 1837 to 1847. Prepared by Edward Needles" (Phil-adelphia: Merrihew and Thompson, 1849); "A Statistical Inquiry into the Condition of the People of Colour, of the City and Districts of Philadelphia" (Philadelphia: Kite and Walton, 1849); "The Mysteries and Miseries of Philadelphia, as Exhibited and Illustrated by a Late Presentment of the Grand Jury, and by a Sketch of the Condition of the Most Degraded Classes in the City" (Philadelphia, 1853); and Benjamin C. Bacon, "Statistics of the Colored People of Philadelphia. Taken by Benjamin C. Bacon, and Published by Order of the Board of Education of 'The Pennsylvania Society for Promoting the Abolition of Slavery,' etc." (Philadelphia: T. Ellwood Chapman, 1856) and its second edition (Philadel-phia: Reprinted by Order of the Board of Education, 1859). Subsequent references to these reports will be given in parentheses.

66. W. E. B. DuBois, *The Souls of Black Folk* (1903); in *Writings: The Suppression of the African Slave-Trade, The Souls of Black Folk, Dusk of Dawn, Essays*, ed. Nathan Huggins (New York: Library of America, 1986), 363. DuBois discusses the mid-nineteenth-century censuses and reports in *The Philadelphia Negro*, 43–44. On the circumstances of DuBois's study and his responses, see W. E. B. DuBois, *Dusk of Dawn: An Essay toward an Autobiography of a Race Concept* (1940; rpt. New York: Schocken, 1968), 58–63; David Levering Lewis, *W. E. B. DuBois: Biography of a Race, 1868–1919* (New York: Henry Holt, 1993), 188–89 (including the quote from DuBois's patrons); and Elijah Anderson's introduction to *The Philadelphia Negro*.

67. On the African American concentration in Moyamensing in the late 1840s, see DuBois, *Philadelphia Negro*, 302–3, and Geffen, "Industrial Development and Social Crisis," 309. For examples of generic mysteries of Philadelphia, see *Mysteries of Philadelphia, or: Scenes of Real Life in the Quaker City* (1848); [Joseph A. Nunes Jr.], *Aristocracy; or, Life in the City. By a Member of the Philadelphia Bar* (Philadelphia: S. G. Sherman, 1848); [George Thompson], *Mysteries and Miseries of Philadelphia. By a Member of the Pennsylvania Bar* (New York: Williams, [185?]; and *The Homeless Heir; or, Life in Bedford Street; A Mystery of Philadelphia. By John the Outcast* (Philadelphia: J. H. C. Whiting, 1856). Elliott Shore discusses the first (and so far only) discovered installment of a German-language Philadelphia city mystery, published in 1850, which takes up issues of class, geography, and racial encounter (depicting an Irish tavern with African American customers). See Shore's "The Mysteries of Philadelphia in 1850: The German American Context," in *New Directions in German-American Studies*, vol. 2, *German? American? Literature?* ed. Winfried Fluck and Werner Sollors (New York: Peter Lang, 2002), 93–112.

68. Theodore Hershberg, "Free Blacks in Antebellum Philadelphia: A Study of Ex-Slaves, Freeborn, and Socioeconomic Decline" (1971), rpt. in *African Americans in Pennsylvania: Shifting Historical Perspectives*, ed. Joe William Trotter Jr. and Eric Ledell Smith (Harrisburg and University Park: Pennsylvania Historical and Museum Commission and Pennsylvania State University Press, 1997), 123–47; E. J. Lapsansky, *Neighborhoods in Transition*, 149–50.

69. Hershberg, "Free Blacks in Antebellum Philadelphia," 126; DuBois, *Philadelphia Negro*, 44.

70. In *The Philadelphia Negro* (1899), DuBois analyzes how waves of European immigrants in the nineteenth century restricted the development of an African American middle class. Wages were depressed by supply, many employers preferred to hire whites, and immigrants often refused to work with blacks.

71. In *The Philadelphia Negro*, citing evidence of "the crime, filth, and poverty of this district [in Moyamensing]" (304), DuBois makes no distinction between the 1849 Society of Friends "Statistical Inquiry" and the 1853 "Mysteries and Miseries of Philadelphia."

Chapter Four

1. John F. Denny, *An Enquiry into the Political Grade of the Free Coloured Population, under the Constitution of the United States, and the Constitution of Pennsylvania: in Three Parts. By a Member of the Chambersburg Bar* (Chambersburg, Pa.: J. Pritts, 1834), 21–23.

2. Mary Howard Schoolcraft, "Letters on the Condition of the African Race in the United States, by a Southern Lady" (Philadelphia: T. K. and P. G. Collins, 1852), 25.

3. Schoolcraft, "Letters on the Condition," 26, 27; Benjamin H. Coates, "On the Effects of Secluded and Gloomy Imprisonment on Individuals of the African Variety of Mankind, in the Production of Disease" (Philadelphia: John C. Clark, 1843), 12.

4. "A Statistical Inquiry into the Condition of the People of Colour, of the City and Districts of Philadelphia" (Philadelphia: Kite and Walton, 1849), 39; Schoolcraft, "Letters," 25, 8, 27.

5. Thomas F. Gossett briefly discusses *Liberia* as a response to *Uncle Tom's Cabin* in *Uncle Tom's Cabin and American Culture* (Dallas, Tex.: Southern Methodist University Press, 1985), 235–36. See also Susan M. Ryan, "Errand into Africa: Colonization and Nation Building in Sarah J. Hale's *Liberia*," *New England Quarterly* 68.4 (December 1995): 559–66.

6. Ryan, "Errand into Africa," 564. Only recently have critics attended to Hale's novel, and they tend to take the Philadelphia chapter for granted, concentrating instead on issues surrounding Liberia; see Nina Baym, *Feminism and American Literary History* (New Brunswick, N.J.: Rutgers University Press, 1992), 167–82; Ryan, "Errand into Africa"; Amy Kaplan, "Manifest Domesticity," *American Literature* 70.3 (September 1998): 581–606; and Etsuko Taketani, "Postcolonial Liberia: Sarah Josepha Hale's Africa," *American Literary History* 14.3 (Fall 2002): 479–504.

7. Sarah Josepha Hale, *Liberia* (1853; rpt. Upper Saddle River, N.J.: Gregg, 1968), 76, 78. Subsequent references will be given in parentheses. Hale instances Clay more faithfully in the portrait of Clara's daughter Madge, who accompanies her on Chestnut Street and is decked out in stockings, gray boots, and a hat adorned with blue streamers.

8. Saidiya V. Hartman, *Scenes of Subjection: Terror, Slavery, and Self-Making in Nineteenth-Century America* (New York: Oxford University Press, 1997), 115–25.

9. Martin Robison Delany, *The Condition, Elevation, Emigration, and Destiny of the Colored People of the United States*, ed. Toyin Falola (1852; rpt. Amherst, N.Y.: Humanity Books, 2004), 38. In the late 1850s and early 1860s, Delany explored the possibility of establishing black American settlements in the Niger Valley; in the 1870s, he unsuccessfully tried to obtain a ministerial post in Liberia.

10. Construed most broadly, Delany's inventory of black achievement includes chapters 7–12. The catalogue of economic success is given mostly in chapter 10, with the Philadelphians clustering at the beginning (114–16, 119–20). As I have outlined the development of Delany's *Condition*, his turn from "elevation" to "emigration" may not be as "odd and arguably contradictory" as Robert S. Levine suggests; see his *Martin Delany, Frederick Douglass, and the Politics of Representative Identity* (Chapel Hill: University of North Carolina Press, 1997), 65. Henry Highland Garnet's "The Past and the Present Condition, and the Destiny, of the Colored Race" (1848) probably served as one of the texts Delany reworked in his *Condition*. For Garnet, at least in this 1848 address, prejudice is directed against condition, not complexion, and the "destiny of the colored race" lies in America. In the following year, Garnet publicly endorsed colonization. On Delany's *Condition*, see Victor Ullman, *Martin R. Delany: The Beginnings of Black Nationalism* (Boston: Beacon, 1971), 142–50; Floyd J. Miller, *The Search for a Black Nationality: Black Emigration and Colonization, 1787–1863* (Urbana: University of Illinois Press, 1975), 125–33; Robert M. Kahn, "The Political Ideology of Martin Delany," *Journal of Black Studies* 14.4 (June 1984): 415–40; Nell Irvin Painter, "Martin R. Delany: Elitism and Black Nationalism," in *Black Leaders of the Nineteenth Century*, ed. Leon Litwack and August Meier (Urbana: University of Illinois Press, 1988), 149–71; Levine, *Martin Delany and Frederick Douglass*,

63–71; and John Ernest, *Liberation Historiography: African American Writers and the Challenge of History, 1794–1861* (Chapel Hill: University of North Carolina Press, 2004), 113–32.

11. William Whipper, letter to the editor, *Frederick Douglass' Paper* (November 3, 1854), rpt. in *The Black Abolitionist Papers*, vol. 4, *The United States, 1847–1858*, ed. C. Peter Ripley et al. (Chapel Hill: University of North Carolina Press, 1991), 242–44.

12. James McCune Smith (writing under the pseudonym "Communipaw"), letter to the editor, *Frederick Douglass' Paper* (April 16, 1858): 3.

13. The Whipper quotations in this and the preceding paragraph are taken from William Whipper, letter to the editor, *Frederick Douglass' Paper* (June 4, 1858): 3. Samuel Cornish made his remarks on the Philadelphia leaders in "Moral Reform Convention," *Colored American* (August 26, 1837). Whipper's mood also may reflect the diminished national authority of Philadelphia's African American leaders in the 1850s; on the shift in leadership away from Philadelphia, see Winch, *Philadelphia's Black Elite* (Philadelphia: Temple University Press, 1988), 129, 152–66.

14. William Whipper, letter to the editor, *Frederick Douglass' Paper* (July 2, 1858): 3. I am grateful to the Douglass Collection, Lavery Library, St. John Fisher College, Rochester, N. Y., for access to this issue and permission to quote from it.

15. James McCune Smith (writing as "Communipaw"), letter to the editor, *Frederick Douglass' Paper* (August 12, 1858): 3.

16. William Whipper, "'Colored History' of Pennsylvania," *Frederick Douglass' Paper* (September 3, 1858): 3; James McCune Smith (writing as "Communipaw"), letter to the editor, *Frederick Douglass' Paper* (January 21, 1859): 3.

17. *Athenaeum* (September 5, 1857): 1129; *Lloyd's Weekly Newspaper* (September 13, 1857): 10. Webb's novel was widely advertised in British periodicals.

18. On Webb's biography, about which much remains to be learned, see Phillip S. Lapsansky, "Afro-Americana: Frank J. Webb and His Friends," in *The Annual Report of the Library Company of Philadelphia for the Year 1990* (Philadelphia: Library Company of Philadelphia, 1991), 27–38; Rosemary F. Crockett, "*The Garies and Their Friends*: A Study of Frank J. Webb and His Novel," Ph.D. diss., Harvard University, 1998, 17–42, and "Frank J. Webb: The Shift to Color Discrimination," in *The Black Columbiad: Defining Moments in African American Literature and Culture*, ed. Werner Sollors and Maria Diedrich (Cambridge, Mass.: Harvard University Press, 1994), 112–22; Allan Austin, "Frank J. Webb," in *The Encyclopedia of African-American Culture and History*, ed. Jack Salzman, David Lionel Smith, and Cornel West (New York: Macmillan Library Reference USA/Simon and Shuster Macmillan, 1996), 5: 2796; and Eric Gardner, "'A Gentleman of Superior Cultivation and Refinement': Recovering the Biography of Frank J. Webb," *African American Review* 35.2 (Summer 2001): 297–308. Webb mentions his second novel, *Paul Sumner*, in a letter to the journalist Mary Wager Fisher, dated May 5, 1870, reprinted in *Frank J. Webb: Fiction, Essays, Poetry*, ed. Werner Sollors (New Milford, Conn.: Toby, 2004), 432. Sollors also reproduces the two daguerreotypes, which are held in the collections of the Harriet Beecher Stowe Center in Hartford, Conn. (this image includes a third figure, a man), and the Amistad Foundation at the Wadsworth Atheneum Museum of Art.

19. Frank J. Webb, *The Garies and Their Friends* (London and New York: G. Routledge and Co., 1857); three subsequent editions have been published in the United States in the twentieth century, by Arno Press and the New York Times in 1969, Johns Hopkins University Press in 1997, and Toby Press in 2004. The 1969 and 1997 editions reproduce the pages of the more expensive volume issued by Routledge in 1857. The texts are the same in the two 1857 British editions, but the cheaper "yellowback" has been printed from different plates with smaller type and totals 298 pages, compared with 392 pages in the cloth. I will quote in parentheses from *The Garies and Their Friends*, ed. and intro. Robert Reid-Pharr (Baltimore: Johns Hopkins University Press, 1997). Rosemary Crockett discusses the original publishing arrangements and Routledge's role in marketing American authors in "*The Garies and Their Friends*," 203–5. The review in *Frederick Douglass' Paper* (December 4, 1857): 1–2 originally appeared in the London *Daily News* (October 9, 1857): 2. Webb is described as the author of *The Garies* in the *New Era* on January 13, 1870 (the first issue): 3, 4; see also *New Era* (March 31, 1870): 4. Phillip S. Lapsansky speculates that the novel had "a sub rosa career among black readers," in "Afro-Americana: Frank J. Webb and His Friends," 28. Webb seems to have influenced at least one antiracist work, Anna E. Dickinson's uneven *What Answer?* (1868). This novel shares with *The Garies* plots, settings, a crucial riot (for Dickinson, the New York City draft riots of 1863), and backing from Harriet Beecher Stowe. Dickinson was a native Philadelphian whose family was acquainted with the Fortens and the Purvises. She was a precocious writer (publishing an antislavery essay in *The Liberator* at age thirteen) and, during the 1860s, a celebrated orator. Her only novel has been reprinted with an introduction by J. Matthew Gallman (Amherst, N.Y.: Humanity Books, 2003).

20. Available in English and American editions, *Bleak House*, first published as a book in 1853, was serialized in its entirety in *Frederick Douglass' Paper* between April 1852 and December 1853. Webb is connected with Dickens by James H. DeVries, "The Tradition of the Sentimental Novel in *The Garies and Their Friends*," *CLA Journal* 17.2 (December 1973): 243–44, and by Crockett, "*The Garies and Their Friends*," 84–87.

21. Benjamin Brawley, *The Negro Genius: A New Appraisal of the Achievement of the American Negro in Literature and the Fine Arts* (1937; rpt. New York: Biblio and Tannen, 1969), 69; Arthur P. Davis, preface to *The Garies and Their Friends* (New York: Arno Press and the New York Times, 1969), v–vi, viii–ix, xii, xi. Davis softens some of his criticisms in a revised version of his preface, which he published as "*The Garies and Their Friends*: A Neglected Pioneer Novel," *CLA Journal* 13.1 (September 1969): 27–34. Critics who follow Davis in faulting *The Garies* for its purported counsel of assimilation include Robert A. Bone, *The Negro Novel in America* (New Haven, Conn.: Yale University Press, 1958), 31; DeVries, "Tradition of the Sentimental Novel in *The Garies*," 241–49; Addison Gayle Jr., *The Way of the New World: The Black Novel in America* (Garden City, N.Y.: Anchor Press/Doubleday, 1975), 11–17; and Arlene A. Elder, *The Hindered Hand: Cultural Implications of Early African American Fiction* (Westport, Conn.: Greenwood, 1978), 12, 53. Robert Reid-Pharr considers the difficulties that the novel has posed for its critics in the introduction to his 1997 reprint (vii–ix). No excerpt from Webb's novel was included in the canon-making *Norton Anthology of African American Literature* (1997).

22. Blyden Jackson, *A History of Afro-American Literature*, vol. I, *The Long Beginning, 1746–1895* (Baton Rouge: Louisiana State University Press, 1989), 348; Lapsansky, "Frank J. Webb and His Friends," 28. In recent years, several critics have analyzed Webb's novel, rather than diagnosed its limits. For examples, see Lapsansky, "Frank J. Webb and His Friends"; Carla L Peterson, "Capitalism, Black (Under)development, and the Production of the African-American Novel in the 1850s," *American Literary History* 4.4 (Winter 1992): 559–83, and *"Doers of the Word": African American Women Speakers and Writers in the North (1830–1880)* (New York: Oxford University Press, 1995), 173–75; Robert S. Levine, "Disturbing Boundaries: Temperance, Black Elevation, and Violence in Frank J. Webb's *The Garies and Their Friends*," *Prospects* 19 (1994): 349–74; Robert Reid-Pharr, introduction to *The Garies and their Friends*, and *Conjugal Union: The Body, the House, and the Black American* (New York: Oxford University Press, 1999), 65–88; M. Giulia Fabi, *Passing and the Rise of the African American Novel* (Urbana: University of Illinois Press, 2001), 28–43; Amy Schrager Lang, *The Syntax of Class: Writing Inequality in Nineteenth-Century America* (Princeton, N.J.: Princeton University Press, 2003), 46–63; Stephen Knadler, "Traumatized Racial Performativity: Passing in Nineteenth-Century African-American Testimonies," *Cultural Critique* 55 (Fall 2003): 63–100; and Diane Helen Matlock, "The Sentimental Novel and the Transformation of Antebellum Print and Material Cultures," Ph.D. diss., University of California, Berkeley (in progress).

23. Frank J. Webb, "Biographical Sketch," in *The Christian Slave: A Drama, Founded on a Portion of Uncle Tom's Cabin; Dramatised by Harriet Beecher Stowe, Expressly for the Readings of Mrs. Mary E. Webb; Arranged, with a Short Biographical Sketch of the Reader, by F. J. Webb* (London: Sampson Low, 1856), iii, iv. An edition had been published in Boston a year earlier, without Webb's preface. A copy of the London *Christian Slave*, inscribed to Mary Webb from H. B. Stowe, along with pencil markings, some of which may have been made by Mary and served as prompts, can be found at the Harriet Beecher Stowe Center in Hartford, Conn. Stowe may have responded to what she perceived as similarities in background and appearance between Mary Webb and her character Cassy, featuring Cassy's long autobiographical speech from chapter 34 of *Uncle Tom's Cabin* in the third act of *The Christian Slave*. Stowe wrote letters of introduction for the Webbs to Lady Hatherton, May 24, 1856, and to Mr. and Mrs. Baines, May 24, 1856, now held in the collections of the Stowe Center in Hartford. On Stowe and the Webbs, see Edward Wagenknecht, *Harriet Beecher Stowe: The Known and the Unknown* (New York: Oxford University Press, 1965), 132, 235 n. 11; Joan D. Hedrick, *Harriet Beecher Stowe: A Life* (New York: Oxford University Press, 1994), 249–50; Susan F. Clark, "Solo Black Performance before the Civil War: Mr. Stowe, Mrs. Webb, and 'The Christian Slave,'" *New Theatre Quarterly* 13.52 (November 1997): 339–48; and Eric Gardner, "Stowe Takes the Stage: Harriet Beecher Stowe's *The Christian Slave*," *Legacy* 15.1 (1998): 78–84, and "'A Nobler End': Mary Webb and the Victorian Platform," *Nineteenth-Century Prose* 29.1 (Spring 2002): 103–16. Elisa Tamarkin describes the Anglicization of U. S. antislavery efforts in *Anglophilia: Deference, Devotion, and Antebellum America* (Chicago: University of Chicago Press, 2008), 178–246.

24. "The Garies," *Sunday Times* (September 27, 1857): 2; "The Garies and Their Friends," *Athenaeum* 1565 (October 24, 1857): 1320.

25. "*The Garies and Their Friends*," London *Daily News* (Oct. 9, 1857): 2; rpt. in *Frederick Douglass' Paper* (Dec. 4, 1857): 1.

26. Harriet Beecher Stowe, *A Key to Uncle Tom's Cabin* (1853; rpt. New York: Arno Press and the New York Times, 1969), v, and *Uncle Tom's Cabin; or, Life Among the Lowly*, ed. Elizabeth Ammons (1852; rpt. New York: W. W. Norton, 1994), 206, 177.

27. I analyze Stowe's racial trials in "Stowe and Race," in *The Cambridge Companion to Harriet Beecher Stowe*, ed. Cindy A. Weinstein (New York: Cambridge University Press, 2004), 15–38.

28. Hale, *Liberia*, 77; Whipper, Cornish, Douglass, and Willson, as discussed in chapter 2; Robert Montgomery Bird, *Sheppard Lee, Written by Himself*, 2 vols., intro. Christopher Looby (1836; rpt. New York: New York Review Books, 2008), 422. I have relied on the Oxford English Dictionary for my discussion of "peculiar."

29. For some examples of Webb's riffs on "peculiar," see *The Garies and Their Friends*, 1, 21, 41, 138, 184, 186, 208, 265, 275, 337, 350, 356. W. E. B. DuBois frequently uses the term "peculiar" to describe the situation in *The Philadelphia Negro* (1899), and the adjective is conspicuous in his famous account of "a peculiar sensation, this double-consciousness, this sense of always looking at oneself through the eyes of others, of measuring one's soul by the tape of a world that looks on in amused contempt and pity," in *The Souls of Black Folk* (1903). See his *Writings: The Suppression of the African Slave-Trade, The Souls of Black Folk, Dusk of Dawn, Essays, and Articles*, ed. Nathan Huggins (New York: Library of America, 1986), 364.

30. Cassy names her price in Stowe, *Uncle Tom's Cabin*, 315, and *Christian Slave*, 51. Only a few critics have attended to Webb's narrative strategies in the opening scene. See Levine, "Disturbing Boundaries," 352–53, and Henry Golemba, "Frank Webb's *The Garies and Their Friends* Contextualized within African American Slave Narratives," in *Lives Out of Letters: Essays on American Literary Biography and Documentation, in Honor of Robert N. Hudspeth*, ed. Robert D. Habich (Teaneck, N.J.: Fairleigh Dickinson University Press, 2004), 130. Some critics miss the narrative distance in the opening chapters. Arthur P. Davis claims that one of Webb's plantation scenes "could have been written by Thomas Nelson Page," the late-nineteenth-century literary defender of the old South, in his introduction to *The Garies and Their Friends*, xii. Werner Sollors writes that Clarence and Emily "live in the most beautiful paradise of a Georgia plantation setting," in *Neither Black nor White yet Both: Thematic Explorations of Interracial Literature* (New York: Oxford University Press, 1997), 213. Dickson D. Bruce Jr. maintains that the novel "begins with the legitimation of a relationship between the white Garie and the beautiful Emily," in *The Origins of African American Literature, 1680–1865* (Charlottesville: University Press of Virginia, 2001), 295.

31. The book's eccentric title allows Webb to reverse the usual order in the philanthropic cliché "the friends of the colored people." In his title, the "colored people"— that is, the Ellises and Walters—are cast as the "friends" of the imperiled mixed-race family.

32. On Philadelphia history in *The Garies and Their Friends*, see Lapsansky, "Frank J. Webb and His Friends"; Levine, "Disturbing Boundaries" (the phrase I have quoted is on page 355), and Crockett, "*The Garies and Their Friends*," 150–202.

33. My thanks to Phil Lapsansky at the Library Company of Philadelphia for his assistance in charting the streets in the novel.

34. Joseph Willson, *Sketches of the Higher Classes of Colored Society in Philadelphia. By a Southerner* (1841); rpt. as *The Elite of Our People: Joseph Willson's Sketches of Black Upper-Class Life in Antebellum Philadelphia*, ed. Julie Winch (University Park, Pa.: Pennsylvania State University Press, 2000), 103.

35. Robert Reid-Pharr argues that Webb's main concern is "black purity" and that as a literary artist he practices "a sort of domestic eugenics, one in which the goal is to produce properly socialized modern individuals who maintain proper racial and domestic distinctions"; see his introduction to *The Garies and Their Friends*, vii–xviii, and *Conjugal Union*, 65–88 (the quoted phrases are from xii and 69). As will become evident, I argue that Webb troubles, rather than endorses, such distinctions.

36. "Address to the Free People of Colour of These United States" (1830), signed by Richard Allen, in "Constitution of the American Society of Free Persons of Colour, for Improving Their Condition in the United States; for Purchasing Lands; and for the Establishment of a Settlement in Upper Canada. Also the Proceedings of the Convention, with Their Address to the Free Persons of Colour in the United States," rpt. in *Minutes of the Proceedings of the National Negro Conventions, 1830–1864*, ed. Howard Holman Bell (New York: Arno Press and the New York Times, 1969), 11; "Report of the Proceedings of the Colored National Convention, Held at Cleveland, Ohio, on Wednesday, September 6, 1848," rpt. in Bell, ed., *Minutes*, 5, and see also 6 and 13 (the phrase "badge of degradation" is used in the "Address to the Colored People of the United States" on 19); Delany, *Condition, Elevation, Emigration, and Destiny*, 211–20; Frederick Douglass, "Learn Trades or Starve" (1853), rpt. in *The Life and Writings of Frederick Douglass*, vol. 2, *Pre-Civil War Decade*, ed. Philip S. Foner (New York: International Publishers, 1950), 223–25. Patrick Rael examines the debates over labor at the 1848 and 1853 national conventions in *Black Identity and Black Protest in the Antebellum North* (Chapel Hill: University of North Carolina Press, 2002), 35–37.

37. Anna Mae Duane interprets Caddy's housekeeping as wrathful, a bitter response to "the maddening knowledge that blackness nullifies the very claim to the sentimental womanhood she nonetheless feels compelled to emulate"; see "Remaking Black Motherhood in Frank J. Webb's *The Garies and Their Friends*," *African American Review* 38.2 (Summer 2004): 207. This seems a partial reading, acknowledging one aspect of the character's industry but reducing her conduct to a balked attempt at assimilation (as Webb does not) and avoiding his humor.

38. George Lippard, *The Quaker City; or, the Monks of Monk Hall: A Romance of Philadelphia Life, Mystery, and Crime*, ed. and intro. David S. Reynolds (1845; rpt. Amherst: University of Massachusetts Press, 1995), 60–61, 120–22.

39. Bryan Wagner analyzes the fierce response to the "visible signs of African American prosperity" depicted in Charles W. Chesnutt's novel *The Marrow of Tradition* (Boston: Houghton, Mifflin, 1901). Like Webb's *Garies*, Chesnutt's *Marrow* is a trenchant retelling of urban racial violence, based on historical events (for Chesnutt, the Wilmington, North Carolina, riots of 1898), whose attentiveness to social behavior and class distinction has

often been misunderstood as evading, rather than addressing, politics. See Bryan Wagner, "Charles Chesnutt and the Epistemology of Racial Violence," *American Literature* 73.2 (June 2001): 311–37. I have quoted from page 320. Given the affinities, one wonders if Chesnutt read Webb's earlier novel.

40. [Joseph A. Nunes Jr.], *Aristocracy; or, Life in the City. By a Member of the Philadelphia Bar* (Philadelphia: S. G. Sherman, 1848), 249.

41. Diane Helen Matlock analyzes the scenes in Walters's parlor and compares this domestic space with Uncle Tom's cabin, in "The Sentimental Novel."

42. Stowe, *Key to Uncle Tom's Cabin*, 89.

43. On possible historical sources for Walters, see Lapsansky, "Frank J. Webb and His Friends," 31, and Crockett, "*The Garies and Their Friends*," 177–78. For details of Forten's and Purvis's lives that echo Webb's portrayal of Walters, see Julie Winch, *A Gentleman of Color: The Life of James Forten* (New York: Oxford University Press, 2002), 5, 290, 351, 375. The character of Walters has become a touchstone in evaluations of Webb's novel.

44. T. Morris Chester, "Negro Self-Respect and Pride of Race, Delivered at the Twenty-Ninth Anniversary of the Philadelphia Library Company, December 9, 1862," rpt. in *Pamphlets of Protest: An Anthology of Early African American Protest Literature, 1790–1860*, ed. Richard Newman, Patrick Rael, and Phillip Lapsansky (New York: Routledge, 2001), 308; Stowe, *Uncle Tom's Cabin*, 18; Hale, *Liberia*, 80. Eric Gardner envisions the Toussaint portrait as Walters's test of Garie, in "Philadelphia and Haiti in American Literature," a talk delivered at the Modern Language Association convention in Philadelphia in December 2004. On appeal to black northerners Toussaint's, see Rael, *Black Identity and Black Protest*, 224.

45. Several critics have argued for a link in *The Garies* between black economic development and self-defense. See, for examples, Levine, "Disturbing Boundaries," 355; Peterson, "Capitalism, Black (Under)development," 577–80; and Fabi, *Passing*, 35–36.

46. Phillip S. Lapsansky speculates that Frank Webb's father may have been a victim of the 1834 riot. After that year, his name is absent from the city directories. See Lapsansky's letter to Allan Austin, July 17, 1991, in the collections of the Library Company of Philadelphia.

47. "*The Garies and Their Friends*," *Daily News* (October 9, 1857): 2; rpt. in *Frederick Douglass' Paper* (December 4, 1857): 1–2; "*The Garies*," *Sunday Times* (September 27, 1852): 2.

48. Smith's Beneficial Hall was located on Lombard Street between Seventh and Eighth, approximately three-quarters of a mile south from the site of Pennsylvania Hall, which was at Sixth and Haines, below Sassafras or Race Street.

49. On Philadelphia's role in the struggle over the Second Bank of the United States, see Nicholas B. Wainwright, "The Age of Nicholas Biddle, 1825–1841," in *Philadelphia, A 300-Year History*, ed. Russell F. Weigley et al. (New York: W. W. Norton, 1982), 301–6.

50. The figure of the chained and kneeling slave, raising his hands in entreaty, was originally adopted by the Quaker-led Society for Effecting the Abolition of the Slave Trade in England in 1787. The image and motto circulated widely among transatlantic abolitionists.

51. For analyses of the riot in *The Garies*, see Levine, "Disturbing Boundaries," 355–62; Reid-Pharr, *Conjugal Union*, 77–88; and Fabi, *Passing*, 31–32, 41–42.

52. "*The Garies and Their Friends*," *Daily News* (October 9, 1857): 2; rpt. in *Frederick Douglass' Paper* (December 4, 1857): 1–2.

53. Delany, *Condition*, 119–20. On Philadelphia cuisine and the city's prominent black caterers, see Mary Anne Hines, Gordon Marshall, and Willam Woys Weaver, *The Larder Invaded: Reflections on Three Centuries of Philadelphia Food and Drink* (Philadelphia: Winchell Company of Philadelphia, 1987), 21–22, 50, 65; Winch, *Philadelphia's Black Elite*, 21; and W. E. B. DuBois, *The Philadelphia Negro: A Social Study*, intro. Elijah Anderson (1899; rpt. Philadelphia: University of Pennsylvania Press, 1996), 32–35. For DuBois, the black caterers in nineteenth-century Philadelphia, who had transformed the legacy of domestic service into an independent, reputable, and lucrative profession, constituted "as remarkable a trade guild as ever ruled in a medieval city" (32).

54. Willson, *Sketches*, rpt. as *The Elite of Our People*, 62–63. Gary B. Nash describes a "reciprocal influence" between black popular and high culture in early-nineteenth-century Philadelphia, with the elaborate balls and parties serving as the counterpart to street frolics, in *Forging Freedom: The Formation of Philadelphia's Black Community* (Cambridge, Mass.: Harvard University Press, 1988), 221–23. Levine argues that the parallels between the opening and closing meals suggest continued black oppression, in "Disturbing Boundaries," 367; Golemba sees a movement from illusory racial integration to a "triumph over hardship" and "a secular communion of the American Dream," in "Frank Webb's *The Garies*," 130–32; and Matlock describes a shift from southern domination to northern "communal integrity," in "The Sentimental Novel." Sustained readings of Webb's scenes are rare.

55. Robert S. Levine is the only critic to have remarked on the plantation inheritance, describing it as "a rather chilling blind spot in the text," in "Disturbing Boundaries," 368.

56. Alcée Fortier records a late-nineteenth-century version of the story in *Louisiana Folk-Tales in French Dialect and English Translation* (Boston: Published for the American Folk-Lore Society by Houghton, Mifflin, 1895), 61.

57. Eliza Leslie, *New Receipts for Cooking* (Philadelphia: T. B. Peterson, 1854), 104–5. On Leslie's influential volumes and for a brief biography, see Hines, Gordon, and Weaver, *The Larder Invaded*, 28, 67. My thanks to Margaret Ronda for locating Leslie's recipe and to Ian Thomas-Bignami for cooking it.

58. Stowe, *Uncle Tom's Cabin*, 122.

59. James Fenimore Cooper, *The Pioneers, or the Sources of the Susquehanna; A Descriptive Tale*, ed. James Franklin Beard, Lance Schachterle, and Kenneth M. Andersen Jr. (1823; rpt. Albany: State University of New York Press, 1980), 107–8.

60. Washington Irving, *The Sketch Book of Geoffrey Crayon, Gent.* (1820), vol. 8 of *The Complete Works of Washington Irving*, ed. Haskell Springer (Boston: Twayne, 1978), 279.

61. Norbert Elias, *The Civilizing Process: Sociogenetic and Psychogenetic Investigations* (1939); ed. Eric Dunning, Johan Goodsblom, and Stephen Mennell, trans. Edmund Jephcott (Malden, Mass.: Blackwell, 2000), 102, 104.

62. Bentley argues that James and Wharton, familiar with late-nineteenth-century ethnography, linked table and tribal manners. Wharton "revises and exhibits manners as the essential, sometimes disguised, rites of social cohesion and punishment rather than as inherent standards of propriety"; see Nancy Bentley, *The Ethnography of Manners: Hawthorne, James, Wharton* (New York: Cambridge University Press, 1995). I have quoted from page 2. Webb's *Garies* may be considered a precursor to such late-century analyses of manners, with some important differences. He draws on early sociology (such as the reports on the "condition" of Philadelphia's African American residents and Joseph Willson's *Sketches of the Higher Classes*), rather than tribal ethnography; he is deeply interested in questions of propriety, even as he rejects "inherent standards"; and he ties manners to actual, as well as figurative, violence.

63. Herman Melville, "The Paradise of Bachelors and the Tartarus of Maids" (1855), in *The Piazza Tales and Other Prose Pieces, 1839–1860*, vol. 9 of *The Writings of Herman Melville*, ed. Harrison Hayford, Alma A. MacDougall, G. Thomas Tanselle, et al. (Evanston and Chicago: Northwestern University Press and the Newberry Library, 1987), 327, 322, 323. Melville's narrator resembles Irving's Geoffrey Crayon not only in his banquet inventories but also in his journey to England and portrayal of insular, fraternal extravagance.

64. Petronius, *The Satyricon*, trans. and intro. P. G. Walsh (Oxford: Clarendon, 1996), 21–66; *Erotica: The Elegies of Propertius, The Satyricon of Petronius Arbiter, and The Kisses of Johannes Secundus*, ed. Walter K. Kelley (London: Henry G. Bohn, 1854), 218–79.

65. For examples of Dutch still lifes, see Ingvar Bergström, *Dutch Still-Life Painting in the Seventeenth Century*, trans. Christina Hedström and Gerald Taylor (New York: Thomas Yoseloff, 1956).

66. Alexander Nemerov, *The Body of Raphaelle Peale: Still Life and Selfhood, 1812–1824* (Berkeley: University of California Press, 2001). On the Peale family still lifes, see John I. H. Baur, "The Peales and the Development of American Still Life," *Art Quarterly* 3.1 (Winter 1940): 81–92; E. H. Dwight, "Still Life Paintings by the Peale Family," in *The Peale Family: Three Generations of American Artists*, ed. Charles H. Elam (Detroit: Detroit Institute of Arts, 1967), 35–38; and Brandon Brame Fortune, "A Delicate Balance: Raphaelle Peale's Still-Life Paintings and the Ideal of Temperance," in *The Peale Family: Creation of a Legacy, 1770–1870*, ed. Lillian B. Miller (New York: Abbeville, 1996), 134–49. On Philadelphia as the center of still-life painting in the United States, see Robert Devlin Schwarz, *150 Years of Philadelphia Still-Life Painting* (Philadelphia: Schwarz Gallery, 1997).

67. Frederick Douglass, "The Claims of the Negro Ethnologically Considered" (1854), in *The Frederick Douglass Papers, Series One: Speeches, Debates, and Interviews*, vol. 2, *1847–54*, ed. John W. Blassingame et al. (New Haven, Conn.: Yale University Press, 1982), 497–525; James McCune Smith, "On the Fourteenth Query of Thomas Jefferson's Notes on Virginia" (1859), in *The Works of James McCune Smith, Black Intellectual and Abolitionist*, ed. John Stauffer (New York: Oxford University Press, 2006), 264–81; Harriet A. Jacobs, *Incidents in the Life of a Slave Girl, Written by Herself*, ed. and intro. Jean Fagan Yellin (1861; rpt. Cambridge, Mass.: Harvard University Press, 2000), 201.

68. Rael, *Black Identity and Black Protest*, 283.

69. Werner Sollors, introduction to *Frank J. Webb: Fiction, Essays, Poetry* (New Milford, Conn.: Toby, 2004), 4.

70. For an influential theoretical statement distinguishing between "form and manner" and "substance," which focuses on a contrast between working-class and bourgeois meals, see Pierre Bourdieu, *Distinction: A Social Critique of the Judgement of Taste*, trans. Richard Nice (Cambridge, Mass.: Harvard University Press, 1984), 194–96.

71. *Benito Cereno* was originally published in the October, November, and December 1855 issues of *Putnam's Monthly Magazine.* The differences between this serial publication and the version published in the 1856 *Piazza Tales* are recorded in *The Piazza Tales and Other Prose Pieces*, ed. Harrison Hayford et al., 595–97. The story appears on pages 46–117. I will cite this edition in parentheses when discussing the novella.

72. Melville's works had some currency in African American periodicals in the late 1840s and 1850s: A long excerpt from his first book, *Typee*, was published in Frederick Douglass's *North Star* in 1848, and *Moby-Dick* was quoted by James McCune Smith in an 1856 essay on American politics in *Frederick Douglass's Paper.* See Elizabeth McHenry, *Forgotten Readers: Recovering the Lost History of African American Literary Societies* (Durham, N.C.: Duke University Press, 2002), 123, and Stauffer, ed., *The Works of James McCune Smith*, 143–48.

73. Amasa Delano, *A Narrative of Voyages and Travels in the Northern and Southern Hemispheres: Comprising Three Voyages round the World; Together with a Voyage of Survey and Discovery, in the Pacific Ocean and Oriental Islands* (1817); chapter 18 is reproduced in facsimile in *Piazza Tales and Other Prose Pieces, 1839–1860*, ed. Hayford et al., 810–47. I have quoted from page 817. Melville may have read either the first (1817) or second (1818) printing of Delano's book. Lea Bertani Vozar Newman lists Melville's changes to Delano's chapter 18 in *A Reader's Guide to the Short Stories of Herman Melville* (Boston: G. K. Hall, 1986), 98–100.

74. Leslie A. Fiedler, *Love and Death in the American Novel* (New York: Criterion, 1960), 383. On Melville's distance from his African characters, see F. O. Matthiessen, *American Renaissance: Art and Expression in the Age of Emerson and Whitman* (New York: Oxford University Press, 1941), 507–8; Gerald Early, *Tuxedo Junction: Essays on American Culture* (New York: Ecco, 1989), 215–30; Robert S. Levine, *Conspiracy and Romance: Studies in Brockden Brown, Cooper, Hawthorne, and Melville* (New York: Cambridge University Press, 1989), 210–23; Eric J. Sundquist, *To Wake the Nations: Race in the Making of American Literature* (Cambridge, Mass.: Harvard University Press, 1993), 175–82; Dana D. Nelson, *The Word in Black and White: Reading "Race" in American Literature, 1638–1867* (New York: Oxford University Press, 1993), 123–30, and her revised argument in *National Manhood: Capitalist Citizenship and the Imagined Fraternity of White Men* (Durham, N.C.: Duke University Press, 1998), 197–203; and Maggie Montesinos Sale, *The Slumbering Volcano: American Slave Ship Revolts and the Production of Rebellious Masculinity* (Durham, N.C.: Duke University Press, 1997), 161–72. On Melville's rhetoric, see Carolyn L. Karcher, *Shadow over the Promised Land: Slavery, Race, and Violence in Melville's America* (Baton Rouge: Louisiana State University Press, 1980), 131–34; Eric J. Sundquist, "Suspense and Tautology in *Benito Cereno*," *Glyph* 8 (1981): 103–26; and Philip Fisher, *Still the New World: American Literature in a Culture of Creative Destruction* (Cambridge, Mass.: Harvard University Press, 1999), 105–10. On the power of irony,

see Marvin Fisher, *Going Under: Melville's Short Fiction and the American 1850s* (Baton Rouge: Louisiana State University Press, 1977), 104–17; Charles Swann, "Whodunit? Or, Who Did What? *Benito Cereno* and the Politics of Narrative Structure," in *American Studies in Transition,* ed. David E. Nye and Christen Kold Thomsen (Odense, Denmark: Odense University Press, 1985), 199–234, and "*Benito Cereno:* Melville's De(con)struction of the Southern Reader," *Literature and History* 12 (1986): 3–15; James H. Kavanagh, "That Hive of Subtlety: 'Benito Cereno' and the Liberal Hero," in *Ideology and Classic American Literature,* ed. Sacvan Bercovitch and Myra Jehlen (New York: Cambridge University Press, 1986), 352–83; James Duban, "Chipping with a Chisel: The Ideology of Melville's Narrators," *Texas Studies in Literature and Language* 31.3 (Fall 1989): 341–85; and H. Bruce Franklin, "Past, Present, and Future Seemed One," in *Critical Essays on Melville's Benito Cereno,* ed. Robert Burkholder (New York: G. K. Hall, 1992), 230–46. On the limits of irony, see Sundquist, "Suspense and Tautology"; Levine, *Conspiracy and Romance,* 165–230; Charles Martin and James Snead, "Reading through Blackness: Colorless Signifiers in *Benito Cereno,*" *Yale Journal of Criticism* 4.1 (Fall 1990): 231–51; Sale, *Slumbering Volcano,* 146–72; Paul Downes, "Melville's *Benito Cereno* and the Politics of Humanitarian Intervention," *South Atlantic Quarterly* 103:2/3 (Spring/Summer 2004): 465–88; and Jonathan Elmer, "Babo's Razor; or, Discerning the Event in an Age of Differences," *Differences: A Journal of Feminist Cultural Studies* 19.2 (2008): 54–81.

75. "Fever" makes an appearance in *Benito Cereno,* when Cereno, only nominally in command, falsely and anxiously explains to the visiting Delano that so many more whites than blacks had perished on his ship as a result of the differential effects of "scurvy and fever": "He made random reference to the different constitution of races, enabling one to offer more resistance to certain maladies than another" (90).

76. The shift from "Spaniards" to "whites" and "Spanish" to "white" is documented in *Piazza Tales,* ed. Hayford et al., 80, 98, 596. Melville probably was responsible for the changes, since they are rhetorical.

77. Among the few critics who take account of the comic aspects of the story are Sundquist, "Suspense and Tautology," 114–15, and Kavanagh, "That Hive of Subtlety," 363.

78. For Higginson's memories of Douglass's encounter with the New York political organizer Isaiah Rynders, see his *American Orators and Oratory: Being a Report of Lectures Delivered by Thomas Wentworth Higginson, at Western Reserve University* (Cleveland, Ohio: Imperial, 1901), 87–89. Robert K. Wallace speculates that Melville may have known about or even witnessed the event; see his *Douglass and Melville: Anchored Together in Neighborly Style* (New Bedford, Mass.: Spinner, 2005), 111–14.

79. "Speech of Rev. T. W. Higginson," *Liberator* (May 28, 1858): 22.

80. Cyprian Clamorgan, *The Colored Aristocracy of St. Louis,* ed. and intro. Julie Winch (1858; rpt. Columbia: University of Missouri Press, 1999), 52.

81. On Melville's shaving scene, see Sundquist, "Suspense and Tautology," 112–20, and *To Wake the Nations,* 158–63; and William Bartley, "'The Creature of His Own Tasteful Hands': Herman Melville's 'Benito Cereno' and the 'Empire of Might,'" *Modern Philology* 93.4 (May 1996): 460–64.

82. Sundquist, "Suspense and Tautology," 118, 119; *To Wake the Nations*, 138; see also Michael Paul Rogin, *Subversive Genealogy: The Politics and Art of Herman Melville* (New York: Alfred A. Knopf, 1983): "The shaving 'play' . . . is finally so disturbing . . . not because Babo controls the blade but because he cannot use it" (217).

83. I have quoted key terms from Sundquist, "Suspense and Tautology"; Kavanagh, "That Hive of Subtlety," 359; Levine, *Conspiracy and Romance*, 223; Nelson, *Word in Black and White*, 110; and Fisher, *Still the New World*, 102.

84. William Bartley analyzes Babo's "intimate attention to small details . . . a tenderness, a minuteness of passionate surveillance that overwhelms imposture," in "'The Creature of His Own Tasteful Hands,'" 464–65.

85. Frantz Fanon, *The Wretched of the Earth* (1961); trans. Constance Farrington (New York: Grove, 1963), 29–83; see also Edward W. Said, *Culture and Imperialism* (New York: Vintage, 1994), 266–71. On Babo as author and artist, see Sundquist, "Suspense and Tautology," 109–12, 122–25, and *To Wake the Nations*, 150–51, 181–82; Bartley, "'The Creature of His Own Tasteful Hands,'" 460–66; and Downes, "*Benito Cereno* and the Politics of Humanitarian Intervention," 476–83. Both Sundquist and Downes analyze the Babo-like aspects of Melville's narrator.

86. Melville writes in *Benito Cereno*: "Upon gaining that vicinity, might not the San Dominick, like a slumbering volcano, suddenly let loose energies now hid?" (68); Frederick Douglass, "Slavery, The Slumbering Volcano: An Address Delivered in New York, New York, on 23 April 1849," in *The Frederick Douglass Papers, Series One: Speeches, Debates, and Interviews*, vol. 2, *1847–54*, ed. John W. Blassingame et al. (New Haven, Conn.: Yale University Press, 1982), 148–58. Douglass's speech was reprinted in 1849 in the *National Anti-Slavery Standard*, the *Pennsylvania Freeman*, the *Liberator*, and the *North Star*. See also his poem "The Tyrants' Jubilee!" line 113: "The pathway of tyrants lies over volcanoes." The poem appeared in *Frederick Douglass' Paper* (January 16, 1857): 2 and is reprinted in William Gleason, "Volcanoes and Meteors: Douglass, Melville, and the Poetics of Insurrection," in *Frederick Douglass and Herman Melville: Essays in Relation*, ed. Robert S. Levine and Samuel Otter (Chapel Hill: University of North Carolina Press, 2008), 127–30. I have noted Henry James's invocation in the Philadelphia section of *The American Scene*; see chapter 3. Gleason explains that the metaphor of the volcano was used by some observers, such as William Lloyd Garrison, to describe slaveholders' dangerous appetites; by others, such as Douglass, to warn of black insurrection and white psychic upheaval; and by others to portray the unstable system of slavery itself (119). See also Sale, *Slumbering Volcano*. The image is at the center of Melville's 1866 Civil War poem about ruptured surfaces, "The Apparition (A Retrospect.)": "So, then, Solidity's a crust—/The core of fire below." See *Published Poems: Battle-Pieces, John Marr, Timoleon*, vol. 11 of *The Writings of Herman Melville*, ed. Robert C. Ryan, Harrison Hayford, Alma MacDougall Reising, and G. Thomas Tanselle (Evanston and Chicago: Northwestern University Press and the Newberry Library, 2009), 116. The trope of the slumbering volcano may have as one of its sources the compound of sin, guilt, and threat figured in such sermons as Jonathan Edwards's "Sinners in the Hands of an Angry God": "Unconverted men walk over the pit of hell on a rotten covering, and there are innumerable places in this covering so weak

340 Notes to Pages 276–281

that they won't bear their weight, and these places are not seen." See Jonathan Edwards, *Sermons and Discourses, 1739–1742,* ed. Harry S. Stout and Nathan O. Hatch (New Haven: Yale University Press, 2003), 407.

87. Fisher, *Still the New World,* 102. Although I have a different sense of the freedom portrayed in Melville's novel from the "listlessness and paralysis" described by Fisher, he captures the unusual temporality of *Benito Cereno,* which superimposes the past on the future to describe a present as though in aftermath. Paul Downes analyzes the "economy of vulnerability" in *Benito Cereno*: "Melville's Delano is followed throughout his adventure by the disembodied narrative presence of a consciousness that, in retrospect, if not at once, reveals itself to be continually aware of the precariousness of his situation"; see "*Benito Cereno* and the Politics of Humanitarian Intervention," 480, 476.

88. For the Forten, Grimké, and Whipper citations, see chapter 2 of this book. For other instances in which writers invoke the foot on the neck, see David Paul Brown's "Oration" and John Pierpont's poem "The Tocsin," collected in *The History of Pennsylvania Hall* (Philadelphia: Merrihew and Gunn, 1838), 15, 171, and "An Appeal to the Colored Citizens of Pennsylvania," issued by the 1848 Harrisburg "Convention of the Coloured Citizens of Pennsylvania," in *Proceedings of the Black State Conventions, 1840–1865,* ed. Philip S. Foner and George E. Walker (Philadelphia: Temple University Press, 1979), 1:132. In fashioning his stern piece and the image of Delano overpowering Babo, Melville may have had in mind the alabaster carvings at the Hôtel de Cluny in Paris, which he visited during an 1849 trip. In these carvings, Christ emerges from his tomb and steps with his right foot on the prostrate body of a Roman soldier. See Andrew Delbanco, *Melville: His World and Work* (New York: Alfred A. Knopf, 2005), 239–40. With its vertiginous masquerades, *Benito Cereno* might be seen as a forerunner of such twentieth-century racial satires as Jean Genet's *The Blacks: A Clown Show* (1960), Brian DePalma's film *Hi, Mom* (1970), Ishmael Reed's novel *Flight to Canada* (1976), the history paintings of Robert Colescott, and the silhouettes of Kara Walker.

Coda

1. Owen Wister, *Romney and Other New Works about Philadelphia,* ed. James A. Butler (University Park, Pa.: Pennsylvania State University Press, 2001), 28; Thomas Pynchon, *Mason & Dixon* (New York: Henry Holt, 1997), 258. Carlo Rotella surveys Philadelphia's postwar "South Street literature" in *October Cities: The Redevelopment of Urban Literature* (Berkeley: University of California Press, 1998), 119–201.

2. On MOVE and Philadelphia, see John Anderson and Hilary Hevenor, *Burning Down the House: MOVE and the Tragedy of Philadelphia* (New York: W. W. Norton, 1987), and Robin Wagner-Pacifici, *Discourse and Destruction: The City of Philadelphia versus MOVE* (Chicago: University of Chicago Press, 1994). Describing John Africa in his novel *Two Cities* (1998), Wideman avoids popular caricature and official reproach. See John Edgar Wideman, *Two Cities* (Houghton Mifflin, 1998), 6–13, 216–18, 227–33.

3. Wideman talks about his interest in the yellow fever epidemic of 1793 and his attempts to write about it in a 1996 interview conducted by Laura Miller; see "The

Salon Interview: John Edgar Wideman," at www.salonmag.com/nov96/interview961111. html. He discusses 1793 and 1985 in the exchange with Miller and in a 1989 interview with Charles H. Rowell and a 1995 interview with Arnold E. Sabatelli, collected in *Conversations with John Edgar Wideman*, ed. Bonnie TuSmith (Jackson: University Press of Mississippi, 1998), 99–100, 147–48. The other U.S. city that absorbs Wideman's concern as a writer is Pittsburgh, and especially the predominantly African American neighborhood of Homewood, where he spent most of the first twelve years of his life. See Wideman's trilogy *Hiding Place* (1981), *Damballah* (1981), and *Sent for You Yesterday* (1983). Pittsburgh and Philadelphia are superimposed in his 1998 novel *Two Cities*, which, like *Philadelphia Fire*, is concerned with the MOVE events. Wideman's fictional inquiries into race and history come with a personal edge and often include autobiographical details, as he reflects upon his own position as an African American writer and academic and the life sentences being served in prison by his brother and his son. In 1975, Wideman's brother Robert was convicted of murder for his role in an armed robbery during which a man was shot to death. Wideman's sixteen-year-old son, Jacob, was convicted of stabbing and killing a friend while on a camping trip in 1986. His nephew Omar was murdered in Pittsburgh in 1993. Wideman confronts family history in *Brothers and Keepers* (New York: Holt, Rinehart and Winston, 1984) and *Fatheralong: A Meditation on Fathers and Sons, Race and Society* (New York: Pantheon, 1994).

4. John Edgar Wideman, "Fever," in *Fever: Twelve Stories* (New York: Henry Holt, 1989), 160–61, 127, 163. Subsequent references will be given parenthetically.

5. Wideman discusses the "ogbanje" in "'It Was Like Meeting an Old Friend': An Interview with John Edgar Wideman," by Chris Okonkwo, *Callaloo* 29.2 (Spring 2006): 347–60.

6. John Edgar Wideman, *Philadelphia Fire* (New York: Henry Holt, 1990), 8, 97. Subsequent references will be given parenthetically. On MOVE in *Philadelphia Fire*, see Madhu Dubey, "Literature and Urban Crisis: John Edgar Wideman's *Philadelphia Fire*," *African American Review* 32.4 (Winter 1998): 579–95. On the Xhosa slaughter, see J. B. Peires, *The Dead Will Arise: Nongqawuse and the Great Xhosa Cattle-Killing Movement of 1856–7* (Bloomington: Indiana University Press, 1989). The stock already had been diminished by an infection caught from British herds.

7. Wideman describes the "archetypal configuration" in his Salon.com interview with Laura Miller. He discusses Richard Allen as a model for his preacher in *The Cattle Killing* in a 1996 interview with Derek McGinty; see *Conversations with Wideman*, ed. TuSmith, 185–86.

8. Lisa Lynch compares "Fever" and *The Cattle Killing* in "The Fever Next Time: The Race of Disease and the Disease of Racism in John Edgar Wideman," *American Literary History* 14.4 (Winter 2002): 776–804. Benjamin Rush appears as a character in "Fever" and is a source for "Benjamin Thrush" in *The Cattle Killing*. In this novel, Wideman includes passages from Rush's actual letters written during the 1793 epidemic. The year 1793 in Philadelphia is resonant for Wideman because of the yellow fever and also because of the events that preceded it: the first balloon ascent from American soil, in January, which began in the yard of the Walnut Street jail; the breaking of ground for St. Thomas's

Episcopal, the first African church, in March; and the roof-raising ceremony in August, when blacks and whites alternately served one another, while the fever began to spread. These events, in sequence and various amalgams, recur in Wideman's Philadelphia fiction. He gathers many of the references in the few pages of his "Ascent by Balloon from the Yard of Walnut Street Jail," *Callaloo* 19.1 (Winter 1996): 1–5.

9. John Edgar Wideman, *The Cattle Killing* (New York: Houghton Mifflin, 1996), 35. Subsequent references will be given parenthetically.

10. For briefer mentions of the grid in Wideman's fiction, see "Fever," 138, and "Ascent by Balloon," 3.

BIBLIOGRAPHY

Primary Sources

Abdy, Edward S. *Journal of a Residence and Tour in the United States of North America, from April, 1833, to October, 1834.* Vol. 3. London: John Murray, 1835.

Allen, Richard, et al. "Address to the Free People of Colour of These United States." 1830. In "Constitution of the American Society of Free Persons of Colour, for Improving Their Condition in the United States; for Purchasing Lands; and for the Establishment of a Settlement in Upper Canada. Also the Proceedings of the Convention, with Their Address to the Free Persons of Colour in the United States." Reprinted in *Minutes of the Proceedings of the National Negro Conventions, 1830–1864.* Edited by Howard Holman Bell, 9–12. New York: Arno Press and the New York Times, 1969.

————. "Confession of John Joyce, alias Davis, Who Was Executed on Monday, the 14th of March, 1808, for the Murder of Mrs. Sarah Cross; with an Address to the Public, and People of Colour, Together with the Substance of the Trial and the Address of Chief Justice Tilghman, on His Condemnation." Philadelphia: Printed for the Benefit of the Bethel Church, 1808.

————. "Confession of Peter Matthias, alias Mathews, Who Was Executed on Monday, the 14th of March, 1808, for the Murder of Mrs. Sarah Cross; with an Address to the Public, and People of Colour, Together with the Substance of the Trial and the Address of Chief Justice Tilghman, on His Condemnation." Philadelphia: Printed for the Benefit of the Bethel Church, 1808.

Bacon, Benjamin C. "Statistics of the Colored People of Philadelphia. Taken by Benjamin C. Bacon, and Published by Order of the Board of Education of 'The Pennsylvania Society for Promoting the Abolition of Slavery,' etc." Philadelphia: T. Ellwood Chapman, 1856.

Banneker, Benjamin. "Banneker's Almanac for the Year 1795: Being the Third after Leap Year. Containing (Besides Every Thing Necessary in an Almanac,) An Account of the Yellow Fever, Lately Prevalent in Philadelphia, with the Number of Those Who Died, from the First of August till the Ninth of November, 1793." Philadelphia: William Young, 1793.

Bell, Howard Holman, ed. *Minutes of the Proceedings of the National Negro Conventions, 1830–1864.* New York: Arno Press and the New York Times, 1969.

———. *A Survey of the Negro Convention Movement, 1830–1861.* 1953. New York: Arno Press and The New York Times, 1969.

Bird, Robert Montgomery. *The Adventures of Robin Day.* Philadelphia: Lea and Blanchard, 1839.

———. *The City Looking Glass: A Philadelphia Comedy in Five Acts.* 1828. Edited by Arthur Hobson Quinn. New York: Colophon, 1933.

———. *Nick of the Woods, or The Jibbenainosay. A Tale of Kentucky.* 1837. Edited by Curtis Dahl. New Haven, Conn: College and University Press, 1967.

———. *Sheppard Lee, Written By Himself.* 1836. Introduction by Christopher Looby. New York: New York Review of Books, 2008.

Brackenridge, Hugh Henry. *Modern Chivalry.* 1792–1815. Edited by Claude M. Newlin. New York: Hafner, 1968.

———. "Thoughts on the Enfranchisement of the Negroes." 1779. Excerpted in *A Hugh Henry Brackenridge Reader, 1770–1885.* Edited by Daniel Marder, 103–4. Pittsburgh: University of Pittsburgh Press, 1970.

Brown, Charles Brockden. *Address to the Government of the United States, on the Cession of Louisiana to the French.* Philadelphia: John Conrad, 1803.

———. *Arthur Mervyn; or Memoirs of the Year 1793.* 1799–1800. Vol. 3 of *The Novels and Related Works of Charles Brockden Brown.* Edited by Sydney J. Krause and S. W. Reid. Kent, Ohio: Kent State University Press, 1980.

———. *Ormond; or, the Secret Witness.* 1799. Edited by Mary Chapman. Peterborough, Ontario: Broadview, 1999.

———. *The Rhapsodist and Other Uncollected Writings.* Edited by Harry R. Warfel. New York: Scholars' Facsimiles and Reprints, 1943.

Brown, Henry Box. *Narrative of the Life of Henry Box Brown, Written by Himself.* 1851. Edited by John Ernest. Chapel Hill: University of North Carolina Press, 2008.

Caldwell, Charles. *Autobiography of Charles Caldwell.* Philadelphia: Lippincott, Grambo, 1855.

Carey, Mathew. "Address of M. Carey to the Public." Philadelphia: Matthew Clark, 1794.

———. *Autobiography.* 1833–34. New York: Research Classics, 1942.

———. *A Brief Account of the Malignant Fever Which Prevailed in Philadelphia, in the Year 1793: with a Statement of Proceedings That Took Place on the Subject, in Different Parts of the United States, Fifth Edition, Improved.* Philadelphia: Clark and Raser, 1830.

———. "A Desultory Account of the Yellow Fever, Prevalent in Philadelphia, and of the Present State of the City." Philadelphia: Mathew Carey, 1793.

———. *A Short Account of the Malignant Fever, Lately Prevalent in Philadelphia: with a Statement of the Proceedings That Took Place on the Subject in Different Parts of the United States.* 4 editions. Philadelphia: Mathew Carey, November 14, 23, 30, 1793; January 16, 1794.

Chester, T. Morris Chester. "Negro Self-Respect and Pride of Race, Delivered at the Twenty-Ninth Anniversary of the Philadelphia Library Company, December 9, 1862."

Reprinted in *Pamphlets of Protest: An Anthology of Early African American Protest Literature, 1790–1860.* Edited by Richard Newman, Patrick Rael, and Phillip Lapsansky, 304–10. New York: Routledge, 2001.

Clamorgan, Cyprian. *The Colored Aristocracy of St. Louis.* 1858. Edited by Julie Winch. Columbia: University of Missouri Press, 1999.

Coates, Benjamin H. "On the Effects of Secluded and Gloomy Imprisonment on Individuals of the African Variety of Mankind, in the Production of Disease." Philadelphia: John C. Clark, 1843.

Cooper, James Fenimore. *Notions of the Americans: Picked Up by a Travelling Bachelor.* 1828. Edited by Gary Williams. Albany: State University of New York Press, 1991.

———. *The Pioneers, or the Sources of the Susquehanna; A Descriptive Tale.* 1823. Edited by James Franklin Beard, Lance Schachterle, and Kenneth M. Andersen Jr. Albany: State University of New York Press, 1980.

Cornish, Samuel E. "Moral Reform Convention." *Colored American,* August 26, 1837.

———. "Our Brethren in the Free States." *Colored American,* April 22, 1837.

———. Response to William Whipper. *Colored American,* March 29, 1838.

———. "Responsibility of Colored People in the Free States." March 4, 1837. Reprinted in *The Black Abolitionist Papers.* Vol. 3, *The United States, 1830–1846.* Edited by C. Peter Ripley et al., 219–20. Chapel Hill: University of North Carolina Press, 1991.

Crèvecoeur, J. Hector St. Jean de. *Letters from an American Farmer.* 1782. Edited by Albert E. Stone. New York: Penguin, 1981.

[Currie, William.] "Respecting Dr. Rush's Conduct and Transactions during the Prevalence of the Malignant Fever of 1793." *Gazette of the United States and Philadelphia Daily Advertiser,* October 6, 1797.

Davis, Samuel H. "Address." 1843. In "Minutes of the National Convention of Colored Citizens: Held at Buffalo, on the 15th, 16th 17th, 18th, and 19th of August 1843." Reprinted in *Minutes of the Proceedings of the National Negro Conventions, 1830–1864.* Edited by Howard Holman Bell, 4–7. New York: Arno Press and The New York Times, 1969.

Delany, Martin Robison. *The Condition, Elevation, Emigration, and Destiny of the Colored People of the United States.* 1852. Edited by Toyin Falola. Amherst, N.Y.: Humanity Books, 2002.

Denny, John F. *An Enquiry into the Political Grade of the Free Coloured Population, under the Constitution of the United States, and the Constitution of Pennsylvania: in Three Parts. By a Member of the Chambersburg Bar.* Chambersburg, Pa.: J. Pritts, 1834.

Dickens, Charles. *American Notes for General Circulation.* 1842. Edited by Patricia Ingham. New York: Penguin, 2000.

Dickinson, Anna E. *What Answer?* 1868. Amherst, N.Y.: Humanity Books, 2003.

Douglass, Frederick. "The Black Man's Future in the Southern States: An Address Delivered in Boston, Massachusetts, on 5 February 1862." 1862. Reprinted in *The Frederick Douglass Papers, Series One: Speeches, Debates, and Interviews.* Vol. 3, *1855–63.* Edited by John Blassingame et al., 489–508. New Haven, Conn.: Yale University Press, 1985.

———. "The Claims of the Negro Ethnologically Considered." 1854. Reprinted in *The Frederick Douglass Papers, Series One: Speeches, Debates, and Interviews.* Vol. 2, *1847–54.* Edited by John W. Blassingame et al., 497–525. New Haven, Conn.: Yale University Press, 1982.

———. "Colorphobia in New York!" 1849. Reprinted in *Frederick Douglass: Selected Speeches and Writings*. Edited by Philip S. Foner and Yuval Taylor, 141–43. Chicago: Lawrence Hill, 1999.

———. "Learn Trades or Starve." 1852. Reprinted in *The Life and Writings of Frederick Douglass*. Vol. 2, *Pre–Civil War Decade*. Edited by Philip S. Foner, 223–25. New York: International Publishers, 1950.

———, Alexander Crummell, John Lyle, and Thomas Van Rensselaer. "Report of the Committee on Abolition." 1847. In "Proceedings of the National Convention of Colored People and Their Friends, Held in Troy, N. Y., on the 6th, 7th, 8th, and 9th October 1847." Reprinted in *Minutes of the Proceedings of the National Negro Conventions, 1830–1864*. Edited by Howard Holman Bell, 31–32. New York: Arno Press and The New York Times, 1969.

———. "Slavery, the Slumbering Volcano: An Address Delivered in New York, New York, on 23 April 1849." 1849. Reprinted in *The Frederick Douglass Papers, Series One: Speeches, Debates, and Interviews*. Vol. 2, *1847–54*. Edited by John W. Blassingame et al., 148–58. New Haven, Conn.: Yale University Press, 1982.

———. "Visit to Philadelphia." *The North Star*, October 13, 1848.

DuBois, W. E. B. *Dusk of Dawn: An Essay toward an Autobiography of a Race Concept*. 1940. New York: Schocken, 1968.

———. *The Philadelphia Negro: A Social Study*. 1899. Edited by Elijah Anderson. Philadelphia: University of Pennsylvania Press, 1996.

———. *Writings: The Suppression of the African Slave-Trade, The Souls of Black Folk, Dusk of Dawn, Essays*. Edited by Nathan Huggins. New York: Library of America, 1987.

Early American Book Illustrators and Wood Engravers, 1670–1870: A Catalogue of a Collection of American Books Illustrated for the Most Part with Woodcuts and Wood Engravings in the Princeton University Library. Introduction by Sinclair Hamilton. Princeton, N.J.: Princeton University Library, 1958.

Dunlap, William. *The Life of Charles Brockden Brown: Together with Selections from the Rarest of His Printed Works, from His Original Letters, and from His Manuscripts before Unpublished*. 2 Vols. Philadelphia: James P. Parke, 1815.

Edwards, Jonathan. "Sinners in the Hands of an Angry God." 1841. Reprinted in *Sermons and Discourses, 1739–1742*. Vol. 22 of *The Works of Jonathan Edwards*. Edited by Harry S. Stout and Nathan O. Hatch, 400–18. New Haven: Yale University Press, 2003.

A Familiar Exposition of the Constitution of Pennsylvania: For the Use of Schools and for the People. Philadelphia: Uriah Hunt, 1840.

"The Fate of Murderers: A Faithful Narrative of the Murder of Mrs. Sarah Cross, with the Trial, Sentence and Confession of John Joyce and Peter Mathias, Who Were Executed Near Philadelphia on Monday 14, March 1808." Philadelphia: Printed for the Purchasers, 1808.

Foner, Philip, and George E. Walker, eds. *Proceedings of the Black State Conventions, 1840–1865*. 2 Vols. Philadelphia: Temple University Press, 1979, 1980.

Forten, James, Jr. "An Address Delivered before the American Moral Reform Society, Philadelphia, August 17th, 1837." Reprinted in *Early Negro Writing, 1760–1837.* Edited by Dorothy Porter, 225–41. 1971. Baltimore: Black Classic Press, 1995.

Fortier, Alcée, ed. *Louisiana Folk-Tales in French Dialect and English Translation.* Boston: Published for the American Folk-Lore Society by Houghton, Mifflin, 1895.

Foster, George G. *New York by Gas-Light.* 1850. Reprinted in *New York by Gas-Light and Other Urban Sketches.* Edited by Stuart M. Blumin. Berkeley: University of California Press, 1990.

———. "Philadelphia in Slices." 1848–49. Reprinted in *Pennsylvania Magazine of History and Biography* 93.1 (January 1969): 22–72.

Franklin, Benjamin. *Autobiography.* Edited by J. A. Leo Lemay and P. M. Zall. New York: W. W. Norton, 1986.

Freneau, Philip. *Poems Written between the Years 1768 & 1794: A New Edition, Revised and Corrected by the Author.* Monmouth, N. J.: Printed at the Press of the Author, 1795.

Godwin, William. *The Adventures of Caleb Williams.* 1794. Edited by Maurice Hindle. London: Penguin, 1988.

"*The Garies.*" Review in London *Sunday Times*, September 27, 1857.

"*The Garies and Their Friends.*" Review in London *Daily News*, October 9, 1857; reprinted in *Frederick Douglass' Paper*, December 4, 1858.

"*The Garies and Their Friends.*" Review in London *Athenaeum*, October 24, 1857.

Grimké, Charlotte Forten. *Journals of Charlotte Forten Grimke.* Edited by Brenda Stevenson. New York: Oxford University Press, 1988.

Grimké, Sarah. "Letter II: Woman Subject Only to God." 1838. Reprinted in *Letters on the Equality of the Sexes, and the Condition of Women.* Edited by Elizabeth Ann Bartlett, 34–37. New Haven, Conn.: Yale University Press, 1988.

Hale, Sarah Josepha. *Liberia; or, Mr. Peyton's Experiments.* 1853. Upper Saddle River, N.J.: Gregg, 1968.

Hall, Mrs. Basil. *The Aristocratic Journey: Being the Outspoken Letters of Mrs. Basil Hall, Written during a Fourteen Months' Sojourn in America, 1827–1828.* Edited by Una Pope-Hennessy. New York: Knickerbocker Press, 1931.

Hamilton, Thomas. *Men and Manners in America.* 1833. New York: Augustus M. Kelley, 1968.

[Hardie, James.] "An Account of the Rise, Progress, and Termination of the Malignant Fever, Lately Prevalent in Philadelphia. Briefly Stated from Authentic Documents." Philadelphia: Benjamin Johnson, 1793.

Hawthorne, Nathaniel. *The Marble Faun: or, The Romance of Monte Beni.* 1860. Vol. 4 of *The Centenary Edition of the Works of Nathaniel Hawthorne.* Edited by William Charvat et al. Columbus: Ohio State University Press, 1968.

Helmuth, J. Henry C. "A Short Account of the Yellow Fever in Philadelphia, for the Reflecting Christian." Translated by Charles Erdmann. Philadelphia: Jones, Hoff, and Derrick, 1794.

Hugo, Victor. Preface to *Cromwell.* 1827. Excerpted in *European Literature from Romanticism to Postmodernism: A Reader in Aesthetic Practice.* Edited and translated by Martin Travers, 45–47. New York: Continuum, 2001.

Higginson, Thomas Wentworth. *American Orators and Oratory: Being a Report of Lectures Delivered by Thomas Wentworth Higginson, at Western Reserve University.* Cleveland: Imperial, 1901.

Irving, Washington. *The Sketch-Book of Geoffrey Crayon, Gent.* 1820. Vol. 8 of *The Complete Works of Washington Irving.* Edited by Haskell Springer. Boston: Twayne, 1978.

Jacobs, Harriet A. *Incidents in the Life of a Slave Girl, Written By Herself.* 1861. Edited by Jean Fagan Yellin. 2nd ed. Cambridge, Mass.: Harvard University Press, 2000.

James, Henry. *The American Scene.* 1907. In *Collected Travel Writings: Great Britain and America.* Edited by Richard Howard, 351–736. New York: Library of America, 1993.

———. *Hawthorne.* 1879. Edited by Dan McCall. Ithaca, N.Y.: Cornell University Press, 1997.

Jefferson, Thomas. *Notes on the State of Virginia.* 1787. Edited by William Peden. Chapel Hill: University of North Carolina Press, 1982.

Johnstone, Abraham. "The Address of Abraham Johnstone, A Black Man, Who Was Hanged at Woodbury, in the County of Glocester, and State of New Jersey, on Saturday the 8th Day of July Last; To the People of Colour. To which Is Added His Dying Confession or Declaration; Also a Copy of a Letter to His Wife, Written the Day Previous to the Execution." Philadelphia: Printed for the Purchasers, 1797.

Jones, Absalom, and Richard Allen. "A Narrative of the Proceedings of the Black People, during the Late Awful Calamity in Philadelphia, in the Year 1793: and A Refutation of Some Censures, Thrown upon Them in Some Late Publications." 1794. In *Negro Protest Pamphlets.* Edited by Dorothy Porter, 1–24. New York: Arno Press and the New York Times, 1969.

Jones, John Beauchamp. *The City Merchant; or, The Mysterious Failure.* Philadelphia: Lippincott, Grambo, 1851.

Leland, Charles Godfrey. *Memoirs.* New York: D. Appleton, 1893.

Leslie, Eliza. *New Receipts for Cooking.* Philadelphia: T. B. Peterson, 1854.

Lippard, George. *The Bank Director's Son, a Real and Intensely Interesting Revelation of City Life. Containing an Authentic Account of the Wonderful Escape of the Beautiful Kate Watson, from a Flaming Building in the City of Philadelphia.* Philadelphia: E. E. Barclay and A. R. Orton, 1851.

———. "Eleanor; or, Slave Catching in the Quaker City." Philadelphia *Sunday Mercury,* January 29–March 12, 1854.

———. *The Empire City; or, New York by Night and Day, Its Aristocracy and Its Dollars.* 1850. Philadelphia: T. B. Peterson, 1864.

———. *George Lippard, Prophet of Protest: Writings of an American Radical, 1822–1854.* Edited by David S. Reynolds. New York: Peter Lang, 1986.

———. *The Life and Adventures of Charles Anderson Chester, the Notorious Leader of the Philadelphia Killers, Who Was Murdered, While Engaged in the Destruction of the California House, on Election Night, October 11, 1849.* Philadelphia: Yates and Smith, 1850.

———. *The Killers. A Narrative of Real Life in Philadelphia, in Which the Deeds of the Killers, and the Great Riot of Election Night, October 10, 1849, are Minutely Described. Also, the Adventures of Three Notorious Individuals, Who Took Part in That Riot, to Wit: Cromwell D. Z. Hicks, the Leader of the Killers, Don Jorge, One of the Leaders of the Cuban Expedition, and "The Bulgine," the Celebrated Negro Desperado of Moyamensing.* Philadelphia: Hankinson and Bartholomew, 1850.

―――. *The Nazarene; or, The Last of the Washingtons, A Revelation of Philadelphia, New York, and Washington, in the Year 1844.* Philadelphia: G. Lippard, 1846.

―――. *The Quaker City; or, the Monks of Monk Hall: A Romance of Philadelphia Life, Mystery, and Crime.* 1845. Edited by David S. Reynolds. Amherst: University of Massachusetts Press, 1995.

[Lovell, Laura.] "Report of a Delegate to the Anti-Slavery Convention of American Women, Held in Philadelphia, May, 1838; Including an Account of Other Meetings Held In Pennsylvania Hall, and of the Riot. Addressed to the Fall River Female Anti-Slavery Society, and Published by Its Request." Boston: I. Knapp, 1838.

Marryat, Frederick. *A Diary in America, with Remarks on Its Institutions.* 1839. Edited by Sydney Jackman. New York: Alfred A. Knopf, 1962.

Melville, Herman. *Battle-Pieces and Aspects of the War.* 1866. In *Published Poems: Battle-Pieces, John Marr, Timoleon. Vol.* 11 of *The Writings of Herman Melville.* Edited by Robert C. Ryan, Harrison Hayford, Alma MacDougall Reising, and G. Thomas Tanselle, 1–188. Evanston and Chicago: Northwestern University Press and the Newberry Library, 2009.

―――. *The Confidence-Man: His Masquerade.* 1857. Vol. 10 of *The Writings of Herman Melville.* Edited by Harrison Hayford, Hershel Parker, and G. Thomas Tanselle. Evanston and Chicago: Northwestern University Press and the Newberry Library, 1984.

―――. *The Piazza Tales and Other Prose Pieces, 1839–1860.* Vol. 9 of *The Writings of Herman Melville.* Edited by Harrison Hayford, Alma A. MacDougall, G. Thomas Tanselle, et al. Evanston and Chicago: Northwestern University Press and the Newberry Library, 1987.

"Memorial of Thirty Thousand Disfranchised Citizens of Philadelphia to the Honorable Senate and House of Representatives." Philadelphia: Printed for the Memorialists, 1855.

Mountain, Joseph. "Sketches of the Life of Joseph Mountain, a Negro, Who Was Executed at New-Haven, on the 20th Day of October, 1790, for a Rape, Committed on the 26th Day of May Last." 1790. Reprinted in *Pillars of Salt: An Anthology of Early American Criminal Narratives.* Edited by Daniel E. Williams, 288–307. Madison, Wisc.: Madison House, 1993.

Mysteries of Philadelphia, or: Scenes of Real Life in the Quaker City, Containing an Accurate History of This Great Moral World. It Gives a Faithful Expose, Laying Bare the Vices and Iniquities of the Fashionable World. By an Old Amateur. Philadelphia: n.p. 1848.

Needles, Edward. "Ten Years' Progress: or a Comparison of the State and Condition of the Colored People in the City and County of Philadelphia from 1837 to 1847. Prepared by Edward Needles." Philadelphia: Merrihew and Thompson, 1849.

Nell, William Cooper. *The Colored Patriots of the American Revolution, with Sketches of Several Distinguished Colored Persons: To Which Is Added a Brief Survey of the Condition and Prospects of Colored Americans.* Boston: Robert F. Walcutt, 1855.

The New Comic Annual, Illustrated with One Hundred Highly Amusing Cuts. London: Hurst, Chance, n.d. [1834?]

[Nunes, Joseph A., Jr.]. *Aristocracy; or, Life in the City. By a Member of the Philadelphia Bar.* Philadelphia: S. G. Sherman, 1848.

Peale, Charles Willson. *The Selected Papers of Charles Willson Peale and His Family,* Vol. 2, Part I, *The Artist as Museum Keeper, 1791–1810.* Edited by Lillian B. Miller. New Haven, Conn.: Yale University Press, 1988.

Peale, Rembrandt. "Notes and Queries: The Physiognotrace." In *The Crayon: A Journal Devoted to the Graphic Arts, and the Literature Related to Them,* Vol. 4, 307–8. New York: Stillman and Durand, 1857.

Pearson, Elizabeth Ware, ed. *Letters from Port Royal, Written at the Time of the Civil War.* 1906. Reprinted as *Letters from Port Royal, 1862–1868.* New York: Arno Press and the New York Times, 1969.

Penn, William. "A Letter from William Penn, Proprietary and Governor of Pennsylvania in America, to the Committee of the Free Society of Traders of that Province, residing in London." 1683. Reprinted in *William Penn and the Founding of Pennsylvania: A Documentary History.* Edited by Jean R. Soderlund, 308–24. Philadelphia: University of Pennsylvania Press, 1983.

Pennsylvania Abolition Society. "The Present State and Condition of the Free People of Color, of the City of Philadelphia and Adjoining Districts, as Exhibited by the Report of a Committee of the Pennsylvania Society for Promoting the Abolition of Slavery, &c." Philadelphia: Merrihew and Gunn, 1838.

———. "Register of the Trades of the Colored People in the City of Philadelphia and Districts." Philadelphia: Merrihew and Gunn, 1838.

———. "A Statistical Inquiry into the Condition of the People of Colour, of the City and Districts of Philadelphia." Philadelphia: Kite and Walton, 1849.

Pennsylvania Archives: Fourth Series, Vols. 4 and 6. Edited by George Reed. Harrisburg: State of Pennsylvania, 1900.

Petronius. *Satyricon.* In *Elegies of Propertius, Satyricon of Petronius Arbiter, Kisses of Johannes Secundus, Love Epistles of Aristaenetus.* Edited by Walter K. Kelley, 189–365. London: Henry G. Bohn, 1854.

———. *The Satyricon.* Translated by P. G. Walsh. Oxford: Clarendon, 1996.

The Philadelphia Book; or Specimens of Metropolitan Literature. Philadelphia: Key and Biddle, 1836.

Pierpont, John. *Airs of Palestine and Other Poems.* Boston: J. Munroe, 1840.

———. *The Anti-Slavery Poems of John Pierpont.* Boston: Oliver Johnson, 1843.

Poe, Edgar Allan. *Collected Works of Edgar Allan Poe.* Vol. 2, *Tales and Sketches, 1831–1842.* Edited by Thomas Ollive Mabbott. Cambridge, Mass.: Harvard University Press, 1978.

———. *Collected Works of Edgar Allan Poe.* Vol. 3, *Tales and Sketches, 1843–1849.* Edited by Thomas Ollive Mabbott. Cambridge, Mass.: Belknap Press of Harvard University Press, 1978.

———. *Essays and Reviews.* Edited by G. R. Thompson. New York: Library of America, 1984.

———. "Morning on the Wissahiccon." In *The Opal: A Pure Gift for the Holy Days.* Edited by N. P. Willis and illustrated by J. G. Chapman, 249–56. New York: John C. Riker, 1844.

————. *Poetry and Tales.* Edited by Patrick F. Quinn. New York: Library of America, 1984.

Porter, Dorothy, ed. *Early Negro Writing, 1760–1837.* 1971. Baltimore: Black Classic, 1995.

Purvis, Robert. "Appeal of Forty Thousand Citizens, Threatened with Disfranchisement, to the People of Pennsylvania." Philadelphia: Merrihew and Gunn, 1838.

Pynchon, Thomas. *Mason & Dixon.* New York: Henry Holt, 1997.

Ripley, C. Peter, et al., eds. *The Black Abolitionist Papers.* Vol. 3, *The United States, 1830–1846.* Chapel Hill: University of North Carolina Press, 1991.

————. *The Black Abolitionist Papers.* Vol. 4, *The United States, 1847–1858.* Chapel Hill: University of North Carolina Press, 1991.

Rush, Benjamin. *An Account of the Bilious Remitting Yellow Fever as It Appeared in the City of Philadelphia, in the Year 1793.* Philadelphia: Thomas Dobson, 1794.

————. *The Autobiography of Benjamin Rush: His "Travels through Life" Together with His Commonplace Book for 1789–1883.* Edited by George W. Corner. Princeton, N.J.: Princeton University Press, 1948.

————. *Letters of Benjamin Rush.* Vol. 2, *1793–1813.* Edited by L. H. Butterfield. Princeton, N.J.: Princeton University Press, 1951.

————. "Observations Intended to Favour a Supposition That the Black Color (as It Is Called) of the Negroes Is Derived from the Leprosy." *Transactions of the American Philosophical Society* 4 (1799): 289–97.

Schoolcraft, Mary Howard. *Letters on the Condition of the African Race in the United States, by a Southern Lady.* Philadelphia: T. K. and P. G. Collins, 1852.

[Sidney]. "William Whipper's Letters." *Colored American Magazine,* February 13, February 20, March 6, March 13, 1841. Reprinted as "Four Letters by Sidney" in *The Ideological Origins of Black Nationalism.* Edited by Sterling Stuckey, 149–64. Boston: Beacon, 1972.

Smith, James McCune. [Communipaw, pseud.]. Letters to the editor. *Frederick Douglass' Paper,* April 16, August 12, 1858; January 21, 1859.

————. "On the Fourteenth Query of Thomas Jefferson's Notes on Virginia." 1859. Reprinted in *The Works of James McCune Smith, Black Intellectual and Abolitionist.* Edited by John Stauffer, 264–81. New York: Oxford University Press, 2006.

Souder, Casper. "The Mysteries and Miseries of Philadelphia, as Exhibited and Illustrated by a Late Presentment of the Grand Jury, and by a Sketch of the Condition of the Most Degraded Classes in the City." Philadelphia: n.p., 1853.

Still, William. *The Underground Railroad: A Record of Facts, Authentic Narratives, Letters, & c., Narrating the Hardships, Hair-breadth Escapes, and Death Struggles of the Slaves in Their Efforts for Freedom, as Related by Themselves and Others, or Witnessed by the Author.* 1871. Chicago: Johnson, 1970.

Stowe, Harriet Beecher. *The Christian Slave: A Drama, Founded on a Portion of Uncle Tom's Cabin; Dramatised by Harriet Beecher Stowe, Expressly for the Readings of Mrs. Mary E. Webb; Arranged, with a Short Biographical Sketch of the Reader, by F. J. Webb.* London: Sampson Low, 1856.

————. *Dred: A Tale of the Great Dismal Swamp.* 1856. Edited by Robert S. Levine. Chapel Hill: University of North Carolina Press, 2000.

————. *A Key to Uncle Tom's Cabin.* 1853. New York: Arno Press and the New York Times, 1969.

————. *Uncle Tom's Cabin; or, Life among the Lowly.* 1852. Edited by Elizabeth Ammons. New York: W. W. Norton, 1994.

Sturge, Joseph. *A Visit to the United States in 1841.* London: Hamilton, Adams, 1842.

Tanner, H. S. *The Stranger's Guide to the Public Buildings, Places of Amusement, Streets, Lanes, Alleys, Roads, Avenues, Courts, Wharves, Principal Hotels, Steam-Boat Landings, Stage Offices, Etc. Etc. of the City of Philadelphia and Adjoining Districts, with References for Finding Their Situations on the Accompanying Plan of the City: The Whole Alphabetically Arranged and Forming a Complete Guide to Everything Interesting in the City and Suburbs of Philadelphia.* Philadelphia: H. S. Tanner, 1828.

Tocqueville, Alexis de. *Democracy in America.* 1835, 1840. Translated and edited by Harvey C. Mansfield and Delba Winthrop. Chicago: University of Chicago Press, 2000.

Trollope, Frances. *Domestic Manners of the Americans.* 1832. Edited by Donald Smalley. New York: Vintage Books, 1949.

Webb, Frank J. "Biographical Sketch." In *The Christian Slave: A Drama, Founded on a Portion of Uncle Tom's Cabin; Dramatised by Harriet Beecher Stowe, Expressly for the Readings of Mrs. Mary E. Webb; Arranged, with a Short Biographical Sketch of the Reader, by F. J. Webb.* London: Sampson Low, 1856.

————. *Frank J. Webb: Fiction, Essays, Poetry.* Edited by Werner Sollors. New Milford, Conn.: Toby, 2004.

————. *The Garies and Their Friends.* London: G. Routledge, 1857.

————. *The Garies and Their Friends.* 1857. Edited by Robert Reid-Pharr. Baltimore: Johns Hopkins University Press, 1997.

[Webb, Samuel.] *History of Pennsylvania Hall, Which Was Destroyed By a Mob, on the 17th of May, 1838.* Philadelphia: Merrihew and Gunn, 1838.

Weld, Angelina Grimké. "Antislavery Speech at Pennsylvania Hall, Philadelphia, May 16, 1838." 1838. Reprinted in *American Speeches: Political Oratory from the Revolution to the Civil War.* Edited by Ted Widmer, 308–13. New York: Library of America, 2002.

Whipper, William. "An Address, Delivered in Wesley Church on the Evening of June 12, before the Colored Reading Society of Philadelphia, for Mental Improvement." 1828. Reprinted in *Early Negro Writing, 1760–1837.* Edited by Dorothy Porter, 105–19. 1971. Baltimore: Black Classic, 1995.

————. "Appeal to the Colored Citizens of Pennsylvania." 1848. Reprinted in *Proceedings of the Black State Conventions, 1840–1865.* Vol. I. Edited by Philip Foner and George E. Walker, 126–33. Philadelphia: Temple University Press, 1979.

————. "'Colored History' of Pennsylvania." *Frederick Douglass' Paper,* September 3, 1858.

————. "Controversies." *National Reformer* 1.7, March 1839.

————. "Convention." *National Reformer* 1.6, February 1839.

————. Letter to Charles B. Ray. *Colored American,* Jan. 30, 1841. Reprinted in *The Ideological Origins of Black Nationalism.* Edited by Sterling Stuckey, 252–54. Boston: Beacon, 1972.

————. Letters to the editor. *Frederick Douglass' Paper*, November 3, 1854; June 4, July 2, 1858.

————. Letter to the editor. *Frederick Douglass' Paper*, November 3, 1854. Reprinted in *The Black Abolitionist Papers*. Vol. 4, *The United States, 1847–1858*. Edited by C. Peter Ripley et al., 242–44. Chapel Hill: University of North Carolina Press, 1991.

————. "The New Year." *National Reformer* 1.5, January 1839.

————. "Our Elevation." *National Reformer* 1.12, December 1839.

————. "Speech Delivered before the Colored Temperance Society of Philadelphia." 1834. Reprinted in *The Black Abolitionist Papers*. Vol. 3, *The United States, 1830–1846*. Edited by C. Peter Ripley et al., 119–31. Chapel Hill: University of North Carolina Press, 1991.

————. "To the American People." 1835. In "Minutes of the Fifth Annual Convention for the Improvement of the Free People of Colour in the United States, Held by Adjournments, in the Wesley Church Philadelphia, from the First to the Fifth of June, Inclusive, 1835." Reprinted in *Minutes of the Proceedings of the National Negro Conventions, 1830–1864*. Edited by Howard Holman Bell, 25–31. New York: Arno Press and The New York Times, 1969.

————. "To the American People." 1837. Reprinted in *Early Negro Writing, 1760–1837*. Edited by Dorothy Porter, 204–9. 1971. Baltimore: Black Classic Press, 1995.

Whittier, John Greenleaf. "Address Read at the Opening of the Pennsylvania Hall on the 15th of Fifth Month, 1838." Philadelphia: Merrihew and Gunn, 1838.

Wideman, John Edgar. "Ascent by Balloon from the Yard of Walnut Street Jail." *Callaloo* 19.1 (Winter 1996): 1–5.

————. *The Cattle Killing*. New York: Houghton Mifflin, 1996.

————. *Conversations with John Edgar Wideman*. Edited by Bonnie TuSmith. Jackson: University Press of Mississippi, 1998.

————. "Fever." In *Fever: Twelve Stories*, 127–61. New York: Henry Holt, 1989.

————. "Modern Voices: John Edgar Wideman on the Yellow Fever Epidemic." "Africans in America" Web site: http://www.pbs.org/wgbh/aia/part3/3i3110. html.

————. *Philadelphia Fire*. New York: Henry Holt, 1990.

————. "The Salon Interview: John Edgar Wideman." Interview by Laura Miller. *Salon* Web site: http://www.salonmag.com/nov96/interview961111.

————. *Two Cities*. New York: Houghton Mifflin, 1998.

Wild, John Caspar. *Panorama and Views of Philadelphia and Its Vicinity*. Philadelphia: J. C. Wild and J. B. Chevalier, 1838.

Willis, Nathaniel Parker. "Pencillings by the Way." *United States Gazette*. November 21, 1831.

Willson, Joseph. *Sketches of the Higher Classes of Colored Society in Philadelphia. By a Southerner*. Reprinted as *The Elite of Our People: Joseph Willson's Sketches of Black Upper-Class Life in Antebellum Philadelphia*. Edited by Julie Winch. University Park, Pa.: Pennsylvania State University Press, 2000.

Winthrop, John. "A Modell of Christian Charity." 1630. In *American Sermons: The Pilgrims to Martin Luther King Jr*. Edited by Michael Warner, 28–43. New York: Library of America, 1999.

Wister, Owen. *Romney and Other New Works about Philadelphia*. Edited by James A Butler. University Park, Pa.: Pennsylvania State University Press, 2001.

Wright, Frances. *Views of Society and Manners in America*. 1819. Edited by Paul R. Baker. Cambridge, Mass.: Harvard University Press, 1963.

Zola, Emile. "The Experimental Novel." 1880. Reprinted in *Documents of Modern Literary Realism*. Edited and translated by George J. Becker, 162–96. Princeton, N.J.: Princeton University Press, 1963.

Secondary Sources

Adams, Paul C., Steven Hoelscher, and Karen E. Till. "Place in Context: Rethinking Humanist Geographies." In *Textures of Place: Exploring Humanist Geographies*. Edited by Paul C. Adams, Steven Hoelscher, and Karen E. Till, xiii-xxxiii. Minneapolis: University of Minnesota Press, 2001.

Agnew, John. *Place and Politics: The Geographical Mediation of State and Society*. Boston: Allen and Unwin, 1987.

Akagi, Roy H. "The Pennsylvania Constitution of 1838." *Pennsylvania Magazine of History and Biography* 48.4 (October 1924): 301–33.

Anderson, John, and Hilary Hevenor. *Burning Down the House: MOVE and the Tragedy of Philadelphia*. New York: W. W. Norton, 1987.

Andrews, William. *To Tell a Free Story: The First Century of Afro-American Autobiography, 1760–1865*. Urbana: University of Illinois Press, 1988.

Austin, Allan. "Frank J. Webb." In *The Encyclopedia of African-American Culture and History*. Volume 5. Edited by Jack Salzman, David Lionel Smith, and Cornel West, 296. New York: Macmillan Library Reference USA/Simon and Shuster, 1996.

Bacon, Margaret Hope. *But One Race: The Life of Robert Purvis*. Albany: State University of New York Press, 2007.

———. "'The Double Curse of Sex and Color': Robert Purvis and Human Rights." *Pennsylvania Magazine of History and Biography* 121.1/2 (January–April 1997): 53–76.

Banta, Martha. "'Strange Deserts': Hotels, Hospitals, Country Clubs, Prisons, and the City of Brotherly Love." *Henry James Review* 17.1 (1996): 1–10.

Barrett, Lindon. "Presence of Mind: Detection and Racialization in 'The Murders in the Rue Morgue.'" In *Romancing the Shadow: Poe and Race*. Edited by J. Gerald Kennedy and Liliane Weissberg, 177–204. New York: Oxford University Press, 2001.

Bartley, William. "'The Creature of His Own Tasteful Hands': Herman Melville's 'Benito Cereno' and the 'Empire of Might.'" *Modern Philology* 93.4 (May 1996): 445–67.

Baur, John I. H. "The Peales and the Development of American Still Life." *Art Quarterly* 3.1 (Winter 1940): 81–92.

Baym, Nina. *Feminism and American Literary History*. New Brunswick, N.J.: Rutgers University Press, 1992.

Bell, Howard Holman. *A Survey of the Negro Convention Movement, 1830–1861*. 1953. New York: Arno Press and the New York Times, 1969.

Bellion, Wendy. "Heads of State: Profiles and Politics in Jeffersonian America." In *New Media, 1740–1915.* Edited by Lisa Gitelman and Geoffrey B. Pingree, 31–59. Cambridge, Mass.: MIT Press, 2003.

———. "The Mechanization of Likeness in Jeffersonian America." MIT Communications Forum: http://web.mit.edu/comm-forum/papers/bellion.html.

Bentley, Nancy. *The Ethnography of Manners: Hawthorne, James, Wharton.* New York: Cambridge University Press, 1995.

Bergmann, Hans. *God in the Street: New York Writing from the Penny Press to Melville.* Philadelphia: Temple University Press, 1995.

Bergstrom, Ingvar. *Dutch Still-Life Painting in the Seventeenth Century.* Translated by Christina Hedström and Gerald Taylor. New York: Thomas Yoseloff, 1956.

Berthoff, Warner. Introduction to *Arthur Mervyn; or Memoirs of the Year 1793,* by Charles Brockden Brown. Edited by Warner Berthoff, vii-xxiv. New York: Holt, Rinehart, and Winston, 1962.

Blair, Sara. "Cultural Geography and the Place of the Literary." *American Literary History* 10 (1998): 544–67.

Blumin, Stuart M. *The Emergence of the Middle Class: Social Experience in the American City, 1760–1900.* New York: Cambridge University Press, 1989.

Bone, Robert A. *The Negro Novel in America.* New Haven, Conn.: Yale University Press, 1958.

Bourdieu, Pierre. *Distinction: A Social Critique of the Judgement of Taste.* Translated by Richard Nice. Cambridge, Mass.: Harvard University Press, 1984.

Brawley, Benjamin. *The Negro Genius: A New Appraisal of the Achievement of the American Negro in Literature and the Fine Arts.* 1937. New York: Biblio and Tannen, 1969.

Brigham, David. *Public Culture in the Early Republic: Peale's Museum and Its Audience.* Washington, D.C.: Smithsonian Institution Press, 1995.

Brooks, Joanna. *American Lazarus: Religion and the Rise of African-American and Native American Literatures.* New York: Oxford University Press, 2003.

Brown, Ira V. "Racism and Sexism: The Case of Pennsylvania Hall." *Phylon* 37.2 (1976): 126–36.

Bruce, Dickson D. *The Origins of African American Literature, 1680–1865.* Charlottesville: University Press of Virginia, 2001.

Buelens, Gert, "Henry James's Oblique Possession: Plottings of Desire and Mastery in *The American Scene.*" *PMLA* 116.2 (March 2001): 300–313.

———. "James's 'Aliens': Consuming, Performing, and Judging the American Scene." *Modern Philology* 96.3 (February 1999): 347–63.

———. "Pleasurable 'Presences': Sites, Buildings, and 'Aliens' in James's *American Scene.*" *Texas Studies in Literature and Language* 42.4 (Winter 2000): 408–30.

———. "Possessing the American Scene: Race and Vulgarity, Seduction and Judgment." In *Enacting History in Henry James.* Edited by Gert Buelens, 166–92. New York: Cambridge University Press, 1997.

Burdick, Michael. "George Lippard." In the *Dictionary of Literary Biography.* Vol. 202, *Nineteenth-Century American Fiction Writers.* Edited by Kent P. Ljungquist, 173–78. Detroit: Gale Research, 1999.

Burt, Nathaniel and Wallace E. Davies. "The Iron Age, 1876–1905." In *Philadelphia: A 300-Year History*. Edited by Russell F. Weigley et al., 471–523. New York: W. W. Norton, 1982.

Cameron, Sharon. *Thinking in Henry James*. Chicago: University of Chicago Press, 1989.

Castiglia, Christopher. *Interior States: Institutional Consciousness and the Inner Life of Democracy in the Antebellum United States*. Durham, N.C.: Duke University Press, 2008.

Chase, Richard. *The American Novel and Its Tradition*. New York: Doubleday, 1957.

Christopherson, Bill. *The Apparition in the Glass: Charles Brockden Brown's American Gothic*. Athens: University of Georgia Press, 1993.

Clark, Susan F. "Solo Black Performance before the Civil War: Mr. Stowe, Mrs. Webb, and 'The Christian Slave.'" *New Theatre Quarterly* 13.52 (November 1997): 339–48.

Cooper, Frederick. "Elevating the Race: The Social Thought of Black Leaders, 1827–50." *American Quarterly* 24 (1972): 604–25.

Corner, George W. "Appendix I: Rush's Medical Theories." In *The Autobiography of Benjamin Rush: His "Travels through Life" Together with His Commonplace Book for 1789–1883*. Edited by George W. Corner, 361–66. Princeton, N.J.: Princeton University Press, 1948.

Cresswell, Tim. *Place: A Short Introduction*. Oxford: Blackwell, 2004.

Crockett, Rosemary F. "Frank J. Webb: The Shift to Color Discrimination." In *The Black Columbiad: Defining Moments in African American Literature and Culture*. Edited by Werner Sollors and Maria Diedrich, 112–22. Cambridge, Mass.: Harvard University Press, 1994.

———. "*The Garies and Their Friends*: A Study of Frank J. Webb and His Novel." Ph.D. dissertation, Harvard University, 1998.

Curtin, Michael. "A Question of Manners: Status and Gender in Etiquette and Courtesy." *Journal of Modern History* 57 (September 1985): 395–423.

Curtis, Julia. "Philadelphia in an Uproar: *The Monks of Monk Hall*, 1844." *Theatre History Studies* 5 (1985): 41–47.

Davidson, Cathy. *Revolution and the Word: The Rise of the Novel in America*. New York: Oxford University Press, 1986.

Davis, Arthur P. "*The Garies and Their Friends*: A Neglected Pioneer Novel." *CLA Journal* 13.1 (September 1969): 27–34.

———. Preface to *The Garies and Their Friends*. Edited by Arthur P. Davis, v–xiii. New York: Annu Press and the New York Times, 1969.

Davison, Nancy Reynolds. "E. W. Clay: American Political Caricaturist of the Jacksonian Era." Ph.D. dissertation, University of Michigan, 1980.

Dayan, Joan. "Poe, Persons, and Property." In *Romancing the Shadow: Poe and Race*. Edited by J. Gerald Kennedy and Liliane Weissberg, 106–126. New York: Oxford University Press, 2001.

Delbanco, Andrew. *Melville: His World and Work*. New York: Alfred A. Knopf, 2005.

Denning, Michael. *Mechanic Accents: Dime Novels and Working-Class Culture in America*. New York: Verso, 1987.

DeVries, James H. "The Tradition of the Sentimental Novel in *The Garies and Their Friends*." *CLA Journal* 17.2 (December 1973): 241–49.

Dimock, Wai Chee and Michael T. Gilmore, eds. *Rethinking Class: Literary Studies and Social Formations*. New York: Columbia University Press, 1994.

Dixon, Annette, ed. *Kara Walker: Pictures from Another Time.* Ann Arbor: University of Michigan Museum of Art, 2002.

Downes, Paul. "Melville's *Benito Cereno* and the Politics of Humanitarian Intervention." *South Atlantic Quarterly* 103:2/3 (Spring–Summer 2004): 465–88.

Duane, Anna Mae. "Remaking Black Motherhood in Frank J. Webb's *The Garies and Their Friends.*" *African American Review* 38.2 (Summer 2004): 201–12.

Duban, James. "Chipping with a Chisel: The Ideology of Melville's Narrators." *Texas Studies in Literature and Language* 31.3 (Fall 1989): 341–85.

Dubey, Madhu. "Literature and Urban Crisis: John Edgar Wideman's *Philadelphia Fire.*" *African American Review* 32.4 (Winter 1998): 579–95.

duCille, Ann. *The Coupling Convention: Sex, Text, and Tradition in Black Women's Fiction.* New York: Oxford University Press, 1993.

Dunbar, Erica Armstrong. *A Fragile Freedom: African American Women and Emancipation in the Antebellum City.* New Haven: Yale University Press, 2008.

Dwight, E. H. "Still Life Paintings by the Peale Family." In *The Peale Family: Three Generations of American Artists.* Edited by Charles H. Elam, 35–117. Detroit: Detroit Institute of Arts, 1967.

Early, Gerard. *Tuxedo Junction: Essays on American Culture.* New York: Ecco, 1989.

Ehrlich, Heyward. "'The Mysteries' of Philadelphia: Lippard's *Quaker City* and 'Urban' Gothic." *ESQ: A Journal of the American Renaissance* 18 (1st Quarter 1972): 50–65.

Eiselein, Gregory. "Humanitarianism and Uncertainty in *Arthur Mervyn.*" *Essays in Literature* 22.2 (1995): 215–26.

Elder, Arlene A. *The Hindered Hand: Cultural Implications of Early African American Fiction.* Westport, Conn.: Greenwood, 1978.

Elias, Norbert. *The Civilizing Process: Sociogenetic and Psychogenetic Investigations.* 1939. Translated by Edmund Jephcott. Malden, Mass.: Blackwell, 2000.

Elliott, Emory. "Narrative Unity and Moral Resolution in *Arthur Mervyn.*" In *Critical Essays on Charles Brockden Brown.* Edited by Bernard Rosenthal, 142–63. Boston: G. K. Hall, 1981.

Ellison, Ralph. *Shadow and Act.* New York: Random House, 1964.

———. "Society, Morality, and the Novel." In *The Living Novel: A Symposium.* Edited by Granville Hicks, 58–91. New York: Macmillan, 1957.

Elmer, Jonathan. "Babo's Razor; or, Discerning the Event in an Age of Differences." *Differences: A Journal of Feminist Cultural Studies* 19.2 (2008): 54–81.

Erickson, Paul. "Welcome to Sodom: The Cultural Work of City-Mysteries Fiction in Antebellum America." Ph.D. dissertation, University of Texas at Austin, 2005.

Ernest, John. *Liberation Historiography: African American Writers and the Challenge of History, 1794–1861.* Chapel Hill: University of North Carolina Press, 2004.

Estes, J. Worth. "Introduction: The Yellow Fever Syndrome and Its Treatment in Philadelphia, 1793." In *A Melancholy Scene of Devastation: The Public Response to the 1793 Philadelphia Yellow Fever Epidemic.* Edited by J. Worth Estes and Billy G. Smith, 1–17. Sagamore Beach, Mass.: Science History Publications, 1997.

————, and Billy G. Smith, eds. *A Melancholy Scene of Devastation: The Public Response to the 1793 Philadelphia Yellow Fever Epidemic.* Sagamore Beach, Mass.: Science History Publications, 1997.

Fabi, M. Giulia. *Passing and the Rise of the African American Novel.* Urbana: University of Illinois Press, 2001.

Faflik, David. "Authorship, Ownership, and the Case for *Charles Anderson Chester.*" *Book History* 11 (2008): 149–67.

Fanon, Frantz. *The Wretched of the Earth.* 1961. Translated by Constance Farrington. New York: Grove, 1963.

Feldberg, Michael. *The Philadelphia Riots of 1844: A Study of Ethnic Conflict.* Westport, Conn.: Greenwood, 1975.

Ferguson, Robert A. "Yellow Fever and Charles Brockden Brown: The Context of the Emerging Novelist." *Early American Literature* 14.3 (1979–80): 293–305.

Fiedler, Leslie A. Introduction to *The Monks of Monk Hall,* by George Lippard. Edited by Leslie A. Fiedler, vii-xxxii. New York: Odyssey Press, 1970.

————. *Love and Death in the American Novel.* New York: Criterion, 1960.

Fisher, Marvin. *Going Under: Melville's Short Fiction and the American 1850s.* Baton Rouge: Louisiana State University Press, 1977.

Fisher, Philip. *Still the New World: American Literature in a Culture of Creative Destruction.* Cambridge, Mass.: Harvard University Press, 1999.

Fortune, Brandon Brame. "A Delicate Balance: Raphaelle Peale's Still-Life Paintings and the Ideal of Temperance." In *The Peale Family: Creation of a Legacy, 1770–1870.* Edited by Lillian B. Miller, 134–49. New York: Abbeville, 1996.

Franklin, H. Bruce. "Past, Present, and Future Seemed One." In *Critical Essays on Melville's Benito Cereno.* Edited by Robert Burkholder, 230–46. New York: G. K. Hall, 1992.

Franklin, Wayne and Michael Steiner. "Taking Place: Toward the Regrounding of American Studies." In *Mapping American Culture.* Edited by Wayne Franklin and Michael Steiner, 3–23. Iowa City: University of Iowa Press, 1992.

Frazier, E. Franklin. *Black Bourgeoisie.* 1957. New York: Free Press, 1997.

Gaines, Kevin K. *Uplifting the Race: Black Leadership, Politics, and Culture in the Twentieth Century.* Chapel Hill: University of North Carolina Press, 1996.

Gallagher, Catherine. "George Eliot: Immanent Victorian." *Representations* 90 (April 2005): 61–74.

Gardner, Eric. "'A Gentleman of Superior Cultivation and Refinement': Recovering the Biography of Frank J. Webb." *African American Review* 35.2 (Summer 2001): 297–308.

————. "'A Nobler End': Mary Webb and the Victorian Platform." *Nineteenth-Century Prose* 29.1 (Spring 2002): 103–16.

————. "Stowe Takes the Stage: Harriet Beecher Stowe's *The Christian Slave.*" *Legacy* 15.1 (1998): 78–84.

Gayle, Addison. *The Way of the New World: The Black Novel in America.* Garden City, N.Y.: Anchor Press/Doubleday, 1975.

Geffen, Elizabeth M. "Industrial Development and Social Crisis, 1841–1854." In *Philadelphia, A 300-Year History.* Edited by Russell F. Weigley et al., 307–62. New York: W. W. Norton, 1982.

———. "Violence in Philadelphia in the 1840s and 1850s." *Pennsylvania History* 36 (October 1969): 381–410.

Gladman, Kimberly R. "Upper Tens and Lower Millions: City Mysteries Fiction and Class in the Mid-Nineteenth Century." Ph. D. dissertation, New York University, 2001.

Glaude, Eddie, Jr. *Exodus! Religion, Race, and Nation in Early Nineteenth-Century Black America.* Chicago: University of Chicago Press, 2000.

Gleason, William. "Volcanoes and Meteors: Douglass, Melville, and the Poetics of Insurrection." In *Frederick Douglass and Herman Melville: Essays in Relation.* Edited by Robert S. Levine and Samuel Otter, 110–33. Chapel Hill: University of North Carolina Press, 2008.

Goddu, Teresa. *Gothic America: Narrative, History, and Nation.* New York: Columbia University Press, 1997.

Golemba, Henry. "Frank Webb's *The Garies and Their Friends* Contextualized within African American Slave Narratives." In *Lives Out of Letters: Essays on American Literary Biography and Documentation, in Honor of Robert N. Hudspeth.* Edited by Robert. D. Habich, 114–42. Teaneck, N.J.: Fairleigh Dickinson University Press, 2004.

Goodman, Susan. *Civil Wars: American Novelists and Manners, 1880–1940.* Baltimore: Johns Hopkins University Press, 2003.

Gossett, Thomas H. *Uncle Tom's Cabin and American Culture.* Dallas: Southern Methodist University Press, 1985.

Goudie, Sean X. "On the Origins of American Specie(s): The West Indies, Classification, and the Emergence of Supremacist Consciousness in *Arthur Mervyn.*" In *Revising Charles Brockden Brown: Culture, Politics, and Sexuality in the Early Republic.* Edited by Philip Barnard, Mark L. Kamrath, and Stephen Shapiro, 60–87. Knoxville: University of Tennessee Press, 2004.

Gould, Philip. "Race, Commerce, and the Literature of Yellow Fever in Early National Philadelphia." *Early American Literature* 35.2 (2000): 157–86.

Grabo, Norman S. *The Coincidental Art of Charles Brockden Brown.* Chapel Hill: University of North Carolina Press, 1981.

———. "Historical Essay." In *Arthur Mervyn; or Memoirs of the Year 1793.* Vol. 3 of *The Novels and Related Works of Charles Brockden Brown.* Edited by Sydney J. Krause and S. W. Reid, 447–75. Kent, Ohio: Kent State University Press, 1980.

Green, James N. and Peter Stallybrass. *Benjamin Franklin: Writer and Printer.* New Castle, De.: Oak Knoll Press, 2006

———. "Mathew Carey." In *Dictionary of Literary Biography.* Vol. 73, *American Magazine Journalists, 1741–1850.* Edited by Sam G. Riley, 56–64. Detroit: Gale Research, 1988.

Grey, Robin. "John Beauchamp Jones." In *Dictionary of Literary Biography.* Vol. 202, *Nineteenth-Century American Fiction Writers.* Edited by Kent Ljungquist, 147–58. Detroit: Gale Research, 1999.

———. "Patronage, Southern Politics, and the Road Not Taken: Edgar Allan Poe and John Beauchamp Jones." In *Poe Writing/Writing Poe.* Edited by Jana Argersinger and Richard Kopley. New York: AMS Press (forthcoming).

Griffith, Sally F. "'A Total Dissolution of the Bonds of Society': Community Death and Regeneration in Mathew Carey's *Short Account of the Malignant Fever.*" In *A Melancholy Scene of Devastation: The Public Response to the 1793 Philadelphia Yellow Fever Epidemic.* Edited by

J. Worth Estes and Billy G. Smith, 45–59. Sagamore Beach, Mass.: Science History Publications, 1997.

Grimstead, David. "Rioting in Its Jacksonian Setting." *American Historical Review* 77.2 (April 1972): 361–97.

Hale, Dorothy J. "Profits of Altruism: Caleb Williams and Arthur Mervyn." *Eighteenth-Century Studies* 22 (1988): 47–69.

Halttunen, Karen. *Confidence Men and Painted Women: A Study of Middle-Class Culture in America, 1830–1870.* New Haven, Conn.: Yale University Press, 1982.

Hartman, Saidiya V. *Scenes of Subjection: Terror, Slavery, and Self-Making in Nineteenth-Century America.* New York: Oxford University Press, 1997.

Harvey, David. *The Condition of Postmodernity: An Enquiry into the Origins of Cultural Change.* Oxford: Blackwell, 1989.

Hedges, William L. "Benjamin Rush, Charles Brockden Brown, and the American Plague Year." *Early American Literature* 8.3 (1974): 295–311.

Hedrick, Joan D. *Harriet Beecher Stowe: A Life.* New York: Oxford University Press, 1994.

Hershberg, Theodore. "Free Blacks in Antebellum Philadelphia: A Study of Ex-Slaves, Freeborn, and Socioeconomic Decline." 1971. In *African Americans in Pennsylvania: Shifting Historical Perspectives.* Edited by Joe William Trotter Jr. and Eric Ledell Smith, 123–47. Harrisburg and University Park, Pa.: Pennsylvania Historical and Museum Commission and Pennsylvania State University Press, 1997.

Hewitt, Rosalie. "Henry James's *The American Scene:* Its Genesis and Its Reception, 1905–1977." *Henry James Review* 1.2 (Winter 1980): 179–96.

———. "Henry James, the Harpers, and *The American Scene.*" *American Literature* 55.1 (March 1983): 41–47.

Higginbotham, Evelyn Brooks. *Righteous Discontent: The Women's Movement in the Black Baptist Church, 1880–1920.* Cambridge, Mass.: Harvard University Press, 1993.

Hines, Mary Anne, Gordon Marshall, and Willam Woys Weaver. *The Larder Invaded: Reflections on Three Centuries of Philadelphia Food and Drink.* Philadelphia: Winchell Company of Philadelphia, 1987.

Hoffa, William R. "The Language of Rogues and Fools in Brackenridge's *Modern Chivalry.*" *Studies in the Novel* 12.4 (Winter 1980): 289–300.

Horton, James Oliver, and Lois E. Horton. *In Hope of Liberty: Culture, Community and Protest among Northern Free Blacks, 1700–1860.* New York: Oxford University Press, 1997.

Humphries, Margaret. "Appendix II: Yellow Fever Since 1793: History and Historiography." In *A Melancholy Scene of Devastation: The Public Response to the 1793 Philadelphia Yellow Fever Epidemic.* Edited by J. Worth Estes and Billy G. Smith, 183–98. Sagamore Beach, Mass.: Science History Publications, 1997.

Hunter, Donna Denise. "Dead Men Talking: Africans and the Law in New England's Eighteenth-Century Execution Sermons and Crime Narratives." Ph.D. dissertation, University of California, Berkeley, 2000.

Ignatiev, Noel. *How the Irish Became White.* New York: Routledge, 1995.

Jackson, Blyden. *A History of Afro-American Literature.* Vol. 1, *The Long Beginning, 1746–1895.* Baton Rouge: Louisiana State University Press, 1989.

Jones, Martha S. *All Bound Up Together: The Woman Question in African American Public Culture, 1830–1900.* Chapel Hill: University of North Carolina Press, 2007

Kahn, Robert M. "The Political Ideology of Martin Delany." *Journal of Black Studies* 14.4 (June 1984): 415–40.

Kaplan, Amy. "Manifest Domesticity." *American Literature* 70.3 (September 1998): 581–606.

Karcher, Carolyn. *Shadow over the Promised Land: Slavery, Race, and Violence in Melville's America.* Baton Rouge: Louisiana State University Press, 1980.

Kasson, John F. *Rudeness and Civility: Manners in Nineteenth-Century America.* New York: Hill and Wang, 1990.

Katz, Michael B., and Thomas J. Sugrue, eds. *W. E. B. DuBois, Race, and the City: The Philadelphia Negro and Its Legacy.* Philadelphia: University of Pennsylvania Press, 1998.

Kavanagh, James H. "That Hive of Subtlety: 'Benito Cereno' and the Liberal Hero." In *Ideology and Classic American Literature.* Edited by Sacvan Bercovitch and Myra Jehlen, 352–83. New York: Cambridge University Press, 1986.

Klepp, Susan E. "Appendix I: 'How Many Precious Souls Are Fled'?: The Magnitude of the 1793 Yellow Fever Epidemic." In *A Melancholy Scene of Devastation: The Public Response to the 1793 Philadelphia Yellow Fever Epidemic.* Edited by J. Worth Estes and Billy G. Smith, 163–82. Sagamore Beach, Mass.: Science History Publications, 1997.

Knadler, Stephen. "Traumatized Racial Performativity: Passing in Nineteenth-Century African-American Testimonies." *Cultural Critique* 55 (Fall Autumn 2003): 63–100.

Lang, Amy Schrager. *The Syntax of Class: Writing Inequality in Nineteenth-Century America.* Princeton, N.J.: Princeton University Press, 2003.

Lapsansky, Emma Jones. "Friends, Wives, and Strivings: Networks and Community Values among Nineteenth-Century Philadelphia Afroamerican Elites." *Pennsylvania Magazine of History and Biography* 108.1 (January 1984): 3–24.

———. *Neighborhoods in Transition: William Penn's Dream and Urban Reality.* New York: Garland, 1994.

———. "'Since They Got Those Separate Churches': Afro-Americans and Racism in Jacksonian Philadelphia." *American Quarterly* 32.1 (Spring 1980): 54–78.

Lapsansky, Phillip. "'Abigail, a Negress.'" In *A Melancholy Scene of Devastation: The Public Response to the 1793 Philadelphia Yellow Fever Epidemic.* Edited by J. Worth Estes and Billy G. Smith, 61–78. Sagamore Beach, Mass.: Science History Publications, 1997.

———. "Afro-Americana: Frank J. Webb and His Friends." In *The Annual Report of the Library Company of Philadelphia for the Year 1990,* 27–38. Philadelphia: Library Company of Philadelphia, 1991.

———. "Graphic Discord: Abolitionist and Antiabolitionist Images." In *The Abolitionist Sisterhood: Women's Political Culture in Antebellum America.* Edited by Jean Fagan Yellin and John C. Van Horne, 201–30. Ithaca, N.Y.: Cornell University Press, 1994.

Larson, David M. "*Arthur Mervyn, Edgar Huntly,* and the Critics." *Essays in Literature* 15 (1988): 207–19.

Laurie, Bruce. *Working People of Philadelphia, 1800–1850.* Philadelphia: Temple University Press, 1980.

Lawrence, D.H. *Studies in Classic American Literature.* 1923. Edited by Ezra Greenspan, Lindeth Vasey, and John Worthen. New York: Cambridge University Press, 2003.

Lefebvre, Henri. *The Production of Space.* Translated by Donald Nicholson-Smith. Oxford: Blackwell, 1991.

Lehan, Richard. *The City in Literature: An Intellectual and Cultural History.* Berkeley: University of California Press, 1998.

Lemire, Elise. *"Miscegenation": Mixing Race in America.* Philadelphia: University of Pennsylvania Press, 2002.

Levine, Robert S. *Conspiracy and Romance: Studies in Brockden Brown, Cooper, Hawthorne, and Melville.* New York: Cambridge University Press, 1989.

———. "Disturbing Boundaries: Temperance, Black Elevation, and Violence in Frank J. Webb's *The Garies and Their Friends.*" *Prospects* 19 (1994): 349–74.

———. *Martin Delany, Frederick Douglass, and the Politics of Representative Identity.* Chapel Hill: University of North Carolina Press, 1997.

———. "Race and Nation in Brown's Louisiana Writings of 1803." In *Revising Charles Brockden Brown: Culture, Politics, and Sexuality in the Early Republic.* Edited by Philip Barnard, Mark L. Kamrath, and Stephen Shapiro, 332–53. Knoxville: University of Tennessee Press, 2004.

Lewis, David Levering. *W. E. B. DuBois: Biography of a Race, 1868–1919.* New York: Henry Holt, 1993.

Lewis, R. W. B. *The American Adam: Innocence, Tragedy, and Tradition in the Nineteenth Century.* Chicago: University of Chicago Press, 1955.

Looby, Christopher. Introduction to *Sheppard Lee, Written By Himself.* 1836. Edited by Christopher Looby, xv–xliii. New York: New York Review of Books, 2008.

———. *Voicing America: Language, Literary Form, and the Origins of the United States.* Chicago: University of Chicago Press, 1996.

Lukasik, Christopher. "The Face of the Public." *American Literature* 39.3 (2004): 413–64.

Lynch, Lisa. "The Fever Next Time: The Race of Disease and the Disease of Racism in John Edgar Wideman." *American Literary History* 14.4 (Winter 2002): 776–804.

Marder, Daniel. *Hugh Henry Brackenridge.* New York: Twayne, 1967.

Martin, Charles, and James Snead. "Reading through Blackness: Colorless Signifiers in *Benito Cereno.*" *Yale Journal of Criticism* 4.1 (Fall 1990): 231–51.

Martinez, Katherine, and Page Talbott, eds. *Philadelphia's Cultural Landscape: The Sartain Family Legacy.* Philadelphia: Temple University Press, 2000.

Massey, Doreen. *Space, Place, and Gender.* Minneapolis: University of Minnesota Press, 1994.

Masur, Louis P. "Benjamin Rush." In *Dictionary of Literary Biography.* Vol. 37, *American Writers of the Early Republic.* Edited by Emory Elliott, 259–65. Detroit: Gale Research, 1985.

Matlock, Diane Helen. "The Sentimental Novel and the Transformation of Antebellum Print and Material Cultures." Ph.D. dissertation, University of California, Berkeley (in progress).

Matthiessen, F. O. *American Renaissance: Art and Expression in the Age of Emerson and Whitman.* New York: Oxford University Press, 1941.

Mayer, Henry. *All on Fire: William Lloyd Garrison and the Abolition of Slavery.* New York: St. Martin's Press, 1998.

McBride, David. "Black Protest against Racial Politics: Gardner, Hinton and Their Memorial of 1838." *Pennsylvania History* 46 (April 1979): 149–62.

McCormack, Richard P. "William Whipper: Moral Reformer." *Pennsylvania History* 43 (January 1976): 23–47.

McHenry, Elizabeth. *Forgotten Readers: Recovering the Lost History of African American Literary Societies.* Durham, N.C.: Duke University Press, 2002.

Miller, Floyd J. *The Search for a Black Nationality: Black Emigration and Colonization, 1787–1863.* Urbana: University of Illinois Press, 1975.

Miller, Jacquelyn C. "The Body Politic: Passions, Pestilence, and Political Culture in the Age of the American Revolution." Ph.D. dissertation, Rutgers University, 1995.

———. "Passions and Politics: The Multiple Meanings of Benjamin Rush's Treatment for Yellow Fever." In *A Melancholy Scene of Devastation: The Public Response to the 1793 Philadelphia Yellow Fever Epidemic.* Edited by J. Worth Estes and Billy G. Smith, 79–95. Sagamore Beach, Mass.: Science History Publications, 1997.

Montgomery, David. "The Shuttle and the Cross: Weavers and Artisans in the Kensington Riots of 1844." In *Workers in the Industrial Revolution: Recent Studies of Labor in the United States and Europe.* Edited by Peter N. Stearns and Daniel J. Walkowitz, 44–74. New Brunswick, N.J.: Transaction, 1974.

Morrison, Toni. "Unspeakable Things Unspoken: The Afro-American Presence in American Literature." *Michigan Quarterly Review* 28.1 (Winter 1989): 1–35.

Nash, Gary. *First City: Philadelphia and the Forging of Historical Memory.* Philadelphia: University of Pennsylvania Press, 2002.

———. *Forging Freedom: The Formation of Philadelphia's Black Community.* Cambridge, Mass.: Harvard University Press, 1988.

———and Jean R. Soderlund. *Freedom by Degrees: Emancipation in Pennsylvania and Its Aftermath.* New York: Oxford University Press, 1991.

Nelson, Dana. "'Indications of the Public Will': *Modern Chivalry*'s Theory of Democratic Representation." *ANQ* 15.1 (Winter 2002): 23–39.

———. *National Manhood: Capitalist Citizenship and the Imagined Fraternity of White Men.* Durham, N.C.: Duke University Press, 1998.

———. *The Word in Black and White: Reading "Race" in American Literature, 1638–1867.* New York: Oxford University Press, 1993.

Nemerov, Alexander. *The Body of Raphaelle Peale: Still Life and Selfhood, 1812–1824.* Berkeley: University of California Press, 2001.

Newlin, Claude M. Introduction to *Modern Chivalry*, by Hugh Henry Brackenridge. Edited by Claude M. Newlin, ix–xl. New York, Hafner, 1968.

Newman, Lea Bertani Vozar. *A Reader's Guide to the Short Stories of Herman Melville.* Boston: G. K. Hall, 1986.

Newman, Richard S. *Freedom's Prophet: Bishop Richard Allen, the AME Church, and the Black Founding Fathers.* New York: New York University Press, 2008.

————. Patrick Rael, and Phillip Lapansky. Introduction to *Pamphlets of Protest: An Anthology of Early African American Protest Literature, 1790–1860.* Edited by Richard Newman, Patrick Rael, and Phillip Lapsansky, 1–31. New York: Routledge, 2001.

Newton, Sarah E. *Learning to Behave: A Guide to American Conduct Books before 1900.* Westport, Conn.: Greenwood, 1994.

Oberholtzer, Ellis Paxson. *The Literary History of Philadelphia.* Philadelphia: George W. Jacobs, 1906.

Okonkwo, Chris. "'It Was Like Meeting an Old Friend': An Interview with John Edgar Wideman." *Callaloo* 29.2 (Spring 2006): 347–60.

O'Malley, Michael. "Specie and Species: Race and the Money Question in Nineteenth-Century America." *American Historical Review* 99.2 (April 1994): 369–95.

Otter, Samuel. "Stowe and Race." In *The Cambridge Companion to Harriet Beecher Stowe.* Edited by Cindy A. Weinstein, 15–38. New York: Cambridge University Press, 2004.

Painter, Nell Irvin. "Martin R. Delany: Elitism and Black Nationalism." In *Black Leaders of the Nineteenth Century.* Edited by Leon Litwack and August Meier, 149–71. Urbana: University of Illinois Press, 1988.

Pease, Jane, and William H. Pease. "The Negro Convention Movement." In *Key Issues in the Afro-American Experience.* Vol. 1, *To 1877.* Edited by Nathan I. Huggins, Martin Kilson, and Daniel M. Fox, 191–205. New York: Harcourt Brace Jovanovich, 1971.

————. "Negro Conventions and the Problem of Black Leadership." *Journal of Black Studies* 2.1 (September 1971): 29–44.

————. *They Who Would Be Free: Blacks' Search for Freedom, 1830–1861.* New York: Atheneum, 1974.

Peires, J. B. *The Dead Will Arise: Nongqawuse and the Great Xhosa Cattle-Killing Movement of 1856–7.* Bloomington: Indiana University Press, 1989.

Pernick, Martin S. "Politics, Parties, and Pestilence: Epidemic Yellow Fever in Philadelphia and the Rise of the First Party System." In *A Melancholy Scene of Devastation: The Public Response to the 1793 Philadelphia Yellow Fever Epidemic.* Edited by J. Worth Estes and Billy G. Smith, 119–46. Sagamore Beach, Mass.: Science History Publications, 1997.

Peterson, Carla L. "Capitalism, Black (Under)development, and the Production of the African American Novel in the 1850s." *American Literary History* 4.4 (Winter 1992): 559–83.

————. *"Doers of the Word": African American Women Speakers and Writers in the North (1830–1880).* New York: Oxford University Press, 1995.

Phan, Hoang. "The Labors of Difference: Race, Citizenship, and the Transformation of Legal and Literary Form." Ph.D. dissertation, University of California, Berkeley, 2004.

Pollin, Burton R. "Edgar Allan Poe and John G. Chapman: Their Treatment of the Dismal Swamp and the Wissahickon." In *Studies in the American Renaissance.* Edited by Joel Myerson, 254–74. Charlottesville: University Press of Virginia, 1983.

Posnock, Ross. "Affirming the Alien: The Pragmatist Pluralism of *The American Scene.*" In *The Cambridge Companion to Henry James.* Edited by Jonathan Freedman, 224–46. New York: Cambridge University Press, 1998.

————. "Henry James and the Limits of Historicism." *Henry James Review* 16.3 (Fall 1995): 273–77.

Powell, J. M. *Bring Out Your Dead: The Great Plague of Yellow Fever in Philadelphia in 1793.* 1949. Introduction by Kenneth R. Foster, Mary F. Jenkins, and Anna Coxe Toogood. Philadelphia: University of Pennsylvania Press, 1993.

Prince, Carl E. "The Great 'Riot Year': Jacksonian Democracy and Patterns of Violence in 1834." *Journal of the Early Republic* 5.1 (Spring 1985): 1–19.

Quinn, Arthur Hobson. *Edgar Allan Poe: A Critical Biography.* Baltimore: Johns Hopkins University Press, 1998.

Rael, Patrick. *Black Identity and Black Protest in the Antebellum North.* Chapel Hill: University of North Carolina Press, 2002.

Reid-Pharr, Robert F. *Conjugal Union: The Body, the House, and the Black American.* New York: Oxford University Press, 1999.

————. Introduction to *The Garies and Their Friends.* Edited by Robert Reid-Pharr, vii-xviii. Baltimore: Johns Hopkins University Press, 1997.

Remer, Rosalind. *Printers and Men of Capital: Philadelphia Book Publishers in the New Republic.* Philadelphia: University of Pennsylvania Press, 1996.

Renza, Louis A. "'Ut Pictura Poe': Poetic Politics in 'The Island of the Fay' and 'Morning on the Wissahiccon.'" In *The American Face of Edgar Allan Poe.* Edited by Shawn Rosenheim and Stephen Rachman, 305–29. Baltimore: Johns Hopkins University Press, 1995.

Reynolds, David S. *George Lippard.* Boston: Twayne, 1982.

————. *Beneath the American Renaissance: The Subversive Imagination in the Age of Emerson and Melville.* New York: Alfred A. Knopf, 1988.

Rhodes, Jane. "At the Boundaries of Abolitionism, Feminism, and Black Nationalism: The Activism of Mary Ann Shadd Cary." In *Women's Rights and Transatlantic Antislavery in the Era of Emancipation.* Edited by Kathryn Kish Sklar and James Brewer Stewart, 346–66. New Haven, Conn.: Yale University Press, 2007.

Rice, Grantland S. "*Modern Chivalry* and the Resistance to Textual Authority." *American Literature* 67.2 (June 1995): 257–81.

Richards, Leonard L. *"Gentlemen of Property and Standing": Anti-Abolition Mobs in Jacksonian America.* New York: Oxford University Press, 1970.

Rigal, Laura. *The American Manufactory: Art, Labor, and the World of Things in the Early Republic.* Princeton, N.J.: Princeton University Press, 1998.

Robinson, Arthur Thomas. "The Third Horseman of the Apocalypse: A Multi-Disciplinary Social History of the 1793 Yellow Fever Epidemic in Philadelphia." Ph.D. dissertation, Washington State University, 1993.

Rogin, Michael Paul. *Subversive Genealogy: The Politics and Art of Herman Melville.* New York: Alfred A. Knopf, 1983.

Rose, Willie Lee. *Rehearsal for Reconstruction: The Port Royal Experiment.* Indianapolis: Bobbs-Merrill, 1964.

Rotella, Carlo. *October Cities: The Redevelopment of Urban Literature.* Berkeley: University of California Press, 1998.

Runcie, John. "'Hunting the Nigs' in Philadelphia: The Race Riot of August 1834." *Pennsylvania History* 39 (April 1972): 187–218.

Ryan, Mary P. *Civic Wars: Democracy and Public Life in the American City during the Nineteenth Century.* Berkeley: University of California Press, 1997.

Ryan, Susan M. "Errand into Africa: Colonization and Nation Building in Sarah J. Hale's *Liberia." New England Quarterly* 68.4 (December 1995): 559–66.

Sacco, Ellen. "Racial Theory, Museum Practice: The Colored World of Charles Willson Peale." *Museum Anthropology* 20.2 (Fall 1996): 25–32.

Said, Edward W. *Culture and Imperialism.* New York: Vintage, 1994.

Sale, Maggie Montesinos. *The Slumbering Volcano: American Slave Ship Revolts and the Production of Rebellious Masculinity.* Durham, N.C.: Duke University Press, 1997.

Samuels, Shirley. "Plague and Politics in 1793: *Arthur Mervyn." Criticism* 27.3 (Summer 1985): 225–46.

———. *Romances of the Republic: Women, the Family, and Violence in the Literature of the Early American Nation.* New York: Oxford University Press, 1996.

Scharf, J. Thomas, and Thompson Westcott. *History of Philadelphia.* Vol. 1, *1609–1884.* Philadelphia: L. H. Everts, 1884.

Schwarz, Robert Devlin. *150 Years of Philadelphia Still-Life Painting.* Philadelphia: Schwarz Gallery, 1997.

Scruggs, Charles. *Sweet Home: Invisible Cities in the Afro-American Novel.* Baltimore: Johns Hopkins University Press, 1993.

Sellers, Charles Coleman. *Mr. Peale's Museum: Charles Willson Peale and the First Popular Museum of Natural Science and Art.* New York: W. W. Norton, 1980.

Seltzer, Mark. *Henry James and the Art of Power.* Ithaca, N.Y.: Cornell University Press, 1984.

Shaw, Gwendolyn DuBois. *Portraits of a People: Picturing African Americans in the Nineteenth Century.* Andover, Mass. and Seattle, Wash.: Addison Gallery of American Art and University of Washington Press, 2006.

———. *Seeing the Unspeakable: The Art of Kara Walker.* Durham, N.C.: Duke University Press, 2004.

Shore, Elliott. "The Mysteries of Philadelphia in 1850: The German American Context." In *New Directions in German-American Studies.* Vol. 2, *German? American? Literature?* Edited by Winfried Fluck and Werner Sollors, 92–112. New York: Peter Lang, 2002.

Shuffleton, Frank. "Juries of the Common Reader: Crime and Judgment in the Novels of Charles Brockden Brown." In *Revising Charles Brockden Brown: Culture, Politics, and Sexuality in the Early Republic.* Edited by Philip Barnard, Mark L. Kamrath, and Stephen Shapiro, 88–114. Knoxville: University of Tennessee Press, 2004.

Silva, Cristobal Selenite. "Monstrous Plots: An Epidemiology of American Narrative." Ph.D. dissertation, New York University, 2003.

Silverman, Kenneth. *Edgar Allan Poe: Mournful and Never-Ending Remembrance.* New York: Harper Collins, 1991.

Slotkin, Richard. "Narratives of Negro Crime in New England, 1675–1800." *American Quarterly* 25.1 (March 1973): 3–31.

Smith, Billy G. "Comment: Disease and Community." In *A Melancholy Scene of Devastation: The Public Response to the 1793 Philadelphia Yellow Fever Epidemic.* Edited by J. Worth Estes and Billy G. Smith, 147–62. Sagamore Beach, Mass.: Science History Publications, 1997.

Smith, Eric Ledell. "The End of Black Voting Rights in Pennsylvania: African Americans and the Pennsylvania Constitutional Convention of 1837–1838." *Pennsylvania History* 65 (Summer 1998): 279–99.

———. "The Pittsburgh Memorial: A Forgotten Document of Pittsburgh History." *Pittsburgh History* (Fall 1997): 106–11.

Smith-Rosenberg, Carroll. "Black Gothic: The Shadowy Origins of the American Bourgeoisie." In *Possible Pasts: Becoming Colonial in Early America.* Edited by Robert Blair St. George, 243–69. Ithaca, N.Y.: Cornell University Press, 2000.

Snyder, Charles McCool. *The Jacksonian Heritage: Pennsylvania Politics, 1833–1848.* Harrisburg: Pennsylvania Historical and Museum Commission, 1958.

Snyder, Martin P. "J. C. Wild and His Philadelphia Views." *Pennsylvania Magazine of History and Biography* 77.1 (January 1953): 32–75.

Soja, Edward. *Postmodern Geographies: The Reassertion of Space in Critical Social Theory.* London: Verso, 1989.

———. *Thirdspace: Journeys to Los Angeles and Other Real-and-Imagined Places.* Oxford: Blackwell, 1996.

Sollors, Werner. Introduction to *Frank J. Webb: Fiction, Essays, Poetry.* Edited by Werner Sollors, 1–13. New Milford, Conn.: Toby, 2004.

Stafford, Barbara Maria. *Body Criticism: Imaging the Unseen in Enlightenment Art and Medicine.* Cambridge, Mass.: MIT Press, 1991.

Stanton, William. *The Leopard's Spots: Scientific Attitudes toward Race in America.* Chicago: University of Chicago Press, 1960.

Stern, Julia. *The Plight of Feeling: Sympathy and Dissent in the Early American Novel.* Chicago: University of Chicago Press, 1997.

Streeby, Shelley. *American Sensations: Class, Empire, and the Production of Popular Culture.* Berkeley: University of California Press, 2002.

Stuckey, Sterling. *Slave Culture: Nationalist Theory and the Foundations of Black America.* New York: Oxford University Press, 1987.

Sundquist, Eric J. "Suspense and Tautology in *Benito Cereno.*" *Glyph* 8 (1981): 103–26.

———. *To Wake the Nations: Race in the Making of American Literature.* Cambridge, Mass.: Harvard University Press, 1993.

Swann, Charles. "*Benito Cereno:* Melville's De(con)struction of the Southern Reader." *Literature and History* 12 (1986): 3–15.

———. "Whodunit? Or, Who Did What? *Benito Cereno* and the Politics of Narrative Structure." In *American Studies in Transition.* Edited by David E. Nye and Christen Kold Thomsen, 199–234. Odense, Denmark: Odense University Press, 1985.

Tamarkin, Elisa. *Anglophilia: Deference, Devotion, and Antebellum America.* Chicago: University of Chicago Press, 2008.

Tate, Claudia. *Domestic Allegories of Political Desire: The Black Heroine's Text at the Turn of the Century.* New York: Oxford University Press, 1992.

Thompson, Peter. *Rum Punch and Revolution: Taverngoing and Public Life in Eighteenth-Century Philadelphia.* Philadelphia: University of Pennsylvania Press, 1999.

Tompkins, Jane. *Sensational Designs: The Cultural Work of American Fiction, 1790–1860*. New York: Oxford University Press, 1985.

Trilling, Lionel. *The Liberal Imagination: Essays on Literature and Society*. New York: Viking, 1950.

Tuan, Yi-Fu. *Space and Place: The Perspective of Experience*. Minneapolis: University of Minnesota Press, 1977.

Turner, Edmund Raymond. *The Negro in Pennsylvania: Slavery—Servitude—Freedom, 1639–1861*. 1911. New York: Arno Press and the New York Times, 1969.

Tuttleton, James. *The Novel of Manners in America*. Chapel Hill: University of North Carolina Press, 1972.

Ullman, Victor. *Martin R. Delany: The Beginnings of Black Nationalism*. Boston: Beacon, 1971.

Wagenknecht, Edward. *Harriet Beecher Stowe: The Known and the Unknown*. New York: Oxford University Press, 1965.

Wagner, Bryan. "Charles Chesnutt and the Epistemology of Racial Violence." *American Literature* 73.2 (June 2001): 311–37.

Wagner-Pacifici, Robin. *Discourse and Destruction: The City of Philadelphia versus MOVE*. Chicago: University of Chicago Press, 1994.

Wainwright, Nicholas B. "The Age of Nicholas Biddle, 1825–1841." In *Philadelphia: a 300-Year History*. Edited by Russell F. Weigley et al., 258–306. New York: W. W. Norton, 1982.

——. *Philadelphia in the Romantic Age of Lithography: An Illustrated History of Early Lithography in Philadelphia with a Descriptive List of Philadelphia Scenes Made by Philadelphia Lithographers before 1866*. Philadelphia: Historical Society of Pennsylvania, 1958.

Walker, Clarence E. "The American Negro as Historical Outsider, 1836–1935." *Canadian Review of American Studies* 17.2 (Summer 1986): 137–54.

Wallace, Robert K. *Douglass and Melville: Anchored Together in Neighborly Style*. New Bedford, Mass.: Spinner, 2005.

Wallach, Allan. "Thomas Cole: Landscape and the Course of American Empire." In *Thomas Cole: Landscape into History*. Edited by William H. Truettner and Alan Wallach, 23–111. Washington, D.C.: National Museum of American Art, 1994.

Ward, David C. "Democratic Culture: The Peale Museums, 1784–1850." In *The Peale Family: Creation of a Legacy, 1770–1870*. Edited by Lillian B. Miller, 260–75. New York: Abbeville, 1996.

Warner, Michael. *The Letters of the Republic: Publication and the Public Sphere in Eighteenth-Century America*. Cambridge, Mass.: Harvard University Press, 1990.

Warner, Sam Bass, Jr. *The Private City: Philadelphia in Three Periods of Its Growth*, 2nd ed. Philadelphia: University of Pennsylvania Press, 1987.

Warren, Kenneth W. *Black and White Strangers: Race and American Literary Realism*. Chicago: University of Chicago Press, 1993.

Waterman, Bryan. "*Arthur Mervyn*'s Medical Repository and the Early Republic's Knowledge Industries." *American Literary History* 15.2 (2003): 213–47.

——. *Republic of Intellect: The Friendly Club of New York City and the Making of American Literature*. Baltimore: Johns Hopkins University Press, 2007.

Watts, Edward. *Writing and Postcolonialism in the Early Republic.* Charlottesville: University Press of Virginia, 1998.

Weigley, Russell F., et al., eds. *Philadelphia: A 300-Year History.* New York: W. W. Norton, 1982.

White, Shane, and Graham White. *Stylin': African American Expressive Culture from Its Beginnings to the Zoot Suit.* Ithaca, N.Y.: Cornell University Press, 1998.

Williams, Raymond. *Keywords: A Vocabulary of Culture and Society,* rev. ed. New York: Oxford University Press, 1985.

Winch, Julie. *A Gentleman of Color: The Life of James Forten.* New York: Oxford University Press, 2002.

—————. Introduction to *The Elite of Our People: Joseph Willson's Sketches of Black Upper-Class Life in Antebellum Philadelphia.* Edited by Julie Winch, 1–73. University Park: Pennsylvania State University Press, 2000.

—————. *Philadelphia's Black Elite: Activism, Accommodation, and the Struggle for Autonomy.* Philadelphia: Temple University Press, 1988.

—————. "Sarah Forten's Anti-Slavery Networks." In *Women's Rights and Transatlantic Antislavery in the Era of Emancipation.* Edited by Kathryn Kish Sklar and James Brewer Stewart, 143–57. New Haven, Conn.: Yale University Press, 2007.

Wood, Sarah F. *Quixotic Fictions of the USA, 1792–1815.* New York: Oxford University Press, 2005.

Zboray, Ronald, and Mary Saracino Zboray. "The Mysteries of New England: Eugène Sue's American 'Imitators,' 1844." *Nineteenth-Century Contexts* 22 (2000): 457–92.

Ziff, Larzer. *Literary Democracy: The Declaration of Cultural Independence in America.* New York: Viking, 1981.

Index

Page numbers in italics refer to illustrations.

abolition, abolitionists, 5, 8, 14, 50, 84,
 98, 104, 109, 114, 120, 134, 149, 194,
 200, 263; antiabolition mobs vs., 20,
 99, 131, 142, 195, 198, 201; Delany
 on, 218; English, 196, 225, 290n4,
 334n50; fanaticism of, 213; Forten and,
 113, 290n4; *The Garies and Their Friends*
 (Webb) and, 225, 227; images of, 151;
 associated with miscegenation, 83, 196;
 laws supporting, 5, 77, 81; Lippard
 and, 181; Melville on, 150; politics and,
 195; rejection of, 212; social engineering
 and, 202. *See also* antislavery; Garrison,
 William Lloyd; Pennsylvania Act for
 the Gradual Abolition of Slavery;
 Pennsylvania Hall; riots and mobs in
 Philadelphia: antiabolitionist
Abu-Jamal, Mumia, 279, 283; *Live from
 Death Row* (1995), 279
Account of the Bilious Remitting Yellow Fever
 (Rush, 1794), 26, 27, 46–49, 61,
 297n18, 300n38; on mosquitoes,
 299n36; quotations from, 31, 35, 50,
 297n18
Adams, John Quincy, 87, 148–50
aesthetics, 170, 172; of place, 21, 165,
 168; power of, 4; urban, 169
Africa, Africans, 31, 269; folktales of,
 255–56, 282; Niger, 328n9

African American higher classes, 20, 83,
 87, 107, 113, 123–30, 134, 179, 181,
 201–2, 217, 219, 262; Webb and, 225,
 227. *See also Sketches of the Higher Classes of
 Colored Society*
African Americans, 6–8, 110, 125–26,
 171, 174, 176, 194, 222; aspirations
 and ambitions of, 7, 73, 86–87, 95,
 103, 214, 217; associations of, 30–31,
 112; as barbers, 271–73; caricatures
 of, 82, 85, 88, 102, 104, 125, 126;
 in *The City Merchant* (Jones), 194,
 199–200; as criminals, 40–46, 83;
 education of, 199, 220, 221, 238;
 finery of, 82, 85, 85–87, 106, 214,
 215, 216; Freemasonry and, 87, 114,
 134; furnishings of, 147, 215, 239–40,
 262; Irish vs., 8, 201, 191, 196–97,
 198, 279; in *Liberia* (Hale), 213–18;
 literature of, 293n16; Pennsylvania Hall
 and, 147, 199; poverty of, 8, 22, 181;
 religion and, 5, 134, 135, 136, 238,
 239; in Revolutionary War, 113; rights
 of, 78, 113, 114, 115, 116, 117, 119,
 199; as servants, 51, 239; in *Sheppard Lee*
 (Bird), 98–99, 102–3; silhouettes of,
 91, 92, 93, 93, 95; social performance
 of, 20, 82, 87, 88, 95, 196, 216. *See
 also* conventions of African Americans;
 disfranchisement; elevation; free
 blacks; mulattos; Philadelphia African

African Americans (*continued*)
    Americans; racial violence; slaves, slavery;
    yellow fever epidemic: blacks and
African Methodist Episcopal Church, 108,
    238, 283
Allen, Richard, 52, 54, 162, 186, 239,
    240, 297n16, 298n22; *Autobiography*
    (1833), 27, 54; Bethel Church and,
    135; as bishop of AME church, 108;
    Carey vs. Jones and, 19, 27, 28–40, 43,
    52–54, 58, 68, 119, 148, 154; catches
    yellow fever, 27, 31, 50; character of, 46;
    "The Confession of John Joyce" (1808),
    43–46, 115, 150; "The Confession of
    Peter Matthias" (1808), 43–46, 115,
    150, 151, 299n29; execution sermons
    of, 43–45; Free African Society and, 5,
    30–31; Wideman and, 23, 281, 283. *See
    also* "Narrative of the Proceedings of the
    Black People"
American Colonization Society, 108, 217,
    218, 221, 263. *See also* colonization;
    Liberia
American Moral Reform Society, 113,
    116, 220; minutes of, 126, 313n55;
    organizers of, 108, 114; Whipper and,
    110, 115, 128, 312n48
American Philosophical Society, 5, 75–78,
    186; race and, 204, 297n13
American Revolution, 5, 15, 16, 166, 169,
    177; blacks in, 113; Fathers of, 153–54,
    164, 197; Philadelphia as symbol of,
    28; political rights and, 117. *See also*
    Declaration of Independence
"American school" of ethnology, 7, 31,
    170
American studies, 13, 292n11
Amistad revolt (1839), 267
antislavery, 14, 149, 196, 205; fairs, 216,
    217; Garrison and, 222; petitions to
    Congress on, 148; poets, 153; Quakers
    and, 4–5, 77, 181–82, 290n4; riots
    against, 181; societies for, 8, 134, 141,

272, 320n24; women and, 134. *See also*
    abolition, abolitionists
architecture, 15; bird's-eye perspective
    and, 178; of City Hall, 286; Georgian,
    173; in gothic fiction, 138; grid and,
    140; Independence and, 164–65;
    Lippard and, 166, 173; neoclassical,
    173; Pennsylvania Hall and, 147, 152;
    Victorian, 286
Arthur Mervyn; or, Memoirs of the Year 1793
    (Brown, 1799–1800), 19, 31, 49,
    58–69, 159, 166, 304n66; African
    Americans in, 61–62, 303n58; Arthur
    Mervyn in, 58, 61–69, 304n63;
    Carey and, 59, 63–64; character in,
    64–68; characters in, 59–62, 64–69;
    as experimental republican novel, 68;
    narrator of (Dr. Stevens), 58–59, 61,
    63–65, 68–69; organicism in, 67; parts
    1 and 2 of, 60–61, 64, 68; Philadelphia
    in, 186; quotations from, 61, 62,
    64, 65, 67–69; race in, 31, 63–64;
    Rush and, 59, 61, 66, 67; scenes in,
    62–67, 304n63; scholars on, 61, 65; as
    sentimental comedy, 68–69; serialization
    of, 301n50; sources of, 64; yellow fever
    in, 31, 58–62, 68
Athenaeum (London), 225, 228

Baltimore, 56, 194; in *Arthur Mervyn*, 62–65
Banneker, Benjamin, 31, 297n12
Beaumont, Gustave de, 290n4
Benezet, Anthony, 5, 121
Benito Cereno (Melville, 1855–56), 22, 23,
    171, 267, 340n87; Babo in, 268–69,
    270–71, 273–75, 339n82, 339n84,
    340n88; Cereno in, 268–71, 273–75,
    338n75; characters in, 267–70, 274;
    constraint in, 271, 275; Delano in,
    267–71, 273–75, 283, 338n75,
    340n88; fever in, 338n75; freedom in,
    273; *The Garies and Their Friends* (Webb)

and, 266–67, 273, 275; manners and gestures in, 22, 266, 268, 274; narrator in, 268–69, 274; performance in, 268; as Philadelphia story, 268, 271; publication of, 266; quotations from, 269–71, 273–74; racial assumptions in, 267–68; *San Dominick* in, 267, 269, 271, 274, 339n86; scenes in, 269, 271; shaving in, 271–75, 339n82; social experiment in, 266–78; sources of, 267

Benjamin Franklin Parkway, 286, *287*

Bentley, Nancy, 260, 336n62

Berthoff, Warner, 65

Bible: allusions to, 4, 47, 52, 77, 177, 178 198, 215, 220; in public schools, 182

Biddle, Nicholas, 195

Bird, Robert Montgomery, 16, 129, 172, 180, 199, 230, 268, 288; *The Adventures of Robin Day* (1839), 106–7, 310n29; career of, 95–96; *The City Looking Glass* (1828), 96, 98, 99, 105–6; death of, 321n32; *The Gladiator* (1831), 105; *Nick of the Woods, or The Jibbenainosay* (1837), 101–2. See also *Sheppard Lee, Written by Himself*

black dandy and dandizette, 83, 88, 106, 107, 167

blacks. *See* African Americans; conventions of African Americans; disfranchisement; elevation; free blacks; Philadelphia African Americans; slaves, slavery; yellow fever epidemic: blacks and

Blumin, Stuart M., 124

Bogle, Robert, 254

Bordley, John Beale, 52–53, 300n42, 301n45

Boston, 3, 13, 14, 153, 167, 168

Bowen, J. T., 319n18; "Destruction by Fire of Pennsylvania Hall" (lithograph), 144–47, *145*, 152–53, 198

Brackenridge, Hugh Henry, 16, 115, 306n7; linguistic self-consciousness of, 15; *The Modern Chevalier*, 79; personal history of, 74; on slavery, 306n8. See also *Modern Chivalry*

Bradley, David, *South Street* (1975), 279

Brawley, Benjamin, 227

Brigham, David R., 95, 309n24

broadsides, 41, 145, 182, 183

Brooks, Joanna, 28

Brotherhood of the Union, 166

Brougham, Henry, Lord, preface to *The Garies and Their Friends* (Webb), 225–26, 228–29, 262

Brown, Charles Brockden, 159; *Edgar Huntly*, 166; fever and, 59, 302n51; genres of, 16, 138; linguistic self-consciousness of, 15; Lippard and, 166, 170; *Ormond, or, the Secret Witness* (1799), 59, 60, 302n52, 303n59, 303n60, 304n63; "The Man at Home" (1798), 59, 60; "Somnambulism" (1805), 293n16; "Walstein's School of History" (1799), 65, 67–68; *Wieland*, 166. See also *Arthur Mervyn; or, Memoirs of the Year 1793*

Brown, David Paul, 149, 150

Brown, Henry "Box," 6

Brown, Thomas, 100

Brown, William Wells, 221; *Clotel*, 225

Bunyan, John, *The Pilgrim's Progress*, 6

Cameron, Sharon, 161

Canada, blacks and, 108, 213, 214, 217, 229, 311n41, 333n36

Carey, Mathew, 16, 26, 46, 50, 51, 186; *Autobiography* (1833–34), 27, 296n7; birth and career of, 29; Jones and Allen vs., 19, 27, 28–40, 43, 52–54, 58, 68, 119, 148, 154; racism of, 29; yellow fever epidemic of 1793 and, 52–58, 59, 281, 297n17. *See also* "Desultory Account of the Yellow Fever, Prevalent in Philadelphia"; *Short Account of the Malignant Fever*

Caribbean, 6, 190. *See also* Saint Domingue; West Indies

caricature, 98, 209; of African Americans, 82–83, 88, 102, 125–26; dramatic, 180; silhouette vs., 91

Cassey, Joseph, 127, 219, 247

Catholics, Catholicism, 29, 58, 195; anti-Catholicism and, 146, 170, 178, 180, 182–87, 195, 201–2; churches of, 182; Irish immigrants as, 131–32, 137, 182, 250; in *The Nazarene* (Lippard), 183; seminary of, 185. *See also* Irish Americans

Central America, 21, 218, 221

Cervantes, Saavedra, Miguel de, in *Modern Chivalry*, 74

character, 13, 17, 18, 22, 117; of Allen, 46; of African Americans, 126–27, 204, 207, 220; in *Arthur Mervyn* (Brown), 64–68; in *Benito Cereno* (Melville), 271; civic, 8; conduct and, 117, 118; Cornish on, 112, 113; exhibition of, 15; Franklin and, 72–73; in *The Garies and Their Friends* (Webb), 145; legislation and, 19; manners and, 71, 88; of middle class, 130; in *Modern Chivalry* (Brackenridge), 74, 75; of Rush, 46; in *Sheppard Lee* (Bird), 95, 96, 97, 100–3; silhouettes and, 91, 94; trials and tests of, 20, 212, 224; in U.S. national literature, 4; urban environment and, 170; Whipper on, 111–14, 116, 223; yellow fever epidemic and, 6, 45, 64

Chase, Richard, 72, 305n3

Chesnutt, Charles W., *The Marrow of Tradition* (1901), 333–34n39

Chester, T. Morris, "Negro Self-Respect and Pride of Race" (address, 1862), 247

chiasmus, of freedom and slavery, 14, 151

Cincinnati, Ohio, 107–8, 156, 167, 311n41

citizens, citizenship, 74, 80–81, 106–7, 117–19; free blacks and, 30, 119–20;
130, 211, 218–20, 222, 224; race and, 107, 134, 228, 306n5; virtue and, 115; Whipper on, 116. *See also* civil rights

City Merchant, The, or, The Mysterious Failure (Jones, 1851), 21, 137, 139, 153, 217, 237, 249, 251; African Americans in, 194, 199; characters in, 195, 196, 197, 198, 199, 200, 202; narrator of, 194, 195, 196, 200, 201; Pennsylvania Hall in, 139, 194, 195, 197–99; plots of, 194–96, 198–201, 202; preface of, 194; quotations from, 194, 195, 196, 197, 200, 201; as racist novel, 194, 201–2, 325n61; riots in, 194–202, 251

civil rights: of African Americans, 109, 128, 149, 218; Civil Rights movement and, 23, 267, 283, 284; laws restricting, 108; moral improvement and, 111, 115–16; Philadelphia experiment and, 74. *See also* citizens, citizenship

Civil War, 88, 92, 122; draft riots of, 14; emancipation and, 4

Clamorgan, Cyprian, *The Colored Aristocracy of St. Louis* (1858), 130, 272

Clarkson, Mayor Mathew, 31, 39

class, 123, 124, 126, 337n70; ambiguity of, 125; antagonism and discord, 178, 183; boundaries of, 125, 207; differences of, 282, 312n50; higher, 262; politics of, 183; race and, 214, 215, 220, 241. *See also* African American higher classes; elites; laboring class; lower class; middle class; working class; upper class

classicism, 89, 144; Classical Library, 260; neo-, 173; of Pennsylvania Hall, 143, 146

Clay, Edward Williams, 16, 91, 92, 95, 97, 115, 129, 171, 180, 214, 229; "Going Home from a Tea-Fight" (1825), 83; "Practical Amalgamation" (lithographs, 1825), 83; silhouette of, 91, 94. *See also* "Life in Philadelphia"

Coates, Dr. Benjamin, 203, 204, 213
Cole, Thomas, *The Course of Empire*
    (paintings, 1834–36), 144, 319n17
colonization, 21, 83, 134, 152, 217,
    238; benevolent paternalism and, 214;
    Garnet and, 328n10; resistance to, 108;
    supporters of, 313n58. *See also* American
    Colonization Society; Liberia; *Liberia; or,
    Mr. Peyton's Experiments*
Colored American, The (New York), 108, 109,
    111–13, 222
Colored Aristocracy of St. Louis, The
    (Clamorgan, 1858), 130, 272
"complexion." See "condition" vs.
    "complexion" debate
Compromise of 1850, 181, 194
"condition" vs. "complexion" debate,
    109–10, 113, 116–17; Delany and,
    219–21; in *The Garies and Their Friends*
    (Webb), 212; Whipper and, 221
conspiracy, conspiracies, 190; in *Benito
    Cereno* (Melville), 270; of elites, 173,
    184; fever and, 60; gothic, 179; riots
    and, 133, 156, 165, 184, 201–2; white
    violence and, 102
conventions of African Americans, 7, 16,
    20, 69, 73, 107–18, 127, 220; minutes
    of, 205; in Philadelphia, 7, 20, 107,
    108
Cooper, James Fenimore, 15–16, 71; *The
    Last of the Mohicans*, 293n16; *The Pioneers*,
    258, 293n16
Cornish, Samuel E.: on character,
    112, 113; American Moral Reform
    convention and, 108; on status of
    African Americans, 109, 230; Whipper
    vs., 110, 222–23
corruption, 100, 144, 177, 183–84, 190;
    of city, 164, 166, 212, 279; of heart,
    152; Lippard and, 137, 179; political,
    133, 161–63, 165–66; of slavery, 77,
    104. *See also* conspiracy, conspiracies
Creole, slave revolt on (1841), 267

Crèvecoeur, Hector St. Jean de, *Letters from
    an American Farmer* (1782), 71
crime, criminals, narratives of, 40–46

danse macabre, 178
Davis, Arthur P., 227, 332n30
Davis, Samuel H., 122–23
Dayan, Joan, 172–73
Declaration of Independence, 6, 27, 51,
    114, 148; African Americans and, 116,
    119, 120; in *The American Scene* (James),
    165; freedom and rights in, 14, 104,
    110, 116, 119–20; symbolic space of,
    66, 144, 147, 212, 286
"Declaration of Sentiment" (1835, 1837),
    114–15, 313n55
decorum, 18–19, 22, 40, 115, 123,
    130, 215, 242, 257–60; of African
    Americans, 290n4; breaches of, 168;
    verbal, 128. *See also* manners
Defoe, Daniel, *Journal of the Plague Year*
    (1722), 46–47, 299n33
Delano, Captain Amasa, *Narrative of
    Voyages and Travels in the Southern and
    Northern Hemispheres* (1817), 267, 270,
    272
Delany, Martin Robison, 16, 194, 212,
    223, 263, 276; colonization and,
    328n9; *Condition, Elevation, Emigration, and
    Destiny of the Colored People of the United
    States* (1852), 21–22, 218–21, 240,
    254, 316n78, 328n10; Whipper and,
    221
Delaware, 32, 43
Delaware River, 9, *10*, 131, 134, 136, 157,
    175, 177, *189*, 310n30
democracy, 79, 80; character of, 123;
    critique of, 144; excess of, 74; manners
    and, 71; republicanism vs., 306n7;
    slaveholding, 217
Denning, Michael, 166, 174, 183
Denny, John F., 211, 219

"Destruction by Fire of Pennsylvania Hall, on the night of the 17th of May" (lithograph, 1838), 144–47, *145*, 319n18; *The City Merchant* (Jones) and, 153

"Desultory Account of the Yellow Fever, Prevalent in Philadelphia, and of the Present State of the City" (Carey, 1793) 29, 30, 47, 52, 53, 57, 297n16, 301n46

Dexter, Pete, *God's Pocket* (1983), 107, 279

Dickens, Charles, 185, 208, 243; *Bleak House* (1852–53), 226; *A Christmas Carol* (1843), 177; deportment and respectability in, 226; on Eastern State Penitentiary, 164, 325n59; on Philadelphia, 11

Dickinson, Anna E., *What Answer?* (1868), 330n19

disfranchisement (1838), 7, 15, 18–22, 73, 107, 110, 115, 118–25, 194, 199, 211, 219–20, 237; aftermath of, 137, 239, 262, 264; Delany on, 221; destruction of Pennsylvania Hall and, 134–35, 150; exclusion and, 238; Pennsylvania Abolition Society and, 204; racial prejudice and, 117, 123; referendum on, 118, 119, 135, 222. *See also* citizens, citizenship; civil rights

Dixon, Jeremiah, 4, 280

Douglass, Frederick, 148, 253, 271, 275; "The Black Man's Future in the Southern States" (speech, 1862), 3, 4; in *The City Merchant* (Jones), 196; "Claims of the Negro Ethnologically Considered" (1854), 263; "Learn Trades or Starve" (1853), 240; *Narrative of the Life* (1845), 151; *North Star*, 337n72; use of term "peculiar" by, 230. See also *Frederick Douglass' Paper*

Dred Scott case and decision, 119, 222

DuBois, W. E. B., 129, 161; *The Philadelphia Negro: A Social Study* (1899), 9, 122, 161, 203–4, 284, 291n7, 332n29, 335n53; *The Souls of Black Folk* (1903), 161, 203,

332n29; sources of, 21, 203, 205, 315n69, 315n72, 327nn70–71

duCille, Ann, 264, 294n20

Dunbar, Erica Armstrong, 4

Dunphy, Jack, *John Fury* (1946), 107, 279

Eastern State Penitentiary (Philadelphia): in *The American Scene* (James), 164; blacks in, 213; Dickens on, 164, 325n59; fugitive slaves in, 201; Poe and, 172–73; Tocqueville on, 164

elevation, 113, 115, 120, 130, 156, 239; Delany on, 219, 220, 221; ironies of, 223; political, 224; as submission, 264. *See also* uplift

Elias, Norbert, *The Civilizing Process* (1939), 259

elites: Anglo, 8, 142, *145*, 146, 260; complicity of, 201; corruption and, 166; home ownership and, 125; in *The Quaker City* (Lippard), 166, 170, 173. *See also* African American higher classes; *Sketches of the Higher Classes of Colored Society*; upper class

emancipation, 30, 46, 151, 199, 272; Civil War and, 4; emblems of, 317n6; immediate, 134, 149; subordination and, 216; in West Indies, 135

Emerson, Ralph Waldo, 98

emigration of free blacks, 238, 263; conventions and, 7, 109; Delany and, 21, 218–20; Whipper and, 111

England, English, 172, 290n4; Henry James in, 159; immigrants from, 6, 89; in Philadelphia, 133; society of, 71–72; Webbs in, 225, 227. *See also* London

engravings and prints, 15, 172, 193, 197; in books and pamphlets, 45, 172, 188, 235, *236*, 319n21, 323n42; comic, 178; on display, 215; etchings, 20; in Lippard's fiction, 188–89; mezzotints, 138, 141, 142, 144, 146, 152, 233, 318n14; wood engravings,

83, 138, 141, 142, 144, 152. *See also*
    "Life in Philadelphia"; lithographs,
    lithographers; Pennsylvania Hall: images
    of, "View of the City of Brotherly
    Love"
Episcopal Church 5, 238, 341–42n8
Equiano, Olaudah, 293n16
ethnology, ethnologists, 7, 62, 78, 126,
    213, 263, 267
Europe: Canada and, 221; gothic fiction of,
    167, 168; Henry James in, 159; history
    of, 144; immigrants from, 6, 160, 165,
    171, 204, 206, 327n70
experiment in freedom: in *Benito Cereno*
    (Melville), 266–78; from black
    perspective, 229; failure of, 194, 212; in
    The Garies and Their Friends (Webb), 212,
    228–30, 237–66; in *Liberia* (Hale), 213–
    18; in Philadelphia, 3–9, 11, 14, 16,
    17, 18–24, 28, 39, 66–68, 74–76, 110,
    113, 116–17, 125, 138, 181, 194, 201,
    202, 209, 212, 213, 224, 229, 284–85,
    290-91n5; at Port Royal, 291n5

Faflik, David, 187, 193
"Fate of Murderers, The: A Faithful
    Narrative of the Murder of Mrs. Sarah
    Cross" (1808), 45–46
Faulkner, William, *Absalom, Absalom!*, 31
Fauset, Jesse, works of, 279
Federal Procession (July 4, 1788), 251
"Fever" (Wideman short story, 1989), 19,
    23, 31
Fiedler, Leslie A., 168, 267
Findley, William, vs. Brackenridge, 74, 79
Fogg, William, case of, 119, 121
food: American suppers, 258–60, 261; as
    medium of struggle, 231; at wedding
    feast in *The Garies and Their Friends*
    (Webb), 230, 252–66
formalism, 18, 45, 60, 73, 148, 294n18
Forten, James, Jr., 113, 116, 127, 134,
    219, 276, 330n19

Forten, James E., Sr., 113, 117, 120, 121,
    127, 134, 238, 247, 313n53
Foster, George G., 167, 174, 212;
    "Philadelphia in Slices" (1848–49), 181
Fourth of July, 6, 251
France, French: in "Life in Philadelphia"
    etchings (Clay), 85, 86; in *Modern
    Chivalry* (Brackenridge), 75, 76, 78–79;
    Orientalism of, 81–82; Paris, 82, 167,
    171, 208; Saint Domingue and, 31,
    62–63
Franklin, Aretha, "Who's Zoomin' Who,"
    286
Franklin, Benjamin, 29, 47, 88, 286,
    291n9, 296n7, 310n29; African
    Americans and, 5, 312n51; in
    The American Scene (James), 165;
    autobiography, 11, *12*, 13, 15, 73,
    96, 291–92n8, 305n4; character and,
    11–13, 72–73, 101, 112, 160; images
    of, 160
Frederick Douglass' Paper, 4, 22; review of *The
    Garies and Their Friends* (Webb) in, 226,
    228; Smith, James McCune, in, 222,
    337n72; Troy, N.Y., convention (1847)
    and, 108; Whipper in, 221–24
Free African Society, 5, 30–31
free blacks, 3, 6–7, 98, 102, 105, 117,
    123, 130, 180–81, 228, 282, 284;
    apathy of despair of, 222, 223, 224,
    263; "burdened individuality" of, 216;
    enterprise of, 219; organizations of,
    5, 30–31, 107–8; peculiar status of,
    109–10, 230; Pennsylvania constitution
    (1790) and, 109–10, 118; reports on,
    121–22, 202–9; rights of, 108–9, 211,
    218, 222–24; voluntary emigration
    and resettlement of, 218–20. *See also*
    African Americans; disfranchisement;
    Philadelphia African Americans
freedom, 19, 22, 117–18, 122, 151, 181,
    202, 264; in *Benito Cereno* (Melville),
    270, 273; Declaration of Independence
    and, 14, 51–52, 104, 110, 114, 116;

freedom (*continued*)
elevation and, 113; emptiness of,
147–48; as experiment, 4, 5, 76, 95,
100, 110, 117, 170, 171, 201; in *The
Garies and Their Friends* (Webb), 228,
234, 235, 265; as imperfect, 211; as
insolence, 107; liberty and, 194; literary
debates on, 209; in North, 87, 109–10,
218; Pennsylvania Hall and, 139, 142,
143, 144, 147; Philadelphia and, 4–9,
6, 8, 51, 209, 265; progress of, 223;
race and, 21, 66, 200, 263; rhetoric
of, 17; slavery and, 149, 221; spaces
of, 229; as suicidal, 213; trials in, 285;
untenability of, 220–21; volatility of,
224. *See also* experiment in freedom; free
blacks; quasi-freedom
Freedom's Journal, 124
Freneau, Philip, 26, 297n17,
300n39
Fugitive Slave Act (1793), 78, 218,
301n47
Fugitive Slave Act (1850), 109, 212, 218;
Compromise of 1850 and, 181, 194;
Delany on, 21–22, 218–21; kidnapping
and, 109; Lippard on, 181–82;
resistance to, 238; Smith, James McCune,
on, 222
fugitive slaves, 6, 109, 176, 184; Allen as,
43; in *The City Merchant* (Jones), 200;
rescue of, 111, 134, 238; rights of,
121; Schoolcraft on, 212; in *Sheppard
Lee* (Bird), 102; in *Uncle Tom's Cabin*
(Stowe), 258. *See also* Fugitive Slave Act;
Underground Railroad
fugitives, 6, 201; Philadelphians as, 52–58,
64, 136, 200, 301n46. *See also* fugitive
slaves

Gaines, Kevin K., 124
gangs, 137, 187, 188, 192–93, 198, 200,
201, 217, 248. *See also* Killers, The
Gardner, Charles W., 120

Garies and Their Friends, The (Webb, 1857),
22, 23, 125, 211–12, 224–25, 227,
237, 249, 266; *Benito Cereno* (Melville)
and, 266–68, 273; *Bleak House* and,
226; Caroline (Caddy) Ellis, 226, 238,
240–43, 248, 252, 333n37; characters
in, 226, 227, 240, 246, 264; Charles
Ellis in, 226, 230, 248–49, 255, 258,
262; Charles (Charlie) Ellis Jr. in, 226,
238–44, 252, 262; Clarence Garie
in, 226–27, 232–35, *236*, 238–39,
244–51, 255; Clarence Garie Jr. in,
226–27, 233, 235, *236*, 239, 249, 257;
"condition" vs. "complexion" debate in,
212; cover illustration of, 234–35, *236*;
critics on, 227; as "curious protest,"
227; domestic scenes in, 215, 244–48,
262; Emily Garie in, 226, 227, 231–35,
236, 238–39, 244, 249, 251; Emily
Garie (daughter) in, 226–27, 233,
235, *236*, 249, 252; Esther Ellis in,
226, 242, 248, 252; freedom in, 229,
252–66; George Stevens in, 226–27,
237, 240, 243–44, 249, 252, 254, 257,
262; George Winston in, 232, 238–42;
history and farce in, 217, 237–44;
irony in, 246; Kinch in, 240–43, 253,
262; manners in, 227, 240, 244–48;
McCloskey in, 226, 237, 249, 255;
narrator of, 163, 212, 225, 227, 231,
239, 241–43, 246, 248, 255, 258, 260,
264; parlors in, 229, 233, 241, 244,
245–48; Philadelphia as experiment in,
234–35, 252; Philadelphia genres and,
224; physical bearing and gestures in,
215, 240, 241, 265; plot of, 226–27;
preface to, 225–26, 228–29; publishing
history of, 224–28, 330n19; quotations
from, 211, 228–34, 239, 242–48,
252, 258; race and, 31, 218, 225–26,
267; reviews of, 226, 228, 249, 253;
riots and mobs in, 147, 226, 239–44,
248–52, 258, 262; scenes in, 230–34,
239–40, 242–43, 248–49; servants

in, 240–41; as *the* Philadelphia story, 19, 212; title of, 332n31; use of term "peculiar" in, 230; *vanitas* in, 261–62; Walters in, 226, 237, 238, 240, 244–48, 252, 262; wedding supper in, 230, 252–66

Garnet, Henry Highland, 328n10; "Address to the Slaves of the United States of America" (1843), 108, 314n62

Garrison, William Lloyd, 134, 149–52, 222; Garrisonians and, 110, 112; *The Liberator* and, 317n6

genre, genres, 207; autobiography, 96; black idealist history, 41; city mystery novel, 21, 165, 166, 167, 171, 173, 184, 188, 207, 322n35, 327n67; comedy of manners, 96, 98, 99; conversion narrative, 47; cookbook, 256; criminal confession, 40–46; documentary collection, 137, 207; epistolary novel, 47; essay, 20; experimental novel, 67; fever narrative, 17, 55, 59, 67, 68, 186; gallows literature, 41; gothic novel, 138–39, 167, 173, 209; historical novel, 15, 153, 194, 198, 207, 224; joke, 292n9, 310n29; of Lippard, 174; metempsychic novel, 69, 95–107, 230, 282; minutes of conventions, 69, 109, 114, 115, 126, 205, 311n43, 313n55; narrative forms, 16; narrative of violence, 224; novel, 19, 227; novella, 22, 187, 190, 266, 270, 273; novel of circulation, 100; novel of manners, 20, 71, 72, 96, 101, 266; petition, 40–41, 205; Philadelphia and, 22, 76, 224; Philadelphia novel, 137, 158, 187, 213–14; picaresque narrative, 20, 99; plague narrative, 40; plantation fiction, 235; prison writing, 279; protest pamphlet, 41; recipe, 16; report, 137, 202–8; riot novel, 16, 97, 137; romance, 72; satire, 77, 171, 279; sentimental comedy, 68, 305n67; sentimental narrative, 40, 103; sermon,

40, 41, 44; sketch of manners, 125–27, 129–30; slave narrative, 96; speech, 20; travel narratives, 137, 164; urban gothic, 158, 166, 183, 208–9; Wideman's, 281

geography, 13, 14, 168, 184, 327n67. *See also* place; space

Georgia, 123, 153; in *The Garies and Their Friends* (Webb), 230–36; slavery in, 226, 255

Germany, Germans, 6, 133, 322n34, 327n67

Gibson, John Bannister (Pennsylvania Supreme Court Chief Justice), 119, 218

Gilbert, R. S., 225n16; wood engraving of Pennsylvania Hall by, 141, 142–43, *143*, 152. *See also* Woodside, John Archibald, Jr.

Girard, Stephen, 177; Lippard and, 183

Girard Bank, 175

Girard College, 177

Glaude, Eddie S., Jr., 23, 111, 264, 312n48, 314n62

Goddu, Teresa, 61

Godey's Lady's Book, 215

Godwin, William, 65: *The Adventures of Caleb Williams*, 64–66, 303n59, 304n62

Goode, Mayor Wilson, 23, 280, 284

Goodis, David, *Down There* (1956), 279

gothic, the, 15, 138–39, 152, 186, 207, 208; American, 303n56; conspiracy in, 179; devices of, 178; of Eastern State Penitentiary, 164, 172; European, 167; Lippard and, 21, 173, 180; of Philadelphia literature, 17, 166, 168, 170; plots of, 184. *See also* urban gothic

Goudie, Sean X., 61, 63, 303n58, 305n68

Gould, Philip, 28

Grabo, Norman, 61, 65

Gray, William, and yellow fever epidemic of 1793, 32–33, 35–37, 52–53, 297n16

grid of Philadelphia, 9, *10*, 13, 17, 131, 137, 186, *189*, 189–90, 202, 264, 285, *287*; Benjamin Franklin Parkway

grid of Philadelphia (*continued*)
    and, 286; comparison of, to Franklin's
    charts, 13; creation of, 291n7; gap
    between ideal of and reality, 157–60,
    178, 208; James on, 159–60;
    Lippard and, 169–70, 173, 174;
    metaphors of, 292n9; pattern of black
    regressive advance compared to, 164;
    Pennsylvania Hall and, 140; rigidity
    of, 9, 11; skewing of, 17; Wideman
    on, 23, 285, *287*; writers on, 20,
    157, 169, 173. *See also* Philadelphia:
    maps of; Penn, William: Philadelphia
    grid and; "Portraiture of the City of
    Philadelphia"
Grimké, Angelina. *See* Weld, Angelina
    Grimké
Grimké, Sarah, 134, 276; *Letters on the
    Equality of the Sexes and Condition of Women*
    (1838), 116
grotesque, 168–69; -sublime, 168, 178

Haitian revolution, 60, 247, 267
Hale, Dorothy J., 65, 66
Hale, Sarah Josepha, 194, 204, 213, 215,
    263; as Southern sympathizer, 214,
    217. See also *Liberia; or, Mr. Peyton's
    Experiments*
Hammond, Charles, 156, 157
Hardie, James, 297n18
Harper, Frances E. W., *Trial and Triumph*
    (1888–89), 31, 40, 279
Harrisburg, Pennsylvania, 120; black
    conventions in, 108, 115, 116
Hartman, Saidya V., 22, 216
Hawthorne, Nathaniel, *The Marble Faun: or,
    The Romance of Monte Beni* (1860), 71–72,
    321n30
Helmuth, J. Henry C., 55, 300n44
Hershberg, Theodore, 204–5
Hibernian Hose Company, 182, 185
Higginbotham, Evelyn Brooks, 111, 264
Higginson, Thomas Wentworth, 271, 272

Hinton, Frederick A., 120, 127
historicism, 18, 165, 237
history, historians, 23, 170, 172; cycle of,
    144; Lippard and, 173; literature and,
    19; local, 178
*History of Pennsylvania Hall, Which Was Destroyed
    By a Mob, on the 17th of May, 1838* (1838),
    20–21, 138–57, 197, 201; appendix
    to, 152–57, 198; close reading of,
    138–44, 154–57; counternarrative to,
    270; intentions of compilers of, 138,
    154; prints in, *139*, 139–44, *141*,
    143, 145, 146, 147, 318n12, 318n14,
    319n18; quotations from, 153–56, 198;
    typography of, 154–55; use of term
    "peculiar institution" in, 230
Holme, Thomas, Philadelphia grid and, 9,
    10, 13, 140, 157–60, 190, 264, 285,
    291n7
Hugo, Victor, 168

Ichabod Crane (Irving, "Legend of Sleepy
    Hollow"), 258–59
immigration, immigrants, 6, 28, 74, 164,
    171, 204, 206, 327n70; in *The American
    Scene* (James), 160–62, 165; Dutch,
    133; Irish Catholic, 131–32, 158,
    250
Incidents in the Life of a Slave Girl (Jacobs,
    1861), 6, 263
Independence Hall, 88, 89, 147, 153;
    bell of, 175; as landmark, 186; in *The
    Quaker City* (Lippard), 175, 177. *See also*
    Pennsylvania State House
industrialization, 133; domestic
    manufacturing and, 185; factories and,
    184, 186
interracial socializing, 134, 135, 137;
    danger of, 216; in *The Garies and Their
    Friends* (Webb), 233
Irish Americans, 6, 28, 131–33, 136, 158,
    182, 185, 250, 260; African Americans
    vs., 8, 21, 187, 191, 196–98, 279;

blamed for riots (1844), 183, 317n4;
in *The City Merchant* (Jones), 195; as
dockworkers, 136; gangs of, 137, 187,
198, 201, 217; in *The Garies and Their
Friends* (Webb), 226, 237; in *Modern
Chivalry* (Brackenridge), 20, 74, 78, 79.
See also Carey, Mathew; Philadelphia:
Irish in; Scots-Irish
Irving, Washington, 15, 260, 293n16;
"Legend of Sleepy Hollow" (1820),
258–59; *The Sketch Book of Geoffrey
Crayon, Gent.* (1820), 258, 293n16,
336n63

Jackson, Andrew, 87, 183, 195, 247
Jackson, Blyden, *History of Afro-American
Literature* (1989), 227
Jacobs, Harriet, 40; *Incidents in the Life of a
Slave Girl* (1861), 6, 263–64
Jamaica, 60, 225, 263
James, Henry, 16, 21, 159–65, 168–69,
193, 284, 321n30, 336n62; dinner
tables in, 260; on Hawthorne, 72; on
texture of society, 71; travels of, 159.
See also *American Scene, The* (1907)
Jay, William, 147, 148
Jefferson, Thomas, 32, *90*; Land Ordinance
of 1785 and, 291n7; *Notes on the State of
Virginia* (1787), 63, 71, 104–5,
263
Jews, 69, 98, 174, 183, 283
Johnstone, Abraham, "The Address of
Abraham Johnstone, A Black Man"
(1797), 42–43, 57
Jones, Absalom, 52, 54, 162, 186, 297n16;
Carey vs. Allen and, 19, 27, 28–40, 43,
52–54, 58, 68, 119, 148, 154; Free
African Society and, 5, 30–31. *See also*
"Narrative of the Proceedings of the
Black People"
Jones, John Beauchamp, 16, 204, 263, 268,
326n63; *Border War: A Tale of Disunion*
(1859), 325n60; life and career of,

194; racial politics of, 196. See also *City
Merchant, The*
Journal of the Plague Year (Defoe, 1722),
46–47, 299n33
Joyce, John, 43–46, 150

Kasson, John F., 178
Kelley, Abby, 196
Kentucky, 102, 194, 212
Killers, The (Philadelphia gang), 187–91,
198, 217
Killers, The (Lippard, 1850), 21, 137, 184,
201, 206; characters in, 187, 190,
192, 200; engravings in, 188; narrator
of, 190–92; plots of, 192; quotations
from, 190–91; reprinting of, as *The Bank
Director's Son*, 187; riots in, 174, 178,
186–88, 191–93, 252; title page of,
187
knots, Gordian, 277–78

labor, organized, 166, 185
laboring class. *See* working class
Lapsansky, Emma Jones, 4, 133, 291n7;
on Cedar neighborhood, 7, 205, 316n2,
325n59
Lapsansky, Phillip S., 28, 311n47,
333n33; on Carey, 38, 58; on *The Garies*
(Webb), 227, 330n19, 334n46
Lavater, Johann Casper, *Essays on Physiognomy*
(1775–78), 89, 95
Le Sage, Alain René, 48, 74
Leslie, Eliza, *New Receipts for Cooking* (1854),
256, 257
Levine, Robert S., 237, 303n58, 328n10,
335nn54–55
Lewis, Matthew, *The Monk* (1796), 138,
166
Lewis, R. W. B., 65
Liberator, The, 157, 158, 272, 317n6
Liberia: colonization of free blacks in, 21,
213, 214, 311n41; Delany and, 218,

Liberia (*continued*)
221, 328n9; founding documents of,
214; as nation, 217. See also *Liberia; or,*
Mr. Peyton's Experiments
Liberia; or, Mr. Peyton's Experiments (Hale,
1853), 21, 199, 218; African Americans
in, 213–18; appendix to, 214; Ben in,
214–18; characters in, 214–18, 230,
241; Charles Peyton in, 213–15; Clara
in, 214–17, 328n7; narrator of, 215;
Philadelphia in, 214–17; physical
bearing and gestures in, 215; plot of,
213–14; quotations from, 214,
216–17, 248; scenes in, 214–17,
230
Library Company of Philadelphia,
10, 47, 84, 85, 91, 92, 93, 132, 189,
287
"Life in Philadelphia" series (Clay
etchings, 1828–30), 20, 69, 73,
81–88, 95, 100, 106–7, 126, 214,
240, 271; ambition and aspiration in,
81, 82, 86–88, 95, 180, 229; coloring
of, 308n16; exhibition of Hunt's
versions of, 88; "Have you any *flesh*
coloured silk stockings, young man?"
(plate 11, 1829) in, 82, 85–87, 85;
misattributions of, 308n18; New
Comic Annual (London) version of,
83–84; other versions of, 307n14;
plates of, 83, 84, 85, 85, 86–87, 215;
sources of, 81–82
Lining, Dr., on yellow fever, 30, 31, 53
Lippard, George, 15–16, 164–67, 172–73,
200–204, 212, 284, 321n32; *The Bank*
Director's Son (1851), 187–88; "Eleanor;
or, Slave-Catching in the Quaker City"
(1854), 139, 166, 181, 321n32; *Empire*
City (1850), 176–77, 181; *Herbert Tracy*
(1844), 170; *The Ladye Annabel* (1844),
170; *The Life and Adventures of Charles*
Anderson Chester (1850), 187–90; novels
of, 165–66, 170; Philadelphia riots and,
158, 165, 174, 178–80, 182, 191–92;

Poe and, 165, 170, 173–74; on upper
class, 162, 170; as urban novelist, 176,
208. See also *Killers, The; Nazarene, The;*
Quaker City, The
literary critics, 15, 23, 71–72, 227–28,
264–65, 331n22
literary genre. See genre, genres
literary societies, black, 126, 127, 215
literature, literary history, 15–16, 19,
293n16; of Philadelphia, 8, 14–18,
23–24, 46, 173, 215, 286; race and,
4, 16; U.S. national, 3–4, 15–16, 130,
168, 214
lithographs, lithographers, 139–40, 182,
198, 249, *250*; by Clay, 83, 307n14; in
History of Pennsylvania Hall, 138, 139–40,
144, 318n12; of Philadelphia, 178,
249, 324n47; of Shiffler's death, 146,
182, 324n52
London, 41, 64, 83, 227; city mysteries
of, 167, 208; in "Man of the Crowd"
(Poe), 170; newspapers in, 226, 228,
249, 253; publication of *The Garies and*
Their Friends (Webb) in, 224–25, 228
Looby, Christopher, 310n30, 311n40;
Voicing America (1996), 15,
306n7
Louisiana, 98, 303n58
Lovejoy, Elijah, murder of, 148
lower class: black, 133, 134; immigrant,
171

magazines and periodicals, 29, 139,
161–62, 170, 172, 266; African
American, 108, 110
manners, 18, 20, 71–73, 115, 130; action
vs., 110; African Americans and, 82,
87, 107, 111; in *The American Scene*
(James), 162; in *Benito Cereno* (Melville),
22, 266, 268, 274; character and, 88;
discourse of, 111; in *The Garies and Their*
Friends (Webb), 227, 230–31, 240,
246; Jefferson on, 71; in *Modern Chivalry*

(Brackenridge), 78; nature vs., 76, 101; novel of, 20, 71, 72, 96, 101, 266; Philadelphia's genres of, 69, 73, 81; physical bearing and gestures as, 215; politics and, 117; satires of, 279; in *Sketches of the Higher Classes of Colored Society* (Willson), 129–30; violence and, 162, 168, 240, 285. *See also* decorum

Mansfield, William Murray, First Earl of, and Somersett decision (1772), 117

Martin, Benjamin, 119, 120

Marx, Karl, 124

Maryland, 36, 52, 56, 111, 196

Mason, Charles, 4, 280

Mason-Dixon line, 4, 110, 111; Pynchon and, 279–80

Massachusetts, 3, 136, 161, 167, 267, 291n5

Massey, Doreen, 13

Matthias, Peter, 43–46, 150–51

McKinney-Whetstone, Diane, *Tumbling* (1996), 279

Melville, Herman, 16; on accommodationism, 150; *Clarel* (1876), 272–73; *The Confidence-Man: His Masquerade* (1857), 292n9; *Moby-Dick* (1851), 252–53, 337n72; "The Paradise of the Bachelors and the Tartarus of Maids" (1855), 260, 336n63; *The Piazza Tales*, 266, 268, 336n62; on shaving, 271–74; Webb and, 22–23, 266–68, 270, 275–78. *See also* Benito Cereno

memento mori, 19, 95, 164, 186

"Memorial of the Free Citizens of Color in Pittsburgh and Its Vicinity Relative to the Right of Suffrage" (1837), 120, 122

"Memorial of Thirty Thousand Disfranchised Citizens of Philadelphia, to the Honorable Senate and House of Representatives" (1855), 122, 205

"Memorial to the Honorable, the Delegates of the People of Pennsylvania in Convention at Philadelphia Assembled" (1838), 120–21, 122

Mercer, Singleton, 173, 180

metempsychosis, 310n32; *Sheppard Lee* and, 20, 69, 95, 97, 100, 101, 230, 282

Methodism, Methodists, 5, 33, 108, 238, 239, 283

middle class, 303n58; black, 6, 20, 14, 133, 181, 201, 327n70; bourgeoisie, 124; character of, 130; white, 124

Milton, John, 45; *Paradise Lost*, 142

minstrel shows, 83

Minton, Henry, 219, 254

miscegenation, 77, 83; black voting rights and, 119; in *The Garies and Their Friends* (Webb), 226, 227, 232–33; riot and, 7, 134, 137, 187, 196

Missouri Compromise (1820), 4

mobs. *See* Pennsylvania Hall: destruction of; racial violence; riots and mobs in Philadelphia

Modern Chivalry (Brackenridge, 1792–1815), 20, 69, 73–81, 99; animals in, 75, 78, 80, 81; blacks in, 76–78, 81; Cervantes in, 74; character in, 74, 75; characters in, 75, 76, 79; Captain John Farrago in, 74–77, 79–80; literary experiments in, 74; manners in, 78, 240; narrator of, 73–74, 78, 79, 81; Philadelphia in, 74, 75, 186; political satire in, 76, 79–80; quotations from, 74, 77, 79, 80; race in, 75–78, 81; Teague O'Regan in, 73–80, 88, 95, 97

moral reform, moral regeneration, 20, 110, 124, 220, 238; DuBois and, 204; legacy of, 223; Second Great Awakening and, 112; Whipper on, 114–16, 222–23, 247. *See also* American Moral Reform Society

Morrison, Toni, "Unspeakable Things Unspoken," 57

Morton, Samuel George, 7, 170–71

Mott, Lucretia, 134, 196

Mountain, Joseph, "Sketches of the Life of Joseph Mountain" (1790), 41–42

MOVE ("The Movement"): bombing (1985), 23, 280–81, 283–84; compared to burning of Pennsylvania Hall (1838), 280; as genocide, 282; Wideman on, 282–83, 284, 285; yellow fever epidemic (1793) and, 282–85

mulattos, 51, 134, 137, 187, 244; in *The City Merchant* (Jones), 196, 198, 199; in *The Garies and Their Friends* (Webb), 226, 232, 238

mysteries of the city, 166, 167, 171–73, 322n35; James and, 162, 165; of Paris, 166; of Philadelphia, 158, 165–67, 184–93, 204, 207–9, 327n67. *See also* Reynolds, G. W. M., *Mysteries of London*; Sue, Eugène, *Les Mystères de Paris*

Mysteries of Philadelphia, The (1848), 158

"Narrative of the Proceedings of the Black People, during the Late Awful Calamity in Philadelphia, in the Year 1793" (Jones and Allen, 1794), 19, 27, 30, 40–42, 46, 50–54, 58, 61, 66, 114–15; addresses in, 38–40; biblical allusions in, 50; Carey vs., 27, 54–55; compared to criminal narratives, 42, 46; influences on, 40–41; Wideman and, 281

Nash, Gary B., 4, 290–91n5, 308n17, 312n50, 335n54

National Era, 212

National Reformer, Whipper and, 110, 115

Native Americans, 75, 102, 134, 151, 183

nativism, nativists, 170, 182, 250, 317n4, 325n56; in *The Nazarene* (Lippard), 183, 185

Nazarene, The; or, The Last of the Washingtons, A Revelation of Philadelphia, New York, and Washington, in the Year 1844 (Lippard, 1846), 21, 137, 168, 178, 182–86,

193; narrator of, 184, 185, 186; Philadelphia in, 174, 184–86; plot of, 183–84; publishing history of, 187; *The Quaker City* (Lippard) and, 165, 182, 184; quotations from, 182, 184, 185; riots in, 182–87

Needles, Edward, "Ten Years' Progress," 203

Nemerov, Alexander, 261–62

New Comic Annual (London), 83–84

New England, 13, 150, 293n16; in *The American Scene* (James), 159; factories in, 260; Puritans and Calvinists of, 16, 229, 339n86; Yankee peddlers from, 98

New Era, 225; Webb's pieces in, 226

New Jersey, 43, 175; as refuge, 27, 46, 56, 134, 136, 200; in *Sheppard Lee* (Bird), 97, 99–100, 103–5

New Orleans, 153, 289n2; city mysteries of, 167; newspapers in, 153; in *Uncle Tom's Cabin* (Stowe), 212, 229

New York Anti-Slavery Society, 272

New York by Gaslight (Foster, 1850), 167

New York City, 13, 83, 227, 238, 255; African Americans in, 14, 148, 220; in *The American Scene* (James), 159, 160, 165, 168; dance halls in, 167; Douglass in, 196; Five Points in, 208; mysteries of, 166; national black conventions in, 108, 109; Philadelphia and, 6, 167, 176–77, 224; Poe and, 170, 171; press in, 108, 110, 167, 174, 222; U.S. literary history and, 3; yellow fever in, 59

newspapers and journalists, 30, 79, 153, 156, 165, 167; in London, 226, 228, 249, 253; in New York, 108, 110, 134, 167, 174, 222; in Philadelphia, 49, 135, 136, 146, 187, 192, 317n4; weeklies, 165, 225

North, the: African Americans in, 22, 108, 110, 171, 227; cities in, 14;

freedom and, 6, 87, 109–10, 213, 218; intolerance in, 216, 221; Philadelphia and, 13; politicians in, 196; prejudice in, 224; scapegoating of, 217; South vs., 186, 194, 196; urban, 215. *See also* New England

North Carolina, 6, 333n39

Notes on the State of Virginia (Jefferson, 1787), 63, 71, 104–5, 263

Oberholtzer, Ellis Paxson, *The Literary History of Philadelphia* (1906), 15, 139

Ohio, 107, 108, 124

Panic of 1837, 8, 194, 199, 202

parades, 15, 87; black temperance, 135–36, 170, 249. *See also* Federal Procession

passing as white, in *The Garies and Their Friends* (Webb), 226, 227, 238–40, 257

Peale, Charles Willson, *90*, 91; children of, 89–90, 261; museum of, 16, 89, 309n24; "Profile Book" of, 90; silhouettes and, 16, 73, 89–95, *93–95*

Peale, Raphaelle, 91, *92*; still lifes of, 261–62

Peale, Rembrandt, 91, 308n21

Peale's Museum, 16, 89, 309n24

"peculiar" (term), 109–10, 230, 262; Banneker's use of, 297n12; Delany's use of, 218; DuBois's use of, 332n29; etymology of, 230; Melville's use of, 271, 276; in Philadelphia literature, 215; slavery as peculiar institution, 153; Stowe's use of, 229, 230, 246

Penn, William, 4–5; in *The American Scene* (James), 164; city of, 138, 147, 148, 157, 169; images and icons of, 249, *250*, 251, 285, 286; Philadelphia grid and, 9, 11, 13, 131, 140, 157–60,

190, 264, 285, 291n7. *See also* Holme, Thomas

Pennsylvania, 4–5, 6–7; constitutions of, 7, 78, 109–10, 120, 150, 204; "Frame of Government" (1776), 211; history of, in *Modern Chivalry* (Brackenridge), 74; legislature of, 5, 40–41, 205, 315n71; state militia of, 182, 191, 200. *See also* disfranchisement

Pennsylvania Abolition Society. *See* Pennsylvania Society for Promoting the Abolition of Slavery

Pennsylvania Academy of Fine Arts, 262

Pennsylvania Act for the Gradual Abolition of Slavery (1780), 77, 81, 91, 119, 199

Pennsylvania Anti-Slavery Society, 8, 134

Pennsylvania Freeman, 123; Whittier as editor of, 155

Pennsylvania Hall, 138–40, 147, 334n48; abolitionists and, 139, 146–47, 152–53, 156, 204, 319n18; in *The City Merchant* (Jones), 195–99; counterhistory of, 197; dedication of, 134, 138, 147, 217, 244; destruction of, 7, 20, 134–46, *141*, *145*, 152–53, 170, 179, 181, 194–99, 204, 244; images of, 138, *139*, 139–47, *141*, *143*, *145*, 152, 197, 198, 249, *250*, 280, 318n12, 318n14, 318n16, 319n18, 324n47; psychological and political significance of, 138–39; ruins of, 135, *143*, *143*; as symbol of African American progress, 156; as temple of freedom, 142, 144; Whittier on, 140, 143–44, 151, 155–56, 318n13. See also *History of Pennsylvania Hall*

Pennsylvania Society for Promoting the Abolition of Slavery (Pennsylvania Abolition Society), 5, 87, 315n69; committees of, 203; reports by, 7, 16, 21, 121, 129, 137–38, 203–6

Pennsylvania State House, 88, 153, 174, 325n56; in *The Garies and Their Friends*

Pennsylvania State House (*continued*)
(Webb), 237; Peale's Museum in, 89,
91; in *The Quaker City* (Lippard), 174,
175, 186; U.S. founding documents and,
6, 144, 164–65. *See also* Independence
Hall

Pennsylvania Supreme Court, 74, 78, 119,
136, 218

performance, social, 73, 83, 88, 95; in
Benito Cereno (Melville), 267, 268–70,
271-75; civic recognition and, 162–63;
compared in *Benito Cereno* and *The Garies
and Their Friends*, 275–77, 278; in *The
Garies and Their Friends* (Webb), 240–43,
252–66

Peterson, Carla L., 23, 264

Petronius, "Trimalchio's Banquet," in the
Satyricon, 260–61

Philadelphia: antislavery in, 4–5, 8, 134,
141, 320n24; in *Adventures of Robin Day*
(Bird), 106–7; in *Arthur Mervyn* (Brown),
59–60, 66, 67, 166; border status of,
6, 8, 13–14, 229, 288; boundaries of,
14, 15, 19, 28, 56, 131, 166, 168, 184,
193; buildings in, 20, 133, 136, 137,
139, 160, 164, 173–75, 185, 186, 249,
250; character of, 21, 28, 173, 212–24;
churches in, 5, 8, 58, 132, 134–36,
178, 180, 182, 185, 239, 341–42n8;
city hall in, 285, 286, *287*; criminals in,
43–46; economic panic and depression
in, 8, 133, 158, 194, 195, 199; factories
in, 184, 186; fashion in, 82, 86, 97; as
federal capital, 5–6, 26, 28, 76, 286;
fires and firemen in, 135, 137, *141,
141*, 142, *145*, 145–46, 178–88, 191,
197, 200, 216, 240, *250*, 280; food
culture of, 254; founding of, 4, 11, 15,
285; gothic tradition of, 166; James on,
159–65; jokes about, 292n9; in *Liberia*
(Hale), 214–17; libraries in, 47, 127;
literary history and, 3–4, 15; maps and
atlases of, 9, *10*, 11, *132*, 186, *189*,
189–90, *287*; merchants of, 136, 170,
190; militia of, 136, 137, 182, 200;
ministers in, 5, 28, 43, 135, 233, 238;
in *Modern Chivalry* (Brackenridge), 74, 75,
186; narratives of, 6, 16–17; the nation
and, 14, 280; national conventions of
blacks in, 7, 16, 20, 69, 73, 108, 220,
224, 238; in *The Nazarene* (Lippard),
174, 184–86; New York and, 6,
167, 176–77, 224; physicians in, 19,
30, 31, 46–48, 170, 203–4; police
and watchmen in, 21, 135–38, 144,
154–57, 197, 200, 251–52, 279–80;
poverty in, 8, 83, 133, 191; printers
and publishers in, 8, 28, 170; in *The
Quaker City* (Lippard), 169, 173–77;
racial violence in, 6, 14, 21, 22, 122,
128, 131, 133–35; in *Sheppard Lee* (Bird),
97, 100, 101, 102, 186; slavery and,
4, 6, 14, 148, 163; taverns and dance
halls in, 137, 184, 187, 188; U.S.
Constitution and, 6, 14, 66, 212, 286;
voluntary associations in, 5, 8, 30–31,
112, 133, 135, 215; West Indies and,
59–60. *See also* grid of Philadelphia;
MOVE bombing; Philadelphia African
Americans; Philadelphia as symbol and
metaphor; Philadelphia
literature; Philadelphia mayors;
Philadelphia streets and neighborhoods;
Philadelphia writers; riots and mobs
in Philadelphia; yellow fever epidemic

Philadelphia: A 300-Year History (Weigley
et al., eds., 1992), 15

Philadelphia African Americans, 3–8, 106,
113, 179, 255; in Cedar or South Street
neighborhood, 7, 9, 20, 124, 132–33,
135–38, 204, 205, 316n2, 325n59;
censuses of, 203, 204–5; churches of,
135, 136, 203; crime and, 43–46, 203,
208; distinctive experience of, 262; as
entrepreneurs, 21–22, 219; executions
of, 42–46; exile of, 200; as former

slaves, 214; geographic settlement of, 7, 9, 97, 132, 133, 158, 191, 204; home ownership amongst, 125–26; in hospitality and catering industries, 254, 335n53; institutions of, 5, 8, 112, 181, 203, 206; leaders of, 112–13, 219, 220, 223, 240, 264; mortality of, 204, 213; pattern of regressive advance for, 264; poverty of, 8, 190, 191, 203–4, 206, 208, 223; as problem, 203–4, 204; reports on status of, 203–8; as servants, 204; social mobility of, 171; success of, 228; Tocqueville and, 290n4; as unskilled laborers, 204; as voters, 120; yellow fever and, 5, 26–31, 45, 47, 50–55, 264, 281, 283, 297n12, 298n18, 300n43. *See also* African American higher classes; African Americans; free blacks; riots and mobs in Philadelphia: African Americans as target of

Philadelphia Anti-Slavery Society, 141, 146

Philadelphia as It Is, 186

Philadelphia Book, The; or Specimens of Metropolitan Literature (1836), 172

Philadelphia County, 131, 137, 183, 237; African Americans in, 120, 191, 203–4

Philadelphia literature, 8, 14–18, 23–24, 172, 286; city mysteries in, 166, 167, 171–73, 327n67; freedom and, 209, 212; genres of, 22, 224; instability of, 18; maps in, 190; Southern medical students in, 199; start of, 46; travel accounts, 9, 11, 164, 290n4. *See also* Philadelphia writers

Philadelphia mayors, 26, 28, 31, 32, 39, 44, 134–36, 152, 155, 180, 197, 237, 252, 280–82; African American, 23, 280, 284; committee appointed by, during yellow fever epidemic, 29, 36, 37. *See also under names of individual mayors*

Philadelphia Museum of Art, 285, 286, 287

Philadelphia Negro, The: A Social Study (DuBois, 1899), 9, 161, 203–4, 284, 332n29, 335n53; sources of, 21, 203, 205, 291n7, 315nn69, 72, 327nn70–71

Philadelphia streets, neighborhoods, and suburbs, *10*, 11, 20, 60, 73, 82, 106, 124, *132*, 166, 178, 186, *189*, 190, *287*; alleys, 158, 169, 173–75, 184, 223; in *Arthur Mervyn* (Brown), 59–60, 66, 67, 166, Baker Street, 133, 207, 208, 237; Bedford Street, 133, 136, 191, 237; Benjamin Franklin Parkway, 286, *287*; Bush Hill, 27, 33, 55, 61, 251; Cadwallader Street, 185–86; Cedar or South Street neighborhood, 7, 9, 20, 124, 131–33, 135–38, 158, 175, 178, 181, 190, 198, 200, 204, 205, 208, 215, 237, 251, 252, 316n2, 325n59; Chestnut Street, 97, 134, 174–75, 180, 186, 196, 214, 237, 250, 325n56, 328n7; Eighth Street, 174, 204, 237, 334n48; Fifth Street, 136, 204; Fourth Street, 136, 174, 175; Front Street, 174, 194; in *The Garies and Their Friends* (Webb), 237–38; Germantown Road, 185–86; Haines Street, 134, 139, 142, 334n48; James on, 159–60; Jefferson Street, 185–86; Kensington, 132, 178, 180–86, 250, 325n56; Little Green Street, 237, 238; Lombard Street, 133, 135–36, 181, 238, 334n48; Market Street, 73, 100, 194–95, 197; Moyamensing, 132–34, 158, 173, 184, 186, *189*, 189–92, 204–8, 213, 217, 223; in *The Nazarene* (Lippard), 184–86; Northern Liberties, 97, 131–32, 182, 186; Osage Avenue, 280, 285; in *The Quaker City* (Lippard), 174–75, 177; Race or Sassafras Street, 134, 334n48; St. Mary's Street, 133, 136–37, 190–191, 199, 207; Seventh Street, 133, 174, 237, 334n48; Sixth Street, 134–35, 137, 139, 142,

Philadelphia streets (*continued*)
190–91, 194, 196, 199, 237, 334n48;
South Street, 7, 15, 131–32, 175, 204,
215, 279, 325n59, 340n1; southern, 7,
131, 158, 173–74, 186, 199, 208, 216;
Southwark, 97, 132, 136, 158, 167, 169,
173–75, 182, 184, 186, *189*, 189–90;
Spring Garden district, 123–24, 205;
Third Street, 174–75, 251; Thirteenth
Street, 196, 199; Walnut Street, 174, 190,
199; Washington Square, 87, 177, 190;
Washington Street, 185–86; west, 280;
Winter Street, 237–38, 248; working-
class suburbs, 158. *See also* Philadelphia
grid; Philadelphia African Americans: in
Cedar or South Street neighborhood
Philadelphia as symbol and metaphor, 6, 8;
of American Revolution, 28; as Camelot,
284; as City of Brotherly Love, 106,
158, 214, 249, *250*, 251–52; as coin,
159, 161, 164; as experiment in freedom,
3–9, 11, 14, 16, 17, 18–24, 28, 39,
66–68, 74–76, 110, 113, 116–17, 125,
138, 181, 194, 201, 202, 209, 212,
213, 224, 229, 284–85, 290–91n5;
as Holy Experiment, 4–5; as queen of
American cities, 158; as Sodom, 177; as
specimen, 20; as synedoche for nation,
280; as volcano, 163
Philadelphia writers, 8, 11, 17, 157, 165;
on corruption, 161–63; in 1850s, 280.
See also Allen, Richard; Bird, Robert
Montgomery; Brackenridge, Hugh
Henry; Brown, Charles Brockden; Carey,
Mathew; Cornish, Samuel E.; Delany,
Martin Robison; DuBois, W. E. B.;
Franklin, Benjamin; Hale, Sarah Josepha;
Jones, Absalom; Jones, John Beauchamp;
Leslie, Eliza; Lippard, George; Poe,
Edgar Allan; Purvis, Robert; Rush,
Benjamin; Schoolcraft, Mary Howard;
Webb, Frank J.; Whipper, William;
Willson, Joseph; Wideman, John Edgar

physiognomy, 64, 89, 102, 303n60
physiognotrace, 89–91, *90*, 93, 95. *See also*
silhouettes
Pierpont, John, "The Tocsin," 153–54,
320n25
Pittsburgh, 79, 108, 109, 110, 120, 288,
341n3
place, 13–14, 170–73, 292nn10, 12;
aesthetics of, 21, 165, 168; close textual
reading and, 13, 17–18; concept and,
19; literary, 13, 18; Poe and, 172–73;
space vs., 13
Poe, Edgar Allan, 16, 104, 296n7; "The
Fall of the House of Usher" (1839),
138–39, 152, 318n10; "King Pest"
(1835), 170; "Ligeia" (1838), 170;
Lippard and, 165, 170, 173, 174; "The
Man of the Crowd" (1840), 170, 171;
"The Man That Was Used Up" (1839),
174; "The Masque of the Red Death"
(1842), 170, 323n40; metempsychosis
and, 101, 310n32; "Metzengerstein"
(1832), 310n32; "Morning on the
Wissahiccon" (1844), 172, 323n42;
"The Murders in the Rue Morgue"
(1841), 171; "The Mystery of Mary
Rogêt" (1842–43), 171; as Philadelphia
writer, 15, 21, 138, 170–73, 322n39,
323n40; "The System of Doctor Tarr
and Professor Fether" (1845), 170, 171,
323n41; "The Wissahiccon" (1835), 172
politics, 4–5, 13; in *The City Merchant*
(Jones), 196; of class, 183; Democratic-
Republicans, 49; Democrats, 87, 148,
195; Federalists, 49; of information,
130, 263; in Lippard's fiction, 188;
Philadelphia novels and, 213–14;
Whigs, 195. *See also* corruption:
political
"Portraiture of the City of Philadelphia"
(Penn and Holme, 1683), 9, *10*, 11,
157, 285, 291n7; riffs on, 159. *See also*
grid of Philadelphia

prejudice, racial, 3, 4, 20, 112–13, 128, 150, 156, 187, 204, 213, 214, 239, 263, 290n4, 328n10; bigotry and bias and, 184, 220; blackness equated with criminality, 41; black rights vs., 116; disfranchisement and, 117; employment and, 226; fear of fever compared to, 57; as force of black cohesion, 110; history of, 221; internalization of, 282; in North, 21, 224, 265; overcoming, 109, 124; tenacity of, 262; victims of, 217

"Present State and Condition of the Free People of Color, of the City of Philadelphia and Adjoining District" (1838), 121–22

prints. See engravings and prints

Puritans and Calvinists, 16, 178

Purvis, Harriet Forten, 134, 244, 330n19

Purvis, Robert, 127, 134, 148, 180, 244, 330n19; American Moral Reform convention and, 108; "Appeal of Forty Thousand Citizens Threatened with Disfranchisement, to the People of Pennsylvania" (1838), 73, 121–23, 135; riot of 1842 and, 136, 247, 317n5

Pynchon, Thomas, Mason & Dixon (1997), 279–80

Quaker City, The; or, the Monks of Monk Hall: A Romance of Philadelphia Life, Mystery, and Crime (Lippard, 1845), 21, 137, 165, 167, 168, 173, 199, 204, 207; back wrappers of, 167; Byrnewood Arlington in, 173–75, 177, 180, 244; characters in, 173–75; crimes in, 173–75; Devil-Bug in, 168–69, 173–75, 177, 180, 193, 208; free blacks in, 180; Gus Lorrimer in, 173, 174; inscription to Brown in, 166; Luke Harvey in, 179, 180; metaphors in, 174, 176; Monk Hall in, 166–70, 173–77, 243–44; narrator of, 168–69, 177,

181; Pennsylvania Hall in, 139, 179; Philadelphia social experiment in, 173, 181; plots of, 173–75; quotations from, 169–70, 175–76, 178–80; riots in, 178–81, 252; scenes in, 174–76; theatrical production of, 180; title of, 169; translations of, 322n34; trapdoors in, 175–78, 243–44, 276; urban apocalypse in, 177–78, 208, 283

Quakers, 58, 102, 164; antislavery of, 4–5, 77, 181–82, 290n4; founding of Philadelphia by, 4, 11, 177; ideals of, 177; orphanage of, 135; Pennsylvania Hall Association and, 138; in Sheppard Lee (Bird), 98; in Uncle Tom's Cabin (Stowe), 258

quasi-freedom, 199, 211, 212, 284

race and ethnicity, 13, 43, 183, 194, 198, 199, 201, 267, 282, 284; in The American Scene (James), 320n29; citizenship and, 107, 119, 134, 228, 306n5; class and, 214, 215, 241; environmental view of, 5, 77; equality of, 151, 196, 212; freedom and, 21, 66, 200, 263; identity based on, 235; intimacy of, 191, 208; logic of, 201; in Modern Chivalry (Brackenridge), 75–78, 81; racial allegory of Poe and, 171; racial passing and, 226–27, 238–40, 243, 247, 257; science of, 7, 31, 63, 77, 170; sexual contact across, 6, 7, 77, 83, 119, 123, 134, 137, 156, 187, 196, 226–27, 232–33; in Sheppard Lee (Bird), 20; yellow fever epidemic and, 6, 26, 29–40, 43, 57. See also ethnicity; prejudice, racial; racial status; racial violence; racism; segregation, racial

racial status: caste and, 109, 110, 149; in Benito Cereno (Melville), 270; of free blacks, 198, 199; hierarchy of, 194;

racial status (*continued*)
  natural "inferiority" of blacks, 119, 199,
    212, 263; in North, 14, 20, 109–10;
    subordination and, 197, 216, 220; white
    "superiority" and, 214
racial violence: in Philadelphia, 6–8, 14,
    18, 20, 21–22, 122, 128, 131, 133–35,
    179, 200, 249; blacks as putative cause
    of, 251–52; in *The City Merchant* (Jones),
    199–202; in Lippard's fiction, 187–93;
    in New York City, 14, 133. *See also* riots
    and mobs in Philadelphia: African
    Americans as target of
racism: of Carey, 29; color lines and, 16;
    Delany on, 219; as limiting African
    American progress, 217–18; northern,
    214; politics of respectability vs., 111;
    racialist terms and, 181; romantic
    racialism and, 21; tropes of, 110. *See
    also* prejudice, racial; race and ethnicity;
    racial status; racial violence
Rael, Patrick, 23, 111, 312n50; *Black
    Identity and Black Protest in the Antebellum
    North* (2002), 264–65
railroads, 6, 176–77
Reconstruction, 279
religion: of African Americans, 5, 108,
    238; Christianity, 110, 115, 274;
    divine approval, 197; God, 114, 157,
    175, 198, 199, 283; Jesus Christ,
    185; Providence, 49. *See also* Bible, the;
    *and under names of religions and religious
    denominations*
reports on African Americans in
    Philadelphia, 121–22, 203–8, 213,
    224; "The Mysteries and Miseries
    of Philadelphia, as Exhibited and
    Illustrated by a Late Presentment of the
    Grand Jury," (1853), 203, 207–9; "On
    the Effects of Secluded and Gloomy
    Imprisonment on Individuals of the
    African Variety of Mankind, in the
    Production of Disease" (Coates, 1843),
    203, 213; "The Present State and

Condition of the Free People of Color"
    (Pennsylvania Abolition Society, 1838),
    121–22, 203; "A Statistical Inquiry into
    the Condition of the People of Colour"
    (Society of Friends, 1849), 203,
    205–7, 213; "Statistics of the Colored
    People of Philadelphia" (Pennsylvania
    Abolition Society, 1856, 1859),
    203, 205; "Ten Years' Progress: or A
    Comparison of the State and Condition
    of the Colored People in the City and
    County of Philadelphia from 1837 to
    1847" (Needles, for the Pennsylvania
    Abolition Society), 203, 205–7; "Trades
    of the Colored People" (Pennsylvania
    Abolition Society, 1838), 203
Reynolds, G. W. M., *Mysteries of London*
    (1844–56), 166, 167, 171, 207
Richards, Leonard L., 142
Richmond, Virginia, 161, 217; in *The
    American Scene* (James), 168
Rigal, Laura, 15
riots and mobs in Philadelphia, 15, 18–19,
    21, 73, 107, 114, 131, 166, 217–19,
    250; African Americans as target of,
    7–8, 14, 20, 114, 128, 133–38, 147,
    156, 170, 178–79, 183, 190, 200, 201,
    216, 217, 226; antiabolitionist (1838),
    20, 99, 131, 142, 156–58, 181,
    195–96, 198, 201, 225, 251, 322n39;
    anti-Catholic (1844), 146, 170, 178,
    180, 182–87, 195, 201–2, 317n4,
    322n39; as antidote for freedom, 202;
    archive of, 194; black resistance to, 21,
    200–201, 252; at California House,
    187–88, 190–91, 193, 198, 217, 252;
    causes of, 133, 165, 183–84; in *The City
    Merchant* (Jones), 194–202; conspiracy
    and, 202; of 1842, 158, 206, 225, 237,
    248–49; of 1849, 158, 186–88,
    191–93, 199, 204, 206, 225, 248;
    fiction of, 182–202; in *The Garies and
    Their Friends* (Webb), 22, 226, 237,
    239–40, 242–44, 248–52; in *The Killers*

(Lippard), 178, 186–88, 191–93; landscape of, 158; Lippard and, 168–69, 177–79, 182–93; MOVE bombing as, 282; in *The Nazarene* (Lippard), 182–87; against performance of *The Quaker City* (1844), 180; popular images of, 147; in *The Quaker City* (Lippard), 178–81; reports on African Americans and, 204, 206; in *Sheppard Lee* (Bird), 102; state militia vs., 182. *See also* Pennsylvania Hall: destruction of; racial violence: in Philadelphia

Rizzo, Mayor Frank, 280

Rocky (movie, 1976), 286

Rodgers, John, 49, 51

Rotella, Carlo, 15

Routledge, G., as publisher of *The Garies and Their Friends* (Webb), 224, 235, 236

Rush, Benjamin, 44, 46–52, 186, 300n41, 302n52; correspondence of, 16, 19, 27–28, 31, 35, 46–53, 61, 66, 299n33, 304n63; critics of, 49; *Journal of the Plague Year* (Defoe, 1722) and, 46–47, 299n33; pupils of, 295n4, 299n34; as signer of Declaration of Independence, 27, 51; *Travels through Life* (autobiography), 27, 28, 46; yellow fever epidemic and, 5, 28, 30, 46–52, 59, 68, 281, 304n63. *See also Account of the Bilious Remitting Yellow Fever*

Rush, Julia, and Benjamin Rush, 19, 27–28, 31, 35, 46–52, 58, 300n41, 304n63

Rush, Rebecca, *Kelroy* (1812), 16, 99, 310n30

Ryan, Mary P., 4

Ryan, Susan M., 214

Saint Domingue, 268; heroes of, 272; refugees from, 6, 62; revolution in, 63, 136, 153, 247–48; yellow fever epidemic and, 26, 59, 62. *See also* Haitian Revolution; Toussaint L'Ouverture

St. George's Methodist Church, 239, 283

St. Louis: black elite in, 130, 272; city mysteries of, 167; newspapers in, 153

St. Michael's Catholic Church, 182, 185

San Francisco, 167, 289n2

Sansay, Leonora, 16, 310n30

Sartain, John, and Pennsylvania Hall engravings, 141, *141*, 142, 146, 152, 318n14, 319n18

Savannah, Georgia, 231, 232

Schoolcraft, Henry Rowe, 212–13

Schoolcraft, Mary Howard, 194; "Letters on the Condition of the African Race in the United States" (1852), 21, 212, 214, 218; on Philadelphia, 212–13

Schuylkill River, 9, 97, 131, 157; docks on, 136

Scots-Irish, 74, 123

Second African Presbyterian Church, 178, 179

Second Bank of the United States, 8, 173, 195, 250, *250*

segregation, racial, 6, 176, 205, 238, 262

sexuality, sexual contact: interracial, 6, 7, 77, 83, 119, 123, 134, 137, 156, 187, 196, 208, 226–27, 232–33; in *The Garies and Their Friends* (Webb), 257, 260; in *The Quaker City* (Lippard), 174; seduction and, 168; struggles over, 133. *See also* miscegenation; violence: rape

Shakespeare, William, 45, 72, 75, 243

shaving, 271–75, 276, 339n82

Shaw, Gwendolyn DuBois, 91, 308n21, 309nn22, 24, 26–27

Sheppard Lee, Written by Himself (Bird, 1836), 20, 69, 73, 95–107, 115, 199, 240, 288; Abram Skinner in, 98, 101–3; African Americans in, 180; character in, 95–97, 100–103, 107; characters in, 99, 102; editions of, 310n29; identification in, 102–3, 105, 115; Isaac Dulmer Dawkins in, 97–98, 100,

Sheppard Lee, Written by Himself (continued)
102; John Hazelwood Higginson in, 97,
100, 102; as metempsychic novel, 69,
95–107, 230, 282; narrator (Sheppard
Lee) of, 95–102, 107, 230, 310n31;
Philadelphia in, 97, 100, 101, 102, 186;
Poe on, 101, 104; quotations from, 96,
100–103, 105; soul/spirit vs. bodies
in, 95–97, 100–101, 103–4; Tom
(Tommy, Thomas) in, 98–99, 102–5,
107; Zachariah Longstraw in, 98,
101–3, 105
Shiffler, George, as Protestant martyr, 146,
182
Short Account of the Malignant Fever (Carey),
19, 52, 61, 66, 281, 296n8, 301n49;
African Americans in, 27–28; critics on,
301n49; editions of 1793, 19, 25, 27,
29–30, 52–53, 55–58; edition of 1794,
19, 27, 29–30, 53, 300n43, 301n46;
edition of 1830, 19, 27, 54, 57, 59,
391n48; "Narrative of the Proceedings"
(Jones and Allen) vs., 27–28;
quotations from, 25, 27–30. *See also*
Carey, Mathew
silhouettes: as alternative to oil portraits,
89; character and, 91, 94; as memento
mori, 95; at Peale's Museum, 16,
73, 89–95, 92, 93, 94. *See also*
physiognotrace
Simms, William Gilmore, 326n63
"Singing Bones, The" (African folktale),
255–56
*Sketches of the Higher Classes of Colored Society in
Philadelphia* (Willson, 1841), 20, 69, 73,
133, 202, 227, 247, 254, 263, 336n62;
manners in, 117, 123,
127–30, 246; nature of, 129–30;
parlors in, 127–28, perspective in, 123,
126-27; quotations from, 123–28;
readerships of, 124–25, 127; social class
in, 124–25, 129. *See also* Winch, Julie
slave trade, 5, 95, 190, 192; auctions and,
232

slaves, slavery, 14, 60, 105, 118, 163,
187, 197; African customs under, 231;
ascendancy of, 222; in *Benito Cereno*
(Melville), 266–70; chattel, 181, 230;
children as, 234; defenders of, 212; evils
of, 182; as experiment, 4; freedom and,
5, 23, 37, 112–13, 221; in *The Garies and
Their Friends* (Webb), 227, 254–56, 262–
64; Jefferson on, 104–5; legacy of, 204;
Lord Mansfield's 1772 decision on, 117;
maritime mutinies of, 266–67, 270;
in *Modern Chivalry* (Brackenridge), 77;
overseers and, 235, 236; owners of, 226;
as peculiar institution, 230; Pennsylvania
Hall and debates on, 139, 149, 156;
in *The Quaker City* (Lippard), 177, 181;
revolution of, 273; in *Sheppard Lee* (Bird),
98–99, 102–5, 107; slave power and,
218, 221; in South, 22, 111, 153, 171,
196, 199, 229, 265; spirit of, 152; in
territories, 222; U.S. Constitution and,
37, 221; as volcano, 275–76; wage,
181; in West Indies, 302n54. *See also*
abolition, abolitionists; antislavery;
freedom; fugitive slaves; slave trade
Smith, James McCune, 276, 277, 337n72;
"On the Fourteenth Query of Thomas
Jefferson's Notes on Virginia" (1859),
263; Whipper vs., 22, 222–24
Smith, Samuel Stanhope, *Essay on the Causes
of the Variety of Complexion and Figure
in the Human Species* (1787, 1810),
5, 77
Smith, Stephen, 111, 136, 247; as
entrepreneur, 219; Smith's Beneficial
Hall and, 249, 252, 334n48
Smith, William Gardner, *South Street* (1954),
279
Smith-Rosenberg, Carroll, 61, 303n58,
304n63
social performance, 18–23; of African
Americans, 73, 83, 87–88
social reform, 20, 195, 204; Pennsylvania
Hall and, 134

Society of Friends, 7, 21, 203–4, 205–7, 213, 327n71. *See also* Quakers

Sollors, Werner, 265, 329n18, 332n30

Somersett decision, 117, 118

Souder, Casper, Jr., 208, 223, 237

South, Southerners, 31, 98, 152, 153, 213; North vs., 186, 194, 196; Philadelphia and, 13, 198, 199; romantic racialism in, 21; slavery in, 105, 153, 171, 229; sympathizers of, 214, 217, 332n30

South America, 21, 218, 221, 266, 267 in *Benito Cereno* (Melville), 269, 274, 276

South Carolina, 30, 152, 161, 212, 229, 231, 291n6

space, spaces: figurative, in *The Nazarene* (Lippard), 184; of freedom, 229; in *The Garies and Their Friends* (Webb), 237; geographic, of riots, 191; instabilities of, 186; place vs., 13; literary, 162; symbolic, 66, 138; urban, 165, 172, 185, 252; Wideman on, 288

Spain, Spanish, 167; in *Benito Cereno* (Melville), 268, 269, 274

Steffens, Lincoln, *The Shame of the Cities* (1904), 161–62

Stern, Julia, 28, 302n52

Still, William, *The Underground Railroad* (1872), 6

still-life painting, 261; *The Garies and Their Friends* (Webb) and, 257, 261–62, 264; in Philadelphia, 261–62. See also *vanitas*

Stowe, Harriet Beecher, 212, 214; *The Christian Slave*, 227–28, 232, 331n23; *Dred: A Tale of the Great Dismal Swamp* (1856), 229; *The Key to Uncle Tom's Cabin*, 229, 246; preface to *The Garies and Their Friends* (Webb) by, 225–29, 235, 262; *What Answer?* (Dickinson) and, 330n19. See also *Uncle Tom's Cabin*

Stranger's Guides to Philadelphia (Tanner), 186, 324n55

Sturge, Joseph, 290n4, 317n5, 320n23

sublime, 48, 59, 260, 276; American, 172; grotesque-, 168, 169, 178; urban gothic, 169

Sue, Eugène, *Les Mystères de Paris* (1842–43), 166–67, 171, 207, 208

Sundquist, Eric J., 273, 294n18, 338n77, 339n85

surfaces, 17–18; in *Benito Cereno* (Melville), 274; in *The Garies and Their Friends* (Webb), 261–62, 265–66; of Philadelphia, 160, 284–85; urban, 161; volatile, 178; vulnerable, 175

Swift, Mayor John, 134–36, 152

Tate, Claudia, 264, 294n20

temperance, 134, 151, 254; African Americans and, 7, 108, 112, 135–36, 138, 170, 179, 221, 244, 249, 252, 264

temporality, temporalities, 16–17; disrupted, 176; layered, 223; manipulated, 251; multiple, 18; regressive advance and, 264

Tenney, Tabitha Gilman, *Female Quixotism* (1801), 16, 99, 310n30

texture, 17, 44; literary, 164; narrative, 46; of Philadelphia experiment, 117; of representation, 176; rhetorical, 137; social, 22, 71, 72, 164, 212; spatial, 169, 252; verbal, 157, 265, 277; visual, 83

Tocqueville, Alexis de, 71, 164, 290n4

toleration, tolerance: city of, 138, 157, 169; religious, 4

Toussaint L'Ouverture, 247–48

Trilling, Lionel, 72, 305n3

trope, tropes: Calvinist, 178; character as unstable, 96; of colonial innocence, 72; of constraint, 154; of Exodus, 220; of grid, 11; inversion of, by Ellison, 72; in Philadelphia writing, 19; of racism, 110;

trope, tropes: Calvinist (*continued*)
    of urban exposure, 167; of volcano,
    163, 339n86; Wideman's, 281, 282
Truffaut, Francois, *Shoot the Piano Player*
    (film), 279
Turner, Nat, 203, 217
Twain, Mark, *Pudd'nhead Wilson*, 151
Tyler, Royall, *The Algerine Captive* (1797), 99

Uncle Tom's Cabin (Stowe), 212, 225,
    247–48, 258, 266; characters in, 229,
    232; domestic scenes in, 215; *Liberia*
    (Hale) and, 214; performances of, 225,
    227; Schoolcraft and, 214
Underground Railroad, 6, 14, 111, 247
United States: African Americans and,
    37, 119, 221; Bill of Rights and, 116;
    federal government of, 221; flag of, 235;
    Philadelphia as capital of, 5–6, 26, 28,
    76; racial destiny of, 14; symbolic space
    of, 66, 212, 286
U.S. Constitution, 6, 14, 74, 144, 251,
    286. *See also* Federal Procession
U.S. Congress: House of Representatives,
    148, 152; Senate, 148
U.S. Supreme Court, 222
University of Pennsylvania, 95, 281, 284
uplift, 23, 40, 111, 264–65. *See also*
    elevation
upper class, corruption and, 162, 183–84
urban gothic, 158, 166, 183, 208–9. *See
    also* mysteries of the city
urban place: aesthetics of, 169; apocalypse
    of, 177–78; decay of, 175; disorder of,
    20, 190, 198, 206, 282; exposure of,
    207; metaphors of, 176; perspectives on,
    177–78; Poe and, 172; riot and, 237;
    Romance and, 168; scenery of, 172

Van Buren, Martin, 195, 196, 199
vanitas, 144, 260, 261–62

"View of the City of Brotherly Love"
    (lithograph, ca. 1842), 249–52, *250*;
    The Garies and Their Friends (Webb) and,
    251–52
violence, 15, 20, 73, 102, 146, 212,
    326n63; in *Benito Cereno* (Melville),
    270, 271; character and, 8, 22; civic,
    281; ethnic, 182; in *The Garies and
    Their Friends* (Webb), 244, 248–49,
    257–58; historical, 178, 249–50;
    intimacy of, 266; in Lippard's works,
    176, 178, 190, 191, 193; manners
    and, 18–19, 22, 106–7, 127–28, 130,
    162, 168, 216, 240, 244–52, 275;
    murder, 43–46, 173, 175, 182,
    191–93, 226, 257–58; omnipresence
    of, 262; in Philadelphia fiction, 107,
    131, 173, 175, 186, 239; rape, 41–42,
    173, 257; religious, 182; sacred, 194;
    shaving and, 271–74; slavery and,
    276; upper class and, 183–84, 250; in
    "A View of the City of Brotherly Love,"
    249–52. *See also* gangs; MOVE bombing;
    Pennsylvania Hall: destruction of; racial
    violence; riots and mobs in Philadelphia
Virginia, Virginians, 56, 98, 99, 100,
    199, 200, 202; disputes of, with
    Pennsylvania, 301n47; in *Liberia* (Hale),
    213, 214; slavery and, 4, 6, 102, 103,
    107, 199; slave uprisings in, 217

wage slavery, 181–82, 184
Wainwright, Nicholas B., 15, 318n12,
    319n18
Walker, David, 293n16, 314n62
Warner, Michael, 65
Warner, Sam Bass, Jr., 183, 325n56
Washington, D.C., 14, 212, 217, 225
Washington, George, portraits of, 247
Waterman, Bryan, 61, 65
Webb, Frank J., 16, 147, 161–64, 172,
    201, 204, 223, 227, 265, 284, 334n46;

emigration of, to Jamaica, 263;
    Melville and, 22–23, 266–68, 270,
    275–78; *Paul Sumner*, 225; Wideman
    and, 280, 284. See also *Garies and Their
    Friends, The*
Webb, Mary, 225; as performer of Stowe's
    The Christian Slave, 227–28, 232
Webb, Samuel, as author of *History of
    Pennsylvania Hall*, 138, 194
Weld, Angelina Grimké, 134, 135, 152
Weld, Theodore Dwight, 147–48
West Indies, 21, 31, 60, 218, 221;
    emancipation in, 135, 249; slavery in,
    302n54; yellow fever and, 46, 59. *See also*
    Caribbean
Wharton, Edith, 260, 336n62
Whipper, William, 16, 20, 107, 118,
    127, 162, 212, 219–20, 222, 263–66,
    276; American Moral Reform Society
    and, 108, 111, 114, 312n48, 313n55;
    "Appeal to the Colored Citizens
    of Pennsylvania" (1848), 115–17,
    313–14n59; on character, 111–14, 116;
    "condition" vs. "complexion" debate
    and, 110–12; Cornish vs., 110, 222–23;
    Delany and, 221; on elevation, 113,
    115, 239, 247; fatalism of, 224; "Our
    Elevation" (1839), 115–16; on slavery,
    163; Smith, James McCune, vs., 22,
    222–24; Smith, Steven, and, 249; "To
    the American People" (1835), 114–15,
    313n55; use of term "peculiar" by, 109,
    230
Whiskey Rebellion (1794), 74, 75
White, Graham, 87, 308n18
White, Shane, 87, 308n18
Whittier, John Greenleaf, 155, 319n22;
    Pennsylvania Hall and, 140, 143–44,
    151, 155–56, 318n13
Wideman, John Edgar, 16; career of, 281;
    The Cattle Killing (1996), 23, 31–32,
    280–84, 288; "Fever" (short story,
    1989), 19, 23, 31, 280–83; *The Lynchers*

(1973), 281; narrators of, 282–83;
    Philadelphia of, 286–88; *Philadelphia Fire*
    (1990), 23, 159, 280, 284–86; Webb
    and, 280, 284
Wild, John Caspar, and Pennsylvania Hall
    prints, 139, *139*, 145, 318n12, 319n18,
    324n47
Williams, Moses, as silhouette maker, 91,
    92, *92*, *93*
Willson, Joseph, 83, 162, 202, 205, 212,
    217–18, 238, 254, 265, 316n78; on
    African American higher classes, 8, 87,
    107; *The Garies and Their Friends* (Webb)
    and, 227; life and career of, 123–24;
    use of term "peculiar" by, 230. See also
    *Sketches of the Higher Classes of Colored Society
    in Philadelphia*
Wilson, Harriet, *Our Nig* (1859), 31
Winch, Julie, 4, 311n47, 312n49; as
    editor of Willson's book, 124–25, 127,
    315nn72–73, 75; on Philadelphia's
    African Americans, 120, 125, 313n56,
    316n77
Wister, Owen: *Romney* (1912–15), 279; *The
    Virginian* (1902),15
women: antislavery and, 134; despotism of
    gender and, 116; employment of, 226; as
    factory workers, 260; female seminaries
    and, 182; as novelists, 99; in Philadelphia,
    scholarship on, 289n2; as public speakers,
    152; in *The Quaker City* (Lippard), 173,
    174; rights of, 134; as slaves, 232; as
    victims of violent crime, 41–44, 173,
    190, 192, 196, 198–99, 249
Woodside, John Archibald, Jr., 318n16;
    wood engraving of Pennsylvania Hall by,
    141, 142–43, *143*, 152
working class: black, 280; conspiracy
    against, 201; economic rivalry within,
    182; gangs of, 200; Irish, 158, 183,
    237; as rioters, 260; suburbs of, 158;
    white, 133, 134, 136, 181, 183, 185,
    201, 216

Wright, Frances, on Philadelphia, 11, 290n4

yellow fever epidemic (1793), 5, 15, 18, 28, 55, 119, 295n4; blacks and, 5, 6, 26, 30, 43, 45, 47, 51–55, 116, 122, 264, 281, 283; Bush Hill hospital and, 25, 27, 33, 55, 61; Carey and, 52–58; character and, 6, 45, 64, 72; deaths in, 26, 57–58, 299n33; debates on, 19, 26, 47–49; fear and, 55–58; mosquitoes and, 26, 46, 48, 299n36; MOVE bombing and, 282–85; narratives of, 17, 55, 59; Poe and, 170; race and, 29–40, 43; refugees from, 55–56; Rush and, 5, 46–52; Saint Domingue and, 26, 31; societal dissolution and, 26–28, 51, 54–55, 58; sources of, 26, 46, 59, 60; as symbol, 60; treatments of, 28, 46–49; Wideman on, 23, 280–84. *See also* Carey, Mathew; "Narrative of the Proceedings of the Black People"; Rush, Benjamin; *Short Account of the Malignant Fever*
Young Men's Vigilant Association, 135

Zola, Emile, "The Experimental Novel" (1880), 67